ALSO BY GAIL LEVIN

Edward Hopper: A Catalogue Raisonné

The Poetry of Solitude: A Tribute to Edward Hopper (editor)

Theme and Improvisation: Kandinsky and the American Avant-garde,
    1912–1950 (principal co-author)

Marsden Hartley in Bavaria

Twentieth-Century American Painting, The Thyssen-Bornemisza Collection

Hopper's Places

Edward Hopper

Edward Hopper: The Art and the Artist

Edward Hopper as Illustrator

Edward Hopper: The Complete Prints

Abstract Expressionism: The Formative Years (co-author)

Synchromism and American Color Abstraction, 1910–1925

EDWARD HOPPER

Arnold Newman, Edward and Jo Hopper in South Truro, *1960. Photograph © 1974, Arnold Newman.*

EDWARD HOPPER

An Intimate Biography

GAIL LEVIN

Alfred A. Knopf New York 1995

THIS IS A BORZOI BOOK
PUBLISHED BY ALFRED A. KNOPF, INC.

Copyright © 1995 by Gail Levin

All rights reserved under International and Pan-American Copyright Conventions. Published in the United States by Alfred A. Knopf, Inc., New York, and simultaneously in Canada by Random House of Canada Limited, Toronto. Distributed by Random House, Inc., New York.

Frontispiece photograph © 1974, Arnold Newman; photograph on page 347 © 1995, Arnold Newman.

Owing to limitations of space, all acknowledgments for permission to reprint previously published and unpublished material may be found following the index.

Library of Congress Cataloging-in-Publication Data

Levin, Gail, [date]

Edward Hopper : an intimate biography / Gail Levin. — 1st ed.

p. cm.

ISBN 0-394-54664-4

1. Hopper, Edward, 1882–1967.

2. Artists — United States — Biography. I. Title.

N6537.H6L48 1995

760'.092 — dc20

[B] 95-2114 CIP

Manufactured in the United States of America

First Edition

For John Babcock Van Sickle

CONTENTS

Introduction: Truth and Pain   x i

The Roots of Conflict: 1882–1899   3

Defining the Talent: 1899–1906   2 7

Seductive Paris: 1906–1907   4 9

The Ambivalent American: 1907–1910   7 2

In Search of a Style: 1911–1915   8 4

The Detour through Etching: 1915–1918   1 0 2

The Deeper Hunger: 1918–1923   1 2 3

The Leading Lady   1 4 6

First Success: 1923–1924   1 6 7

CONTENTS

Getting Established: 1925–1927   1 8 8

On the Road to America: 1928–1929   2 1 2

Recognition: 1930–1933   2 2 7

First Retrospective and the Truro House: 1933–1935   2 5 1

An Intellectual Self-Portrait   2 7 2

Consequences of Success: 1936–1938   2 8 3

The Struggle to Paint: 1939   3 0 7

The War Begins: 1940   3 2 0

Failed Odyssey: 1941   3 3 3

Nighthawks: *1942*   3 4 8

Mexico: 1943   3 5 8

War on the Home Front: 1944   3 6 7

The Aesthetic Divide: 1945   3 7 5

Anxiety: 1946–1947   3 8 5

Illness and Loss: 1948   4 0 0

Melancholy Reflection: 1949   4 0 8

A Retrospective Year: 1950   4 2 1

Mexico Again: 1951   4 3 6

Planning Reality: *1952*   4 4 5

Reality: *1953*   4 5 5

Taking Stock: 1954   4 7 4

Personal Vision: 1955   4 8 2

Time *Cover Story: 1956*   4 9 4

Toward Reconciliation: 1957–1958   5 0 8

Excursion into Philosophy: *1959*   5 2 0

Protest: 1960   5 2 9

Prints Again: 1961–1962   5 4 3

Last Rehearsal: 1963–1964   5 5 4

Final Curtain: 1965–1967   5 6 9

Bibliographical Notes   5 8 1

Notes   5 8 3

Acknowledgments   6 4 5

Index   6 4 7

INTRODUCTION
TRUTH AND PAIN

IN THE LAST DECADE of her life, Jo Hopper was planning to write two books: one on Arthur, her alley cat, strayed some thirty years before, and one on Edward, her husband. "Some day I'm going to write the real story of Edward Hopper," she told an interviewer, adding with emphasis, "No one else can do it. The man from *The New Yorker* wanted to do a Silhouette of Eddie, but finally gave up. He just couldn't get the material. You'll never get the whole story. It's pure Dostoevsky. Oh, the shattering bitterness!"[1]

Jo's boast was a feint to intimidate the inquirer. She never wrote "the real story of Edward Hopper." But through the years, from the early 1930s until her eyesight failed not long before she died in 1968, she did keep diaries. Often she wrote to express herself when Edward shunned conversation. She told of her frustration at his silence: "Sometimes talking with Eddie is just like dropping a stone in a well except that it doesn't thump when it hits bottom."[2] As time passed, the entries became more introspective and purposeful. She began to imagine a future audience. On a page dated Wednesday, March 29, 1950, a great blot of ink stands out like some enigmatic Rorschach test. Envisioning a prospective reader who might be tempted to see too much, Jo verified suddenly: "This no emotional crisis—just reversing ink bottle to fill side chamber for filling fountain pen."[3]

On a typical day, Jo began by complaining of her week shut in with a cold:

> Read Reader Dig. & New Yorker . . . not like reading a fine book—
> Radio out of tune too. E. has made such sketches at a burlesque & is
> juggling with advisability of attempting a canvas, but wants to see
> things more clearly—wants to make sure he is really interested be-
> fore starting off. Ed is reading a translation of Paul Valerie Criticism
> & reads me bits on Beaudelaire & Stendahl. E. does not want to go to
> bed anymore—wants to sit up & then leaps up at 7—must be all those
> vitamins he's taking Benzarine, Cebeose & Bottalin. . . . E wants to sit
> up and read, read, read. Never wants to talk about anything. Try to
> devise ways of making our lives gayer, "richer" D. calls it. Not that I
> need to go places, but I do like to look at people or discuss circum-
> stances as they are, not like him, a clout with no consciousness of the
> passing of hours, days, weeks, lives.[4]

Not only the man from *The New Yorker* pursued in vain the secrets of life
chez Hopper. Would-be chroniclers multiplied as Edward's reputation grew.
The invaders had to confront not only his storied reticence but Jo. She made
herself notorious for the obstacles she threw in the way of those who hoped
to write about her husband. Purposefully, energetically, and with his full
complicity, she engineered his legend as a recluse. All the while, she kept filling the diaries with the detailed personal record that would permit the kind
of biography both she and he approved.

In their opinions about the requirements for biography, the couple con-
verged for once. Jo was defying an outsider when she claimed that only she
could tell "the real story." Edward put off another outsider and asserted that
artists' lives should be "written by people very close to them." That Hopper
expressed his opinion at all is a tribute to Katharine Kuh. She provoked him
in a 1960 interview by claiming he had "suggested that a book dealing exclusively with the lives of artists would be valuable." Evidently she touched a
nerve. He virtually jumped to set her straight and pushed on with uncharacteristic openness to spell out a tenet of his faith about art: "I didn't mean that.
I meant with their character—whether weak or strong, whether emotional
or cold—written by people very close to them. The man's the work. Something doesn't come out of nothing."[5]

The importance of the man in the art was a theme Hopper stressed repeatedly. He once explained to Selden Rodman: "Originality is neither a matter of inventiveness nor method—in particular a fashionable method. It is far
deeper than that, and it is the essence of personality."[6] Hopper had voiced the
same thought years earlier at a moment of personal triumph. In 1933, for the

catalogue of his first retrospective at the Museum of Modern Art, he wrote: "I believe that the great painters, with their intellect as master, have attempted to force this unwilling medium of paint and canvas into a record of their emotions. I find any digression from this large aim leads me to boredom."[7] The conviction surfaced again when Hopper was asked to explain why he chose certain subjects over others: "I do not exactly know, unless it is that I believe them to be the best mediums for a synthesis of my inner experience."[8]

This belief in the personal grounding of his art links Hopper to the confessional mode of certain writers among his contemporaries. Hopper belongs to the tradition of spiritual autobiography.[9] His search for personal expression through his work suggests analogies with what occurs in modern literature, particularly in writers like Marcel Proust, Thomas Mann, and André Gide, all of whom Hopper read. Hopper, too, is one of the disaffected. His lonely and uneasy figures in everyday situations and common settings suggest "spiritual crisis within the framework of realistic characters, real places" in the manner typical of modernism.[10]

Believing in art as a medium for inner experience, Hopper naturally shied away whenever pressed to comment on the content of his own work. To speak would have risked putting his innermost emotions on display. Many an interviewer was sent packing in frustration. Even Lloyd Goodrich, his early and persistent partisan, who organized two retrospective exhibitions of Hopper's work, was kept at arm's length.

Hopper's defenses were more subtle in the case of the chronicler at home. He knew perfectly well that Jo was keeping diaries. She made no secret of the fact. They were enough of a fixture in her life to provoke his teasing. An ironic attack on diarists comes in just those bits about "Beaudelaire and Stendahl" that Edward chose to read her from the essays by Valéry. It must have been with a certain sardonic glee that he purveyed to the house diarist remarks like the following:

> The authors of confessions or memoirs or private diaries are invariably taken in by their own desire to shock; and we ourselves are the dupes of such dupes. It is never one's self that anyone wants to present; we know perfectly well that a real person has very little to tell us about what he is. He therefore writes the confessions of somebody else who is more impressive, purer, blacker, livelier, more sensitive, and ever more himself than is permissible, for the self has its degrees. Anyone who confesses is a liar and is running away from what is really true, which is something null or shapeless and, in general, blurred. But every confession has an ulterior motive: fame, scandal, an excuse, or propaganda.[11]

Wicked Edward! Poor Jo! Yet she gives little sign of the ulterior motives Valéry ascribed. So much of what she wrote impressed not even herself. She never rereads and regroups, focuses and builds. Even in the end, she took no thought to arrange, preserve, or publish. The diaries were found stored in an old metal box. The writing served as an outlet for that desire to "look at people and discuss circumstances" which she found so lacking in her "clout with no consciousness" of a husband. Her chatter, day in and day out, filled some of the emptiness and sometimes vented the bitterness and pain.

Protective as Hopper was about his privacy in life, he was skeptical about the prospects of later fame for artists: "Ninety percent of them are forgotten ten minutes after they're dead."[12] Nevertheless, his lack of more than ironic awareness of Jo's diaries goes beyond mere generic diffidence. Edward could not imagine that anything Jo produced might have a significant impact. Yet the diaries grew in importance in her mind. She even asked Edward to write a foreword during a trip and recorded his response: "Record of a woman's wandering mind & wandering thru the U.S. & Mex. There is no excuse or justification for such an effusion, only God will be allowed to see what has there been written & I think it will not please him greatly."[13] Secure in his own sardonic humor, he took for granted that the diaries would have no interest and no real public. Not the last man to underestimate Jo, he felt no need to know, let alone censor, what she might choose to record. He left the way open and she provided the means for someone to discover what it would entail to tell "the real story of Edward Hopper" reckoning with the viewpoint of someone really "very close."

By way of story material, the diaries offer long and often tiresomely repetitive stretches of daily movements or inaction, but then unique facts like paintings planned or executed together appear, and the moments of what she meant by "emotional crisis"—the bursts of resentful hurt. Often facts can be checked and corroborated, sometimes through letters in which intimates discussed the couple. The passions and conflicts came through only too often to interviewers and friends. As years wore on, Jo would pause more and more frequently to look back and take stock. By and large her recollections, too, turn out to have been reliable, although now and then she confused dates or conflated events. Reliability, bolstered by repeated verifications, lends credibility to the rest.

The general reliability of the diaries is especially welcome, given the absence, even willful destruction, of many other sources of evidence. Few contemporaries were left to be interviewed when Hopper died in 1967, aged nearly eighty-five. No children resulted from the marriage. The sole siblings on both sides were childless and already dead. But these are minor impediments to history by comparison with what happened next.

At Edward's death, Jo inherited everything. Virtually blind, ill, and facing her own death, she was in no condition to alter her husband's wish that his art go to the Whitney Museum of American Art. Lacking a viable alternative, she included in the bequest the bulk of her own work as well, although she disliked and distrusted the Whitney. To Lloyd Goodrich personally, she willed the record books of Edward's work she had kept meticulously for years.

Comprising more than three thousand paintings, drawings, watercolors, and prints of Edward's alone, to say nothing of Jo's, the bequest took the museum by surprise. Almost three years passed from the time of Jo's death until March 19, 1971, when a Whitney press release announced the gift of "the entire artistic estate of the late Edward Hopper"—with no mention of Jo's work. The Whitney's director, John I. H. Baur, called the collection "an asset beyond valuation." Plans for the future of the bequest soon appeared. Goodrich, the museum's advisory director, told *The New York Times,* "We want collectors and other museums to have access to it, so we'll put it on the market eventually."[14] Denouncing as a scandal this "contemplated disposal of the Hopper bequest," the *Times* critic Hilton Kramer characterized the museum as "a major institution suffering from . . . a feeble sense of its own identity and purpose." Kramer accused the Whitney of trying to destroy the value of the bequest as a permanent archive.[15] Baur retorted that the Whitney had itself not yet reached a decision on what part of the bequest it would keep.[16] Some sales did take place, including etchings and watercolors. A list drawn up by Lloyd Goodrich as late as June 6, 1974, indicates that he recommended selling twenty-five drawings—even though Hopper had produced these drawings during the 1920s at the museum's forerunner, the Whitney Studio Club. Eventually, under the pressure of intense public scrutiny and growing indignation, the museum stopped selling items from the bequest.

The controversy over sales only scratched the surface of disregard for the nature and value of the bequest as a permanent archive. To this day the public record gives no hint of the full extent of history's loss. My own awareness began when I started work on a catalogue raisonné of Hopper in 1976. By definition, a catalogue raisonné employs methodical scholarship to gather and digest in systematic form all that can be known of an artist's work and life. Beginning the project at the museum, I expected to find Hopper's papers, including the letters he kept, the photographs, books, and phonograph records that he and his wife owned: in short the evidence of his intellectual and cultural activity. I searched in vain. Soon I learned that neither Goodrich nor anyone else from the museum had sought to obtain this material, either directly from Jo after Edward's death, or, later, from the executor of her estate. The opportunity had been missed to conserve basic materials for a history of the artist and his production. This, despite the fact that in 1964 Jo wrote on the subject of "pack rats" to Margaret McKellar of the Whitney at the time when the museum was producing the catalogue for the last retrospective exhibition during Edward's life: "Pack rats might not like to be associated with the Rat Family even—however honorably antiquarian. Of course I keep everything from way, *way* back—letters to his mother from French people E. stayed with—when in Paris to say E. such a very good boy in 1906. His mother gave them to me. She a pack rat too."[17]

Compounding the dearth of expected documents, a different lack began to emerge. In going through the Hopper collection, I expected to see Jo's art as well as Edward's. I had read James Mellow's article in the *Times,* describing canvases by Jo in the bequest as "generally pleasant, lightweight works: flowers, sweet-faced children, gaily colored scenic views."[18] But I found nothing. Dealing with the bequest, Baur naturally looked for advice to Goodrich, his immediate predecessor as director and Hopper's recognized interpreter and friend. Together Baur and Goodrich rejected Jo's work as unworthy of the museum. They arranged for some of her paintings to be given away; they simply discarded the rest. They saw no need to invest even in archival photographs. Ironically, the only paintings from this group that can now be traced are four that went to New York University, which had troubled the Hoppers for years with efforts to evict them from their home.

In all, only three works by Jo were added to the Whitney's permanent collection. None was ever exhibited. All three had disappeared by the time I began work in 1976. None has ever turned up. Others managed to escape destruction by passing as Edward's: these included a few of Jo's drawings, several early small oil paintings, and some watercolors, all mistakenly identified as his. As curator of the Hopper collection, I convinced Hopper's dealer, the late John Clancy, to give the museum a portrait of Edward painted by Jo. This picture, now the only mature oil by Jo Hopper at the museum, has never been accessioned for the permanent collection. Today, most of Jo's paintings and drawings are known only by photographs that she had taken during her lifetime. The sole survivors are a few works she sold or gave away.

The men at the Whitney took for granted that Jo's work had no significance, but not all opinion was so shortsighted. Her qualities had not escaped the one interviewer who also became a friend in her last years. Concerning her, Brian O'Doherty wrote, "Josephine Verstille Nivison Hopper was one of the most extraordinary women any artist ever married."[19] He also made no bones about the tension in the marriage: "He and she were so opposed to each other in temperament that they were a continuous source of life and dismay to each other. Opinions are much divided as to her role. One view holds that Mrs. Hopper persecuted her husband. Another claims that she stung him to life."[20] A still more incisive estimate of Jo appeared in O'Doherty's 1971 review of the first exhibition from the Hopper bequest. He wrote that she

> must receive considerable attention in future Hopper studies. The Bequest reveals that the sinewy, female bodies in the paintings all belonged to his wife, who devoted herself to insuring that her husband's exposure to mankind in general (of which she had a low opinion) would be kept within the boundaries of her own person. Since Josephine Hopper had wit but no humor, she has hitherto been treated with a farcical indulgence which she herself invited. But she was a woman of genuine if frustrated talents, extremely well-read, and at her best a brilliant and eccentrically original conversationalist.[21]

O'Doherty's prescription for Hopper studies proved prescient. My research went on to demonstrate how Jo's activity as an artist intertwined with Edward's. Not only did she insist on modeling for his nudes—that was the least of it. She, like him, had studied painting with Robert Henri at the New York School of Art. Starting in courtship, she and he made art together. Often they used the same studio or worked at the same locations. When he suffered from painter's block, as frequently happened, she would goad him into action by beginning to paint first. They shared the routines of every day and the laborious travels north or west or south in quest of subjects. They absorbed and discussed the same books, plays, and films, exchanging *billets-doux* in French. With her help his career took wing. Her career withered, ignored when not discouraged by him. As she recorded and remembered, her resentment welled up again and again.

It is time, then, to acknowledge Jo Hopper's role not only as her husband's wife and model, but as the intellectual peer and fellow painter who both stimulated and challenged her more gifted colleague. The "whole story" needs them both together. There is her chronicle of paintings, quarrels, and tea parties laced with bitter pain. There is her challenge that the truth would be worthy of a tragic narrator. No less there is Edward's belief in the personal core of his work and his resulting evasive posture. Together, their testimony suggests a story of acute anguish in personal life transmuted into gripping art. The pain and the craft create the uncanny tension through which his paintings speak. Their pictorial idiom, at once familiar and estranged, touches our memories, hopes, uncertainties—the yearning and disquiet of modern lives.

EDWARD HOPPER

THE ROOTS OF CONFLICT: 1882–1899

THE ROOTS OF Edward Hopper reach back to the old Dutch settlements that punctuate the wooded bluffs and promontories along the lower Hudson River. The conflict in his character mirrors the tension in those communities, where local and traditional values faced the horizons opened by technology and science and new waves of migration. Hopper's childhood spanned the end of the Victorian age and the dawn of the new century with its momentous disruptions and displacements. The decade of the 1880s saw great scientific and social transformations: Hopper was born just weeks after commercial electric lights made their debut in New York. Less than a year later the first telephone line would connect New York with Chicago.

At the time of Edward's birth on July 22, 1882, his home town of Nyack counted a population of about four thousand. Light manufacturing included shoes, carriages, and pianos. Service industries flourished, especially those related to tourism and resort development along the river.[1] Incorporated as late as 1872, Nyack was considered a healthful resort. The streets were paved and there was no threat of malarial mosquitoes. Nearby on the Hudson the promontory of Hook Mountain offered a noble prospect. At "the pond," ice was cut in the winter and recreation such as boating was available all summer. Along the river affluent captains of industry lived in elaborate Victorian elegance. The area had been populated primarily by people of Dutch extraction well into the 1820s, when more settlers, including Hopper's forebears, began arriving from New Jersey, New York City, and abroad. When later immigrants came, they included refugees from the potato famine in Ireland.[2]

Change in Nyack had begun in earnest when the railroad linked it with New York City in 1870. Growing rail traffic in both passengers and freight prompted an upgrading of the local country roads. The improvements also caused dislocation, gradually driving out of business the local steamboat lines and the industry that built the boats. Still, during Edward's boyhood, the port remained relatively prosperous and a thriving shipyard turned out racing yachts. The last riverboats steamed up and down and across the Hudson. The lad could spend Saturdays "in the Nyack shipyards where he studied the building and rigging of yachts with a boy's enthusiastic attention to detail," reported Alfred Barr, who interviewed Hopper in 1933.[3] When only five or six Edward learned to row on Rockland Lake, the local "pond." He went on to gain community notice from a boating accident on Hackensack Creek. While rowing with a chum, Ralph Bedell, he attempted to take off his coat and fell overboard, capsizing the boat. For once his height stood him in good stead: "It was no stunt for Edward to stand up and keep his head out of water and at the same time to lend a helping hand to Ralph," reported the local paper. "The boys got a wetting, but no further damage was done."[4] In deeper water, Edward excelled at swimming and enjoyed it all his life.[5]

Edward and his friends, Harold Green, Louis Blauvelt, and Harry MacArthur, spent much of their free time near the docks or on the river, particularly at John P. Smith's boatyard at the foot of Fourth Avenue.[6] The Baptist minister's daughter, Lois Saunier, remembered the lanky boy and his friends coming to borrow her father's boat.[7] They would sail on the Tappan Zee, where the Hudson River broadens out between Irvington, south of Nyack, and Croton Point, ten miles to the north.[8]

Eddie and three pals formed the Boys' Yacht Club, for which he designed plaques with the names of the members' boats: one version sported *Glorianna, Mary M.,* and *Bubble,* which were traditionally feminine, but upbeat and innocuous.[9] Edward's choice, *Water Witch,* telegraphs his love of books. *The Water-Witch,* James Fenimore Cooper's 1830 novel, tells how the "exploits, mysterious character, and daring of the Water-Witch, and of him who sailed her, were, in that day, the frequent subjects of anger, admiration, and surprise. . . . All wondered at the success and intelligence with which her movements were controlled."[10] Also, Cooper's character Tom Tiller declares, "A ship is a seaman's mistress."[11] Where the title of Edward's fantasy suggests derring-do and mastery even in the mystery of sex, the boat he actually built was something else. At age fifteen he received the wood and tools as a gift from his father, but the resulting cat boat "wasn't very good," its maker recalled. "I had put the center board well too far aft and she wouldn't sail up-wind very well."[12] One story held that the boat sank, another that it was sold for scrap.[13] Up in the attic on North Broadway, Edward also built a canoe, which he depicted in drawings as the vessel of the Indians. To an interviewer he once related: "I thought at one time I'd like to be a naval architect because I am interested in boats, but I got to be a painter instead."[14]

The circumstances of Edward's immediate family were comfortably middle class. He was the first and only son, but the second child; his sole sister, Marion Louise, had been born on August 8, 1880. Their parents' marriage was marked by dominance on the female side. When Garret Henry Hopper, twenty-six, married Elizabeth Griffiths Smith, twenty-three, on March 26, 1879, the ceremony took place in the house where Elizabeth grew up and the new couple settled there under the wing of Elizabeth's widowed mother, since Garret had no means of providing an independent dwelling. The home on North Broadway was a constant reminder that Elizabeth had married less well than her mother. Her father, John DeWint Smith, had built the house for his wife on coming to Nyack six years after their marriage in 1852. Smith had also acquired two other houses in Nyack, and his mother's family, the DeWints, owned historic houses in Tappan. The DeWints traced their origin to a wealthy sugar plantation owner who had emigrated from the Caribbean island of St. Thomas.

In her roles as mother-in-law to Garret Hopper and grandmother to little Edward, Martha Griffiths Smith wielded more than just the authority derived from providing their home. She was the daughter of a moral force in the community. Her father, the Reverend Joseph W. Griffiths (1782–1860), had organized the Baptist congregation in Nyack in 1854. His story became a part of family lore and stuck in the memory of his great-grandson: even at age seventy-two, Edward Hopper still spoke of the ancestor who "married a French girl—Lozier—when he came to America."[15] In fact, Griffiths came as a young man in his twenties from England to New York, where he worked in a foundry. In the new surroundings, Griffiths left his Anglican origins for an evangelical sect. He became a Baptist, founded a Sunday School, and soon was called to the ministry. He had retired from a long career when he helped to propagate the Baptist persuasion in Nyack. The woman he married was Elizabeth Lozier, descended from Le Sueurs, Huguenots who came to America from Dieppe in 1657. Their Protestant heritage led them to the Dutch Reformed Church and they soon simplified their French name beyond recognition.[16] Yet when Edward remembered the story, he thought of his great-grandmother as "French," emphasizing the trace in his family tree of his favorite culture. Another time, he told Katharine Kuh: "Like most Americans I'm an amalgam of many races. Perhaps all of them influenced me—

John DeWint Smith,
Edward's maternal
grandfather.

Martha Griffiths Smith,
Edward's maternal
grandmother.

Dutch, French, possibly some Welsh. Hudson River Dutch—not Amsterdam Dutch."[17]

The namesake and granddaughter of Elizabeth Lozier Griffiths, Edward's mother Elizabeth, was born to Martha Griffiths and John Smith in Blauvelt, New York, before her parents moved to Nyack and built the house where all of them lived and died and where Edward grew up. Elizabeth enjoyed the privilege of attending private school at the Rockland Female Academy. She was remembered as "full of charm and a complete extrovert, generous, witty, handsome, gay of spirit, natural hostess, always full of concern for friends."[18] Expressive of her feelings, she was said to "rave" when she was angry.[19] Elegant, feminine, yet formidable-looking, she wore her long hair swept up in a chignon. A photograph shows strong features like those that made her son a distinctive subject for portraits. He, when painting her portrait, emphasized her determined stare. Elizabeth showed her skill with children when the new minister arrived at the Baptist church, as his daughter recalled:

Our great favorite was a delightful white-haired lady named Elizabeth Hopper. As soon as we became acquainted, she suggested that we call her "Auntie" Hopper which we were glad to do. She was such fun to be with, always ready to laugh and joke with us and take interest in what we were doing. To join a game of tag or help us dress a doll, seemed to give her as much pleasure as it did us.[20]

On the paternal side, Edward's family had been prosperous traders and farmers, more exclusively Dutch. There were Hoppen mayors and aldermen in fifteenth-century Amsterdam. Andries Hoppen came to New Amsterdam in 1652, where he succeeded in shipping and trade. When he died prematurely, aged only thirty-three, his widow and five children went to New Jersey, where they flourished around Hackensack and Ho-ho-kus, once known as Hopper Town. Edward's great-grandfather Christian, born in 1826, married Charity Blauvelt in Paramus on April 17, 1851. Although Charity's

Elizabeth Lozier Griffiths, Edward's maternal great-grandmother.

Reverend Joseph W. Griffiths, Edward's maternal great-grandfather.

parents, the cousins Abraham Blauvelt (1789–1864) and Marie Blauvelt (1793–1882), came from a Dutch family, they baptized their daughter in the Methodist church of Waldwick, New Jersey, turning to the evangelical sect of English working-class origin.[21] Thus the strains of a rigorous evangelical Protestantism took over from more established religious traditions in both sets of Edward's great-grandparents. The effects were felt even to the third generation.

Evangelical austerity displaced the more festive way of life the early Dutch settlers in the new world had kept up in the style of the old world taverns of genre painters like Jan Steen. Beer and rough games had been favorites. This is why Hopper emphasized that he was descended from "Hudson River Dutch—not Amsterdam Dutch." Baptized into the sobriety of the Methodist church, Charity Blauvelt Hopper remained a forbidding figure all her life: Edward, writing home from the relative liberty of Paris, said he wanted no more letters from such disagreeable old ladies. In fairness, it must be admitted that Charity's life was unlucky and hard. Her husband Christian died on April 20, 1854, in an accident with a runaway horse when their son was only two years old. Unlike Andries Hoppen in the first generation, Christian did not leave his heirs secured. Charity took the little Garret to New York City to live with her parents, Abraham and Marie.[22] Grandfather Blauvelt died when the boy was only twelve, forcing him to curtail his education and go to work to support his widowed mother. Barred from his natural talent for study, lacking the commercial knack of his ancestors, deprived of paternal guidance, Garret Hopper drifted until a further chance brought him to Nyack and a strong mooring with Elizabeth Griffiths Smith.

In 1878 Garret Hopper went into business in Nyack; four years later, he identified himself on Edward's birth certificate as "Salesman."[23] In 1890, Garret purchased Morris and Minnerly, a dry goods store not far from the family home. In the shop, which became known as "G. H. Hopper," he sold table linens, towels, fabrics, notions, kid gloves, hosiery, underwear, and other items of clothing. Elizabeth Hopper made dresses for herself and her daughter from the fabrics procured by her husband. The fact that "G. H. Hopper" sold men's and boys' underwear may account for the young Edward's otherwise inexplicably detailed reports on the condition of his underwear when he wrote letters home. Garry, as people called him, was active in community affairs. He wore a short, pointed Van Dyck beard and a mustache; he resembled Thomas G. Masaryk, the first president of Czechoslovakia, his son recalled. At the end, Garret was remembered as "kind-hearted and of a genial disposition, with a large circle of friends."[24] He was also reputedly "the most polite, gracious person."[25]

Christian Hopper, Edward's paternal grandfather.

Charity Blauvelt Hopper, Edward's paternal grandmother.

Garret made every effort to succeed. He advertised regularly in the Nyack *Evening Journal* and in the *Fair Journal*, published by the ladies' auxiliary at the YMCA. He promoted business with periodic sales, claiming to offer the "lowest New York City prices." (The metropolis at the other end of the rail line was already undercutting local autonomy.) He enlarged his business in April 1892, buying out his local competitor, William O. Blauvelt. But Garret's heart was not in commerce. He closed shop about 1901, aged only forty-nine, when his son was already studying in the city.

Garret Hopper's failure to live up to his forebears' mercantile prowess did not undermine the household's standard of living, thanks to the inheritance of his wife, who owned and received rents from two houses and held mortgages on other properties. Upon Edward's birth in 1882, the Hoppers built a new wing onto the north side of their home. About two years later, they enlarged the wing with a second story and bay window. They frequently redecorated, paid for repairs and yard work, and sent their laundry out to be done. They also ran charge accounts with the local grocer, butcher, baker, and confectionery, and they hired horses and carriages from Blauvelt's Livery Stable. In keeping with this lifestyle, they also employed an Irish maid from the population of newer immigrants.

Comfortable circumstances permitted private school for Edward and Marion, as for their mother before.[26] Then they went to the public school on Liberty Street. Eddie was a prankster. He dipped girls' braids in inkwells, the classic torment in times when every desk in school held a supply of ink. Marion, as the elder, remembered that he was "a dreadful tease" when little.[27] Lois Saunier described a mortifying occasion when she was the Hoppers' guest for Sunday dinner.

> When we were ready to eat Auntie Hopper was seated at one end of the table, with the daughter Marion at the other and Ed was seated opposite me. I had been seated on a hassock which was on a dining room chair, a napkin tied around my neck, grace had been said and we were ready to eat. At this point Ed decided to have a bit of fun— fun for him, that is—so he stretched his long legs under the table, curled his feet around my hassock and gave a quick pull. Of course I went down with a bang, hitting my chin lightly on the table's edge and injuring my vanity more than anything else. I looked to Marion and Auntie Hopper for consolation but saw that they were trying not to laugh so I knew that I too must take it as a joke, tho' I was truly embarrassed. Auntie Hopper said Ed was a bad boy to do such a thing and to punish him she would call him "Eddie" all the rest of the day knowing he disliked the name.[28]

Marion Hopper also recalled that her brother "couldn't stand it if he didn't win every game he entered into—checkers, whatever children played."[29] Edward's high spirits paid off in schoolwork, as attested by a surviving report card from January 1890, when he was only seven: he received a grade of ninety for his numbers, but scored a perfect one hundred for geography, reading, spelling, punctuality, and behavior, for an overall average of ninety-eight.

When Edward moved up to Nyack High School on the top floor of the elementary school, he did not maintain such standards. He received honors on the New York State Regents Examinations only in drawing and plane geometry. Although there were then no art classes in Nyack schools, Edward's ability to draw came in handy at least once, recalled his sister, when, stymied for words to answer a question on an exam, he illustrated it, impressing and satisfying his teacher.[30] No particular teacher, however, ever won credit for encouraging him. His French notebooks attest to his diligence

Elizabeth Griffiths Smith,
Edward's mother.

Garret Henry Hopper,
Edward's father.

in studying the language that he later knew well and continued to read all his life. He also studied spelling, reading, geography, writing, English, U.S. history, arithmetic, algebra, German, botany, zoology, and economics.

§

THE HOPPER FAMILY did travel out of Nyack, taking trains and ferryboats to New York City to attend cultural events, although Nyack also had its own opera house and a hall for other performances. The Hoppers even kept scrapbooks of the operas and plays they attended. (Edward's father's first cousin Lillian Blauvelt was an accomplished opera singer.) Sports too interested the family. As an adult, Hopper expressed some interest in baseball, remarking: "Used to go to a game once in a while when I was a boy."[31] Garret Hopper took Eddie to visit his relatives in Ridgewood, New Jersey, traveling in rented equipment as they did not own their own horse and buggy.

Each August, the family spent a week on the Jersey shore, where the Christian religious camp meetings of the 1870s had evolved into summer colonies where no liquor was allowed and evangelical "surf meetings" attracted devout crowds. In 1895, when Edward was thirteen, the Hoppers stayed at the Sunset Lodge in Ocean Grove; the following year they were at Norwood Hall in Asbury Park, to which they returned in 1897, staying this time at the Edgemere Inn.[32] Inspired by the change of scene, as he often would be in later years, Edward made drawings on these trips.

For religious education during the rest of the year, Hopper's parents sent him just up the street to the Baptist Sunday school, in the tradition of Great-grandfather Griffiths. The Sunday afternoon classes taught the gospels, temperance, and the whole range of moral discipline: values ingrained in Edward, especially frugality and the willingness to postpone gratification, not to mention emotional reticence and sexual inhibition.[33]

As strict Baptists, the Hoppers could be expected to use corporal punishment to discipline their children. Their church, like generations of evangelical Protestants, cited biblical rationales for the use of the rod.[34] No direct evidence proves that Edward's pranks ever provoked a thrashing. He did, however, in adulthood develop symptoms of depression like those sometimes traced to overzealous punishment in childhood: some argue that often depression is "a delayed response to the suppression of childhood anger that usually results from being physically hit and hurt in the act of discipline by adults whom the child loves and on whom he or she depends for nurturance and life itself."[35] Whether or not the mild Garret resorted to the razor strop and woodshed to check his son's prankishness, Edward showed signs already in adolescence of the introverted nature that would become his trademark as an adult.

The decade of Hopper's adolescence, the 1890s, was a "watershed" in American history.[36] Seen with hindsight, the "gay nineties" mark the passage from the strong moral principles of rural and small-town America into the beginning of urban and industrial development that eroded traditional ways of life and produced growing alienation. Across the nation, Americans were facing a challenge to their most basic assumptions and beliefs.[37] These changes had little effect on Garret and Elizabeth Hopper, insulated as they were by their economic security and religious principles. Indeed, the nineties saw Garret Hopper not only befriend the minister but twice serve as a church trustee.

Neither precept nor example sufficed to transmit a confident faith to Edward. Growing up ill at ease and feeling different, he took his distance from the religion-centered community by becoming a skeptic. Late in life, he spoke approvingly of a couple who, having finally formalized their alliance with a church ceremony, proceeded to rear their first child as a Catholic, the second as a Protestant, and the third as a Jew.[38] Skepticism had personal and social roots. By the time he was about twelve years old, Edward had suddenly shot

*Eddie at the Liberty Street School, Nyack
(seated on the left in the second row from the front).*

up to over six feet. His height and skinny, awkward physique set him apart from his contemporaries. "Grasshopper" they taunted him at school. Social discomfort reinforced a mind-set already independent. He took refuge in solitary pursuits. He had discovered early his talent for drawing. In art he found a private and unique ability to deal with the world confidently on terms more nearly his own. Both parents encouraged him to develop his gift, although his father, concerned that the boy was too reclusive, also tried to suggest outdoor activity, as when he promoted the scheme of the ill-fated cat boat.

Garret's most profound and lasting influence took place indoors. The prognosis for paternal imprint was not good, Garret never having known a father himself and failing to live up to conventional expectations of the male role, what with his meek demeanor and lack of business acumen, all overshadowed by his wife, with her inherited moral authority and wealth, her hold on the purse strings, and her confident and outgoing character. Yet this very diffidence toward business made its effect on Edward, who used to help out in the store after school, and soon realized where his father's true passion lay: "An incipient intellectual who never quite made it," Edward sized him up,[39] opining that his father should have become a scholar, being that he was less at home with his books of accounts than with Montaigne's *Essays*.[40] Garret set his most telling example to his son through his reading. The boy read

Eddie and his sister, Marion.

avidly and always remembered his father's library as well stocked with "the English classics and a lot of French and Russian in translation."[41]

Citing Montaigne to exemplify his father's intellectual interests, Edward evokes a world shaped by the influence of Ralph Waldo Emerson, who made Montaigne represent "the skeptic" in one of the six essays in *Representative Men* (the other five examples being Plato, Swedenborg, Shakespeare, Goethe, and Napoleon). Emerson was read in America by men of Garret Hopper's intellectual pretensions and Emerson commended Montaigne's prose: "Cut these words and they would bleed; they are vascular and alive."[42] Three of Emerson's representative men—Plato, Shakespeare, and Goethe—were the only figures of world literature that Hopper ever related to pictures he painted. The concept of "the skeptic" provided a philosophical peg for his own development as he outgrew his religious upbringing. Although rooted in the Puritan background, Emerson rejected formal religion in favor of intuitive spiritual experience. He traced an American rite of passage that Hopper could recognize in his own difficult transition. He had far to go from his parents' community of belief to create a life that was largely secular yet profoundly devoted to the search, through art, for inner truth.[43] For Hopper, Emerson's belief in the harmony of man and nature was fundamental, providing a matrix for his considered view that painting would eventually "attempt to grasp again the surprise and accidents of nature, and a more intimate and sympathetic study of its moods, together with a renewed wonder and humility on the part of such as are still capable of these basic reactions."[44]

For the situation of Garret Hopper and his son, Montaigne's essay "Affection of Fathers" seems ironically apt: "It is right to leave the administration of affairs to mothers while the children are not yet of legal age to take over on their own. But the father has brought them up very badly if he cannot hope that at that age they will have more wisdom and ability than his wife, seeing the ordinary weakness of the sex."[45] Affirmations of male superiority were as common in serious writing as they were at variance with the reality of the Hopper ménage.

Also in vogue at the time were the "French and Russian in translation," recalled by Edward, who spoke of reading Turgenev and Tolstoy, the two most popular Russian novelists then translated. Turgenev's American reception was fostered by William Dean Howells and Henry James, who advertised what they called his "dramatic or pictorial method."[46] Howells soon became an even more fervent proponent of Tolstoy for the "reality" of his fictions, which "seem the truth always."[47] James remained partial to Turgenev, whom he knew in Paris: "M. Turgenev's pessimism," James argued, "seems to us of two sorts—a spontaneous melancholy and a wanton melancholy. Sometimes, in a sad story, it is the problem, the question, the idea, that strikes him; sometimes it is simply the picture."[48] As James describes the narrative process, he thinks of a conflict between the "picture" and the ideas. Hopper came to define his art as a constant struggle to master the pictorial in order to record inner truth.

The work of Turgenev read most widely in America was the novel *Fathers and Sons*.[49] Reading about its themes of conflict and love between generations may have offered a means of unspoken communication between Edward and his father.[50] Garret Hopper appears, in the somewhat contemptuous caricatures and sketches produced by his son, as a man afraid of emotional expression. He found a surrogate voice by urging on his son the literature he loved. Edward took the lesson to heart. Extremely shy, he also had difficulty voicing his feelings. Not only did he withdraw by reading, but, as an adult, he would often read aloud some literary passage that he admired instead of directly uttering his own emotions and ideas. He found this a less intimidating and less revelatory means of communicating.[51]

Among French novelists, Hopper knew Victor Hugo, whom he later illustrated, being attracted especially to *Les Misérables,* with its dramatic twists and vivid descriptions of Paris. Other French classics commonly translated and read in America in Hopper's youth were Gustave Flaubert's *Madame Bovary* (with its unromanticized observation of life and nature and its defiance of convention), and Emile Zola's naturalistic novels of the Rougon-Macquart series, such as *Nana*. Further readings and sympathies can be inferred from illustrations Hopper eventually produced in art school: there were novels by Charles Dickens, including *Barnaby Rudge, Oliver Twist, Bleak House,* and *A Tale of Two Cities,* as well as Sir Arthur Conan Doyle's *The Exploits of Brigadier Gerard.* Edward also sketched Rudyard Kipling's Private Mulvaney from the cycle of soldier stories that made its author famous. Kipling's work made such an impression on the young Hopper that even when he wrote as an adult, he referred to the poetry.[52] Nor can he have missed Kipling's misogyny, which could only reinforce prejudices gained elsewhere.

If Garret Hopper's legacy was literature, his wife's was art. Elizabeth had pursued art as a child, and some of her drawings survived among the family papers. She took pride in a history of artists in her family. Her grandmother and namesake, Elizabeth Lozier Griffiths, had a brother, Jacob Lozier, whose drawings survive from the 1830s. And François Le Sueur, a civil engineer, had transplanted the family to America two years after the death of his brother Eustache (1616–1655), who painted religious and mythological subjects and won election to the French Academy.

Both of Elizabeth's children drew from an early age and she saved their work, much of her son's and some of her less-gifted daughter's. Marion's creative efforts focused on staging puppet shows and plays, often assisted by her brother. As she later told an interviewer, "the paper dolls with which she played were not paper dolls cut out of magazines with which little girls of her day and succeeding generations have played," but objects that her brother, "often taken for her twin, drew and colored."[53] Once after going to a play, she said, Edward fashioned a model theater; another time, after a family excursion to Coney Island, he built "a miniature pictorial fireworks display," patterned after one seen on the trip.[54] Theater would provide a field for his imagination all his life.

Even when he was "a tiny lad," Edward's gift was recognized and the family "gave him every encouragement," Marion remembered.[55] He began drawing at the age of five and for Christmas at age seven he received the blackboard that became his first easel.[56] He made cutout soldiers and decorated the cover of his paint box, which he inscribed prophetically "WOULD-BE ARTIST."

When he was about ten, he was given books or magazines of drawing instruction. For the next year or so, Edward diligently practiced drawing and shading geometric shapes, such as spheres and cylinders, and objects, such as vases, bowls, and boxes. Already these sketches in charcoal and white chalk

Edward Hopper, Three Birds on a Branch, *signed and dated May 23, 1893. Charcoal on paper, 9½ × 12¾″ (24.1 × 32.4 cm.).*

focus on the importance of light, a concern that remained important to him all his life. He also practiced drawing birds, horses, dogs, hunters, soldiers, guns, athletes, trains, boats, and bells in church towers. For school, he produced particularly competent drawings for geography and zoology classes.

Elizabeth Hopper also procured illustrated books and magazines to stimulate and shape her children's imaginations. A deluxe edition, *Masterpieces from the Works of Gustave Doré,* was one of Edward's treasures.[57] From Doré's illustration of *The Enchantment of Don Quixote,* Edward in his teens copied the head of the Don. His later depictions of Quixote on horseback may also have been inspired by this source.

Art supplies were never scarce in the Hopper home, thanks to a running charge account at Dutcher Brothers, the Nyack stationer. Elizabeth kept receipts for crayons, ink, chalk, paste, pens, pads of paper, and frames, as well as books and magazines: *Black Cat* (fiction), *Cosmopolitan, Delineator, Harper's* (for reprints of British literature), *Ladies' Home Journal, McClure's, Metropolitan, Munsey's, Quarterly Illustrator, St. Nicholas* (illustrated, for children), *Strand,* and *Puck* (weekly humor and social commentary).[58] The issue of *Puck* for November 13, 1889, contains doodles of heads in profile and the printed name "EDDIE."

By the age of ten, Edward was signing and dating drawings. The large quantity preserved testifies to his own enthusiasm and his mother's foresighted appreciation of talent. The drawings document a childhood that Hopper barely referred to in interviews and for which there are few written records. Some scenes show remarkable sophistication and anticipate style. A realistic rendition of brick shop fronts along North Broadway, with Callahan Brothers (the grocery store that the Hopper family patronized) and its delivery wagon, suggests the composition of his 1930 masterpiece, *Early Sunday Morning.* Hopper made a clear compositional choice of a long horizontal format, preferring to leave blank the bottom of the page rather than draw a square picture. A restaurant interior populated with diners and waiters suggests paintings of his maturity. Besides drawing, Hopper experimented with watercolor; one of a sailboat is signed and dated 1895, when he was thirteen. Using small pieces of ordinary paper he painted a range of subjects similar to his drawings: not only sailboats and ships, but also soldiers, trees, holly, a lion at play, a still life. By 1899, he had attained some command over the medium, managing to paint an aggressive soldier with a drawn gun and two ballet dancers. Around this time, he painted his father's portrait in gouache. The paternal figure looks a little scared.

A few amateurish attempts at oil painting also survive. Initially Hopper wanted to paint landscapes. At thirteen, he painted a rowboat moored in a cove, his first surviving signed and dated oil on canvas. In a later pen-and-ink sketch of his studio space in his boyhood home, he depicts his own painting of the old ice pond at Nyack on an easel with his paint box lying beneath it on the floor. Another oil, painted while he was still in high school, attempted a favorite subject of the early drawings, a sailing scene.

Hopper also experimented with ink as a medium. As early as 1895, he made a drawing of the British transatlantic steamship, the *Great Eastern.* He must have been motivated to try pen and ink by reading the illustrated magazines. Joseph Pennell, a popular illustrator, claimed that pen drawing, "as an art in itself," only began to flourish in America about 1880.[59] This was in part due to the development of a new photographic engraving process suitable for the reproduction of pen-and-ink drawings. Hopper emulated the technique as it appeared in magazines like *St. Nicholas, Puck, Harper's,* and the *Century.* He developed such facility with pen and ink that this alone might have suggested to his parents that he pursue a career as a commercial illustrator. From the drawing manuals and the popular illustrations in magazines and books, Edward absorbed the current repertoire of attitudes, styles and themes, along with late Victorian values. A Christmas gift from his father of toy soldiers in-

Edward Hopper, THERES TROUBLE COMIN', *1898. Pen and ink
on paper, 10 × 8" (25.4 × 20.3 cm.).*

spired him to cut out his own, painting them in careful detail in watercolor, and he would draw soldiers, often in action. Historic uniforms caught his eye and he conceived a particular fascination for American history. The War between the States had defined the collective memory of his father's generation;[60] Garret, born in 1852, had felt the repercussions at first hand, living through the terror and danger of the 1863 draft riots in New York, garnering memories to open the boy's eyes.[61] The war lived in documentary photographs and works of art, from Winslow Homer's illustrations and paintings to commemorative sculpture, also in public ceremonies and festive reenactments. Already by 1890, the event was "becoming a romantic memory."[62] Civil War monuments and museums and the photographs of Mathew Brady would interest Hopper in later years.

An American revolutionary soldier standing with his bayonet before the fire at an encampment appears in *At Valley Forge,* an especially competent drawing made by Hopper in 1895, aged thirteen, in which he took care to render accurately the folds in the soldier's coat and the wrinkles on his leggings.

In February 1898, when he was fifteen, Hopper was swept up in the wave of collective fervor caused by the sinking of the battleship *Maine,* which went down in Havana harbor with the loss of 266 men. Devouring headlines and illustrations, he used pen and ink for his own versions of the events that led to the Spanish-American War: *DESTRUCTION OF THE MAINE; FEBRUARY 15, 1898; HAVANA HARBOR; U.S.S. Maine;* and an image of Uncle Sam captioned *THERES [sic] TROUBLE COMIN'.* Thrilling to the patriotic rhetoric of President William McKinley and the brilliant naval displays, Hopper also portrayed *Shelling Havana.*

Less dramatically, Edward absorbed other contemporary preoccupations and prejudices. By the 1890s the country was sharply divided over its ability to assimilate the increasing influx of immigrants, and the debate also split the Baptists.[63] Stereotypes flourished, tending to depict a threat by alien and radical forces to a status quo represented as Anglo-Saxon, Protestant, and, *tout court,* the real America. This nativist ideology underlies Hopper's sketch of a grotesquely bearded, long-haired man, captioned *Anarchism* and resembling the popular stereotype of recent immigrants from Eastern Europe.[64] A similar ideology informs several other drawings of this period. In one he portrays eight male figures, endowed with exaggerated attributes of anatomy, dress, and occupation to suggest ethnic types. Others depict a Chinese man in a junk, Africans dancing around white men tied to a stake near a cooking pot, and stock scenes of African-American life.

Cultural stereotypes also surface in Edward's first surviving doggerel, which is cast in language that echoes hymns from church and lessons from Sunday school:

Edward Hopper, Anarchism, *1899. Pen and ink on paper, (detail on sheet) 9⅞ × 7¾" (25.1 × 19.7 cm.).*

On the Late Chinese War

A pagan race may downward trod the path to hell
While from their multitudinous throats there swell
A hoarse cry raised in boistrous praise
Of images of brass and stone
But can the Christian race with fire and sword
Choke down their throats the Gospel of our Lord
The wrath of God will surely fall on these presumptious puppets
Who bestow their iconsistant efforts on the heathen horde.
[below are sketches of three heads with Chinese features][65]

Alluding to Chinese resistance to foreign domination in the 1890s, which culminated in the Boxer rebellion of 1900, Edward uses religious jargon versified, subversively and awkwardly groping his way through jingoism toward the irony of a skeptic.[66]

Irony and satire become a characteristic mode, evident in numerous drawings. The new vogue of the bicycle quickly caught Hopper's eye and inspired satire: a woman speeds out of control toward the viewer; typically for Hopper danger comes in female guise. Satirizing himself, he sketched a couple courting, with the caption *LANDSCAPE AFTER HOPPER,* alluding to

Edward Hopper, Eight Male Figures of Different Nationalities and Occupations, *c. 1897. Pencil on paper, 10 × 8″ (25.4 × 20.3 cm.).*

himself ironically with the formula reserved for old masters. Portraying courtship again, he used the caption "A Snapshot," showing an early and timely awareness of photography: "snap shot" referred to hand-held photography and first came into use around 1890. He made a satirical drawing of a man posing for a photograph at the studio of "Prof. Meryon Clark Hypo Durkee Esq."

Hopper's prankish sense of humor frequently surfaces, encouraged by his love for the cartoons of the popular British caricaturist Philip May. The scene of a baseball player at bat is captioned *THIS IS A COMIC PICTURE* and another, of a catcher in a mask, repeats this assertion and commands, "You must laugh." Humorously he combines scientific awareness with ethnic prejudice in a sketch from 1899: a man with simian features, dressed in a suit and top hat, looks at a monkey in a cage at the zoo. The caption reads: "Pat— And they say we're descended from those beasts, faith! I don't see any resemblance." The name Pat invokes the stereotype of the Irish Catholics, who were among the most recent immigrants in Nyack. For its punch the joke depends upon Darwin and takes sides in the conflict between religious fundamentalism, from Sunday school, and the mounting scientific fervor for Darwin's theories, coming down humorously on the side of secular knowledge. Human beings with simian features appear also in other humorous sketches he made at the time.

Knowledge of Darwin might reinforce negative stereotypes of women. Readers of *The Descent of Man* encounter such statements as "Man is more powerful in body and mind than woman, and in the savage state he keeps her in a far more abject state of bondage than does the male of any other animal."[67] Darwin also asserted that men have a "greater intellectual vigor and power of invention" than women.[68]

If ideas of male superiority were in the air, they could hardly be taken for granted in the Hopper ménage. Edward's father was not in charge. Frequently he found reason to be at the store or at church, leaving his son alone in a household in which he was overwhelmed by females: his mother, his sister, his grandmother, and the maid. When the presence of all these women became too threatening, Edward would retreat to read or draw in the solitary retreats of his bedroom or the attic. When he resorted to his insensitive pranks, his targets were often female, suggesting equal parts of resentment at domination and desire to be noticed. These were patterns he never outgrew.

Out of the disparity between male and female roles in the Hopper household came some remarkable examples of Edward's joking vein. Satirical sketches, made at about fourteen, show first a thin, weak man with a beard fending off a stout woman; then the thin man submitting with evident reluctance to the woman's smothering embrace; and finally, the man in flight, pur-

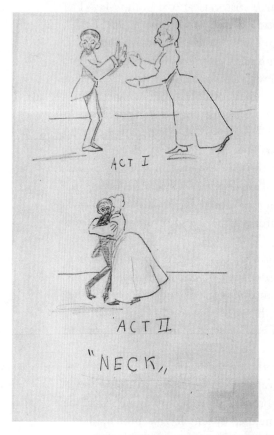 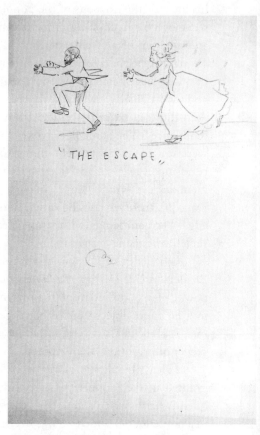

Edward Hopper, ACT I, ACT II NECK, THE ESCAPE, *c. 1896.*
Pencil on paper.

sued by the woman with arms outstretched, over the captions *ACT I, ACT II NECK, THE ESCAPE.* The images caricature Hopper's parents and the narrative conveys his adolescent sense of an imbalanced and threatening relationship between male and female. His mother represents both attraction to and fear of the demonstrative and domineering female, while his father foreshadows the insecure, retiring male he himself became.

Another cartoon narrative, *A Misinterpreted Command,* represents Mrs. Henpeck instructing her husband: "Now John, I'm going out and I'll leave the fire in your hands." Her husband, identified as Mr. Henpeck, timidly replies: "Oh, no, you'd better leave it in the stove." Again the images record contemporary stereotypes while suggesting specifically Hopper's observation and experience at home.

In a similar vein, he produced a card for his father captioned *MERRY CHRISTMAS POP,* with a pen-and-ink drawing of Garret in great surprise at his gift, a quill pen. The paternal figure stands awkwardly, wearing house slippers with his suit, his hair shaggy and disheveled on his balding head, weak and even pathetic.

These caricatures make clear that Hopper's male role model lacked the authority expected by the culture and the son. His parents' inversion of psychological roles may have caused him to resent willful women. But in the end, like his father, he was drawn to an outgoing woman like his mother, whose garrulous personality contrasted with his own introversion.

§

HOPPER'S SENIOR CLASS produced a newspaper, *The Graduate,* which trumpeted itself: the seniors of 1899 in Nyack High School far exceeded "in number [seventeen] and in scholarship any graduating class in former years." Nyack was "one of the eight best high schools in the 'Empire State' " and boasted twenty-nine faculty members. In the issue for March 1899, G. H. Hopper Dry Goods ran an ad. Edward served on the advertising committee. In fact the school's programs were limited. Sports were not offered. Hopper had a rowing machine and a punching bag at home in the attic where he sometimes played with friends. (With one, Ralph Bedell, he also used to draw.)

Repeatedly in these years Hopper painted and sketched himself. These self-portraits, often in the form of rather casually executed caricatures, reveal much about his personality, self-image, and concerns. In one drawing, on a sheet together with two sketches of boxers, he portrays himself with a grim expression, bent over and dressed in boyish knickers, as if he had not grown up, standing awkwardly with large ungainly feet. In another, his thin lanky body resembles a pole supporting a cylindrical neck supporting his head, with large ears protruding in an ungainly manner and his arm extended at an angle. This caricature is placed in the middle of a sheet crowded with other male images, including a shepherd with his staff, a man with a sword, a native with a spear, a policeman with a drawn gun. Only the awkward scrawny figure in the center seems helpless, without a weapon to face the world.

Throughout his youth Hopper represented himself with homely, distorted features, indicating his dislike of his thick lips and large ears. He also appears as a skinny, ungraceful nude with stooped shoulders, seated on the edge of a tub or pool. When he appears riding a bicycle, his figure is struggling and scrawny. But he repeated this theme, indicating that he could work up speed, and rewarded himself for the workout with a halo, the conventional symbol of virtuousness that would become a staple in his portrayals of himself in situations of conflict.

When he graduated from high school in 1899, he sketched himself in pen and ink: clad in cap and gown and holding his diploma, he walks out the door representing the security of home toward a distant mountain labeled "FAME." A caption reads, *OUT INTO THE COLD WORLD.* Once again he resorts to the style of caricature and to stereotypical themes in seeking to express his own complex emotions. His confidence in his talent induces him to use pictorial means to express inner conflict. The sketch reveals that in the moment of passage, his mind is set on the ambition raised and justified by his experience of art, even while insecurity dictates reference to the risk. His artistic talent, discovered and nurtured in the home, had already proved a refuge and a resource. Now it pointed him outward beyond the community that was so familiar and assuring, yet narrow and inhibiting. His feelings show again in another sketch on the same sheet, in a frontal self-portrait with an anxious, wrinkled brow under the mortarboard of the graduate.

Hopper longed to be an artist, but he had to contend with his parents' fears for his future security. His father's own failure in business did not instill confidence. His mother, although cultivated and aware of his talent, was anxious and over-protective. She knew how much their tenor of life depended on her resources and feared the father's fecklessness in the son. Both parents implored Edward to go to school for illustration. Mindful of economic risk, forgetful of the confident enterprise of Elizabeth's own grandfather in his adopted land, they counseled the route made familiar by myriad books and journals. Virtues stamped with prudence and predicated on mediocrity prevailed. Edward was prey to the same considerations, haunted by his father's inability and dependence, in no position to be certain of his powers. Doubt and the history of failure wrote frustration and depression into the script from the start.

DEFINING THE TALENT: 1899–1906

IN THE FALL OF 1899, Hopper began formal training at the New York School of Illustrating. The school has left scant trace in the annals of American art, apart from advertisements on crumbling pages of old magazines. Hopper's receipts for the monthly ten-dollar fee took their place with the childhood sketches and keepsakes treasured in the attic. His parents paid the bills and conditioned the choice. Rearing him, they had provided art supplies and illustrated magazines to stimulate and shape his imagination. That very cultural opening came back to delimit their horizon, narrowing their vision of where talent like their son's might lead.

Clues to what the Hoppers wanted to obtain by sending Edward to a school for illustration can be gathered from the surviving advertisements. The hopes dangled and the expertise professed belong to the eternal come-ons of commercial colleges, even while they document the lively image market in late Victorian America.

Just when Edward was graduating from high school, the issue of *Brush and Pencil* for June 1899 carried an advertisement featuring a youth in bow tie with pad and pens:

CORRESPONDENCE SCHOOL
OF ILLUSTRATING

LEARN TO DRAW BY MAIL

Home instruction in drawing for newspapers and magazines by successful illustrators. Requires spare time only. Adapted to young and
old, men and women, beginners and advanced students. An opportunity to enter a highly profitable profession. No such practical instruction given elsewhere. By our methods students have become
well-known illustrators.

Full information free.[1]

During the summer, the school had changed location and expanded to offer
classes in-house.[2] It advertised again in September in the *International Studio*
with a new name and different spiel:

N.Y. SCHOOL OF ILLUSTRATING

teaches drawing for newspapers, magazines, books. Practical instruction in all modern methods.

Instructors: CHAS. HOPE PROVOST (known as a contribu-
tor to *Life, Truth, Scribner's, N.Y. Herald, St. Nicholas,* etc.); M. DE
LIPMAN (former Art Editor *N.Y. Journal,* and contributor to *N.Y.
Herald*); R. L. CURRAN (photography contributor to *Cosmopolitan,
Truth, Illustrated American,* etc.); MISS JANIE ZIMMER (pupil of
W. L. Metcalf, Douglas Volk, and Francis C. Jones).

Classes day and evening. No such practical teaching elsewhere.
Call or write for full information.

N.Y. SCHOOL OF ILLUSTRATING
114 West 34th Street, New York[3]

Hopper's receipts bear the school's old name and new address. He enrolled by the month for lessons "Every Day," returning each evening to the
house on North Broadway, taking the ferry to Hoboken and the train to
Nyack.[4] The family took the school at face value. It sounded like a way into
the world they knew from print. Nothing in Nyack prepared them to consider
that this faculty was not in fact big-time. An ad in *Scribner's Magazine* October
1899 issue states that the "School is [the] outgrowth of illustrating classes
formed seven years ago by Mr. Chas. Hope Provost."[5] Further outgrowth
came in the form of books, *A Treatise on How to Illustrate for Newspapers,
Books, Magazines, etc.* (1903) and *Simplified Illustrating* (1911),[6] which describes
the methods Provost used and Hopper met in school: "Practise sheets similar
to those which accompany this text book were devised by me in 1893, and first

used in my classes then located at 9 West 14th Street, New York City. . . . A part of my program for each student's work is liberal practise-sheet training."[7] Provost advised the would-be illustrator to copy carefully a number of charts, and himself boasted he had "drawn thousands of illustrations" for many magazines, including *Harper's Monthly, Harper's Weekly, Vogue, Ainslee's,* and *Ladies World.*[8]

The 1903 book addressed the "Commercial Side of Illustration," returning to a favorite theme of its author: "Commercial art is extremely profitable when treated as a business."[9] Profit was a proven selling point, worth repeating. "A highly profitable profession" was what Provost advertised in June of 1899. Yet the profit motive does not grip everyone, as even Provost is forced to admit: "To many students of an extremely artistic temperament all commercial work is distasteful. They should try the publishers." That would not satisfy the likes of Edward Hopper. Whatever practice sheets and charts might give him technically, the school's most valuable lesson was a more precise understanding of the nature and implication of his gift. Illustration school taught him that commercial work was as alien to his natural bent as business was to his father's. With growing self-knowledge came resentment that lingered and surfaced at a great remove. In the 1930s Hopper confided the story of his departure from home and initial disappointment with rare openness to a supporter of his work, Homer Saint-Gaudens, director of the Department of Fine Arts at the Carnegie Institute. According to Saint-Gaudens: "So continuously did he draw, that after graduation from high school his parents sent him to a commercial art establishment in New York City. That gave scant satisfaction."[10]

The later memory of discontent must be weighed against the signs of what engaged Hopper at the time. It was the "Golden Age" of illustration, when the most famous practitioners commanded impressive fees. The paragon of illustrators caught his fancy: he made a pen-and-ink sketch of Charles Dana Gibson, palette in hand, elegantly attired.[11]

Themes suitable for publishers predominate in his earliest work. He had copied an illustration by Doré for Coleridge's "The Rime of the Ancient Mariner"; now he sketched other literary characters in pen and ink: from Dickens, the simple-minded youth in *Barnaby Rudge,* Fagin and Oliver in *Oliver Twist,* Tulkinghorn the inscrutable lawyer in *Bleak House*, and Sydney Carton in *A Tale of Two Cities;* from Conan Doyle, the hero of *The Exploits of Brigadier Gerard;* from Hawthorne's *The Scarlet Letter,* the adulterous Hester Prynne. He penciled an illustration for Thomas Hood's poem "The Bridge of Sighs," about a young woman's suicide. He also sketched from his old favorites Kipling and Hugo as well as from Ibsen and Cervantes.

Less likely to represent assignments, other sketches show devils' heads with the caption "Studies for Devil in 'Miser,'" although Satan is not a character in the Molière drama. Hopper expands on the devil theme with a small, boldly colored panel in oil, signed and dated 1900: a meditative figure, chin reflectively on one hand, is dressed in accordance with old German tradition, all in red, with a cape of stiff silk and a cock's feather in his cap, a long pointed sword barely visible in the other hand. Surrounded by a hint of flames, this Mephistopheles image suggests nothing so much as a drawing for the theater, perhaps for Goethe's *Faust,* which came to be seen as emblematic of German Romantic consciousness. Hopper later refers to Goethe (one of Emerson's "representative men") as a writer whose ideas shaped his aesthetics.

Even while honing techniques in the city, Hopper continued to sketch ordinary settings at home. Working in graphite or ink, he drew a woman in a rocking chair, the house on North Broadway, Smith's dock, a colonial tombstone, a cat boat that he saw in neighboring Piermont, more studies of boats, rocks, and buildings in the landscape, and sketches of his family and friends. In the spring of 1900 he also experimented with ink wash, for him a new medium, one that was gaining currency with some illustrators and might be expected in an up-to-date school. Ink wash, like painting, could be reproduced by the new process of printing from a half-tone screen and seemed to some an easier alternative to the exacting discipline of line. Although Hopper had no fear of line drawing, he used wash to depict a music box, a revolver, a satchel, a figure of a boy, and a United States naval vessel, the *Ship of the Great White Fleet.* The latter he rendered in loving detail, characteristic of the boy who grew up around boats and remembered the *Maine* in youthful drawings. He continued to take pride in the new fleet, which was modernized under the expansionist presidency of McKinley and painted white in a boast of power to the world.

With his penchant for caricature, Hopper should have heard willingly the views on "humor in art" of the school's head, Provost, who later wrote:

> Broadly speaking, all humorous art is exaggeration of nature. A little lengthening of line, a little shortening of that one, an almost imperceptible twist to a curve—these and similar devices make what is called a caricature. But—these intentional deviations from nature must be guided by a brain that has a true conception of humor; and the hand that draws a caricature must first learn to draw an object as it is. Copying the works of comic artists of ability will help to give an insight into approved methods of caricaturing.[12]

With or without such advice, Hopper found an able comic artist and began to copy. The brilliant English illustrator Phil May drew *East End Loafers* for the Christmas number of the *Century* magazine for 1899.[13] Soon after, one of

May's three down-and-out male figures before a shop front was copied by Hopper, who also acquired *Phil May's Sketchbook* with fifty cartoons;[14] likewise he made two pen-and-ink sketches entitled *Phil May's Singer,* depicting a scruffy street musician.

When Hopper returned home for the summer he selected and delineated local sights in precise sketches that suggest the effect of "liberal practise-sheet" training: *The Creek at Hogencamps, Old Church on New City Road, Deserted House on Mountain,* and *Camp Nyack, Greenwood Lake.* He also ventured a naturalistic watercolor of the most famous and grandiose local landmark, *Hook Mountain, Nyack.* Looming above the Tappan Zee, the promontory had inspired an ambitious oil by Sanford Robinson Gifford in 1866. Other grand vistas nearby were painted with similarly romantic vision during the second half of the century by Albert Bierstadt, who lived and worked just across the river from Nyack in Irvington-on-Hudson. Widely reproduced in the illustrated press, the Hudson River painters formed part of the visual culture that permeated the Hopper home. Their vision must have been in Edward's mind as he viewed their scenes. Gifford's calm view of the double peak above the water emphasized light and atmosphere, looking south from Haverstraw Bay. Hopper looked north from Nyack, centering his composition not on the double peaks but on a bare rock face: against the light rock a dark smokestack stands out, above a mill with dark windows. Below, trestles and hints of works and docks invade the green slopes and encroach on the river. Typically, he undercuts the romantic.

Choosing to draw at Greenwood Lake, Hopper invited comparison with another Hudson River painter. Jasper Cropsey, whose home overlooked the Tappan Zee, had painted the lake in the 1860s. When Hopper camped there with friends, he recorded the experience in drawings: two show the tent and campsite in meticulous detail, with a bicycle wheel suspended in the tent, cans littering the foreground, milk crate benches, and laundry hung out to dry. A third sketch (at the end of the letter he wrote home) shows not only the campsite, but the way home. Beneath the caption *ON THE WATCH,* Hopper depicts his father sitting on the roof of the house squinting through a telescope, spying on his son. The boys stayed out for a week or more: his mother preserved a fungus on which he inscribed: "Edward Hopper, Camp Nyack, Greenwood Lake, N.Y., July 24, 1900." Two days later he wrote his earliest surviving letter:

Dear Mama,
In the first place it's raining "to beat the band," which prevents us from going outside very much and that is why I am writing for I said I should not. I am feeling well and having a good time and have

Edward Hopper, Camp Nyack, Greenwood Lake, *1900. Pen and ink on paper,*
9½ × 13¾″ (24.1 × 34.9 cm.).

plenty of clothes and underwear, having worn my underclothes in
the lake yesterday which was a regular washday for us.

On Tuesday, while some of us were out in the woods, I found a
beautiful fungus as white as snow and have scratched my name on it.
We have been fishing but have had poor luck. We have only had one
mess of fish since we came and they were rather small.[15]

At eighteen, Hopper still felt under surveillance. His mother had wanted reports. He had resisted. Rain persuades where she could not: characteristic but
hardly gracious. He knows the topics mothers want, health and hygiene, underwear. To judge from the sketch, the garment washed in the swim was
striped.

Among the friends who camped that summer at Greenwood Lake was
Wallace Tremper, who in his own way was to deal with the transformations
of the early twentieth century more deftly than Hopper, going from black-
smith to plumber and finally to gas station operator in Nyack.[16] Hopper portrayed Wallace and himself boxing in a format inspired very directly by Phil
May, who had lampooned himself boxing in his *Record of the Famous Fight
between Phil May and Fatty Coleman,* setting his own scrawny, awkward figure against Coleman's rotund brawn.[17] Hopper made a like sketch of himself
taking a beating from the more muscular Tremper. Hopper's body is long

and skinny, his posture awkward and graceless, his face delicate but distorted with a fearful grimace. Tremper's belly bulges out over his boxer shorts, while Hopper's striped shorts are ornamented with a flowerlike bow suggesting effeminate qualities. A variant shows the virile Tremper with his strong right arm scoring a knockout as Hopper falls to the floor. Again a comic narrative expresses a deep truth about Hopper's emotional life and, here, his insecurity about himself.

The year in the city had sharpened Edward's awareness of his natural bent and of the art scene. In the fall of 1900 he persuaded his parents to let him transfer to a much more famous and distinguished school, which offered a full range of instruction not only in commercial but also in fine art. They agreed to pay fifteen dollars a month, half again as much as before. Edward, for his part, would continue to study illustration. But now the next step would be shorter. The examples with which he was beginning to identify would be close at hand. The New York School of Art was on the second floor of a ramshackle brick building at 57 West Fifty-seventh Street, at the northeast corner of Sixth Avenue. Founded as the Chase School by the painter William Merritt Chase, in 1900 it was owned and run by Douglas John Con-

Edward Hopper, Edward Hopper Boxing with Wallace Tremper, *1900. Pen and ink on paper.*

nah, a painter who worked in a style strongly influenced by Chase. Admission required no tests, an exceptional laxity. Anyone familiar with drawing would be eligible for the painting class. Beginning students worked immediately from life rather than from classic works in plaster casts. Drawing and color were taught together. The whole thrust was antiacademic. By comparison with more staid academies, the place was boisterous, even chaotic. When the instructors were not in the studio, the students boxed with the models; ran races while seated on chairs, hopping about the room; and chinned themselves on the lintels.[18] New students could enroll at any time of year as long as space was available in the dilapidated studios. Unsuspecting entrants were greeted by whistling, singing, smoking, and teasing classmates. A former student recalled:

> One of the peculiarities of the Chase School is a Bohemian way they have of wiping palate scrapings at the end of the day on the walls, and sometimes on the chairs. The paint is two inches thick from floor to the highest a man can reach, most of it dry, but you can never tell. It is in great close velvety gobs, laid on by the knife full and indeed a curious sight to a stranger and every Chase student has an accidental patch of red paint on the brow of his pants.[19]

Vivacity and pranks went hand in hand with serious work. The school held regular public *concours* and student exhibitions. Every year there were ten free tuition scholarships, five each for men and women. Cash prizes for the best studies in the several classes were also handed out monthly.

A remarkable number of Hopper's classmates went on to make names more or less vivid in the story of twentieth-century American art: Guy Pène du Bois, George Bellows, Rockwell Kent, Glenn O. Coleman, Gifford Beal, Homer Boss, Arnold Friedman, Walter Pach, C. K. Chatterton, Carl Sprinchorn, Edmund William Graecen, Randall Davey, Walter Tittle, Patrick Henry Bruce, Clarence Coles Phillips, and Eugene Speicher. A much younger student, Webb P. Hollenbeck, then called Robin, or sometimes "Robin Red Nose," became the actor Clifton Webb.[20] Another, Vachel Lindsay, took the advice of the popular teacher Robert Henri and gave up painting for poetry, although he continued to illustrate his own poems.[21]

Illustration was taught by Arthur Ignatius Keller, whose realistic figure sketches emphasized character, unlike Hopper's work before this time. Keller, renowned for the brilliant facility of his technique, had trained in New York at the National Academy of Design and in Munich at the Alte Akademie. He created an impression of spontaneity through the judicious use of passages of light and tonal subtlety. Also, Keller had published an illustration in the issue of *Century* magazine from which Hopper copied Phil May.[22] Hopper's work of this period makes it clear that Keller's students focused on the figure, sketching costumed models as an aid to their imagination and to improve their drawing. Hopper had already begun to study anatomy seriously, concentrating on just one part of the body, such as a hand or a foot. He also investigated the drawings of Vesalius. A fellow student recorded his impression of Hopper as "tall, big-boned and solemn, but with nice flashes of dry humor."[23] Clarence K. Chatterton, known as Chat, was a classmate in illustration, two years older than Edward and a "tall and good looking"[24] young man, also from along the Hudson, at Newburgh, New York. Chatterton recalled that Hopper looked up to him like an older brother, always sitting next to him in class.

Another year passed before Hopper developed the further self-confidence and awareness to make the leap from illustration to painting. The intensity of his newly acquired resolve emerges from an anecdote told by Chatterton, who was still training as an illustrator. One day late in the fall of 1901, Hopper came into the class where Chatterton was drawing and handed him a palette and brushes: "It's time you started to paint."[25] For one of Hopper's timidity and reserve, it was an enormous self-revelation and commitment. He could do no less than share his own new sense of higher purpose with the man who had come to fill the place in his affections of the brother he never had. Hopper's determination so impressed Chatterton that he accepted the challenge. He became a painter and a lifelong friend.

In that period at the school, fine arts students chose from a range of teachers, all of whom deferred to Chase as the founder and leading teacher. Other faculty members included J. Carroll Beckwith and F. Luis Mora, both of whom, like Chase, taught drawing and painting, and Frank Vincent du Mond, who taught painting and composition. Beckwith's name is inscribed on one of Hopper's early drawings of a female nude, perhaps because he assisted Chase and may have taught one of Hopper's classes in Chase's absence. Hopper's favorite teacher was Kenneth Hayes Miller, with whom he studied drawing.

Chase was Hopper's first teacher in painting. Born in Indiana, but trained at the Royal Academy in Munich, Chase commanded admiration as "the leading spirit and chief instructor" at the school, to which he brought his European urbanity.[26] In February 1901, Chase, then fifty-two, claimed to have three hundred students, about sixty percent of whom were women. He insisted that he warned his students: "Shake off the influence of the school as quickly as you can. Cultivate individuality. Strive to express your own environment according to your own lights, in your own way."[27] He explained: "Many students stay too long in art school . . . The average period of study is about three years. . . . Not more than one-tenth of the art students follow art as a life career, and this, perhaps, is just as well."[28] He felt that a student needed art school only to gain technique and mechanical facility. Hopper, heartened by prizes and scholarships, stayed six years, twice what Chase prescribed.

The great man "was always impeccably dressed—white carnation in his lapel buttonhole, pearl-grey vest, his tie run through a ring, spats," Chatterton recalled.[29] Every Monday, Chase gave a public evaluation of all the students' work in a large studio, and once a month, he painted a study from the model in front of his students as a "practical demonstration of his method."[30] Chatterton called Chase's criticisms "theatrical triumphs" and noted: "He punctuated his remarks by running his fingers through his large moustache while he gazed intently at the student whose work he was considering through glasses, or a monocle which hung around his neck on a wide black ribbon. He was a great showman, and he had a great following. The women, particularly, hung on his every word."[31] Chase accompanied his students on occasional visits to the Metropolitan Museum of Art, where he hoped that they would be inspired. Vachel Lindsay told how Chase implored students to go to the galleries at least once a month.[32] They also went to exhibitions held nearby at the Lenox Library, which in the fall of 1903 was showing Japanese prints and Whistler etchings.[33] These excursions are documented by Hopper's sketches of three men in a museum gallery carefully studying the paintings.

Sculpture, too, caught Hopper's attention. Most of the figures he sketched were in the cast gallery, then a permanent installation at the Metropolitan. His eye fell on the *Heracles* from the east pediment of the Parthenon, the *Laocoön*, Lysippos's *Apoxyomenos,* Boëthus's *Boy Strangling a Goose,* the Venus de Milo, the Apollo Belvedere, Michelangelo's *David* and his *Moses,* Johann Dannecker's *Ariadne,* Thorvaldsen's *Venus,* and Rodin's *La Vieille Femme.* He also sketched from reproductions in art books that he bought, particularly *Masters of Art,* the inexpensive magazinelike series then popular. Hopper even copied part of the letterhead of this series on one of his drawings.

Chase defended the need to assimilate the advances made by others: "Absolute originality in art can only be found in a man who has been locked in a dark room from babyhood. . . . Since we are dependent on others, let us frankly and openly take in all that we can. . . . The man who does that with judgment will produce an original picture that will have value."[34] And he encouraged his students to synthesize and adapt motifs from famous works of art, advising: "Study a few pictures at a time and try to understand them and find out what you most like in them. I should not mind you imitating the master whose work most pleases you, in order to find out what you like in it and try to do it yourself."[35]

In line with Chase's teaching, Hopper produced a number of sketches after other artists, revealing a wide range of interests and a student's open-minded curiosity. He sketched details more often than the entire work, attempting to understand better whatever features interested him most. His sources were old masters, such as Hals, Rubens, and Velázquez; he also found the nineteenth-century artists appealing. His taste included both academics such as Sir Edwin Landseer, Henri Alexandre Georges Regnault, Mariano Fortuny y Carbo, and Frederick Lord Leighton, and more vanguard artists such as Edouard Manet. Hopper even used oil to copy Manet's *Woman with a Parrot,* instead of the usual pen or pencil sketches, which he made of Manet's *The Fifer* and *Olympia.* He also sketched Jean-François Millet's *Man with a Hoe,* which was much reproduced at the time. With his characteristic wit, Hopper combined elements of Ingres's *Comtesse d'Haussonville* with Manet's *Bar at the Folies-Bergères* into a single sketch of Miss Flora McFlimsey, a character from a popular poem of the pre–Civil War period. That Chase influenced Hopper by example, too, is evident in Hopper's earliest student paintings. Chase painted in an elegant realist style, characterized by broad sweeping brush strokes with a loaded paintbrush, achieving surface virtuosity. He taught separate life classes for men and women, where students drew and painted from nude models, although male models wore loincloths when posing for women. Chase held portrait and still-life classes where students worked from costume models or set-ups. He liked to show that he could limn a fish so rapidly that it could go back, still fresh, to the market around the corner when he was done. Students labored over less perishable objects such as copper pots and ceramic jugs, contrasting the textures and degrees of surface reflection. In 1903, Hopper painted a series of still lifes for Chase, who reminded students that "it is not the subject, but what the painter makes of his subject that constitutes great painting."[36]

An untitled oil portrait of a young girl from this period must represent Chase's daughter Dorothy, whom her father portrayed in a similar pose about 1902. Either she posed in class, or Hopper copied Chase's work. Hopper also painted a fellow student before her easel in what must be an observation from Chase's class in portrait and still life. Observed unaware from behind, this young blonde is painted with elegance worthy of one of Chase's depictions of women in interiors.

While studying with Chase and Miller, Hopper produced many drawings. In 1901, he frequently drew clothed and costumed models: American Indians, a chef, and figures wearing various historical garb. He drew the nude models in life classes over and over again. One favorite male model, Jimmy Corsi, boasted of his heroic poses for John Singer Sargent at the Boston Public Library.[37] Hopper drew him both nude and costumed as a fisherman or a historical figure, also portraying him in rather somber oils. Hopper's work on anatomical details and figures in movement reflects his conscientious attention to specific classroom exercises.

It was in 1902 at the school that Hopper made his first prints—his only monotypes ever—probably after seeing monotype portraits by Chase, who may have had his students try the medium in class. Chase felt strongly about the communion of the brain and the hand and stressed the spontaneity necessary for this technique. Monotype, in which the image is painted, rubbed, or wiped in a slow-drying oil paint or ink directly on a metal or glass plate and printed before it dries, is not really compatible with Hopper's very deliberate way of working. His five surviving monotypes, all portraits on small scraps of paper or discarded envelopes, appear to have been experiments quickly forgotten. Fashion in the art world shifted and Chase's work came to be viewed as regressive by the time Hopper matured. Hence he often omitted mentioning that he had ever studied with Chase. In a rare reference, the lanky, diffident, laconic, and misogynistic pupil dryly undercut the short swaggering master, whose talk was said to be as dazzling as his demeanor: "Men didn't get much from Chase. There were mostly women in the class."[38]

Hopper's shift to painting had marked a decisive break with his past, and life in that free society encouraged other developments as well. Only two years after his transfer to the New York School, he found himself in a position to make fun of someone more provincial than himself. Walter Tittle, a year younger than Hopper, came from farther away and from an even more controlling background. Tittle's father in Springfield, Ohio, presumed to require what never crossed the mind of the meek Garret Hopper. Tittle was constrained to apply to Douglas Connah, as head of the school, for a special dispensation to take the life class only when a male model was posing.[39] No sketches of nude women, like those that went to take their place among the boyish sketches and the receipts stored up in Nyack, were wanted back in Ohio. Edward's reaction to this contretemps gained him what was perhaps his first entry in a diary: for on October 28, 1902, Walter recorded:

Hopper, at school today, got up a verse about me this afternoon.

> There was a young fellow named Tittle
> Who worked in the life-class a little
>   When a female they hired,
>   he quickly retired—
> Back, back to the woods, Mr. Tittle.[40]

In his younger schoolmate Hopper recognized and ridiculed values that he himself was in the process of rejecting, not without the inevitable conflict.

Among all the riotous students, Hopper's intensity prompted the words that Tittle recorded. Limericks are to poetry as caricature is to art. Here again Hopper resorts to a reductive form when touched in a deep nerve.

Adjusting to life classes may have been unsettling for Hopper. Just getting it right with male anatomy was challenging enough, but female models provided his first view of a woman without clothes. Flesh was not exposed in Baptist circles in Nyack. Something of what the young men felt and talked about among themselves may be gathered from Guy Pène du Bois, Hopper's schoolmate, confidant, and lifelong friend, who described his own shock at first sketching a female nude: "His face was hot, and he knew, with a feeling of desperation, that it was redder than it had ever been before in his life. He could have stood this better, he thought, with fewer men in the room, but without any others he could not have stayed at all." On returning home in a flurry, du Bois blurted to his mother: "I know how you look when you are undressed."[41]

In the fall of 1902, as Hopper started his third year at the school, he was about to encounter a new teacher who would give new definition to his ideas about art and, incidentally, prolong his stay in school. In November Frank Vincent du Mond moved across Fifty-seventh Street to the Art Students League. He was replaced by Robert Henri, then thirty-seven, who had trained in Philadelphia at the Pennsylvania Academy of the Fine Arts, under Thomas Anshutz, a disciple of Thomas Eakins, and had also studied and worked in Europe. Tall, broad-shouldered, casually dressed, Henri taught life classes, portraits, and composition, and made himself exceedingly popular with his students. Warm personally, he advised them to study the life around them and to express forthrightly their own ideas. Stressing that art should communicate character and emotions, he emphasized a philosophy of aesthetics more than the craft of painting or drawing.

"Completely overturned the apple cart: displaced art by life, discarded technic, broke the prevailing gods as easily as brittle porcelain," wrote du Bois, who underscored Henri's challenge to the reigning philosophy and master with metaphors of revolution.[42] Henri's class was "the seat of the sedition among the young. Chase . . . preached art for art's sake; Henri, art for life's sake. The difference was monumental."[43] When the newcomer delivered his first criticism in class on November 7, Walter Tittle exclaimed: "He is simply burning with art enthusiasm and is the most original man I've yet had as an instructor. He talks in a forceful and animated manner, and can be heard all over the room."[44]

From the start, Henri taught his "Special Composition Class," devoted "to a critical study of the principles of pictorial and decorative composition, with a view to their practical application in painting, illustrating, and designing." The course also covered "the theory and history of art."[45] In his portrait class, Henri, according to Vachel Lindsay, "paints the face of a portrait all through in half an hour—but does it over and over ten or thirty times till he has mastered every passing expression of the sitter's countenance—then at the last moment he dashes in the expression that he thinks the profoundest expression of the sitter's personality."[46] Henri demanded "force, likeness, and life" in the portraits the students produced.[47]

In spite of the perceived revolution, Henri shared much with Chase. Both admired Manet. Henri encouraged his students to study Manet's *Woman with a Parrot* and *Boy with a Sword* at the Metropolitan Museum, where he, like Chase, often took groups of students. He also stressed that Manet had admired Velázquez, Goya, and Hals. Hopper recalled: "At the Chase school we had painted like Manet. Henri was a great admirer of Manet and Manet had been influenced by the Spaniards, flat, low tones, dark."[48]

Henri resembled Chase, too, in using somber colors with painterly brushstrokes reminiscent of Manet's work, which he praised: "Manet's stroke was ample, full, and flowed with a gracious continuity, was never flip or clever. His 'Olympia' has a supreme elegance."[49] Henri also agreed with Chase in encouraging spontaneity of paint application. Du Bois, who served as the class monitor, recalled that Henri "forbade his students the use of small brushes."[50] This prohibition ultimately helped Hopper to develop a style of painting in which he grouped large masses of forms, emphasizing figure-ground relationships.

Henri's presence soon affected the direction of Hopper's student work. Although Hopper did not make radical changes in subject matter, he never again returned to the still lifes Chase stressed. He continued to make portraits of models and friends such as du Bois, often depicting his fellow students at their easels. He also continued to paint oils that portray nude models shown seated or standing on the classroom platform. Henri instructed his students that the purpose of studying from the model was "mainly to get experience," explaining, "Your composition is the expression of your interests and in making your composition you apply what you learn when working from the model."[51]

Even after Henri's arrival, Hopper continued to paint with the somber palette he had developed under Chase, including when he chose subjects outside of the classroom, such as his men in an orchestra pit (which clearly borrows its composition, but not its palette, from the work of Edgar Degas). Hopper also painted several pictures of his bedroom in Nyack, a lone figure in a dimly lit theater interior, as well as colorless views of a ferry slip and sailboats. Henri had taught his students to experiment with "black and white modeling," explaining that it "was largely practiced by the old masters who relieved themselves of a double difficulty by building up their pictures in monochrome and later applying glazes of transparent color. Form was almost wholly dependent on the monochrome substructure."[52] Life in Henri's classes, however, was anything but somber. Henri did not seem to mind student pranks as long as he was not present. In his men's life class, a custom evolved that upon the arrival of a student new to the school, he would be goaded into treating the entire class to a beer and cheese party. There was also an elaborate charade in which one older student pretended to be Henri himself, variously commenting on the students' work only to lavish elaborate encomiums on the neophyte's tentative drawing.[53] The pretender would then look at the drawing of the best student, who was Hopper, and fly into a fractious rage, even attempting to destroy it. At this juncture, it was Hopper's role to strike the *faux* Henri, seconded by the others, with the exception of Rockwell Kent, who took the teacher's part.

In class, Henri's style of criticism differed from that of Chase. He would line up a group of drawings against the large, dirty studio walls with their layers of smeared and spattered paint, student sketches, and caricatures. Opening a discussion, Henri pointed out both good and bad features, praising individual expression over technical proficiency. Where Chase scrawled a bold X over work he disapproved, it was Henri's custom to paint a red dot on pictures as a sign of approval; many of Hopper's student paintings earned the mark.

Hopper's long hours of reading and intellectual curiosity made him, more than many of his fellows, a ready audience for Henri's philosophy and its revolutionary difference from Chase and academic art. Henri spoke inspirationally on a wide range of topics, including contemporary theater. He frequently quoted from French authors such as Zola, Jean-Jacques Rousseau, and Guy de Maupassant, not that he wanted his students to impose a European aesthetic on their work.[54] Like Walt Whitman and Emerson, he found value in American subject matter; he wanted his students to develop personal, native means of expression. Among his diverse enthusiasms were Emerson, Tolstoy, and Whitman, whom he praised as a model for the artist: "Walt Whitman was such as I have proposed the real art student should be. His work is an autobiography—not of haps and mishaps, but of his deepest thought, his life indeed."[55]

The excitement Henri evoked in the writings of others could hardly be expected of Hopper: too far from character. His recollections provide estimates that are balanced and nuanced: "Henri wasn't a very good painter, at least I don't think so. He was a better teacher than painter. His wife was an Irish woman with red hair. Beautiful and tough."[56] Hopper picked up little in the way of style from Henri, but he began to develop his own philosophy of painting under his teacher's influence. He defined Henri's central princi-

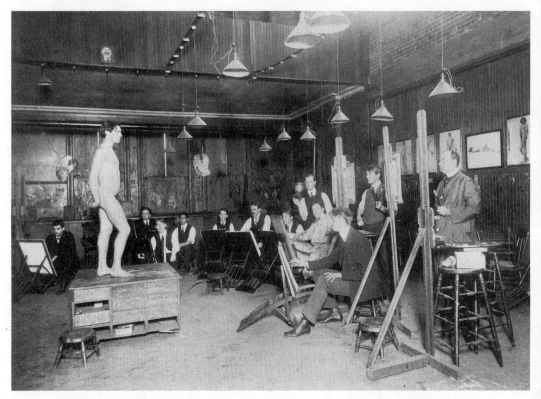

Edward Hopper in Robert Henri's Life Drawing Class at the New York School of Art,
c. 1903–1904 (seated in foreground at right).

ple as: "Art is life, an expression of life, an expression of the artist and an interpretation of life."[57] "Henri was a good teacher. He taught broadly. He dealt
not just with the meticulous things of painting but related painting to life.
The technical side was a little weak. He was sold to the economy of means in
painting, which led to a certain meretriciousness of brush work."[58]

Walter Tittle noted that Henri predicted a renaissance: "A school of
artists will arise who will paint their personalities, and not the same old
thing."[59] It was this that Hopper echoed when he asserted that an artist expresses nothing so much as his own personality in art. Hopper later wrote of
Henri's "courage and energy," which he believed did much to "shape the
course of art in this country." He asserted: "No single figure in recent American art has been so instrumental in setting free the hidden forces that can make
the art of this country a living expression of its character and its people."[60]

Henri's command that his students interpret life around them coincided
with the goals of the Muckrakers, the group of contemporary writers who
sought to arouse public opinion by exposing greed, corruption, and social
evils such as slums and prostitution. Their sensational stories, featured in

popular magazines like *Cosmopolitan* and *McClure's,* ultimately had an effect
on both art and literature. Their efforts served to reinforce Henri's suggestion
that any subject was possible for a painting.

Henri's real-world concerns were balanced by Hopper's other important
teacher, Kenneth Hayes Miller. Only six years older than Hopper, Miller had
begun his study at the Art Students League under the conservative teacher
Kenyon Cox, but he and several other male students were expelled in 1896 for
bursting in on the women's life class, which was strictly segregated.[61] The of-
fenders sought out Chase, who was then considered a progressive and who no
longer taught at the League, which he regarded as too conservative. These
students became the nucleus of the Chase School of Art.

Since 1899, the year before Hopper's arrival, Miller had taught sketching,
composition, and life classes, as well as illustration. He stressed spatial organization, recession, modeling forms "in the round," and a consideration of
the picture plane. Hopper later credited Miller with having "a fine sober influence on much of our contemporary painting."[62] Miller might critique the
work of his students in his life class daily as they worked before the model,
and then Chase would view the same work the following Monday.[63] Vachel
Lindsay recounted that Miller told him that he believed in "more old fashioned drawing than the school allows him to teach."[64]

Walter Tittle described Miller as "quite conservative then in his requirements that students learn to draw in a sound, academic way before trying
their wings in real flight."[65] Miller did not have the dominating personality of
either Chase or Henri. Rockwell Kent later compared their three teachers,
explaining that Chase had taught the students to use their eyes, Henri to en-
list their hearts, while Miller insisted that they use their heads. Kent believed
that Miller emphasized the importance of style and saw this as a corrective to
Henri's neglect of it.

> Utterly disregardful of the emotional values which Henri was so in-
> sistent upon, and contemptuous of both the surface realism and vir-
> tuosity of Chase, Miller, an artist in a far more precious sense than
> either, exacted a recognition of the tactile qualities of paint and of the
> elements of composition—line and mass—not as a means toward the
> recreation of life but as the fulfillment of an end, aesthetic pleasure.[66]

Miller's emphasis on aesthetics may have reinforced Hopper's reluctance to
discuss the implicit content of his work.

Hopper's abilities were recognized by both his teachers and his fellow
students. Kent remembered him as "the John Singer Sargent of the class"
who could be counted upon to turn out "an obviously brilliant drawing" on

Edward Hopper, [Nude Female Model Posing in Class, The New York School of Art], *c. 1900–1903.*

the occasions when the older students mocked a neophyte.[67] This was no slight compliment, for Sargent was one of the painters most revered. Hopper's humor repeatedly won him friends. He was one of a group, which also included Tittle, Morie Ogiwara, Tod Lindenmuth, and others, who received tickets to a Rodin show at the National Arts Club in May 1903 from Henri, who believed that "Rodin had unusual understanding."[68] The next week, Tittle noted that Hopper and two other students had "made some burlesques of Rodin," among them Hopper's drawing after the sculptor's *La Vieille Femme.*[69] Walter Pach recalled that Ogiwara, who took Rodin more seriously than Hopper, produced "drawings of immense fineness, of delicate sentiment and humor" and that Henri had singled out Ogiwara's drawing of a nude woman, claiming that "only a Japanese could have done it."[70] Ogiwara left for Paris the following autumn, where he became a disciple of Rodin's. A sculptor in his own right, he eventually pioneered in introducing Western-style sculpture to Japan.[71]

Far from leaving school, Hopper was encouraged to stay by growing recognition. At the annual spring *concours* of 1903, he won a scholarship in life drawing along with Patrick Henry Bruce and Hilda Belcher.[72] Bruce left school to go to Paris in late 1903; in a letter to Henri in February 1904 he said that he had expected Hopper to receive the painting prize, evidently acknowledging news received in a letter from Henri.[73] Hopper had won first prize in oil painting, while du Bois got first mention.[74] Then Hopper's drawing of a woman opening an umbrella was selected by the faculty for reproduction in an article on the school published in the *Sketch Book* of April 1904.[75] In another letter to Henri from Paris, Bruce responded to Henri's account of the year's final *concours,* saying he wished he could have been there to have seen the work, "especially Hopper's," and inquiring: "What kind of special scholarship did he get, and will he continue at the School another year?"[76] In fact, Hopper would continue for two more years. He received not only encouragement, scholarships, and prizes, but also the opportunity to teach at the school.

Further evidence survives of Bruce's affection for Hopper. When he left for Paris, he gave Hopper an unfinished painting. The canvas bears the name Bruce boldly, painted across its entire back. On its face, the thrifty Hopper painted his own self-portrait in another direction, covering up Bruce's unfinished portrait study.[77]

Beginning in the autumn of 1904, Hopper taught Saturday classes, including drawing from life, painting, sketching, and composition. His fellow faculty members for this all-day session were Douglas Connah, the owner-director, and Wladyslaw Theodor Benda, another Henri student and, later, an illustrator whom Hopper would encounter at the Penguin Club. Although Saturday students were considered less serious than the regulars, this appointment represented important recognition for Hopper.

He recalled attending fights at Brown's gymnasium with a fellow student; perhaps it was George Bellows, who painted his first boxing picture, *Club Night,* in 1907.[78] Although Hopper enjoyed boxing, which seemed to embody masculinity and power, he did not like to paint action. He confined this interest to the humorous sketches, never developing the theme into a painting. Even though he admitted attending baseball games as a child, he did not join Bellows, du Bois, Kent, and the others who fielded a baseball team against their arch rivals, the Art Students League, or the school of the National Academy of Design.[79]

Student enthusiasm extended to political and aesthetic debates in the corridors and classrooms. Ibsen, Tolstoy, and Shaw were of special interest, and Rockwell Kent remembered that "Eugène Sue, Verlaine, and Baudelaire and the French Decadents in general were read and admired."[80] The milieu was congenial to Hopper, with his reading of Russians in translation, particularly Turgenev and Tolstoy.[81] About 1903, he made several pen and ink drawings for poems by Edgar Allan Poe, "The Raven" and "The Bells." Given the students' attraction to the French Symbolists and Decadents, it is not surprising to find Hopper reading Poe, whom the Symbolists admired more than any other American. Poe's theme of anguish at death in "The Raven," and the gloomy bird Hopper depicts, recall the absorption with death already discernible in Hopper's childhood sketches and recurrent throughout his life.

Neither ringleader nor hermit, Hopper was one of "the fellows" a friend would miss when venturing abroad to retrace the steps of Henri to Paris.[82] He could be counted on for a limerick and the regular charade to haze new students. Yet unlike some of the more independent spirits, who lived at the YMCA or boarding houses, he continued to go back each evening to his mother's bed and board, at least for the first few years. It was hard to stay in town for the theater or perhaps even the school dances. When at last he managed to find a small studio on Fourteenth Street, which he described as "a terrible place,"[83] it was not much of a habitation.

At the school dances, female students were provided with cards for prearranging a partner for each dance. "Ho" appears several times on two of Emma Story's undated dance cards.[84] The socials were held in the school building. The big sliding doors between the men's and women's studios were opened for the occasion; cookies and lemonade, but no liquor, were served. Hopper, Glenn Coleman, and possibly others designed posters for the Arts and Crafts Dance, a masquerade ball, held there on January 29, 1905.

Hopper, as paintings and drawings show, continued and developed his childhood fascination with theater, encouraged now by Henri's enthusiasm. Hopper probably went to see Ethel Barrymore as Nora in Ibsen's *A Doll's House,* which his classmate Vachel Lindsay saw in May 1905.[85] Henri especially admired Ibsen for portraying "a state of life and questions as to the future of the race."[86] Hopper made several early illustrations referring to the Norwegian playwright and he later continued to admire his works. He may also have seen Charlie Chaplin at the Colonial Vaudeville Theatre, a performance Emma Story recalled.[87] Apart from Emma, who would marry George Bellows in 1910, the names of the women who frequented the New York School in Hopper's day are difficult to trace. Women faced many obstacles to success in the art world. None of the female members of Henri's classes achieved fame comparable to the men. In addition to Emma and Josephine Nivison, whom Henri portrayed in student guise and Hopper married much later, it is possible at least to document the lives of Edith Bell, Amy Londoner, Ellen Ravencroft, Madge Huntington, Edith Haworth, Ethel Louise Paddock, and Mary Rogers. Ethel Klinck Myers, like Nivison, found her own career subordinated to that of her husband, the painter Jerome Myers. Nivison never specified the exact years she studied at the school because she tried to conceal her age and pretended to others that she was much younger than Edward. It is certain, however, that she was at the school between 1904 and 1906, when Henri painted her portrait (page 152).

Women students found Hopper attractive. Emma Story, who came from Upper Montclair, New Jersey, recalled that she first met him while crossing the Hudson on the ferry.[88] Although she considered him talented and promising, she fell for the attentions of the dashing, athletic Bellows. Hopper also knew Edith Bell, who like him came from Nyack, and he may have first met Jo through her. Hopper asked another young woman, Hetty Dureyea, to pose for several portraits that he painted in oil. Dureyea was responsible for arranging an exhibition of Japanese prints that took place at the school. But she apparently developed an interest in a fellow named Connaugh, because later Hopper's mother wrote to him in Paris with news that made him respond that he was "sorry to hear that Connaugh has 'done' Hetty in," calling him "a born crook."[89]

Ever introspective, Hopper often contemplated himself at this time, frequently filtering his observations through his sardonic wit. Numerous oil self-portraits reveal that he reflected seriously upon his self-image, but many caricature sketches on paper poke fun at his appearance. He wittily depicted himself as a diligent art student hard at work, showing himself, in one example, with his ungainly body chained to the floor so that he could concentrate on his drawing board while seated on one of the uncomfortably low stools that were a part of the school furniture.

By late May 1905, Hopper was growing restless in school and was eager to earn some money. Classmates such as Walter Tittle and Clarence Coles Phillips had already begun working as illustrators. Tittle reported that "Ed Hopper down at school has decided to try illustrating. He has been in school for years."[90] Hopper began to work part-time for C. C. Phillips and Company, a New York advertising agency founded by Coles Phillips, who had attended the New York School of Art in 1905. Working in the new agency's offices at 24 East Twenty-second Street, Hopper produced cover designs for trade magazines such as the *Bulletin* of the New York Edison, where he illustrated the advantages of electric light in the home by depicting a man in colonial dress struggling to read by candlelight. Phillips closed his agency the next year to pursue his own very successful career as an illustrator.

Hopper's last experience with a new teacher was in the spring of 1906, when John Sloan taught classes for Henri to free his friend to work on a portrait commission. This was Hopper's first meeting with Sloan, whose work he admired and later wrote about. From March 14 through April 13, Sloan, who, like Henri, had studied with Anshutz, took Henri's place criticizing the men's morning life class, the afternoon portrait class, and the men's evening life class. He noted in his diary: "The pupils show the results of Henri's tremendous ability as a teacher."[91] Seven years had transformed Hopper's generic talent into a vocation for painting, validated by intense practice and exchange, by praise and scholarships from teachers, and by the affectionate esteem of peers. He had diligently studied and found himself at home, staying twice as long at the New York School of Art as the founder thought fit. For the moment he had acquired a palette. More far-reaching, his philosophy about his calling had been permanently enriched and shaped. One of his teachers reputedly said that he "is the kind of artist who could not be taught anything; he had to learn it for himself."[92]

The example of teachers like Chase and Henri and friends like Bruce, du Bois, and Edmund Graecen suggested the next step. Hopper's horizons had grown from the world of illustrators to encompass Hals, Rembrandt, and Velázquez, as well as the moderns like Courbet, Millet, Daumier, and Manet, who were touted by Henri and Chase. His accomplishment in New York had also educated his parents, who now understood more clearly where his talent could lead. With their financial support, Hopper embarked for Paris in the fall of 1906. Not even Henri and the intensity of student life had prepared him for the challenges to his character and values that awaited in the world capital of art.

SEDUCTIVE PARIS: 1906–1907

EDWARD ARRIVED IN PARIS in the autumn of 1906, when he was twenty-four. It was not to be a grand tour conducted through letters of introduction to academies or *grandes personnes,* still less an escapade. If Edward had been prone to *la vie bohème* he would already have had occasion in New York. The family network was religious. Through their church, Elizabeth and Garret Hopper found Edward lodgings in the Baptist mission in Paris, the Eglise Evangélique Baptiste, located at 48, rue de Lille. A widow named Louise Jammes lived with two teenaged sons in rooms at the top of the building. It would be the perfect home away from home. Reaching the rue de Lille on October 24, Edward found time by the thirtieth for his first letter home, which he addressed with nothing so generic as "Dear ones" or "Folks" or "My dear parents" but simply to his mother:

> I write you this from Madame Jammes where I have a good room and plenty to eat.
>
> Paris is a very graceful and beautiful city, almost too formal and sweet after the raw disorder of New York. Everything seems to have been planned with the purpose of forming a most harmonious whole which has certainly been done. Not even one jarring note of color is

there to break the dismal tone of the house front, which is a universal grey or buff.

Then too, the trains and buses work with a regularity and precision which can only have been obtained after years of experience.

The streets are remarkable for their cleanliness and their shop-windows which are undeniably attractive and seem to be right upon the street itself. As much time and thought seems to have been spent on every little tobacco or butcher shop as is spent for the window of a department store in New York and they are all supremely clean.

Every street here is alive with all sorts and condition of people, priests, nuns, students, and always the little soldiers with wide red pants.

The Frenchmen for the most part are small and have poor physiques. You will not see here as you do on "Broadway" the finely built young fellows with their strong, well cut features. However, the French must conceal "the goods" somehow or other, as we know they are on the spot when the time comes, in spite of their little beards & long shoes.

The climate here seems very mild to me. I do not believe they have the biting cold of New York, nor do you see here the deep blue sky and gorgeous sparkle of color we have at home. Everything seems to be pitched in a milder key.

I have just run to the "Autumn Salon" and found it for the most part very bad, although it is much more liberal in its aims than the shows at home.

I hope you are doing as well as could be expected and remain

Your son & heir

E. Hopper[1]

Calmly Edward supposes that his mother's real interest will be in his impressions of Paris. Having sought to reassure her that he is properly settled, Edward looks outward to make his first sketch of the city. Almost by the book, he checks off the topics expected of the traveler: the general form and color, some particulars of transport, streets, shops, picturesque types, the French physique and character, climate, light and color again, with a first glance at the art scene. The whole and some parts sound more than a little academic, yet hints emerge already of his particular vision. For the first time the boy from Nyack shows what he had seen and felt in the passage to New York—"raw disorder." The consciousness of contrast quickens his imagination. Similar shocks and images of contrast would accompany each further crossing and confrontation in his life. The shocks would register in his art as dissociation and ironic dissonance.

The contrast between New York and Paris organizes other perceptions. Edward picks out that which merits praise in Paris by explicit or implicit polarity with its opposite in New York: transport, the streets, and shops—the details of daily urban life that would have escaped notice by an academic painter but fascinated Hopper and other students of Henri. New types of people strike the eye that always sought out human quirks and dramas, right down to the soldier in red pants.

On one score the values get reversed. With his usual penchant for caricature, Edward contrasts the "Broadway" stage image of American masculinity with the street reality of scrawny French who nonetheless "are on the spot when the time comes." Edward, the buff of military history, may well have meant to underscore a contrast between unprepossessing physique and national military prowess. Yet his language, structurally and metaphorically, flirts with the theme of French renown in love. His irony brings him willy-nilly to a subject that neither he nor his mother would wish to address directly. Sexuality was there, always, in expectation because of the common image of French mores and bohemian Paris. The first glimpse of strange little men in curious shoes prompted elaborate recall of theatrical images in New York that grazed the issue of sexuality. And this was only the start. Far deeper and more provocative spurs to imagination lay in wait and not only in the streets outside the Baptist mission.

Edward's even tone shows how far he was from imagining the state of his mother's feelings, how deep her anxiety would run and to what lengths it would drive her. Three days before Edward found time for his first dispatch, his mother had written in a way that provoked a mixture of affection and ironical self-defense in another letter:

> I received yours of the twenty-seventh and read the contents carefully. I find in it a tendency towards sentimentality which is not consistent with your hardy Anglo-Saxon nature. The little incident of my room is told with much tenderness and pathos, but if you persist in so exposing your true heart, our friendship must cease.
> Hoping that you are bearing it bravely, I remain
> Your male child
> E. Hopper.[2]

Invoking his mother's "hardy Anglo-Saxon nature," a cultural commonplace for stern and repressive character, in order to check her feelings, Edward betrays its presence in himself. He is uneasy with emotions, hers and his. Later, as he hesitated on the threshold of adult life, his friend du Bois would identify the same stereotype in his character and see it as an obstacle to Edward's personal and artistic growth.[3]

The Hoppers' plan had reckoned with neither anxiety nor illness. Edward was slow to realize the gravity of both. On November 16, he answered simply:

> I write you this in order to let you know that I am well and having a good time. I hope you are improving and will be able to go some-where this winter. I am sure it would do you good. Tell Marion to write if she cares to as I should like to hear from her or father. Do not give yourself a lot of useless worry about me as I never felt better in my life.[4]

For him, "never felt better" sounds uncharacteristically sweeping and confident. Paris tempts him to hyperbole, weighing and revising his view of all that went before. The assessment was hardly well calculated to have the desired effect, for Elizabeth Hopper redoubled her doubts. One week later, Edward felt obliged to write yet again:

> I am still at Madam Jammes, as I have been painting out-of-doors and do not need a studio as yet. The weather has been very mild and would be pleasant were it not for the rain which comes down at the most unexpected moments, even out of a clear sky. The Parisiens don't seem to mind it though as they are in the streets and cafés at all times. The people here in fact seem to live in the streets, which are alive from morning until night not as they are in New York with that never ending determination for the "long green," but with a pleasure loving crowd that doesn't care what it does or where it goes, so that it has a good time.
>
> Remember me to your husband and tell Marion to write.
>
> Yours truly, E. Hopper.[5]

The young man's attention has clearly shifted from the general harmony and the scattered Parisian types to the phenomenon of the café and the crowds, and to their motives. Again his vision doubles, comparing New York and Paris. The "Anglo-Saxon" sense of discipline and duty bristles at the spectacle of people bustling about not for business but for pleasure.

Edward's dispatches did not avail. Elizabeth Hopper suffered a crisis of confidence. Losing faith in her Baptist friends, she kept demanding further credentials, until Edward felt driven to write his sister:

My dear Marion:

Mother has been so persistent in her inquiries about Madam Jamme [sic], that I feel that I should answer although it's an awful bore.

Madam Jamme I think at one time was in very good circumstances, but through some misfortune has lost everything. This same misfortune drove her mother insane and finally killed her. It, I believe, was also responsible for the death of her husband. So you see that she has suffered a great deal. Her bad fortune however has not embittered her as she has an extremely kind heart and a very fine sense of humor. Her sons, who are sixteen and eighteen years old are very tall and look much older. The little French lady [another boarder] is not French but an Irish American whose home is in San Francisco. She has lived in Europe and known Madam Jamme for a long time. I hope this will suffice regarding my domestic affairs.[6]

Suffice it did not. Elizabeth had the minister's wife, Ada Saunier, write to Louise Jammes, who replied reassuringly at the beginning of December:

More than a month has passed over since your young friend Mr. Hopper has arrived in our home. We all like him & we think that he is a good American fellow. He seems happy in beautiful Paris & has begun his work & as his dear mother is so far away Miss Cuniffe [the Irish American boarder] & I try to be mothers to him so that he must not ever feel homesake. We three went together to Sevre on the boat, if the wether were only fine we would go to ever so many places, but, in this season of the year the days begin to be short & wise people must be contented in all circumstances even in la belle France.

Mr. Hopper's mother must not be anxious of her son for he is very quiet & so reserve & has a most delicate soul of refinement & with his sweet smile & his true look in his eyes will make friends all over the globe. For his mother's sake I sincerely hope that he will become master over master is a son not the crown of its mother's head?

Our best souvenirs to your dear husband. . . . I shall write a line to Mrs Hopper.[7]

Between one mother in Nyack and two in Paris, Edward was well tended. His discovery of the city would profit from the enthusiasm of eager and generous guides, with a "kind heart and a very fine sense of humor" as he said of Louise Jammes. The flutter of confidences the boy inspired took on a life of its own. Elizabeth wrote Louise, who replied in February of the next year:

Your letter deserved an earlier answer, but, were it not for all the buts, you should had long ago the acknowledgement of thanks & gratitude for having placed on this Hemisphere such a fine boy as your son.

I have a friend who makes her home with us she is an American Lady & her name is Miss Cuniffe well we call your son mama's boy & we both are his mothers since his arrival. My two boys are also very fond of Mr. Hopper. You ought to see your son how well he looks. He parlez français like a french man you would be astonished to hear him converse if he continues you may call him with the time Victor Hugo.

Dear Mrs Hopper why don't you come to Paris it would be recreation for you to accompany your son in our Musées to admire the Chef d'Oeuvre of the ancients gods & also to bow to Luxor have you not his brother in your Central Park?

Should you see Mrs or Mr Saunier . . . would you kindly present them our most gracious souvenirs until then & ever more believe me a sister in the One whose blood was shed for us.

Mr. Hopper is already in bed otherwise he would send love & kisses to his dear mama & papa & sister.[8]

At twenty-four, Edward was still a "fine boy" and "mama's boy," as indeed he perceived himself, fortunate to have fallen in with friends not only affectionate but generous, proud of French culture and eager to show it around. Louise Jammes turned out to be more than his family had bargained. No one projected the transfer of Elizabeth Hopper to Paris, nor that the intended studio would fade before the unexpected comforts of home on the rue de Lille.

Edward opened an almost jocular vein seeing that his mother was getting over an illness that had required both a nurse and confinement indoors: "I hope you are well, fat, and jolly as usual."[9] A bit later, he struck a nasty note: "I was glad to learn that you are in New York again, as it must be intolerably stupid at home."[10] What the son and the mother both found to despise in Nyack, and where Elizabeth took refuge in New York, is not clear.[11] His mother answered his solicitude and expressed impatience with his reports of the city and the weather, in her inquiries about his person, which he parried, not about to bare his soul:

You ask me always to tell about myself and I suppose it is my health and my clothes that concerns you,—therefore—as follows:
1. buttons are still on underwear
2. heavy underwear is fast going to pieces
3. light underwear still in good condition.

4. new necktie must be bought soon
5. old clothes are fast becoming covered with paint—green spots predominating (owing to spring)
6. have turned band on hat
7. hairs have ceased to fall out in such large quantities
8. had moustache for two weeks
9. cut it off
10. this is it [sketch of mustache]
11. have been darning hose (which is proper side to do it on?—) have tried both inside and out.
12. am fat in the face

I never have received a letter from "Charity," so it is very probable that the French postal officials have been unable to decipher her hieroglyphics, or it is very possible it has gone on to China or Japan. In either case I would not encourage her to write again as I haven't any time to waste on disagreeable old ladies.[12]

The ironic charm of his checklist, with its touches of self-satire, gets overshadowed by the close. Breaking his usual decorum, Edward refers to his long-widowed grandmother Charity Blauvelt Hopper, enclosing her first name in quotes as if to suggest that her personality did not live up to it. His manner jars, and his tone matches the "awful bore" and "intolerably stupid" of previous letters in suggesting a dimension of Hopper very different from the "mama's boy" admired by Louise Jammes for his "delicate soul."

Years later Alfred Barr, after interviewing Hopper, reported that he had "lived in a respectable French family studying French, reading extensively in French literature, and avoiding bohemia."[13] The painter himself once admitted that his only concession to his surroundings near the Latin Quarter was a thin red mustache which he grew in April 1907 but soon shaved off because "it looked silly."[14]

Secure in his home base, encouraged by his solicitous guides, Hopper gradually reached out, though he soon learned that rain could limit work outside. The weather, as much as his training with Henri and Chase, affected his palette. It was a wet and cool autumn, even for Paris. Adapting to the circumstances of *la belle France,* he started by painting at home: small somber panels of the courtyard, the interior staircase leading to Mme. Jammes's apartment, a view of windows and a mansard roof seen across a window railing. In the roof, he found a familiar shape that he had admired in Nyack, on houses built in the American version of Second Empire style just before his birth.

From the rue de Lille, he ventured into the near neighborhood, turning the corner into the rue de Bac and walking the block to the Seine, where he painted the embankments with bridges and stairways, a sculpture on a pedestal seen before a corner of the Louvre, and a street scene. The latter, rendered in a simple but dramatic blue-gray tonality, reflects the impression of his new surroundings that he described for his sister:

> Paris as you must know is a most paintable city, particularly on and around the Ile du Cite, upon which was the first Paris. Here the streets are very old and narrow and many of the houses slope back from the top of the first story which gives them a most imposing and solid appearance. The wine shops and stores beneath are dark red or green, contrasting strongly with the plaster or stone above. On the roofs hundreds of pipes and chimney pots stick up into the air giving the sky line a most peculiar appearance. The roofs are all of the Mansard type and either of grey slate or zinc. On a day that's overcast, this same blue-grey permeates everything. It's at the end of the streets, and the open windows of the houses in the trees, and under the arches of the bridges. Even a man's coat becomes a deep blue grey at a few yards distance. This may all mean nothing to you, but I if could give you a glimpse of the real Paris I would be doing well. For it must be seen to be understood. And it will have a different meaning for each.
>
> Yours truly. Ed.[15]

After the academic generality of his first bulletin, the painter has spent the month working with his eyes. By now he is so absorbed in the concreteness of Parisian shapes and colors that he no longer thinks primarily of comparison with New York. Paris so captivates him that he speaks in terms of an ideal, a kind of absolute, how "paintable" the city is in itself. This is what sweeps him up and focuses his mind. He passes from an academic sense of general harmony to more specific observation, in the manner encouraged by Henri, of what lies around him close to hand. The loving detail of his report reveals acute visual sensibility: what Hopper saw usually became more important for him than whom he met or what he did.

Hopper's eyes and their affair with Paris preempt the next week's letter as well:

> Here in the Grand Palais we have an automobile show, and the illumination of the building is most beautiful. Last night the search light on the Eiffel tower was playing all over the city, and as the tower itself could not be seen it looked like nothing so much as a gigantic comet away up in the air. I do not believe there is another city on

earth so beautiful as Paris, nor another people with such an appreciation of the beautiful as the French. There is always some sort of an
exhibition going on here either of pictures sculpture or the industries
and everybody is interested the rich and the poor alike.

I wish that I could make you to know the importance the public
institutions have for the people and the veneration and respect in
which they hold them. Coming from a place where everybody is for
himself—it is hard to grasp.

The Boulevard des Capucines is another wonderful place at night
with its theatres and coloured lights. The crowd here is so thick in the
evening that one can hardly get through. It is also lined with cafés
where the Demimondaines sit with the silk hatted boulevardiers.[16]

To Marion the previous week he had described forms and colors along streets
imagined virtually empty. Earlier to his mother he had sketched, in social
more than visual terms, the crowds forever looking for pleasure. Now he
finds a social dimension to admire, again by contrast with America: appreciation of the beautiful and veneration for institutions of culture. At the same
time he makes no secret of the growing vividness and concreteness of his perception of street life: the animated and illuminated boulevard, and now the
defining form of its inhabitants. Scarcely into his second month, his eye fixes
on a set of figures that would have a long and intense history in his imagination: the café and the couples of the demimonde. He knows their names in
French. As for the great tower, unlike his contemporary, the French modernist painter Robert Delaunay, Hopper preferred it invisible and never
painted or sketched it.

Spring gave new play to the eye: Straw hats had been out for about a
week. The Tuileries Gardens were very fine with the sun and blue sky: "in
fact the whole city is alive with color now. The women have blue and red
parasols."[17] The most tumultuous sight came latest:

We have just had the carnival of the Mi-Carême, it is one of the important fetes of the year. Everyone goes to the "Grands Boulevards"
and lets himself loose. The confetti lies four inches deep in the street,
the dust arising from this fills the air so that it seems to be a foggy
day—this dust enveloped crowd and the confetti falling every where
like colored snow is a sight unique. The crowd finds the sidewalks
too narrow for its horseplay and takes to the road also. Do not picture these in costume, they are not for the most part, but here and
they you will see them, perhaps a clown with a big nose or two girls
with bare necks and short skirts trying to escape the confetti which

half a dozen bearded frenchmen are playfully forcing them to eat. Here too are always the students—perhaps a crowd of art students wearing their gowns, and endeavoring to keep up their reputation of wild bohemianism—but mere boys for the most part and not very formidable after all.

The parade of the queens of the halles (markets) is also one of the events. They go through the streets on various floats—some are pretty but look awkward in their silk dresses and crowns, particularly as the broad sun displays their defects—perhaps a neck too thin or a painted face which shows ghastly white in the sunlight.

Withal it is a tractable and peaceful crowd and does not overstep the bounds of decency—(possibly because the bounds are very wide here) nevertheless there is little drunkenness and less fighting. Given the same liberties, I am afraid an American crowd would not comport itself so well.[18]

Before May was over, Edward had one last spectacle to report: the king and queen of Norway on parade instead of the queens of the halles:

Their entry was quite an occasion and a beautiful sight. There were many troops along the route. The French cavelry always make a good showing with their helmets and cuirasses, quite in contrast to the infantry who are usually small and have rather ugly uniforms. The houses are decorated with the flags of the nations. The German flag, however, is never seen. The "grand old rag" shows itself here and there.[19]

This spectacle does not bring out the moral censor and the defensive ironist as Carnival had. Edward can focus on the uniforms that had fascinated him since boyhood and remark on the political omen of the absent flag. He resorts to a mild irony only where affections are most nearly involved, as he identifies the sign of home by playing with the phrase from the patriotic song, "It's a grand old flag."

The original agenda included not only the city but its art. Edward came predisposed to fall in with the local penchant for exhibitions. He had not been in Paris a week before he had "just run to the 'Autumn Salon' and found it for the most part very bad." What he saw was his first extensive exposure to Courbet and Cézanne. Among the thirty works in Courbet's retrospective was a variation of Frans Hals's grotesque old woman *Malle Babbe,* which Hopper had sketched in art school. Years later he admitted that he admired Courbet, citing his mechanical strength, but disliked

Cézanne, who was represented in the Salon by ten works, which Hopper thought lacked substance and had a papery quality.[20] Another time, he complained: "Many Cézannes are very thin."[21] As Hopper developed his own volumetric sense, he rejected Cézanne's flattened forms in favor of Courbet's more traditional modeling in order to delineate conventional relationships in space. That same quick tour exposed Hopper to works by Albert Marquet, Félix Vallotton, and Walter Richard Sickert, three artists who used themes that Hopper subsequently explored. Marquet presented prosaic views of Paris and summary treatment of figures;[22] Sickert and Vallotton offered intimate interior views with psychological drama. Hopper also had the opportunity to see the work of several young American artists who managed to get into the Salon: his fond classmate, Patrick Henry Bruce, along with Max Weber and Maurice Sterne.

Bruce was among the first people Hopper saw outside the rue de Lille. Before he had been in Paris two weeks, he visited Bruce several times, one evening as a guest for dinner.[23] The year before Bruce had married another veteran of the New York School, Helen Kibbey. The couple lived in a charming garden on the boulevard Arago, where they entertained generously on a modest budget. After Christmas, Hopper wrote to his mother: "The Bruces have been very cordial whenever I have called and Bruce is very much more agreeable than formerly."[24] At the Bruces', Americans had a habit of dropping by. "Here art was talked of seriously, frowningly, with no funny business,"[25] wrote Guy Pène du Bois, also Edward's familiar in art school but now called back prematurely to America because of his father's death. Others, less close, were frequent visitors: Walter Pach, a classmate, Maurice Sterne, Daniel Putnam Brinley, Arthur Burdett Frost, Jr., and Samuel Halpert. Edmund Graecen, another classmate, settled in Paris with his wife, Ethol, a few months prior to the birth of their son in December 1906. The Bruces followed suit with a son in April. Domestic focus pinched hospitality and shrank camaraderie. Du Bois, of French heritage and lively, open demeanor, would have been a better facilitator and guide.

In the autumn of 1906, around the time of Edward's arrival, the Bruces first met the celebrated Stein family from Baltimore. Gertrude, her brothers Leo and Michael, and Michael's wife, Sarah, all admired and collected modern art. Gertrude and Leo held salons on Saturday evenings that many young artists attended. Hopper later credited Bruce with introducing him to the work of the Impressionists in Paris, "especially Sisley, Renoir, and Pissarro,"[26] and certainly could have met the Steins through Bruce, had he been so inclined. "Whom did I meet? Nobody," he later remarked. "I'd heard of Gertrude Stein, but I don't recall having heard of Picasso at all. I used to go to the cafés at night and sit and watch. I went to the theatre a little. Paris had no great or immediate impact on me."[27] Another time he repeated that he had heard of Stein, but insisted: "I wasn't important enough for her to know me. About the only important person I knew was Jo Davidson, and he was willing to look at me only because I knew the girl he was going to marry, met her on the boat going over."[28] The woman in question was Yvonne de Kerstrat, an American actress.

Often, the young American artists who went to Paris attended famous art schools, such as the Académie Julian or even the Ecole des Beaux Arts. They also congregated at the American Art Association, a social club on the rue Notre Dame des Champs sponsored by Rodman Wanamaker. Hopper never mentioned this organization, yet he must have visited its numerous exhibitions. American artists abounded in Paris at the time: besides Jo Davidson and Max Weber, there were Lyonel Feininger, Stanton MacDonald-Wright, John Marin, Alfred Maurer, Lyman Säyen, Morton Schamberg, Edward Steichen, and Abraham Walkowitz. In 1906, the expatriate community were talking about the work of Whistler (dead in 1903), whose portrait of his mother they studied at the Luxembourg Gallery along with the Caillebotte collection of Impressionists.

American and English artists frequented the Café du Dôme in Montparnasse, within walking distance from Hopper's place on the rue de Lille. Unlike the long evenings with the Bruces, where talk flowed "seriously, frowningly, with no funny business," and babies were on the way or just born, talk by the artists in the cafés often ran to the turbulent dramas they created with the mistresses they found among young French working girls, *les grisettes*. Café life was bohemian and sexual drama was a staple. It is no accident, then, that Hopper so pointedly deprecated bohemia in writing, while taking its women as frequent subjects for his art.

Fascinated, but divided between longing and fear, Hopper made a pen-and-ink sketch of a shapely nude woman endowed with a devil's tail and pursued by several overly eager men: his scenario recalls the carnival sight of men forcing confetti down the throats of scantily clad girls. He also depicted a nude standing provocatively by an open window, holding her hand to her face in a contemplative pose that anticipates certain images in paintings of his maturity. The sketches confirm the impression conveyed by one or two letters that sexuality was on his mind. Despite his strict upbringing, or perhaps because of it, he was particularly drawn and repelled by the variety of prostitutes in the streets of Paris.

While Louise Jammes was writing to Elizabeth Hopper about the cultural values of Paris and the refined soul of "mama's boy," Edward's eye was sizing up *les filles de joie*. He did not come to the encounter free from prejudice or expectation. Experience with French art and literature and with New York conditioned what he perceived and drew. At this time in the United States, noisy public campaigns against prostitution were being organized. Antivice agitators held outdoor prayer meetings and marches in the heart of urban red-light districts.[29] Congress passed legislation banning the importation of women for the purposes of prostitution in 1903 and would do so again in 1907. During the later years of art school, Edward had rented a studio on Fourteenth Street, where solicitation was aggressive and frequent.[30]

But the Anglo-Saxon puritan in him could only wonder at the conspicuously lax attitude toward prostitution he found in France in 1906. The prostitutes' demeanor also impressed him. Hopper represented several in cafés, staring right out at the spectator, the artist himself, with a distinctly come-hither look. The sketches suggest that Paris produced in him a kind of sexual awakening.

As often when facing an excess of emotion, Hopper resorted to caricature, using watercolors to depict various types and degrees of sexually available women: *La Pierreuse, Fille de Joie, Type de Belleville, La Grisette,* and *Une Demi-mondaine. La pierreuse* is slang for a street-walker, "she of the paving stones." *Fille de joie,* "daughter of joy," refers to a tart, prostitute, or any woman of loose morals. *Type de Belleville* refers to a disheveled working-class woman from the colorful area that became for Hopper the French equivalent of the New York district that attracted artists like John Sloan, who also depicted prostitutes.[31]

La grisette was a term with roots in the social displacement caused by industrial development, which attracted rural labor to the cities in search of work. The sobriquet refers to a working girl, usually a young dressmaker or a milliner, who typically came to Paris from rural communities where a certain sexual freedom was countenanced, but in a framework where marriage would naturally ensue. Translated to the isolation and anonymity of the city, where bourgeois morality generally prevailed, these country mores conferred on their bearers a romantic aura in the eyes of the students and artists of the Latin Quarter, who sought them out as mistresses.[32]

The easy virtue of Rigolette *la grisette* had been featured in *Mysteries of Paris* by Eugène Sue, a novel read by the boys at art school.[33] Sue also described and expressed fear of female sexuality, which he embodied in the character of Cecily, who exercises power to dominate and subdue the defenseless male.[34] The theme clearly preoccupied Edward, to judge from the sketch of the woman with the devil's tail and his boyhood sketches of the engulfing woman and frail man. The term *grisette* even migrated into English, in popular accounts such as the chapter "The Ghost of the Grisette" in George Augustus Sala's *Paris Herself Again:*

Edward Hopper, Fille de Joie, *1906–1907. Watercolor on composition board, 11⅛ × 9⅜" (30.2 × 23.8 cm.).*

Her manner of walking was matchlessly graceful and agile. The narrow streets of old Paris were, in those days, infamously paved. There was no foot pavement. The kennel was often in the centre of the street, and down it rolled a great black torrent of impurities fearsome to sight and smell.... The manner in which the grisette would pick her way over the jagged stones, and the dexterity with which she would avoid soiling her neat shoes and stockings when venturing on the very brink of that crashing plashing kennel, were wonderous and delightful to view. She had an inimitable way, too, of whisking the end of her skirt over her arm as she trotted along.[35]

Sala also discussed other Parisian types that Hopper portrayed, including the *sergents de ville,* the concierge, and the demi-mondaine.

Not only literature, but art suggested the theme of prostitution to an apprentice painter. As a student, Hopper based a sketch in pen and ink on a reproduction of Manet's *Olympia,* that scandalous Parisian courtesan. At the Metropolitan Museum, he had also sketched the seductive figure of Henri

Regnault's *Salomé,* which had been compared to a courtesan when exhibited in Paris in the Salon of 1870.[36] Besides these two admired images, there were representations of prostitutes everywhere—from the academic paintings in the salons to works by Toulouse-Lautrec, as well as in many of the caricatures that appeared in satirical magazines like *L'Assiette au Beurre.*[37] Prostitutes also appeared in novels by Honoré de Balzac, Victor Hugo, and Emile Zola. For an avid reader like Hopper, books raised expectations through names that experience would connect with sights. Within a month of his arrival, Edward had recognized and was describing the demi-mondaines with the "silk hatted boulevardiers" to his mother.

Edward often went to cafés to observe and to sketch the pleasure seekers he described as just people smoking, talking, or at their ease. He made many quick pen-and-ink figure sketches filled with images that range from fashionable women to soldiers and priests. Occasionally he included little French phrases such as "Tout le monde debarque" or "Les Americans." Assimilating at least imaginatively to the scene, he sketched himself in hats such as boaters or derbies. He even purchased a tweed suit especially to dress up to go to the opera.[38] In a theater, he recorded an elegantly coiffed woman peering through her lorgnette. He loved to watch the boatmen working along the river in their wooden shoes, cummerbunds, and berets. A more finished group of pen-and-ink sketches of individual figures includes a muscular workman, an *ouvrier* with cigarette and bottle of cheap wine, the soldier known as a Piou-Piou, and a French cavalry officer in full regalia.

The visual excitement he expressed in letters led to a number of elaborate drawings, in which he combined pencil, Conté, charcoal, wash, and touches of white paint. He focused on groups of people in typical settings: travelers boarding the train in a railroad station, poor people drinking beneath a bridge along the Seine, elegant shoppers along a street with its characteristic kiosk and mansard-roofed houses. He drew a horse-drawn carriage making its way along the narrow Paris street, and elsewhere the impressive dome of the Pantheon looming above the city, as seen from the Seine. By far the most poignant is a drawing entitled *On the Quai: The Suicide,* which depicts four figures standing on the walkway along the river around the body of someone who has jumped to death from a bridge, from which a spectator now looks down. Hopper's choice of the macabre subject recalls his earlier illustration of Thomas Hood's poem about suicide, "The Bridge of Sighs." Ever alert to difference, in manners as in appearance, and disaffected from the values of New York, Edward ventured a political report:

> The church and the state are getting into another mix-up here and the papers are full of it. Would I read French & could tell you about

Edward Hopper, On the Quai: The Suicide, *1906. Conté, wash, and touches of white, 17½ × 14⅝″ (44.5 × 37.1 cm.).*

it. In fact though the French are a very mild mannered people, they burst into flame at the slightest provocation. A short time ago one of the professors of the Sorbonne was nearly killed by the students for some unguarded words about Joan of Arc, thus do they fight for the sake of an idea—quite in contrast to those at home who only are roused when their pockets are endangered.[39]

(This controversy over Joan of Arc was instigated by the right, who tried to turn her into an asset for the Nationalists: they confronted Catholics with the fact that she had been burned by the Church, and Royalists with the king's abandonment of her cause.[40])

Expanding on his judgment of French character, Hopper wrote to his father:

The workman here seems to be in a perpetual state of protest against his employer and the administration—therefore the many strikes of this winter, electricians, bakers, and even the waiters of the cafés. The Frenchman in fact is a hard man to keep down and will have his say, if not with official permission, then without it, such as anti-militia proclamations which were torn down by the police re-cently—the signers of which were arrested.[41]

He sent his father a broadside announcing a lecture by the prominent liber-tarian philosopher and anarchist Sébastien Faure attacking "La Dictature Clemenceau" and reported that the notice "was given to me at Belleville one of the districts of Paris near the wall."[42] Faure's struggle against the con-straints of authority appealed to Hopper's contrarian nature. Hopper also asked his family whether they had formed an opinion on "the Japanese ques-tion," noting "I have none. There are many Japanese students here. I saw a bunch of them in a café a few nights ago, and they looked strangely out of place. I wondered what they thought about it and about the music."[43] Evi-dently Hopper had lost touch with his Japanese classmate, Morie Ogiwara, who was also then living in Paris.[44] His comments were made in response to the intensive local news coverage of the defeat of France's ally, Russia, in the Russo-Japanese War.

Taking advantage of the inexpensive ticket prices, Hopper also fre-quented the theater, much as he had in New York: "I have been to the opera and saw Julius Caesar at the Odéon—they are both supported by the govern-ment as is the Théâtre Français."[45] Another time he reported: "I saw Co-quelin in Cyrano de Bergerac—he looked pretty good to me,"[46] referring to the celebrated French actor, Contant-Benoit Coquelin.

Spring turned Hopper's somber palette to lighter tones and covered his painting clothes with green. After a cold, wet winter, the new season seemed especially glorious, the sunlight incredible: "The light was different from anything I had known. The shadows were luminous, more reflected light. Even under the bridges, there was a certain luminosity."[47] As the weather warmed, he wrote: "I am well, in fact I've never felt better."[48] Delighted to be able to work outdoors, he noted: "Paris is very beautiful in the sun and the people never miss a clear day to be out in the street and the parks."[49] He usually set up his easel along the Seine.

By this time, Hopper was showing the influence of the Impressionists. The pastel tonalities of Renoir, Sisley, and Monet encouraged his move to a lighter palette, away from the teaching of Henri. He later recalled:

I went to Paris when the pointillist period was just dying out. I was somewhat influenced by it. Perhaps I thought it was the thing I should do. So the things I did in Paris—the first things [i.e., large paintings: he never showed the earlier, darker, smaller works of the fall]—had a rather pointillist [i.e., Impressionist] method. But later [on the 1909 trip] I got over that and later things done in Paris were more the kind of things I do now.[50]

He could see Impressionist paintings in the galleries and salons, and in the Caillebotte collection at the Luxembourg. Under their influence, he not only lightened his palette, but he also painted with shorter, more broken brushstrokes, as is apparent in works of 1907 such as *Tugboat at Boulevard Saint Michel* and *Le Louvre et la Seine.* That year, he produced light-hued paintings with pink, blues, lavenders and yellows predominant, such as *Pont du Carrousel* and *Gare d'Orléans, Après-midi de Juin,* and *Pont du Carrousel in the Fog.* The latter suggests that he was familiar with Monet's Waterloo bridge series, begun in 1900, some of which he probably saw at the Durand-Ruel gallery.

Hopper's mention of "pointillist influence" was misleading, for he was not directly affected by the painting of such artists as Seurat or Signac. Despite his later denial, he seems, however, to have been interested in the work of Albert Marquet, who followed up his part in the autumn Salon with a one-man exhibition at the Galerie Druet in February 1907. Marquet painted several of the sites that Hopper would depict in the next few months, including *Notre-Dame, Quai des Grands-Augustins, Quai du Louvre,* and *Pont Neuf, Temps de Pluie.* After Hopper switched to a more subdued palette and took a prosaic simplified approach to his subjects, the results resemble Marquet's ordinary, nondramatic views of Paris. Like Marquet, he also adopted a style of summarizing the human figure with a quick brushstroke as can be seen in *Le Pont des Arts* of 1907.

Another interest that Hopper developed in Paris was photography. Years later he admitted that he had once bought a camera and taken pictures of architectural details, but he lamented "the camera sees things from a different angle, not like the eye."[51] Yet he was amazed "by how much personality a good photographer can get into a picture."[52] He later avowed admiration for the photography of Eugène Atget,[53] who was then active in Paris producing the "documents pour artistes" that he supplied to artists looking for subject matter, among them Dunoyer de Segonzac, André Derain, and Man Ray. Like Atget, Hopper created a mood of melancholy and tended to convey a feeling of solitude. Both he and Atget depicted such subjects as an interior stairway, Left Bank streets, and bridges along the Seine. Hopper even took the boat to nearby Saint-Cloud, where his painting of the staircase in the park suggests familiarity with the photographs Atget made there. Both artists emphasized the sloping terrain and the rhythmic angularity of the architectural forms. The painter, however, chose to compress this space through the use of a characteristically flattened perspective.

Hopper reveled in the Paris spring. He watched the children playing in the Luxembourg Gardens and went to hear music in the garden of the Tuileries.[54] He enjoyed the students on parade in the Luxembourg Gardens every Friday afternoon when the French army band played and all sorts of colorful bohemian types emerged to join in the festivities.[55] It was a young American gawker's delight. He went to the Salon des Indépendants, which he commented was not "particularly good."[56] If he noticed the works by John Marin and the ever-present Max Weber, as well as European avant-garde artists ranging from Henri Rousseau to Vassily Kandinsky, he gave no sign. Perhaps he liked the three landscapes by Marquet.

In late May, he reported: "I am painting out-of-doors all the time now, often taking the boat to St. Cloud or Charenton."[57] These were the excursions on which he produced *Canal Lock at Charenton; Gateway and Fence, Saint Cloud; Le Parc de Saint-Cloud;* and other scenes along the Seine. These three canvases are all painted in a rather harsh midday light, stressing muted greens and grays. Hopper recalled that Paris was "the apex of everything. I liked the physical aspect of the city. I worked by myself in the streets, along the river, painting under the influence of Impressionism, painting everything in a high key for nearly a year. It was probably not a strong, lasting influence, after all. Other than to lighten tones for me. Henri's students painted very dark."[58] The hooks were set deeper than he cared to admit. The neighborhood of the rue de Lille stayed with him and became a place of

Edward Hopper in Paris, 1907.

imagination: "I could just go a few steps and I'd see the Louvre across the river. From the corner of the Rues de Bac and Lille, you could see Sacré-Coeur. It hung like a great vision in the air above the city."[59] His feet turned the familiar corner toward the broad, open vistas along the Seine and his imagination soared.

Before Christmas, when Edward wrote his mother about his first holiday away from home, the occasion moved him to a confidence of which the implication seems to have escaped even her vigilant eye:

> On Christmas evening I went to a dinner at an English chapel "after which games were played and a pleasant evening enjoyed" spin the platter; etc. I went with a very bright Welsh girl, a student at the Sorbonne, and we derived considerable amusement from the evening's programme, which consisted chiefly of sentimental songs with the h's omitted.[60]

Enid Marion Saies was a brilliant young woman who also boarded with Mme. Jammes. Her family had lived in Wales, but were actually English, not Welsh, a distinction initially lost on Hopper. Enid was three years younger than he, tall like him (five feet eight inches), slender, and pretty, with dark brown hair and bright brown eyes. She was charming, had a delightful speaking voice and an infectious laugh.[61] An intellectual, she was then in her second year at the Sorbonne, where she studied French literature and history. She had a gift for languages and loved literature; she may have introduced Edward to various French authors. Like him, she cared little for religion, but her mother was intensely religious, which explains how she, too, came to board above Eglise Evangélique Baptiste. (Her strict family had sent her to a Quaker school in England.[62]) Once, when an interviewer asked him about visiting Great Britain, Hopper, who was then in his early eighties, recalled: "I knew an English girl there I'd met in Paris and we went around a little, not much."[63]

When Enid wrote to Edward many years after their meeting and asked if he remembered her, he answered: "I remember going to Versailles with you and to the Opera to see 'Manon,' I think it was." He added: "I have not forgotten Mme. Jammes kitchen with Miss Cuniffe speaking fluent, but bad French and drinking too much tea—I remember the two gangling boys and mud all over Paris—but a wonderful city just the same."[64] Hopper took Saies, whom he liked to tease, on a number of excursions to tourist attractions such as Versailles. They enjoyed each other's company and she recalled how much he made her laugh. At the age of twenty-one, she had just finished her studies at the Sorbonne and was ticketed for marriage. A Frenchman was in pursuit, one M. Premier, who had already proposed. As summer approached, Saies returned to her family in London. Years later she told her daughter that Hopper was "in love with her"; he even "followed her to London and wanted to marry her."[65]

To his mother Edward wrote only to propose expanding their original project with travel to Madrid, England, Holland, Italy, and Germany, even if he had to ask for money: "I feel that since I am here I might as well see all I can as I may not have another chance."[66] When he left Paris on June 27, it was not for Madrid, Holland, Italy, or Germany. In London, he found lodging in one of the cheap hotels in Bloomsbury, at 55 Gower Street, not far from the British Museum. His later memory of the city was not favorable. Writing to his family, he extended the series of comparisons across cultures that Paris had instigated: "London deserves its bad name as regards weather and gloom. . . . [It] has a sort of squat dingy strength to it, that is quite in contrast to the gay sparkle of Paris. It is like New York, essentially a commercial city."[67] He did not paint: he rejected the Thames as a subject, saying he found it "very swift and very muddy—the bridges also are higher and larger then those over the Seine. The banks are lined with factories and ware houses except where the 'embankments' are."[68]

Enid Saies.

Setting out to visit museums, he judged that the National Gallery had finer examples than the Louvre, also going to the Wallace Collection, which he especially admired, the British Museum, and other galleries. He found the interior of Westminster Abbey "very interesting" and "tremendously English," but the Francophile missed the charm of Parisian streets, which he referred to as "the peoples playground."[69] Paris still loomed large, especially French food: "I have discovered a little French restaurant on Soho Street where I eat cheaply and well. You see I could not forget the French cooking (there is nothing like it)."[70] What had brought Edward directly to London was Enid. He took her to "dinner at an Italian restaurant in Soho,"[71] and they sat together in her family's garden while she embroidered a waistcoat for her French suitor and intended husband. Edward was helping her by biting off the threads, she recalled, when he suddenly recoiled and said he wasn't "going to do that for another man."[72] He let her know that he loved her and wanted to marry her, as she told her daughter. He had the examples of his friends in Paris, Bruce and Graecen, with their newborn sons. Nothing came of it. He waited in London only until money arrived from his parents on July 18, leaving the next day for Amsterdam, about nine days earlier than originally planned.

In Holland, Hopper spent only four or five days. He visited Amsterdam and Haarlem, where his favorite teacher, Robert Henri, was conducting a summer school for American students, among them Josephine Nivison, Elizabeth Fisher, Hartman K. Harris, Clara Perry, Louise Pope, and Helen Niles. Every Sunday, Henri took his students to look at works by Rembrandt and Hals in Amsterdam's Rijksmuseum. Hopper saw Hals's paintings in the town hall in Haarlem, but it was Rembrandt's *Nightwatch* in the Rijksmuseum that impressed him as "the most wonderful thing of his I have seen, it's past belief in its reality—it almost amounts to deception."[73]

The next stop was Berlin, where he arrived July 26 and stayed at Eichberg's Hotel on Charlottenstrasse. He commented that the prosperity of the countryside through which he had passed on the train from Holland reminded him of America: "Immense wheat fields, railroads and factories."[74] By the first of August, he was in Brussels, "a fine little city, but very much like Paris—everything is French, even the soldiers look so and as you know, French is spoken almost altogether. The teutonic traits of the Flemish seem to have been entirely extinguished."[75] He did not think much of the museum and spent only two days in the Belgian capital, staying at the Monopole Hotel. While there, however, he seems to have had a good time, as he posed for a photograph with two male friends.

Hopper arrived back in Paris on August 3. He wrote to his father five days later, hoping that he was "gaining strength daily"—which suggests that Garret was suffering from a rather serious illness.[76] Hopper had planned a trip to Madrid, but reconsidered and sailed home on the Majestic from Cherbourg on August 21, a sudden decision that was surely connected to his father's health. Yet, he also must have recognized that it was imperative that he return to America and begin to make his mark as an artist. How to go about this remained unclear. Abruptly he cut short the voyage of self-discovery that had indelibly altered his life and his art.

THE AMBIVALENT AMERICAN: 1907–1910

EUROPE, WHICH HAD STRENGTHENED Robert Henri and propelled him to new heights of influence on his return, caused only confusion in his pupil. Edward Hopper's talent fell prey to conflicting claims, enticed by the newly discovered charms of Paris, yet beleaguered by the outcry back in New York for an American art. Among the strongest proponents of the value of native roots was Henri himself, whose own successes in Europe had been one of the original spurs to Hopper's pilgrimage abroad. Henri's message now was, do as I say, not as I did.

To compound confusion, the economic outlook for a young artist in America in the autumn of 1907 was not auspicious. The previous spring the stock market had plunged. Business failures multiplied as the panic of 1907 revealed flaws in the currency and credit structure. Given the economic uncertainty, no gallery or patron could be expected to take a chance on an unknown painter. The alternative was only too familiar to Hopper. He had arrived on the New York scene by way of commercial art, only to outgrow it for the ideal of the free artist. Now his very survival in the art world seemed to depend on the commercial work he had come to scorn. At stake, too, was a growing, if tardy, desire for independence from his family. Back from France and the Baptist mission, Hopper was determined to live on his own in New York City, rather than return to his parents and sister in Nyack.[1] From the pressures and uncertainties of New York, his mind fled to the happier past. He wrote to his Paris companion Enid Saies, who replied from England thanking him for his "lengthy and interesting letter" and confiding her depression in the face of her impending marriage. Expressing deep disappointment about her fiancé, she reminisced fondly about the confidences shared with Edward in Paris:

> We decided, the day you said goodbye, do you remember, that I should like Monsieur Premier. I was quite in love with him for 6 days 18 months ago. He is 10 years older than I, & seems more. . . . I suppose I've made a hash pretty generally of my life, but I'm not going back now, & perhaps for a "child of impulse & of passion" it's safer & wiser—well, I suppose I lived & had a good time during my "gay student life" in Paris. But Oh! I'm miserable. I don't know why I'm telling you all this. But you are the only one to whom I need not pretend that I'm gliding through a period of engaged bliss—& we were good pals, weren't we? I like to think that.[2]

If Enid hoped that Edward would come to the rescue, she did not know him well enough. Years later his friend Guy Pène du Bois would remark that Hopper preferred "able dissection of the human species" to romance. Enid's letter did not stir Edward to action and her ensuing story was far from tragic. She eluded her *monsieur,* and in 1909 married a Swede named Nils Buhre, moved to Malmö, and had four children.

Her 1907 confidence elicited no response. Only in 1948 did Enid renew the correspondence, when she read of Hopper in *Time:* "I wonder if you can remember the very unsophisticated English girl you used to make fun of & take for excursions to Versailles etc.," she wrote. "You used to make me laugh a lot."[3] He was so pleased to hear from her that he not only answered her letter, but sent her a monograph on his work. The exceptionally warm and lengthy, for him, response suggests how special she had been: "Of course I remember you Enid Saies. . . . It was good to hear from you after so many years."[4]

Having broken his one personal link with Europe, Hopper faced life in New York. Simply to keep himself in the city, he looked for work, which he found doing illustrations by the piece for an advertising agency, Sherman and Bryan. They were to prove a mainstay for longer than he could hope or fear. For the agency in 1908 he designed the next season's ads for Brigham Hopkins straw hats: modishly he aped the silhouettes and curvilinear forms of contemporary Art Nouveau. Neither personally distinctive nor innovative, his output makes no secret of the fact that his heart had other designs.

In the midst of nostalgia and financial necessity, Hopper lost no time catching up with old friends from the New York School of Art. In his absence, they had been busy seeking avenues for their work, inspired by their teacher Henri, out to circumvent not merely the general hard times but the dominance of the conservative National Academy of Design. The ringleaders, Arnold Friedman, Julius Golz, Jr., and Glenn Coleman, assembled a show of fifteen artists, Exhibition of Paintings and Drawings by Contemporary American Artists. They rented the top floor of a former club building at 43–45 West Forty-second Street from March 9 through 31, 1908.

Besides the organizers, two of Hopper's friends gave a special hand: George Bellows worked to improve the decoration of the hall and Guy du Bois gave early proof of the gift for publicity and social connections that he would use unselfishly and assiduously to aid Hopper. Friedman recalled du Bois's lending "support to our faltering spirits by interesting the newspapermen and other Bigwigs."[5] As for Hopper, Friedman spoke of him only as "recently returned from Paris" and "enthusiastic," but noted no active participation.[6] Since work began on this exhibition in the late winter of 1906, right after Hopper's departure for Europe, his inclusion after his return in the autumn of 1907 indicates a certain amount of effective networking and suggests that his peers continued to hold him in esteem, as they had in school. The participants came from the circle of Henri's male students and comprised some of the most promising artists of the next generation: besides Friedman, Golz, Coleman, Bellows, du Bois, and Hopper, there were Rockwell Kent, Carl Sprinchorn, and seven more.[7]

As a gesture against the predominance of academic art, the show by students of Henri took inspiration from the master himself. Henri had recently achieved a controversial success against academic art: the famous show of "The Eight," as they became known—besides himself, they were John Sloan, George Luks, Ernest Lawson, Everett Shinn, William Glackens, Arthur B. Davies, and Maurice Prendergast—which opened at the Macbeth Gallery, 450 Fifth Avenue, on February 3, 1908. The success of Henri, in both sales and notoriety, was not duplicated by the younger group. The headline in the *Evening Mail* proclaimed "The Eight Out-Eighted." The reviewer meant no compliment: "Having had 'The Eight', we now have their direful consequences." He singled out Bellows as "a coming man all right," but pontificated that most of these "youths," whose work he found too derivative of Henri, "belong to a future that is never going to happen at all."[8]

On March 13, Sloan and Henri came to see the show: "Good lot of stuff and full of interest," Sloan remarked. "I'd like to be rich enough to buy some of these things by Golz, Dresser, Keefe, etc. They would be fine to own, so different from the 'regular picture game'."[9] The artists he singled out never made a particular mark, and if he recognized any special talent in Hopper, he gave no evidence of it at the time. More than a decade would pass before Sloan came to think highly of Hopper. As for Henri, Hopper recalled that his old teacher "didn't like my Paris paintings. They were too light. He used to say that the only excuse for a light painting was to hang on a light wall."[10]

Hopper contributed three canvases done in Paris, using English titles *The Louvre and Seine, The Bridge of the Arts,* and *The Park at St. Cloud.* All employed a light palette and a freedom of brushstroke inspired by his encounter with Impressionism. He showed, too, one of his Paris caricatures in water-color, *Une Demi-mondaine.* Besides Hopper, three of the fifteen artists ventured to exhibit French subjects in a show billed as "American": du Bois's Paris painting *Gaité Montparnasse* shared its subject with a painting that Shinn had exhibited a month earlier with "The Eight." G. Leroy Williams and Harry Daugherty showed illustrations from Flaubert's *Madame Bovary.* The other artists mainly showed scenes painted in and around New York and portraits employing the dark palette favored at the New York School of Art.

Ignoring this marginal French contingent, the *New York American* trumpeted that the exhibition represented "one step nearer to a national art."[11] Hopper was not in step. His entries betrayed his allegiance to Paris in both content and style. When the show opened, seven months after his return from Europe, he was still full of the experience of France and the late-nineteenth-century tradition of French art, even though he desperately wanted to find acceptance at home and enough support to enable him to pursue a career as a painter.

For the rest of 1908 Hopper's paintings avoided French subjects: *Tramp Steamer, The El Station* (based on his memory of the Ninth Avenue El at Christopher Street), *Railroad Train,* and *Tugboat with Black Smokestack.* He seemed to be following Henri's reiterated calls for "progress in our national art" and "an appreciation of the great ideas native to the country and then the achievement of a masterly freedom in expressing them."[12] In reality, Hopper derived *Tramp Steamer* from his memory of a British ship observed in the English Channel. All the pictures share the theme of transportation and suggest preoccupation with getting away. Hopper was biding his time until illustrating and frugality would let him save up enough to go back to Paris. Money not spent in convivial evenings of drink and talk with other artists could speed his departure. He was more keen on getting back to something indefinable than on being one of the boys. Then, too, there was the model of Henri, who still took his summers abroad.

For the second journey, the initiative came from Edward. This time there was no careful advance planning by Elizabeth Hopper, laying the groundwork to provide her son a home away from home. Everyone in the family seems to have taken for granted that one could simply reappear on the doorstep at 48 rue de Lille and pick up where things had left off nearly two years before. On March 17, 1909, the R.M.S. *Majestic* arrived in Plymouth bearing Edward Hopper. Via train from Cherbourg he proceeded directly on to Paris. He presented himself in the rue de Lille, only to discover that things were not as expected: he was forced to seek "an hotel in the latin quarter (Hotel St. Malo)," he reported to his mother on March 24, because "Madame Jammes has been ill and in bed for some months—today she left for a sanatorium on the outskirts of Paris."[13] Suddenly having to fend for himself, he had looked near the university, where lodgings would be cheap. His heart remained set on the rooms above the Baptist mission. By April 2, when he wrote again, he had been able to reinstall himself there. Familiarity was uppermost in his mind; he had no thought of any possible risk of infection. On April 16 he reported that Madame Jammes was still at the hospital in Courbevoie, a Parisian suburb, and looking better;[14] on April 28, she died of consumption.[15] Hopper wrote the next day, saying that he thought Madame would be buried sometime the day after, but he was not certain. His comment made years later to Enid Saies clarifies his concern for their old landlady: "Mme. Jammes was ill then and died while I was there. I went to her burial at Courbevoie."[16]

To his family in Nyack, Hopper showed little emotion at the death of the woman who had so mothered him and sheltered both him and Enid. He had come to know her sons, too, yet his only expressed feeling was concern regarding the apartment: would the sons keep it? If not, "I shall try to get a room near here as I like this part of the city. I am hoping to see some riots the first of May, although it is hardly possible as there has been no serious trouble for some time."[17]

The Jammes boys decided to keep the rooms above the mission until October. Hopper could feel secure in his familiar base. He warmed up to the surroundings, repeatedly praised "the splendid weather," wrote his father, "The boulevards and parks are looking fine, and the men are wearing straw hats."[18] Taking advantage of the season and his proximity to the Seine and the Louvre, he painted out-of-doors along the river almost every day. It was the line of least resistance. As a result his paintings differ little in theme from those of the previous trip: *Le Pavillon de Flore* of the Louvre and, hard by, *Le Pont Royal.* His style did evolve to a degree: he utilized much more dramatically the contrast of light and shadow; he modified his palette into more subdued tones, without the high-key pastels of his earlier canvases. Gradually he freed himself from the impact of the Impressionists: his brushstrokes were no longer as choppy.

Socially Hopper was rather busy during this second stay in Paris. He told his mother that he had run into several "fellows" whom he knew from New York, probably classmates such as Patrick Henry Bruce, Oliver N. Chaffee, or Walter Pach, still living in Paris.[19] And he reported, "All Paris is decorated in honor of Jeanne d'Arc as she has recently been canonized in Rome—it looks very fine."[20] Some occasion brought him to lunch at the home of a French family, which he found awkward, given his inability to speak much French.[21]

Late in May, the "splendid weather" began to change. Years later Hopper chose to forget the sunny spring and dwell on the negative. He wrote to Guy du Bois, who could appreciate the point: "It is hard for an American to get used to Paris weather. The low clouds and the rain. 'Showers are still probable' used to be the daily weather report when I was there in summer. I never got used to it."[22] No longer able to work at his ease in the neighborhood of the rue de Lille, he was forced to turn to excursions. To his mother he reported again: "I am far from feeble. I went to Fontainebleau yesterday with a friend of mine and had a very good time although it rained now and then. The Gorge de Franchard in the forest is very fine as is also the forest itself."[23] Elizabeth herself had been feeble, but made a recovery, as Edward's next letter shows:

> Dear Mother,
>   I am glad to hear you are growing stout—I had guessed as much from your handwriting—you know it is comparatively easy to detect the writing of a fat lady. I hope however that you won't rise over two hundred. In spite of that you should be thankful that you are feeling so much better.[24]

His bent for caricature did not stop at his father and himself. After this sally, he announces a further excursion: "I am going to try to go to Chartres in a few days to see the cathedral supposed to be one of the finest in France."

Work interrupted by weather, Hopper began taking stock and making plans, as he explained to his mother:

> I suppose you want a letter from me not having had one lately.
>   I have been thinking of going down to Madrid for about a month, as I want very much to see the gallery there, and return through Paris to England & Holland. Of course I should like to see Italy & Germany, but don't believe I will be able to, even as it is I may have to ask you for money in a month or two. You know of course that I do not want to do so, but I feel that since I am here I might as well see all I can as I may not have another chance. Should I remain

in Paris I would have ample enough to last me until December, but I don't think I shall stay that long.

I took your cousins to hear the music in the Tuileries a few nights ago, and they seemed to enjoy it very much. I find them very agreeable, though I suspect Helen might prove to be otherwise on a closer acquaintance, however she has been very nice to me the few times I have met her.

I hope you are well and thriving.

Your son

E. Hopper[25]

Velázquez, Goya, and Manet had been favorites of his teachers at the New York School. The lesson remained and prompted the ideal itinerary. He had glimpsed Germany, England, the Netherlands on the previous round; now he would see the Prado, and he was well aware that Italy was the classic tour. His mother's cousins had proved a diversion. He sounds surprisingly sociable, aware of what to do and where, interested in music, sensitive to nuance. Money was a delicate subject, the province of his mother. With his father two days later, he took a different tack:

G. H. Hopper.

Dear Sir:

We are still having fine weather here and also many English and Americans although not as many Americans as usual. It is said also that they are not casting their coin about as freely as in former times, and that many shops are feeling the effects of it.

A few nights ago I went to see the pictures (cinematograph) of the Burns-Johnson fight—it looked as if Burns didn't even have a "look in" from the start although he seemed as good a boxer but not so big or powerful. He probably lacked "the punch."

On Monday of this week I went to St. Germain en Laye a town on the Seine near Paris. There is a very fine view here of the country surrounding Paris, as it is up on quite a hill. A high "Terrace" extends for a mile and a half along the river at a height of two or three hundred feet, flanked by an absolutely straight line of enormous trees. It's very imposing. In the town there is also an old Chateau which has a moat and contains the usual collection of antiques more or less interesting.

Give my regards to your wife and child.

Yours respectfully

E. Hopper[26]

The American Jack Johnson had defeated the Canadian Tommy Burns in a knockout, prompting racial tensions as promoters searched for a "great white hope" to humble the new champion. Hopper leaves unspoken the dominant view of victory by a Negro and delivers a practiced estimate of the bout. He assumes that his father will be interested and follow his points, which he expresses in boxing jargon vividly set off by quotation marks, as if to say, this is not our language but the way they put it. Boxing had been a topic of mutual interest since the days of the punching bag in the attic, one of their few male bonds. Hopper had to explain to his father that by "the pictures," he meant the cinema, a form of mass entertainment that was not yet considered respectable back in Nyack for those of the Hoppers' background and station.[27]

Without missing a beat, Hopper switches to one of his excursions. Again he gives a practiced estimate, this time from a painter's point of view. In clear language he sketches the layout and principal features of the place, as much to consolidate the memory for himself as to communicate it to someone else.

In the end the weather, rain "that I do not believe could be beaten in London," as much as any lack of funds, put off further projects to paint or travel. Hopper embarked July 31 on the *Ryndam* of the Holland-American Line, arriving in Hoboken August 9.[28]

Vivid reminders of his roots awaited his return. Plans were under way for the Hudson-Fulton Celebration, jointly commemorating the passage of 300 years since Henry Hudson sailed up the river and 102 years since Robert Fulton's similar voyage by steamboat. Hopper's classmate Clarence K. Chatterton had been commissioned to design a booklet and several posters promoting his hometown of Newburgh. Hopper, too, produced a black-and-white poster design for the event (whether on commission or not is unclear). Nyack held its own parade with floats that landed at the Main Street dock, where they were joined by local groups, including the Baptist Boys' Brigade and neighboring fire companies.[29] The Metropolitan Museum mounted a Hudson-Fulton exhibition, which focused on the Dutch settlers of New York and featured seventeenth-century Dutch artists, notably Rembrandt, Hals, and Vermeer.[30]

Ancestry was all very well, but even before his second trip Hopper had made the move from Nyack to New York. He had no intention of giving up and going back. Again his only way to independence was illustrating, and he returned to Sherman and Bryan for advertising commissions. At the same time, he threw himself into his painting with renewed ambition. In his new canvases, he staked out fresh territory as he grappled with old and new memories of France and his own renewed feel for his American roots.

In spite of the rain, the five months in France had reinforced his attachment and planted visions. He set about painting from memory the landscape he had sketched so precisely in the letter to his father.[31] His words had captured the view in language his father would understand. The "Terrace" in France recalled the Palisades along the Hudson south of Nyack. Thinking back and beginning to paint *Valley of the Seine,* he uses a visual language that mingles memory of the place in France with recollection of other painters' visions. He had grown up with the river and learned to see it as interpreted in the landscapes of the Hudson River School. A masterpiece of the school, Thomas Cole's *The Oxbow,* had come to the Metropolitan Museum in 1908. Advertising it as "one of the most important productions in pure landscape painting," the museum that December featured *The Oxbow* in the Accessions Room.[32] For Hopper it became a matrix and a foil as he shaped *Valley of the Seine.* In the manner of Cole, Hopper commands a vast space, with the river winding in the distance. But Cole boldly fixed his eye on a highly detailed tree set close on the left in the foreground of the picture, before sweeping across and out to the panorama and the sinuous river. Hopper instead places himself at a distance back from the picture plane and "up on quite a hill." He, too, carries the eye across from the left and out, but by means of a gleaming white viaduct for the railroad that curves down the center of the valley and the picture toward the dim city. The arches and the city at the limits of sight suggest a traditional French image of Italian landscape, stretching past some dilapidated and weedy aqueduct toward Rome. In complexity and scope *Valley of the Seine* represents a new departure for Hopper.

Also in 1909, Hopper painted *Le Bistro,* a dramatic evocation of intimacy and vastness, dark and light in Paris: on the edge of shadow to the left, at the foot of dark facades, a couple sits at a round table, immobile, with glasses and a bottle, while the eye moves out and center, back to imaginary cypresses that bend above a preternaturally white bridge with arches stretching to the right. Hopper remembers a possible intimacy on the margin, set against the brightness of a scene that is monumental and picturesque. He had absorbed the spring sunlight, but never saw such trees in walking out from the rue de Lille.

In a third canvas of this period, Hopper shifts to imagine something certainly not drawn from spring mornings along the Seine. He creates a vignette of erotic tension and loneliness indoors: *Summer Interior.* Again the eye moves diagonally from the foreground across and back, taking in a woman flung down next to an unmade bed on a trailing bedsheet: dressed only in a sleeveless blouse, her head cast down, her right elbow supporting her body against the bed, her left arm drooping limp, the hand invisible between her thighs, her bare leg touching a carpet of light from an unseen window. The figure's partial nudity, facelessness, abandoned posture, and visually emphasized sexuality imply the disconsolate aftermath of an encounter in the demimonde. Formally the composition, with abrupt diagonals and a tilted green floor, as well as the intimate theme, suggests that Hopper had been looking at Degas. The intensity of feeling reveals a further way in which the second Parisian trip renewed and deepened Hopper's experience and his inner conflict with puritan values. All his life, he preferred to paint "from the fact," whether from memory or from posed models. But here, as in the other two canvases of this autumn of 1909, he paints in a way without precedent for him. The return to Paris had provoked, not placated, his erotic sensibility. Coming after and out of his experience there, *Summer Interior* looks toward works of his maturity: the loneliness of recurrent tense interiors, the sexual undercurrent, and the perspective of the voyeur.

Besides Degas, the composition of *Summer Interior* also shows signs of Hopper's growing interest in contemporary French illustration. He brought back three issues of *Les Maîtres Humoristes,* illustrated by Albert Guillaume and Jean-Louis Forain, as well as a copy of *Le Sourire,* a humor magazine. From Guillaume, Hopper adapted an illustration of a French couple seated on an embankment, using similar architecture, curb stones, and grassy slope, but exaggerating the drinking of wine, including three empty bottles. Hopper changed the mood as well, conveying melancholy rather than ironic humor, more in line with Anglo-Saxon puritanism than Latin freedom.

Not until early 1910 did the old school network afford Hopper another opportunity to show. Unlike two years before, he now appeared not only with Henri's legions but with the leader himself. Henri and Sloan were among the chief organizers of the "Exhibition of Independent Artists," which took place from April 1 through 27 in galleries improvised in a vacant commercial warehouse on West Thirty-fifth Street. The dates overlapped with the annual spring exhibition at the National Academy of Design and called its authority into question. Each artist could enter one work for ten dollars, two for eighteen. Frugal as ever, Hopper spent for only one, *Le Louvre et la Seine.* No doubt the fee was a factor, and possibly also his dissatisfaction with the results of his recent experiments, or sensitivity about his French themes in the face of Henri's American bent. Hopper did not sell and no critic singled him out among the 344 entries, although the show commanded many reviews. The tireless Guy du Bois both took part and reviewed for the *New York American.* Eager to emphasize the public impact of the initiative, he reported that more than two thousand people showed up for opening night, so that the "promoters find it necessary to adopt police regulations for handling crowds."[33]

Once again on the margins, outside the fanfare, Hopper nursed his French aesthetic and lived by commercial illustrations. He did not know how to fit in. He produced advertisements for the "Wearing Apparel, Textile and Fashion Show," a national trade exhibition that took place in Chicago in March 1910. As the symbol for the show, he designed an Atlas-like figure stooped under the weight of the show's name. Atlas provides an apt metaphor for Hopper's own sense of the burden he felt in his obligatory work. He continued to scrimp and dream of escape. The ideal itinerary, rained out the summer before, loomed in his mind, though even less than the year before does he seem to have made a careful plan to carry it out. Ever present was the enthusiasm of Henri, who spent the summers of 1906, 1908, and 1910 in Spain and painted the common people and especially their heroes, the fighters of bulls.[34]

Hopper's move does not have the air of a regular summer expedition. As soon as he had saved the minimum, he embarked. On May 11, 1910, he arrived in Plymouth aboard the R.M.S. *Adriatic,* and made a beeline for Paris. For the first time he knew he was on his own, and could not expect to find the homelike setting securely linked with Nyack. The experience of the previous year had taught him to look in the Latin Quarter for lodgings he could afford. He settled on a name that reflected the place: Hôtel des Ecoles, 15 rue Delambre. He looked up the Jammes boys, and the younger informed him that the elder had entered the army and was stationed near what Hopper translated as "the German frontier." That was all he bothered to relate to his mother. Years later, he filled in more for Enid Saies: "I have often wondered if the sons [of Mme. Jammes] survived the first World War. Casimir was doing his service in the cavalry the last I heard of him and that is just where he did not want to be—he was afraid of horses—and he must have had plenty of them."[35]

Toward the end of his stay the year before, Hopper had written of a half year's worth of work still to be done in Paris, besides ambitious travel. In fact in May 1910 he tarried in Paris only a week or so. He told his mother: "I left Paris on the 26th of May and spent 28 hours on the train to Madrid and am staying at a very good pension in the centre of the city. The trip on the train through the Pyrenees and the north of Spain is very remarkable—I have never seen such wonderful clear views and sunshine."[36]

To his father he described Madrid: "Not very large but is quite modern with exception of the means for transportation. The trams are very slow and ox and mule carts seem to be the thing for drawing freight."[37] Ever alert to landscape, he reported that "the country roundabout the city is very fine—there is a big range of snow-capped mountains toward the northwest of which I have forgotten the name—they look good without the name, however."[38]

For his sister he reserved his longest and most vivid letter:

I went to a bull fight last Sunday and found it much worse than I thought it would be. The killing of the horses by the bull is very horrible, much more so as they have no chance to escape and are ridden up to the bull to be butchered. It is not what I would call an exciting sport, merely brutal and horrible sickening.

The entry of the bull into the ring however is very beautiful, his surprise and the very first charges he makes are very pretty.

I have also been out to Toledo—, a most wonderful old town, and wandered about under a very hot sun for a day after which I came back to Madrid.[39]

The bull's entry was the only part that later, perhaps in deference to both Goya and Manet, he made the subject of an etching. Nothing else from his trip to Spain made its way into his art. He would not ape Henri. His eye and heart were already engaged.

For Spain, after all, eleven days sufficed. Originally he had justified venturing Spain by invoking the Prado to his mother—"I want very much to see the gallery there"[40]—but no museums figure in the extant letters. By June 10 he was back in Paris. Before leaving he had booked a hotel inhabited by Miss Cuniffe, his fellow former resident with Mme. Jammes. He remained scarcely three weeks: on July 1 he sailed from Cherbourg for New York on the *Cincinnati* of the Hamburg-American line. The third venture across the ocean had been the shortest, less than two months all told, the least well conceived and least lucky. Not even the truncated new itinerary had broken new ground. Whatever Hopper had hoped to recapture or acquire did not materialize. He would feel no need to pursue the rest of his ideal tour. He had exorcised the lure of European success, the treacherous example of Henri— and he never tried Europe again.

If the literal yearning had been quenched, the original impact endured. More than two decades later, Hopper wrote in the space labeled "where studied" on an exhibition entry form: "New York City and in Europe."[41] On another occasion he sounded more ambivalent: "The life over there is entirely different from the life here. In Europe life is ordered; here it is disordered. And, with the exception of Spain, the light there is different. Those countries don't have the clear skies and sunlight we have here."[42] In the end he admitted: "It seemed awfully crude and raw here when I got back. It took me ten years to get over Europe."[43]

IN SEARCH OF A STYLE: 1911–1915

SUDDENLY HOME AGAIN in the summer of 1910, Hopper had re-
solved nothing. At most his hasty third trip to Europe had tarnished, not broken, the spell. At twenty-eight, his reasons for inner conflict were as acute as
ever. He vacillated, feeling nostalgia for French themes and a new attraction
to the style of the expatriate Whistler, and yet aware of the challenge
launched by the apostles of truly American art. Unable to sort himself out and
settle down to a distinctive style of his own, he could hardly hope to persuade
galleries and buyers. Nor was he any closer to decisiveness and settling down
in his emotional life.

He took a practical initiative, finding a studio at 53 East Fifty-ninth Street,
not far from the brownstone of Robert Henri. Here he would at least have
more than the inadequate space he had suffered on Fourteenth Street, and be
free of the annoyance of being accosted by the streetwalkers who swarmed
there. In the absence of any outlet for his paintings, the need for financial independence continued to press. Momentarily he despaired of his dream.

In the city directory for 1911, he listed his profession as "salesman."[1] It
was a low point. "Salesman" would satirize the function of commercial art
and the burden upon the artist to drum up business by selling his skill. It
may have been a bitter joke made at his own expense; quite in character, it
would top the long line of caricatures of himself. Hopper was reduced again

to canvassing offices and peddling his skill. "You had to sell yourself, with a portfolio under your arm, just like Edward Hopper. It was hard and demeaning," recalled James Ormsbee Chapin, another artist and illustrator."[2] Hopper himself spoke frankly of his reluctance and embarrassment: "Sometimes I'd walk around the block a couple of times before I'd go in, wanting the job for money and at the same time hoping to hell I wouldn't get the lousy thing."[3] He never tired of reiterating his antipathy: "Illustration didn't really interest me. I was forced into it in an effort to make some money. That's all. I tried to force myself to have some interest in it. But it wasn't very real."[4] Besides the advertising agencies, Hopper sought out magazines. By the end of 1911, he was illustrating for *Everybody's,* a magazine active in the muckraking movement, then edited by Trumbull White. Hopper's work, all of it in black and white, consisted at first of line drawings for stories about young boys.

The business of earning left little time for painting. Only two works survive from 1911: *Sailing,* which recalls his boyhood enthusiasm for boats and the yachts built in Nyack, and *Blackwell's Island,* depicting a body of land that lay in the East River, a few minutes from his studio. The latter had a specific recent history in art that might attract and provoke. In 1901 Robert Henri, who had returned from his successes in Europe and settled in New York, had painted *Blackwell's Island, East River,* from his East Fifty-eighth Street window: a close view of ice floes and snow-topped buildings, with a long glance downriver. Henri's star pupil George Bellows returned to the theme in 1909, shifting the focus to the dramatic innovation on the scene: *The Bridge, Blackwell's Island.* At center, light rakes the massive pier of the new Queensborough Bridge, one of the three engineering marvels recently built to supplement the famous old span to Brooklyn. In characteristic fashion, Bellows crowds the foreground with city life: a Manhattan quay, barge, dory, sight-seers in silhouette, gas streetlight. On the water a tugboat chugs upriver. In 1910, a third Blackwell's Island painting won praise for another veteran of Henri's classes, Julius Golz; at the Independents exhibition, it moved the critic for the *New York Mail and Express* to speak of "work of compelling earnestness."[5] Hopper, too, had paid his ten dollars for the Independents, but his *Le Louvre et la Seine* had gone unremarked: evidently he had chosen the wrong river. Now his decision to paint the East River island looks suspiciously like an effort to move in on an American subject, to emulate success and overcome his own obscurity and isolation. Already he had moved into Henri's neighborhood near the bridge.

For his own version of Blackwell's Island, Hopper used a soft, blue-gray palette which reflects his interest in Whistler, whose tonalist paintings and pastels had been shown at the Metropolitan Museum in the spring of 1910.[6]

In a further departure from Bellows, Hopper establishes a viewpoint high up in the bridge itself, its dark tower and light roadway hugging the left like the facades and figures in *Le Bistro*. The island huddles darkly beneath, with a suggestion of the villages in *Valley of the Seine*. In the distance, a tiny tugboat stands in outline. The moon shimmers on the band of blue before Queens. The bump on the far horizon could be Montmartre.

For *Sailing* Hopper emphasizes tone over color in the contrast of light and shade. So strained were his financial circumstances that he frugally painted the new image over one of his old portraits. He worked indoors from memory, either in Nyack, or, more likely, in his studio. Recalling that he was inspired by "boyhood boating on the Tappan Zee,"[7] he referred to his subject as a "knockabout sloop rig" and noted that the jib and mainsail take up most of the canvas.[8]

Toward the end of 1911 or the beginning of 1912, as a favor to Arthur Cederquist, a friend and art school classmate, Hopper produced a group of illustrations for *Melange,* the 1912 yearbook of Lafayette College in Easton, Pennsylvania. (Arthur's younger brother Milton was the art editor for the yearbook. He had asked his brother to provide illustrations, but Arthur felt that he was not familiar enough with college life, and persuaded Hopper to take the project.[9]) For the athletics section, Hopper created another Atlas, this time dressed in gym shorts and shirt, kneeling in order to support the weight of the Lafayette College emblem. Hopper's flat black-and-white motifs are the most innovative illustrations he had yet produced. Although he was not paid, the assignment represented recognition of his abilities, which must have given him confidence.

Nearly two years had passed since the show of Independent Artists. For Hopper, this had been the most abject period he had known. When relief came at last, early in 1912, it derived from the same source. The Independents had been Henri's initiative. Now, to give fuller and more regular embodiment to his ideas about exhibitions, he created a plan for group shows at the MacDowell Club (108 West Fifty-fifth Street), which had been founded in memory of the composer Edward MacDowell.[10] Henri envisioned a series of nonjuried exhibitions in which groups of eight to twelve artists would show for two-week intervals.[11] As one of the regulars, Leon Kroll, remembered: "We had this group that used to exhibit at the MacDowell Club, which had a beautiful gallery at the time. It was a self-chosen group: you had to be elected by the other ten. Hopper was in it, and Speicher, John Sloan, as well as Henri, Glackens, and Luks—it was a very good group of the best artists. I felt very pleased because I was an Academy product, which was anathema to those people."[12]

The first show took place in November 1911. Hopper was invited for the group that showed from February 22 to March 5, 1912; his cohorts were Guy du Bois, who more than likely saw to his inclusion, and Bellows, Kroll, Mountfort Coolidge, Randall Davey, Rufus J. Dryer, and May Wilson Preston. If he considered the politics of the venue, Hopper betrayed little sign in his choice of works to present: of the five oils, only one, *Sailing,* did not specifically depict a European scene. By showing the French *Riverboat, Valley of the Seine, The Wine Shop* (which was *Le Bistro,* only superficially disguised under the title), and *British Steamer,* Hopper flew in the face of Henri's American agenda. His new *Blackwell's Island* would have made a different statement. One might blame intransigence and unwillingness to adjust to the flow. He neither sold pictures nor received any significant attention in the press.

Hopper turned again to advertising work for a regular client. His plight struck a sympathetic chord in James Chapin, who took a salaried job at the agency before going on to work free-lance as an illustrator: "I used to see Edward Hopper; he used to come down to Sherman & Bryan looking for work. . . . Before he was known as a painter, he was in the same boat I was, trying to make a living, trying to be an artist on the side."[13] Early in 1912, Hopper received commissions to illustrate a play for the July issue of the *Metropolitan Magazine* and articles for the August and September issues of *System, the Magazine of Business,* a periodical for which he would continue to work. For *System* he depicted the offices that years later he would develop into themes for his paintings. He now listed himself as an "illustrator" in the city directory.

With cash and confidence enhanced by multiple assignments, Hopper began to think of travel again. He did not look back to his old agenda. The most successful of his friends and classmates were not wandering in exile. They were colonizing the New England coasts, and Hopper, though more of a loner, felt drawn to emulate them.

For his first try, he picked Gloucester. Whether by chance or not, he fell in again with Leon Kroll. Younger by two years, as chatty as Hopper was taciturn, short as Hopper was tall, and Jewish as Hopper was Baptist, Kroll lived long enough and spoke so well as to inspire an oral history, which registered—along with comments on the streetwalkers on Fourteenth Street, bouts of debate over aesthetics with Bellows, and much else—that "Hopper was never conversational, nor was he exactly in the group as much as the rest of us were. . . . Henri was in, of course. He was the great, respected leader."[14] Like Hopper, Kroll had worked in Paris and traveled through Europe. As a painter, Kroll, too, was a realist, painting scenes that he observed around him. Unlike Hopper, Kroll claimed: "I don't have to wait for inspiration. An

Illustration for "Your Business Tomorrow," in System, *September 1913.*

artist's vision is working at all times."[15] For his part, Hopper opined: "Well, maybe there is such a thing as inspiration. Maybe it's the culmination of a thought process. But it's hard for me to decide what I want to paint. I go for months without finding it sometimes. It comes slowly."[16] (Nor did Kroll share Hopper's other inhibitions. He would soon fall in love with a French woman of good family and marry her within months.)

During their summer in Gloucester, the two worked on canvases of approximately the same scale. Kroll painted *Good Harbor Beach, Bridge at Bass Rock,* and other views of the picturesque rocky shore. He populated his canvases with dense crowds, while Hopper's were nearly figureless. Yet Kroll's lively optimism must have helped Hopper, who had a particularly productive summer.[17] He was painting out-of-doors for the first time in America, and his subjects included *Briar Neck,* where the white surf of the waves breaks energetically against the rocks; *Gloucester Harbor,* seen in an overview; *Tall Masts,* with boats and a typical fishing shack; the lighthouse in Annisquam known as *Squam Light;* and *Italian Quarter,* with its colorful wood-frame houses tucked in against the rocky shore. As for the latter canvas, Hopper recalled Kroll's claiming that the modernists would like the angular rocks in the foreground, but insisted that he had no thought of Cézanne or anyone else when he painted them: "The angularity was just natural to me; I liked those angles."[18]

That fall in New York, Hopper produced a single picture, *American Village,* a dark, brooding view that he said was inspired by various towns he saw from the train on his way back from Gloucester. He adapted a vantage point from which he looked down over the railing of a railroad viaduct to a small-town street below. His perspective, simultaneously emphasizing the immediate foreground and the distant view, suggests the influence of French Impressionist painters such as Gustave Caillebotte or Camille Pissarro. (As late as 1962, Hopper remarked about himself: "I think I'm still an impressionist."[19]) After the far-sweeping viaduct and distant villages in *Valley of the Seine,* and the perspective of *Blackwell's Island,* this picture marks a dramatic shift in scope, although similar in adopting an elevated viewpoint and moving the eye across and back from the left.

January 1913 found Hopper taking a second turn at the MacDowell Club. The cohort for this show included the dominant Henri and favorite Bellows, along with Hopper and Kroll, besides eight others. Hopper presented only two paintings, this time balancing his Parisian repertoire with Henri's Americanism: *Squam Light* was new, but *La Berge* looked back to his beloved banks of the Seine. Balance availed nothing; neither painting sold nor attracted mention. No relief from illustrating was in sight. Besides his work for *System,* Hopper had begun to sell regularly to *Associated Sunday Magazine,* a newspaper tabloid featuring serialized fiction and carried by papers in such major markets as Chicago and Philadelphia. Those were cities with vigorous cultural elites and institutions of fine art, his future clients, but for the moment another world for Hopper.

§

THE YEAR 1913 marked a turning point in the history of art in America. February saw the opening of the vast International Exhibition of Modern Art, popularly known as the Armory Show because it took place in the Sixty-ninth Regiment Armory at Twenty-fifth Street and Lexington Avenue. It would travel to Chicago and Boston, causing reverberations as it went. The arguments and polemics belong to the growing pains of American culture, but the show occasioned a more insidious kind of pain for Hopper.

The show's General Executive Committee included two of his friends, Guy du Bois and George Bellows; the network, however, did not function, and he was not invited to submit. Immediate control lay in the hands of the Domestic Exhibition Committee, chaired by William Glackens, Henri's ally in the famous show of "Eight" and also a MacDowell regular, but his own man. His panel gave offense by omission and commission, requesting that those it deigned to invite enter "works in which the personal note is distinctly sounded."[20] Protest led the committee to adopt more liberal procedures, allowing uninvited artists to submit. Hopper brought his two works of 1911, *Sailing* and *Blackwell's Island;* only the former placed. Others forced to volunteer included names that became more or less famous in American art: Stuart Davis, Bernard Karfiol, and Marguerite and William Zorach.[21] None of the other men placed only a single work, the more humiliation for Marguerite and Edward, who had to be content to make the show at all.

The Armory Show drew huge crowds. Hopper remembered seeing his former teacher, William Merritt Chase, dressed in frock coat, top hat, and boutonniere, making the rounds, "reviling everything."[22] Remarkably, given the attention to representatives of the European avant-garde, such as Matisse, Picabia, Kandinsky, Brancusi, and Duchamp, *Sailing* was purchased by Manhattan textile manufacturer Thomas F. Vietor for $250 (although the listed price was $300).[23] It was Hopper's very first sale of a painting, and he accepted the offer at once.[24] This sale was clearly a momentous event in Hopper's life. After pursuing the quest that had led him with growing assurance to New York and Paris, only to result in confusion, Hopper seemed to find new vigor that directed him toward freedom. At last he had something beyond school prizes to show his parents. He was barely in time: on September 18, 1913, Garret Hopper died.

Death brought the survivors together in the house at 53 North Broadway. Elizabeth and Marion garnered the obituary notice, with its kind opinions, for the archive that also preserved Edward's drawings, with their caricatures of the ineffectual husband and over-protective father. Garret's illness over his last summer could hardly have occasioned a burst of painting from his son. Perhaps only after his return from Nyack did Edward once again look in the direction of Blackwell's Island, this time placing himself to envision the whole span of piers and suspension towers marching off into an ever bluer distance—hence the title, *Queensborough Bridge.* He places himself low, on the Manhattan shore. With none of the urban busyness of Bellows, his gaze rises calmly and reaches further. Hopper worked in oil, again with the tonalist palette influenced by Whistler. He painted in his studio from a color sketch that he made at the site, a method that he seldom employed. He did not save the color sketch.

Scarcely two months after Garret's death, no doubt taking courage from the Armory sale, his son began to write in a large ledger bound in cloth, perhaps left unused by his father, its cover embossed with a border and an ornamented title, "MEMORANDUM." From left to right the four unequal columns march, with space that Edward used to register respectively the date, the client, quantity, medium, commission title, and the relevant dollars and cents:

1913		160
Nov. 13th	Asc. Sunday Magazines	35
	2 line drawings	195
	"The Iron Stickpin"	20 00
	"Wayland"	20 00
Nov. 22nd	Rec'd by check	$40 00

The entries advance in their regularly articulated and informative array until March 23, 1967. He had bought better than he knew. Only two and a half pages were left over when he died.

Where keeping accounts was concerned, Edward certainly shared his father's preference for other kinds of reading. Yet for more than fifty-three years, five times Garret's life in business for himself, Edward carefully husbanded these books. With never a change in emphasis or an aside, he registered his fortunes, at first the results of trudging about with his portfolio, screwing up courage to knock on doors, the runs of work for certain clients, and the sudden disappearances of familiar names and the arrival of new ones that document the relentless necessity to drum up sales.

The clientele and their orders reflect the ongoing tastes and functions of the world that had oriented Edward and his parents toward horizons beyond Nyack. Ironically for Edward, who aspired to be a "world" painter, the range of themes and topics that parade through the ledger falls within limits drawn to appeal to the folks back home in that narrower world. Titles embody a spectrum of popular fears, prejudices, and hopes: "It Walks & Talks, The Midnight Thieves, An Eery Hunt for Gold, Home-Sweet-Home, Baseball Matches, How I Caught an Outlaw, What a Word's Worth in Wall Street, My First Order, Making a Million in Wall Street." To be illustrated they have to be read, digested, and regurgitated in visual formulas recognizable and welcome in every parlor and country kitchen. The reduction to a common visual idiom particularly galled Hopper: "There were certain conventions in illustrating in those days that you had to observe. For instance, there was this story in which the woman had a bearded lover. I did a scene that showed the woman and her bearded lover, but they made me remove the beard. Lovers weren't supposed to be bearded. It was all right in the story but not in the illustration."[25] The subservience to such standards and the need to read trash insulted the boy who loved Emerson and Montaigne.

The very chains of economic and cultural necessity, which Edward yearned to break, find intellectual and material embodiment in the discrete entries in the ledger, with their exacting and repetitive form, always firmly, broadly, and neatly penned, with never a sign of either resentment or celebration. The discipline once set goes on, with no change in emphasis or form to take in stride the first step toward freedom by the sale of something besides commercial art. Keeping good books remains a baseline and reminder of upbringing and deep-rooted habit. The books become emblematic of the old-fashioned character and its stand-off with the changing world.

The summer's event had called a halt at the moment when forward steps seemed possible. Not even his father's death slowed Edward's new sense of purpose for long. Nothing could have made him suspect how much more time would pass before he sold a painting again. Stirred by his first sale, no doubt buoyed by the commercial income he so meticulously registered, he set out to find a more appropriate studio. It was time. He was past thirty, and had seen the careers of friends catch on. What he settled on speaks more than a diary about his ambition for his own career and his judgment of the art scene in New York.

In December 1913 Hopper left Fifty-ninth Street for Greenwich Village, where he would live and work until his death. Three Washington Square North forms part of the handsome Greek revival "Row," erected during the 1830s on the northeast side of the square. In 1884, the building was converted into studios for artists and enlarged by the addition of an extra story, making it stand apart in The Row.[26] Although quite run-down, it was sought out by its inhabitants because of the park-side location, high ceilings, modest rents, and the community of artists who swarmed in its studios. At first Hopper occupied the back room on the top floor of the four-story walk-up, a climb of seventy-four steps.[27] He had neither central heating nor a private bathroom, but the light from the large skylight was exceptional.

The building could point to a distinguished history; not only had Thomas Eakins (whom Hopper especially admired) painted there, but the roster of former tenants included Abbott Thayer, Thomas W. Dewing, Will H. Low, Augustus Saint-Gaudens, Walter Shirlaw, and William Glackens.[28] Another artist-tenant was Frederick W. Stokes, who had accompanied Admiral Peary to the North Pole. Nearly thirty years later, Homer Saint-Gaudens observed that Hopper's studio had once been Dewing's: "It is a matter of nostalgic contemplation to me that today I may climb those same creaking back stairs to find in the same apartment another huge blond man of talent, Edward Hopper."[29] Hopper's other neighbors under the roof, with whom he shared the hall bathroom, were also "confirmed bachelors": Walter Tittle and Colin Cruikshank.[30] Tittle had taken a studio in the back of the building, overlooking Washington Mews and University Place in March 1909.[31] He both lived and worked there for a year, until "social activities of the building's inhabitants developed to a degree utterly incompatible with my rather spotty capacity for sleep. Night was too frequently turned into carnival, and though I was always greeted with acclaim if I wandered into the center of the festivities clad in pajamas and dressing gown, this solution hardly provided energy for the next day's work."[32] Hopper, who had never shared in the bohemian side of artistic life, was not about to begin. He must have been a sounder sleeper than Tittle, since he both worked and lived on the premises for the rest of his days.

Hopper's arrival prompted a new entry in Tittle's diary: "Bobby Edward's old studio, next to mine, is now occupied by Edward ('Pop') Hopper, who was in art school with me."[33] The nickname hints at good-natured ribbing between the two since the time Hopper wrote the limerick teasing Tittle for eschewing work with female nudes. The missed life classes had not kept Tittle from early success as an illustrator. Generously he began to assist his neighbor in getting further commissions.

Hopper left the neighborhood of Henri and the MacDowell Club for the run-down and riotous province of Irish and Italians, where cheap housing was attracting a new influx of immigrants. Hopper's choice of Greenwich Village did not lack irony. Bohemian life in Paris had never seduced him, although it captivated his eye and brush and pen; nor did he demonstrate any taste for the convivial life or ever show any inclination for vanguards. He did not yearn for access to the famous salons of Gertrude Stein's friend Mabel Dodge, who had returned from Europe and set up a house of cultural innovation not far up Fifth Avenue from Washington Square, at the corner of Ninth Street. Neither the free talk of radical politics and aesthetics, nor the free sexuality, appealed to Hopper. Psychoanalysis, another current topic, did arouse his intellectual interest. He did not hear Sigmund Freud's disciple, Dr. A. A. Brill, speak on the unconscious, yet Freud's theories were frequently discussed in the popular press of the day. Even if Hopper missed the earliest of these articles, there was "Exploring the Soul and Healing the Body," by Max Eastman, a defining spirit of Village culture, in the June 1915 issue of *Everybody's* magazine[34] that contained Hopper's illustrations for "The Hero Business," a story by Edith Mirrielees.

Eastman discussed Freud and Jung as heading two schools of psychoanalysis. Both their names appear on books under the arm of a skinny figure with outsized fetal head and huge eyeglasses that Hopper sketched, in what looks like a self-caricature as both an impressionable infant, vulnerable to neuroses, and an adult "voracious reader" fascinated with the latest fashion for dissecting the human species—as his ironic and satirical bent would be described by Guy du Bois.[35] Hopper later spoke of his interest in Freud's ideas.[36] However, although he would complain of troubling dreams, he never sought professional counseling, true to his philosophy that the emotions are the proper subject of painting.

The move to the Village brought no immediate change. One sale did not lead to another. The carnival atmosphere in the new quarters neither distracted nor inspired. The ranks of commissions continued their march. Over and over Hopper penned neatly "Asc. Sunday Magazines, 2 line drawings," with the typical reading and imaging of "An Obstreperous Roommate, Diamonds and Junk." He could even identify with the theme of "An Emergency Sideline." And all the while he painted. Later Hopper insisted he had kept commercial work in bounds by limiting himself to three days of it per week: "Besides, even if I had wanted to work full time at commercial art, I did not have the skill or the facility and I never would have done well at it."[37]

Meanwhile the art press urged its nationalist campaign in tandem with the popular mentality. One authoritative voice could ask "whether American artists are doing their duty to their country by remaining abroad the greater part of their lives instead of seeking motives and subjects in America";[38] and assert in a similar vein, "The American artist who has made a permanent home abroad cannot paint pictures with the real American atmosphere and feeling. Very little, consequently, can be expected from him that will help to build up the national art."[39]

By now a regular at the MacDowell Club, Hopper took part in his third group show in January 1914. At last he decided to present only works painted in America on American subjects: two oils, *Gloucester Harbor* and *The Bridge*. In spite of their common national origin, his divergent styles show that his new emphasis on America did not reflect the achievement of a distinctive manner and personal vision. He continued to vacillate between the Whistlerian palette of *The Bridge* and the crisply rendered forms in bright sunlight of *Gloucester Harbor*. Readiness of material, rather than any further vacillation, must account for his reversion to exclusively French subject matter and works made in France for a group drawing show at the MacDowell in April. (He showed *On the Quai, Land of Fog, The Railroad, The Port,* and *Street in Paris*.) No sales and no significant recognition resulted from either his American or his French themes.

In the background he chalked up entries to the ledger. Besides the usual magazine dreadfuls, on March 4 he began a series of movie posters for "U.S. Printing & Litho Co." A drawing for a poster meant ten dollars to the far column. Time for watching the movies added two more. In range of plot and theme, the silent films Hopper was paid to watch and promote resemble the magazine commissions. Both aim at the expectations and interests of the popular audience: *Dance of Mammon, Mendel Beilis under Arrest, The Master Criminal, She of the Wolf's Brood, The Lunatics, Petrof the Vassal, The Horrors*

of War, Whom the Gods Destroy, Chasing a Million, and The Gape of Death.
Most were produced by Eclair, The Société Française des Films et Cinématographes, which acquired a reputation for excellent photography.[40] Eclair
had a studio and factory in Fort Lee, New Jersey, from 1911 until March
1914, when fire destroyed it. (No copies of the films for which Hopper made
posters appear to have survived.) When war broke out in August 1914, film
production ceased and Hopper lost a good client.

Reading dreadfuls was one thing, but Hopper liked watching movies.
Here, too, he complained of the rules laid down for making the posters, rules
like those for illustration meant to assure acceptance by a broad American
public: "Say the movie was about the Napoleonic wars. I'd do the soldiers in
French uniforms of that period. They'd make me re-do them and put them
in khaki uniforms and campaign hats like American soldiers."[41] Catering to
the stereotypes of a mass market would never be his forte. He had nothing
but contempt for a Norman Rockwell: "Does everything from photos; they
look it, too."[42] Pandering went against the grain of Hopper's self-conscious
irony, his deep transformation of reality, and his study since boyhood of soldiers and war. Of cinema, he became a true aficionado, like his classmate
Vachel Lindsay, who wrote a book on it, *The Art of Moving Pictures,* published
in 1915. Both had absorbed Robert Henri's emphasis on theater and his openness to new forms of expression.

"The Gape of Death," Hopper's last poster for U.S. Printing and Eclair,
was delivered on May 23, 1914. Earlier in the month he had done two others
on war and fate. The ledger had been filling nicely, and steady employment
made it possible to think of retreating again in the summer to focus on artists
and art. The sleepy fishing village of Ogunquit was becoming popular with
New York artists. In the previous year, *American Art News* had described it
as "adjacent to Prout's Neck where Winslow Homer lived his hermit's life for
so many years" and as "an attractive Maine coast resort."[43]

Hopper passed July and part of August at a boarding house on Shore Road
run by Mrs. Daniel Perkins, known affectionately to her many lodgers as Ma.
Communal meals were served, at which Hopper mingled with the other
guests. They included acquaintances from art school, among them the petite
and talkative Jo Nivison. Room and board can have cost no more than eight
dollars a week, which was all that Hopper had to pay even the following year.[44]

Links with the New York art world had been forged by a wealthy painter,
critic, and collector of modern art, Hamilton Easter Field, who in 1911
founded the Ogunquit School of Painting and Sculpture. A protégé of Field's,
the New York artist Bernard Karfiol, may have originally directed Hopper's
attention to the colony. Karfiol produced figurative paintings with outdoor
Ogunquit settings and, like Hopper, had worked in Paris and exhibited in the

Armory Show. In such a small community as Ogunquit, Hopper inevitably met the faculty and students from the school, even though much of Field's teaching took place indoors before a model. Even before New York, Boston had begun to colonize Ogunquit. In 1898 the Boston painter Charles Wood-bury had founded a school that stressed impressionist methods. Hopper can-not have failed to observe Woodbury's students out making small eight-by-ten-inch *pochades* (rough sketches) of a particular scene at different times of the day.[45] Indeed, one of the rare oil studies Hopper made for a larger painting, a ten-by-twelve-inch sketch on canvas board for the larger canvas called *The Dories, Ogunquit,* was probably prompted by Woodbury's methods.

Hopper's treatment of *The Dories* assumes a lofty vantage point and moves the eye from a gloomy cliff in the left foreground across to warm or-ange rocks and out to the boats gleaming in light, sketched crescents that float high on intense blue water, with a headland, sea, and sky beyond. The con-trast and movement recall the drama of canvases from several years before. More sober and tranquil, almost emphatically understated in down-east style, *Rocks and Houses* places a yellow flowering plant against a warm brown hump of stone, from behind which peep in linear geometry two farmhouses and the concise cupola of a barn. The humble viewpoint and spare rendering make a striking contrast with works like *American Village* or *Gloucester Harbor* of 1912, with their more commanding viewpoints, various and vital colors, and blurred lines.

During this first stay in Ogunquit, Hopper painted his earliest view of a lonely deserted road, *Road in Maine,* as well as views of the stony terrain and coastline, and the clapboard New England houses. The rugged shore and the stark and barren rocks offered him the chance to create picturesque forms seen through the drama of sunlight. As Karfiol described Ogunquit, "It has a character quite different from inland country. One never feels closed in. . . . The view was wonderful . . . the cove with colored dories at anchor or sailing in and out among the fine rock formations."[46]

That fall "Asc. Sunday Magazine" kept ringing its changes on the theme of Wall Street—"Breaking into . . . , Keeping your Wits in . . . , Making a Million in . . . , The Wolves of . . ." Among Hopper's clients, only *Everybody's* magazine with its social and political agenda commissioned him to look beyond American myths to imagine the menacing and brutal reality abroad: "Uhlans charging, Infantry attack, German gun in action, French in trenches."[47]

The autumn of 1914 brought Hopper his first opportunity to show in a commercial gallery, the Montross, at 550 Fifth Avenue (above Forty-fifth Street). He found himself in a company larger and more diverse than at the MacDowell Club, although Bellows did take part. Since Guy du Bois placed four works in the show, his influence may be behind the invitation to Hopper, who chose to present his new canvas, *Road in Maine,* putting behind him works already shown without success. Du Bois used his position as editor of *Arts and Decoration* to publicize the show. Tactfully eschewing mention of himself, he did not hesitate to inform the public about the oil painting contributed by his friend:

> Mr. Edward Hopper showed a "Road in Maine" of considerable austerity and baldness. He carries elimination sometimes to unfortunate extremes—those wireless telegraph poles stuck in this bleak country, that barren untraveled road, however, are given life and warmth by a color that rings with sincerity and truth. This is where the painter has returned more than he took away.[48]

Du Bois singles out features—"austerity and baldness"—that were to become stylistic trademarks of Hopper's mature art and commonplaces in Hopper criticism. Yet the terms also smack of familiar wit on the part of an old school chum, for whom the painter's character and physique had long been distinguishing marks, ripe for affectionate caricature. Playfully no doubt, yet unerringly and with the instincts of someone very close to the subject, du Bois makes the connection between person and art that he and Hopper had drawn from their teacher Henri and that Hopper himself would come to theorize and reluctantly discuss. Praising the artist for "color that rings with sincerity and truth," du Bois enters an aesthetic judgment with pronounced psychological and ethical tones. He ascribes to the art a seriousness and gravity of character that he would later describe and applaud in the man. Terms like "austerity and baldness, . . . sincerity and truth" do credit to du Bois as the first penetrating critic of Hopper. They also signal Hopper's progress toward focusing and defining a personal style.[49] Not accidentally, the qualities du Bois perceived belong to the world of values associated then as now with a Puritan strain in America.

In spite of du Bois's perceptive praise, the show might have fed resentment in Hopper. Not only did his one painting fail to find a buyer, but the previous January the Montross Gallery had devoted an entire show to paintings done in Maine by George Bellows. Critics had not been unanimous about the quality of Bellows's work, although *American Art News* suggested that he followed "in Winslow Homer's footsteps . . . like Rockwell Kent" and produced "with remarkable strength and sympathy, the scenery, the sea and the humans of the stern and rock bound Maine coast."[50] The examples of Kent and Bellows, both classmates from the New York School, may have contributed to Hopper's choice of Maine in the first place, only to leave him even more acutely aware of the diversity of their fortune from his.

Du Bois had cause to return to the defense two months later. In another group show at the MacDowell Club, in February 1915, Hopper—undeterred by earlier failures or the pressure of cultural fashion—had thrown himself into an even more ambitious French composition, *Soir Bleu*. This he showed with *New York Corner,* a lively urban street scene, like those he had observed in Paris, but unexceptionally American. For once the critics paid attention. Their judgments split: "Edward Hopper is not quite successful with his 'Soir Bleu,' a group of hardened Parisian absinthe drinkers, but he is entirely so with his 'New York Corner' "; and again, "in Edward Hopper's 'New York Corner,' there is a completeness of expression that is scarcely discoverable in his ambitious fantasy, 'Soir Bleu.' "[51]

Soir Bleu shows Hopper's persistent fascination with the forbidden Paris he had discovered as a rather innocent, timid young man. What he saw titillated; it provoked what was to become a recurrent taste for observing what he himself did not dare to grasp. The only surviving drawing for this work, a sketch for the man on the far left, is captioned "un Maquereau," literally, "a mackerel," which is French slang for a procurer, intimating that the erect woman with the heavily painted face is a prostitute who seeks clientele in the soldier, the clown, and beret-clad artist seated in the outdoor café.

Hopper knew exactly what he was after when he painted such a theme. From his newly rented vantage point in the American Bohemia, he meant to shock the conservative audience and provoke the uptown critics, impelling them to sit up and take notice at last. He invoked themes that were the center of public controversy. The term "French macquereaux" was notorious. In New York alone, they were said to be operating in force: one report claimed that four hundred "French macquereaux" were "known to have women in houses" of prostitution, explained that many of the houses were "run under the guise of massage parlors," and declared that "many of the women in these houses are French."[52] Echoes appeared in the popular muckraking magazines and in books such as Reverend Ernest A. Bell's *Fighting the Traffic in Young Girls or War on the White Slave Trade* published in 1911.[53] The theme engaged the theater, where *Little Lost Sister* attracted crowds in 1913. Movies such as *Traffic in Souls* capitalized on the scandal.[54] Between 1908 and 1914, there was a panic over "white slavery," the discussion of which itself produced a frisson even while fueling public discourse on sexuality.[55] As a result, movies, restaurants, and even ice-cream parlors were declared to be "dangerous places for young girls to attend unescorted."[56] For the popular American mind, Paris was "The Modern Babylon," the capital of "debauchery," and the "headquarters of the world-wide white slave trade of the present time."[57]

The panic symptomized a deeper social change, which Hopper and his generation lived at first hand. In 1914 the sexual values of the American mid-

Edward Hopper, Soir Bleu, *1914. Oil on canvas, 36 × 72" (91.4 × 182.9 cm.).*

dle class were on the threshold of a decisive transformation. There was at best an uneasy balance between the old and new, causing strife between the last of the proper Victorians and the proponents of radically new social behavior. The critics who preferred *New York Corner* to *Soir Bleu* sensed the import of the theme of illicit seduction and threatening sexuality. The critic who presumed that the figures in the café were "hardened Parisian absinthe drinkers" was projecting a cultural stereotype that linked prostitution with compulsive drinking. The theme was current in the preaching of reformers such as the Women's Christian Temperance Union, as well as the 1909 United States Senate report that made foreigners the scapegoats for sexual anxieties, claiming "the vilest practices are brought here from continental Europe."[58]

Hopper himself lived the conflict between his own Victorian values and the new society, which assailed him in New York and especially in Paris. Asked years later whether in Paris he had seen the cabaret singer Yvette Guilbert, whom writers like Zola described as the "incarnation of decadence,"[59] Hopper said he had only heard of her. Pressed for details, he temporized in a defensive tone: "I'd rather not say what I heard about her."[60] The reticence testifies to the strength of the fascination, as did, in their fashion, the subject and even the exceptional size (3 × 6′) of *Soir Bleu*. Hopper did not need a Max Eastman to introduce him to the tensions and contradictions beneath the "Anglo-Saxon" facade.

The Frenchness that left the other critics cold did not faze Guy du Bois. In the face of puritanical sexual mores, the growing wave of cultural nationalism, and critical xenophobia, only du Bois, of French descent, proud of his early exposure to French language and culture, could comprehend what Paris meant to Hopper. Confirming and amplifying the vision of his review the previous December, du Bois saw through the contrasting subjects into the artistic quality both works shared:

> Mr. Hopper's "New York Corner" and "Soir Bleu" are the work of an Anglo-Saxon spirit that avoids show of enthusiasm and spends the language of art with an economy that one might compare to parsimony were it not so coldly judicious. If Mr. Hopper has a predominant fault it is self-consciousness, but not, however, lack of individuality.[61]

A different slant emerges fifteen years later, when du Bois had not seen *Soir Bleu* for some time. Then he dwells less on Hopper's artistic engagement and more on the overall impression conveyed through authenticity of detail: "I remember one of those Parisian scenes very vividly. . . . It is of a little café, isolated, in a barren landscape, near the fortifications certainly, in which two or three figures sit stolidly at little round tables."[62] Du Bois does not impose on the scene the stereotype of French wickedness found by the New York critic, whose ideas of what to expect in a Paris scene would be formed by the clamor in the press, as well perhaps by familiarity with such paintings as *L'Absinthe,* by Degas. Instead du Bois allows his personal experience and nostalgia to distort the painting in his own way, so that for him it evokes a certain atmosphere in a familiar and beloved *quartier.* His simplification serves to highlight a sense of atmosphere and mood that Hopper himself hinted through his choice of title. *Soir Bleu* means literally "blue evening" but refers idiomatically to the twilight hour that captured the imagination of poets such as Arthur Rimbaud and Paul Verlaine, both favorites of Hopper.

Verlaine evoked the twilight hour in a poem that Hopper loved to quote throughout his life, "La Lune Blanche."[63] Verlaine's image suggests both gradually enveloping quiet and satisfaction and the palette of sunset colors on the sky. Into this scene Hopper injects the unsettling social drama that reflects his own fascination, ambivalence and pain. With the very phrase "blue evenings of summer," Rimbaud opens the poem "Sensation," in which he meditates on the senses, love, and pain.[64] His "blue summer evening" is a fantasy of escape into the felt touches of the countryside, annihilating speech and thought, but freeing the surge from within of a great indistinct love; it will be like wandering far in nature, happy, as with a woman: "as *if* with," not *with* her.

Hopper dispenses with Rimbaud's idyll. His "blue evening" transpires under lights in a precise space set off by a formal balustrade from an indistinct world. One woman dominates, statuesque and masklike, alluring and menacing against the sky. The other woman, even more bare-shouldered than the first, hair elegant in chignon, bends a little to her male companion, whose open lips in shadow are the only sign of animation in the work. The rest seem frozen into their separate roles and places by the light. What captures the momentary spectacle is the eye of the viewer, the painter in the assumed role of a voyeur. He remains detached, suspended between hope and fear that the woman's opaque impassive visage may break into a gesturing glance. The only action under way, the shadowy conversation, implies an intimacy that shuts the viewer out. In effect, Hopper has imagined a scene of bohemian life as felt by a nonparticipant who is suspended between deep desire and disgust. Memory of his own earliest experience of Bohemia dictates the Paris setting, filtered through the compositions of Renoir and Degas. Yet the experience and visual memory force themselves to the surface and lay claim to public attention only when Hopper settles in the midst of Bohemia in New York. The stylized theatricality of the figures and the opaque ground suggest, too, not merely theater but the silent screen. Conversely, then, Rimbaud's self-image as "bohémien" free wanderer in nature represents an idea of anarchist freedom abstracted from the license of bohemian life within the urban social scene.[65] The figures Hopper summons come from the actual demimonde he brings himself to skirt but not ignore.

The critic who called *Soir Bleu* an "ambitious fantasy" hit the mark. It is for Hopper's development what, seven years before, *Les Demoiselles d'Avignon* had been for Picasso. Like the Spaniard's monumental bordello, Hopper's theatrical café is a threshold work. Each artist dramatizes the relationship of temptress and tempted, as imagined from the viewpoint of a prospective client: the painter casts himself as potential participant and actual looker-on. For Hopper, as for Picasso, the large canvas on this theme heralded important developments to come. *Soir Bleu* pioneers Hopper's later exploration of psychological states and emotional interaction through painted figures. Looking back to the segment of Parisian life that most beckoned and repelled, he synthesized a tension that would capture an ever-growing public in his mature work.

On the threshold of his mature concerns, Hopper stumbled. He placed considerable stock in his fantasy, to judge from the fact that *Soir Bleu* is the largest painting he had yet produced. He took the critical disapproval to heart. Never again did he attempt to show *Soir Bleu*. At his death more than a half-century later his magnum opus remained unidentified, unstretched and rolled up, to be partially exhumed by Lloyd Goodrich as a "Café Scene" of unknown date.[66] Never again would Hopper paint a specifically French theme. Blocked in one of his boldest projects, he would have to reflect and once again reinvent his art.

THE DETOUR THROUGH ETCHING: 1915–1918

THE ARMORY SALE RECEDED. There was another set of pictures to haul home and carry up the steps. The debacle of *Soir Bleu* posed more urgently than ever the question of what and even if to paint. What would issue from this long affair with France? As a practical matter, the ledger had to be fed. Help continued to be forthcoming from Walter Tittle, who was enjoying a certain success as an illustrator. He introduced Hopper to Nathaniel Pousette-Dart, the art director of the *Farmer's Wife,* and commissions resulted in February and March: "Trail's End, Queer Old Rob." In April 1915, the farm wives of America were treated to an article featuring six of the magazine's illustrators, among them Tittle and Hopper. Although Pousette-Dart had also studied with Henri at the New York School of Art, he later claimed that he only became familiar with Hopper's work at this time.[1]

Uncertain of direction in his painting, Hopper put his artistic energy into a new medium, tentatively at first, but then with increasing confidence. The detour proved serendipitous. His vision and purpose sharpened, his imagination opened, and he began to find an audience for his art. Etching was enjoying a revival in America, attracting new and more numerous collectors and offering artists more frequent opportunities to show. Asked why he made the move, Hopper gave a typical answer—opaque and matter of fact: "Etching? I don't know why I started. I wanted to etch, that's all."[2]

*Edward Hopper and
Walter Tittle from the*
Farmer's Wife.

He had never formally studied etching, although briefly and casually in 1902, at the New York School, he had tried monotype prints. His later fame gave rise to contention over who gave him the start. C. K. Chatterton, who had begun to etch by 1913, maintained it was he who first interested Edward in the medium. "Hopper," he contended, "would never have started etching if it hadn't been for me."[3] That would have been fair return, since it had been Edward who converted Chat to painting, after his own escape from illustration, bursting into the illustration class and thrusting palette and brushes into the hands of his astonished friend. Hopper spoke of picking up some basic technical points on etching from another friend and contemporary, Martin Lewis, an Australian émigré, who also supported himself by working as a commercial artist and illustrator. Since Lewis had only just started etching himself, he could offer Hopper little more than the most general knowledge plus encouragement and a shared experience.

Through the new medium Hopper sifted memory and the sights he had been absorbing in the city, on vacation, or on visits home. His earliest etchings reflect his continuing division between the cities, Paris and New York, his old love and his present life, as well as his habitual excursions. He recaptures Paris streets, with a focus on one or another typical figure, a bent head and enveloping cape, or an urchin's broad cap. He begins to translate his observations of New York into the etcher's lines. Business had moved him through the city in search of sales; now he went for views. He found immigrant women chatting beneath a locksmith's sign on Carmine Street in lower Greenwich Village and a bosky view from St. Nicholas Terrace far uptown. He also reached back into memories of earlier drawing and reading for imaginary themes, such as Don Quixote, who had previously figured in his sketches and unpublished literary illustrations. In a similar manner he revives a distant Spanish experience of his own, *The Bull Fight,* which also repeats the theme of an earlier unpublished illustration.

In the first half of 1915, the commissions from *Farmer's Wife* were welcome, but other sales were scarce. Tittle's help was not enough. Hopper found it necessary to go back to selling directly, making the rounds with his portfolio under his arm, knowing he needed the money, even when he hated the work. One day in July he walked to the offices of the Wells Fargo *Messenger,* the house organ of the famous express company, at 65 Broadway. A member of the editorial staff, Elsie Scott, recalled well into her nineties that Edward Hopper had been glad to get what she offered for two drawings.[4] In the ledger for July 16 he entered, with his customary lack of emphasis, "2 line drawings 'Some Boy' Bill Rendered $25." He never indicated ease or difficulty. They were all sales.

The fact that Hopper was peddling drawings in mid-July suggests that he was feeling pinched financially right in the season when successful artists, his fellows at the MacDowell Club, had left the city for privileged enclaves to paint. His return to the hated soliciting and promoting puts in perspective the earnings he had recorded up to that time in the year: $240, all paid up promptly. Yet he felt constrained to sell more before getting away.

The previous year's experience told for Ogunquit. This year the pre-season banter among the MacDowell regulars might have offered a further incentive. Ogunquit was catching on with the group; for once, Hopper had preceded the pack. This was the season that George Bellows left Monhegan Island for Ogunquit, and attracted Robert Henri. The master had stopped summering in Spain after 1912, triumphantly toured the native Ireland of his wife in 1913, and reverted to America at last in 1914, exploring southern California.[5]

The newcomers' style of living quite outshone Hopper's. Successful and prosperous, accompanied by their wives, and in Bellows's case, two small children, they could afford to rent their own summer cottages. When the weather thwarted painting *en plein air,* which it did to an unusual degree that summer, they could pay for indoor studios and models. Emma Bellows was at the center of social and artistic life, hostess to dinners and long evening conversations. More than a decade had passed since Emma Story from Montclair and Edward Hopper from upriver had taken the ferry to New York to school and Emma had "Ho" written on her dance card. The little community was joined by that other veteran of MacDowell shows, Leon Kroll, who had painted with Hopper in Gloucester in 1912. Kroll was freshly returned from Europe, where he had become intimate with such avant-garde artists as Robert and Sonia Delaunay. That summer in Ogunquit he set out to paint landscapes and still lifes.

In the foggy weather, Bellows and Henri were content to stay inside, hiring models and painting figures. Hopper could pay for neither studio nor models. Yet the fog muted colors, impeded views, and generally made working out-of-doors uncomfortable. Discouraged from trying to paint, he turned to sketching local subjects with an eye to small etching plates. He sketched a lighthouse, a house behind a picket fence, a fisherman and a dory, and bathers both male and female, the last of which resemble those of Bernard Karfiol, a regular at Ogunquit.

The financial worry that drove Hopper to the doorstep of Wells Fargo in July did not abate in the fall of 1915. If anything, his bad luck with the weather and his failure to paint increased his depression and forced him to dredge deeper to imagine some new expedient. Teaching might do the trick. He had some experience of that. Prize students were often invited to teach at off-hours in the art schools, and Hopper had done so at the New York School of Art. Chat Chatterton was teaching in a girls' school at home in Newburgh. (In fact he ended his career across the river in Poughkeepsie as the first artist-in-residence at Vassar College.) Edward, too, would look homeward, although he no longer turned to his mother for money. He advertised Saturday morning art classes in Nyack. He had cards printed, in a sober style, adopting advertising conventions, which were familiar from the days when the family scoured the ads in search of a school for him:

DRAWING PAINTING ILLUSTRATION
Mr. Edward Hopper will give instruction in drawing, painting, illustration and the composition of pictures at 53 North Broadway, Nyack, N.Y. on and after October 2nd every Saturday morning from 9 to 12. Mr. Hopper was a pupil of Chase, Henri, K.H. Miller and others and is a former instructor of the Chase School. For terms address 53 North Broadway, Nyack, or 3 Washington Square North, New York.

The entrepreneur received support from his mother. Elizabeth served lemonade and cookies to the students, who included several neighborhood teenagers. Sitting in her rocking chair, she also posed for the class, which was held inside the house in a room off the front parlor. Working first from large plaster casts of portrait busts, the students sketched in charcoal on large sheets of paper. Hopper only permitted them to work in oil after they had sketched for a time. A student evaluation was positive. The youngest pupil, who was only ten or eleven years old at the time, Elizabeth Cornell (sister of the artist Joseph Cornell) recalled taking the class together with several other girls who were "quite a bit older." She remembered Hopper as "a tall, serious person," and "a patient, wonderful teacher who let nothing go by," and recalled her great disappointment when Hopper, who never could relate to children, told her father that she was too "silly" to continue.[6]

True to type, Hopper would not sacrifice sincerity even to his need for enrollments. When Leon Kroll taught at the National Academy of Design, he would help out the prettiest girls with their classic drawings to get them to come into his life class.[7] Not Hopper. He would deliver jaundiced comments about teaching: "I don't know a single man in this country who hasn't had to teach, paint signs, shovel coal or something."[8] Another time, he opined: "Teaching is of course a great strain on the poise of a man of temperament, and to one who never or rarely ever compromises to ingratiate himself with others, might require some adjustment to fellow instructors or those about him."[9] Understatement, for Hopper, was a fine art.

The urgency that made Hopper think of teaching also inspired one of his typical self-caricatures. He satirized the idea of himself as teacher in a French parody of the all-too-familiar clichés of advertising, even inventing a heraldic company symbol in which he replaces the traditional date of founding with the year of his own birth:

[a ribbon with bands descending right and left is inscribed]

HOPPER
MAISON FONDEE 1882

[on an escutcheon, halved, a globe whose axis is pierced by a hammer]

MAISON E. HOPPER
OBJETS D'ART ET D'UTILITE

Peinture a l'huile, gravures, eaux fortes, cours de peinture, de dessein et de litterature, reparation des lampes electrique et des fenetres, en-levement et transportation des malles, guide de campagne, charpen-tier, blanchisseur, coiffeur, pompier, transportation d'arbres et de fleurs, salles de noces et de banquets, lectures, encyclopedie d'art et de science, mecanicien, guerison rapide pour les maladies de l'esprit tel que la legerete, la frivolite et l'amour propre. Prix reduits pour les veuves et les orphelines. Echantillons sur demande. Exigez la mar-que de fabrique

Maison E Hopper 3 Place Washington

[translated as:]

E. Hopper. Firm Founded in 1882
Firm E. Hopper
Objects of art and utility

Edward Hopper's mother,
Elizabeth Griffiths Hopper,
in front of his painting from
Ogunquit, c. 1915.

Oil paintings, engravings, etchings, courses in painting, drawing and literature, repair of electric lamps and windows, removal and transportation of trunks, guide in the countryside, carpenter, laundry man, hair dresser, fireman, transportation of trees and flowers, wedding and banquet halls, readings, encyclopedia of art and science, mechanic, rapid cure for illnesses of the spirit such as flightiness, frivolity, and pride. Reduced prices for widows and orphans. Samples on request. Demand the registered trademark.
  Firm E. Hopper, 3 Washington Square

The wit reflects his reading and his ruefulness: "art" couples with "utility," bridging a hoary antithesis. The skills include his familiar painting and drawing, with his new enthusiasm for etching, his reading and handiness at repairs (which was quite real), but then a comic expansion. The offer of "rapid cure for illnesses of the spirit such as flightiness, frivolity, and pride" sounds like both a satirical thrust at the rage for psychoanalysis around him in the Village and an ironical reflection on his own character.

The confident plan to paint again in Maine had fallen flat. Teaching was not something you cared to admit to the art world. Hopper lamented the bad summer and the need to get back to commercial work. At least that was the impression he conveyed years later to Alfred Barr, who was arranging Hopper's first retrospective for the Museum of Modern Art. "After a mediocre summer's work in 1915, [Hopper] began to devote most of his time to pot boiling illustration."[10] Barr's word became gospel. The actual story was more complex.

The pot had been boiling for some time, as the ledger shows, and would continue to boil. Yet the budget of time continued religiously to include painting, and now etching as well. Some of the time in the fall of 1915 went to planning with the usual MacDowell cohort a show for November: the inevitable Henri, Bellows, Kroll, Sloan, and Chatterton and the rest. When it came to the usual questions, "Where did you go *this* summer? How did it go? Who was there?" Bellows, Henri, Kroll, and Hopper could answer Ogunquit. More than that would embarrass Hopper. How to explain why he had little to show? They all had suffered the great fog. Did anyone underline who could afford to pay for studios and models and who could not? In Hopper's ever-hypercritical judgment, nothing he did that summer was worth hauling down four flights of stairs and up to Fifty-fifth Street to put on the wall to compare with Bellows and Henri and Kroll and Sloan. He pulled out three older works: *American Village* of 1912, and two Ogunquit paintings completed his first, more fortunate, sunny, and productive year: *Dories* and *Rocks and Houses.* And yet, although he avoided the risks attendant on French subjects after the reviews for *Soir Bleu,* his slice of a simpler America failed to repeat the success of *New York Corner.*

As usual, Hopper sold nothing at the MacDowell. Nor did the fall bring much improvement in his earnings from illustration, even though *Adventure* again sent along an entire number with titles to read and illustrate like "L'il Son of a Gun, Wild Bill in Deadwood Gulch, Too Much Business, Ethics." Through it all, Hopper kept up his friendly relations with du Bois. Together they cooked up a new scheme. Guy would showcase Edward from a new perspective and obtain in the bargain a nice item for *Arts and Decoration.* Thus in February 1916 he published, as a full-page feature, eight of Hopper's Parisian caricatures, watercolors that had been stored away for nearly a decade. Evidently both men decided they could catch the public eye and give Edward a boost, as Guy wrote: "The drawings of Parisian types on the right hand page are by E. Hopper, to whom the exhibition galleries, for no very plausible reason, have rarely been opened. None of these pictures has hitherto been shown or published elsewhere."[11] (By this time, Edward had given up working in watercolor, but perhaps the feature did serve as a stimulus and showcase. By the end of 1916, he was producing color covers for his clients at Wells Fargo, and 1918 brought him a new client, *Morse Dry Dock Dial,* the house organ of a company in Bay Ridge, Brooklyn, which was then engaged in fitting and repairing battleships.)

Hopper's collaboration with du Bois comes in an unusually long interval between MacDowell shows—all of 1916: he reappears with his regular cohort in February 1917, making an interval of fourteen months instead of only eight, nine, and two, in earlier years. Even when not taking part in shows, however, Hopper made the rounds of galleries. It was a habit acquired in art school and kept up by anyone still seriously engaged, especially one still on the outside looking for ways to get in. On April 13, 1916, he and Tittle descended from their top floor to see two shows, which Tittle entered in his diary:

> Hopper and I went to see some modernist pictures at the Bourgeois Gallery. Walter Pach, an old school mate of ours, who got up the show, was there. He showed us around. Our old teacher, Kenneth Hayes Miller, joined us too. Pach had a lot of his own stuff there and several others of our old crowd had their things there, including Stella, Gleizes. Cézanne, Matisse, Duchamp, and a lot of the famous "queer ones" were represented. Not that I am classing Cézanne as queer. I like most of his things. We saw at Durand Ruel's some paintings by Manet, Degas, Pissarro, Monet, Sisley, Renoir, etc.[12]

Veterans of the New York School of Art did not forget their old teachers and companions. Teachers did not forget their students: Miller makes the rounds, as Henri did and Sloan. Breathlessly Tittle runs his American friends together with the foreigners. For all the "queer ones" at the Bourgeois (including Cézanne), Hopper had no time. He had long admired and felt the influence of Durand-Ruel's stable, especially Monet, Degas, and Renoir. Traces of that influence surface again in the development of the etchings.

In 1916, as in the previous year, the ledger got off to a slow start, until a new client approached Hopper. From Philadelphia *The Country Gentleman* commissioned "3 half tone drawings 'Lightening the Work' $90," which was followed in June by "1 line drawing 'The Slave of the Lamp' $8" and in July by "1 half tone drawing 'Good Times on the Farm' $35." In the process, Hopper struck up a friendship with A. N. Hosking, the art editor of the magazine. Hosking saw Hopper's frustration with illustrating and pushed him to develop his etching skills. Along with skill came enthusiasm. Hopper acquired a New York Banknote press to print his plates and he began to proselytize his neighbor Tittle, who recalled:

> Being swamped with commissions, my good intentions needed Edward Hopper's active aid . . . before I was launched into the endless

beguiling and difficult intricacies of this exacting art. . . . My neighbor was busy messing about with bottles of acid, porcelain trays, balls
of ground, etc., with an eagerness born of new interest. Occasionally
he would show me his experiments, and use me as a model for his
plates. He urged me to try this medium, pursuing his propaganda in
this direction with remarkable persistence. He adopted a cookoo-
clock technique, popping his head through our connecting door with
monotonously repeated advice: "Make an etching, make an etching,"
and so on indefinitely. The door would slam to escape a missile or bar
a rush, then open again: "Buy a copper plate, buy a plate, buy a
plate!" As drops of water wear away stone, he forced me into an activity that I had really craved for a long time.[13]

The story repeats the incident with Chatterton at the New York School,
when Hopper first switched to painting himself, then dragooned his friend.

After a slow start, business picked up. The entry for June 3, 1916, records
$225 from adventures such as "Snuffy and the Monster, Guiding Clementine,
In Grip of the Minotaur." Joined with a previous $200, the total would reduce
Hopper's anxiety about a third sojourn in Maine. After the depressing fog of
Ogunquit, he turned further north to Monhegan Island, where Bellows and
Emma had been in earlier seasons. For Edward it was the first of several visits to a place that provided an opportunity for spectacular plein-air painting.
Small but extraordinary, with towering headlands, granite ledges, powerful
breezes, and thundering surf, Monhegan offered him an exceptional variety
of dramatic seascapes to paint. Again there were his beloved boats for drawing and etching. He had heard the island praised by Henri and several of his
former classmates: Rockwell Kent and Julius Golz, who in 1910 ran an art
school there, and Randall Davey, besides Bellows, who had first painted with
Henri on Monhegan in 1911, and again in 1913 and 1914.

With parsimony honed by memory of only-too-recent need, Hopper put
up at Monhegan House, an inn with communal meals. He both sketched and
painted outdoors, carrying small wooden panels up the narrow, rocky paths
to the headlands that offered the best vistas. From Whitehead, stretching out
150 feet above the sea, he found his favorite view, the stunning panorama of
the adjoining headland, Blackhead, surrounded by emerald eddies, rocky
cliffs, and the turbulent, changing sea. He also painted other island land-
marks, including Gull Rock, and many views of the craggy coastline. Portraying the play of light and shadow across the irregular shapes of the rocks,
these Monhegan paintings sometimes appear to be nearly abstract, a quality
that perhaps explains his later reluctance to show them, even excluding them
from his retrospectives.

After pressing for new and more challenging subjects and pushing his style to a new extreme, Hopper returned in the fall of 1916 to the demands of the ledger: Wells Fargo, *Farmer's Wife,* and *Country Gentleman.* The latter especially were commissioning subjects that required a different slant: "Washing Machine, Vacuum Cleaner, Fire Prevention for Farm, Electric Iron, Stove, Helping the Hired Girl." Brought up in the ways of an older America, he was employed to help push change. His parents believed in progress; he was not so sure. All his life Hopper felt acutely the conflicts between traditional and modern, rural and urban, American and foreign ways. He would return to explore them again and again in his work.

In the fall of 1916, the MacDowell did not offer the show that might have been expected. Compensation of a sort came from Tittle, who persuaded his MacDowell friends and colleagues to allow their works to travel as far as his Ohio hometown. The result was not the local equivalent of the Armory Show, unleashing scandal. Respect for New York and the native son prevailed: "Prominent Paintings Are Shown" headlined the Springfield *Daily News* for January 29, 1917. The exhibition, sponsored by the City Federation of Women's Clubs, took place in the auditorium of the Young Women's Christian Association and lasted only a week. Tittle wangled from his old schoolmates Bellows and Hopper two paintings each, from his teacher Henri three. The native son sent four.[14] Among the "prominent paintings" actually mentioned in the press were none by Hopper.

Tittle's list suggests that the MacDowell network was still in action. In February 1917, the usual Henri, Bellows, Davey, Kroll, and Sloan organized an exhibition. Hopper's three entries betray continuing uncertainty. He was working in several directions, if not at cross-purposes: a *Portrait of Mrs. Sullivan,* in the manner of Henri; *Rocks and Sand,* painted on Monhegan; and *Summer Street,* a colorful view of Yonkers with an uncharacteristically bright, almost Fauvist, palette from which he applied paint more thickly than usual. *American Art News* reviewed the show and labeled it the work of "a group of clever painters of the Henri type," citing works by Henri, Kroll, Sloan, Chatterton, Dasburg, and Bellows. Only the list of "other painters represented" mentioned Hopper.[15]

All the while Hopper had kept up his correspondence with A. N. Hosking and his experiments with prints. In February, Hosking printed one of Hopper's small plates in his Philadelphia studio and sent him several proofs. Hopper replied on March 7, pronouncing the results "very good" and praising Hosking's skill by contrast to his own relative ignorance of printing: "I did not think you would be able to do so much. . . . They are certainly better than I could pull with my present knowledge of printing. I can see that my plates are too incomplete to be wiped clean and get the best result."[16] The self-doubt again is typical. Events were about to give it the lie.

Doubt had not kept Hopper from tormenting Tittle to learn to print. His new enthusiasm was hardly kept under a bushel. Word had gone out along the MacDowell grapevine, and Hopper received an invitation to show in the First Annual Exhibition of the Painter-Gravers of America, held at Frederick Keppel and Company from March 27 through April 28, 1917. The organization aimed to improve the general quality of prints in America.[17] It was the first to encourage Hopper's prints, thanks to Bellows, who was a member of the board of governors. The three prints Hopper sent were small and, as he might be expected to feel, insignificant: the portrait of Tittle as illustrator and two French subjects, *Les Poilus,* which showed three French soldiers interrogating a woman in the countryside, and *Evening, the Seine.* The former belonged to the embattled France Hopper was illustrating in the magazines, the latter was set in the Parisian neighborhood he loved. To his mentor Hosking, he expressed anxiety: "Hoping they stack up well but feel they are very slight and do not represent me as yet."[18] Yet he looked to the future with redoubled purpose: "When I am through with the pot-boilers I have on hand I am going at it in earnest." These first prints did not engage the critics. Again Guy du Bois came to the rescue with his French sympathies and his friendly editorial hunger: in the issue of *Arts and Decoration* for March 1917 he reproduced *Les Poilus.*[19]

In April 1917, true to his word, Hopper went at it in earnest. What that meant for him could be predicted from his gallery rounds with Tittle the previous spring. Now he studied etchings at galleries and at the Metropolitan, as he told Hosking: "There are three large rooms full—most of the big names of the eighteenth and nineteenth centuries: Girtin, Turner, Whistler, Jongkind, Goya, Hayden, Palmer, Meryon, Braquemond, etc."[20] He later remarked of Goya: "He had strength, he had a vision."[21] And he was particularly fond of the work of Charles Meryon, the nineteenth-century Frenchman who etched such enchanting views of Paris; he also praised "a fine show of drawings and prints by Meryon at Knoedler's."[22] Later Hopper remembered Meryon's *Tourelle de la rue de la Tixéranderie* as a particular favorite: "One called *The Street of the Weavers.* Marvelous rendition of sunlight. To me. Romantic sunlight. He had a terrible life. He was a little bastard. Father was English. Was a doctor—related to Hester Stanhope, that crazy woman who went to the Orient."[23] The praise was rare from someone who seldom expressed admiration for others' work; the sketch of life reveals the reader and ironist.

On April 13, Tittle noted in his diary: "Hopper and I pulled etchings this morning."[24] Hopper depicted Tittle in an etching, as *The Illustrator,* and, eventually, in a drawing and a drypoint. When Henri, who saw a lot of Tittle at this time, came to his studio on May 1, he was "astonished" at the etchings "and exceedingly enthusiastic about them."[25] He offered to sit so that Tittle could make a drypoint portrait of him, which Tittle finished in a few hours. Henri admired the resulting print, pulled on Hopper's press next door, comparing it to Rodin's portrait of Victor Hugo. The master made too much of Walter, too little of Edward, thought the latter. Resentment festered for years.

"Sour" was the way Hopper remembered feeling about the treatment he received from Henri and Tittle, and from Bellows, Kroll, and Davey besides. He mentioned feeling excluded from some exhibitions, particularly those organized at the MacDowell Club, which he described as in those days practically the only show in town.[26] Yet the old catalogues list him in the shows annually from a few months after they started in 1912. Evidently Kroll's perception of Hopper as a MacDowell regular was not shared by Edward himself. There was that fourteen-month interval between fall 1915, when they all came back from foggy Ogunquit, and the show of February 1917. For whatever reason, Hopper chose to dwell on circumstances in general that made it hard to get a toehold:

> In those days art schools did little or nothing to help their former students get established. The young artist didn't have much of a chance. There weren't nearly as many galleries as there are now, and very few could take the work of a young artist. Almost any young artist, unless he happened to be admitted to the Academy, had to do pot boilers to get along.[27]

The idea of "pot boilers" sticks in his craw. Despite the neat entries and growing sums in the ledger, the necessity rankled: the compulsion to walk the streets and accost strangers, lug the portfolio and spread it out. The point of pride was not to be beholden or compromised, to be able to make art freely, suit himself, be an artist among artists. Years later, he would make it quite clear to his wife, who knew plenty about the ins and outs of Grub Street and perfectly captured Edward's gist:

> He certainly did do plenty of pot boiling—but was never a wage slave. He had no one to support and could live such manner of frugal life as he pleased. He was so accomplished a draftsman that he could easily turn his hand to illustration—such illustration as he could get without compromise—he never did that and could not do pretty girls—he'd get locomotives etc. Did covers of ship yards— express companies etc.—all very much in character. . . . He did work hard—when he was working—but no one could make him work more than three days a week—the rest he painted in his own studio

to suit himself. His illustration or any of his commercial work was a thing apart—only pot boiling—and strictly his own affair. Same as our washing the dishes or washing out silk underwear—nobody's business—not our career. He didn't even runabout with the illustration profession. His friends were the painters.[28]

Edward was no Charles Dana Gibson, the popular illustrator known for pretty girls. That was only too clear to the person who knew him best before Jo, Guy du Bois: "He made a meager living, meager because of his inability to meet editors' ideals in feminine beauty, doing illustrations."[29]

Hopper's resentment toward illustrating even dictated a different working process than he used for painting or etching: "When I did illustration I sometimes photographed the model and used it instead of a sketch."[30] He was not willing to accept such short cuts for his painting: "I once got a little camera to use for details of architecture and so forth, but the photo was always so different from the perspective the eye gives, I gave it up."[31]

The first invitation to show prints had been an excellent omen. Now Hopper took work to the year's most important show: the First Annual Exhibition of the American Society of Independent Artists, held from April 10 through May 6 at the Grand Central Palace. One of the prime movers was Walter Pach, the classmate who had organized the modernist show that Hopper and Tittle had visited the previous April. The new show was not juried; works were hung alphabetically in accordance with democratic principles.

Hopper brought two canvases. Painted only two years apart, *American Village* (1912) and *Sea at Ogunquit* (1914) could have been produced by different artists. The two demonstrate no sense of clear or coherent direction. They produced a familiar result: neither attention nor sales. *American Village,* with its perspective raked downward from the railroad bridge, was hardly traditional—no Currier and Ives. *Sea at Ogunquit* was brighter and more conventional, a sunlit landscape with more sharply defined forms. To no avail.

Even though Hopper's painting seemed invisible for the moment, critics like Henry McBride of the New York *Sun* were once again suggesting the need for a more original American art: "Here and there, sticking out all over the exhibition, are little signals of aspirants who may later gain complete control of our melting pot to shape the national spirit into new forms."[32]

In the summer of 1917, Hopper wrote once more to Hosking, asking if anyone from Philadelphia would like to sublet his New York studio for August and September at thirty dollars a month (which was less than his actual rent) so that he could afford to go on vacation.[33] He opted for Monhegan once more. It was during one of these first summers there that he again ran into Josephine Nivison. As she remembered it, "We were both at Monhegan and he said 'hi' to me on the wharf. But he was shy. He had good dancing legs but he wouldn't dance."[34] On Monhegan in 1917, Hopper certainly met an old and a new friend, Rockwell Kent and Carl Zigrosser, a young man then working at Frederick Keppel and Company in New York, where Hopper had first shown prints that spring.[35]

The fall of 1917 brought no further invitations. Even work for the ledger was slow. "The Am. Red Cross" commissioned a wagon poster for thirty dollars, Wells Fargo assured "Safe Sure & Speedy Service." Wells Fargo also was reacting to American involvement in the war. Women took men's places in the office, money orders went back and forth between home and camp: "Doing his Bit, Your Boy and Mine, U. S. Camp money order, Girl & Soldier, War Worker, Good Bye Jim." From January 1918, covers in color become frequent, both for Wells Fargo and the new client, *Morse Dry Dock Dial.* With a change of staff, *The Country Gentleman* disappeared from the ledger, but Hopper kept his promise to its former art editor Hosking. His studies in the galleries and museums and his experiments were producing a respectable store of etchings and a reputation. The results would emerge in the new year.

The earnest pursuit of etching through the autumn and winter bore fruit in the spring of 1918. The advantages of the widespread vogue began to make themselves clear. From Chicago came an opportunity to exhibit a print at the Art Institute with the Chicago Society of Etchers: Hopper renamed and sent *Les Poilus,* which he had shown and du Bois had published the previous spring. The new title, *Somewhere in France,* for the image of the soldiers and the woman in wooden shoes, shifts from the foreign name that would be difficult for most viewers to a caption in the manner of the popular press that suggests an actual situation during the war. This season, there had been no chance to show paintings at the MacDowell Club. But some of the regular group organized a show of watercolors, pastels, and drawings. On April 26, Tittle recorded in his diary that he, Henri, Sloan, Davey, Hopper, Theresa Bernstein, and others had spent most of the day hanging the show.[36] Hopper brought eight items: another copy of *Somewhere in France,* and *Evening, the Seine,* both of which he had first shown in 1917, and also some results of the winter. Maine figures in this new work: *Cow on Monhegan, Bathers,* and *The Monhegan Boat,* in which a sailboat heels gracefully behind the perfectly flat, plodding island ferry lined with tourists looking like huddled immigrants. Hopper's eye for ironic contrast adapts well to the new medium. New York is the locale of *Night, the El Train* and *The Open Window,* while *The Bull Fight* looks back to his experience in Spain.

In a review, Guy du Bois singled Hopper out for special praise, calling his etchings "masterpieces in conclusive statement . . . especially the decorative handling of his *Bull Fight* and the note of life that he has breathed into *Night, the El Train.*"[37] Again Hopper's most loyal and perceptive critic scores. If *Bull Fight* appears decorative, the effect must represent a strong effort to deal with emotion, even at a distance: Hopper had reported to his sister his revulsion from the actual fight, above all the evisceration of the horses that he chooses to depict. Pointing to the vitality of *Night, the El Train,* du Bois also shows how well he is attuned to Hopper. The print supposes a viewer observing a couple seated in a corner of an elevated railway car in intimate conversation, the man bent toward the woman, a boater on his knee, his face masklike, the woman relaxed under a broad round hat, one foot hooked over the other, in no hurry to get up. The theme of intimacy spied upon, taken unawares by the painter-viewer as voyeur, appears already in *Soir Bleu,* with a rather similar couple, where, as here, the man is the active, tense figure. Likewise *The Open Window* represents a nude woman seen from behind seated quietly on a bed faced toward the window, where wind moves the curtains. Hopper later varied the theme, fixing on the sight of a woman variously peering around or gazing out, while exposing herself potentially to another's sight. Whether from memory, models, or experience, this initial image also defines a focus for Hopper's imaginative growth. The range of Hopper's prints at the MacDowell show testifies to the progress made in his year of study and experiment. He also reaped a return for dragging Tittle into the act. On May 11, Tittle started a drypoint head of Hopper, which he finished on May 20, capturing his neighbor's bald head, pince-nez, and glum expression.

Tittle later sketched Hopper in words, giving what may be the earliest eyewitness report of the depressions that would constantly recur: "he suffered from long periods of unconquerable inertia, sitting for days at a time before his easel in helpless unhappiness, unable to raise a hand to break the spell."[38] Recalling Hopper's "semi-funereal solemnity," Tittle thought that only a very individual sense of humor—laced with "puckish nonsense" and "practical jokes"—saved his friend from descending into unendurable "blues." Tittle told of recoiling at the sight of a family of bedbugs on his pillow, only to discover that they were watercolors painted with horrific accuracy and cut out by Hopper. To settle the score, Tittle told Hopper that the bugs were "the best things he had ever produced" and prophesied that now at last having found his metier, he would become the preeminent "painter of bed bugs."

In fact, it was illustration, despite progress in printmaking and persistence in painting, that won Hopper his first kind of fame. His French loyalties, his American patriotism, and his experience as an illustrator played a part in the feat. Bert Edward Barnes, editor of the *Morse Dry Dock Dial,* liked his work and probably persuaded him to enter the contest for a propaganda poster sponsored by the United States Shipping Board Emergency Fleet Corporation

Edward Hopper, The Bull Fight, *1917. Etching, 4⅞ × 7″ (12.4 × 17.8 cm.).*

in 1918. The agency had been created in September 1916 with the authority to build, purchase, lease, or requisition vessels needed for the war effort.

Barnes encouraged Hopper to visit the shipyard to get the right feel, and volunteered one of his employees, Pete Shea, to model for the poster. He also had Shea photographed in the pose and gave a print to Hopper, who recalled in an ironical sketch: "I got this big Irishman to pose for me in the shipyards, with a background of ship's ribs, that sort of thing. I had him swinging a maul, and the maul was aimed at a bloody bayonet sticking up in one corner. I titled it 'Smash the Hun'; it was pretty awful and I don't think it was ever published."[39] In fact, Hopper's design appeared on the cover of the *Morse Dry Dock Dial* for February 1919.

The four-color poster won Hopper the three-hundred-dollar first prize among fourteen hundred contestants. This was a considerable sum at a time when his annual rent had risen to $540.[40] Since armistice was declared before the poster could be reproduced for mass distribution, Hopper's fame came from the exhibition of *Smash the Hun* along with nineteen other finalists in August 1918, in the window of Gimbel's department store on Broadway, where according to the press, "thousands" saw the "stirring pictures placed on view."[41] The papers reported that the wave of popular excitement swept up Hopper's model, Shea: he enlisted in the Navy.[42]

Walter Tittle, Portrait of Edward Hopper, *1918. Drypoint,*
3½ × 3⅞" (8.9 × 9.8 cm.).

All at once Hopper was the center of a great deal of attention in the press. With the journalistic necessity to pigeonhole, they identified him as a "well-known illustrator." It was ironic praise for one who detested the work. Even more insulting was the organizers' declaration that the contest had not been judged on "purely artistic considerations" or style, but on a combination of "a powerful, inspiring idea with a strong artistic conception and good technical workmanship"; the "idea held greater importance than art."[43] Although fame on these terms irritated him, Hopper was delighted with the cash and "took the prize and went off to Monhegan to paint."[44] The ledger records with only the slightest sign of possible excitement (as Hopper misstated and then corrected the date), "July 24 'U.S. Shipping Board' 1 poster 'Smash the Hun' rec'd by check $300." No bill was rendered. The curious slip in the date had to be fixed. The sum was by far the largest to appear in the sober columns since their beginning in 1913.

Hopper had taken an uncharacteristically aggressive position in regard to this contest. He wrote a letter to the *Sun,* the newspaper promoting the competition. Responding to the officials' call for "American posters" and op-

Edward Hopper, c. 1918.

posing the "German commercial art idea," he demonstrated a sophisticated understanding of the traditions of poster art in Germany, France, and England. He emphasized the potential for the poster artist in America, while admitting to influences from abroad: "Poster technic in Germany has been carried to a perfection that has been attained in no other country, but it has been made of rather more importance than idea . . . the French have been unequalled in fire and vivacity."[45]

Hopper's later sensitivity to a figure's posture as an expressive force is already evident in his poster design, and his consciousness of this formal element for conveying content is apparent in a statement he made upon winning the award:

> In my poster I tried to show the real menace to this country as symbolized by the bloody German bayonets. The resistance of the worker to that menace is evident, I think, in his pose and the design. The way the worker's feet are spread out has a meaning to me of a certain solidity and force. They are set there for all time against this threatened invasion. The work to which the special appeal is directed is typified by a silhouette of a shipyard, smokestack and smoke.[46]

This patriotic gesture represented Hopper's personal contribution to the war effort; aged thirty-five when the United States entered the conflict in 1917, he was five years too old to register for military service under the Selective Service Act of May 1917. However, when the act was amended in August 1918, it was extended to require the registration of all men between the ages of eighteen and forty-five. Hopper returned to register as a Nyack resident, listing himself as a self-employed illustrator whose place of business was 3 Washington Square, North, in New York City. He was described as tall, slender, and having no physical disqualifications. But as the sole son, if not the support, of a widowed mother, he was not a likely choice for the draft.

At the moment of his first fame, Hopper's decision to make yet another excursion to Monhegan acquired new weight. He had become enough of a celebrity that a Portland newspaper interviewed him on his way through to the island. Asked his reasons for coming to vacation in Maine, he produced comments generic enough to be interchangeable with some of his old reports to his mother from Paris: "Maine is so beautiful and the weather is so fine in the summer—that's why I come up here to rest and to paint a little, too."[47] But the preseason networking would have informed him that Henri intended to return to Monhegan that summer. For Hopper it would be a welcome, rare occasion to be remarked and praised.

In 1918, Hopper also produced a poster for the benefit of the American Red Cross. *With the Refugees,* showing a Red Cross worker aiding the wounded while an armed soldier looks on, was exhibited along Fifth Avenue from December 16 to 23, during the organization's annual fund-raising drive. Having worked out a small study on illustration board, Hopper, like the fifty-one others who participated, painted the final version of his poster on a large canvas seven by ten feet. Each artist executed his own design in the chaotic atmosphere at the Penguin Club in the parlor floor of a brownstone at 8 East Fifteenth Street. The club, which sponsored the event and provided the materials, was a group of artists in rebellion against the National Academy. It had been organized by Walt Kuhn, famous for his role in arranging the Armory Show of 1913, and head of the art department of the Red Cross. The Penguin Club was said to include "practically every well known illustrator in New York,"[48] which explains how Hopper, who had won acclaim for *Smash the Hun,* was invited to take part. Hopper even managed to have his name mentioned in the press in connection with this patriotic event, along with other well-known participants such as Arthur B. Davies, James Montgomery Flagg, Maxfield Parrish, and Charles Dana Gibson.[49]

Working at the Penguin, Hopper ran into both old and new acquaintances: Guy du Bois, faithful and ubiquitous, as well as W. T. Benda, who had taught Saturday classes at the New York School of Art with Edward, and Louis Bouché, employed for the duration at the Navy's camouflage department, who recalled: "A tall taciturn character was painting along side of me. I had never laid eyes on him before. Later I learned that it was Edward Hopper. No waste there. He knew exactly what he was doing, and how much paint would be required. On the other side of the improvised studio was Guy Pène du Bois at work."[50]

The Penguin was not a natural habitat for Hopper. He never mentioned the club's exhibitions or weekly evening sketching classes. Ambivalent as he was toward anything bohemian, he was not likely to enjoy their annual costume balls. Given his strong desire to associate with painters rather than illustrators, he would not relish the company of such members as Flagg, Parrish, or Gibson, all famed for their commercial work. Nor, with his insistence on realism, did he care for the modernists who exhibited at the Penguin, painters like Arthur Dove, Man Ray, Francis Picabia, Wyndham Lewis, and John Marin, as well as Albert Gleizes and Joseph Stella, the members of the "old crowd," whom Tittle, gallery-hopping with Hopper in 1916, had counted among the modernist "queers."

Fame fostered Hopper's career in illustration. In September 1918, he began to sell to *Scribner's,* a cut above his usual clients. Walter Tittle claimed the credit for the first assignment: "I succeeded in getting him a bit of work from Scribner's magazine almost by brow-beating my old friend [Joseph Hawley] Chapin [the art editor], insisting that here was a man really too good for him."[51] Hopper's wife came on the scene in time to observe: "Scribner's were wonderful to him—let him go his own gait—careful not to give him things not his kind to do."[52] His kind: the first story they gave him to read was "The Hearing Ear," by Henry Van Dyke, which dealt with heroic rescue in the war. The two drawings, which appeared in the issue of December 1918, added one hundred dollars to Edward's books. The next assignment was even more congenial. They asked him to read *The Emperor's Ghost* by Temple Bailey, which he could do with a certain feeling: to rescue France in her time of trouble Napoleon comes back, rising from the mist before the trenches: "C'est l'empereur! He returns to lead us"; but also on the home front, a quintessentially French "for love, mademoiselle, and truth and constancy." For these attempts to depict French stereotypes, he entered $175, as he would for another six commissions from *Scribner's,* down virtually to his last illustration.[53] None of the others risked such ironic revisions of his memories of France. His last for *Scribner's* shows two women in intimate conversation by a window.[54] It presented an opportunity to revise and domesticate the conception through which his imagination had achieved such powerful development in the detour through etchings toward his mature style in paint.

THE DEEPER HUNGER: 1918-1923

FIVE YEARS HAD PASSED since the whiff of success at the Armory Show, three since the debacle of *Soir Bleu*. Hopper's nostalgia for France gave way little by little to wandering through New York City, often in hope of sales, and brief escapes to the New England coasts in search of scenes to paint. The group shows and old school fellows, the assiduous rounds of galleries, had not produced a breakthrough. The poster brought prestige in the wrong career. Etching began to hold out promise, but not in the medium he most prized. After the one sale at the Armory, no one bought any more paintings; no one paid much notice in print.

Nobody that is, but Hopper's companion from those heady days at the New York School of Art, who believed in his talent and went to bat for it at every turn. Guy Pène du Bois—affable and socially dexterous where Edward was diffident and awkward, brightly witty where Edward was ironic if not morose and bordering on malign, a cosmopolitan from New Orleans where Edward bore the stamp of Sunday school and Nyack—had made himself a dual career as a painter and a writer about art. Generous and outgoing, Guy offered private stimulus and repeated public occasions for Edward to show work. From the vantage point of long familiarity and comradeship, the talk of studio and life, he had been the first to write significantly of Edward Hopper, the man and the work. Now in his diary for

C. K. Chatterton, Guy Pène du Bois, and Edward Hopper on Monhegan Island,
summer 1919.

November 30, 1918, he caught the whole drama of Hopper's character and
stalled career:

> E. Hopper is a long lean friend of mine who began doing some illus-
> trating a few years back and is still at it. I've been seeing quite a little
> of him lately. He is a voracious reader. Gone through all the modern
> French productions, read a lot Russian, a lot of German. Loves able
> dissection of the human species. Hates romance? Timid as an Eng-
> lish school boy himself. Long and lean—face great prominent mas-
> ticating muscles, strong teeth, big mouth, full lipped but not
> sensuous.
>
> Cool about his painting. Blocks out things. Hardly any freedom
> in handling. Carries out his plan. Thinks of spacing. Takes little ad-
> vantage of accident. Static pictures. Loves the romance of uniforms.
>
> The best man we had at school. A capable man still—but in the
> present condition not an artist. Not free enough for that.
>
> To[o] much Anglo-Saxon reserve. And he does not like it a bit.
> Loves the freedom of the Latins rather.
>
> Should be married. But can't imagine to what kind of a woman.
> The hunger of that man.

He always makes me feel like tripping sentences together reck-lessly. But he's far from dull though he makes me feel like a papier or a foolish butterfly—either or both. Such sincerity.

But the hunger of him, the hunger of him! I'd [like] to see him out of his present condition. I'd like to see him happy.[1]

The features Guy describes appeared in the drypoint etching (page 118) that Walter Tittle produced in May: the same thick, protruding lips, defi-nitely "not sensuous," along with Edward's wire-rimmed spectacles and pre-cocious baldness, always inviting caricature. Guy foreshadows a story of suspense. Will Latin freedom rescue the puritan? Will imagination free the failed artist, satisfy hopes and expectations, answer yearnings and realize tal-ent, recover the past and project it into the future? The story sounds rather like the popular titles that Edward had to read and use his imagination to il-lustrate, with the difference that he had been slow to imagine for himself.

The ledger filled strongly the following year. By the end of June 1919, Hopper had recorded payments of $665. He would have no need to drum up business to assure a summer vacation. In the past, he had left largely to chance any companionship for painting, although his choice of destination had been conditioned by shop talk and imponderable influences from grander Mac-Dowell regulars. The vacation in 1919 would be different, happier. Edward went to Monhegan again, but now in company with du Bois and C. K. Chat-terton. Edward sketched Chat painting in his room, with a chair for an easel, and outdoors, seated along the rocky shore. He portrayed Guy twice, once alone, but also on a single sheet with a woman wearing a middy blouse and skirt—probably Floy, Guy's wife. Guy in turn sketched Edward with the "not sensuous" lips. It was a round-robin like the old days in art school. Med-ical students take the pulse, artists the likeness, of each other. Guy and Ed-ward both liked to look beneath the surface: they shared the love for "able dissection of the human species," which was Guy's medical metaphor for Ed-ward's mind.

Hopper's ledger did less well in the third and fourth quarters of the year, still grazing one thousand dollars for the year. France America Corporation commissioned a colored cover for their magazine promoting goodwill be-tween the two countries: a view over Paris complete with gargoyle, not the sort of thing Edward saw from the rue de Lille but indebted to an etching by Meryon, whom he had singled out for special praise during his burst of study-ing prints at the Metropolitan Museum in 1917. The winter of 1919–1920 tes-tifies directly and emphatically to Hopper's growing engagement with etching. In December, his big folio ledger acquired a companion one-fourth its size, devoted to keeping track of prints and other fine art consigned to gal-

Edward Hopper, Guy Pène du Bois, *1919. Sanguine on paper, 21 × 16″*
(53.3 × 40.6 cm.).

leries and exhibitions. The new notebook shows how decisively he had overcome his earlier self-doubt. In the year and a half since his last show, he had
found a potential market for his etchings; but success had made him realize
how hard it was to keep track of work in a medium that produces multiple
exemplars. A painting might be more trouble up and down the stairs, but at
least each was unique.

The first recorded shipment went to Carl Smalley, McPherson,
Kansas—within range of the influence of Chicago, where Hopper had
shown in 1918 at the burgeoning Art Institute with the Society of Etchers.

Edward Hopper, C. K. Chatterton on Monhegan, *1919. Charcoal on paper, 9⅛ × 12″ (23.2 × 30.5 cm.).*

The selection included older prints—*The Bull Fight* and *Don Quixote, Somewhere in France,* and *The Monhegan Boat*—and two new ones, *The Bay Window* and *A Corner.* In the latter two women huddle in conversation on a field starkly divided by a pole that casts a shadow on the swinging doors of a corner saloon. In the pared-down quality, isolated figures, dramatic light, detailed doors, Hopper moves from his bent for caricature and dissection into vision: again in a print he crystallizes elements of his mature style. Similarly, in *The Bay Window* he pursues his fascination with isolated female figures taken unawares in a setting where the presence of the window implicitly, and more often expressly, suggests possibilities and risks of seeing and being seen: in this case, he captures a rather stout, older woman sewing in a scene that mingles the sight of his mother at work upstairs at home in Nyack with the memory of compositions by Degas.

In the two months after McPherson, Hopper consigned his prints to more prominent places: C. W. Kraushaar Art Galleries at 680 Fifth Avenue, twice to the Chicago Society of Etchers at the Art Institute, to the Print Makers of Los Angeles, and to the National Arts Club in New York's Gramercy Park. The network spread at home and reached from coast to coast, as never yet with his paintings. He relied most on his old standby, *The Monhegan Boat,* sending it to New York, Chicago, McPherson, and Los Angeles. He shipped three copies of *Bull Fight,* two of *A Corner,* but only one of *Night, the El Train.* Nor did he merely sit back to await results. Prints had been claiming most of the time left over from making covers for the *Dry Dock Dial* and illustrating "Negro Cabin," "The Magic Carpet," "Thrift." Yet painting remained his ultimate agenda: it had run like a thread through the past conversations with du Bois, and again during the summer evenings they spent together with Chatterton and Floy on Monhegan. The camaraderie in Maine led to a new conspiracy in New York, as Guy and Edward put their heads together to cook up yet another scheme. Guy might not be able to imagine the right wife for Edward; but he understood the longing to be an artist and would help as only he could.

Guy had become a close friend of the socialite sculptor Gertrude Vanderbilt Whitney. In the spring of 1918 she founded the Whitney Studio Club at 147 West Fourth Street, the latest outpost of the new Bohemia in Greenwich Village. Artist members could drop by to read or use the Ouija board in the library, draw from life or play at billiards, and eventually show their works. Members could also nominate new members. In November 1918 Guy obtained a one-man show for himself, at the moment when his diary shows his intense concern for Edward's failure to free himself as an artist. True to form, Guy argued Edward's case with the club director, Juliana Force, who agreed to membership and a show of his paintings. Opening in January 1920, it was Hopper's first one-man show. He had not exhibited any paintings at all since April 1917.

The venue inspired reviews, with help from a concurrent show of drawings and prints by Kenneth Hayes Miller, who had taught both Guy and Edward at the New York School. Miller chose to emphasize female nudes, which were called "if not inspiring . . . faithful artistic performances" by an unsigned squib in *American Art News* that gave more attention to Hopper: "The oils of Mr. Hopper, for the most part views in Paris, are truthful and sympathetic, carefully and thoughtfully executed and in good color. Stronger, and as truthful, are the portrayals of the rocky Monhegan cliffs and the weather-beaten old houses of the Maine island."[2] The teacher and his former pupil received more equal treatment from Royal Cortissoz in the New York *Tribune:* "Both artists express unusual talent and their work is well worth a visit."[3]

A reviewer's respect for Paris but preference for Maine should not have surprised Hopper after the 1915 praise for *New York Corner* and ill fate of *Soir*

Bleu. Since then he had virtually banished French themes from the paintings he showed, except for the Paris watercolors Guy published in 1916. Yet when given the chance for a major statement at last, Hopper forgot or ignored the warnings. He paraded Paris all over again, eleven oils out of sixteen, entering the titles in his new little notebook, heading the page "1920 Jan 14 The Whitney Club 146 W 4th St": *Le Bistro, Le Pont des Arts, Le Pont-Neuf, Notre Dame de Paris, Juin, Après-midi de Printemps, Le Parc de St. Cloud, Le Quai des Grands Augustins, Le Louvre et la Seine, Les Lavoirs, Blackhead Monhegan, The Little Cove Monhegan, Rocks and Houses, Squam Light, La Cité, Road in Maine.*

Unrepentantly, Hopper reached back. He sorted through, pulled out, and dusted off. Some had to be unrolled, the canvas stretched and tacked all over again, and framed. He carried through deliberately. The list of titles in French sounds like a Baedeker for Paris: some of the pictures look like what a young American interested in boats would see on a fine morning when he strolled around to the river from the rue de Lille. Only one, *Le Bistro,* done in America in 1909, represents his later Paris, imagined, retrospective, and more forced, focusing on a couple frozen between shadow and light. The critic was right to speak of care and thought and color. If only the paintings had been able to tap the American market for French art. For Edward, they held up. And why not? Efforts to sell American themes in all the years since *Soir Bleu* had achieved neither notice nor sales.

Guy later remembered the show as "composed entirely—curiously enough for a man now so well-known specifically for his renderings of the American scene—of pictures done in Paris";[4] although he went on to penetrate beneath the surface content in his usual manner, arguing that "their spirit continues in his present work," and asserting, "The America that Hopper records is, as it should be, in his own heart. That heart, unlike those of some now remorseful wanderers, would resist foreign contamination anywhere and under the most alluring temptations." Again Guy takes a psychological and ethical line. He insists on Edward's sincerity and truth to himself, also his self-contained and unbending character. In the end he comes to praise the very stiffness he had reproached for inhibiting the artist and frustrating the man. He foreshortens the resistance, as if Edward's heart had never wandered or been strangely touched. He praises Edward for standing up to "alluring temptations" in aesthetics where, in reality, the foreign models of art had tugged and pulled together with sexuality to produce the tension of the experiments that came to a head in *Soir Bleu* and were about to take a forced detour into the medium of the prints.

The Whitney show was de facto a retrospective: the artist as seen by himself. Du Bois claims neither blame nor credit for the selection. The critics at least paid lip service and gave reasonable praise, but demand did not materialize. Du Bois had done his best for Hopper's painting, but the show did not live up to his hopes. Hopper revealed his present condition as a painter with work that was preponderantly old and French. The rest recapitulated newer excursions and summers: Gloucester, Ogunquit, Monhegan, but the place where he had been working, selling, glimpsing day after day did not show. He left in storage the *Queensborough Bridge* and *Blackwell's Island* and pulled three bridges from Paris. He presented nothing painted in the actual context where his imagination was growing freer. New York remained oddly elsewhere, off there in the etchings. Nostalgia had its last hurrah. In the notebook, after the list of titles, he wrote "returned." Although he opened 1920 looking backward, for the rest of the year he moved on. The surge of nostalgia for the past, painfully obvious at the Whitney, flowed ever more strongly into the alternate medium, where it merged with the deeper hunger that Edward revealed to Guy. Their shared beliefs about the bond between an artist's emotions and his work illuminate Edward's next steps, which were new prints that registered the bitter hunger, the need to get free, and, increasingly, began to display the daring to imagine ways to achieve his artistic goals. Edward himself later looked back on what etching meant: "The goal of the etcher must still be the more complete development of his personality"; for him, "the etcher's job was . . . to draw honestly on the plate his vision of life."[5] Sincerely and openly, though masking personal feeling in the discreet forms of generalization, he invited the sensitive and empathetic attention to his etchings that he ultimately desired for both his art and his life.

After the Whitney show, the artist's notebook entries for 1920 proceed with prints already in stock. On January 27 *The Monhegan Boat* went out to Los Angeles at $18.00. On May 17 Hopper registered payment at the original place in the notebook: $16.20. He also wrote in the ledger, "@ $18. less 10% 16.20." The entry stands at the top of a new page, otherwise indistinguishable in format and emphasis. It follows after "Americanization Campaign 1 half tone drawing 'Woman & Liberty Bond' $75" and it stands before "Norma Talmadge Film Corp. 1 four colour drawing 'Town Tell-Tales' $75." The sum is modest, the implication immense.

For the rest of 1920, the only other follow-up entry in the notebook is that eloquent "returned" for the paintings from the Whitney, but the consignments are joined very soon by new prints. *Cow and Rocks* places front and center the posterior of a rather rocky cow in a rocky Maine landscape: the scene makes an ironic departure from the soft pastoral views of traditional landscape. Hopper borrowed the cow from a painting by Jacob Jordaens, the seventeenth-century Flemish artist. He was not the first artist to find cows by Jordaens very suggestive: in 1890 Van Gogh had copied Jordaens's entire bucolic composition.[6] *House by a River* shows what looks like a tall Victorian mansion on the Hudson near Nyack—an inscrutable house towering over a dwarfed, pensive man, who stands with hands in pockets, arms akimbo. The feel for vernacular architecture and for the psychology of loneliness crystallize yet another of Hopper's mature visions. Years later, he responded to a suggestion that "loneliness" was one of his main themes by explaining: "It isn't at all conscious. I probably am a lonely one."[7] In 1920 he consigned seven prints, and as many more the following two years.

Another new offering of 1920, *Summer Twilight,* shows a woman and a man on a raised lawn before a cavernous house. She sits motionless in a rocking chair, a fan held limply on her lap, a dog inert behind her. The man stands stiffly, his elegant dark jacket pushed back by hands thrust into the pockets of white pants. The title suggests both the time of day and the state of the relationship portrayed: fading of the affective bond. Similarly in later works, like *Summer Evening* (1947), Hopper depicts not merely an hour but a personal crisis, when romance goes sour. The choice of subject is painful and clear. The hour is that of *Soir Bleu* and this couple resembles the one depicted there in stylized dress and disparity of attitudes: the ambience, now, is closer to home, again a suggestion of Nyack Victorian, but the looming houses are like a backdrop and the terraced lawn a stage.

In *House by a River* and *Summer Twilight* Hopper develops an interest in vernacular architecture that was already evident in paintings like *Rocks and Houses* from his days at Ogunquit. He represents America and evokes its past. Similarly, in *House on a Hill* of 1920, which he also called *The Buggy,* he depicted architecture from the last century and included a horse and wagon at a time when automobiles had become the rage. He would eventually portray this powerful theme of attachment to the past and alienation from modern urban life with great success in his paintings, but he first explored it in other prints such as *Night Shadows* and *Night in the Park,* which he distributed in 1921. When asked years later if nostalgia was a theme in his work, Hopper replied: "As for nostalgia, that isn't conscious. . . . But why shouldn't there be nostalgia in art? I have no conscious themes."[8]

Before 1920 was out, public approval began to accrue. In October, when Hopper showed four etchings in a group show at the Touchstone Galleries, the critic of the New York *Herald* singled out *House by a River* to praise the artist's "architectural studies" for their "breadth and personal touch."[9] Earnings remained modest: Hopper's 1920 tax return indicates an income of $1594.20, out of which he deducted $680 for rent of his studio, $150 for materials, $75 for rail transportation to business, and $75 for "bad debts," leaving a net of only $614.20.[10] On November 27, he registered in the ledger but not the notebook that Carl Smalley paid for *Somewhere in France:* "@ $12 less 33½% 8." McPherson and Los Angeles caught on sooner than New York.

As the year 1921 opened, painting remained on Hopper's mind. On January 13 he sent *The Park Entrance* to the Pennsylvania Academy of the Fine Arts, priced at $300. On May 11 the same work, still priced $300, together with *Pont Royal,* $350, went to the Whitney Club for the members' annual spring show. In imagining a park, Hopper recalled subjects he had painted in Paris using a light palette, frontal vision, and limpid, impersonal forms. Now his tones are darker and his viewpoint unrealistic, looking down on a shadowy monument to heroic struggle that looms over light, curving paths that are dotted with tiny human figures framed against dark woods. Hopper focuses on the paradox of urban culture and dim historical memory imposed on the natural setting. He later said this painting was improvised in his studio and represented no specific place. Its monumental sculpture and generalized figures could suggest either New York or Paris. In bringing out *Pont Royal* Hopper chose another work from his first visits to Paris, like those he had revived for his retrospective the previous January, which did not sell. He was learning no lessons and scarcely breaking new ground. Signs of dramatic change emerge, instead, in the etchings that enter his notebook in 1921. A first group reveals the final developments of work in 1920: on January 5, he shipped *Night Shadows* to Chicago, and on January 28, *Evening Wind* and *Maine Coast* to Los Angeles. By late spring, he goes further: on May 3, to the Weyhe Gallery in New York, Hopper consigned *Les Deux Pigeons, Train and Bathers,* and *Night in the Park.* On November 10 he sent to Brooklyn two final results of the year: *American Landscape* and *Soldier Reading.* In *Night Shadows,* Hopper intensifies the vision tested in *A Corner* the previous year, shifting to a high viewpoint for a steep glance down on a single figure that is ominously set off in an urban landscape by the dramatic play of shadow and light. The fabric of architecture, figure, shadow, and light moves yet further toward Hopper's later vision.

Toward the end of January he first shipped the print that he would distribute most frequently, twenty-one times, in the following two years. With *Evening Wind* he explores and develops the themes of intimacy and sexuality that figured in *Night, the El Train* and *Open Window* (1918), and in *Summer Twilight* (1919). In particular he returns to dramatize a situation like that of *Open Window.* In *Evening Wind* a nude woman half-crouches on the edge of an unmade bed, hair partly veiling her breasts, head turned abruptly away toward the unexpected touch of a curtain blown in from an open window by an intrusive wind. What the viewer sees is a drama of violation and sexual surprise, imagined between the woman, who is shown as vulnerable, naked before an unprotected window, and the wind, metaphorically the aggressive male. Neither French nor American per se, the theme in Hopper's repertoire transforms the situation of the painting *Summer Interior* of 1909. There light from a window dramatized the dejection of a woman, as if in the aftermath of alienating sexual relations. Here the implicit attitude seems rather of fear or expectation, poised for what, momentarily, the wind is made to mean. No vouchers or paid receipts indicate a model's name and no diaries record the day or the place of the work. As in *Open Window,* the situation does not suggest the model or the studio, or the memory of youth in Paris. Rather Hopper appears to be stretching his imagination in the direction envisioned as his way to freedom and self-realization by du Bois.

By contrast, two etchings consigned in May look backward and evoke the history of Edward's hunger. *Les Deux Pigeons* is pointedly not present-day New York. The scene is a belvedere above a handsome gorge. Nobody looks at the view. A couple kisses obliviously, wholly absorbed in fresh passion. A seated soldier and whiskered man seem set in their own concerns. A waiter ogles the lovers, who are the very picture of the kind of sensual freedom Hopper so painfully lacked and which was pointedly absent in *Summer Twilight,* etched the year before. There the troubled artist might identify with the estrangement, here with the onlooking voyeur, as in *Soir Bleu.* At the same time, Hopper's choice of yet another French title opens further dimensions of meaning.

The French words underline the distance of the scene in time and place, pointing in memory back to Paris, where besides the fascination and affront of blatant public sexuality registered in *Soir Bleu,* Hopper had known the exhilaration (if also the ultimate disappointment) of his friendship with Enid Saies. He took the title "Two Pigeons" from a popular fable of La Fontaine's that might well have lingered in his mind: the story of a dove straying foolishly, nearly perishing, before reunion with her love, but the whole tale framed by the narrator pointing the moral in nostalgia for his own past love:

> Hélas! quand reviendront de semblables moments?
> Faut-il que tant d'objets si doux et si charmants
> Me laissent vivre au gré de mon âme inquiète?
> Ah! si mon coeur osait encore se renflammer!
> Ne sentirai-je plus de charme qui m'arrête?
> Ai-je passé le temps d'aimer?
>
> Shall ecstasy return that was, alas, my own?
> Are lost delights that made life sweet forever gone,
> Forsaking my soul in its dejected state?
> Ah! might my heart take fire once more in the old way,
> Alert even now to love's spark and, elate,
> Beat fast as in a former day.[11]

Edward Hopper, Les Deux Pigeons, *1921. Etching, 8½ × 10″ (21.6 × 25.4 cm.).*

Last words have their way of sticking in memory. These of this fable must have transfixed Hopper. At the time he made *Les Deux Pigeons,* he did not know what had become of Enid. Nor could he find again the freedom and the person for new love.

The French framework for the scene was crucial to Hopper's imagination. He had seen lovers in public nearer home: he places couples on elegant lawns like the one in *Summer Twilight* and on the "El Train." He registered the remarkable changes in public behavior in America that were taking place in the 1920s. In the press he would have read the reformers' alarmed complaints, even though he did not go to dance halls where bodily contact was now the rule.[12] At the same time, his own standards of public behavior remained rooted in his small-town Victorian and Baptist past. His images of couples in American settings do not suggest freedom or mutual delight.

When he pictures oblivious happy lovers, he locates them at a distance, in France, where he had not been for more than a decade, but where he had seen and, perhaps, experienced passion. His nostalgia and his hunger merge in the new medium to recall and project the past.

A French background also lies behind a second etching consigned on May 3, *Train and Bathers*. A French locomotive lurches from a wooded background onto a viaduct over a stream, puffing smoke, impetuous, almost jumping the rails. The onset has startled two women who were taking a swim. One clambers up the bank, showing ample hips and buttocks, the other half-turns, glancing furtively, before whirling to flee into the woods. The seductive, sensuous forms of the women and their natural setting contrast starkly with the aggressive, mechanistic force of the train, which hurtles past and beyond, without contact with the desirable, yet elusive, females.[13] The engine is endowed with eyelike fixtures—circular bumpers, headlight, window in the cab—although no engineer or fireman leers. Once again drawn to a sexual theme, Hopper finds a paradoxical variation in the image of excitement, fear, exposure, even aggressive masculinity, all of which are suggested as forces alienated from a human connection.

With typical irony, Hopper has constructed his story with French forms, in particular those of the Impressionists who had earlier left their impact on his painting. Why he chose to depict "a French locomotive, when the American locomotives were so much more interesting to draw," was a question put to Hopper by Martin Lewis, as Carl Zigrosser recalled.[14] The train with its steaming engine echoes repeated motifs of Monet. The two female bathers along the water's edge evoke the frequent subjects of both Renoir and Cézanne. Hopper's etching is neither just the Impressionists' train, nor their bathers in the landscape, but instead, it effects an unlikely combination of the two that brings to mind his pastiche in art school, when he combined Ingres and Manet to produce Flora McFlimsey. Yet again, as always when he displays sardonic wit and turns to satire or caricature, the reductive game deflects and masks deep emotions. Here again he adopts the viewpoint of a voyeur that is implied in so many of these defining etchings and will recur in his later work.

The final innovations for 1921 went to Brooklyn in November. In *American Landscape,* cows meander home across a railroad track that horizontally bisects the entire plane; in the background a lonely farmhouse reaches starkly above the horizon. The tracks encroach on the countryside and connect it to urban life. The whole treatment undercuts the traditions of pastoral landscape even more emphatically than *Cows and Rocks* of the year before. The solitary house by the train tracks will reappear, too, in the memorable 1925 painting *House by the Railroad,* although harshly and dramatically stripped of anecdotal details such as trees or cows. Unwittingly Hopper played a small part in the urban assault on the country through his drawings in farm journals to advertise modern conveniences and lighten work. His vision of the country, then, is anything but sentimental. In his irony, he resembles Robert Frost, whom he admired, and whose bitter New England pastoral sequence, *North of Boston,* had appeared in 1914.

Hopper went on in subsequent years to develop these ironies in a series of etchings, such as *The Railroad* and *The Locomotive,* and in two drypoints, *Railroad Crossing,* where a man leading a cow is blocked by a lowered barrier from crossing tracks, and *House in Tarrytown,* where tracks again cut across the plane, isolating a staring house set next to smokestacks and a tall steel signal pole. A related focus on urban desolation appears in *The Lonely House,* where two children play alone in a vacant lot under the blank wall of a narrow, isolated structure—an urban row house without its flanking neighbors. Here Hopper recalled a building that stood near his family's in Nyack; a house resembling the one in the etching is visible in an 1884 pictorial map of the area.[15] His eye turns the neighborhood into a site of alienation.

In 1921, the number of consignments rose to thirteen, and the total number of prints shipped was forty-four. The sales recorded were four. There had been only eight consignments in 1920, although the total was fifty-one prints, with two registered sales. In 1922, consignments would reach twenty-nine, and the quantity would rise to 115. As Hopper's reputation and the demand for his work grew, so did the quality and variety of exhibitors: in 1920, besides Chicago and Los Angeles, there had been the Canadian National Exhibition and the Brooklyn Society of Etchers. In 1921, there were again Brooklyn, Chicago, and Los Angeles. At home in New York, he penetrated the defenses of the ancient foe of the young rebels from the New York School of Art: the National Academy of Design had consistently rejected his paintings, but he was able to place prints in its spring and winter shows. On May 11, the Academy sent a check for $19.80 for one $22 sale of *Bull Fight.* At ten percent, not only their prestige but their commission rate was advantageous; forty percent had been retained by the Weyhe Gallery for the dramatic consignment of May 3. By September, on one page of the ledger, out of four items, two were payments for prints, two for illustrations: the respective totals, $73 and $250. Similar pages were few as yet, and the sums still slight; but the tide was creeping up.

On November 1, 1921, Hopper followed up his breakthrough of the spring by sending a second round of etchings to the Academy for its winter exhibition, chosing *Train and Bathers, Night Shadows, House by a River, Night in the Park,* and *Evening Wind.* The group provoked an unsigned article in *The New York Times* comparing Hopper's work with that of Childe Hassam, a member of the Academy, whose nude bathers appeared to be "an excuse for

Edward Hopper, Evening Wind, *1921. Etching, 7 × 8⅜″ (17.8 × 21.3 cm.).*

the play of light and shadow and the statement of certain elegance of proportion, both classic reasons for art," while Hopper's etchings were "an excuse for a little research into human anatomy, the display of an orientalized sense of pattern, a genius for finding beauty in ugliness."[16] The writer falls rather short of Hopper's acute parody in *Train and Bathers,* and shorter still of the erotic imagination in *Evening Wind.* Less penetrating than Guy du Bois, the critic did at least get at something in perceiving "research" and "pattern" and "ugliness." Hopper is perfecting his characteristic delight in making the apparently commonplace do the trick of his peculiar vision.

On November 23, 1921, Hopper made another consequential consignment: *Evening Wind, Night in the Park,* and *Les Deux Pigeons* to Frank K. M. Rehn at 33⅓ percent. It was his first transaction with an important dealer whom he hoped would represent him. Rehn had opened his gallery three years before after working for E. and A. Milch, dealers in American painting and framing. Gregarious and personable, a man who learned "to play golf with the swells," Rehn had also worked as an art salesman for the Salmagundi Club and had written art criticism for newspapers.[17] Since Rehn's father, Frank Knox Morton Rehn, had been a painter, the dealer had a sympathetic understanding of the profession.[18] Going to Rehn at the suggestion of his former classmate Edmund Graecen, Hopper took some of his old French canvases. Rehn could see that they were too much influenced by others and lacked their own distinctive style. Still, he must have perceived talent, for he took the consignment of prints. Thanking Graecen for suggesting Rehn, Hopper reported that the art critic of the New York *Tribune* "[Royal] Cortissoz came in while I was there and was enthusiastic about the things I have at the Academy."[19]

On January 25, 1922, Hopper first consigned the etching called *East Side Interior,* which views from within a room a woman, dressed lightly in a slip, who looks up startled from a sewing machine to glance toward a window that opens onto the plinth and ionic column and curved end of a railing at the top of a front stoop. Her dishabille look and attitude of surprise clearly relate her to the growing constellation of prints in which Hopper has been exploring sexuality through varying nuances of position and gaze. Hopper himself deflected one kind of inference in a typically ironic commentary years later:

> There is little to tell about it. It was entirely improvised from memories of glimpses of rooms seen from the streets in the eastside in my walks in that part of the city. No implication was intended with any ideology concerning the poor and oppressed. The interior itself was my main interest—simply a piece of New York, the city that interests me so much, nor is there any derivation from the so called "Ash Can School" with which my name has at times been erroneously associated.[20]

He denies political or social significance and focuses on the disparate sources of materials, with no word of what it was psychologically that his imagination improvised: a moment of intimate drama captured by an intruding eye.

Hopper showed *East Side Interior* with *Evening Wind* and seven other prints in the American Etchers Salon at Brown-Robertson Galleries in New York on February 21. Henry McBride, then the critic for the New York *Herald,* lauded Hopper's work in a review of the show that reproduced *East Side Interior:* "A little known etcher who stands out in the present exhibition is Edward Hopper, whose 'Evening Wind' and 'Eastside Interior' show positive promise. The 'Evening Wind,' in particular, is full of spirit, composed with a sense of the dramatic possibilities of ordinary materials and is well etched."[21] Hopper was so thrilled that he presented McBride with a gift of *East Side Interior* soon after the review appeared.[22] McBride's praise helped the gallery sell two copies of *Evening Wind,* for eighteen dollars apiece (netting twelve dollars each for the artist). Hopper was able to sell other etchings in New York that year at the Whitney Studio Club, the Sardeau Gallery, Brown-Robertson Galleries, and the Brooklyn Society of Etchers.

Hopper's imagination thrived on these dramas of women surprised in intimate interiors, and through them he forged the breakthrough to painting in what became his mature style. As Hopper himself later realized, there was a definite continuity between prints and paintings: "After I took up etching, my painting seemed to crystallize."[23] On March 27, he consigned a new painting to the Whitney Studio Club for three hundred dollars. In *New York Interior,* Hopper once again assumes the viewpoint of a watcher, looking at the back of a woman seated, her shoulders bare above a tight bodice and full skirt, like an evening gown, her right arm raised in a gesture, drawing a thread through a needle like the old woman in *The Bay Window.* The total absorption of the gesture and the reddish hair falling loose in front of her shoulders convey an image of defenselessness like that in *Evening Wind* and *East Side Interior.*

Even closer to *Evening Wind* is a second painting of this period, *Moonlight Interior,* in which the viewer looks from within a room at a nude woman with long auburn hair who, unaware of being observed, moves forward in a crouched position, away from an open window, her hands reaching out toward a bed, while wind moves a curtain: strangely warm light emphasizes the curve of her back and the color of her hair while picking out highlights and shadows on a tall, gabled house outside. In outline, the house recalls the Victorian structures in etchings such as *House on a Hill.* Again, as in all this series of scenes, the observer catches a glimpse of motion, here away from the line of sight. The different degree of intimacy and vision suggests that Hopper has reached a further stage in unfolding and freeing his imagination.

Hopper's return to painting the figure is all the more remarkable because of his expressed weariness at having to depict the human body for his illustration jobs: "I was always interested in architecture, but the editors wanted people waving their arms."[24] He insisted that he was "a rotten illustrator—or mediocre anyway," explaining his dislike of drawing people "grimacing and posturing. Maybe I am not very human," he added. "What I wanted to do was to paint sunlight on the side of a house."[25]

In April 1922, at the First International Exhibition of Etching organized at the Anderson Galleries by the Brooklyn Society of Etchers, Hopper showed *Night Shadows.* William V. Graff (a fellow artist whom Hopper had depicted in at least four drawings, a drypoint, and an etching) showed his *Portrait of Edward Hopper,* an image of an intense, balding man conscientiously at work on an etching. Among Hopper's other friends who had prints in this exhibition were Pach, Tittle, Sloan, and Miller. Later that month, a critic for the *Evening Post* featured Hopper's work under the headline "An O. Henry of the Needle," and compared the painter's use of Manhattan themes to the writer's. Of the painting *New York Interior,* he wrote: "The cramped quarters in which life is led in such a city as this are not so much stated as felt in this canvas."[26]

Sometime in 1922 Nathaniel Pousette-Dart paid a visit to Hopper's studio; he had become the art director of the George L. Dyer Company, which had been a good customer for illustrations by Hopper: "He showed me a few oil paintings, but he was not satisfied with them. As I remember them they were not at all like his later paintings. These canvases were frankly in the Henri tradition."[27] In October Guy du Bois took stock of the rise in Edward's fortunes and pronounced a positive judgment. His long piece in the magazine *Shadowland* stressed that Hopper was not merely an etcher, but an artist.[28] Clearly he read in Edward's new purpose and success a significant change from the "present condition" that he had sketched in his diary three years earlier.

About this time, John Dos Passos, who was then both writing and painting, along with another writer friend, Dudley Poore, had moved into rooms three floors below Hopper's on Washington Square.[29] Although it is not certain when Hopper and Dos Passos first became acquainted, both were showing at the Whitney Studio Club: Dos Passos in January 1923, and Hopper the previous October, when he presented ten of his Parisian watercolor caricatures and a group of his prints.

In 1923 the Club moved to larger quarters at 10 West Eighth Street and continued to hold evening sketching sessions, which Hopper attended. These were life drawing classes, where a model posed and artists paid a fee of twenty-five cents to attend. Hopper's surviving sketches from these classes indicate that the model was usually female. Others who took part were du Bois and other friends, such as Louis Bouché, Arthur E. Cederquist, Martin Lewis, Leon Kroll, and Richard F. Lahey. Caricatures of the sketch classes by both Mabel Dwight (who also worked for the Club) and Peggy Bacon document Hopper's presence. Although not especially social, he liked the Club, not only for the life classes, but for the plentiful refreshments, especially at the opening parties for exhibitions.

Hopper's renewed interest in the figure is evident in *New York Restaurant,* a canvas of about 1922 that he showed in 1923 in both the annual exhibition at the Pennsylvania Academy of the Fine Arts in Philadelphia and the Ninth Corcoran Biennial of American paintings in Washington. At the latter show, Edward Redfield, identified in the press as an "outspoken enemy of modern art," served as the chief adviser to the director, C. Powell Minnigerode, and as chairman of the selection jury, which included Hopper's classmate Rockwell Kent. George Bellows won the first William A. Clark prize of two thousand dollars, but one alert critic, who lamented how excessively conservative the show was, remarked, "Edward Hopper's 'Restaurant,' a small interior with figures, strikes a vivid and positive note on an otherwise rather tame wall."[30]

Hopper later expressed his intentions for *New York Restaurant:* "In a specific and concrete sense the idea was to attempt to make visual the crowded glamour of a New York restaurant during the noon hour. I am hoping that ideas less easy to define have, perhaps, crept in also."[31] For once he admitted his wish to convey content beyond that apparent in outward appearances, a goal he would pursue throughout his career. This picture also reveals Hopper's continuing interest in Manet, whose painting *Luncheon in the Studio* he would have known in reproduction. Hopper has rendered the same abruptly cropped ceiling, tall potted plant before a geometric design of windowpanes, and table tilted forward in a shallow space.

Figures also punctuated *Aux Fortifications,* an etching that Hopper produced in 1923, which pictures people congregating on the old ramparts surrounding Paris, where the working classes gathered to socialize. He vividly recalled the colorfully uniformed soldiers and the seductively dressed women with their elaborate topknot coiffures. In *Girl on a Bridge,* a solitary young woman, clad in coat and hat, stands in a breeze overlooking an urban scene that might be Paris or New York.

Hopper found many opportunities to exhibit his etchings in 1923, the last year he produced any. He showed in New York at Frederick Keppel and Company, Sardeau Gallery, Brown-Robertson Galleries, Anderson Galleries, and the Belmaison Gallery at Wanamaker's, as well as at the National Academy of Design and the National Arts Club. Some of the shows elicited further critical attention. In January, a critic responded to his three prints at Keppel, finding "both strength and beauty" and commenting of Hopper: "Would that some one could persuade him to do more! There are originality and vitality in these plates which the power of line and balance of color intensify."[32] In February, after seeing Hopper's prints at Sardeau, the critic for the New York *Evening Sun* enthused:

> Edward Hopper does etchings of city life in an understandable thorough-going way. . . . He takes what he sees almost as is. A couple on an elevated train late at night, a railroad track and telegraph poles, a street corner seen from the third story above—this choice of subjects means that Edward Hopper lives in an actual world and knows its odd shape. His character and his sincerity carry well in black and white.[33]

The critic for *The New York Times* also responded to Hopper's etchings at Sardeau, citing his "firm workmanship and clear understanding" and noting presciently: "In each of them lurks a certain philosophy of seeing that makes a difference between dull literal transcription and a definitely personal point of view."[34]

When Hopper simultaneously showed *East Side Interior* at the Art Institute of Chicago and at the Los Angeles Museum, he was awarded the twenty-five-dollar Logan Prize by the former, and then the Mr. and Mrs. William Alanson Bryan Prize for the Best American Print, from the Print Makers Society of California. He was so proud of winning the Logan Prize that he wrote to Henry McBride—to whom he had given a copy of the print—telling him of the award and quipping: "I don't suppose you believe in the giving of prizes, nor do I except when they are given to me. However now that my fall has been accomplished there is nothing to be done."[35] In April he wrote to Carl Zigrosser, at the Weyhe Gallery, and raised two prices: *East Side Interior* was now twenty-five dollars and *Evening Wind* was twenty-two dollars.[36]

Hopper's ever-increasing success in the print medium runs hand in hand with the growing and varying imagination that reaches, also, to shape the moods and attitudes of his painting. Through the successive images of interiors and of women caught in intimacy, he moves toward greater freedom from his Anglo-Saxon reserve. He later identified some of these intimate images when he told Carl Zigrosser that an etched portrait of a woman wearing a fashionable fur-trimmed hat and coat was "Jeanne Cheruy." He also labeled and kept sketches of her from the front, back, and in profile. The sketch from the back shows her reading. From her appearance, with her long hair worn pinned up in a chignon at the nape of her neck, it is also clear that she was the model for the etched plate of a woman, clad only in a slip, seated sideways in a chair, also holding a book.

These images of Chéruy suggest a link to a sequence of intimate interior scenes. A drypoint, *Nude in a Chair,* appears to depict Chéruy. Likewise she must have been the model for the long-haired female nude in several other preparatory sketches for never-executed etchings of figures posed at the window. To the same type belong *Open Window* of 1918 and *Evening Wind* of 1921. Another recognizable sketch shows Chéruy lying in bed asleep. (Hopper later depicted his wife asleep in virtually the same intimate pose.) Out of this growing life in imagination comes the leap to painting, *New York Interior* and *Moonlight Interior:* in both, the woman's long hair is auburn.

Hopper referred to Chéruy always as Madame, which suggests, in accordance with French usage, either that she was or had been married, or was of a certain age. Not burdened with middle-class American mores, she offered

Edward Hopper, Madame Cheruy, *1922. Pencil on paper, 12 × 9½″ (30.5 × 24.1 cm.).*

an opportunity for Hopper to realize his French fantasy, perhaps to recover the happiness imagined in *Les Deux Pigeons:*

> Ah! si mon coeur osait encore se renflammer!
>
> Ah! might my heart take fire once more in the old way!

No fuller document of this affair seems likely to emerge. The very parsimony of data lends poignance: the man and the artist who remembers Paris and who lacks freedom, who struggles with his emotions through his art, finds his way through carefully etched lines, so slight, so intensely felt, so late, toward a new engagement with the figure and with life. Not for Hopper the precocious and repetitive promiscuity of Bohemia, advertised and cheapened by hectic correspondence in cosmopolitan circles up and down Fifth Avenue. In Hopper, the meeting between America and Europe is more difficult and finer, more full of meaning because more rare.

The single most revealing fact may be that Hopper through all his life kept her images as well as his Christmas gift in 1922 from Chéruy—a volume in French of Paul Verlaine's poetry inscribed "Souvenir d'amitié Jeanne

Edward Hopper, [Jeanne Chéruy Asleep], *1922. Sanguine on paper, 11 × 15″ (27.9 × 38.1 cm.).*

Chéruy 10/12–22." Many of the poems contain erotic themes: "ecstasy," "strange voices in her heart," "gay erotic things," or "purple as our souls' desire, as blood stolen from our hearts when I burn and you catch fire."[37] The intensity matches the fantasy of *Les Deux Pigeons* and ministers to the hunger.

Must be in want of a wife, du Bois had thought: "Can't imagine to what kind of woman." Hopper's imagination, freed and strengthened, was on its way to overcoming its defect. He would choose an American who had traveled to France and loved its literature and language as much as he did himself. She would also be a fellow artist who stimulated his work. Nearly a decade had passed since the failure of *Soir Bleu*. With her help he would at long last get off to the right start.

THE LEADING LADY

NO INHERITED HOUSE and "pack rat" mother enshrined the early years of Josephine Verstille Nivison. The Nivisons, Mary Ann and Eldorado, rented, and never for long at one place. They were living in their third apartment in as many years when Jo was born on March 18, 1883, at 312 West Twentieth Street in Manhattan.[1] They moved in quick succession through a series of other buildings ever further uptown as Jo was growing up.[2] With the constant moves came other forms of domestic instability. "My home life when I had one, was anything but peaceful," Jo recalled. "My father was a terror to live with. As a child, my mother permitted a fat, garrulous aunt to live with us.[3] She kept my father and me always at concert pitch."[4] On the other hand, Mary Ann's permissive attitude also extended to her daughter, who referred to her affectionately as "the Mother Bird," remembering family lore: "My mother was well before the Freudians. One day a friend was visiting when I was one and a half and I put on a show. At that age there could be no compromises. I yelled. 'What a temper,' said my mother's friend. 'You'll have to break that!' 'I'll do nothing of the sort,' said my mother. 'She may need it sometime.' "[5]

In a moment of introspection, Jo attributed her loquacious and outspoken nature to her Celtic and Gallic blood.[6] Her mother was a first-generation American, born Mary Ann McGrath to Irish immigrants in 1848 in Liberty,

Josephine Verstille Nivison as a young girl.

New York. Jo's father, Eldorado, had been born in Texas in 1849.[7] From his mother, who was French, came his daughter's middle name, Verstille. Jo recalled that her grandmother "had kept slaves," and that her two "uncles had fought under" General Lee.[8] A music teacher, Eldorado Nivison, was "a brilliant tho unsuccessful pianist" who encouraged Jo to study dance, French, and art.[9] While she fondly recalled growing up "in an atmosphere of music," and remembered how splendidly her father had played works such as Mendelssohn's "Wedding March" from *A Midsummer Night's Dream,* she had to admit that he made her home life difficult.[10] Recounting that her father had no paternal instincts,[11] she described him as very self-involved, so much so that it kept "his parental ties from developing into anything more than rudimentary."[12]

The troubled household produced three children. There was one elder sibling, who died in childhood sometime after Jo's birth. A younger brother, Charles E. Nivison, was born the year after Jo (December 8, 1884). Absorbing neither his mother's independent spirit nor his father's cultural ambition, without his sister's drive and talent, he worked at rather menial jobs and eventually became an alcoholic.[13] Perhaps as a direct result, Jo would never touch alcohol. Despite the turbulence, perhaps in compensation, Jo early took an interest in books. Years later, she speculated that "books kept me back

*Josephine Verstille Nivison
in the Normal College
Drama Club, 1903.*

OPPOSITE: *Josephine
Verstille Nivison,* Class of
*1903, 1903. Drawing re-
produced in the* Wistarion,
Normal College of New
York *yearbook.*

from reality. What a shock for me to find out life not like books, I who had done Shakespeare at 10 & loved ideas for themselves—with no background for digestion, so ideas stayed ideas & fastened themselves to my backbone."[14]

Looking back, she later emphasized the positive side of these years: "It was my great good fortune to grow up in New York and not have to move mountains and lakes and hencoops and relations in an effort to get there."[15] For a woman with no endowment but intelligence, energy, and bookishness, the city offered an opportunity that was unavailable to Hopper's sister in Nyack. The Normal College of the City of New York had been founded as a free institution to provide women with higher education and the city with trained and competent teachers.[16] Located even then at Sixty-eighth Street and Park Avenue, the college was led by President Thomas Hunter, whose name it would bear after 1914. The directors maintained strict discipline and closely monitored attendance in order to determine the "moral fitness" of the students for the work of teaching.[17] Josephine Nivison enrolled in the fall of 1900, at age seventeen.

Nivison was an average student, earning grades of B and C.[18] She must have been ill during her last two years, for she had sixteen and forty-one excused absences respectively, and received the Bachelor of Arts degree six months late, in December 1904. She pursued a rigorous and challenging course of study, encompassing Latin, which included readings in Cicero, Livy, and Horace, and French, with selections ranging from Montaigne and Descartes to Molière and Balzac. By the time she finished college, she had studied Latin for five years and French for more than six.[19] Her English literature requirements included Shakespeare, Milton, Wordsworth, and a sur-

vey of English prose. She also took civics, with an "intensive study of American History," psychology and principles of education, and the history of education. Her formal education was thus much broader than what Hopper received at art school.

While attending college, Nivison demonstrated unusual inventiveness, energy, and drive. In extracurricular activities, she found outlets for her creativity and forged the positive self-image as an artist that propelled her long after she received her degree. Some of her energies expressed themselves through drama. She appeared in several productions of the Merry Makers, the school's drama club.[20] A hint of her vitality appears in the quotation that accompanies her senior yearbook entry: "The Gods Give us Joy!—*As You Like It.*"[21]

Nivison's other creative focus was the visual arts. Her drawings appeared in the two school publications, the *Echo,* a magazine, and the *Wistarion,* the school yearbook. In November 1901, during her sophomore year, an entire page in the *Echo* was devoted to her ink drawing captioned " 'At Last!' Quote 1902," depicting a student in graduation cap and gown.[22] The *Wistarion* for 1902, listing her as one of five "special artists" who contributed drawings, featured two of her delicate sketches in pen and ink signed with her now characteristic signature in a vertical format: "JVN 04."[23] One depicts a young woman in cap and gown sitting on a high stool and the other portrays a dreamy young woman, dressed in ordinary attire, contemplating her reflection in a mirror by candlelight, where she appears in her graduation cap and gown. The yearbook of 1903 once again listed Nivison as a "special artist," and published two of her drawings of young women.[24] She was also the *Echo*'s special reporter for her section that year.

All told, Nivison's first published works reveal the considerable charm of a young talent already stretching beyond the austere aims and methods of the limited art taught at the college, where the main intention was "to enable teachers to illustrate on the black-board with ease and facility, and cultivate the eye and hand with the view of preparing pupils for industrial pursuits."[25] The drawing classes, taught by tutors Gertrude P. Harrington and Sarah E. Beach, under the direction of Superintendent M. Christine W. Reid, offered some instruction in modeling, perspective, and illustrating solid geometry. A photograph of the drawing classroom, with its casts of ancient sculptures such as the Winged Victory of Samothrace, demonstrates how academic and conservative the teaching methods were.[26] The alumnae of the Normal College were expected to repay society for their free education by laboring to train the children of the immigrant masses to become fit for "industrial pursuits." Nivison felt a different calling. She decided to study art. Reacting against the academic narrowness of her training, she chose the school with the most innovative and liberal reputation and the most controversial teachers.

At the New York School of Art, she soon caught the attention of Robert Henri. In December 1905 he asked Nivison to pose for a portrait as *The Art Student*.[27] He recorded the impression she made on him:

> She was standing in her old paint-spattered apron at the close of a lesson, with her paint brushes clutched firmly in her little fist, listening to a conversation. She seemed a little human question mark, and everything about her, every line of her dress, suggested the idea. I wanted to paint her just as she was, and I asked her to pose for me the next day. I was afraid she couldn't assume the same pose and the same look, but it happened that as she entered my studio she fell into the same energetic, questioning attitude. I had to paint very rapidly to get it.[28]

Henri captured Nivison's determined gaze, her intensity, and her winsomeness. Her face is framed by brown ringlets that spill across her forehead. She arches her right brow with a natural coquettishness. Beneath the dark smock, which has slipped down below her shoulders, her red dress stands out with its large white lace-trimmed collar against the dark ground. She has precisely ornamented herself with a locket on a ribbon worn round her neck and a ring on her finger. As she grasps her paintbrushes she seems to bear witness: "I will be an artist." Though weighing in at a mere ninety pounds, she looks as though she would swat anyone who tried to stand in her way.

Nivison adored Henri as a teacher and found him generous and inspiring. She considered him her most important mentor, calling him "a great prophet of our age."[29] Although she had also enjoyed her study of painting with Kenneth Hayes Miller, she praised Henri most profusely: "His teaching was so broad. It amounted to a philosophy of life, a religion, and was never confined merely to putting paint on canvas. The search for character was a dominating interest in the treatment of a subject. . . . The student . . . was left pretty much to himself to carve out his own technique."[30] Posing for Henri was in itself instructive, for Nivison was then studying portraiture, in which she maintained an interest throughout her life.

In February 1906, a month after Henri painted her portrait, Nivison entered her delayed career in the public schools, at a salary of six hundred dollars a year. She began teaching the boys' classes at P.S. 188, an elementary school on the Lower East Side, then populated by an East European immigrant population who often perceived public school teachers as "sexless saints" and "the most wonderful people in the world."[31] That fall, she was transferred to P.S. 64, also on the Lower East Side, where she continued teaching through the spring of 1912.[32] Nivison was part of a small group of middle-class women of her generation who received a college education that offered them alternatives to marriage and motherhood. In 1904, the year of her graduation, a prominent psychologist, G. Stanley Hall, warned that higher education was threatening to produce women who were "functionally castrated . . . deplore the necessity of childbearing . . . and abhor the limits of married life."[33] An extraordinarily high percentage of female college graduates of Nivison's generation never married and, even among those who did, a significant proportion never had children.[34]

Nivison, like many of her fellow graduates, felt a sense of mission, and was not eager to exchange her new possibilities for household duties. Her own mother produced children late (she was thirty-four or thirty-five when Jo was born), while her father's difficult personality and uncertain accomplishments would have made clear the folly of total dependence on a male. Furthermore, men of her generation did not understand the encouragement that women's colleges gave to their students to use their talents in the world.[35] Men had little sympathy for female aspirations, typically expecting that even women with college degrees would become dutiful wives tending the home.

Even while teaching, Nivison kept in touch with the artistic world. In the summer of 1907, after her first full year of work, she traveled to Holland to take Henri's landscape and portrait classes in Haarlem.[36] Years later she recalled how she "had worked very hard all winter helping to drum up mem-

Robert Henri with his painting of Miss Josephine Nivison as The Art Student, *1906.*

bers for a summer class abroad with the hope of getting into it myself by way of commissions."[37] Two small oil panels that Nivison painted that summer survive. One, of the harbor in Volendam, is not unlike the work Henri himself produced there. The other depicts the town of Haarlem with its Grote Kirk. Once abroad, Nivison also visited France, as well as Italy, which her future husband never saw. She later mentioned seeing "the more modern painters in Paris" of whom Hopper claimed he was unaware during his visits in the same period.[38] Nivison may have gone on to Paris and Italy with some of Henri's other students and the school's administrator, Douglas Connah, who accompanied them when the class in Haarlem ended in mid-August.[39]

After her father's death about 1909, Nivison, her mother, and her brother continued their frequent relocation, each time moving further uptown, first to 60 West Seventy-fifth Street, then to 2 West Ninety-fifth Street. By 1911, they had gone as far as West 141st Street, which gave her an extremely long subway trip to work. In the fall of 1912, she transferred to P.S. 192, an elementary school at Amsterdam Avenue and 136th Street, also known as The Hebrew Orphan Asylum of the City of New York.

Giving up this new proximity to her job, in 1913 Nivison moved to a studio on the top floor of 30 West Fifty-ninth Street, where she would remain for the next six years. Now aged thirty, she no longer lodged with her mother and brother, who moved to Warren, Rhode Island, to live with the mother's two maiden sisters. At first, Charles worked as a bookkeeper in a cotton mill in Warren.[40] After his drinking intensified, he worked as a clerk and a farm helper. In 1931 he died, aged forty-six, in a state infirmary in Howard, Rhode Island, of chronic pulmonary tuberculosis and alcoholism.[41]

At thirty, Nivison was free from her family for the first time. She shared her new quarters with a friend, Susie Belden, who was then studying voice at Carnegie Hall.[42] Nivison came to adore this tiny one-room space on the top floor of an old house situated between the Plaza Hotel and the New York Athletic Club.[43] In settling outside her family, Nivison chose an alternative that was becoming increasingly common among college-educated daughters of business and professional families.[44] Social conventions were shifting rapidly; for example, chaperons for respectable young women were becoming passé.[45] Nivison's social life was active and she had a stimulating circle of friends through whom she found links to bohemian life in Greenwich Village and became acquainted with many people who were involved in radical thought. Despite her employment as a school teacher, her outgoing personality enabled her to forge friendships with those who could help advance her career in the arts. In fact, it was her work as a teacher that put her into contact with the vanguard dealer and photographer Alfred Stieglitz.

In the spring of 1912, Stieglitz held the first of two exhibitions of the art of children at his 291 Fifth Avenue gallery. Published accounts credit the artist Abraham Walkowitz with obtaining the children's pictures from "an east side settlement house,"[46] yet Nivison's later diaries make clear that the drawings came from her students. (She taught art classes at a settlement house in addition to her regular teaching job.) Even years later, whenever she encountered Walkowitz, she would bring up "my children's drawings of long ago." She recorded that Walkowitz "hung that show & that Stieglitz probably doesn't know where they are—in storage somewhere—& that's why I can get nothing out of him when I want them back—nothing but crazy harangues."[47]

Around this time, Nivison was taking courses at the Independent School of Art, which succeeded the Henri School of Art that Henri founded in 1909 in two rooms on the top floor of the Lincoln Arcade at Sixty-sixth Street and Broadway. Henri had created his own school after withdrawing from the New York School of Art. By 1912, he was teaching much less, but still giving criticism to students. His associate and former student, Homer Boss, began to run the school. Boss emphasized vanguard trends after the Armory Show in early 1913 and Henri soon left the school entirely. When Henri began lecturing at the Art Students League in the fall of 1915, Nivison, ever the faithful disciple, attended.[48]

Nivison counted among her friends Alfred "Krimmie" Kreymborg, "an emaciated-looking, bespectacled"[49] young poet who edited the vanguard little magazine *The Glebe* and sent her one of his poems for Christmas in 1913. Kreymborg, the painter Marsden Hartley, and the poet Alanson Hartpence, a friend of Krimmie's, then stayed in a rooming house on Fourteenth Street and ate frequently at Kiel's, a German bakery on West Fifteenth Street.[50] Lance Hartpence worked for Charles Daniel, a former saloon-keeper who had started the Daniel Gallery at Fifth Avenue and Forty-seventh Street. Hartpence was said to have had a strong critical sense and to have exerted a special influence on the important collector of modern American art Fernand Howald of Columbus, Ohio. Later, Nivison gratefully recalled how "Lance Hartpence tried to make a wee crack for me at the Daniel."[51] In December 1914, she had exhibited with a number of Kreymborg's friends in a group show of sixty-four "Small Oils by American Artists" at the Daniel Gallery. Kreymborg's other intimates in this show were all modernist painters, including Man Ray, Samuel Halpert, William Zorach, and Hartley. Among the remaining participants were Stuart Davis, Preston Dickinson, Maurice Prendergast, Leon Kroll, and Charles Demuth.[52] The *New York Times* review mentioned Nivison as a participant and commented in general: "The work is unequal, but it holds together coherently, and not one of the artists has written down to the size of his canvas."[53]

Nivison had been brought up to value individuality over conformity, and her life consistently reflected this. She contributed an illustration on this theme to the revolutionary, Socialist-oriented magazine *The Masses* when its art editor was John Sloan, whom she may have first met in 1906 at the New York School of Art. Her drawing, captioned *"THE PUNISH LINE: Where the Individualists in Public Schools Spend their Recess,"* appeared in July 1914, on the same page as an unrelated article by the radical journalist John Reed. Clearly inspired by her own work as a teacher, the illustration suggests that Nivison both sympathized and identified with nonconformist children.

Even when *The Masses* began publishing more doctrinaire pacifist propaganda after the beginning of World War I, disillusioning Sloan and others, Nivison continued to contribute (literally, for neither artists nor writers received compensation) her work. After Sloan's resignation in 1916, the art editors Robert Minor and Boardman Robinson gave more space to political cartoons. Another of her drawings of children appeared in the issue of January 1917. Identified as "Non-Combatants Sketched by Jo Nivison," it was captioned: "Strikers' children entertained at luncheon by the Authors League while their fathers are fighting for more wages and better conditions."[54]

Nivison must have been sympathetic to many of the positions supported by *The Masses,* particularly feminist issues such as Margaret Sanger's battle to disseminate information on birth control. As for her own behavior, she was hardly a radical, in contrast to some of the women with whom she associated in the Village. Her conservative family background and, perhaps, her fears of breaking with their values led her to cling tenaciously to her virginity, even past her fortieth birthday.

Nivison published more of her drawings, which were sometimes on humanitarian themes, in newspapers such as the Chicago *Herald Examiner,* the *Evening Post,* and the New York *Tribune.*[55] She also pursued her love of dance, sketching the notorious Isadora Duncan when she performed in New York in the spring of 1915 and the celebrated Nijinsky when he danced with Diaghilev's Ballets Russes at the Metropolitan Opera House in New York in April 1916. She recalled how she had "strutted in as one of the musicians in Cleopatra—& how Nijinski had offered to pose for me—& all the enchantment of those nights in the wings snatching at so quick sketches."[56] Another time, she described these drawings as "just breaths, gasped from the wings where I was allowed to hover while the Nijinsky ballet was here—oh such a heavenly experience—to draw to music—grab what one could."[57]

Nivison associated with some of the many feminists active in Greenwich Village, particularly when she performed in the productions of the Washington Square Players.[58] She knew one of its founders, Ida Rauh (a feminist, socialist, and former sculpture student of Jo Davidson), who was then married to Max

Josephine Verstille Nivison, THE PUNISH LINE. *Drawing reproduced in* The Masses, *July 1914.*

Eastman, the editor of *The Masses*.[59] This little avant-garde group had begun by performing an occasional play at the Liberal Club, located in the ground floor of a Macdougal Street brownstone. Alfred Kreymborg recalled that their plays, initially performed without scenery, often treated the new theme, "sex," and, except for some chairs and an occasional table, "props were taboo."[60]

By 1915, while still teaching school and earning a yearly salary of $1,080, Nivison had joined the Players and appeared in their first productions, which were moved uptown to the Bandbox Theatre on Fifty-seventh Street near Third Avenue. She characteristically played supporting roles and, like the others, initially worked without pay.[61] During the company's first season, which opened in February 1915, she played a "Passerby in the Flesh" in *Another Interior,* which served as a divertissement to Maurice Maeterlinck's poetic *Interior.* This highly praised anonymous gastronomic allegory consisted of a mise-en-scène that represented "the inside of a man's stomach, in which various foods portrayed by the actors, passed through the esophagus."[62] In another role that first season, Nivison played Valentine in Maeterlinck's ironic comedy *Miracle of St. Anthony,* which debuted in May 1915.

Nivison appeared on the first bill of the Players' second season as "a boy" in Percy MacKaye's Yankee fantasy *The Antick,* in October 1915.[63] The play, about a group of French Canadians, starred the famous Russian ballerina Lydia Lopokova. By this time, the actors were earning twenty-five dollars a week and the company had gone from two to seven performances weekly, a heavy commitment for Nivison, who had to support herself as an elementary school teacher.[64] She next played one of the slaves of the princess in Holland

Hudson's one-act play *Shepherd in the Distance* (which she later described as a "black and white Beardsley pantomime"[65]), both in New York beginning in May 1915, and at the Little Theatre in Philadelphia the following month. In February 1916, she was cast as Lisetta, Filippa's lovely handmaiden, in *The Red Cloak,* which was billed as "A Sort of Marionet Pantomime by Josephine A. Meyer and Lawrence Langner."

In 1917, Nivison played the role of "Katie, His daughter" in Leonid Andreyev's *Love of One's Neighbor,* a play that her pal Kreymborg had first published in translation from the Russian in *The Glebe.* The sets were designed by Lee Simonson, who later recounted that "everything was plentiful at the Washington Square Players except money" and remembered going to "the family saloon at the corner of Third Avenue where everyone met after the week-end performances."[66]

During the summers, Nivison tried out the various art colonies in New England. "Cape Cod was no impossible distance from New York," she recalled, "and my mother, who loved Provincetown, saw that we spent many summers there as well as some in Gloucester, Ogunquit and Monhegan."[67] She fondly remembered that during her art school days, about 1906, in company with her mother, she made her first trip to Provincetown, the picturesque fishing settlement at the tip of Cape Cod. They stayed at the boarding house of Mrs. Mary Turner, who arranged to let her use an old "cellarway" under a shoemaker's shop for her studio.[68] Long afterward Hopper poked fun at her early artistic endeavors by making a caricature of *Jo's "Cellar-way" Studio at Provincetown years ago.* He drew six figures peeking in the trap door, making comments such as "CUTE," "ADORABLE!!!," "BROMIDE," "GORGEOUS," and "ANOTHER SET OF VALUES."

On several of these summer jaunts Nivison encountered Hopper, whom she remembered from art school.[69] She later recollected that they stayed at the same boarding house in Ogunquit in 1914. But Hopper was then either too shy, as Nivison suspected, or too financially strapped to make the overtures of a relationship. Her memory of him on Monhegan focused on her disappointment, since she adored dancing, that in spite of his great dancing legs, he didn't dance. On one occasion in Provincetown, Nivison enrolled in the Summer School of Painting that Ambrose Webster had started in 1900. A pioneer champion of modernism, Webster had studied for two years in Paris, where he discovered Impressionism. A small shy man, then in his thirties, who spoke with a lisp, Webster had less influence than Henri on Nivison: she rarely mentioned her study with him.[70] Webster exhibited in the Armory Show in 1913, which Jo very surely saw, for she recalled that the modern art on view inspired her mother to make a rag rug, a craft that Nivison later enjoyed herself.[71]

Edward Hopper, Jo's "Cellar-way" Studio at Provincetown years ago, *c. 1932. Pencil on paper, 11 × 8½″ (27.9 × 21.6 cm.).*

In Provincetown in the summer of 1915, when she stayed in an ill-equipped fishhouse, Nivison received unexpected warmth and hospitality from the feminist writer Susan Glaspell and her husband, the writer George Cram "Jig" Cook.[72] Glaspell and Cook gathered their Village friends together in a wharf house in Provincetown that belonged to the feminist writer Mary Heaton Vorse and produced their first play, *Suppressed Desires,* a satire on psychoanalysis that the Washington Square Players had considered too esoteric.[73] The activities that summer led to the founding of the Provincetown Players, but Nivison did not join the new company, continuing to perform with the Washington Square Players instead. She later recalled that "Mary Heaton Vorse has had a lovely little house at Provincetown all her married life & has had it full of visiting friends who complained of her cooking, criticized the way she brought up her children etc. Now she opens her house to the travelling public, charming people who appreciate everything & pay her good money."[74] Nivison remembered "a gay summer with many costumes & much dancing."[75] She recollected her fondness for Glaspell, Cook, and his "valiant & delightful little mother, Mamie."[76] Among the others there that summer were the set designer Robert Edmond Jones, the writers Neith Boyce and Hutchins Hapgood, the radical socialite Mabel Dodge, and many artists, among them Marguerite and William Zorach, and Charles Demuth, who, like Nivison, worked in watercolor. The Provincetown Art Association, founded the previous season, numbered 147 members.[77]

Back in New York, Nivison fondly recalled giving "big teas at my studio.... When Orrick Johns married Peggy Baird ... all there for tea and never a drop of anything stronger than White Rose Tea."[78] Nivison probably met Johns, a poet who came to Greenwich Village from St. Louis, through his wife, who was an artist from Babylon, New York; they were all friends of Kreymborg and belonged to the circle of the Washington Square Players, the Liberal Club, and *The Masses*.[79] Johns recalled his wife's fondness for people, cats, and flowers, all enthusiasms that she shared with Nivison.[80]

Growing restless, Nivison sought to go abroad in the summer of 1918, although the war was still on. She unsuccessfully applied for a job with the Red Cross. Then, at the Teachers College of Columbia University, she saw a cable from General Pershing seeking to recruit reconstruction aides for the medical department of the American Expeditionary Forces. She was immediately attracted by the idea of this government program for wounded and disabled men in U.S. army hospitals in both France and the United States.[81]

Nivison hoped not just for a change of scene and a new job, but for a husband as well. She volunteered to teach occupational therapy, asserting that she would "bring to the work a zeal and breadth of experience that you will find of real value."[82] So eager for this position was she that she presented three letters of recommendation, even though they were not required. She had evidently gathered them when she had applied to work for the Red Cross.

Her colleague at the Hebrew Orphan Asylum wrote a strong recommendation, claiming that "she has proven herself to be very capable, her ideals are of the highest and she is an inspiration to the children under her charge."[83] Nonetheless, Nivison felt compelled to add in her own hand: "Altho I have worked among them, I am not a Hebrew. The Hebrews are too clever a people to discriminate against Gentiles when their service can be of value to them." She also had her friend Arthur Warner, the acting city editor at the New York *Evening Post,* which had published her illustrations, recommend her. He noted of Nivison that "for many years she has been the virtual head of her family, carrying its responsibilities and looking after its business; and that, more than once she has been called upon to pass through the Slough of Despond, and has emerged with unruffled patience and undiminished courage."[84] Nivison's mother had been suffering from breast cancer that recurred after an operation and she died in Warren, Rhode Island, on August 25.

Taking a leave of absence from the New York City public schools, Nivison signed up. She hoped to teach both handicrafts and academic subjects in France.[85] The government interviewer noted that she "had a slight mannerism which might be a handicap" and commented that she was "very anxious to fit herself in every way—Thinks she would be able to handle hospital work without any difficulty."[86] Her art background was considered an asset. Nivison was delighted to be accepted, and by October 9 she reported that she had "packed up my studio & disposed of my affairs."[87] On the eleventh, she was mobilized; she embarked for France on the tenth of November. Years later, she recalled going "overseas for World War I" in the new leather coat given her by her favorite aunt, Anita, to mark this momentous event.[88]

Nivison was assigned to work in occupational therapy on the U.S.S. *Sierra* in Bordeaux, in the base hospital at Beau Desert in Saverney in Brittany, and in Brest. By December 14, 1918, she was ill with acute bronchitis and was herself admitted to the hospital at Beau Desert. She was sent home on the S.S. *Melita* and arrived in Boston on January 22, 1919. On February 28, Anne E. Radford, the chief nurse, reported that Nivison "was considered temperamentally and physically unfit for service" in the AEF. She was assigned to continue as a reconstruction aide in the Medical Department at Large at Walter Reed General Hospital in Washington. In June 1919, she was sent to New York, where she was discharged by the Surgeon General.

On her return to New York, Nivison found that she had lost her teaching position, which the Board of Education had not held for her during her leave of absence. She was desperate to find another job. She had also given up her cherished studio, where she had lived since 1913. She later spoke of having had to endure a broken heart, her mother's death, and the loss of both her home and her job in rapid succession.[89] It is not known who broke her heart.

By the fall of 1919, Nivison still had no job. Homeless and unemployed, she was initially unable to obtain shelter she could afford, but she finally found a studio in a private house at 3 University Place in Greenwich Village. Located above the TallyRand Pericord Chapel, the studio was next to the Church of the Ascension, where an old sexton had taken pity on Jo after he came upon her weeping in the church.[90] She later recalled nearly freezing to death from the cold during the winter she spent in that studio.[91]

Nivison remembered herself at this time as "the most forlorn church mouse in the world," who counted her friends by the beads on the rosary she made of leftover supplies from her work in occupational therapy.[92] She remembered: "Monty Coolidge highly approved & wanted to be one bead. E. Hopper sniffed as would be expected but said he 'wanted to be that cranberry of a big red one.' "[93] Her comment, recorded years later, is one of the few clues that Nivison and Hopper had established a friendship that predated their actual courtship during the summer of 1923.

Among Nivison's other friends was Henrietta Rodman. Her acquaintance with such feminists as Rauh and Rodman and the issues they raised contributed to her vision of herself as an artist. Despite the fact that few women were able to show and sell their paintings, much less earn their living as visual artists, Nivison was determined to make art her profession, no matter how much she had to maneuver and sacrifice. She was ready and willing to take risks. She had little to lose. In this moment of crisis, Nivison also renewed her interest in the theater. In 1919, she saw Yvette Guilbert, the great French diseuse who was then performing in New York. Guilbert presented medieval songs as well as the work of French poets that she admired, including Baudelaire's *La Causerie* and Verlaine's *L'Heure Exquise*.[94] Nivison shared her enthusiasm for the actress with her friend from the New York School of Art, the Swedish-born painter Carl Sprinchorn, whose 1919 sketch of Guilbert she saved all her life. Years later, she vividly recalled Guilbert's performance in the fourteenth-century French miracle play, *Guibour*:

> She seemed to be some sort of Madonna of the Annunciation. What she did with that I'd never heard of anyone else doing. The Virgin walks in the garden and meets the angel Gabriel, and Gabriel tells her, not only of the birth of the child, of the life, of the death, but of the finale. . . . Gabriel throws his arms out, the crucifixion, it has been prophesied.[95]

Guibour, the story of the Virgin's intervention to save a devout woman about to be burned at the stake, was performed with sets by Robert Edmond Jones. Nivison's admiration was not shared by the writer and editor Harold Loeb, who later referred to the "perfectly dreadful miracle play . . . presented at the Grand Street Theatre."[96]

Nivison's enthusiasm actually led her to enroll when Guilbert held evening classes at the Hotel Majestic, advertised as "Yvette Guilbert's School of the Theatre" and including such offerings as "Highest Lights of French Literature of the 19th Century" and "Dramatic Interpretation."[97] Edmund Wilson recalled that during Guilbert's years in New York, she had "conducted an original kind of school for actresses, singers, and diseuses."[98] He raved about her abilities: "Her powers of impersonation were equal to any I have ever seen."[99] Hopper, on the other hand, had avoided Guilbert's notorious cabaret performances in Paris, and later expressed embarrassment about her.

No records of Guilbert's school survive, but Nivison later praised her as a teacher who was "theatrically giving," and likened her to Henri, who had been her favorite teacher of art.[100] Nivison also mentioned studying French with Mademoiselle Alice Blum, who taught a course at the school.[101] Nivison's studies at this time are confirmed by her response to the question in the United States Census for 1920 of whether she had attended school at any time since September 1, 1919.[102] Although Nivison could not have met the tuition of five hundred dollars a year, Guilbert allowed students to enroll for any part of the course and even offered some scholarships.[103] Guilbert stressed that the well-rounded actress, in order to learn how to reduce truth to its simplest expression, should make the visual arts her special province; it was a philosophy that must have held special appeal for Nivison.

Around this time, she began to show her work at the Sunwise Turn, a bookshop founded in the spring of 1916 by Madge Jenison and Mary Mowbray-Clarke, then the wife of the sculptor John Mowbray-Clarke.[104] Originally located on Thirty-first Street near Fifth Avenue, not far from Alfred Stieglitz's gallery, the shop moved into the Yale Club building on Forty-fourth Street in 1919, shortly after Harold Loeb bought a third share in it and he and his wife, Marjorie Content, began to work there.[105] The Sunwise Turn also showed many other contemporary artists, including friends of Nivison's like Martha Rhyther, Bertram Hartman, and the Zorachs, both William and Marguerite.[106] The shop also showed Charles Burchfield from 1916 through 1922.[107]

Nivison must have attended some of the Sunwise Turn's evening programs when talks were given on modern art and poetry and plays were read. The bookshop also began publishing its own titles, including an essay on Rodin by Rainer Maria Rilke, *The Dance of Shiva* by Ananda Coomaraswamy, and *Guibour,* the miracle play that Guilbert performed. Jenison remembered that Mme. Guilbert herself came to the shop. Beatrice Wood, who, like Nivison, studied acting with Guilbert, also frequented the Sunwise Turn, where she recalled reciting Amy Lowell's "Patterns" to polite applause.[108] Loeb recounted first making the acquaintance of Alfred Kreymborg, Nivison's old friend, when Kreymborg recited *Lima Beans,* his best-known one-act play, and some of his poems at the shop. Other artists among the regulars attending the evening programs were Arthur B. Davies, Walt Kuhn, Jerome Myers, and Maurice and Charles Prendergast.

In May 1920, Nivison won the right to another job from the Board of Education. She was assigned to teach sick children in a public school classroom at the Willard Parker Hospital, where treatment was given for contagious diseases. She immediately contracted diphtheria during an epidemic.[109]

(Diphtheria, which is transmitted by airborne bacteria, causes inflammation of the heart and nervous system: when not treated, it can be fatal.) Although she spent the summer of 1920 working at Aloha Hive,[110] a religious camp for young children in South Fairlee, Vermont, she continued to suffer the effects of this debilitating illness.

In the meantime, Nivison had clarified her ambition. She was now prepared to propel herself toward a new goal. Although she had specified her occupation as "teacher" in the previous city directories, in 1920 she first listed herself as an "artist," affirming the professional identity she claimed in the 1920 census, when she declared herself an artist who earned her living painting portraits and landscapes. She also began to lie about her age. For the census, she stated that she was twenty-nine, when, in fact, it was taken shortly before her thirty-sixth birthday. In October that same year, she found a tiny room on the top floor of the Vanderbilt Studios at 37 West Ninth Street in the Village. Almost immediately after moving in, she held an exhibition of her work. Years later, the art critic Margaret Breuning recalled coming to Jo's open studio on a deserted Saturday afternoon when only the artist and her cat were present.[111]

Describing the Spartan conditions in her new place, Nivison recalled having to descend four flights, walk through the cellar, and climb to the fourth floor of the adjoining building to wait in line to use the communal bathroom.[112] But despite the daily hardships, she so enjoyed the experience of living with other artists in this building that she affectionately referred to it as "Titmouse Terrace."[113] The cat that Breuning remembered seeing in Nivison's studio became the subject of a feline legend. Soon after she moved, Nivison acquired her "adored pussy cat Arthur," whom she claimed was "sent to live with me."[114] Jo described herself as Arthur's "silly mother" and lavished much wit and affection on him. She avowed that he "knew traffic cops, the maitre d'hotel at the Brevoort, people at the Jefferson Market Court."[115] She also observed: "Someone said he was the reincarnation of some old Village poet—or back (a lot farther)—of François Villon himself."[116]

In the fall of 1920, Nivison was assigned to teach rambunctious young boys at P.S. 122, at Ninth Street and First Avenue. But after more than a decade of working with children for whom she claimed to feel "deep affection," she was physically and emotionally overwhelmed. It would be her last year of teaching.[117] Maintaining that she had not been informed of the health risk at the hospital school, she fought for and won early retirement in the autumn of 1921, receiving lifetime disability payments based on her current annual salary of $1750.[118] Considering that she was able to lead a rather healthy life for more than four more decades, her successful campaign demonstrates her determination and resourcefulness, if not outright manipulation. These payments provided her with more freedom to continue her own art work than she had ever known.

For the summer of 1921, Nivison went to Woodstock, New York, where exhibitions organized by the newly founded Woodstock Artists Association and the annual Maverick Festival were attracting more and more visitors from other art colonies.[119] Her revered teacher, Henri, was there with his second wife, the illustrator Marjorie Organ, as were many other former Henri students, including such successful artists as George Bellows and Eugene Speicher. After returning to New York, Nivison wrote to Henri explaining that she had not been able to accept his invitation to stop by and see his work because she "had to rush off from Woodstock suddenly."[120] She told him:

> To us who haven't been able to keep up the painting much—it's all the same—we're painters & have had it all just the same—to say nothing of the wonderful tribal sense of having belonged. When ever any two of the old crowd meet it's the meeting of spiritual kin you know all about them—that's all that matters—there is an extension of personality, of faith transmitted that is a priceless experience to have.

Nivison proceeded to recount news of her many friends among Henri's former students. She had been both a friend and neighbor of the late Mary Gamble Rogers (1881–1920), whom Henri had eulogized after her early death, and now she reported that the Brooklyn Museum had "come over to get 10 of Mazie Rogers' for a watercolor show there & found they couldn't do with less than 20. We fairly weep with joy—and rage everytime anything comes for Mazie."[121] Nivison revealed something of her politics at the time when she reported that Maurice Becker "is living down in Tioga, Pa. as I suppose you know. What a darling curly headed youngster he still remains. Even Levenworth couldn't spoil him."[122] She had met Becker, a Jewish immigrant who had arrived from Russia at the age of three in 1889, after he joined Henri's evening class in 1909. Then during the 1910s, Nivison and Becker had both contributed illustrations to *The Masses*. A conscientious objector during World War I, Becker was sentenced in 1918 to twenty-five years of hard labor and sent to federal prison in Fort Leavenworth, Kansas.[123] Freed in 1919, after serving only four months, Becker remained a lifelong friend.

Nivison likewise reported on Henrietta Shore, whose work was becoming rather abstract: "Etta Shore is back from Monhegan—it's done her such worlds of good to be there—she came back so freshened up, so much less keyed up."[124] As for herself, Nivison announced proudly that she had "brought back a couple of dozen watercolors," reflecting, "It did one so much good to be back at work & they look rather gay & amusing back here." The titles of some of them survive to suggest their subjects: *Kiddy Party, Hill from Allens, Woodstock Hill out of Window,* and *Woodstock Mountain.*[125]

Nivison also confided that she had just taken some of her drawings of Nijinsky and the Russian Ballet to the *Dial,* which had asked her to leave them for a few days. She felt so encouraged by this "gentler treatment than the usual flat turn down" that she generously suggested that Henri's wife Marjorie might also place her drawings there. At the time, Nivison had received a gift subscription to the *Dial;* she later recalled how she had greatly "cherished" these issues with their reproductions of modern art.[126] It was surely reading the *Dial* that Nivison developed her admiration for the writing of critics such as Van Wyck Brooks, Roger Fry, and Henry McBride.

For the summer of 1922, Nivison returned to Provincetown, where she stayed in the Gingerbread Inn with her cat, Arthur.[127] The social scene included the Zorachs and Gusta and Bertram Hartman; the latter became a close friend. Yet the conservative Nivison could not have approved of the frenetic postwar atmosphere of the Provincetown Players' clique led by the playwright Eugene O'Neill. Wild parties featuring jazz and bathtub gin were not her style.

That December, Nivison and Hopper both exhibited in a group show of interiors at the Belmaison Gallery of Decorative Arts in John Wanamaker's Department Store in New York. Nivison showed one of her Cape Cod watercolors, *The Provincetown Bedroom,* and Hopper showed his etching of an urban scene, *East Side Interior.* This show was organized by their mutual friend Louis Bouché, who directed the gallery and included his own work in the exhibition, as well as that of Hamilton Easter Field, whom Nivison and Hopper both knew from past summers in Ogunquit. Bouché also put Nivison's work in a show that he did of flower painting, which included Joseph Stella, Charles Demuth, Charles Sheeler, Walter Tittle, and many others.[128]

At last Nivison's career was beginning to thrive. When James Rosenberg, a wealthy attorney and painter, opened the New Gallery at 600 Madison Avenue, intending to promote unknown artists to the American art market, he hired Nivison's friend from art school, Carl Sprinchorn, as director.[129] Her watercolors were featured in a large "Holiday Exhibition" in December 1922 along with work by many other artists including Hartley and the Zorachs, Bertram Hartman, Moise Kisling, Modigliani, Picasso, Abraham Walkowitz, and Sprinchorn himself. The catalogue text, which commented, in alphabetical order, on each artist, stated: "The water colors of Nivison add a gay note of color."[130]

The following spring, Nivison was in another group show at the New Gallery that included Florine Stettheimer, Aline Bernstein, Bertram Hartman, and Kees Van Dongen, among others. Her work was mentioned by the reviewer for the *Evening World,* who noted: "Josephine Nivison shows a pair of water colors in which the blues are made prominent."[131] The New Gallery survived for only two seasons, but remained a high point for Nivison. She later recalled to Sprinchorn, "I'll never forget how, soon as you were ensconced in that delightful New Gallery you came & got me! And how pleasantly things were there for a while. I owe you such happy memories for that."[132] With summer came the turning that would make such memories so poignantly bittersweet.

FIRST SUCCESS: 1923-1924

AS THE SUMMER of 1923 approached, Josephine Nivison had reason to feel upbeat. Her circle of loyal friends was giving her access to the art world and her work was at least noticed. Reports circulated of new activity in Gloucester, which was one summer art colony she had not visited recently. Among the other painters who planned to paint there in the 1923 season were Theresa Bernstein and William Meyerowitz, Milton Avery, Charles Allan Winter, and Alice Beach Winter. The previous season, the artists had organized rival groups. The radical Gloucester Society of Artists chaired by Stuart Davis rejected the jury system and took as their motto "Open to all and an equal chance for all" when they organized a summer show; the conservative North Shore Arts Association promoted a traditional juried show.[1] The town itself was celebrating the 300th anniversary of its founding in 1623.

Edward Hopper, who eleven years earlier had painted oils at Gloucester with Leon Kroll, also planned to return. Like Nivison, he had reason to feel optimistic about his work. He was finding an ever-increasing demand for his etchings, which commanded frequent showings and prizes. On the other hand, his productive intimacy with the French woman Jeanne Chéruy had ended sometime after Christmas 1922. He was on the rebound as he made his own plans for the summer of 1923.

Hopper turned forty-one in July; Nivison was just forty. In appearance and personality two people could hardly have been more different. She was not quite five feet one inch tall and weighed about a hundred pounds, while he stood nearly six feet five inches and was as skinny as ever. Years later Nivison, who was often described as "lively, vivacious," and "cute," recalled that "no one had ever called him either handsome or distinguished when I married him. It was the 'long, lean & hungry' that got me."[2] She admitted that she had "always found tall men exciting."[3] She was gregarious, outgoing, sociable, and talkative, while he was shy, quiet, solitary, and introspective: "He's known to be pure gold really—but like the silence that is golden, he seldom opens his mouth. . . . When he does say anything—it's apt to be very witty or very wise—or both."[4]

A pretext to break silence came from Arthur, the alley cat, who shared the trip from Greenwich Village with Nivison: "Hey, I saw your cat yesterday," were the first words Nivison remembered. Then, she said, Edward "sat on a fence and drew a map of Gloucester for me."[5] They began to go out working together, even though Hopper had to make some effort: "The girl I was rooming with didn't like Eddie; so he would come around early in the morning and throw pebbles against my window to wake me up for a sketching trip."[6]

They soon discovered their shared passion for French. Hopper "started quoting Verlaine on Bass Rock in Gloucester" and he was astounded when she took up the poem where he stopped.[7] (Bass Rock is the peak of a small headland, located above the white sandy stretch of Little Good Harbor Beach, where the ocean's waves dash with terrific force upon the jagged rocks.) Hopper years later reminisced about the happy days when they "got together over Verlaine, Verhaeren, etc. etc. etc."[8] Emile Verhaeren was a Belgian symbolist poet and art critic whose collections, *Les Heures Claires, Les Heures d'Après-midi,* and *Les Heures du Soir,* with love poems dedicated to the poet's wife, had particular relevance for a courting couple.[9] An aspect of Verhaeren that parallels the future direction of Hopper's art was described by Amy Lowell: "Verhaeren is no mere descriptive poet. Neither is he a surface realist. His realism contains the psychologic as well as physiologic."[10] Even Verhaeren's titles, with their focus on the qualities of times of day, parallel similar themes and conceptions already emergent in Hopper's work. Love poems by Verlaine, of course, had been Hopper's gift the previous Christmas from Jeanne Chéruy.

The new working friendship induced a momentous change in Hopper's work. After art school and a few Parisian caricatures, he had employed watercolor only for his commercial assignments. That summer in Gloucester, he began to use the medium in a new and freer way. He showed impressive facility, improvising as he went along, faintly outlining his composition in pencil and then applying his pigments with extraordinary control. More than rendering textures he focused on depicting sunlight, applying color directly, without manipulation, painting almost entirely outdoors, recording his most careful observations immediately in the presence of his subjects. In a trice, he made watercolor his most spontaneous medium.

Hopper's new freedom drew stimulus from Nivison, whose accomplishments in the same medium piqued his competitive spirit.[11] They worked together in the Rocky Neck section of Gloucester, where the large old houses of the sea captains were well preserved; on Good Harbor Beach; along the harbor; and in the Italian and Portuguese quarters. They made excursions to nearby Lanesville and Annisquam. Nivison depicted ships, a sailboat in Gloucester harbor, churches, trees, houses, children, and flowers, while Hopper also portrayed ships and harbor views, but concentrated on houses. One watercolor that Nivison painted that summer introduced a theme that later became significant for Hopper: in *Shacks,* she portrayed two houses behind a dead tree, a motif that would recurrently interest him.

It is hardly a surprise, given their contrasting personalities, that they even preferred contrasting formats in their work. The petite Nivison usually chose a vertical orientation, while Hopper, who towered a foot taller, was habitually horizontal, claiming "I just never cared for the vertical."[12] Hopper later commented that he had a "bird's eye view," while Jo had "a worm's eye view."[13] She explained: "Edward likes the surface of the earth, he likes to stay close to it."[14]

Both artists were attracted to the quaint fishermen's church Our Lady of Good Voyage, on Prospect Street in the Portuguese quarter. Hopper eventually painted only distant views of the exterior, but that summer Nivison focused on the figure of the Madonna located at the top of the facade between the two towers. Nivison later recalled "straining one's neck up to paint her," and described the Madonna as having "one arm raised higher to bless, the other holding, not the bambino, but a ship, a 2 masted fishing schooner."[15]

Hopper remembered: "At Gloucester, when everyone else would be painting ships and the waterfront, I'd just go around looking at houses. It is a solid-looking town. The roofs are very bold, the cornices bolder. The dormers cast very positive shadows. The sea captain influence I guess—the boldness of ships."[16] He remembered that he had painted *The Mansard Roof* "in the residential district where the old sea captains had their houses. . . . It interested me because of the variety of roofs and windows, the Mansard roof, which has always interested me. . . . I sat out in the street . . . it was very windy."[17] Actually, he sat away from the street, right on the water's edge,

Jo Nivison Hopper, Our Lady of Good Voyage, Gloucester, *1923 (signed later). Watercolor.*

looking up a hill at the complex protuberances of the Victorian structure, which was located in the Rocky Neck section.[18]

Boats and nautical events also caught Hopper's eye. The year before, he had etched a small sailboat, *The Cat Boat,* like one he sailed on the Hudson as a boy. Now he sketched the *Henry Ford,* a fishing schooner, on August 22, making several drawings, one of which became a study for an etching of the same subject. He depicted a group of spectators standing on the rocks, observing the vessel, which had been launched the previous year to compete against the renowned Canadian *Blue Nose* in the International Fisherman's races. That summer the schooner was generating a lot of interest in Gloucester; by the end of August, she would outsail two other American schooners, the *Elizabeth Howard* and the *Shamrock.*[19] Gradually it became clear to both Edward and Jo that they were courting. They went to Rocky Neck to see a puppet show inspired by the traditional folk song "Frog Went a-Courtin' "[20] and featuring a "long & gangly frog" wooing a female mouse. More than twenty years later, Jo recalled it as a moment of self-revelation and discovery: she and Edward both agreed that the puppets' story could have been made just for them.[21]

§

BACK IN NEW YORK, their romance began to transform their lives. The Brooklyn Museum invited Nivison to show six of her watercolors in a group exhibition of watercolors and drawings by American and European artists. Her work had probably come to the museum's attention in 1921, when curators had come to her Ninth Street studio building to select watercolors by her recently deceased friend Mary Rogers. Nivison generously suggested to the organizers, the director William Henry Fox and his curator William H. Goodyear, that they also consider Hopper's work. She recalled: "I got over there and they liked the stuff and I started writing and talking about Edward Hopper, my neighbor. . . . They knew him as an etcher, but they didn't know he did watercolors."[22] Nivison suggested that Hopper "bring some of his things over for the show."[23]

As a result, the organizers agreed to show six of Hopper's Gloucester watercolors—*Deck of a Beam Trawler, House with a Bay Window, The Mansard Roof, Shacks at Lanesville, Italian Quarter,* and *Beam Trawler Seal*—which were hung next to a more miscellaneous offering by Nivison: watercolors of children, views of Provincetown and Woodstock, and even one of Arthur of Ninth Street, her cat. She remembered that Hopper "carried my stuff back when the time came . . . didn't have me hauling them through the subway, what a sorry sight I'd have made."[24] The critic for *The New York Times,* Elizabeth Luther Cary, remarked on the show: "All the things shown are of good quality but not all of the most expensive cut."[25] She praised "Josephine Nivison's far-away echoes of Mary Rogers," while she relegated Georgia O'Keeffe to a long list of "other Americans," among them John [Singer] Sargent, George Luks, Jerome Myers, Stanton Macdonald-Wright, Max Weber, Abraham Walkowitz, and Thomas [Hart] Benton.[26]

Most critics ignored Nivison and raved about Hopper. "The Hopper group is one of the high spots," wrote Helen Appleton Read, who had also studied painting with Henri. "What vitality, force and directness! Observe what can be done with the homeliest subject, provided one has the seeing eye"; and she went on to compare Hopper's watercolors to those of Winslow Homer in their "authority of big, simple forms over the effect attained by brilliant brush work."[27] Royal Cortissoz found Hopper's watercolors "exhilarating" and exclaimed, "We rejoice that he is using the medium."[28]

After the show, the Brooklyn Museum paid Hopper one hundred dollars for *The Mansard Roof,* a work of which he later allowed only that it was "one of my good watercolors of the early period."[29] Also, in more than one interview, he denied the importance of Nivison's role in procuring him this success.[30] Yet her considerate gesture on his behalf proved decisive for his career. She encouraged and facilitated his new venture in watercolor. She contrived his presence in the show, setting the stage for the critical approbation and the sale. More than ten years had passed between the Armory Show, where Hopper first sold a painting, and this second sale, which was to a major museum. As early as 1920 Nivison had confidently listed herself in the city directory as an artist; only now, through her help, would Hopper feel able to claim the same. Despite the new success, Hopper's income in 1923 still depended largely on illustration. He recorded the sales of only eighteen etchings for a total of $233.40 (including two prizes at $25 each), averaging less than $13 per print after the dealers' commissions. During the same period, his income for illustrations was $1,325. But freedom was on the horizon, if only he could continue to sell watercolors at $100 each.

Lugging their paintings back and forth in the subways between Manhattan and Brooklyn, climbing the endless stairs to their top-floor studios, finding and comparing reviews, unpacking and storing paintings, Hopper and Nivison saw more and more of each other during the fall and winter. They began to frequent a Chinese restaurant at Columbus Circle, later the subject of a 1927 canvas, *Chop Suey.* They went to movies and to the theater. Reciprocating Nivison's support, Hopper wrote to two museum directors "commending" her work.[31] He also courted her with romantic sketches, poetry, and notes in French:

Chere Mlle. Nivison:
    Ci-enclos, le Korn crayon que vous m'avez demandé. J'ai tâché de donner un peu de gaieté et de couleur à ce crayon, dont le noir sombre vous agacerait sans doute, et d'adoucir ses lignes fortes et severes. J'espere qu'il ne vous genera jamais en essayant dessiner la sombre et triste verité de la vie.
tres sincerement
E. Hopper

Dear Miss Nivison:
    Enclosed here, the Korn crayon that you asked for. I have done my best to give a bit of cheer and color to this crayon, since its gloomy black would trouble you no doubt, and soften its strong and stern lines. I hope it will never hinder your efforts to draw the gloomy and sad truth of life.
very sincerely
E. Hopper

Playfully he wrapped the crayon and assigned its color a metaphysical significance, infusing even his usual pessimism with romantic urgency. Jo had captured the imagination so recently freed by Jeanne Chéruy and rooted so long ago in Paris. Words were never Edward's forte. With Chéruy he had registered increasing intimacy through successive visual images. For Jo he designed and painted a Christmas card in 1923 depicting the two of them reclining together, in silhouette before an open window, with the full moon and the spires of Notre-Dame visible in the Paris night outside. All this was pure imagination: he had not been in Paris for thirteen years and their visits there had not coincided. He incorporated her into a new matrix mingling nostalgia with present excitement. Underneath their image as a couple in a Parisian garret, he copied six lines in French from "La Lune Blanche," which Paul Verlaine had composed for his own fiancée:

> Un vaste et tendre
> Apaisement
> Semble descendre
> Du firmament
> Que l'astre irise
> C'est l'heure exquise.

> A huge and gentle
> Peacefulness
> Seems to come
> From the heaven
> That the moon illumines:
> It is the exquisite hour.[32]

French remained the language of romantic imagination for Edward and Jo all their lives, although their travels in search of new subjects would take them ever further south and west in the New World and never back to Paris.

§

LOVE AND RECEIVING recognition for his watercolors buoyed Hopper's confidence. In February he submitted *La Berge,* a picture he had painted in Paris, to the twenty-third International Exhibition of the Carnegie Institute in Pittsburgh.[33] If he imagined that his old Paris works would finally gain acceptance after so many rejections, he was wrong. His scene of the bank of the Seine was rejected and with a notice to pick up the painting at a warehouse in New York warning that it would be "held at your risk and is subject

à Mlle. Jo.
Noël 1923

Un vaste et tendre
Apaisement
Semble descendre

Du firmament
Que l'astre irise
C'est l'heure exquise

Edward Hopper, À Mlle. Jo. Noel, *1923. Gouache on paper, 7 × 8⅝" (17.8 × 21.9 cm.).*

to charges if not called for promptly." Whether or not it was ever reclaimed, the painting does not survive.

Taking to heart his failure in Pittsburgh, at his next chance to show Hopper switched to recent work on a New York theme, sending his 1922 oil painting *New York Restaurant* to the annual Members Exhibition of the Whitney Studio Club in May, where Nivison showed too, with a pastel drawing of an eleven-year-old ballerina, Margaret Van Epps, one of her numerous portraits of children in the medium. (She considered pastel "a good material for doing children where one must get effects fast."[34]) Belonging to the Studio Club placed Nivison in the same orbit as Hopper and his friends Louis Bouché, Arthur Cederquist, John Dos Passos, Leon Kroll, Richard Lahey, and Martin Lewis, all of whom had work in the 1924 annual. Most of her previous associations had been with more vanguard artists. The winter's intimacy presaged a second shared summer. Jo wanted to return to old haunts and friends of hers on Cape Cod, but Edward preferred Gloucester, where he had worked so well. In early July the difference provoked an argument that led to a double agreement: they would go to Gloucester for the summer, as Edward wished, and they would get married that very day.[35] Jo sacrificed old friends for the new bond. The date was July 9, 1924, shortly before Edward's forty-second birthday. On the marriage certificate, Jo gave her age as thirty-seven, though by now she was forty-one. Everything had to be improvised. Nothing had been planned and announced. The decisions and reasons were wholly theirs, with scant regard for the world, setting a pattern for their ensuing life.

About to make such a bold démarche, Edward turned to the person who had most closely supported his work, shared his hopes, and listened to his anxieties since their days together in art school. Guy du Bois had seen Edward's hunger, diagnosed his need for a wife, and felt the difficulty of imagining the right woman. Now Guy found his day suddenly interrupted by Edward asking him to act as best man. Guy had other plans, but he set out with Jo and Edward to look for a minister.[36] A hitch developed. In a succession of neighborhood churches, such as the Ascension, where Jo had survived a chilly winter, or the elegant Fifth Avenue Presbyterian, one minister after another refused to perform the ceremony when Hopper answered inquiries about his denomination only with the obdurate and minimal "Christian" (this in spite of his Baptist roots; Nivison had been raised as an Episcopalian). Guy had to leave to get home to Connecticut. Edward and Jo pressed on as far as West Sixteenth Street, where they found a clergyman to accommodate them. Fittingly, in view of their family roots and shared cultural enthusiasm, he was Paul D. Elsessor of the Eglise Evangélique, the French Huguenot church. Once in the midst of a later quarrel, Jo demanded of Edward: "Why, why did you marry me? Give me three reasons." He responded directly: "You have curly hair. You know some French. And you're an orphan."[37]

For a honeymoon, the newlyweds passed their second season painting watercolors in Gloucester. They found a room in Mrs. Thebaud's boarding house near Bass Rocks, where they had courted a year earlier.[38] Only afterward did Edward get around to taking his wife to meet his family in Nyack. Edward and Jo passed a tense week in the old home with his widowed mother and spinster sister. Elizabeth and Marion made no secret of their disapproval: they thought no one was good enough to marry into their family. Little wonder that Jo later referred to the Hoppers as "a loathsome breed." To her mother-in-law she said that "neither she nor I were Hoppers & she very much a Nivison—fire eater like my daddy, eat 'em alive stock." Jo reported her satisfaction that Elizabeth had been "quite pleased at the fancy."[39]

On Jo's side, there was no family to snub Edward. But she made the point that he "married a woman with a cat, not just a woman. I was taking out a maternity complex on a big warrior alley cat—the scourge of 9th Street. It was alright by the cat. He lapped it all up. Nothing he wanted more than an adoring mother. Think of all a child has been spared by all that went to the

Elizabeth and Marion Hopper.

cat instead."[40] Referring to the cat as "my sainted Arthur,"[41] Jo claimed that he, unlike some spayed animal, "had seen it all except aviation and the Paris I promised him. I married E. H. instead so he didn't have chance to accompany me down the Champs-Elysées on yards and yards of purple wool tape in my blue bead necklace & learn French—even meet Colette!"[42]

The tension between Edward and Arthur was real enough. Jo recalled that her husband and her cat "exchanged glances when there was something about me too utterly utter."[43] Edward felt that Jo catered to Arthur more than to him and his resentment was strong enough to trigger caricature, which since boyhood had been his response to issues that were emotionally charged. In a sketch called *The Great God Arthur* and captioned "Status Quo," he depicted Jo seated at the dinner table across from her cat while her husband crouched catlike on the floor begging for something to eat. *Studio Readjusted* showed how he felt about the cat's intrusion into his studio and his life, with "Eddie's place" as a cramped corner beyond "Arthur's sink, Arthur's fireplace, Arthur's stove, Arthur's chest of drawers."

Jo had foreseen the jealousy and she maintained her studio on Ninth Street for nearly a year following their marriage. Several months after the wedding, she explained her situation to a friend: "It's so difficult trying to live

Edward Hopper, The Great
God Arthur *("Status Quo"),
1932. Charcoal pencil on
paper, 11 × 8½" (27.9 ×
21.6 cm.).*

between two establishments and to keep two males fed, cause Arthur's on
Ninth Street and Ed's on the Square and it seems best to keep them apart and
there is no room for all my junk over there anyway, and it seems wisest to
hold on to my nest."[44] She recalled that Edmund Wilson, who lived on the
first floor, had scowled at her when she moved in "as a bride."[45]

Another of the caricatures engendered by matrimony suggests that Edward must have come into the relationship with never-to-be-realized fantasies of domesticty, of a wife cooking delicious meals for him. In *Meal Time,*
he depicted himself ignored by Jo as she sits in the clouds reading a book
while he, a mere skeleton, begs for food and attention. (One wonders how he
managed to eat during the interminable bachelor years.) While Jo liked to
sew and was very neat about the house, she abhorred the kitchen. When Edward was asked to contribute a favorite recipe to a cookbook of Greenwich
Village artists and writers, Jo characteristically answered for both of them:
"We feel that where there's too much fussy cooking there isn't so much painting. One might say we like to have cans of the friendly bean on the shelf.
Then there is that good Canadian pea soup—Habitant. And the opening of
cans is just bad enough."[46]

Jo suffered her own disappointments. Sociable and gregarious, she had
scarcely returned from the difficult week in Nyack before she was complaining to a friend: "Ed is anything but a social being and he won't bother himself
with people at all. He's not a bit nice and gracious to the people I've introduced
him to—people we meet on the street—he won't go anywhere to meet any of
my friends, which is most selfish of him. But, I suppose they [men] are all selfish."[47] Yet she admitted, "And in a way, I see his point. He says I fritter away

Edward Hopper, Meal Time, *c. 1935. Pencil on paper. 8 × 9⅜″ (20.3 × 23.8 cm.).*

all my time and I get nothing at all done."[48] Jo arranged to have her friends come to the studio on Ninth Street so as not to disturb Edward's solitude.

From his standpoint, Edward, too, raised an issue of selfishness, using caricature to reflect on yet another area of contrast in the marriage. The lover who had imagined himself embracing Jo against the Paris sky above romantic verses by Verlaine now produced *The sacrament of sex (female version),* in which he depicted himself, wearing a halo and a nightshirt tied in an effeminate manner with a sash at the waist, bending double in homage at the foot of a bed, which is imagined as a shrine. Lighted candles adorn the bedposts at the foot, while at the head Jo sits up, clothed in a long-sleeved gown and a bridal veil decorated with flowers and a bow. Beside her stands a lighted candelabrum, a bird perches above her head, and directly beneath her under the bed is a chamber pot. She extends her hands in a gesture of command to the humbled, saintly male. Apart from any emblematic association, the pot testifies to the reality that in Hopper's studio, the bathroom was down the hall.

Unfortunately for Edward's version of sex in marriage, Jo long after in her diaries gave her side of the story. Despite her bohemian associations, she had been a virgin bride. Edward later teased her with a caricature in which he depicted the goat-god Pan crouching among a group of elegantly attired men and pointing lasciviously at Jo, who shyly passes by, drawing her protective cape around herself—the perfect stereotype of Victorian virtue, uninterested in sex, incapable of passion unless artificially stimulated by the male.[49] The caption reads: *There's a virgin—give her the works.* Bitterly Jo recalled the pain she had encountered in what she referred to as "the matter of sex":

> About the first week or so I realized always with amazement, but I knew so little about this basic concern—except to be appalled at prize hog proportions that the whole thing was entirely for him, his benefit. Upon realizing this—& with the world so new & all & I emerged in such vast ignorance—I declared that since that was the status quo of that—let him have it all. I withdrew all my interest— There was my body, let him take it—but I'd not consent to be hurt *too* much—only a certain amount—I'd not be object of sheer sadism. I was forbidden to consult with other women over the mysteries. If he had drawn a lemon, I needn't advertise his misfortune. Then he set forth to build up as neat a little job of inferiority complex for

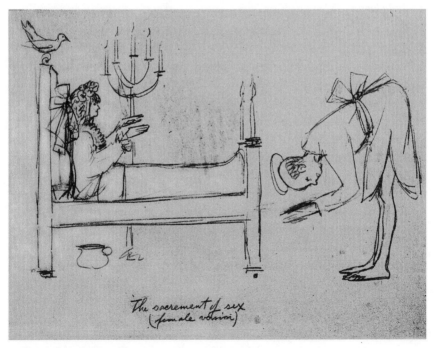

Edward Hopper, The sacrament of sex (female version), *c. 1935. Pencil on paper, 8½ × 11″ (21.6 × 27.9 cm.).*

Edward Hopper, There's a virgin—give her the works, *c. 1932. Pencil on paper, 8½ × 11" (21.6 × 27.9 cm.).*

which I in my ignorance was eligible. I, so subnormal—not enjoying attacks from the rear![50]

Neither Baptist upbringing nor Anglo-Saxon character explain a penchant for "attacks from the rear." As for Jo, she knew the sexual mores of the Village vanguard, which she rejected in spite of all:

> I had at no time shown any inclination to trail off to someone else. My limited idea having been only to give what I could. . . . I couldn't help being a virgin when he married me & if I hadn't been he wouldn't have wished to marry me anyway. Virgins, Christian ladies all so little prized—but he knows when they're not & feels what lacking.[51]

What is remarkable in the face of physical and psychological indignities are Jo's self-denial and devotion.

When Jo wrote another entry on sex after a long interval, her remarks reveal no adjustment or change on Edward's part but her own fuller awareness of "the mysteries" and realization of the damage suffered by her own nature:

> The tensions of this uncanny situation could be harmful for me. My mother was surely very normal specimen, why ever shouldn't I be given the chance. But that not his idea at all. That the Catholic Church idea of need of male & female anatomy, human anatomy. I blamed for not being a 4 foot animal with other arrangements, anatomically. Could this all being part of his intense selfishness—determination to give nothing to anyone—exclude me from that relief of tensions. I such an intense, nervous organism, so highly emotional, fine bate for sadism.[52]

Despite Edward's ban on consulting about "the mysteries" with other women, Jo needed only the example of her own mother and the teachings of the Catholic Church to instance the "normal" sexuality that Edward denied her.

In her ignorance and submission, Jo was only too typical. Most women of her generation entered marriage without sexual experience. According to one pioneering survey conducted in 1929 among women of Jo's age, only half of the respondents reported being "attracted" by the initial experience of marital sex.[53] Twenty-five percent of these women reported that their first sexual experience "repelled" them, although many "came to enjoy conjugal relations after an initial period of adjustment."[54] The study found a high correlation between the absence of sexual instruction, distaste for sex, and unhappiness in marriage: "The wife is ignorant, unprepared, shocked at the strength of her husband's passion; the husband unable to realize this, inconsiderate, uncontrolled; a long period of adjustment—and if this fails, unhappiness for both."[55] Men who applied "brute force" to women in search of their own gratification were vehemently criticized by the birth control advocate Margaret Sanger, whose work Jo certainly knew through her own participation in *The Masses* and from Sanger's much-discussed lectures at the Liberal Club.[56] Even if Edward had made more typical demands and been more open to adjustment, it would have been difficult for one who had so long maintained abstinence in a time and milieu of "free love" suddenly to shed her guilt and fear and find pleasure instantaneously in the union sanctioned by marriage.

Like most middle-class men of his generation, Edward had experienced some premarital sex: if with prostitutes, this would account for his lack of any sense of mutuality or responsibility for his partner's pleasure. Commercialized sex offered a poor training ground for marriage, as one study put it: "To the degree that young men's expectations were based on their encounters with prostitutes, they would bring to the conjugal bedroom a form of sexual expression badly out of line with what their wives might desire."[57] Edward's exclusive concern for himself was still Victorian. Whatever his experience had been in Paris or with Jeanne Chéruy, whatever he had dreamed when quoting Verlaine at Christmas, nothing had freed him from the old, selfish vision of male sexual dominance.

By the 1920s, Victorian marriages based on dominance and submission were seen by feminist critics as emotionally barren.[58] Long-standing biases that women should serve their husbands' needs and pleasures gave way to talk of satisfaction for women in marriage. These new attitudes made sense to Jo, who in marrying Edward had done so for neither of the traditional reasons: to escape parental authority or find economic security. She had already attained the former and Edward offered no promise of the latter when they met. Social scientists like Phyllis Blanchard emphasized the importance of the "sex side of marriage," pointing out that the husband now wanted more than "good natured acquiescence" and the wife expected that he would "arouse ecstasies of sensual pleasure."[59] Clearly the new arguments for mutuality never reached Edward. Nor do they echo explicitly in Jo. She was satisfied to think of her mother and a simple idea of male and female anatomy and common human need, which was more than Edward could. His image of the bride as enshrined priestess humiliating the angelic male recalls his boyhood caricature of a weak male and engulfing female: the model of disparity between the sexes proves impossible for him to outgrow. Put to the test of marriage, Edward's imagination fell short of real freedom from the past.

§

AMIDST FAILURES, constraints, and conflicts, the marriage took shape and endured. Tragedy had to contend with comedy for the upper hand. Jo recalled a quixotic incident in their early days together: "When I came back up the 74 stairs dragging food for dinner & panting with fatigue, he started to tickle me. Could anything be more brutal. I leaped at an open window, anything to escape such torment. I didn't make it, but got out the studio door in time to collapse on the stairs. Eva Cruikshank rescued me & got me into her place."[60] Once, while Edward was trying to take "conciliatory measures," he amused Jo by "cosying up in bed & purring tremendously . . . purring so I'd like him if a cat."[61] As if Edward could ever displace Arthur. On other occasions, wearing his shorts and floating drapes, Edward aped Isadora Duncan. Another memorable pantomime was Edward "in a sun hat à la Chinois and long rope pigtail—doing Cooley with mop rice field." Jo also fondly recalled his "Salomé with head of John the Baptist," in which he employed "grapefruit & hat on tray with dance slouch."[62]

In spite and perhaps because of dramatic tensions, Jo and Edward settled on something of a daily routine. They coped with the physical hardships of the studio, sharing the hall bathroom with their neighbors, hauling up coal in the dumbwaiter for the stove that was their only source of heat, climbing the seventy-four steps, cooking in a tiny closetlike kitchenette with primitive appliances or on the potbellied stove, and having such inadequate closet space that Jo had to store her party dresses in boxes on a high shelf. Above all, they looked forward to annual escapes to rural New England.

It was not long before Jo initiated and maintained new and more extensive record keeping, which Edward soon began to augment with small sketches and occasional comments of his own. Until Jo entered his life, he had been less organized in keeping track of exhibitions of his work, although he carefully recorded income from sales and did note where he showed and consigned his prints. Jo also took over most of her husband's correspondence, including an increasing volume of loan requests. Another caricature was provoked by her habit of conscientiously clipping and saving every article mentioning Edward: *Josie lisant un journal* showed her burying her head in a huge chaotic pile of rumpled newspapers, while exposing her naked buttocks to view. Considering the precise and persistent focus of his sexual attentions of which she complained, the sketch seems particularly pointed and embarrassingly frank.

Though Hopper needed to view his wife as a subordinate and erotic object, she had a separate identity as an artist. It was through her that he had gained access to the Brooklyn Museum even before they married; and the summer of the wedding three of her watercolors (*Petunias, Larkspur,* and *The Picnic*) were included in a large exhibition of American art shown in Paris at the Galerie de la Chambre Syndicale des Beaux-Arts.[63] Although Hopper was not included, a number of the other artists in the show were his friends or former classmates: George Bellows, Gifford Beal, Louis Bouché, Randall Davey, and Rockwell Kent, as well as Leon Kroll and the faithful du Bois.

Around the time of their marriage, Jo made Edward the gift of a newly published French monograph, *Degas,* by Paul Jamot, inscribed "for Edward Hopper from Jo." Hopper, who had admired Degas's work since art school and considered him one of his favorites, seems to have taken some of the biographic text to heart: "In the declining years of a long life devoted entirely to art, Degas was celebrated, but with a celebrity that was mysterious and ill-defined. He could not complain of this obscurity. He did not complain: he concealed his life, he nearly concealed his work. One mentioned his name with respect, with fear. His person was by no means more public than his painting."[64] Jo, who shared Edward's high regard for Degas, appears to have concurred on adopting the French painter's strategy for concealing his per-

Edward Hopper, Josie lisant un journal, *c. 1935. Pencil on paper, 5⅞ × 8½″ (14.9 × 21.6 cm.).*

sonal life. She would later discourage critics who tried to ask Edward prob-
ing questions or who sought private details. She not only helped Hopper to
create a myth for himself modeled after Degas, but she provided him with the
guidelines for the plan by giving him the monograph.

A renewed attention to Degas's painting is also evident in the composition
of Hopper's 1924 canvas *New York Pavements*. As in the etching *House on a
Hill,* Hopper shows the view from above. The dramatic cropping, emphatic
diagonals, and unusual perspective all bring to mind Degas, who made the
framing edge a stylistic hallmark. Its importance for Hopper emerged years
later in an interview: "The frame? I consider it very forcibly."[65] The subject of
New York Pavements, a nurse pushing a baby carriage, is unique in Hopper's
work: although the child is not visible, it is the only suggestion of an infant in
any of his paintings.[66] At the time of his marriage, he must have given the possibility of children some thought—and firmly rejected the idea. He expressed
his fantasy in a caricature that he made for Jo, *Joseddy at age of 6½,* in which he
pessimistically imagined an awkward, bow-legged, but intellectual little girl.
Hopper, who was already jealous of the cat, wanted Jo to focus entirely on him.

Edward Hopper, Joseddy
at age of 6½, *c. 1932. Pencil
on paper, 6¼ × 3¼" (15.9 ×
8.3 cm.).*

§

ALTHOUGH HOPPER'S FORTUNES were shifting, he still lacked a gallery to show his paintings. In the fall of 1924, armed with his new confidence, a crop of watercolors from his Gloucester honeymoon, and a personal recommendation from Guy du Bois, Hopper went to the C. W. Kraushaar Art Galleries, where du Bois showed. John Kraushaar, however, found the work "too stark." Rebuffed and retreating, Hopper happened to pass by the Rehn Gallery in its new and larger quarters at 693 Fifth Avenue, between Fifty-fourth and Fifty-fifth Streets. Spontaneously he decided to pay a second visit.[67] Rehn at the time represented Bellows as well as some artists from the previous generation, such as Childe Hassam and John Twachtman. At first he told Hopper he could not see him. Relenting, he said that if Hopper wanted to spread out his watercolors in the back room, he would look at them when he returned from lunch. Before he left, a customer stopped in front of Hopper's depiction of a Victorian house, remarking with enthusiasm: "Just like my grandmother's." Rehn sold him the picture at once, forgot about lunch, and began to represent Hopper.[68]

With growing excitement, Rehn arranged to hold an exhibition of Hopper's watercolors in "a secondary inner room," during his fall opening show, which was called "Ten American Paintings" and comprised figure pieces by William Merritt Chase, Childe Hassam, Abbott Thayer, Frank Duveneck, George Fuller, Charles W. Hawthorne, R. Sloane Bredin, and Leon Kroll. The Hopper show was both a commercial and a critical success. Sixteen works, eleven exhibited and five additional, were sold at one hundred dollars each. The frugal artist celebrated by going to Brooks Brothers and buying himself a hundred-dollar ulster, the long loose belted overcoat that he favored for New York winters.

Rehn's unbounded enthusiasm for Hopper's work impressed both collectors and critics. The artist himself wrote once again to Henry McBride, telling him: "I am having a show of recent water colors done in New England at the Frank Rehn Gallery and hope you will get to see it."[69] Responding, McBride wrote that Hopper's watercolors had "aroused Mr. Rehn to a pitch beyond his usual enthusiasm, which is always considerable, but has so excited his clients that at this writing more than half of the water colors have been sold."[70] In October, Rehn wrote to a friend, John Fraser of the Rhode Island School of Design: "I am having great good luck with the little group of Edward Hopper water colors now on exhibition. Have sold five out of eleven already and we are hardly started."[71] To one of his best clients, Stephen C. Clark, an heir to the Singer Sewing Machine fortune, Rehn wrote on October 21: "I think you would enjoy . . . seeing the amazing group of little water colors by Edward Hopper now on view—the best things of their kind since Homer."[72] When someone returned one of the pictures on November 4, Rehn was relieved, as "the demand so greatly exceeds the supply—I have just received letters from the Chicago Arts Club and several of the Boston collectors asking if there are any available examples."[73] Returning to Rehn in 1924, Hopper had found a relationship that, like his marriage (if less dramatically), would last the rest of his life.[74]

The major buyers from Hopper's first show were John Taylor Spaulding, a corporate lawyer and trustee of the Museum of Fine Arts in Boston, who took four works in all, and Elizabeth Cameron Blanchard, a New York interior decorator, who purchased three. Spaulding and Bee Blanchard became Hopper's two most important early patrons and the latter also became a friend. When George Bellows bought *Haskell's House* and *House in Italian Quarter* from his own dealer, Hopper's feelings must have been mixed, with gratitude for the friendly solidarity but also ironic recollection that Bellows had not always been so supportive in the difficult years when recognition was elusive.

Eclipsing Rehn's major show of "Ten American Paintings," Hopper received considerable attention in the press, most of it very positive. The headline in the *Sunday World* read "Hopper's Work Is Independent in Aim and Spirit." The reviewer recognized that a significant aspect of Hopper's personality explained the delayed recognition that his work received: "Mr. Hopper has never joined a cause nor been the exponent of a theory. He has never belonged to the Academy or to the 'moderns.' He is quintessentially not a group artist and cannot beat a drum."[75] Several critics, having defined Hopper as a painter of homely native subjects in a realist manner, began to write about his work with increasing enthusiasm.

Margaret Breuning saw him as an "incorrigible romanticist, who finds beauty in the utmost realism, for he sees things with so fresh a vision."[76] But the praise was not unqualified. More reserved, Henry McBride called Hopper "interesting," but stated that he was not yet an artist of "absolute greatness"; he nevertheless concluded that Hopper was "forcefully eloquent upon the hitherto concealed beauty of some supposedly hideous building."[77] McBride and a number of other critics sought to pigeonhole Hopper in an American "school" led by Charles Burchfield. While Elizabeth Luther Cary argued that Burchfield was "unquestionably the greater designer of the two," she admitted that Hopper was "a cleverer technician and a more able painter," who "takes a blatantly hideous structure" and "intensifies his subject."[78]

The success of this exhibition was another decisive turning point in Hopper's career. At last he could do without the illustrating he so despised. His success with watercolor had already led him to stop making etchings. With greater confidence, he began working more frequently in oil, tackling more ambitious canvases, and developing what would become his mature style. He built himself a large, heavy easel on which he continued to paint as long as he lived.[79]

GETTING ESTABLISHED: 1925–1927

THE YEAR 1924 set patterns for a lifetime: the massive easel, the committed dealer, the intense wife, and marital drama. Success bred success. In 1925 Hopper showed his etchings at the Los Angeles Museum, the Art Institute of Chicago, and the Brooklyn Museum, as well as in New York, at the Whitney Studio and National Arts clubs, and also at two important dealers in contemporary American art—Kennedy and Company and Weyhe Gallery. Both the Art Institute of Chicago and the Cleveland Museum exhibited one of his 1923 watercolors from Gloucester, *Portuguese Church*.

As the recognition grew, so did courage for new adventures. No longer constrained by the yoke of commercial assignments, Hopper began expressing his feelings and values through innovative images and themes. The years just after he gave up illustration brought a veritable burst of productivity as he introduced new subjects and experimented with symbols. The confident self-reflection also carried over into writing, where he began to articulate his aesthetic philosophy, although his writing was so introspective, scrupulously weighed and crafted, in a word, demanding, that he would soon give it up.

Hopper opened 1925 on a gloomy note, making a dark, dreary watercolor unique among his works for its somber tones and theme. *Day after the Funeral* shows two female figures in black walking across a bleak wintry street, with a lone lamppost before a bay window. On January 8, 1925, George

Bellows died suddenly from a ruptured appendix. Bellows, who set the standard for rapid and brilliant success, was alone among the students of Robert Henri to have risen to become their old teacher's intimate and peer. Through the years he had used his prominence in the art world to help Hopper place work in occasional shows, and had purchased two watercolors from the Rehn Gallery exhibition; yet his stellar accomplishments had been a constant reminder of Hopper's inability to win recognition as a painter.

Lingering resentment was eclipsed by the sudden loss: "Edward Hopper came through the door that connected our studios in Washington Square. Tears were streaming down his face. He came to tell me that Bellows was dead," remembered Walter Tittle.[1] Edward was not alone in his grief; Jo would recall attending the funeral at the Church of the Ascension: "It was all the most grief stricken community, such sad men followed the coffin down the aisle. Everybody there. . . . Henri weeping wretchedly as we went down centre aisle."[2] She remembered that Edward "kept himself in hand by counting the pipes of the church organ in French, then the floor tiling."[3] For him, the display of emotion was rare.

Not much later in 1925, Hopper gave *Day after the Funeral* to E. P. "Ned" Jennings, a private dealer who handled some of his prints. It was Jennings who succeeded in placing fifteen of Hopper's etchings in the Metropolitan Museum that May and who, according to Jo, "sold etchings of E.H.—Night Shadows to British Mus."[4] The nature of Hopper's gift suggests that Jennings also knew Bellows and perhaps had sold some of his lithographs. Jo identified Jennings as "Fuller Brush man, friend of Robt. Frost—queer Duck."[5] Frost would interest the Hoppers for the rest of their lives.

The sale to the Metropolitan signaled both the arrival and the tardiness of Hopper's success. Bellows had placed his first work in the museum in 1911, living an entire career while his classmate struggled to find himself, only to die just as Hopper finally got going. Not until March of 1925 did Hopper sell an oil painting to a museum. He sent the innovative canvas of 1923, *Apartment Houses,* to the annual show of contemporary art at the Pennsylvania Academy of the Fine Arts, which purchased it. Of the $400 price, $340 went to the artist, after a fifteen percent commission to the Rehn Gallery. Thrilled at this new level of recognition, Hopper wrote a formal note to John Andrew Myers, the academy's director: "I appreciate greatly the Penns. Academy's having selected my canvas 'Apartment Houses' for purchase under the Lambert Bequest."[6]

In May 1925, Hopper showed two oils in the tenth annual exhibition of the Whitney Studio, held at the Anderson Galleries. He reached back into the stockpile for older canvases, not French, however, but American—*New York Corner* of 1913 and *Yonkers* of 1916—holding back his new work for Rehn and no doubt seeking the recognition originally denied these works.

Rejection was not yet a problem for Jo, who was still showing under her maiden name. To the Whitney exhibition she sent two works, *The Josie of Boston* and *A Tree*.[7] About this time, she introduced Edward to the antiquities and art dealer Joseph Brummer, a Hungarian émigré and former sculptor, who was enthusiastic about her work and had encouraged her. (He showed the work of modern sculptors such as Brancusi, Maillol, and Rodin, and painters such as Walter Pach, Jules Pascin, and André Derain.) Bitterly she remembered that Edward had given Brummer a "dirty look,"[8] perhaps resenting any attention paid to Jo, for her an ominous sign.

More adventuresome than the previous year, the Hoppers planned an entirely new departure for the summer of 1925: from June through late September, venturing both longer and farther, they went as far as James Mountain, Colorado, and Santa Fe, New Mexico. They traveled by train, via Niagara Falls and Chicago, and since they planned to splurge on riding lessons, they economized by sharing one lower berth, snuggling together in the narrow space.[9] One night, passing through Kansas, Edward awakened Jo so that she could see "1,000,000 fire flies swimming thru the black velvet of the night." She concluded: "As well that I was right there not to miss it."[10]

Originally they meant to go in time for the Easter holidays, so as to see the famous fiestas, but Jo's beloved tomcat, Arthur, got lost. Reluctant to leave, she eventually had to give up the search.[11] Thereafter, she concerned herself with the welfare of every cat she encountered that might be hungry or otherwise "in distress."[12] Cats were a constant preoccupation in her diaries and figured importantly in her painting.

Arthur's disappearance removed one of the reasons Jo gave for keeping her separate studio. Before departing for Santa Fe, she made the drastic decision to give up her place on Ninth Street and store her belongings (books, early paintings, clothes, and other prized possessions) in the basement of 3 Washington Square.[13] Not only did she relinquish a room of her own, but she cut off from view much of her previous work by making it inaccessible without a great deal of effort. Her conscious motive might have been thrift, but she must also have sensed that moving in completely would make her less independent, thereby cementing her union with Edward. The move certainly did not further her career as a painter.

Santa Fe, like its neighbor Taos, was then popular with New York artists. In 1917 it had attracted Henri and Bellows in one of their frequent summers together, and Henri had made many trips there between 1916 and 1922. Jo had often followed Henri's lead; but it was surely more recent enthusiasm by John Sloan that convinced Hopper to try New Mexico. Appalled at the mounting cost of living in Gloucester and other East Coast art colonies, Sloan and his wife, Dolly, together with Randall Davey and his wife, Florence, had first driven out to Santa Fe during the summer of 1919. By the next summer, the Sloans had purchased a house there. (Taos, with its avant-garde circle around the writer Mabel Dodge, including Andrew Dasburg and Marsden Hartley, did not appeal to Sloan and his friends.) Hopper was also drawn to Santa Fe because he wanted to try Indian baths to help a lame knee.[14]

Surrounded though he was by the picturesque beauty of the southwestern landscape with its intense light, saturated colors, and "gaudy mountains," Hopper had trouble finding subject matter that appealed to his sensibility, as he later admitted to Alfred Barr.[15] The mesas, mountains, and "geometric" hills helped Sloan to "work out the principles of plastic design,"[16] but Hopper was disappointed, insisting that the mountains were "like sand hills," though allowing that they were "better near Albuquerque."[17] Sloan also appreciated Indian culture on visits to surrounding pueblos, but the colorful inhabitants of Santo Domingo and San Ildefonso left Hopper cold. He and Jo witnessed festivities, the "gun shot off from roof at San[to] Domingo, N.M. during that ceremony before the Corn Dance 1925."[18] Yet this most extraordinary of rituals inspired in Hopper no feeling for the way in which art and religion coalesce in Indian culture.[19] Jo was so impressed that a decade later she spoke of the Corn Dance with the painter John Marin and his wife.[20]

Santa Fe in 1925 had yet to acquire street lights or paved roads and this raw, primitive quality held no appeal for Hopper. The entire town seemed cramped. Discouraged, he finally located something familiar: a railroad car from the Denver and Rio Grande Railroad, which became the subject of a watercolor, *D. & R. G. Locomotive.*[21] He was attracted, too, by such atypical structures as St. Michael's College and the Cathedral of St. Francis, with their complex and intricate angles and towers. Eventually he did paint some typical adobe houses, huts, ranch houses, and desert landscapes, as well as the strong silhouette of the local poplar trees.

Hopper was also drawn to the Penitente Order, a secret religious organization of Spanish-Americans, which was notorious for self-flagellation and which dramatized the passion story during Holy Week. The Penitentes must have evoked for him the Spanish mystics shown in paintings by El Greco that he had seen when he had visited Madrid and Toledo in 1910. In *La Penitente,* he presented a singular view of the dark figure of a lone woman in a windy landscape, although generally he tried to avoid the theatrical quality of the New Mexican setting.

While in Santa Fe, Edward had Jo pose for a watercolor called *Interior.* The title recalls the themes of prints and paintings in the period just before his courtship and marriage. In the record book, she described the new composition as "Wife in shirt tail, hair down, foot of oak bed across foreground, bureau top with red powder box-tin, tall." Later Hopper showed this work under the title *Model Reading,* which suggests that he was beginning to see Jo's potential for her lifelong role.

For them, this Santa Fe summer was unusually recreational, with patio parties and their riding scheme, which supplied Edward with a letter home: "Jo and I and some others took a twenty five mile horseback ride through the mountains yesterday. It being only the fifth time I had ridden I thought much more about the hard saddle than I did of the mountains, but they seemed fine when I could look at them"; Jo evidently took to riding more easily than he, for he also wrote: "Jo is all hardened now and prefers a saddle to a plush rocker." There follows the inevitable caricature, with the two of them turned out in newly acquired togs, he towering over her petite frame, with equally disparate horses: "These horses are not drawn to scale, but pretty near it."[22] What Jo recalled was riding

> on my Indian pony, Prince—who was a Prince at that, foregoing an engagement with that evil looking black horse with a bell on his neck that we met on . . . the Barago Trail after the rest had ridden on & left me on the tail end behind. Prince & the Evil One had rubbed noses, I didn't see anything that I could do about it, I always left everything to Prince crossing the arroyos & skirting high cliffs. Now Prince, not in name only, bethought him of the responsibility of having me along & trotted off. . . . In time we caught up with the others, but it was getting dark & not so good if the 2 horses had seen fit to kick me over some abyss & make a night of it.[23]

Clearly, Jo's new husband was not acting like a "prince," protecting his damsel in distress.

Another aspect of Hopper's caricature is especially telling: touching the line of peaks in the background, the sun forms a great ball behind the ten-gallon hat on Jo's head and shoots forth rays: it was the closest he ever came to giving her a halo. The hint of harmony and a sunny vacation with his still new bride may have been meant especially to reassure Hopper's mother. Always anxious and apprehensive, suspicious of Jo, Elizbeth had let them know she was not well, for he added: "Hope you are feeling a lot better."[24]

§

RETURNING TO NEW YORK in late September, Hopper made his final sale of illustrations, to *Scribner's.* In the ledger for September 28, 1925, he recorded $175 for three drawings for a story called "The Distance to Casper,"

which was published in February 1927. At last he felt liberated, enough recognized as a painter to abandon illustration as well as etching. He quickly
produced two watercolors, which he delivered to Rehn on October 15, together with seven painted in Santa Fe. He was evidently dissatisfied with six
other New Mexican watercolors, almost as many as he found acceptable, for
these he never exhibited or sold.

Back in familiar surroundings, he had no trouble finding subjects that
appealed. Continuing his long fascination with the great, and then still new,
spans over the East River, he produced a watercolor of the Manhattan Bridge.
He also used watercolor in *Skyline near Washington Square* to portray an austere rooftop behind which rises a single gaunt, narrow building that dominates the sky. This work at its first showing bore the title *Self-Portrait,* in a
pun on Hopper's own height, which had so often provoked caricature and
comment. The self-referential title, which also appears in the record books,
must have puzzled viewers unfamiliar with Hopper's lanky figure, and he
changed it by the time he sold the work in 1927.

Visual punning may be suspected, too, in his next oil, *The Bootleggers,*
which shows three men in a motorboat passing before a house with a nineteenth-century mansard roof, next to which stands a lone figure. Although
Hopper painted in his studio, he had made etchings of such houses, which still
survive along the Hudson River near Nyack. Prohibition had been in effect
since January 1920 and violations were increasingly common. In February
1925, the Attorney General denounced the large number of foreign vessels
smuggling liquor into the United States.[25] The ships waited off shore to deliver
their cargoes to small boats that transported the illicit goods to shore. It was
one of these small launches or "rummies" in action that Hopper chose to depict. In the record book Jo described the scene as "very early A.M. Water &
cloudy sky blue, white house, pale blue, roof dark, 3 red chimneys. Pale cement wall built on rocks, amber rock weed along edge of water. Ridge back of
house dark dull green. 4 men (one left side of house) dull on dark business."[26]

Painting a forbidden enterprise in the teeth of Prohibition is typical of
Hopper's contrarian bent. Although he never consumed much alcohol, his
cynicism was such that he could not have endorsed the self-righteous vehe-
mence with which the Women's Christian Temperance Union and the Christian evangelical churches supported the Anti-Saloon League. Reacting to his
own strict upbringing, he mistrusted religion. A number of his artist friends,
including Bellows and du Bois, were serious drinkers. Bellows, an early critic
of fundamentalist Christians and their crusades to outlaw "sinful" alcohol,
made such antics the subjects of his art.[27] In this context, one can read Hopper's rendition of the three red chimneys on the house as three crosses, a sub-

Sidney Waintrob, Edward Hopper with "The Bootleggers," *1955.*

tle pun that becomes apparent when one compares them to the chimneys he usually depicted in the same period, as in *The Mansard Roof* (1923) or *House by the Railroad* (1925).

Hopper did not continue to make such specific references to current political debates; in general, he preferred to steer clear of comment. Many years later, when a writer asked him if he believed "that the artist should be engagé in the social and political struggle surrounding him," Hopper insisted that the artist's commitment was to his art, explaining that Daumier "was great in spite of his political explications not because of them." While Hopper felt that art could be critical, he was adamant that it should "never be reduced to sociology."[28]

It was not politics that led Hopper to picture another American Second Empire house in his 1925 canvas *House by the Railroad.* Again, he featured the mansard roof that appealed to him, at least in part because it reminded him of Paris. When John Maass, author of *The Gingerbread Age,* later discovered two similar houses in Haverstraw, just north of Nyack, and wrote to Hopper in the mid-1950s to inquire about the exact location of the house that appears in *House by the Railroad,* Jo responded: "He did it out of his head. He has seen so many of them."[29] In this image of a house bypassed by progress, Hopper evoked an enduring mood of universal loss and a yearning for simpler, less complicated times. The compelling tension of his life was between the Victorian world of his childhood and the uncertain modern world that intruded on him daily.

Hopper was not alone among his contemporaries in his nostalgia for "the virtuous goodness of the American past."[30] By 1921, Bellows had been arranging for his portrait subjects to pose in Victorian dresses in Victorian interiors, in imitation of the conventions of nineteenth-century photographs and lithographs. In *Lady Jean,* which Bellows painted during the summer of 1924, he employed a typical stiff pose and included easily recognizable bits of Americana, a hooked rug and country hutch.[31] Both Bellows and Hopper also recalled the lost values of earlier times in their prints: Bellows in lithographs such as *Sunday 1897* (1921), and Hopper in etchings such as *The Buggy* (1920), with its image of a couple riding in a horse and buggy before an elaborate Victorian house. A few years later, Bellows recalled the weekly carriage rides his family took to church in his lithograph *Sixteen East Gay Street* (1923–1924).

The conflict between the past and "the new generation" was a central theme of Ibsen's *The Master Builder,* which the Hoppers saw in a performance directed by Eva Le Gallienne (who also played Hilda Wangel) on December 15, 1925.[32] Hopper had long admired Ibsen, and now his use of symbol within a context of seeming realism reinforced Hopper's own interest in painting realist pictures with implicit meaning. The painter of the undeclared content of

The Bootleggers, with its mockery of religion in society, must have found compelling the defiant confrontation of Solness, the Master Builder, with God: "Listen to me, Almighty One! From now on I will be a free Master Builder, free in my sphere, just as You are in yours. I will never more build churches for You; only homes for human beings."[33]

Drama was an enthusiasm the couple shared, between his early drawings, later theater-going, and her acting. As theater-going became a habit, he poked fun at her tardiness in a caricature, *À la Route au Theatre,* where he drags her to the theater while she tries to coax the cat Arthur to follow by dangling a fish from a pole. During this period and for some years afterward, Hopper carefully saved each pair of ticket stubs, which he labeled with the plays' titles. Almost always he and she economized by purchasing balcony seats.

Their choice of plays spanned the immense variety then available in New York. They saw modern European drama such as Arthur Schnitzler's *The Call of Life* (October 9, 1925), revival classics such as Shakespeare (*Hamlet* on October 27, with Ethel Barrymore as Ophelia), as well as the work of American contemporaries, such as Channing Pollock's *The Enemy,* an antiwar tract starring Fay Bainter (April 6, 1926). They were adventurous in their taste, even going to see the first English adaptation of the Moscow Habima production of *The Dybbuk* (March 30, 1926), at the Neighborhood Playhouse on Grand Street, where a permanent company had staged experimental theater since 1915. The Hoppers patronized the Theatre Guild, which had its roots in the Washington Square Players with whom Jo had acted and which still employed some of her old acquaintances. They saw a double bill of George Bernard Shaw's *A Man of Destiny* and *Androcles and the Lion* at the Guild's new playhouse, the Klaw Theatre, on December 30, 1925.

Just as their theater-going encompassed both traditional and contemporary drama, Edward's representational style and subtle allusions to the tensions of the modern world appealed to both traditional and modernist tastes. In January 1926, he was one of ten nonmembers invited to participate in the New Society of Artists' Seventh Exhibition at the Anderson Galleries. Among the officers and council for this exhibition were Robert Henri and other established artists such as Joseph Pennell, Gari Melchers, and Stirling Calder. Hopper showed two oils: *New York Pavements* and *House by the Railroad.* Just before the show's opening, the New York *Sunday World* reported that Hopper would present

> his final apotheosis of a Grantian or a Garfieldian house deserted by everything except the railroad track that runs across the bottom of the canvas and also a portrait of the lower facade of a McKinleyan New York apartment house with a blue veiled nurse wheeling a

baby carriage. Mr. Hopper does not intend to be caught being aesthetic, not if he knows the time in which we are living.[34]

A young critic, Lloyd Goodrich, praised *House by the Railroad* as probably "the most striking picture in the exhibition. . . . Without attempting to be anything more than a simple and direct portrait of an ugly house in an ugly place, it succeeded in being one of the most poignant and desolating pieces of realism that we have ever seen."[35] This was the first comment on Hopper by the man who later became the leading proponent of his work.

Goodrich had grown up in Nutley, New Jersey, where he had been a schoolmate of the painter Reginald Marsh. In Goodrich's home there was a painting by Winslow Homer that his grandfather had purchased in the 1880s. Goodrich studied art, both at the Art Students League and at the National Academy of Design.[36] Questioning his own creative abilities, he gave up painting and eventually started to write about art, beginning with book reviews and going on to criticism for *The Arts,* a magazine founded to emphasize contemporary American artists. (Its editor then was Forbes Watson and its sponsor Gertrude Vanderbilt Whitney, also the angel of the Studio Club.)

In 1926, Goodrich was not alone in saluting Hopper's talent. Invitations came to exhibit in February at the Boston Arts Club, where Hopper showed five oils painted in Paris in 1907, and in April at the St. Botolph Club in Boston for a one-man show of nineteen watercolors and twenty-one etchings. In New York, he showed a new oil, *Sunday,* in Rehn's February exhibition called "Today in American Art." At the Whitney Studio annual in March, he also showed only one work, his etching *Aux Fortifications.* Jo exhibited *Guinney Boats,* one of her favorite watercolors, using professionally for the first time the name Josephine Hopper.

To get material for *Sunday,* which depicts a disconsolate man seated on a street curb, Hopper had taken the ferry to Hoboken. Originally he was planning to use the title *Hoboken Facade,* only to settle on something more universal. With this picture, critics began to examine the psychological content of Hopper's work, remarking, for example, that the figure in this painting was "helpless," a "pathetic figure," or "an old barkeep . . . planted in bored dejection on his doorstep."[37] They also began to praise what they saw as the artist's distinct "Americanness." Elizabeth Luther Cary singled out Hopper and Rockwell Kent for the "Americanism of their technique,"[38] while the reviewer for the Brooklyn *Eagle* noted: "No question of the Americanness of this picture both as to treatment and to subject—a street, empty and silent, a worker, clean-shirted and helplessly idle. . . . Out of such commonplaces has Hopper created beauty as well as injected humor and an astute characterization of place and type."[39]

During the spring of 1926, Hopper continued to paint watercolors of lower Manhattan—familiar sites not far from Washington Square: *Manhattan Bridge and Lily Apartments, Manhattan Bridge Entrance, Roofs of Washington Square,* and *Skylights,* the latter depicting the roof of his own studio. Jo specified in the record book that he painted *Manhattan Bridge Entrance* in the studio, noting the change from his usual practice of working in watercolor on location. Two years later, writing to the Hamilton College professor A. P. Saunders, who purchased this work, Hopper remarked: "I am glad that you like the watercolor. It is one of those that I care the most for."[40]

On June 2, Hopper dropped off the four new watercolors at Rehn's. For their third summer, they planned to renew their ties with Gloucester and with haunts they had known separately in Maine. The dealer's attentions to Stephen Clark bore fruit when later that month Rehn sold him *House by the Railroad* for six hundred dollars. Not yet apprised of the sale, Hopper wrote to Rehn from Rockland, Maine:

> We did not like Eastport at all. It has very little of the character of a New England coast town. We left after three days and went to Bangor by rail and then by boat to this town, a very fine old place with lots of good looking houses but not much shipping. I don't know how long we will stay here. Have been thinking of going out to Matinicus Island. I've made two sketches here within two days which is not so bad. We don't know when we will be down (up) your way, but probably not until later in the summer.[41]

Of Jo he added, " 'My best pal and severest critic' sends her best regards and I do also."

The return to New England made Hopper especially prolific. In Rockland alone, he painted about twenty watercolors in seven weeks, including *Mrs. Acorns' Parlor* (at a local boarding house), *Haunted House* ("an old boarded up boarding house near the ship yard"), *Talbot's House* ("a fine white Mansard"), several views of Lime Rock Quarry, the *Lime Rock Railroad, Rockland Harbor,* and the *Civil War Campground,* where ten companies of men recruited in this area of Maine encamped on Tillson's Hill. Once again he takes subjects from the past, favoring images evocative of bygone epochs and lost values, like this *Haunted House,* which serves as a metaphor for the role that the past came to play in his present.

Not all of Hopper's work referred so obviously to former times; he also painted numerous views of local fishing schooners and beam trawlers. He had chanced upon a fleet of these craft, or "lumpy fishing boats equipped with gigantic nets for ground fishing."[42] The beam trawlers had originally been built for the French government during World War I, but after the armistice, they were sold to a large fishing company. For him, however, they allowed a return to the nautical world of his boyhood along the Hudson.

Leaving Rockland for Gloucester, where they courted three years earlier, they stayed on through October. Edward focused on painting watercolors of individual homes in the town's center, only occasionally journeying to other locations. The subjects he chose, such as *Anderson's House, Davis House,* or *Tony's House,* were typical Gloucester residences, in some ways indistinguishable from those he did not paint.

Records of what Jo painted that summer are rather scant. In the fall of 1927, after a summer not spent in Gloucester, she consigned six of her watercolors to the Whitney Studio Club, including *Guinney Fleet in Fog* and *Movie Theatre—Gloucester,* both of which she probably produced a year earlier.[43] Jo's decision to depict a movie theater is noteworthy, for Edward would soon pick up the theme himself, beginning with a drypoint in 1928. But in the summer of 1926, Jo was just another of the countless artists working in Gloucester from whom he tried to stay aloof. Hopper avoided the crowds painting views of the picturesque Universalist Meeting House on Middle Street. Not painting the church, he sat in front of it and painted the *Davis House* across the street. It clearly took him hours to complete this watercolor; as the sun moved, he just kept adding the new shadows, as if there were more than one source of light. Although Hopper generally stayed very close to the boarding house where he and Jo were living, he did manage occasionally to venture farther afield, producing the watercolors *House by Squam River* and *Trees, East Gloucester.* The latter was so atypical in its loose, spontaneous execution that Jo described it in the record book as "wild & wooly."[44]

In September, working in the same neighborhood as he did for *Davis House*, Hopper painted the canvas titled *Gloucester Street,* representing the view at the corner of Church and Pine Streets. The approach closely resembles that of his watercolors, with similar subject matter and composition, depicting buildings cropped by the framing edge on each side of the painting. Characteristically, he chose to render the play of sunlight on the most mundane vernacular architecture, including such details as picket fences and utility poles. After he painted another watercolor, *Abbott's House,* on a cold day in October, he and Jo returned to New York.

That November the Washington collector Duncan Phillips paid six hundred dollars for *Sunday.* The year before, Phillips had been so enthusiastic about discovering Hopper's work that he wrote to Rehn, changing his mind about buying the work of a painter he did not name except to say, "Immediately after leaving your place that day, Mrs. Phillips and I had almost forgotten him, Hopper effacing him so completely."[45] Phillips bought the watercolor *St. Francis Towers* and soon wrote about Hopper in his book *Brief Estimates of the Painters:*

> A NEW type of American painter and etcher. He depicts American architectural horror from the standpoint of the philosophical historian and of the Luminist who is proud of the mitigation afforded by the beauty of light. Hopper defies our preconceptions of the picturesque and unflinchingly accepts the challenge of American subjects which seem almost too far beyond the scope even of the realistic artist's "alchemy." The most hideous, turreted houses of "the sartorial Seventies" have a fascination for this laconic observer.[46]

For Phillips, *Sunday* represented "a Middle Western town," despite the fact that the artist could have told him of its roots in Hoboken, New Jersey. Phillips's geography of Hopper's art was consistently inaccurate; he described the artist's "portrait of a locomotive" as painted "out in romantic California," oblivious of the work's origins in New Mexico.

Phillips asserted that Hopper's art had literary connections: "[He] wishes to make American realism in painting as rank with the odor of our own back streets and as unafraid of the homelier facts about our national life as the novels of Theodore Dreiser, Sinclair Lewis and Sherwood Anderson."[47] Years later Hopper discouraged an interviewer from comparing him to the American realists, claiming, "I think they're a little too mid-western for me."[48] Another time, he called Lewis "a fathead," although admitting that Dreiser was "all right," and with unusual enthusiasm allowed that Anderson was "a good writer."[49] Anderson's stories and novels, such as *Winesburg, Ohio* (1919), with their naturalistic images of emotionally sterile small-town life and of the impersonality of the big city, naturally appealed to Hopper, who readily identified with the puzzled characters who experienced the alienation of contemporary existence.[50] Many of Hopper's subjects share the theme of isolation in the midst of urban life. His solitary figures in either public or private interior settings appear vulnerable. A nude by a window gazes pensively outside; a woman in an Automat turns inward, absorbed in her own thoughts. In Hopper's view of the city itself, the few figures that populate the vast urban space are reduced to insignificance.

§

HOPPER APPRECIATED good literature, in part because he himself found writing difficult. Not long after the sale of *Sunday*, he declined an invitation from Forbes Watson to write for *The Arts*, explaining that his forthcoming show at Rehn's was scheduled for February: "I am trying my best to get some canvases done before that time. It may seem foolish to you that I cannot give a little spare time to writing but I sweat blood when I write and a thing that you could probably do in a day would take me I am sure a week or two."[51] Hopper suggested that he might attempt some reviews later in the winter, after his show opened.

Getting ready for the show, Hopper had been working in his studio on several new oils—*Eleven A.M., Automat,* and *The City.* For the first two he turned again to his in-house model and actress, posing Jo for the first seated in an armchair, nude, gazing out the window, and for the second dressed in a hat and coat, pensively nursing a cup of coffee.

The image of a woman alone in a domestic interior with sunlight streaming through the window, as in *Eleven A.M.,* has affinities with Hopper's transitional etchings. The composition of *Automat* recalls a seventeenth-century Dutch painting, Jan Vermeer's *A Girl Asleep,* which Hopper saw in the Metropolitan Museum, depicting a lone woman across the table from an empty chair. Like Vermeer, Hopper employed background architectural elements and a bowl of fruit to help organize space.

In *The City,* other concerns are apparent, especially Hopper's love of movies and how they look. A cinematic bird's-eye view determines his angle of vision, sharply down from a rooftop, as in *American Village* of 1912. Also at work are his interest in Pissarro and Caillebotte and his fondness for mansard roofs. Signaling another attitude that became typical, he presented a skyscraper "cut off abruptly by the top of the frame," as Alfred Barr later observed, adding that Hopper's "indifference to skyscrapers is remarkable in a painter of New York architecture."[52] Hopper's paintings reveal again and again how much he disliked skyscrapers. If he includes them at all, he makes them out to be interlopers, awkward and misplaced. He shared the climate of opinion that would find voice in critics like Lewis Mumford, who soon published articles with such titles as "Is the Skyscraper Tolerable?" and "Botched Cities."[53] For them, the skyscraper represented everything that was wrong with modern urban America, from the superficiality of material values to the increased standardization of life.[54]

§

HOPPER'S SHOW OPENED at the Rehn Gallery on Valentine's Day, 1927: four oils (*Eleven A.M., Gloucester Street, Automat,* and *The City*), a dozen watercolors, and a group of prints. The press paid attention and the influential Henry McBride proclaimed in the New York *Sun:* "Edward Hopper Adds to His Reputation."[55] Frederick W. Eddy, the critic for the New York *World,* reflected upon the changes that had occurred since American artists had begun imitating French modernists, making Hopper, who once seemed conservative, now appear "much more modern." He noted: "the success of Edward Hopper during the past few years has been the delight of these optimists who believe in the future of American painting."[56] *American Art News* identified Hopper as "one of the foremost American etchers" and allowed that "something of the fine quality of his black and white has been carried into his pictures."[57] Although flaws in the paintings were cited, the review concluded: "If some day all of his abilities are united in one canvas, he will produce something very fine." Helen Appleton Read wrote about Hopper under the now-convenient rubric "The American Scene," an appellation he soon came to despise.[58]

Only the more conservative Royal Cortissoz had serious reservations, despite his admission that he admired certain aspects of Hopper's oeuvre: "Mr. Edward Hopper, at the Rehn Gallery, uses various mediums with varying success. He is a proficient etcher, captivating in his free vivid way of hitting off a subject, and sound in line. He paints well, sometimes in water color. The 'Bow of Beam Trawler Widgeon' is a capital piece."[59] But Cortissoz carped:

> The oils are disappointing for the same reason that makes some of the watercolors unsatisfying, the touch is heavy, almost dragging. In both mediums Mr. Hopper suffers from seeing his subjects with a terribly prosaic literalness. The artist, said Whistler, is known by what he omits. This one makes a kind of dogged statement of fact, giving every detail the fullest possible view.

His complaint that the work was "unnecessarily explicit and sadly drab" seems to have been heeded, as Hopper progressively reduced detail and intensified color in subsequent work.

Cortissoz's strictures aside, the reviews showed that Hopper was catching the wave of nationalism that was sweeping isolationist America. The art critics were writing amidst fears of a foreign conspiracy against the United States and reacting to what many perceived as the threats by extremist elements as epitomized by abstract art. With the execution of Sacco and Vanzetti in August 1927 and the frenzy that ensued, "ethnic" or "foreign" came more and more to be equated with "un-American." Seeking traditional native values, critics more and more would find Hopper's figures, with their seemingly "typical" American faces, and his realist style far less threatening than European-inspired modernist abstraction. Wholly caught up in his exhibition at Rehn's, Hopper did not submit to the Whitney Studio's twelfth annual show. Jo, who entered a work called *Boats,* now added a middle initial to her name and identified herself as Josephine N. Hopper.

The yearly variations in nomenclature suggest that she was searching for her identity as a woman, a wife, and an artist, and attempting to reconcile all three. Her contemporary Theresa Bernstein (likewise the artist wife of an artist, William Meyerowitz) recalled advising Jo to show under her maiden name in order to preserve her professional individuality: "I told her that she had made a mistake. You must have your own name, so that you won't be confused."[60] As Bernstein predicted, Jo's artistic identity eventually became unclear in her own mind as well as in the minds of others. Even as late as 1964, Jo considered further changing the way she signed her pictures. Another friend had suggested that she made an error in dropping not only Nivison, but also her middle name, Verstille, which revealed her French ancestry. The argument was that Jo's pictures were "distinctively French" and that they were "Happy Pictures" that needed to be distinguished from the somber kind of work that Edward did.[61]

On March 7, 1927, Hopper delivered to Rehn a new canvas, *Two on the Aisle*. Jo suggested the name,[62] and she modeled for both the women, elegant patrons with choice seats in a near-empty theater. In the previous months, Jo and Edward had gone to at least eight plays and one major film;[63] it was a season that boasted as many as 268 attractions on Broadway.[64] The subject evokes the Hoppers' shared enthusiasm, not only for drama but for Degas with his theaters, cafés, restaurants, and intimate interior scenes. Even when Hopper pointedly sought indigenous subject matter and abandoned overtly French subjects, he continued to favor such French Impressionist themes.

In the spring of 1927, Jo and Edward had not been married three years and Edward's fame more and more was overshadowing her efforts to maintain her career. The divide only grew with publication of Lloyd Goodrich's "The Paintings of Edward Hopper" in the March issue of *The Arts,* where Goodrich was an editor. Citing qualities of austerity, strong color, and subtle technique, Goodrich called Hopper an "eminently native painter" and predicted even greater achievement.[65] He reflected, "It is hard to think of another painter who is getting more of the quality of America into his canvases than Edward Hopper," reiterating some of the nationalistic tones of the recent reviews. In reply, Hopper wrote the most formal kind of acknowledgment, "I want to thank you for your very appreciative and understanding article on my work in 'The Arts' "; noting that he found the reproductions "unusually successful."[66] The first magazine article ever devoted to Hopper's paintings, this was Goodrich's first full feature on Hopper. The reserve with which Hopper would always treat Goodrich is already apparent. Although clearly appreciating the support, he evidently felt the need to present his desired self-image to the critic. Rarely would he allude to his past as an illustrator, and he failed to mention studying with William Merritt Chase, who had become ever more unfashionable. Goodrich for his part accepted whatever Hopper chose to tell him as the whole truth, never prying or seeking independent corroboration.[67]

In April, Hopper, who was delighted by Goodrich's attention and with the show now behind him, contributed a piece to *The Arts*. The year before he had reviewed a book on prints,[68] but his new article was much more revealing and significant, ostensibly about John Sloan but emphasizing concerns central to Hopper, such as the negative experience of illustrating:

> John Sloan's development has followed the common lot of the painter who through necessity starts his career as a draughtsman and illustrator: first the hard grind and the acquiring sufficient technical skill to make a living, the work at self-expression in spare time, and finally the complete emancipation from the daily job when recognition comes. This hard early training has given to Sloan a facility and a power of invention that the pure painter seldom achieves.[69]

Hopper took the occasion to express his admiration for many artists, as well as for his teachers Henri and Miller (omitting Chase), but he stressed the necessity of developing a "native art," reinforcing the very point Goodrich and the others had been making about his own work by referring to

> certain artists of originality and intelligence who are no longer content to be citizens of the world of art, but believe that now or in the near future American art should be weaned from its French mother. These men in their work are giving concrete expression to their belief. The "tang of the soil" is becoming evident more and more in their painting. . . . We should not be quite certain of the crystallization of the art of America into something native and distinct, were it not that our drama, our literature and our architecture show very evident signs of doing just that thing.[70]

The call for an authentic American art had already sounded in Emerson's essay "Self-Reliance," which Hopper would cite in his next major essay on an American artist:[71]

> And why need we copy the Doric or the Gothic model? Beauty, convenience, grandeur of thought and quaint expression are as near to us as to any, and if the American artist will study with hope and love the precise thing to be done by him, considering the climate, the

soil, the length of the day, the wants of the people, the habit and form
of the government, he will create a house in which all these will find
themselves fitted, and taste and sentiment will be satisfied also.[72]

The two visions of the American artist confine themselves to "him, he" and
"these men." Hopper envisioned no creative role for women, including his
wife. His attitude toward women typifies most male artists of his generation.
He was consistent in his disparagement of women artists in general, viewing
them mainly as dilettantes who painted flowers, dabbled in other trivial subjects, and caused trouble for men in the profession.

In asserting that "our literature" shows evidence of turning "into something native and distinct," Hopper resembles Van Wyck Brooks, who more
than a decade earlier had achieved renown as "the most poised and coherent
theorist of diverse movements in literary nationalism."[73] Hopper later came
to know Brooks well and shared many of his interests, values, and conflicts
about American culture. Brooks believed that "deracination meant ruin" and
he bravely addressed "the question . . . how to change the whole texture of
life at home so that writers and artists might develop there."[74] Although Hopper admitted in his article on Sloan that "generalizations about race are unsatisfying," he considered his own case and asked: "But what of the men of
talent and originality who have until now dutifully spent their apprentice-
ships in Europe and returned with the persistent glamour of the European
scene to confuse and retard their reabsorption into the American?"[75] "The
native qualities are elusive and not easily defined except in their superficial
manifestations. Perhaps these are all that concern us," he continued, explaining, "They are in part due to the artist's visual reaction to his land, directed
and shaped by the more fundamental heritage of race."[76]

Hopper goes on to give further evidence of broad reading and serious reflection: "There are many pitfalls for him who would broach the question of
the racial and the indigenous in art, including the cases of Whistler, Henry
James, Lafcadio Hearn and other tortured and restless expatriates."[77] Hopper
reflects the conflict he himself had felt when forced to repudiate French culture and he suggests his familiarity with Brooks's *The Pilgrimage of Henry
James,* published two years earlier.[78] Brooks, who like Hopper had reluctantly
made the decision to return to work in America, concluded that James erred
in remaining abroad: he published "Henry James: The American Scene," in
the *Dial* for July 1923, reflecting, "To the end of his life, then, and however
disenchanting his experience of Europe may have been, America, to James,
signified failure and destruction. It was the dark country, the sinister country,
where . . . men were turned into machines, where genius was subject to all
sorts of inscrutable catastrophes."[79]

More surprising than mention of Whistler and James is Hopper's reference to Lafcadio Hearn, the writer, translator, and teacher who helped introduce the culture and literature of Japan to the West.[80] (Hearn was born in Greece in 1850, raised in Dublin, and educated in England and France. He wrote in America during the 1880s and moved to Japan in 1890, where he became a Japanese citizen and remained until his death in 1904.) Hopper probably came into contact with Hearn's work during his student years, perhaps through his friend Hetty Dureyea, who worked on an exhibition of Japanese prints in New York, or through Morie Ogiwara, his Japanese classmate.

§

REHN SOLD *Two on the Aisle* within a month for fifteen hundred dollars, Hopper's highest price up to then. Buoyed by the tide of successes, he and Jo decided to splurge, buying their first car, a used 1925 Dodge, and learning to drive near Nyack. A friend, Frank Downs, taught Edward, while Downs's wife, Anne, sat with Jo in the backseat, although Jo too was eager to learn.[81]

The backseat was emblematic. The car came loaded with implications that were dividing men and women in society at large. Driving in the 1920s meant more than just convenient transportation. The introduction of the automobile coincided with a time of rapidly changing roles for women in the workplace, the family, and politics. The auto became a frontier in the women's struggle for equal rights.[82] Driving symbolized female independence and signaled a new assertiveness. But the prospect that women might abandon traditional supportive and subordinate roles was so threatening to men that they promoted a whole folklore with negative stereotypes calculated to discourage women drivers by linking them to poor driving.[83]

The stock arguments asserted "women's inferiority at the wheel: emotional instability, physical weakness, and intellectual deficiencies."[84] The themes found support in Victorian traditionalists, who drew on Darwinian assumptions and reduced the entire question to biology, claiming that women as a whole were unfit to drive, "through no fault of their own. They were born that way."[85] The year the Hoppers bought their car, an article in the *New Statesman* contended that women "do not commonly possess the nervous imperturbability which is essential to good driving. They seem always to be a little self-conscious on the road, a little doubtful about their own powers."[86]

The mythic struggle mapped out roles for which Edward and Jo were only too well prepared. He brought his early acceptance of Darwinism, his childhood appetites for autonomy still unfulfilled, his deep ambivalence toward female forcefulness, and his stubborn streak. She was one of the new breed of independent women, college-educated, responsible for her own employment and housing, and, once she obtained the right to vote, politically

Edward Hopper painting Lighthouse Hill *at Two Lights near Cape Elizabeth, Maine, 1927.*

aware; yet no one ever perceived her as blessed with imperturbable nerves. Jo and Edward would enact the general drama with particular fierceness because they saw the automobile as a principal means to further their art.

This practical vision is manifest already in their first use of the car. Realizing that now they need not depend on public transportation, they set out in search of new subjects, directing their first campaign back to Maine. The lighthouse at Two Lights on Cape Elizabeth caught Edward's eye. Jo found a nearby place to stay. When she remarked that she would paint the same subject, he snapped, "then I won't."[87] In the end, he produced two now famous oils, *Lighthouse Hill* and *Captain Upton's House,* as well as several watercolors.

In retrospect, Jo remembered campaign rigors: she and Edward had "lived curiously for sake of a canvas. *Lighthouse Hill* came out of housekeeping with water from village pump—& the toilet in a shed shared with lobster bait."[88] The small Coast Guard settlement, named, Jo said, because it once had a second lighthouse, enthralled Edward. In addition to *Captain Upton's House,* he depicted the home of another local officer, Captain Berry, in *Hill and Houses.* He was fascinated by—maybe even envious of—their isolation; their job obliged them to live in the station, apart from their families, who occupied the surrounding houses. The rugged old-fashioned lives, lacking modern comforts like running water, also appealed to his imagination. Once again, the culture of the past held particular charm. Probably at Jo's instigation, they actually met the residents of the station and houses.

Free to range about, moving just a little along the coast, Hopper painted several watercolors. *Portland Head-Light* showed the lighthouse and the surrounding buildings viewed from the adjacent bluff; *Rocky Pedestal* focused on the base of the lighthouse, with its foghorn perched on high rocks above the sea. Finally, *Captain Strout's House* gave a frontal view of the keeper's home, with the lighthouse only partially visible behind it: "It is the house of the keeper of the Light at Portland Head & was painted right there from the fact," wrote Jo; "the good Capt. himself very much interested."[89]

The couple spent their third wedding anniversary visiting Chatterton and his wife in Ogunquit.[90] Although Edward and Jo had stayed in the same Ogunquit boarding house, it was their first visit together to the town. The Chattertons always put them in a harmonious mood, perhaps because Annette (as Jo called Chat's wife, Margaret Antoinette[91]) was so kind to Jo. Edward always liked "cutting up" with Chat, a survival from their art school days, and would get unusually boisterous.[92]

Venturing from Ogunquit into Portland, which he considered "our finest New England city,"[93] Hopper painted watercolors of two very uncharacteristic subjects: the *Custom House, Portland,* and *Libby House, Portland.* For the former's nineteenth-century classical architecture, he used a muted

palette and worked in the rain, discovering a use for the parked car and seizing on the contrast between the classical structure and the neighboring rustic
warehouse. Similarly, for the latter he focused on the contrast between the
1859 structure, designed in Italian villa style by the New Haven architect
Henry Austin, and the pedestrian apartment building next door. Pointedly,
in front of the elegant old villa he also emphasized the forms of a rotting tree,
with a metaphorical suggestion of Victorian values in decay.

Leaving Maine in late September, the Hoppers used their new mobility
to go by way of Charlestown, New Hampshire, where they "visited" Mrs.
Katherine Budd, a retired opera singer who lived in what "was formerly the
governor's mansion."[94] That summer, Juliana Force had rented Budd's home
Maxstoke as a summer residence for the Whitney Studio Club. She brought
along Marie Appleton, the club's sales clerk, and every three weeks the exhibitions in the drawing room galleries were changed. Settling in, Hopper used
the car for day trips across the Connecticut River into Vermont, where he
painted several watercolors of horses and barns. It was mid-October before
they got back to New York, risking traffic for the first time to deliver the
summer's output to the gallery on Fifth Avenue before ferrying the car back
to winter quarters in Nyack. Hopper's watercolors were then selling for $250.
When Jo consigned several of her new watercolors to the Whitney Studio
Club shop, she asked only five to fifty dollars each.[95]

In the fall Edward had Jo write to Carl Zigrosser at the Weyhe Gallery
and to some of the other dealers who regularly stocked his prints, raising
prices from eighteen to twenty-five dollars for *American Landscape* and *The
Cat Boat* and to twenty dollars for *The Railroad.*[96] Hopper's fame as an etcher
had just earned him his first mention in a book. Ralph Flint's new monograph on the artist Albert Sterner discussed the earlier exhibition Painter-
Gravers of America, which Sterner had organized with George Bellows, Leo
Mielziner, Childe Hassam, and others. The book listed Hopper as one of the
invited artists who showed together with the charter members.[97]

It was also in the fall of 1927 that Hopper allowed himself to be drawn
briefly back toward the world of prints. Even though he had not etched since
1923, Hopper maintained his connection to printmaker friends such as
Richard Lahey and George "Pop" Hart. When Lahey came to to talk about
forming a new society of printmakers "to include those of a more liberal way
of thinking than those who have usually made up the membership" of etchers' societies, Hopper recommended Hart, with whom he had shared exhibition space at the Sardeau Gallery in February 1923, even writing him to
explain, "There is a need for such a group. The only obstacles that I can see
in the way of forming such a society is the work that all would have to share.
And also to find a way to finance such a thing."[98] Hopper, who admired

Hart's "kindly humor" and "personal expression" and had praised his prints in a book review in 1926, was typically willing to help his male artist friends.[99]

As a result of these contacts, Hopper joined with Lahey and Hart to form the American Print Makers, a society that "eliminated the jury system."[100] Each committee member agreed to serve a three-year term, which Hopper did, although the organization's rules called for four members to retire at the end of each annual exhibition.[101] The group held its first show in December 1927 at the Downtown Gallery run by Edith Halpert at 113 West Thirteenth Street in New York. The etchings Hopper showed came from years earlier: *The Locomotive, The Cat Boat, Night Shadows,* and *Night in the Park.*

One member of the print committee, Rockwell Kent, now occupied the studio next to Hopper. He had arrived earlier in 1927 when Walter Tittle, by then a successful illustrator and printmaker, relocated to more comfortable quarters uptown. Kent, Tittle, and Hopper had all been classmates, but there were by now significant differences in their lives. Kent actually resided in an apartment on a lower floor with a new wife, Frances Lee, together with a child each from their previous marriages. For him it was "a mad, exuberant, licentious time."[102] With his various wives and assorted children, his zest in flaunting his disregard for prohibition, and his radical politics, he had little in common with his austere classmate in the adjoining studio. Busy with drawing advertising for a jewelry firm, besides paintings, engravings, and lithographs, Kent in 1927–1928 employed as an assistant the artist Andrée Ruellan, who recalled that next door Hopper had drawn a "line of demarcation in his studio," indicating his side of the room, which was forbidden to his wife.[103]

Instead of returning to his former medium in the months before the print show, Hopper busied himself in his studio on the oil painting now known as *Drug Store.* What he turned out was a new departure, developing on canvas his preoccupation with nocturnal solitude in the city, the empty spaces, some obscured by shadows and others eerily lit by electric light, a spectral Victorian door emerging from shadow, but a burst of red and blue bunting at the center, set off with white. Nowhere to be seen are figures like those of earlier street scenes, such as *New York Corner* of 1913, the Wells Fargo advertisement of 1917–1918, or certain etchings. Evoking the commercial world, however, are the faded name of the store, "184 SILBERS PHARMACY 184," and the garish advertising strip above the window that dominates the scene: "PRESCRIPTIONS DRUGS" and, in the largest lettering, "EX-LAX."

Underscoring the visual dominance of the brand name for the popular laxative, Hopper called the work *EX-LAX* when he took it to Rehn on December 9, 1927. If he meant to provoke, the reaction was not slow in coming. Rehn's wife Peggy suggested that the title "might have indelicate implications for those whose realism concedes nothing to aesthetics."[104] Indeed, one of Rehn's customers, a Dr. Lyle, had just returned Hopper's watercolor *Two Lights Village* because his wife considered the inclusion of an outhouse to be indelicate. Bowing to pressure, Hopper changed the title to *Drug Store* and altered the spelling of "EX-LAX" (with watercolor over his oil) to "ES LAX." Scarcely a month later, in January 1928, one of Hopper's most eager patrons came to the rescue. John T. Spaulding had purchased four watercolors from Hopper's first show with Rehn, subsequently buying two more. Now he bought *Drug Store* for fifteen hundred dollars. Either Rehn, or Hopper himself, who regretted the censorship, pointed it out. The Boston lawyer would brook no substitutes. The *X* got restored.

Drawing attention to a bodily function at a time when such subjects were taboo in polite company, Hopper meant to provoke, pushing his contrarian streak to a new extreme; his eagerness to restore the original spelling shows that he attached significance to its presence. Nor was it chance that he chose to depict an advertisement when he had only just freed himself from the burden of commercial work (the last illustrations he sold being finally published earlier in the year),[105] and that he emptied the format of figures, as if expressing relief that he no longer had to portray people, as he put it, "grimacing and posturing."[106] He appropriates the commercial frame and repopulates it on his own quizzical terms, reinforcing the role of the corner store as a focus of his imagination. With the flourish of red, white, and blue at the center, he evokes the fashionable theme of Americanism only to tie it to the name of the popular remedy intended to offer relief. Violating proprieties, going beyond even the preference for ugliness that critics had been remarking, he conveys his complex sense of his new freedom, both affirming and undercutting the role of standard-bearer for the American in art.

ON THE ROAD TO AMERICA: 1928–1929

THE CONTRETEMPS OVER *EX-LAX* hardly broke Hopper's stride. But he did suddenly make two prints in quick succession, his first in five years and his last. Although prints had served him well when the way through painting was blocked, he had left behind the mess of etching and printing as soon as the watercolors started selling. For this late and brief return to the print medium, he chose the relatively clean and less complicated technique of drypoint: on January 15, 1928, he produced *The Balcony* or *The Movies,* depicting two women seated in a theater.

Printmaking was on his mind, what with Rockwell Kent in the space next door and his own role in founding the new American Print Makers, even though he had made nothing new when they opened the previous fall. The theme of women in the theater varied *Two on the Aisle* of the year before, and "movies" would come to engage him ever more deeply. Years had passed since he was paid to watch silent films and make poster illustrations; but as recently as 1919, Hopper had been commissioned by the Methodist magazine *World Outlook* to depict a movie house interior, captioned "Movies give cheap, democratic amusement," as an alternative to saloons.[1] In the fall of 1927, Jo had just shown her watercolor of the Gloucester movie house at the Whitney Studio. The same season, the movies themselves had taken an astonishing turn. October saw the release of *The Jazz Singer,* starring Al Jolson. For the first time, a movie came with its own singing and spoken dialogue. As the medium developed during the next decade, its spare forms would inspire Hopper again and again.

On January 20, five days after *The Balcony,* Hopper produced his last print, a drypoint *Portrait of Jo,* who appears in a contemplative mood, with her head cast downward. Although sales of his prints remained strong and his reputation grew, his last etching dated to 1923, nor did he want to print additional examples from the plates. Even the excitement of forming a new venue for printmakers the previous year had not lured him from painting, although he never scorned his prints as he did his commercial illustrations.

Meanwhile, painting remained his real focus. He consigned one picture in early February and another before the end of the month. February 7, 1928, he took to Rehn *Captain Ed Staples.* After the figureless urban imagery of *EX-LAX,* the new picture is remarkable in presenting a figure with a name—an imaginary portrait, said Jo, of one of the Coast Guard officers Edward had met the previous summer:

> Dreamed up by E. himself, . . . the figure is every inch a New Eng. sea capt. conjured up from all the sea farers E. had met there & in Gloucester. The tall bleached grass is a fixture in E.'s consciousness & the house, its clapboards, lamp in window, the prototype of what in 1934 he was to have materialize over his own dissenting head, not Gloucester—that's not Cape Anne, Cape Elizabeth, but Cape Cod.[2]

Jo saw Captain "Ed" Staples as an alter ego for "Ed" Hopper, for she also noted that the house in this painting predicted the actual one that Hopper designed for them in 1934. It was unusual both for Hopper to name a painting after a particular person and for him to paint a theme from his summer travels during the winter. As this canvas was soon destroyed in a rail accident while returning from an exhibition at the Cleveland Museum during the summer of 1929, Hopper had little occasion to comment upon it. Jo did note much later that she had told Peggy Rehn: "If I hadn't married E.H., I'd have married Capt. Ed Staples & she said then I'd have taken on the life of a New England housewife, cook slave, wash tub drudge & regretted the day." Peggy knew only too the well the extent of domestic instinct in Jo.

In the following two weeks of intense work, Hopper turned from memory, personal imagination, and New England back to New York, where again he was drawn to the East River. On February 22, 1928, he finished *From Williamsburg Bridge,* which depicts old, heavily corniced apartment buildings seen from the bridge, with only a solitary figure in one top-floor window. Hopper made his preparatory sketch on the bridge itself and then painted the

Edward Hopper, Portrait of Jo, *1928. Drypoint (exists only as posthumous print),* 6⅞ × 5⅜" (17.5 × 13.7 cm.).

picture in his studio, where he also produced his next picture, *Manhattan Bridge Loop*. For this, he worked with at least three preparatory sketches, which demonstrate how carefully he adjusted the placement of the vertical street lamp to emphasize and accent the long horizontal sweep of empty space. He depicted the elevation where the trolley tracks run, with the trolley scaffolds prominent in the composition.

These studies and this painting occasioned a rare self-revelation by Hopper himself. When in 1939 they became the basis of a teaching exhibition for Andover Academy, Hopper wrote the organizer, Charles Sawyer, describing with unusual frankness how he had invested "a long time on the proportions of the canvas, so that it will do for the design, as nearly as possible what I wish it to do." He also commented expressly on his compositional choices:

> The very long horizontal shape of this picture . . . is an effort to give a sensation of great lateral extent. Carrying the main horizontal lines of the design with little interruption to the edges of the picture, is to enforce this idea and to make one conscious of the spaces and elements beyond the limits of the scene itself. The consciousness of these spaces is always carried by the artist to the very limited space of the subject that he intends to paint, though I believe all painters are not aware of this.[3]

Hopper also described his working process: "The picture was planned very carefully in my mind before starting it, but except for a few small black-and-white sketches made from the fact, I had no other concrete data, but relied on refreshing my memory by looking often at the subject." He characteristically discouraged Sawyer from including the drawings in the show, claiming: "The preliminary sketches would do little for you in explaining the picture. The color, design, and form have all been subjected, consciously or otherwise, to considerable simplification."[4]

While Hopper painted, his dealer organized. For March 1928, Rehn arranged a small show of etchings and watercolors at the Art Society in Utica, New York, where Hopper found a new champion in the person of Edward Root. The son of Elihu Root, who was Theodore Roosevelt's Secretary of State, Root had studied painting with George Luks and taught art appreciation at Hamilton College in nearby Clinton.[5] Two years younger than Hopper, Root was a zealous and dynamic collector of contemporary American art. He wrote a long, enthusiastic letter of article-length to the editor of the local newspaper, extolling Hopper's work and picking out what he considered its distinguishing features:

His feeling for the brilliant sharply defined iconic appearance of the American landscape; his sense of architectural surfaces which enables him to give a stronger suggestion of mass in his pictures of buildings than the buildings themselves are able to give; his ability to eliminate the unessential from each and every part of his picture; his instinct for the effective utilization of the elements of design; his ample, deliberate, but nonetheless emotional method of laying on his paint; his feeling for the quality and carrying power of the paint itself.[6]

Another painter whom Root admired was Charles Burchfield, to whom critics had already compared Hopper. It may, then, have been Root who suggested that the two painters meet and that Hopper write about Burchfield.

Hopper made an approach through the dealer Newman E. Montross, who showed eleven of Burchfield's paintings in a one-man show from March 26 through April 7. Montross had shown Hopper in the group show in 1914 that du Bois reviewed. Now he wrote to Burchfield, encouraging him to grant the interview: "I feel that he would do something important. . . . He is not only a distinguished artist but also an able writer. He would like very much to meet you."[7]

Hopper's article, "Charles Burchfield: American," appeared in the July 1928 issue of *The Arts*. He stressed that Burchfield's work is "decidedly founded, not on art, but on life" and quoted from Emerson's "Self-Reliance," which he praised for its incomparable clarity:

In every work of genius we recognize our own rejected thoughts; they come back to us with a certain alienated majesty. Great works of art have no more affecting lesson for us than this. They teach us to abide by our spontaneous impression with good-humored inflexibility, then most when the cry of voices is on the other side. Else tomorrow a stranger will say with masterly good sense precisely what we have thought and felt all the time, and we shall be forced to take with shame our opinion from another.[8]

Already the year before, in writing about John Sloan (and reflecting on himself), Hopper had echoed Emerson's rejection of European influence: now he placed Burchfield (and himself) squarely in the line of American painters who turned away from Europe, including "Inness, Eakins, Homer, Luks, Sloan, Kent, and Bellows." Their character, he argued, was growing "progressively more native."[9] Even as Hopper was writing about Burchfield, he was also very busy showing his own work. He placed *Eleven A.M.* in the 1928

Whitney Studio Annual, where Jo, exhibiting again as Josephine Hopper, had a watercolor called *Charlestown Tree* in a frame borrowed from Edward. Earlier in the year, she had taken several of her watercolors to the Morton Gallery at 66 West Fifty-third Street, where they were offered for sale at fifty dollars each. The gallery also carried Edward's etchings, by now priced at twenty-five and thirty dollars.

A second campaign with the car hardly seemed urgent given the pace of activity in New York. It was only on June 28, 1928, that the Hoppers arrived in Gloucester. Revisiting the place where they had worked happily together, and exploring with their new vehicle, they enjoyed a prolific season. Edward took fresh looks at familiar subjects: oils of vernacular architecture and other small-town scenes such as *Freight Cars, Gloucester,* a view of the middle of town with the Catholic church steeple behind. In watercolor, he painted a box factory, a circus wagon, railroad gates, Prospect Street with the Portuguese church, and an unusually fine group of local houses. But having the automobile also made it possible to go farther afield. He painted an oil, *Cape Ann Granite,* of a rocky green pasture in back of the summer colony called Riverview, and a related watercolor, *Cape Ann Pasture,* which includes several grazing cows. The remote wilderness of the West had seemed unpredictable and threatening, but he could relate to settled farmland that brought a respite from city life. He painted an oil of *Hodgkin's House,* an 1850 structure on the road to Annisquam. Leaving Gloucester on August 25, the Hoppers drove north and exchanged visits with Chat and Annette, who were summering again in Ogunquit. Their second encounter, as Chat remembered it, showed a side of Hopper that was hardly evident in those years of intense productivity, but would become a pronounced obstacle to his work:

> He was quite depressed because it was the middle of the summer and he hadn't done anything. And I said "What's the matter, anyhow? Plenty of stuff here to do, isn't there?" He said "I can't find it." So we got in the car and rode around, and we came to one spot that looked like the kind of thing he would do. We stopped and looked at it . . . nope, didn't interest him. Wasn't quite right. Something about it wasn't right. But he was that way about it. The thing would have to be made almost perfectly before he would do it, because he wouldn't change a thing. Oh, here and there, yes, but not too much.[10]

Back in New York, Hopper delivered most of the fruits of his summer travel to Rehn on September 27. He began work in his studio on an ambitious oil painting, *Blackwell's Island,* the same East River location he had previously painted in 1911, and took the canvas to Rehn on November 20. Before a low urban skyline of venerable buildings, a small white motorboat headed off to the right is reminiscent of that in the foreground of the 1925 *Bootleggers.* Jo noted in the record book that the "water [was] done over many times from sketches," indicating the struggle that Hopper always had depicting anything moving.[11] While Hopper was at work on *Blackwell's Island,* he and Jo visited their neighbor, the British artist Fred Mories,[12] who had invited them over to hear the broadcast of the election-day returns. To Hopper's satisfaction, Republican Herbert Hoover defeated Democrat Alfred E. Smith. Jo recalled that Mories

> had fine phonograph & put on some Beethoven & when it started something sacred to Isadora [Duncan], I leaped up & started dancing about. Soon Fred Mories joined me—presently E.H. who had gone snapping about the model stand for the "2 yds. of cheese cloth for self expression" (prized by Forbes Watson) lay hold of a pair of much trimmed white drawers. With this scarf effect, E.H. joined us & we had a riot. E. was always so funny with Mories about.[13]

Jo reflected that Edward "had a good gift of comedy when anything brought it out."[14] But their friendship with Mories was marred; "I couldn't endure Mories because he made it clear that as an artist, I was to be snubbed & kept out," she recalled. "But I right there when he all but rubbed his nose into E.'s canvases to make out how he got certain effects—& I not disguising my observations of his efforts."[15] She had no patience with those who courted Edward and bluntly ignored her.

After the rather impersonal *Blackwell's Island,* Hopper began a canvas with a more intimate theme. In *Night Windows* he reveals a woman in her slip, glimpsed from behind, in an illuminated interior observed through windows from the dark. The subject is unaware of being watched, making the viewer into a voyeur, as so often in Hopper's own development of similar themes in his series of transitional etchings. No doubt he took inspiration, too, from John Sloan's 1910 etching of the same name, but he produced a more sensual and more subtle vision. The curtain blowing at the open window seems cinematic, as does the intimacy of the view. In fact, Hopper's voyeurism would find an outlet in his lifelong affair with the cinema.[16]

Night Windows recalls the experience of the voyeur pastor in "The Strength of God," one of Sherwood Anderson's short stories in *Winesburg, Ohio.* From the clergyman's study in the church bell tower, he accidentally discovers that he can see into the bedroom of a young woman in the house next door. He becomes a virtual Peeping Tom, unable to resist being drawn to spy upon the woman in various states of undress. "When the shade of the window to Kate Swift's room was raised he could see, through the hole, directly into her bed."[17] Likewise, Hopper's painting reveals a woman undressing alone in her bedroom at night as she is observed unawares through her raised window shades. Years later, Hopper commented: "The way in which a few objects are arranged on a table, or a curtain billows in the breeze can set the mood and indicate the kind of person who inhabits the room."[18] The choice and shaping of the image also, of course, indicate the kind of imagination that inhabits the artist and attracts the spectator.

Night Windows communicates a mood like that, too, of Anderson's 1923 *Many Marriages,* which was the first of his novels to focus on modern sexual experience.[19] Hopper's acquaintance with it by the time he painted *Night Windows* seems evident: most of it was published serially in the *Dial,* to which Jo subscribed; and in the three months following its publication, the novel sold over nine thousand copies.[20] Anderson's preoccupation in *Many Marriages* is with the symbolic value of nudity, sexual frankness, and the inner emotional life of its characters. In a number of his subsequent oil paintings, Hopper addressed similar issues of voyeurism, temptation, repression, and sexual ennui, continuing the imaginative exploration of the etchings.

After writing about Sloan and Burchfield, Hopper found the tables turned when he himself became the subject of an article written by Forbes Watson for the magazine *Vanity Fair.* The editor, Frank Crowninshield, sent him proofs, to which Hopper responded: "The phrase, 'the greatest possible austerity without loss of emotion' is no child of mine however. Rehn is the real father of this cutey and has tried to hang it on me." He conceded, "It makes no difference, though, as it listens good in type."[21] After the piece appeared in the issue for February 1929, Hopper thanked Watson, telling him, "You've done me proud."[22] Watson wrote that "from the top of his slow-moving lanky body," Hopper had "looked down with infinite disgust upon those who, ceasing to be themselves, were rushing to get aboard the bandwagon of modernism."[23] Admiring the painter's "dry wit" and his "depth of feeling for purely native material," Watson quoted Hopper: "I don't see why people are so crazy to import French paintings when there are so many French paintings being made in America."[24] Hopper was referring to works inspired by French modernism, not only the American Impressionists, but especially the later followers of Cubism. Watson explained: "Hopper, looking like a professor of higher mathematics in an out-of-town college, refused to listen to the noisy demands for professorial painting. His paintings, his water colors and his etchings remained just Hopper."[25]

Amused by the last comment, Hopper quipped: "My wife says I don't look as much like a professor of higher mathematics as Kenneth Miller, but I know her to be prejudiced."[26] According to Watson, time was on Hopper's side: "Unnoticed, except for a few of his fellow painters, the uneasy conditions of that time forced him into doing what is called commercial art. But they could not force him to waver. Consequently when the inevitable reaction set in and people turned from art based on art to art based on life, Hopper was destined to reap the rewards of his incurable honesty."[27] Watson had also recognized Hopper's "originality of invention," "his boldness of selection," "his richly critical mind," and his "lyric imagination."[28] Hopper was so thrilled with Watson's article that he presented a drawing to him and his wife, Nan.[29]

When Hopper delivered *Night Windows* to Rehn on December 28, 1928, it was the culmination of a very successful year. He had earned $8,486, which, except for some sales of prints elsewhere, all came from the gallery, which had sold five oils, fourteen watercolors, and a number of prints. Hopper continued to raise print prices, moving to twenty-five and thirty dollars.[30]

On January 21, 1929, he opened another one-man exhibition at Rehn's. Featuring a dozen oils, ten watercolors, and a group of drawings, the show garnered both critical and commercial success. The reviews carried headlines like "Americanism of Edward Hopper" and "Hopper Interprets America," further sharpening his nationalist image.[31] And the critics now allowed that his reputation as an etcher and a watercolorist was equaled by his work in oil.[32] They also began to define his realism, noting the difference between his art and photography: "This is an art of selection, of proper emphasis, of painstaking arrangement. Nature's sayso is not the artist's affirmation."[33] Edward Alden Jewell, the critic for *The New York Times,* quoted Hopper as seeking "the esthetic confluence of that 'something inside me and something outside . . . to personalize the rainpipe.' "[34]

Just after the opening, Hopper wrote to Forbes Watson about an anonymous American folk painting:

If you are ever in the vicinity of 44th St. and Sixth Ave., I wish that you would look at a picture that I ran across in a little jeweler's shop on 44th St. on the downtown side a few doors west from Sixth Avenue. I discovered it by accident upon looking in the window of the shop. It is American of the 1830's I should say. A portrait of three children done with a simplicity and honesty that is striking. Very large in its values and unaffected in its design. It is not at all naive but done with experience and understanding. I think it's quite a fine thing. The owner of the shop does not know the painter and says he bought it from an estate. I do not know why I wrote you this except that I should like others to enjoy what is to me a quite unusual discovery.[35]

Watson's reply is lost, but with or without his encouragement, Hopper purchased his find, *Calvin Howe and His Two Sisters,* and kept it the rest of his life, arranging with Jo to bequeath it to the Metropolitan Museum.[36] This is the only known instance of Hopper's buying art of the past or having an interest in American folk painting, but the genre was quite popular in the circle of artists associated with the Whitney Studio Club.[37] A tenet of his own aesthetics shows in his praise for the picture's "simplicity and honesty."

Almost immediately Hopper brought Rehn another new canvas, *Chop Suey,* which he had painted in the studio with Jo playing the roles of all three women. The setting recalled the inexpensive, second-floor Chinese restaurant the Hoppers had been frequenting at Columbus Circle. Both the composition and the restaurant theme evolved out of his commercial illustrations, and the bold lettering of the sign outside the window is another link to that earlier work.

While engaged with their own theater in the studio, the Hoppers kept up their enthusiasm for Broadway. Even the dramas they chose now were American: Elmer Rice's *Street Scene,* hailed in the press as "one of the best plays of the season," and Eugene O'Neill's *Strange Interlude,* a marathon performance with nine acts interrupted by a one-hour dinner intermission. Both productions featured sets designed by Jo Mielziner, whose father, the portraitist Leo Mielziner, had helped organize the Painter-Gravers Show in which Hopper took part in 1918. The sets stayed in Hopper's mind.

Confident, prosperous, and engaged with themes of American identity, the Hoppers imagined a new use for the car. On April 1 they embarked on their third and most ambitious campaign, breaking the pattern of returns to familiar territory in New England to explore the old South. What they sought or expected has to be inferred from their itinerary.

They began by making a beeline for Charleston, South Carolina, which enjoyed a specific fame: its renaissance during the 1920s attracted writers and artists, leading a northern journalist to comment in 1928 on the "pilgrims who go that way to worship at the shrine of spring," and to note "the inexhaustible picturesqueness of Charleston, and on everyside an artist set up his easel in devotion."[38] They might have read DuBose Heyward's 1925 novel, *Porgy,* and did go to see the play of the same name the following October. Heyward's Charleston included Negro tenements and other aspects of local culture that succeeded in capitvating Hopper's diffident eye. For a Civil War buff such as Edward, Charleston offered a feast. Fort Sumter, located on a small man-made island at the entrance to the harbor lay under almost constant bombardment by Union forces from 1863 to 1865, and became a symbol for both sides. In Charleston, Hopper made a watercolor of the battery, with its ancient cannons poised among the palm trees and park benches.

The Hoppers boarded with a widow who had three children, one of whom, Gertrude Wulbern Haltiwanger, was then about twenty. She remembers that the Hoppers liked their room on the top floor because of the good north light but did not take meals in, that Edward seemed not overly pleased with Charleston, and that Jo was the more outgoing of the two.[39] She also recalls Hopper seeing a local artist, Alfred Hutty, who had settled in Charleston at the close of World War I, sometimes exhibited in the same print circles, and may also have shared summers in the North.

Hopper's other watercolors included *Ash's House,* a typical local house with a veranda, *Charleston Doorway, Charleston Slum, Folly Beach* (where he spotted a dead deciduous tree among the shaggy palms), and *Negro Cabin,* with a female figure perched in the doorway. About the latter work, he later recounted that the woman seemed willing to pose, but her husband suddenly appeared and frightened him off.[40] Hopper made both a Conté crayon sketch and a watercolor of a second cabin surrounded by trees covered with hanging Spanish moss.

In *Baptistery of Saint John's* Hopper painted an interior view of the empty Lutheran church, which was an early nineteenth-century building located just a few blocks away from the boarding house. He recorded its white marble rail and font and a black-and-white tiled floor. In an unusual gesture, he made a detailed preparatory sketch of the cloth covering the cross on the baptistery font. Perhaps the exceptional focus on a still life subject prompted this exercise. Hopper, who had long since rejected his Baptist upbringing, never painted another church interior. Years later, Jo made a telling comment: "The inanity of early Sunday School predisposes many of us against churches— unless they are beguiling and empty."[41]

The Hoppers were still in Charleston on April 22, when Jo wrote to Miss Masterson of the Whitney Studio Galleries (the Club had been renamed the previous fall) concerning the whereabouts of some of the etchings Edward had consigned for sale there for thirty dollars each. (The Whitney now took a 25 percent commission on sales.) Jo reassured Masterson, telling her, "I'm a very careful secretary," and "Don't worry, that print will turn up in the fall like as not."[42] She noted: "We were desolated to miss the circus. It must have been tremendous! We'll go looking for some one to tell us about it as soon as we get home."[43] Jo referred to a lively group show on the theme of the circus that was held at the Whitney Galleries that spring. The Hoppers' friend Louis Bouché had produced special decorations for the installation.

Leaving Charleston on April 27, the Hoppers drove to Charlottesville, Virginia, making up for the single-mindedness of their journey down. Thomas Jefferson's university campus struck Jo as one of "the most moving places I know of in America—real shrines. And Jefferson's home at Monticello—way way up—infinitely above all the sin & vulgarity & triviality of his age & ours."[44] In the spirit of the nationalism they had been breathing in New York, they turned their trip into a pilgrimage to American shrines.

Driving on to the old capital of the Confederacy at Richmond, Virginia, they visited the Confederate Museum, where Edward displayed "the greatest reverence."[45] Jo added, comparing it with her memories of Rome, "Everything seemed so real, so simple, so from the heart—no Arch of Titus, no bumptiousness—it felt like holy ground." The next day, May 8, they stopped by Surrey Caverns in Virginia. Continuing on through the Shenandoah Valley, they visited the Civil War battlefields at Gettysburg.

Back in the city in early May 1929, the Hoppers lost no time in catching up on theater, getting in the British comedy *Bird in Hand* by John Drinkwater and a war play by R. C. Sheriff, *Journey's End,* before Edward delivered his best Charleston watercolors to Rehn on the twenty-fifth.

With no thought of settling down to work in the city, they started again for Maine, adding along the way a further professional use for the car. From now on it would be easy to detour to touch base with collector-friends, which they did in Topsfield, Massachusetts, staying over with Anne and Sam Tucker, mutual acquaintances of Bee Blanchard, the decorator who had been buying Hoppers since his first show with Rehn. In the course of the visit, Hopper made excursions to nearby towns. In Salem, he drew only a factory with a tall chimney; in Essex, however, he painted two watercolors, *Farm House at Essex* and *Barn at Essex.* The view of the farmhouse includes a typical New England stone wall, cascading into the depth of the composition. The barn view is painted in the pale tones of a gray day with a moist atmosphere.

On June 27 the Hoppers departed for Maine, reaching the coast by July 3, at Pemaquid Point, where Edward painted a watercolor of the lighthouse known as *Pemaquid Light.* They returned to Cape Elizabeth on July 4, where Edward painted another oil of *The Lighthouse at Two Lights,* probably at the urging of the Tuckers, who bought the canvas shortly after its completion. He also painted an oil of the Coast Guard station, which he had previously depicted in two 1927 watercolors.

The major part of Hopper's work in the summer of 1929, however, was in watercolor. He painted the Coast Guard boats, a dory with sails, rocky coves, a house with a vine, and a third version of the *House of the Fog Horn,* which he had depicted twice in 1927. His *Methodist Church* shows the side rear of the graveyard with one gravestone and the square tower of the church looming up, but cropped abruptly by the picture's edge. This watercolor represents another instance of his response to mortality. In fact, the news that their favorite teacher had died disrupted their vacation calm. The July 22 issue of *Time* magazine reported the death of Robert Henri at age sixty-four, omitting from the list of Henri's protégés Hopper, but including his classmates "Rockwell Kent and the late great George Bellows."[46] The slight may have been a larger shock than the death itself; Hopper had long resented the attention paid by Henri to some of his colleagues, although Jo continued to idealize their former teacher for the rest of her life.

Maine kept Edward busy into the autumn. How he worked appears from Jo's later remarks about the watercolor *Light House Village,* "done early in the fall of 1929 on outer edge of the little coast guard settlement called Two Lights":

> Sitting upon the bluff is this light house, the house of its keeper. . . .
> Below are the houses of the families of the coast guard. The men have
> to sleep at the station . . . but these men have their families right there
> at a stone's throw. Life very primitive, water from the village pump.
> The grass in the foreground is timothy. E. Hopper is past master of
> dead grass. He had previously painted all the other items here more
> or less. Singly, but he couldn't resist the timothy, so these other items
> became involved which makes this picture, as I recall it, somewhat of
> catalogue of several canvases and some 2 doz. watercolors.[47]

Edward's health also became an issue: "Mr. Hopper was so little well that summer, dragging his big frame around not learning until later about low thyroid. This may explain the scanty output of his work—all the pictures have vitality enough—a concentration of all he had at the time." He also had broken his little toe, necessitating a drive to Portland on August 9. But despite his injury and fatigue, he completed more than a dozen watercolors and two oils. Her "scanty output" hardly seems a fair summary of the campaign.

Although they were passing their third summer with the car, Jo still was struggling even to learn to drive:

> I had found an empty lot—rough as rocks & weeds could make it—
> dragged about stones to indicate the width of a street, narrow street,
> & practiced turning the old Dodge about in it. Of course things
> couldn't fail to be a little different on a smoothe pavement when no
> such effort would be required. One could be only amazed that the
> car went easily & didn't stall going over bumps.[48]

It later turned out that Edward had refused to have the steering wheel tightened, although it was a quarter turn off, claiming that nothing could be done. When Jo had trouble preventing the car from weaving, one of the myths about women drivers seemed confirmed, although the root of the trouble was his stubborn and misguided claim.

The Hoppers returned to a tense New York on September 30, well in time to experience the panic caused by the stock market crash on October 29. Optimistically, Hopper delivered much of his new work to Rehn and began thinking about his next canvas, for which he made at least one preparatory sketch. Representing late sunset with red and gold clouds, he painted *Railroad Sunset* in his New York studio. With its dark, brooding foreground and dramatic imagery, this work is strikingly atypical. Hopper must have been responding to the agitation and despair in the city around him. He picked out the tall silhouette of a railroad signal tower, a lonely symbol of of technology and modern urban life intruding into the countryside. Surely this sinking sun and hyperbolic sunset mark the end of an epoch and its lost innocence, also reflecting the artist's feel for French Symbolist poems such as Charles Baudelaire's "Harmonie du Soir," which reads: "The sky, like an altar, is sad and magnificent; drowning in curdled blood, the sun sinks lower."[49] Hopper finished this painting and took it to Rehn on December 20. It found no buyer, for many collectors had suffered serious losses in the stock market. (However, during 1929 Hopper sold two oils, fourteen watercolors, and eighty prints for a total of $6,211, slightly less than the record-breaking previous year, but substantial nonetheless.)

In the brief time since 1924, Hopper had established his reputation and won a strong position among America's contemporary artists. James Laver, in his book *A History of British and American Etching,* published in 1929, noted: "Edward Hopper, who is also known for his work in oil and watercolor, is an etcher who is almost puritanical in his refusal of the various tricks of the etching craft."[50]

The recognition came to a head late in 1929 with Hopper's inclusion by the new Museum of Modern Art in its second exhibition, "Paintings by Nineteen Living Americans,"[51] which firmly identified him as a leader among his compatriots. The fourteen trustees of the museum were originally supposed to select fifteen artists from a list of over a hundred, submitted by a committee led by the museum's director, Alfred H. Barr, Jr. When the trustees could not agree upon fifteen names, an additional four were added. Among the trustees, Stephen Clark, Duncan Phillips, Samuel A. Lewisohn, Frank Crowninshield, and Mrs. John D. Rockefeller, Jr., already owned one or more of Hopper's works. Phillips himself had written vivid praise and Crowninshield had published Forbes Watson's enthusiastic article.

The roster of artists and the show's definition of modern American art caused a great deal of controversy. Watson attacked the foreign-born Max Weber for taking "no account of the American tradition" and for being tied to "European standards," but he defended Hopper, Burchfield, Kent, Speicher, and Sloan against those who perceived "a disturbing conservative quality" in their work, while denouncing "American laymen," for whom "the modernity of all art depends upon the degree of success with which it emulates painting in Paris."[52] The review in the New York *Sun* by Hopper's veteran critic Henry McBride was headlined: "Works of Nineteen Best American Artists Exhibited in New Museum's Second Show."[53] That a major New York critic and a major New York museum could place Hopper in such a stellar context indicates beyond any doubt how far he had come from the obscurity in which he had languished so shortly before.

RECOGNITION: 1930-1933

JUST AS THE Great Depression caused hardship for so many, Hopper's career took even greater strides. In January 1930, the Museum of Modern Art accepted *House by the Railroad* as a gift from Stephen Clark, the first painting by any artist to enter the museum's permanent collection. Other coups soon followed. On the big easel, meanwhile, *Early Sunday Morning* was taking shape.[1] Initially called *Seventh Avenue Shops,* the cityscape "was almost a literal translation of Seventh Avenue," Hopper later claimed, allowing, though, that "it wasn't necessarily Sunday. That word was tacked on later by someone else."[2] At first he depicted a figure in one of the windows, but thought better of it and painted it out.[3] Jo remembered how hard it had been for Edward to establish the sense of a third dimension going back into the imagined depth of the canvas: "Only such slight help on that barber pole, hydrant & so little indented door ways & windows. How true that the conception must be in the mind & proceed from there with all the technique of a life of struggle to acquire—All this power with so little effort that is obvious & an appeal that is spontaneous & immense."[4]

The elevated vantage point in *Early Sunday Morning,* looking down to the surface of the sidewalk, has much in common with the view Jo and Edward had from the second balcony when they saw Elmer Rice's *Street Scene* in February 1929. Jo Mielziner's set for the realistic play represents the exterior of a

Edward Hopper with Early Sunday Morning *at the Virginia Museum of Art, Richmond, Virginia, 1953.*

two-story New York apartment house, with its flat facade extending across the width of the stage, like the shallow space in front of the buildings in Hopper's painting. The enthusiasm triggered by the set echoes in a later comment about Mielziner's mother, Ella, who would be the Hoppers' Truro neighbor: "My friend, Mrs. Mielziner . . . the mother of that Street Scene set we loved so much. Jo Mielziner, the artist and Kenneth McKenna, the actor are her sons."[5]

Early Sunday Morning stands out among pictures by both Hopper and his contemporaries. Sunlight warms an old-fashioned two-story row building, set beneath a solid blue band of sky. The only interruption of the horizontal sweep of sky is a dark rectangle in the upper right corner of the composition. This detached vertical shape suggests another dimension beyond the human scale of the foreground. With minimal means, Hopper has represented a skyscraper. Almost an afterthought, seen only in this partial glimpse, it intrudes on the cityscape, projecting none of the majestic grandeur of the new towers as they appear in the work of Georgia O'Keeffe or Charles Sheeler. While accepting the need for a new "American" art that "would wean itself from its French Mother," as he wrote in his essay on Sloan, and thinking that American architecture was developing a native style, he largely disdained the sky-scrapers, industrial structures, and airplanes painted by contemporaries such as Sheeler and O'Keeffe or Joseph Stella and Elsie Driggs. He rarely represented skyscrapers at all, and when he did, he reduced them to fragmentary glimpses or intrusions on the cityscape, as here and in *The City* (1927). His recurrent visual ironies on the manifestations of modern life suggest his highly ambivalent attitude toward the changes occurring in twentieth-century society; it is his profound alienation from contemporary life that makes his art so characteristic of modernity itself.

A few months after its completion, *Early Sunday Morning* was acquired for the newly established Whitney Museum of American Art, placing Hopper in his second museum collection that year and marking the Whitney's most expensive purchase up to that time. The director, Juliana Force, paid three thousand dollars, twice what John T. Spaulding spent for *Drug Store* in January 1928. When the new Whitney actually opened its doors on Eighth Street in November 1931, it featured *Early Sunday Morning*. The poet and critic Horace Gregory recalled: "I saw Hopper's spare figure buttoned up in a Chesterfield topcoat, bending forward, hands clasped behind his back, to examine a canvas painted by a young contemporary. I heard him sigh, scarcely above his breath, 'At last they're all beginning to paint like me.' "[6] While it is difficult to imagine the silent Hopper speaking out loud to himself, he did have reasons for pride. By this time, he had realized a clear vision of who he was and mustered the self-assurance to expect other artists to subscribe to his aesthetic. As for his featured picture, it was destined to be reproduced again and again, becoming emblematic of the museum.[7]

Another boost came from Forbes Watson, Force's sometime paramour, who had solicited Hopper's writing for *The Arts,* where he reviewed *Early Sunday Morning,* and who now was now getting ready to publish a Hopper portfolio. The project provoked an energetic critique from the ever watchful Jo, who wrote Watson, "We are profoundly grateful to you for all your wonderful kindness in promoting the work of E. Hopper," before getting to the point, "That engraver could be kept in jail & whoever tampered with E.H.'s selection of pictures!" although adding, "This letter is a female of the species—spontaneous, spiteful & utterly unreasonable I suppose. Now don't hold it up against E.H. (he's out of the room shaving)—who is busy holding his tongue & prepared to smite me if I don't. Otherwise he's sad & meek & the combination would drive any wife to folly."[8] Edward, who obviously shared his wife's sentiments if not her audacity, subsequently wrote to Watson: "I have just learned of a damn fool letter that my wife sent you regarding the Arts Portfolio on my stuff. Please disregard it, it being entirely female and unofficial and I blush to the seat of my pants when I think of it."[9]

In June 1930, the Hoppers began the summer campaign with an even longer detour, driving upstate to Clinton to see Edward and Grace Root at Hamilton College. Following Root's written appreciation of Hopper in 1928, he had purchased the canvas *Freight Cars, Gloucester* and two watercolors. A believer in spreading good news, Root had also convinced his colleague, Arthur Percy "Stink" Saunders, a distinguished professor of chemistry, and his wife, Louise, to acquire works by Hopper: they bought two watercolors and an etching. It was also Root who collected work by Charles Burchfield and persuaded him to switch to the Rehn Gallery in 1929, where he and Hopper became friends.[10]

The visit lasted a week, in which the Hoppers attended a play produced in the open air on College Hill by the class of the Saunders' children. Jo reported to Bee Blanchard that they "had a lovely time—were taken to tea & dinner parties at houses with Hopper watercolors on the walls. It was such satisfaction to find one's children so well situated. The Roots are the lambiest people to visit."[11] It is not surprising that the Hoppers found Root congenial; he was so focused on artists and teaching about art that he had asked to have his name removed from the social register, remarking that "more of his friends were listed in the Manhattan telephone directory."[12]

For the summer, the car permitted a further departure. At long last Jo would get the wish she had expressed in the summer of 1924, when she settled for Gloucester and Edward. She was a veteran of the avant-garde community of theater and art, where he had never bothered to go, at the tip of Cape Cod in Provincetown. Just below it, Truro, much less developed, with a population of only 500 in 1930, attracted the Hoppers.[13] Like its sisters Provincetown and Wellfleet, Truro had been a great whaling center and this seafaring history appealed to Edward.

The Hoppers rented a cottage on Prince Valley Road on the vast farm of the local postmaster, A. B. Burleigh ("Burly" according to Jo's spelling) Cobb. They adored their tiny place, described by Jo as a "little cottage on the side of a hill in such a wonderful land of bare green sandy hills—so open to the sky & wind-blown & wild."[14] Jo reported that Edward was "very enthusiastic," explaining: "It's so much less spoilt than a lot of the Cape. There are very few houses—they are little houses & far apart—no hotel anywhere, no movies, no stores. One goes to Wellfleet for provisions."[15]

Hopper wrote to his friend Chat, adding a sketch of the South Truro Church at the bottom of his letter: "We like it very much here at South Truro and have taken a cottage for the summer. Fine big hills of sand, a desert on a small scale with fine dune formations, a very open almost treeless country— I think you would like it. I have one canvas and am starting another and have a few punk water colors."[16] In fact, Hopper's first summer on the Cape was quite fruitful. Despite his typical understatement, he produced a number of fine watercolors of the new surroundings, including *Burly Cobb's House* and *Burly Cobb Hen Coop and Barn.* By July 14, Jo reported that Edward had "4 watercolors that he doesn't like much."[17] Other places that he recorded in watercolor that summer were the *North Truro Station, South Truro Post Office, Truro Station Coal Box, Rich's House,* and *Lewis Farm.* He also painted in Wellfleet (*Wellfleet Bridge*) and Provincetown (*House in Provincetown* and *Methodist Church Tower*). Jo later commented that the latter work was "painted in back seat of car parked on Main St., a little to side of the church where shops pile up making fine composition of angles for foreground. Parking has since been prohibited there."[18]

After his experiences in Maine, it was natural for Hopper to size up the local lighthouse.[19] Standing in North Truro at the extreme eastern edge of the Cape, on a dramatic cliff 140 feet above sea level, "It is like being at the masthead of a man-o'-war sixty miles out at sea," wrote Thoreau in 1849, calling the setting "a place of wonders."[20] The position directly across from northern Spain marks the closest one can be to Europe while still on American soil. When Hopper painted his watercolor of *Highland Light* that summer, the structure still functioned with the ancient instrument that had to be rewound by hand three times a night.[21]

Hopper's oils that summer began with *Hills, South Truro,* which, he told Guy du Bois, was "done almost entirely on the spot," when "the mosquitoes were terrible."[22] (A contemporary guide book explained that the recent increase in mosquitoes was the result of cars replacing horses. Since marshes were no longer drained for the harvesting of salt hay, the drainage ditches were not maintained to allow the free flow of tides in and out and, as a result, the water became stagnant and bred mosquitoes.[23])

On July 14, Jo described *Hills, South Truro* in progress as "a canvas that he's grouching over—rather a beauty—hills & hills on over to the sea that he's working on from 6 to 8 P.M."[24] It was already Hopper's practice to work on a painting at the same time every day in order to keep the light consistent, in the manner of the French Impressionists. Jo also noted that Edward hoped to paint six more canvases.[25]

The Hoppers' isolated mode of life on the Cape prevented them from continuing their city routine and caused enormous stress. In New York, Jo did not have to do much cooking, which she despised, for she and Edward often ate out at inexpensive neighborhood diners. But there were no restaurants in Truro, and it was simply too far to Wellfleet or Provincetown to go for meals. At first, Jo was cautiously optimistic about assuming a domestic routine: "There are no stores in S. Truro, no one to feed us, so I've been at it in real earnest—with more equipment for doing than I've ever had, so I've been trying my hand at various things & have accomplished baked mackerel, baked ham, blueberry cake & even 1 blueberry pie. Imagine having even a flour sifter & a rolling pin."[26] This much cooking, she admitted, was much more than she had ever envisioned: "When we came I made a pile of all the baking tins, rolling pins, flour sifter, pie pans etc. & shoved them up on a shelf under the roof. Not for me! But one by one I've hauled each one down— Even a big glass sugar bowl—(to put wild roses in)."[27]

Jo was initially amazed at her competence in the kitchen, but she complained that cooking takes "nearly all one's time," and admitted that it left her tired and cross.[28] Still, she shared Edward's enthusiasm for their little rented abode, noting, "This is the first time we've ever had a little house all to ourselves & we're having great joy of it. It's just a little summer cottage, as primitive as the land it's in. We have our own pump (that works & easily) & a brand new 3 burner oil stove & big oven."[29]

Although Jo did the cooking, Edward shared the laundry chores, as she informed Bee Blanchard: "We have a big nickel kettle & the pump & the stove & tubs & I wash & E.H. rinses & wrings out & the sheets & things looked so white blowing in the wind, we got quite excited over it. But we mean to wash as little as possible—& nearly never iron."[30] When the weather was "glorious," Jo even found it "rather fun to be primitive."[31]

She was pleased by the effect of the Cape on Edward after his weakness in Maine: "He's all brown & his eyes look so blue in the tanned face—& coarse blue cotton shirt & kaki norfolk & elk skin moccasins & kaki duck-hunter hat. He's lots better looking out doors. He is feeling pretty well too—only gets tired more than he used to. But this life seems to agree with him."[32] Nor was there only art and domestic drudgery. They swam in the bay and enjoyed the sandy beach. Jo also painted oils, including *Cape Cod Hills* and *South Truro Church,* the historic Methodist meeting house that Edward subsequently preferred to paint from the opposite side; she worked farther back than he would, near the cemetery, "so as to see the sea beyond row of hills—no close foreground at this distance."[33]

One potential of the car caused an unexpected turn. Edward soon discovered that he could drop Jo off with her easel and leave her to work while he drove off to peace and quiet with a subject of his own. His practice left Jo alone painting the meeting house late one summer morning when she saw a strange car approach. Knowing that there was "nothing, no one for him to come for" and uneasy, she at once stood up only to have a tall red-headed stranger come and sit down on her camp stool, and "all but put his nose into the canvas." She sensed danger. "It was all so peculiar his descending upon me there with deep pit before me—on the Cape this formation called a 'kettle,' formed by glaciers. If tossed down into one of those things, one would never be found until a funeral bought some one to the graveyard in back." Nervously, she kept up "a steady babble to cover his stubborn silence," mentioning "my husband [is] coming to get me soon, he should be painting this church, more in his line than mine, but it must be painted, so I [am] trying my hand." Finally, the intense intruder departed, leaving as silently as he had arrived—declining to give her any explanation for his weird behavior. She reported: "Naturally, I never went back. So the odor of sanctity surrounding that church was not disturbed—& just as well. I added the weathervane later in the studio."[34]

Her "husband . . . should be painting" confirms that she painted this subject before him. Besides the tiny sketch of the church he included on his letter to Chatterton, he made a caricature of Jo, *Painting South Truro Church in the Wind,* poking fun at the problems she had holding on to her canvas. He also painted a small watercolor version of the motif on a birthday card for Bee Blanchard's mother. Only then did he paint his own version of the venerable building, which was a popular subject for local artists.[35]

That summer, he also painted several views of *Cobb's Farm* as well as *Corn Hill,*[36] a high cliff in one of the sandiest areas on the Cape, where, in

Edward Hopper, Painting South Truro Church in the Wind, *1930. Pencil on paper, 8½ × 5½″ (21.6 × 14 cm.).*

1620, sixteen pilgrims under Captain Myles Standish found the Indians' store of corn; they "borrowed" enough to plant their own crop at Plymouth the following spring.[37] The crop saw the pilgrims through the next year. A bronze tablet proclaimed the history of Corn Hill, which was otherwise then just a small summer colony of bleak-looking cottages buffeted by strong winds, even in the heat of the summer. For Hopper, painting outdoors, the cool breeze beckoned and meant fewer mosquitoes.

Other Cape subjects occurred to Jo, who saw her role as facilitator of Edward's painting and often tried unsuccessfully to interest him in one or another. She had seen "the cutest little airplane—called the robin—all bright orange which came to roost on a nearby hill. We went over to visit it—& I tried to get E.H. interested to paint it—but no—not he! Said nothing he could get hold of."[38] With his diffidence toward technological progress, Hopper never did develop an interest in airplanes, either for painting or flying. And he resisted letting Jo suggest subject matter.

Coming from Truro, Jo found New York a "wretched, dirty, noisy city—so vile after being away from it," and she complained of "awful looking people."[39] Before settling in to paint, they drove Edward's mother and sister to Connecticut, which clearly did not thrill Jo. She felt that Marion was merely interested in local "church politics, neighbors, & their reactions to cat, etc.," but not in anyone else. She did recall Edward's mother saying once that "she was learning so much more about him since I married him."[40]

§

EVEN AS HOPPER had been discovering the new scene in the unspoiled backwater that was Truro, the tireless du Bois was preparing to assign him yet further prominence in the firmament of American art, appropriating from James the phrase "American Scene":

> It would be well to examine the American scene. There must have been some original difficulty finding it. It is extremely rare. It is composed of relics. Its active life ceased not later than nineteen hundred. Wherever a town has been progressive, and America is said to be progressive, the American scene has been wiped out of it. Two research men, historical painters, are the straws which are going to save our elephant. They are Edward Hopper and Charles Burchfield.[41]

Du Bois called Hopper a "house painter," noting that "he paints Victorian examples, still as death, as forbidding as their stark surroundings. The American scene is unquestionably ugly."[42] Recognizing the modernization that was

Edward Hopper, South Truro Church, *1930. Watercolor on paper,
3¾ × 9″ (9.5 × 22.5 cm.) (birthday card for Mary Amis Hooper, Bee
Blanchard's mother).*

transforming America, du Bois suggested: "To hide progress might be a good
business move if anybody could be made to believe in it."[43] For du Bois, the
"wealth and luxury" of New York City "might be likened to Rome in its heyday or to Venice in the sixteenth century," but "the American scene is poor,
pallid, stark. The real American painter is a provincial who must manage
keeping his eyes shut before urbane splendours."[44]

   Filling Du Bois's prescription to a T, the canvas Hopper sent to Rehn for
a group show in October was *South Truro Church.* Jo's version of the same
motif, which she called *South Truro Church (Odor of Sanctity),* commanded no
such attention. Meanwhile Edward focused again on the urban scene, with a
large canvas showing a view from the street through a restaurant window,
which presented a voluptuous still life that Jo described: "window display of
grapefruit, gingerale bottles, raw meat (chop) on the plates and century plant
(or what not?) is very handsome—and Bee basket [a gift from Bee Blanchard]
with red apples and the pineapples I'd shopped all over to lay in for the occa-

sion."[45] It appears that her theater experience qualified her not only to act as exclusive model, but to play the set designer and decorator as well.

The resulting picture, *Tables for Ladies,* is another masterpiece of ironic wit. The voluptuous waitress bends enough to reveal a hint of cleavage, which is unambiguously echoed in the row of plump grapefruit and basket heaped with fruit, if anything stretching the sensual note to the point of parody. Just below the waitress's white arms, the two raw chops on the doily suggest a visual pun on the expression "lick your chops," implying "anticipate carnal pleasure." In the background, the figures are more somber and austere, including Hopper's favorite motif of the lonely couple. He alludes in his title to a social development of the 1920s, when some restaurants set aside tables for respectable "ladies," since women unescorted were subject to suspicion as prostitutes and were entirely excluded from some restaurants, while less proper establishments would encourage mingling. The figure of the buxom woman reveals Hopper's continuing interest in seventeenth-century Dutch painters such as Jan Steen and Frans Hals.[46] In Hals's *Merrymakers at Shrove Tide,* which Hopper knew well from the Metropolitan Museum, the display of meat suggests sexual appetite.

The "very blond, fine looking waitress all in white apron with bow in back" received the fictional name of "Olga" in Jo's record for this painting, which also referred to the cashier as "Anne Popebogales in black at desk" and "Max Scherer and wife Sadie at table,"[47] thus inaugurating what became the Hopper's custom of privately naming the characters in his compositions: the fantasies began when Jo either dressed up or stripped to pose for the female figures. Hopper painted the couple in virtually the same pose as that of the more glamorous pair in his illustration for the cover of *Hotel Management* for January 1925. Later, he lamented that *Tables for Ladies* lacked a certain "nobility," but he said he "wanted the vulgar color of cheap restaurants—for local color."[48] A like search for vulgar stereotypes may account for the invention of what sound like parodies of recent immigrant names.

While Jo collaborated productively with Edward on *Tables for Ladies,* she was not satisfied with their relationship. Her growing fury showed in her response to Edward's card for Christmas 1930, which she described as a "lovely mosaic of colored papers" representing St. George and the Dragon: "So then dragon met dragon & his had such lovely silver paws all spread out—the dragons canceled each other."[49] The other dragon was evidently her own persona as an angry woman. Edward also resorted again to caricatures to express his perception of their relationship, representing himself as a tall haloed saint dressed in a choir gown, and Jo as a tiny, pony-tailed little girl dressed in a full skirt who approaches in a catlike pose, attacking him with her claws: he belabored the point with captions, *Non-Anger man* and *Pro-Anger woman.*

Edward Hopper, Non-Anger man, Pro-Anger woman, *c. 1935. Charcoal and pencil on paper, 8½ × 5½" (21.6 × 14 cm.).*

Their squabbles soon began to disturb Edward's congenial relationship with his patrons, some of whom they saw socially. Jo had broken her ankle in a streetcar accident, and when Edward stayed to eat dinner with Anne and Sam Tucker one night and neglected to telephone her until quite late, she complained to Anne: "Of course being cooped up for so long doesn't improve one's disposition—I'm hoping not to see anybody I'm fond of until I've run several miles & got rid of lots of impatience." With Tucker she shared concerns that Edward would have kept close, confiding that he had "pitifully little surplus energy. Not nearly enough for his pictures," although she knew that he loathed "people talking about how little strength he has." She concluded that "It's so much better to let E.H. be the hermit he has always been & do his work with no complications. . . . He's managed to get thru the winter without a bad spell—for which I devoutly grateful. Cod liver pills seem to help & taking the greatest care not to take cold."[50] His chronic fatigue was later diagnosed as "low thyroid," but at this time they did not know the reason why he frequently felt so tired.

One of Jo's first excursions after her injury was to the memorial exhibition of Robert Henri that opened at the Metropolitan Museum on March 9,

1931. Her deep respect and wholehearted admiration for her former teacher compelled her to get up and out again. Edward felt less motivation, since he shared her high opinion of Henri as a teacher but did not consider him a great artist and continued to resent the fact that Henri had criticized his Paris pictures during the period when he was promoting Bellows and other former classmates. Asked about Henri years later, Hopper candidly admitted: "I didn't see much of him. I wasn't a success. I don't think he thought I had much future. He liked Bellows."[51]

Also in March, Hopper received another sign of approbation. The Baltimore Museum of Art in its first Pan-American Exhibition of Contemporary Paintings awarded him honorable mention and a prize of one hundred dollars for the painting *Night Windows.* George Luks, who was on the jury, told Frank Rehn that "Hopper was the best horse in the Rehn stable."[52]

Not only recognition but sales thrived in 1930, totaling $6,885 for the year. Success inspired larger, more ambitious canvases such as *Hotel Room,* which was delivered to Rehn on April 25, 1931.[53] Jo recalled posing for *Hotel Room* in the rear studio at Washington Square: "I posing in a pink shimmy shirt far from the fire place (in a bitter cold room) because E. needed the light on the surface of the bed & top of my head, or whatever—& I must endure."[54] Although Hopper had her model for the solitary woman seated on a bed reading a train timetable, the composition of *Hotel Room* relates to an illustration by Jean-Louis Forain in a 1908 issue of the magazine *Les Maîtres Humoristes* that Hopper brought back from Paris and treasured all his life. His 1927 article on Sloan referred to "the great French delineators of manners, Daumier, Gavarni, Toulouse-Lautrec, and Forain."[55]

In May, the Metropolitan Museum purchased *Tables for Ladies,* paying $4,500. The curator, Bryson Burroughs, was probably responding to growing pressure caused by the museum's director, Edward Robinson, who had recently rejected Gertrude Vanderbilt Whitney's offer to give her collection of American art to the Metropolitan, prompting her to establish a museum of her own. The Metropolitan now needed to acquire some American paintings, and paradoxically, Hopper's billing at the Modern Museum and the Whitney conferred the necessary cachet. Contributing yet again to Hopper's identification as "American," Guy du Bois now published a monograph on Hopper in the new American Artists Series founded by the Whitney.[56] In this, the first book devoted to Hopper, du Bois characterized his old friend as "the most inherently Anglo-Saxon painter of all times . . . with an accent upon the Anglo-Saxon's capacity for Puritanism":

> In America since the advent of Freud inspired demand for sensuality in life and art, Puritanism has been more generally derided than ever

and a good many painters led away from it into byways where they must, because of temperamental exigencies, be lost. Hopper in direct contradiction to these weaklings is so deaf to all faddish chatter that he can, without strain, with no stunting exercise of will, remain himself.[57]

Du Bois went on to argue that Hopper had "turned the Puritan in him into a purist, turned moral rigours into stylistic precisions."[58] Here, for the first time, and early in Hopper's career, a critic defined Hopper as a figure central to American cultural tradition. Du Bois was also the first to grasp that Hopper's precise structure served as a metaphor for his state of repression; his emotions were often present only by inversion. His paint surface was extremely spare, avoiding the sensuous play of brushstrokes through thick paint.

Du Bois's attention elicited more than polite gratitude. Although still characteristically laconic, Hopper's response picked up and underlined du Bois's major thrust: "I think you did a swell job on me as a Puritan in the Whitney Museum book."[59] Instead of the reservations that he usually expressed at having his identity defined, Hopper accepted the du Bois creation, at the same time using the adjective "swell," which, since it can mean "excellent," but also "blustering," or "pompous," allows a margin for Hopper's characteristic self-deprecation and diffidence about any baring of self. His denials, statements such as that he only wanted "to paint sunlight on the side of a house,"[60] were attempts to obscure how much more meaning was implicit in his pictures.

Du Bois's description of Hopper as "the most inherently Anglo-Saxon painter of all times" emphasized a self-consciousness about racial identity and ethnicity that was both inaccurate and exaggerated. In fact, Hopper's ancestry was not mostly Anglo-Saxon, which in an English-speaking nation was then viewed as more "American," but half Dutch and part French. Du Bois may have intended to strike a balance with earlier remarks in which he had stressed the artist's links to France, and to French art and culture. A part of the larger wave of cultural nationalism, the Whitney Museum, sponsor of the American Artists Series, was attempting to correct the significant hold that French art had on collectors and artists in the United States by focusing attention on "American" art. Just a few years later, Forbes Watson would describe the time "when Francomania drove the Americans before it like blind slaves."[61]

Still, du Bois played up the "Puritan" or restrained aspects of Hopper's character to underscore the American. He related a story that was intended to reveal the painter's fear of "the ridiculous": "He had gone to [a tailor] with the intention of ordering a gay suit of clothes, 'something cheerful and of fashionable cut.' To the tailor's 'conservative as usual, sir?' he had found himself replying 'Yes.' The gay suit has never been made to my knowledge. It would not suit him in any case."[62] This tale prompted Hopper to comment: "I am a little puzzled by the anecdote of the tailor. It must have happened some time when I wasn't looking, for I don't remember it very well. It has given me courage however in my dress, and I've just broken loose with a very brilliant black tie."[63]

Du Bois was generous even at this moment when Hopper's success was eclipsing his own. For his part, Hopper considerately assured du Bois of his continuing interest in his art: "I have been meaning to come see you for some time, but I was afraid I might break in on your work. I would like very much to see what you are painting." This must have been comforting to his friend, who still had to write and teach to supplement his income, even though he considered himself a painter. Hopper, for all his new fame, managed to maintain a respectful attitude toward his male peers, as long as they painted in a representational style.

Whatever the conflicts of the winter, Jo and Edward agreed that the expedition to Truro had been a success and they returned for their second tour in early June 1931. The landscape still inspired Edward; working outdoors, he painted *The Camel's Hump* and *New York, New Haven, and Hartford*, depicting the tracks of the railroad line that then ran out along the length of Cape Cod. (Some months later, when the latter painting was acquired by the Heron Art Institute in Indianapolis, he allowed: "If any serious objection arises regarding the title it can be easily changed. In that case let me know and I will send you another," revealing how often he considered a variety of titles before settling on one to use.[64]) He worked with facility in watercolor that summer, painting many localities: *Rich's Barn, Lombard's House, Dead Tree and Side of Lombard House, Roofs of the Cobb Barn, High Road, Captain Kelly's House, Freight Car at Truro, The Schuman House, The Lewis Barn, Railroad Warning, Scrub Pines, House on Dune Edge,* and *Wellfleet Road.* This flurry of watercolors testifies to Hopper's ambition and optimism in this period. Only close scrutiny of his choices might detect any hint of a melancholy side.

On the wave of his summer productivity, in autumn 1931 Hopper started his largest painting yet, *Barber Shop* (5 × 6½'), which emerged from the studio in December. He intensified his palette, placing a sharp yellow-green light on the banister and curtain rod and a green glow on the steps. *Barber Shop* was inspired by a 1915 John Sloan etching of the same subject and title, also depicting a female manicurist at work in this male enclave. Unlike Sloan, however, Hopper imagines the woman as psychologically remote, absorbed in reading, withdrawn into a private space of her own. This is the same kind of psychological distance evident in his caricature *Meal Time* (page 178), showing Jo reading and ignoring him as he begs for food and attention.

In 1931, Hopper sold thirty works for a total of $8,728. Further encouraged and uncharacteristically optimistic, he entered a very productive period. He began 1932 at work in his studio on *Room in Brooklyn,* a new canvas featuring a solitary female figure before a bay window, which "was largely improvised."[65] Explaining the title, Jo later admitted that Edward had "intended to have the Brooklyn Bridge in full view of the window in back. But when he got around to it, he thought that the Bridge would clutter up the picture. He loathes clutter, so left out the Bridge—(& more or less Brooklyn or maybe not.)"[66]

Hopper himself remarked: "In all the work I've done there's only one painting with flowers, *Room in Brooklyn,* a little vase on the table with flowers. . . . The so-called beauty is all there. You can't add anything to them of your own—yourself."[67] His comment reflected his disdain for the flowers that Jo liked to have around the house for her still lifes. He often reminded her that he considered flowers a subject for "lady painters." He did admit: "Manet added something. Of paint quality and pigment. . . . It's what you add that makes it beautiful. No, the unsophisticated think there's something inherent in it (the subject). A pond with lilies or something. There isn't of course."[68]

In February 1932, the Hoppers' domestic tensions made their way into Edward's work. Immediately after delivering *Room in Brooklyn* to Rehn, he shifted to an unusually bright and dissonant palette for a canvas that he called *Room in New York.* The mood of his home life reverberates in this nocturnal scene, which portrays a couple coexisting in the same space but tensely ignoring one another. The man seems preoccupied by his newspaper, as Edward was by his painting, while the woman, apparently bored, halfheartedly begins to strike a key on the piano, a gesture that will command his attention. Like this woman, Jo was feeling discouraged; since her marriage, her artistic endeavors had received much less recognition than formerly, and at the time, she still had no studio of her own. *Room in New York* is only the first of a number of paintings Edward produced depicting couples locked into states of alienation.

Hopper gave a completely external and circumstantial account of the genesis of this painting, which he finished in three weeks. He was able to work as quickly as he did because, he contended, he had had the conception firmly developed in his imagination. Avoiding a discussion of what appears in retrospect to be the obvious personal content of the work, he explained: "The idea had been in my mind a long time before I painted it. It was suggested by glimpses of lighted interiors seen as I walked along city streets at night, probably near the district where I live (Washington Square) although it's no particular street or house but is really a synthesis of many impressions."[69]

Years later, Burchfield wrote of Hopper: "The element of silence that seems to pervade every one of his major works . . . can almost be deadly, as in *Room in New York*."[70] Here the piano serves as a reminder of the lack of spoken communication. It is significant that Burchfield, who was well acquainted with the Hoppers' squabbles, commented on a work that alludes to their relationship. On a more universal level, this painting suggests the fragility of romance, pointing out how easily eros can yield to despair. Moreover, Hopper's conception of this couple reflects popular male-female stereotypes. The man reading his newspaper appears intellectual and pragmatic, while the woman, about to make music, seems more emotional and expressive.

When *Room in New York* was exhibited that autumn in the First Biennial at the new Whitney Museum, Royal Cortissoz singled out Hopper in the *Herald Tribune* as one of the artists who "turn their backs upon imaginative themes and hew close to the line of America in 1932":

> Witness the 'Room in New York' by Edward Hopper. The theme is pure banality and what the artist wreaks himself upon is simply the exact registration of fact. . . . That photographic spirit which Mr. Hopper embodies is all over the place, perceptible in the pictures of experienced painters like John Sloan, Kenneth Hayes Miller, and Walt Kuhn and dominant among scores of the younger men.[71]

For the conservative Cortissoz, Hopper's realism was too modern. He preferred painters who "drive at beauty," pointing to the American Impressionist Childe Hassam among others.

Although Cortissoz still considered Hopper inexperienced, the passage in his career from struggling to successful artist had already taken place. This had been underlined in March 1932, when the members of the National Academy of Design finally elected him an associate member. *The New York Times* reported that this "stronghold of conservatism, departed from its traditional paths last night by electing . . . an artist of the modern school, Edward Hopper."[72] While other now obscure painters such as Robert Brackman and Francis Scott Bradford accepted, Hopper proudly declined the honor, annoyed that the Academy had rejected his paintings in years past while electing his contemporary Bellows to early membership. By now, Hopper concurred with the commonly stated notion that the Academy was "hopelessly old-fashioned and out-of-date."[73] After the press repeatedly urged him to make a statement concerning his decision, the *Art Digest* reported his terse response under the caption "Hopper Will Not Break Silence": "I have decided that it would be better if I made no statement regarding my refusal to become an associate of the National Academy of Design."[74] In his review of the spring exhibition at the Academy, McBride reported that "there was a great deal of whispering at this year's varnishing," which he attributed to

> Mr. Hopper's dreadful act in refusing to be an academician after being elected to be one. Of course, if Mr. Hopper has some other way of making a living than exhibiting in the academy it is difficult to imagine what dire retribution can be visited upon him, especially as, in these days, publicity itself is capitalizable and Mr. Hopper got more publicity by refusing to be an academician than he could dare hope for by accepting. He has now become, like Gutzon Borglum and Jacob Epstein, a "newspaper personality" and henceforth will automatically figure in the news.[75]

The publicity included a feature by Frank Crowninshield in *Vanity Fair* for June 1932.[76] Louise Dahl-Wolfe came to photograph Edward alone and then with Jo in front of their prized folk painting, *Calvin Howe and His Two Sisters.* Dahl-Wolfe cleverly created a visual parallel between Jo and the girl in the back of the portrait, who also looks to the left. For the event, Edward dressed up in a three-piece suit and a dark tie with small polka dots. Jo, who wore two rings, a bracelet, a beaded necklace, and earrings, was clearly decked out for the occasion. Her dress, however, was rather prim, with a white collar and a dark bow. Dahl-Wolfe, who was more than a decade younger than her subjects, caught Jo's apprehensive gaze as she protectively held her husband's right shoulder and draped her hand over his left. Hopper appears pensive and self-absorbed.

Despite his success and the recent attention in the press, Hopper's negative outlook had begun to return. On June 17, he wrote to du Bois: "We're going again this summer to that awful Cape Cod. If you should be again at your daughter's in Orleans, let me know, and I will call for you in the car and show you what a really barren horrible place the Cape really is. You don't know the half of it."[77] By proclaiming the Cape "barren," Hopper, who had already painted most of what he found to be of interest there, anticipated what he feared would be his own condition that summer: he dreaded that he would run out of ideas for paintings as he returned for a third campaign. The car is now second nature, as he offers Guy a tour.

By late June 1932, the Hoppers were once again in Truro. Working outdoors again, they both painted oils of the same nearby site that Edward had rendered in watercolor the previous summer, calling it *Captain Kelly's House* after the original owner. A pencil sketch of the house by Jo also survives, but if she made a watercolor of the motif, it is lost. Jo recalled that while she was working on her picture up the hill, Edward was "at the foot of hill doing this same scene"; she remembered that on three different occasions he stopped work and "dashed up the hill to rescue my easel blown over in sand & bushes while it was painted."[78] As they worked together on their canvases in the late afternoon through "many changes of light til too dark to see," they found the house, which was then up for sale, "peaceful before dark."[79] Edward called his picture *Dauphinée House,* after the new owners, Henry and Constance Dauphinée, who became friends with the Hoppers.

Later that summer, Edward painted a canvas of another neighbor's home, *Mrs. Scott's House.* He captured it in the late afternoon with glorious light, surrounded by its landscape, set in the midst of the tall grasses changing colors at the end of September. Jo both sketched the site in pencil and painted it in watercolor. The Hoppers developed a deep appreciation of nature on the Cape. She later commented: "All Cape Cod grass is special. No weeds grow on Cape Cod, everything that comes out of the ground is beautiful. . . . The house, kept in good repair, is old, it is quite humble, as is the best of this Cape (to our point of view) & doubtlessly built by the people who fished or sailed on its seas, but it is no proud Captain's house."[80] Jo recalled that as Edward worked daily on his canvas, the man in the caboose at the end of the New York, New Haven, and Hartford train would always wave in a friendly fashion.

Hopper also continued to work in watercolor. *Back of Freight Station* is a view of the beach behind the Truro station with a freight car, shed, and "most seaworthy dory" visible.[81] In search of new subjects, he drove to Eastham, a neighboring Cape town beyond Wellfleet, where he produced *House at Eastham.* Jo, characteristically paying attention to people whom Edward ignored, noted that "6 well behaved children lived there & gave no trouble."[82] But usually he worked closer to home, painting *House Back of Dunes* on a gray day; *House with Dead Tree,* a view of the Cobbs' house; *Kelly Jenness House,* the home of another neighbor who came down for the summer from Boston; *Locust Trees,* a view of Frank Lombard's house, a neighbor who became a close friend; *Marshall's House,* a nearby home distinguished by the effect of sunlight falling on the red roof; and *Railroad Embankment,* another view of the Dauphinée house.

A further source of tension between the Hoppers surfaced that summer. Continuing to make Edward's patrons her confidants, Jo complained to Bee Blanchard about having to write "weekly reports to my good mother-in-law, who holds me to it with rigor."[83] Evidently Elizabeth Hopper preferred Jo's really descriptive letters to a few terse lines from Edward. In her own letters to Jo, Mrs. Hopper often enclosed recipes, probably anxious that her son would be well fed, perhaps aware of her daughter-in-law's ambivalence about cooking. Jo had once again assumed her summer routine, reporting to Bee that she had "made several cakes & biscuits" and was "generally hitched

Louise Dahl-Wolfe, Edward and Jo Hopper. *The couple are posed in front of their prized American folk painting,* Calvin Howe and His Two Sisters, *1932. Photograph © 1989 Center for Creative Photography, Arizona Board of Regents.*

up to the cook stove. One doesn't mind it so much here & forever washing out things & hanging them out on the hill."[84]

Fueling Jo's domestic ambivalence was her growing awareness that life with Edward had thwarted her career as a painter. She lamented that her one or two recent attempts were "such dismal failures," complaining to Bee:

> One simply can't divide oneself—the way E.H. can. He can do all the chores, look after the stove, feed it oil, drag water, wash sheets even & string beans & think nothing of it. Go right back to work. For the female of the species, it's a fatal thing for an artist to marry, her consciousness is too much disturbed. She can no longer live sufficiently within her self to produce. But it's hard to accept this.[85]

Jo maintained that worry about Edward disrupted her ability to concentrate on her work. And he was constantly asking, " 'How about a little something to eat?' Do you wonder that I scratch & bite?"[86]

Edward loved the isolation of Truro, while Jo preferred company. When his good friend du Bois took him up on his promise to drive to Orleans, and even recommended some local subjects for Edward to paint, he reneged. Jo concluded that Edward "hates to visit," despite his difficulty in finding "enough to paint that he hasn't already done."[87] Jo said that they had "come back to swim in mild sea waters & to paint if E.H. could, then will try Vermont."[88] But, she concluded, Edward "seems hard to move. We're so settled here. We won't go yet for a while, too much work to pull up stakes."[89] Ultimately, painting in Vermont was postponed indefinitely. In his melancholy, Hopper preferred to contend with boredom rather than adjust to new surroundings.

July 22, 1932, was Edward's fiftieth birthday. To Jo, he looked like a twenty-eight-year-old blue-eyed Viking. Even in the warm summer weather, he insisted that she wear her long hair down and flowing.[90] Clearly physical attraction had survived the battles. She sought to provide comfort as he faced the half-century mark, a milestone that actually bothered her much more than him. Years later Jo recalled that she had arranged to give him "prizes every half hour for consolation: night shirts from Sears Roebuck, New Yorker subscription, home made big chocolate layer cake rushed while E. down at Gas station, P.O., local errands, Brady's photographs of the Civil War, Safari coat from Abercrombie, their electric lantern, etc."[91] The passage of time may have caused her to confuse several birthdays, however, for she recorded her gift of the Brady photographs in a diary entry for 1936.[92]

Jo imagined that she would distract Edward from depression about aging. In reality, she projected her own inability to accept her age, her own fiftieth birthday just eight months off. To a man with growing success, age mattered little, while the woman in his shadow might fear seeming no longer a "cute young thing," but only complex and troublesome. Jo had written Marion suggesting that what Edward would want from his mother was an appreciative letter telling him what a good son he was, pointing out that he did not drink, gamble, or get put in jail for radical politics like others who broke their mothers' hearts.[93] Her initiative suggests that Edward, who so often had tried to please his mother, suffered from too little praise. Jo understood and empathized with his need to feel worthy.

Returning to New York on October 5, Edward rapidly painted *City Roofs,* a view from the rooftop of his studio; partially visible on the back right side of the canvas is the pale yellow skyscraper that had recently been built at One Fifth Avenue. (He had painted a similar view in watercolor, *My Roof,* in 1928.) Once again, Hopper's attitude toward the skyscraper is clearly negative; here it takes up space and air and blocks the view and the light, recalling what Edmund Wilson referred to in 1927 as "The Crushing of Washington Square":

> Returning to New York at the end of the summer, one was shocked to find Washington Square completely transformed since the spring. . . . In the short months of summer, there have been erected on lower Fifth Avenue two monstrous apartment houses—one just south of the Brevoort Hotel and the other between Tenth and Eleventh Streets. They loom over the Village like mountains, and they have suddenly changed its proportions. Their effect is to crush, in Washington Arch and in the row of red façades behind it, whatever these had formerly kept of chaste elegance and decorous pride. The whole Village seems now merely a base for these cubic apartment buildings.[94]

Hopper's painting makes visual Wilson's complaint that "it is impossible to get away from these huge coarse and swollen mounds—blunt, clumsy, bleaching the sunlight with their dismal pale yellow sides."[95] He delivered the new canvas to the gallery on October 12.

With the confidence engendered by sales and recognition, Hopper decided to move into a larger space that comprised both the front studio overlooking Washington Square Park and a small adjacent room, which became his and Jo's bedroom. (Their bathroom remained unchanged, in the public hall; until the spring of 1941, they shared it with neighbors on the same floor.[96]) Some years later, Jo recalled this momentous move down the hall:

> The place had all been done over in fresh white walls & fresh shellac floors & he'd had a mover bring the etching press in, then we had

lugged in the best pieces—old mahogany table & rush bottom chairs & very tall chest, etc., but the elec. not on yet. I remember having been in bath room & not finding him in bed when came back—so looked in front & there he was in his bath robe gloating in the dimness of the park lights outside over the fine effect of the new studio before the necessary junk for living should arrive with us next day. It did look so New England & that press with the long spokes of its wheel so fine against the wall & the fireplace mantel with his great uncle's tall clock & the candle sticks—so serene, uncluttered. But alas—the canvas rack had to come & all the rest of it.[97]

Hopper immediately started to paint his extraordinary new view. He began *November, Washington Square* but, fearful of ruining his composition, did not finish the picture, which lacked only a sky, until 1959. The starkness of bare tree branches in late autumn appealed to the morbid streak in his sensibility as much as the dead trees that he often found so compelling. His canvas depicts the south side of the square with the Judson Memorial Church notable among the "fresh arty grays and pinks" that Wilson had deplored as replacing "the sooty peeling fronts," yet Hopper managed to imbue the scene with something of the "romance and mystery" that Wilson believed lost.[98]

The expansion of their space was followed by another momentous development. In June 1933 Jo casually began to keep diaries. At first she merely recorded the details of summer travels and the most mundane particulars of their daily lives; gradually personal feelings began to enter. Sometimes she noted in detail what Edward said, to her or to others. If she had previously kept journals, they have not come to light. Just what motivated her to begin at this point remains obscure. Perhaps the prospect of Edward's first retrospective, scheduled for the fall at the Museum of Modern Art, stirred in her a sense that they were making history together.

In 1933, as the time approached for a summer campaign, the Hoppers were uncertain. The more ample and attractive studio in New York and an unexpected inheritance from Jo's uncle Harry Woolsonwood made them think of purchasing a permanent summer home, which had to be in a place that appealed to Edward's eye and supplied subjects to paint. The resulting quest filled the diaries with evidence of false starts and shifting hopes.

On one June day they managed to get as far as Charlestown, New Hampshire, where they spent their first night out as guests of Katherine Budd, meeting her new husband, William H. Proctor. The next day, they pushed farther north than ever before, reaching Quebec City, where they stayed for two nights.[99] "We're crazy about Quebec but E.H. doesn't want to paint it," wrote Jo to Katherine, "so we're moving on tomorrow."[100] Jo hoped the Proctors would come to New York to see Edward's retrospective in the fall. William would like Edward's work: "No fear Mr. P. won't fancy it. There is no flapdoodle about either of them, praise be!" She urged Mrs. Proctor to tell her husband: "The art of E. Hopper is so fundamental in its character, it's like Abr. Lincoln or G. Washington—for best American tradition. There is honesty, simplicity, proud appreciation of sound construction, noble mouldings, the kind of land its built on. Reality seen clearly & given its dignity. A God fearing quality."[101]

Pressing north along the St. Lawrence River, Edward found nothing to like and made no paintings, so they quickly pulled back toward known scenes, liking a camp on a lake,[102] but making for Portland and Two Lights, where they found their old Coast Guard friends, but no new inspiration, then hastening on to Gloucester, which for a change put Edward off; they made a quick detour to Magnolia, Massachusetts, to see the Rehns, then a stopover in Boston, where they set about renting their usual cottage on the Cape. This they did with difficulty because their landlord, A. B. Cobb, had died in January. They spent the night with a Cape neighbor, Mrs. Kelly Jenness, in suburban Chestnut Hill, and the next day she took them to Harvard's Fogg Art Museum before they went on to Cape Cod.

Though fond of their primitive rental cottage, they were not pleased with that summer's excessive rain, which often drenched their inside walls, as the new diary recorded: "Our bedroom a little boat we had to keep bailing out. When we got back [from a dinner with Dorothy and Davenport West in Harwichport] it was a lake. Well—decided we couldn't do that again."[103] (The Hoppers knew the Wests from New York, where Davenport was a physician.)

The poor weather let Hopper finish only three watercolors: *Capron House* (the home of a summer colonist down Prince Valley way), *Cottages at Wellfleet,* and *Cold Storage Plant* (a view of a fish-processing plant in North Truro), and one canvas depicting *Ryder's House* (located not far from Cobb's cottage). Some twenty-three years later, Hopper said of this latter painting: "It was done directly from nature," meaning he painted it outdoors.[104] Jo commented: "We are not sure this Ryder House still stands in its acres of deep sand—probably occupied briefly each year by people who had inherited it from some more or less remote ancestor who built it—in the Southern end of South Truro."[105] She proudly told how "some painter coming into the gallery where it was being shown said, 'I can hear the silence.' " She further noted: "This would have to be a day of deep calm, because the sea is very near—beyond a rim of dunes. . . . Edward got stuck in that deep sand surrounding Ryder House & had to be dug out."[106]

The very rainy season convinced the Hoppers that their rented shelter in Truro was inadequate. Bird Cage Cottage they named it, because rain, wind, and animals entered with equal freedom. The cottage was "hanging on the side of a hill that let in rain driven from any direction & field mice that wanted to be adopted & share our meals—especially sweet corn & peaches."[107] Furthermore, the bad weather had prevented Edward from painting outdoors as much as he had hoped and created a more urgent need for an indoor summer studio. They decided to buy land in Truro on which they could build their own home with space enough to paint indoors.

The rationale for such a major investment in the midst of the Depression was the potential benefit for Edward's work, so the new diary explained: "Edward said if he had a study he thought he could make work in doors—compose. Health better on Cape Cod than any where else. We had covered the ground of all known alternatives on way down—Quebec—Malbaie, 2 Lights, Gloucester—None of them pleased E.H.—likes S. Truro better—so that settled."[108] On October 1, 1933, the Hoppers bought the site for their house, with a thousand feet of shoreline along the bay, from the son of L. D. Baker, the founder of the United Fruit Company, who had invested heavily in property on the Cape. They went ahead with the purchase even though at the time of their purchase, Rehn had registered no sales at all, after the run of bumper years.

FIRST RETROSPECTIVE AND THE TRURO HOUSE: 1933–1935

THAT THE CONSERVATIVE Hoppers had the courage, as the Great Depression deepened, to begin building a house must owe something to the vote of confidence for Edward's work by the director of the Museum of Modern Art, Alfred H. Barr, Jr. A champion of modernist abstraction, he had nonetheless decided to organize Hopper's first retrospective for the fall of 1933. Hopper was only the third American artist to receive this honor, after Max Weber and Maurice Sterne. Preparing for the show and dealing with its psychological aftermath only compounded the effect of rain on Cape Cod in reducing Hopper's output for the year.

During the rainy summer, Hopper and Barr corresponded about the details of the exhibition and its catalogue. In answer to a letter from Barr, Hopper confirmed that he would like to have oils, watercolors, and etchings in the show, explaining: "I don't care so much for my drawings."[1] He inquired which of the museum's rooms would be assigned to his show and modestly agreed "to write something of a general character for the catalog, if I can get together something that shows enough penetration to interest people."[2]

When Barr requested a photograph of Hopper working on a picture, Jo was elected to dissuade him from featuring Edward "appearing in the Sunday supplements posed like a monkey before his easel. He's persistently seasick at the thought & how he'd be eternally jeered at by every one who knows him. He'd go hide his head forevermore—& he's hermit enough as it is. You can't ask him to be all that vulgar!"[3]

When it came time for the installation, Barr initially left the sensitive task to Hopper and Frank Rehn, but when they became frustrated, he stepped in and finally arranged the work to their satisfaction.[4] (A separate room was devoted to the etchings and the watercolor character sketches from Paris.[5]) The retrospective, which was seen from November 1 through December 7, 1933, was not an unblemished success, for modernist critics took it as a cause for debate. In anticipation of the show, the *Art Digest* pontificated baldly: "To many, Edward Hopper in art, like Sinclair Lewis in letters, conjures up the thought of Main Street, but unlike the author, the artist portrays the American landscape and architecture without satire."[6]

More acutely, in the *Times* Edward Alden Jewell called the retrospective a "beautiful exhibition beautifully presented" and Hopper "one of America's most vital, original and accomplished artists," characterizing the work as "imaginatively transfigured emotional experiences."[7] The *Herald Tribune* praised the artist for following "his own impulses," for his "draftsmanship," and his "sincerity," and declared: "In the illumination of his subjects Mr. Hopper uses a touch giving him a place apart and it is, moreover, absolutely true and credible. He deserves this exhibition if only for the originality in the bare quietude of his work."[8]

None dissented more vehemently than Ralph Pearson, the critic, educator, and painter, who insisted that Hopper's work was "the reverse of that which characterized the modern movement" because modernism "definitely breaks with all transferring of actual appearance from nature to the picture."[9] Pearson objected to Hopper's statement in the catalogue: "My aim in painting has always been the most exact transcription possible of my most intimate impression of nature. . . . The trend in some of the contemporary movements in art, but by no means all, seems to deny this ideal and to me appears to lead to a purely decorative conception of painting."[10] Although Hopper had refused to accept election to the National Academy, Pearson argued that he was "definitely outside the modern school" and was "definitely within the academic."[11]

The gusto of Pearson's attack may owe something to a grudge as old as 1923, when his work was overshadowed by attention and praise directed to Hopper. A critic reviewing a show of drawings and prints at the National Academy of Design that year mentioned both Pearson and Hopper as "contributors of note," but hailed Hopper as "one of the most impressive of the younger men."[12] Worse still, at the National Arts Club, a reviewer merely mentioned Pearson while singling out Hopper's etching *Evening Wind* as an example of "exceedingly good figure work," commenting "this is a nude by a window with a blowing curtain by Edward Hopper which would establish him, if he were not already rapidly acquiring fame, as one of the best of the younger men."[13]

Hopper's art and Barr's decision to show it were defended by Barr himself, as well as by Lewis Mumford, Horace Gregory, Helen Appleton Read, and others. Barr accused Pearson of trying "to transform a popular and temporary implication of the word modern into an academic and comparatively permanent label."[14] "To like the Cubists now is the expression of a sound conservative taste," quipped Mumford, claiming, "This is just the little joke that one generation plays upon another."[15]

"Racial Quality of Hopper Pictures at Modern . . . American Scene Predominating Theme," declared the *Brooklyn Daily Eagle* headline, over Read's account of her "exhilarating experience" in coming across what she had written ten years earlier about the Brooklyn Museum show that launched Hopper's rise: "The 'seeing eye,' the quality . . . which stirred me in 1923 is again what gives his work its personality and distinction."[16] In support she quoted Hopper's own essay on Burchfield and his quote from Emerson, going on to say that "Edward Hopper's rise to fame, and it has been a rapid one, since in the ten years he has been before the public he has come to be one of the most discussed figures in American art, is partially to be explained by the fact that he has come in on the rising tide of nationalism." Hopper satisfied, she went on to say, "requirements of what was meant by racial quality in American art. Puritan austerity and nothing in excess, an emotional response to his native environment and above all independence of thought and spirit."

When Mumford reviewed the retrospective for *The New Yorker,* he described Hopper as "a fine and capable artist whom one may characterize fairly accurately, and certainly without disparagement, as a second Winslow Homer." As Mumford saw it, Hopper had "caught one phase of America, its loneliness and its visual exhilaration: the loneliness of even occupied houses."[17] Although he found Hopper "a good painter," Mumford could not resist contrasting him with John Marin, who was showing concurrently at An American Place, the gallery of Alfred Stieglitz, and who was, in Mumford's opinion, "a great protean spirit who stands on the level of the best of his contemporaries in any country."[18]

Henry McBride, less enthusiastic about Hopper's painting than he had been about the etching a decade earlier, preferred "the brilliant modernists." He pronounced the work much too static for his taste, but suggested that "with ever so little an effort," Hopper could "do pictures worthy of a machine age."[19] Just where the *Art Digest* stumbled, McBride correctly saw Hopper's art as "faintly tinged with satire," noting, "It developed about the time that all of our young writers and intellectuals discovered that we were far enough away from the 'Gay Nineties' to safely laugh at them."[20] But McBride failed to grasp Hopper's attachment to the values of the past and his alienation from modern urban life.

Hopper confided in Barr that he dismissed McBride's criticism: "I did not convince McBride as you said I might perhaps. But neither has he convinced me."[21] Generally pleased with the show and catalogue, he wrote to the director: "Until now I have not had the opportunity of telling you, how much I liked your estimate of my work in the catalogue, and I am also much pleased with the looks of the whole book."[22] Hopper proudly called Barr's attention to Forbes Watson's recent piece on him: "Perhaps you remember that I told you that Watson was to write about me for the *Brooklyn Eagle Magazine* section. I am enclosing his article, believing it will interest you."[23] Watson and Hopper were well enough acquainted that the critic offered a rather personal view of the artist by comparing him to some of the contemporary artists in his circle:

> Hopper had none of the back-patting gifts of Bellows, none of that singing, ball-playing geniality which always enabled Bellows to be one of the boys in a big way. He never followed Kent to the North or the South Pole. He never made a noise like a two-fisted Luks nor tore his hair over the wrongs committed against Emma Goldman like a John Sloan. He has none of the hypnotic charm of a Henri who could stir his classes into a state of idolatry. Tall, awkward, slower than the renowned molasses, utterly devoid of all the facile graces, his main power to get on, aside from his iron faith and ability, might be said to be his complete lack of all get-on attributes.[24]

Watson also praised Hopper, whom he clearly respected:

> Personally the charm of Hopper lies hidden in his intelligence and in his palpably awkward honesty. It is not merely that he cannot lie but that he could not conceive of any reason for lying, such for instance as the saving of a fellow mortal's feelings. He is uncouthly honest—a great handicap in political circles, and a great asset when the barriers of silence and awkwardness are broken down. People who know Hopper have not the slightest doubt of his sincerity. Only a fool would have. His personal admirers may be few but they are intensely loyal.[25]

Watson also mentioned the sincere admiration Hopper received from his collector friend Edward Root, and from his colleague Charles Burchfield, citing a tale about the latter: "Burchfield, I am told, is never as happy in New York as when he and Hopper stroll through the city streets talking away as noisily as two mutes."[26]

In January of 1934 the retrospective traveled to the Arts Club of Chicago, where it was shown at the same time as a show of the French painter Georges Rouault. Local Chicago critics responded favorably to Hopper. Eleanor Jewett praised his "haunting melancholy beauty," while C. J. Bulliet called him "the poet in paint of loneliness," and applauded his "subtlety of psychology."[27]

It was Jo who had dealt with the complexities of loans, catalogue text, insurance, mats, lighting, and installation. Without Edward's knowledge, she requested of Alice F. Roullier of the Arts Club that he be allowed to check any foreword to the exhibition catalogue for inaccuracies, pointing out "there has been a lot of misunderstanding in his publicity here. Don't believe one word of it, unless corrected by him for you. Please don't reprint the Life from Modern Museum catalogue in yours. It doesn't sound one bit like E. Hopper to anyone who knows him."[28] Jo then gave a lengthy description of the ideal lighting for Hopper's work, insisting: "His gorgeous wind swept blue skies turn grey on you under yellow electric bulbs. Please don't be too stubborn to use blue bulbs for blue skies."[29] She justified her concerns somewhat defensively: "I do hope you won't resent my talking about these pictures like young children, telling about their diet, etc. But I honestly do feel that way about them."[30]

Once again, when Hopper found out what Jo had written on behalf of his presentation, he professed horror, writing at once to retract:

> I have just learned that Mrs. Hopper has written to you regarding the inclusion into the catalogue, which you are to publish for my exhibition, of the first or biographical part of Mr. Barr's foreword. There has been some difference of opinion between Mrs. Hopper and myself in regard to this. I wish that you would disregard what she has written to you about it. Mr. Barr's article seems adequate to me and I should like to have it included, if that has been your intention.[31]

He did add that he would like to approve any abbreviation of Barr's essay. For her part, Jo felt that when Edward wrote letters, he was so formal that "one doesn't get anything out of it that means anything much. A strictly formal answer to me is worth just as much as a grunt however politely formal."[32] Therefore, she appointed herself Hopper's unofficial secretary. Even when he wrote letters, she sometimes added or attached her own comments. Edward did not enjoy writing letters and usually relinquished the task.

Barr had given Hopper only a brief moment in his office to read and approve the biographical essay and chronology, and the artist, not wanting to offend, acquiesced although, in fact, both he and Jo saw certain inaccuracies, particularly the incorrect suggestions that Hopper's first etchings were "made under direction of Martin Lewis," that he "fell into the life of a recluse" as a result of a lack of recognition during the 1910s, and that he had given up painting for "pot boiling illustration" during this period.[33] Years later, Hopper asserted that the essay had been inaccurate: "The idea that I gave up painting is completely wrong. I painted in Gloucester and Ogunquit. I improvised pictures in the studio. Nor did I withdraw from the art world— whatever the hell that is."[34]

Although "one of the most discussed figures in American art" even before the retrospective, Hopper sold only one painting in 1933: *Night Windows* on December 20 for fifteen hundred dollars to John Hay Whitney. The retrospective and its mixed reviews generated stress. His always self-critical nature began to erode the confidence that had been building for a decade. Preparing and viewing the exhibition made it more difficult to paint. Reviewing his work from the past twenty-seven years triggered self-assessment and opened the door to sweeping judgments. After the show closed, he tried going back to finish *Cape Cod Sunset,* begun the previous summer, when the infamous weather slowed him down. Now working in the studio, his mind divided, he produced a weak result, which went to the gallery on January 22, 1934, but never sold.

Still preoccupied with rethinking his art, in late January or early February, he took the unusual step of painting a canvas based on a watercolor, *Prospect Street, Gloucester,* of 1928, a view looking down toward the towers of the Portuguese Church, Our Lady of Good Voyage. He called the oil *Sun on Prospect Street,* but he was never truly satisfied with it. The painting lacks the mood or psychological intensity of his most gripping work.

In late February 1934, Hopper took another unusual tack, resorting to a different past, to produce *Dawn before Gettysburg,* a small canvas that was the first of the only two paintings he ever made about specific historical moments. He had long admired Mathew Brady's Civil War photographs (which he knew even before receiving a book of them from Jo), as well as the Civil War pictures and illustrations of Winslow Homer, whose work he cited for its "simple visual honesty."[35] Also, he and Jo had paid their memorable visit to Gettysburg only five years before. Now he painted the surviving farmhouse that had served as the Union Army's headquarters.

Clearly in need of diversion, Hopper continued to attend the theater. With Jo he saw Walter Huston and Fay Bainter in *Dodsworth,* adapted by Sidney Howard from the 1929 novel by Sinclair Lewis, to whom Hopper would continue to be compared. The story, a sympathetic portrayal of a retired American automobile manufacturer who travels with his faithless and impetuous wife to Europe, did not appeal to Edward. Jo noted that he considered the play "most superficial & that it is about time someone wrote about Americans with more penetration of character—not everything always so from the exterior."[36] Hopper never liked Lewis, even though satire of American society might have been expected to offer a common ground.

Further distraction came from the need to design the new house. Edward took the planning in hand. After celebrating the seventy-ninth birthday of Edward's mother on April 3, they drove to New City and dropped in on the artist Henry Varnum Poor to see the house he had designed and built, which Jo vetted: "Spacious, colorful, delightfully whimsical."[37]

In the cold, raw weather of early spring, Hopper took the ferry to Weehawken, New Jersey, to look at some rather ordinary houses: "Mr. Hopper has just gone over to New Jersey—across the ferry—to gaze at the East Wind in Hoboken where he has found a most bumptious suburban affair whose one merrit is its solidity. E. Hopper can look after that factor," Jo affirmed, even as she lamented: "He has very little strength to drag himself about in the cold & damp. It's a pity he couldn't take some interest in more gracious material nearer home. He goes to make notes but will paint in the studio—fortunately—with that damp East wind blowing about."[38]

Jo failed to see the attraction that Weehawken held for Hopper, yet he focused on houses built along the water thinking toward the construction of his own design overlooking Cape Cod Bay. For his painting, he made eight preparatory sketches and extensive notations about color, probably hoping that he would not to have to return to the scene as often as he usually did. After one last trip to the site on April 12, he delivered *East Wind over Weehawken* to Rehn on April 17.[39] He was now free to focus on his own house.

After Edward had drawn plans and made a model, he and Jo solicited bids. He became so discouraged by the high prices that he spoke about giving up and going to New Mexico.[40] A letter from their future neighbor, Harriet Jenness, encouraged them to persevere. In the end they engaged a Boston contractor, Maurice Dunlavy, who went down to Truro to start work in May 1934. The Hoppers arranged to stay in the empty Jenness house while construction was going on. For this privilege, Hopper painted a watercolor of the house, which had already been one of his subjects.

On May 4, the Hoppers closed the New York studio and went to Nyack for the car, not without an acute outbreak of packing nerves, punctually registered in the diary: "E. feeling watched—All his symptoms to the fore—All negation & prohibition, I driven to scratch & bite, he hinders one so, his insistent driving in of the spurs, every time I glanced at my list."[41] Still, she was relieved that the "tension relaxed" as they departed and noted that Edward "remembered—after all our shoutings & yells—our usual rite of saying goodbye to our happy home for the summer."[42] When they arrived, she observed: "The Cape looks so brilliant. E. sais it is because the shadows aren't dark, like Maine. Shadows light, because of greater density of atmosphere. The brilliant light is diffused. A great deal of reflected light keeps shadows light."[43] Spring was just coming to the Cape, but as they went farther along toward Truro, she noted: "This end spring still sleeping. I always did want to see how the barberry looked in winter—so green & tough looking."[44]

The trip had been good for Edward, who had "a bad spell the week before," Jo wrote Bee Blanchard, but "picked up surprisingly the minute the car left our door."[45] After a week in the Jenness place in Truro, they drove to Boston and spent two days with the Jennesses in suburban Chestnut Hill, observing with approval some of the houses built by their contractor: "chaste looking—like E.H.'s water colors—that is like the style of his water colors."[46]

With work on the house progressing, the Hoppers felt free to drive to visit Georgie and Ambrose Webster in Provincetown. Webster had helped build the reputation of the local art colony and was still running the school where years earlier Jo had studied.[47] As year-round residents, the Websters offered advice on building and on shopping for used furniture.

The new house was tailored to Edward's needs: a large high-ceilinged studio with a north wall penetrated by a huge thirty-six-paned window, also a small bedroom, kitchen, bathroom, cellar, and an open attic landing. The studio contained a red brick chimney, the only note of color in a house where all the rooms were painted white except for light gray in the bedroom and gray on the floors. The exterior shingles were painted white, making the rather bare unadorned structure look almost "Bauhaus modern" in its simplicity. Eventually an odd assortment of comfortable functional furnishings accumulated, such as a chaise longue in the studio and a group of homey antiques picked up here and there for bargain prices. On the bedroom bureau they kept a reproduction of a Degas nude. Edward's large homemade easel completed the clutter.

A door to the west and windows in the studio and the bedroom looked out on the bay. The land dropped off so dramatically that when one was seated, it looked as if one might step directly from the house into the water. The effect was like being on a ship at sea, a feeling Edward loved, since his boyhood dream had been a career as a naval architect.

The house shared one important feature with the larger studio in New York to which he had moved in 1932. In both, Hopper treasured a sense of openness—of openness just outside, that he could look out on, no matter how small his own interior space might be. This was the kind of view he had as a boy in the house at Nyack with its unobstructed command of the river down the hill. His Manhattan studio rose seventy-four steps above Washington Square, and the house on the Cape overlooks the bay from an elevation of seventy feet, commanding a panoramic view across the water to Provincetown.

The afternoon light is extraordinary; the sun setting over the bay is glorious, as Jo once wrote, describing how the "immense ball of flame, big as a beach umbrella . . . looked like a fire on the horizon."[48] No wonder Hopper declined to paint any more sunsets on Cape Cod. No painting could compare with the splendor of his view. He once explained that despite "people around here telling me about beautiful sunsets," he refused to paint them, there being nothing he could add.[49]

Construction brought the inevitable aggravation, complicated in this case by the distance to any missing supplies. Jo feared their little home might look too conventional, suburban. Edward humored her with a caricature, *The HOUSE THAT JO BUILT,* representing her ideal house "standing on its chimney supported by springs & me watering flower beds on the roof & a cat looking to see how it could hop off & a bird house fastened on too & a young bird being fed."[50] She admitted: "There sure is a perversity in me—it isn't as E. said I can't abide by any convenience—it's that I can't abide things not having some individual flavor—some play of wit."[51] She tried to explain her point of view to Bee, pointing out that they would even have an enclosed ironing board:

> Not my idea of a house. This is E. Hopper's house. His, and the dear dead uncle whose money is buying it. My uncle would never stand for anything but the (conventional) best—best plumber, best tailor, best hotel etc. It's rather interesting that his preferences are working themselves out in this little house—No funny business for him—no adorable 3 legged table propped up on box cover dexterously disguised. Nor for E. Hopper either. Tables around here are to have 4 whole legs. Personally I like the reclaimed horse car—or house made out of ex-moving van. Something with a smack of adventure about it.[52]

Jo reflected on her desire for the unusual: "Suppose it comes from having been fetched up on made overs—but such successful made overs—always a little better than other children got at Bests."[53] This certainly explains her lifetime penchant for remodeling her clothes. Some of the endless hours she spent sewing, ripping, and ironing might well have been devoted to painting.

Edward Hopper, The HOUSE THAT JO BUILT, *1934. Pencil on paper, 5⅞ × 8½″ (14.9 × 21.6 cm.).*

But Jo could not bear to throw out a single garment. Indeed, those she could no longer wear she made into rag rugs for the new house or the studio, a craft that she had learned from her mother. She wrote to Bee:

> I'm going to do all the rugs for the little house—so I mortgaging the clothes right off the backs of all my friends—even acquaintances. So please don't give Salvation army any wool jersey of brilliant hue— they'll only clean stoves with it—& fondly I remember a red jersey sport dress that may some day grow too short for present modes. Would you remember me & rugs. I do so sadly need good red.[54]

Edward was mechanically inclined and Jo was very pleased and proud that he was so handy at fixing things around the house. They took delight in discovering resident fauna, including a two-foot-long snake and some mice, which awakened the nurturing instincts Jo once lavished on her cat: she fed them milk. Still, the details of construction provoked conflict. Jo found the detached garage at the bottom of the hill "too tall & important . . . like another house sitting there." Her plan to drag the bathroom fixtures around to see how they might be placed best was sidetracked by the plumber, Horace Snow, who just went ahead and installed them, never seeking advice.

In the end Jo grew discouraged, feeling that Edward showed "determined opposition to every breath I draw . . . I live in the constant expectation of his prohibition," and admitting to "the rage this engenders in me," which she justified: "He complains of my rages as he goes about invoking them. And he objects to being called a sadist."[55] Her report reveals the same kind of conflict that drove and infected their marriage and unequal careers. The tensions that projected their drama into the automobile, reenacting its mythology, now were flowing into the spaces, functions, customs, and expectations of the house. Like the car, the house was meant to serve Edward's art. The studio was the main thing. It was a purpose unlikely to make the house a home.

Her consciousness of frustration was heightened by the approach of their tenth wedding anniversary on July 9, 1934. To Bee, Jo wrote that she had given up the idea of a party because the new house would not be ready.[56] The occasion went uncelebrated but not ignored. Edward drew a sheet of caricatures of four who might have been present at the party that never took place: Jo, Harriet Jenness, Maurice Dunlavy, and Bee. He depicted Jo rather minimally, representing only her hair, eyes, earrings, collar, cuffs, hands, ankles, and feet. He drew Mrs. Jenness wearing a large hat that covered her face and a bathing suit that revealed shapeless drooping breasts. Dunlavy, holding a

Edward Hopper, Caricatures of Jo, Harriet Jenness, Maurice Dunlavy, and Bee Blanchard, *1934. Pencil on paper.*

ruler for measuring right angles, looked skinny and earnest. And for the wealthy patron, Bee Blanchard, he created a stout but highly fashionable fig- ure topped by a hat worn at a rakish angle above a featureless face.

Two days after the anniversary, the house was ready to be occupied. There was still plenty to do, cleaning up after the builders and getting orga- nized, and Edward had not been able to paint since April. Yet his first thought was to get in the car and drive to Nyack to fetch his mother and sis- ter for a visit. Jo blew up: "I do hope it can be accomplished without blood shed."[57] She was horrified at the prospect of setting up beds in the studio or sleeping on the attic floor with Edward while their guests occupied the only bedroom. Above all, what set her off was the idea of feeding four. Cooking was complicated by the lack of electricity or refrigeration and she knew bet- ter than to expect help in the kitchen: her mother-in-law was already using a wheelchair and Marion was never much of a cook.[58] She also knew her own temper: "After I've stayed over the kitchen stove or the sink for about two days, I'm ready to heave a tomahawk."[59]

The tempest was still raging five days after they moved in, when they were invited out for a belated anniversary lunch in Provincetown by Sam and Anne Tucker, who drove up with their family from Chatham. Anne encour- aged Jo to express her anger at the in-laws' prospective visit; as a result, Jo, shaken by her own show of emotion, soon found herself writing Anne:

> Ed is the very center of my universe. . . . If I'm on the point of being very happy, he sees to it that I'm not. If I'm happy ever and not too exhausted, I might want to paint. . . . He's better fed, more blithe- somely fed during the infrequent periods when I do paint. But, it riles him. . . . It's so necessary that he should be allowed to retain a mood while a picture is in process—not be forever disturbed and the mood dispersed. . . . I never scratch and bite when there is a picture coming and I feed him patiently.[60]

She found the proposed visit all the more untimely, since Edward too was un- able to paint: he "has so little vitality to waste."

Painting was the root issue, not only his but hers. The mutuality escaped Anne, who invited Jo to escape the threatened visit by coming to stay with her, but focused on Edward's work, sending Jo's letter to Bee with a note that the Hoppers "had scrapped & it was the worst I've ever seen, . . . they are thrown too much together, & get on one another's nerves. . . . He's not painted a stitch, only the cellar walls."

Jo took the bull by the horns, in a style that was pungent even for her, writing Edward's sister that the little house was "ideal for 2 married. Hell for any more—& both tired to death with both labor & strain. So on the top of everything else—he started that. Our lovely little nest turned boarding house for me to cook for."[61] With only slightly more diplomacy, she also suggested that the visit would be inopportune, because Edward was not doing his best work and needed to concentrate after the distraction of the retrospective the previous autumn; she even evoked the threat to his career of other painters trooping to South Truro from Provincetown in order to paint Edward's hills and the meeting house—his church, as she saw it.

That put Edward's initiative on hold. In reality, house guests would have been an extraordinary departure from the habits of ten years. Jo hesitated even to accept dinner party invitations, because she could never reciprocate. The only entertaining they ever did was having guests for tea, serving rich store-bought cakes. The new kitchen was hardly calculated to change that. Although calling it "cute as the dickens," Jo found it inconvenient in design: "We eat in one corner on a little round table, white plaster walls & pale grey floors—& every day I go crazy over more spots on that floor, all cleaned the day before. The oil stove drives me crazy it's so slow & so far all one's hot water has come out of a tea kettle—which of course you don't go off & leave cooking."[62] Food was never the cement for friendships made among the Truro neighbors. Often Edward painted pictures of their houses. Jo's diaries would record, besides the Jennesses, Mrs. Scott; the Lombards; Ella Mielziner and her two talented sons; Dad Stephens, a retired steel worker, and his son Bob, who worked in advertising on Madison Avenue and was a Sunday painter who emulated Hopper; and the writers John Dos Passos and his wife, Katy Smith.

Not that even their first summer in the house the Hoppers had been hermits. Jo chronicled their guests: Henry Varnum Poor, eager to see what effect his house might have had on Edward's design; also Edward's childhood friend Ralph Bedell; the Websters from Provincetown, returning the Hoppers' visit; another Provincetowner, but from the conservative school, Ross Moffett, a fellow Rehn artist, with his wife, Dorothy Lake Gregory (a former Henri student).

One friend took some of the earliest known photographs of the couple. When Edward needed a snapshot of himself "for Homer St. Gauden's collection of informal snapshots of painters in the [Carnegie] International," he enlisted Dr. Davenport West. On August 30, the vacationing physician drove over from Harwichport with his wife and took "lots of photos."[63] It was already cool enough for Edward to wear both his jacket and the hat with which he liked to cover his baldness as he posed outdoors. West photographed Hopper (and Jo) standing and sitting with the sandy hills over Cape Cod Bay as the background. In one, a beaming Jo, her dress blowing in the sea breeze, nestles her head against Edward's shoulder, while he smiles shyly and, somewhat tenderly, inclines his head in her direction. Hopper was clearly pleased with the results, for he sent four of the snapshots to Saint-Gaudens and asked him to include a credit line for West if any were published.[64]

Only in September did the Hoppers finally settle down enough to start painting again. Edward first produced a watercolor, of a nearby house and barn, *House on Pamet River,* and Jo two watercolors of sunflowers, in the face of Edward's often expressed disdain for the genre. For his next watercolor, *Forked Road,* Edward drove to Wellfleet, typically picking out the railroad tracks and town dump. He worked in the parked car, while Jo sat beside him tying a rag rug. She told herself that only her "bull dog strain" kept her at the rug rather than painting. She tried to convince Edward to paint the hills around their place or the view of it from the south, but he never chose to depict the house he had designed; he left that to Jo, who eventually made both interior and exterior views of what she called, with a touch of their mutual francophilia, "Chez Hopper."

After they had been painting for a while, Jo could write to Bee that Edward had been "wonderful—he's so bright & able about a house & has been so cheerful—putting up with me & my tantrums. But it's taken all his time too & he helps with all I do in the kitchen too. It's only lately that he's been able to paint & we're staying on until he can get something to take home."[65]

Resentment boiled up in the same letter. More immediately and continually than the car, the new house made Jo aware of her dilemma, caught between her shaken identity as an artist and conventional expectations of women's place: "It makes me simply a too devilish hyena to have to cook at all. . . . Building a house is worse than having twins." Yet the real hurt lay deeper: "Time was I considered myself an artist and would accept no other destiny. Now I know myself as a kitchen slave and everything being considered, don't see my way out." Likewise her diaries of 1934 register despair at "kitchen maid duties—with no life beyond—only fatigue & ill-nature—irritability," and again Edward's active discouragement: "he doesn't like me to have any creative impulses."[66] Soon she would admit learning to swallow eggs raw to save the trouble of cooking.[67] Yet she vacillated, occasionally feeling guilt for her anger, telling herself that her dear Eddy shared "all my labors about the house."[68]

In New York, too, Jo frequently did the laundry for them both. She also altered their clothes, often letting out and adjusting new pajamas to fit her husband's nearly six-foot-five-inch frame. There is no evidence that he ever washed out her underwear, a service that she routinely performed for him. Jo also sewed some of her clothes from scratch, but her motivation was more thrift than artistry. Only in the winter, he hauled coal from the cellar on the dumbwaiter and tended the stove. Through the years, Jo's pain would grow as it became clear that Edward's design for the new house made no special provision for her work and that the kitchen would have to double as her studio. As in New York, she was left to make do. She later reflected: "I have produced some good canvases in bedroom & out kitchen window. But the light is difficult."[69]

The neglected anniversary underlined the fact that for the ten years since their marriage Jo's career had been withering, discouraged both by Edward and by his circles in the art world. When she invited their mutual acquaintances over to see her work, she was humiliated by their indifference. For example, Edward's art school friend Arnold Friedman once arrived very late, after most of the daylight was gone. When he returned, he sat with Edward in a stony silence that Jo found "decidedly cruel."[70] Friedman counted on Hopper to write him letters of reference for teaching jobs and grant applications and probably sensed his friend's annoyance with Jo's ambitions as a painter.

Another cause for resentment was the Whitney Museum's reluctance to exhibit work by the artist-wives of the men shown. In this cause, Jo was joined by Marguerite Thompson Zorach, Martha Rhyther Kantor, and Theresa Bernstein. Jo also felt that the museum had failed to recognize the worthy work of women like Agnes Tait and Rosella Hartman. Yet she disdained most of what she saw at the New York Society of Women Artists,[71] a group formed in 1925 in opposition to the older, more conservative National Association of Women Painters and Sculptors, and she had no desire to show with artists she considered inferior. It may be that Jo had absorbed Edward's disdain for women artists and simply did not want her work seen in shows segregated by gender, for some of the artists she respected and admired, such as Marguerite Zorach, did show with this group. Instead, Jo wanted equal opportunity for herself and all women.

§

MAKING UP FOR their tardiness in settling down to paint, the Hoppers lingered in the new house until November. The year's production had been spotty at best, yet sales recovered modestly: by the end of 1934, Edward's total came to $3,550, entirely from watercolors; Jo had sold nothing.

Her increasing resentment was not Edward's only challenge. With growing fame came the need to defend his reputation. In early January 1935, he was dismayed when the art critic Nathaniel Pousette-Dart wrote that Hopper found his "direction and bent when he saw the work of Charles Burchfield."[72] In rebuttal, Hopper argued that his choice of subject matter preceded his knowledge of Burchfield's work, which he openly admired, and he insisted that in his vision and working method, "I am unlike him in almost every respect."[73] To dispute the allegation that his work derived from Burchfield, Hopper called upon his readings in psychology:

> In every artist's development the germ of the later work is always found in the earlier. The nucleus around which the artist's intellect builds his work is himself; the central ego, personality, or whatever it may be called, and this changes little from birth to death. What he was once, he always is, with slight modifications. Changing fashions in methods or subject matter alter him little or not at all.[74]

All of which failed to convince Pousette-Dart, who retorted: "Despite Mr. Hopper's protests, I still feel that he was at one time strongly influenced by Burchfield's work."[75]

Such critical carping was undoubtedly prompted by the huge attention focused on Hopper by the Museum of Modern Art. Yet Hopper was quite proud of the show, and particularly pleased to receive a degree of public acclaim that could be recognized by his elderly mother, confined as she now was to her wheelchair. Hopper could not have forgotten the period during the mid-1910s when his career was hopelessly stalled. When Henri looked to other rising stars among his former students, Elizabeth Hopper resolutely believed in her son, encouraging him to keep on, even preparing refreshments and working as the model for his students in the classes he reluctantly taught in Nyack.

Awareness of his mother's growing frailness may have prompted the painting *House at Dusk,* which he delivered to Rehn in January 1935, with the title *House by Evening Park.* The picture represents an apartment building (perhaps at the edge of Riverside Park on the west side of Manhattan) at the end of day, at the moment just before dark. Behind the building, in which a solitary figure is visible in a lighted window, the woods are already dark. Hopper liked to quote, in both German and the English translation, from Goethe's "Wanderer's Nightsong," an evocative lyric of evening, nature's stillnesses, and impending death, which he described as "an extraordinary visual picture":[76]

> Over all the hills is quiet,
> Over all the dells you can
> hardly hear a sound,
> All the birds are quiet in the woods
> Soon you will rest too.[77]

On January 25, Hopper learned that he had won the Temple Gold Medal from the Pennsylvania Academy of the Fine Arts. Two of the jurors were also artists at the Rehn Gallery, James Chapin and the same Ross Moffett from Provincetown who had visited the new house. The academy pronounced *Mrs. Scott's House* "the best oil painting at its 130th annual exhibition."[78] But joy over the award was interrupted by news of illness and death. From Provincetown came word that Ambrose Webster was dead, at sixty-six: a fine friend, Jo recalled, "dating back to one's early youth." Even Edward "could find no flaw" in him she mused, regretful that "one of the big rich things of the Cape has gone. We'll sure miss him."[79] Less than two weeks later, Edward's mother wrote summoning him to her bedside. According to Jo, he found that Elizabeth was "absolutely wretched when no company around."[80]

As Jo reminisced about her study with Webster and her early artistic career, she was busy posing for Edward. On February 11, she reported that he had "started another head of me—side view reading, hair down—so much for having washed my hair. E. likes me with my hair down & bushing."[81] For the next three days, she continued posing, only to conclude that it was "a saddening experience"; she was quite critical of Edward's efforts to paint her portrait, claiming that he made her "a heavy slouch creature & look like she drank."[82] She recorded that Edward admitted that he "doesn't think it looks like me at all—but he just can't paint the way I am—he hasn't the skill."[83]

Hopper's spirits were lifted when his longtime supporter Edward Alden Jewell reviewed the Whitney Museum's exhibition of abstract art in America; he felt that Jewell's statement vindicated his work and countered the arguments of Ralph Pearson and others who had objected to his show at the Museum of Modern Art. Mentioning that Hopper's painting could be found elsewhere at the Whitney, Jewell wrote: "Every process of true simplification contains a germ of the abstract principle. Such simplification may or may not proceed in the direction of the decorative. In artists such as Hopper and Burchfield, it decidedly partakes of abstraction in the essential sense—as opposed to that of decorative pattern, which predominates in the present exhibition at the Whitney."[84]

Hopper's pleasure at Jewell's continued respect for his work over the brand of abstraction touted by the Whitney was soon disturbed by the further deterioration of his mother's health. Jo's demand that they postpone the potentially oppressive visit to the Cape of Elizabeth and Marion proved to be unfortunate. Claiming that "It would have been *hell* all around," Jo had wanted to put off their trip until the following spring or fall, when accommodations could be had at the Holiday House in Wellfleet at off-season rates.[85] The visit, however, was not to be, for Elizabeth died on March 20, 1935, at the age of eighty-one.

Once again, Jo's attitude disturbed Anne Tucker, who wrote a conde-
scending letter to Bee Blanchard: "Poor little warped thing! Perhaps she'll be
better now that old Mrs. Hopper is gone, but she seems resentful even in her
death, I am afraid she's not been much of a comfort to E.H. in his sorrow. He
adored his mother."[86] Jo saw things differently, for she later noted in her diary
that she had "abiding satisfaction" that she and Edward's mother "got on so
well together," noting that her mother would have been glad of that too.[87]

When Jo wrote about Elizabeth to Marion, she said that she felt convinced "that so much of Ed's work—the character of it, came directly from
her—its color, its integrity."[88] She insisted that she had tried very hard to get
Elizabeth's role mentioned in the Modern's catalogue, but that she had been
dismissed by Barr who "actually resented any intimations of 'class' for Ed."[89]

Losing his only surviving parent made Hopper more intensely aware of
his own mortality. Death becomes an implicit theme in much of his painting.
Just before Elizabeth died, Hopper had gone up to 155th Street to study Macomb's Dam Bridge in Harlem as the subject for his next canvas. He chose a
"more or less grey day to make color notes."[90] Jo recorded in her diary how
Edward had suffered since the shock of his mother's death and noted that the
interruption was taking its toll on his picture. He not only risked losing interest in the theme, but "the March weather has gone—the March light &
March sky that he particularly wanted—not a dull still grey day—but a
March grey day—with some blue in the sky looking thru."[91] Despite his dis-
heartened state, Hopper continued taking the subway uptown and walking
quite a distance to the site itself; sometimes he went there twice in a day, often
discouraged by finding the sunlight too bright or encountering a sudden
shower. It was April 7 before he finally found a sky for the picture.[92] In the
face of such circumstances, his achievement, with its ample yet harmonious
sweep and fine tonalities, lends subtle conviction to Jo's estimate of the virtues
with which Elizabeth Hopper imbued her male child.

The ritual rounds and details of arrangements, entailing tense and tear-
ful stays with Marion, who was now left alone in the old home, generated the
inevitable recriminations. Jo's ill-fated postponement of the family visit could
only exacerbate the usual nerves of packing to leave for the summer. Yet by
June first the Hoppers were able to get away and drive to Truro. Frustrated
in his desire to show his mother the home he designed, Edward now hoped
for a visit from the Chattertons on their way to summer in Maine. Opposed
as she remained to the idea of guests, Jo relented when she saw how intent
Edward was to show off the house to one of his very oldest friends. Yet she
complained of fatigue and was relieved when the Chattertons failed to appear.[93] With Edward's mother gone, Jo finally gave in to the idea of having his
sister visit and even encouraged her to come.[94] But even Marion sensed that

the time was not ripe and again stayed home. Freed from preoccupation with visits, Edward and Jo dug in for their first full summer in the new house. The view to the bay engaged Edward's nautical eye, inspiring a watercolor, *Yawl Riding a Swell,* and an oil, *The Long Leg*—his first sailing pictures since his 1929 visit to Maine. Although he retained his boyhood enthusiasm for sailing, and sailed occasionally with friends, he never had a boat of his own on the Cape. John Clancy of the Rehn Gallery recalled that Jo insisted: "He's too good a man to lose that way."[95]

Edward soon took the car to look for subjects, driving through Wellfleet to Eastham, the town he came to prefer on that end of the Cape. He produced a watercolor called *House with a Big Pine.* He also began a canvas of a clam digger, but it was not going well. Jo wrote to Marion: "I'm trying to save its life for it."[96] By September, Edward felt the need to leave the Cape in search of new subjects and they drove as far as East Montpelier, Vermont. Jo complained to Marion that Edward felt he had already painted everything on the Cape.

Back in New York, they consigned the summer's meager production to Rehn. By November, *Yawl Riding a Swell* had won recognition: the $750 Purchase Prize in watercolor at the Worcester Museum.[97] Meanwhile Edward hunkered down in the studio. He consigned a new oil painting to the gallery on November 21. The picture shows a statue looming over the deserted mall in Central Park, where stark tree branches straggle up in outline against the horizon, which is illuminated by the afterglow of a sunset only interrupted here and there by city structures. Calling the picture *Shakespeare at Dusk,* Hopper identified the silhouetted figure and invited comparison with the famous "visual picture" in a sonnet:

> That time of year thou mayst in me behold
> When yellow leaves, or none, or few, do hang
> Upon those boughs which shake against the cold,
> Bare ruin'd choirs, where late the sweet birds sang.
> In me thou see'st the twilight of such day
> As after sunset fadeth in the west,
> Which by and by black night doth take away,
> Death's second self, that seals up all in rest.[98]

Meditatively, calling up his own visual idioms and epitomizing his reflections on values lost, finding the germ of the later in the earlier, as he put it, Hopper expresses the melancholy brought home to him by his mother's final lesson. In November 1935, the New York *Post* carried a rare intimate report of Edward, after reporter Archer Winsten took the Hoppers by surprise one evening while trying, he said, to locate a friend who had lived in their build-

Edward Hopper, Drawing for "Shakespeare at Dusk," *1935. Conté on paper,*
10½ × 16″ (26.7 × 40.6 cm.).

ing. Telling Jo that he admired her husband's work, he managed to get to
speak with Edward. He described the studio with its huge north skylight, its
coal fire in the grate, its windows facing south, and the bare floor; and he
found Hopper "tall, bald, big, slow-moving and slow-talking."[99] Winsten
managed to extract the information that Hopper "paints less than half dozen
oils a year, working from the subject itself, or from memory, or from sketches
made previously" and reported that Hopper "spends a great deal of time getting ready to work. And he spends a great deal of time walking in the city he
loves and always has loved. He likes to look in windows and see people standing there in the light at night. For this same reason he likes to ride on els."
When Winsten added that Hopper "would like to get into the apartments,
but there's no excuse," he missed a double thrust: the taciturn artist might
yearn to spy, yet lack the means, while the reporter in fact managed to find an
excuse to penetrate the privacy of the Hoppers.

Jo chimed in that there was not much to be written about them: "We're
not spectacular and we're very private, and we don't drink and we hardly
ever smoke." When Winsten asked what Hopper did for fun, he replied "I
get most of my pleasure out of the city itself." Jo vigilantly shunted aside the
question of why Edward painted: he did not "mind thinking out loud, but if

it's for quotation, no. He would sit down and think and write a couple of months to get it down to his own satisfaction."

By December, the Great Depression was again making itself felt: Jo complained to Marion that, except for the recent Purchase Prize, "there hasn't been a thing sold for a long time."[100] In May, the Boston Museum acquired *Room in Brooklyn* for $1,500, which, with the Purchase Prize, made sales of $2,250 for the year. The Hoppers were reduced to drawing on savings and trying to figure out how to cut expenses. Even so, neither ever seriously considered working on any of the arts projects of the WPA (Works Progress Administration), the large-scale national program set up under the New Deal. Edward believed that government funding would merely encourage artistic mediocrity and he condemned Roosevelt and all his works.

AN INTELLECTUAL SELF-PORTRAIT

ABOUT 1936, Edward made a caricature of himself captioned *Le Rêve de Josie*. For the man of "Jo's dream" he sketched himself as an idealized dandy—lanky, elegantly caparisoned in a tweedy suit, swish cape, and sporty hat with a jaunty feather, looking alertly through a monocle, and seated, resting on a walking stick a pair of hands as hairy as the trousers. Below, a sagging sock reveals a scrawny leg. A basket of heavy reading stands beside.

The title employs their language of intimate communication. French had been their emotional liaison and cultural focus ever since they discovered they could quote Symbolist poetry in the original to each other. To Edward, his time in Paris, with its nightlife, had meant sexual liberation: to Jo, Paris brought freedom from the circumscribed life of teaching in New York; and Paris had given them both firsthand experience of the art they learned about in school.

If the nickname Josie also connotes intimacy and affection, intellectual complications emerge from the rest. Edward's self-image combines contrasting values, the veneer of put-on smartness above and the natural gaucherie that sticks out below, suggesting a duality that is implicit also in the idea of "the dream." Both Jo and Edward were well aware of the popular interest in dreams and the vogue for Freud and Jung. Edward "talked Freud most of the time" on one of their evenings out with Bee Blanchard, Jo recorded in her

Edward Hopper, Le Rêve de Josie, *1936. Pencil on paper, 11 × 8½″ (27.9 × 21.6 cm.).*

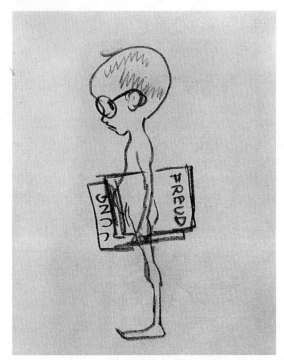

Edward Hopper, Caricature of the artist as a boy holding books by Freud and Jung, *c. 1934. Pencil on paper, 4⅛ × 3⅛″ (10.5 × 7.9 cm.).*

diary for 1935.[1] Freud and Jung figure in yet another self-caricature from around this time, where Hopper sketched himself as an infant with a huge, embryonic head, bespectacled and clutching under his arm books labeled with their names. The pairing recalls the sixth chapter of Jung's own collection of essays addressed to a general public, "Freud and Jung—Contrasts," in which Jung tries to explain the difference between their views.[2] The first essay dealt with the topic of dream analysis that Freud had made popular and stated that "dreams give information about the secrets of the inner life."[3]

Dream images figure, too, in the art of the Surrealists, whose work came to Hopper's attention in this period. He and Jo saw the show "Fantastic Art, Dada and Surrealism" that Alfred Barr organized at the Museum of Modern Art in December 1936, only three years after Hopper's own retrospective. Edward admired the fine color of the Surrealists, some of whom, he told Jo, were better artists than they realized.[4] He was probably pleased when the Chicago critic C. J. Bulliet later commented: "Hopper has imagination, invention and a subtle feeling for what is alive, without exhibitionism. He has the psychological insight of the best of the 'Surrealists' without their circus methods."[5] Psychological introspection lay at the heart of his aesthetic articulated for the retrospective: "I believe that the great painters, with their intellect as master, have attempted to force this unwilling medium of paint and canvas into a record of their emotions. I find any digression from this large aim leads me to boredom."[6]

The Hoppers considered *Le Rêve de Josie* significant enough that they later showed it to the critic Brian O'Doherty, who described the seated figure as "Mrs. Hopper's dream-boy, a Rex Harrison, pipe-smoking, tweedy type with a basketful of Mrs. Hopper's favorite authors."[7] The writers, in fact, interested Edward as well. He and Jo had shared many interests when they met, and by now, after more than a decade of marriage, their intellectual life had long since become synergistic. The basket contains an assortment of books offering clues to the multiplicity of intellectual pursuits that helped shape Hopper and that reverberate through his art. The books are labeled: Ibsen, Henry James, *Poésie de Paul Verlaine,* [Marcel Proust's] *Du Côté de Chez Swann,* and [George Santayana's] *The Last Puritan.* Hopper's own interest in each of these writers is supported by direct references he made to them in his art, his writing, in the quotations he recited in interviews, and by Jo's notations in her diary.

The Last Puritan (1935), which Santayana subtitled *A Memoir in the Form of a Novel,* held a special appeal for Hopper. Jo noted that he was so eager to read it that he immediately seized upon the book when he first spotted it in the Truro library in July 1936.[8] That fall she wrote: "Read Last Puritan— George Santayana. What a delectable prologue!"[9]

Santayana's only novel presents a moral critique of American life in the early twentieth century. As the prologue opens, the narrator is speaking with a man who "was almost my neighbor in Paris, for he lived where the Left Bank ceases to be the Latin Quarter and where it's not yet the Faubourg Saint Germain"[10]—just the neighborhood where Hopper had lived. Speaking of his father, Harold, the narrator reflects: "There were many such Americans de luxe in my generation who prolonged their youth at the Ecole des Beaux-Arts or at Julien's."[11] And his reference to the period when Harold "despaired of becoming a great painter—as he did every other year" can only have revived Hopper's memories of his own struggle for recognition.[12] In the novel, the conversation shifts to a discussion of the narrator's gifted student, the late Oliver Alden, a casualty of the war, for "Oliver was THE LAST PURITAN."[13]

In the dialogue that follows, Santayana examines what is meant by "Puritanism," and establishes that "there will always be puritans," claiming "puritanism is a natural reaction against nature."[14] His interlocutor then explains that Oliver "convinced himself, on puritan grounds, that it was wrong to be a puritan," and that he wanted "to give puritanism up, but couldn't."[15] The discussion concludes with a description of Oliver's character and again comes close to ideas that would have attracted Hopper: "His puritanism . . . was a deep and speculative thing: hatred of all shams, scorn of all the mummeries, a bitter merciless pleasure in the hard facts. And that passion for reality was beautiful in him."[16] This portrayal of puritanism, particularly the "pleasure in the hard facts" and the "passion for reality," invite comparison with what we know about Hopper's attitude toward painting.

The critic Joe Lee Davis has suggested that someone could write a chapter in Santayana's life called "The Last Puritan and the Ghost of Emerson."[17] This points up another aspect of *The Last Puritan* that appealed to Hopper, who once volunteered: "I admire [Emerson] greatly. I read him quite alot. I read him over and over again."[18] Emerson's doctrine of a higher individualism, his ability to dignify the lowly and raise it, to see art everywhere, and his stress on the importance of self-reliance were central to Hopper's thinking. Emerson's emphasis on the truth, revealed intuitively, and on individual thinking were especially significant to Hopper, an individualist if ever there was one. Reading Emerson also encouraged his turn from Europe and his search for a new, American art: "We have listened too long to the courtly muses of Europe," Emerson said. "I ask not for the great, the remote, the romantic . . . I embrace the common, I explore and sit at the feet of the familiar, the low. Give me insight into to-day, and you may have the antique and future worlds."[19]

In *The Last Puritan,* a character named Jim Darley retorts sharply to Oliver's identification of Emerson as "a saint" who loved nature and humanity: "An old barebones like Emerson doesn't love; he isn't a saint. He's simply a distinguished-looking old cleric with a sweet smile and a white tie; he's just honourable and bland and as cold as ice."[20] Emerson's presence pervades the story: Oliver is described as having a "transcendental consciousness," as being "a budding transcendentalist," as having "a transcendental mind"; he visits Concord to look "at the dreadful little house in which Emerson lived"; later he is assigned to live in a room in Harvard's Divinity Hall that was said to have been Emerson's; then, at Oxford, his quarters remind him "of Emerson's room in Divinity Hall."[21] Hopper, who also admired Goethe, must have noted the reference to "the heathen imagination in Goethe and Emerson" by Oliver's father; later Oliver comments: "You mustn't condone nature's crimes, you mustn't become a pagan in your heart. That had been Goethe's mistake."[22] Santayana's novel considers the problem of a spiritual life for the disillusioned thinker, who having rejected all the traditional Platonic and Judeo-Christian ideas of transcendence, tries to reconstruct faith in a purely naturalistic moral order.[23] This, in a sense, was also Hopper's dilemma, one he eventually examined in his 1959 painting *Excursion into Philosophy.*

Hopper's identity as a "puritan" had a number of earlier associations. Five years before, his friend du Bois had written about his "Anglo-Saxon capacity for Puritanism," and asserted that Hopper had "turned the Puritan in him into a purist, turned moral rigours into stylistic precisions."[24] Hopper was certainly familiar, then, with some of the debate over puritanism that became one of the paramount concepts in American letters after 1890. As early as 1896, in an essay on Emerson, John Jay Chapman had argued that puritanism was to blame for preventing the philosopher from fully developing his emotional life.[25] Then in 1908, Van Wyck Brooks first declared in *The Wine of the Puritans* that despite the value of puritanism as idealism, our history was problematic because "we preserve the Puritan idea," leaving us unprepared to cope with the problems of "an advanced cosmopolitan civilization."[26] In book after book, Brooks would search for what he termed a more "useable past."[27] With, as du Bois put it, "the advent of the Freud inspired demand for sensuality in life and art," the theme of liberation and self-expression had resulted in "the denunciation of Puritanism as repressive and hostile to expression."[28] Yet, while Hopper identified with puritanism and even ironically quipped to du Bois that he had done a "swell job" on him "as a Puritan," his interest in Freud qualified his puritanism. Hopper occasionally remarked upon the value of Freudian theory in creative expression. At times, he was even willing to admit that he viewed art as a reflection of his own psyche: "So much of every art is an expression of the subconscious, that it seems to me most of all of the important qualities are put there unconsciously, and little of importance by the conscious intellect."[29] He felt ambivalence, resistance, and respect for this mode of thinking. Once, referring to the short stories of Thomas Mann, he commented: "Rough going. Well depressing. Freudian. A great writer of fiction."[30]

Hopper was not alone in his identification with puritanism at this time. Provoked by the publication of *The Last Puritan*, Henry McBride described the painter Marsden Hartley as "one of the last of the New England Puritans," asserting "George Santayana is mistaken; they are not all yet dead."[31] Hopper's self-image as a "Puritan" is also linked to his familiarity with the work of Henry James, much of which he found meaningful. Late in life, however, he remarked in an interview that "he did not think very much of Henry James because there was no sex in his women," intentionally provoking both Jo and his interviewer to express indignation.[32] When the same interviewer told Hopper that there appeared to be "little sensuality if any" in the women he portrayed, he appeared "amused," no doubt thinking of Jo's monopoly as his model.[33]

In his fiction, James explored the complexity of American puritanism, examining eighteenth-century New Englanders, the nineteenth-century heirs of various aspects of the disintegrating puritan tradition, and the enduring puritan strain in his own time.[34] James also felt the conflicting ideologies of contemporary puritanism, much as Hopper would in his day.

In his early novel *Roderick Hudson,* James examined in considerable detail the puritan boyhood of a character named Rowland Mallet, whose father's asceticism, James suggests, came from fear and a sense of duty rather than positive faith.[35] Rowland is the heir to "a rigid Puritan stock" who "had been brought up to think much more intently of the duties of this life than of its privileges and pleasures."[36] Hopper's own experience paralleled that of Roderick Hudson, who ventures abroad in search of traditions of art unavailable to him at home. He could readily identify with James's description of the artist at work in the intervals between "sterile moods." Hopper's own strict Baptist background made it easy for him to recognize the stern religious legacy, the sharp distinctions between "right and wrong," that James delineated in this novel.

In his comments on Hawthorne and Emerson, James further expanded on the role of puritanism. In a discussion of *The Scarlet Letter,* he wrote: "Puritanism, in a word, is there, not only objectively, as Hawthorne tried to place it there, but subjectively as well. Not, I mean, in his judgment of his characters in any harshness of prejudice, or in the obtrusion of a moral lesson; but in the very quality of his own vision, in the tone of the picture, in a certain coldness and exclusiveness of treatment."[37] In 1899 Hopper had made an illustration of Hester Prynne, so we may assume that he had read *The Scarlet Letter;* perhaps he read James's book on Hawthorne as well.

James saw the limitation of Emerson's puritan heritage. He remarked upon visits that they made together to the galleries of the Louvre and the Vatican, where he noted: "I was struck with the anomaly of a man so refined and intelligent being so little spoken to by works of art. It would be more exact to say that certain chords were wholly absent."[38] James further reflected "how strange" it was that Emerson did not want to read Hawthorne's novels, especially since they were neighbors in Concord for several years: "It was a rare accident that made them live almost side by side so long in the same small New England town, each a fruit of a long Puritan stem, yet with such a difference of taste. Hawthorne's vision was all for the evil and sin of the world, a side of life to which Emerson's eyes were thickly bandaged."[39]

In 1927, Hopper had referred to James in his article on John Sloan, for to him the writer epitomized the question of expatriation and its impact on the search for an "American" art.[40] James must also have interested Hopper on many other levels. It is significant that in his caricature, he does not specify particular works by James (or by Ibsen) as he does for Santayana and Proust. Leon Edel has characterized James as "a veritable bridge from the romantic movement to all that is 'modern' in the literary art of the twentieth century."[41] It is this tension between the romantic and the modern that so held Hopper's attention. James's emphasis on private life as observed or imagined by the artist is parallel to Hopper's depictions of people in interiors. Both men reflect an intimate sphere of existence, the consciousness of the artist who responds to the world around him.

It is not known when Hopper read James's *The American Scene,* published in 1907, but it seems certain that the painter would not have ignored the expatriate novelist's impressions of America made on a visit during 1904–1905 after an absence of a quarter of a century.[42] The year of the book's publication marked Hopper's own experience as an expatriate, his discovery of European culture and of cultural difference. He sustained some of the same reactions as James, both in evaluating America from a European perspective and in coming to terms with some of the rudeness of American urban "progress."

Consider the words Hopper used to describe his first impressions of Paris: "very graceful and beautiful . . . almost too formal after the raw disorder of New York."[43] And he noticed the difference in the people, concluding that the French seemed "to live in the streets," while he characterized New Yorkers as businesslike, "with that never ending determination for the 'long green.' "[44] James had earlier used negative images to describe New York; in various passages, he described New York's "ugliness," and called the city "terrible," even "horrible."[45] Hopper shared with James his despair over modernity.

The rare and deflected apparitions of the skyscraper in Hopper's pictures of New York correspond to James's sentiments about these most American of buildings. James said of the "tall buildings": "Crowned not only with no history, but with no credible possibility of time for history, and consecrated by no uses save the commercial at any cost, they are simply the most piercing notes in that concert of the expensively provisional into which your supreme sense of New York resolves itself."[46] Skyscrapers, he contended: "never begin to speak to you, in the manner of the builded majesties of the world as we have heretofore known such—towers or fortresses or palaces—with the authority of things of permanence or even of things of long duration."[47] Like James, Hopper appreciated palaces; he had painted the Louvre over and over again. And like James, Hopper did not find all towers objectionable; he was drawn to lighthouses and, occasionally, despite his disdain for organized religion, to church towers.

The architectural subjects that Hopper chose to depict suggest that he agreed with another of James's assessments: "Houses of the best taste are like clothes of the best tailors—it takes their age to show us how good they are."[48] In his 1928 essay "Charles Burchfield: American," Hopper anticipated our appreciation of Victorian houses: "Our native architecture with its hideous beauty, its fantastic roofs, pseudo-Gothic, French-Mansard, Colonial, mongrel or what not, with eye-searing color or delicate harmonies of faded paint, shouldering one another along interminable streets that taper off into swamps or dump heaps—these appear again and again, as they should in any honest delineation of the American scene."[49]

If Hopper associated Henry James with his own American aesthetic, he associated the lyrical poetry of Paul Verlaine with his youthful days in Paris and with romance. The Symbolist aesthetic had figured in his *Soir Bleu* of 1914. Verlaine was the principal poet whom he chose to quote during his courtship of Jo, and *Poésie* was the book that Jeanne Chéruy had inscribed and given to him less than a year before he started courting Jo. While Verlaine's expression of erotic longing seems in direct opposition to Hopper's identification as "the last puritan," he clearly felt an enormous clash between the liberation represented by Verlaine and Paris and the ingrained values of his boyhood. The debate over puritanism was more than an intellectual exercise for Hopper; it mirrored a central conflict in his life.

His inclusion of Proust in his caricature, like his love of Verlaine, reaffirms his attachment to French culture. *Du Côté de Chez Swann* ("Swann's Way"), the first part of *A la Recherche du Temps Perdu,* provides a description of the life of Swann as a young man in Paris, including a love affair: "he's always shy with her, and that makes her shy with him. Besides she doesn't care for him in that way, she says; it's an ideal love, 'platonic,' you know . . ."[50] Hopper must have enjoyed the novel for its suggestions of his own Parisian sojourns, but there are also parallels with his later work.

Hopper surely read Proust in the English translation that appeared in 1932, although he could have read the novels earlier in French, discussing both Proust and James with du Bois, who in 1924 commented on the two writers: "The preciousness of thought of James is smaller because . . . of . . . the Puritanism of the nineties. . . . James at his finest, never quite walks out of the parlor, drawing room he would call it, into the street. Proust does this only a little more. No vulgarity due to excessive blood. . . . Both are a little maddening—fussy men, meticulous."[51]

Like Proust's great work, Hopper's paintings combine obsessive memory and meticulous imagination. The passage of time is a theme central to both, although perhaps less immediately apparent in Hopper. Yet the painter's repeated allusions to times of the day (*Soir Bleu, Eleven A.M., Night Windows, Dawn before Gettysburg, Early Sunday Morning,* to name only a few) and, later, to seasons of the year (*Summertime, October on Cape Cod, Summer Evening, Summer in the City*) convey this focus. His many depictions of trains and railroad tracks also suggest the passage of time, but none more so than *House by the Railroad.* Outmoded architecture, passed by and neglected, looms up as a reminder of discarded customs and values forgotten as civilization, like the speeding train, thunders into the modern age.

By 1936, when Hopper included Ibsen in his basket of books, he was surely familiar with most of the Norwegian dramatist's work. But his earliest impressions, made during art school, where the playwright was very much in fashion among the students, must have contributed most to his view of Ibsen. In Robert Henri's book *The Art Spirit,* Ibsen is cited as "supreme order in verbal expression."[52] Around the time he made his illustrations of people at the theater that he captioned *Ibsen,* Hopper had had the opportunity to see *Rosmersholm, Hedda Gabler, When We Dead Awaken,* and *A Doll's House.* He may have read or read about still other plays.

Ibsen's death in May 1906 had brought the dramatist even more attention in the American press, which hailed his "modernity and universality."[53] Hopper too thought of Ibsen as a standard of what was modern. For the "Notes on Painting" for his retrospective, he wrote of "definite personalities that remain forever modern by the fundamental truth that is in them. It makes Molière at his greatest as new as Ibsen."[54]

As early as 1907, an American critic, Jennette Lee, published a book called *The Ibsen Secret: A Key to the Prose Dramas of Henrik Ibsen.*[55] To explain the dramatist's symbolism, she posits that in each of his plays "An object or event is used as a central theme or motive."[56] Lee also stressed that Ibsen "was intensely interested in the life and problems of his own time,"[57] an aspect that certainly appealed to Hopper. Lee compared the plays of Ibsen to the novels of James (who, in fact, admired Ibsen's work): "His plays have plot in abundance, but nothing happens in them, any more than in one of Mr. Henry James's novels. The action takes place in the soul of a character or in the relation between characters."[58] Like Hopper's painting, in Ibsen's dramas, "The action is not progressive, but static; and it is, thus, best revealed, not by events, but by pictures; that is, by symbols. . . . The action of the play is psychological."[59]

Of all of Ibsen's plays, *When We Dead Awaken,* which is thought to be autobiographical, seems to have particular relevance for Hopper. A young sculptor called Rubek has created a major figure group, *The Resurrection Day,* inspired by a beautiful young model, Irene. When Irene realizes that Rubek cares for her, not for herself, but as a model for his work, she leaves him. After a loveless marriage to another, Rubek encounters Irene, to whom he admits: "When I found you, I knew at once how I should use you for my masterpiece." Irene tells him: " 'Resurrection Day' you called it—I called it our child."[60] This passage brings to mind Jo's poignant habit of referring to Hopper's pictures as "their children."

Like Ibsen, Hopper at times utilized specific symbols, for example, *Skyline near Washington Square* with its gangly skyscraper (1925), first called *Self-Portrait.* Other symbols can be found in the clown in *Soir Bleu* (1914), the train tracks and house with a mansard roof in *The House by the Railroad,* the chimneys that look like crosses in *The Bootleggers,* the Ex-Lax advertisement in *Drug Store,* the various foods in the restaurant window in *Tables for Ladies,* the darkness of the tunnel in *Bridle Path* (1939), and the train tracks in *Hotel by a Railroad* (1952), to name just a few.

Under all the teasing, *Le Rêve de Josie* sends a private message to his wife. His shyness and introversion made Edward avoid most personal discourse and all public speaking. Introspective and intellectual, yet distrustful of verbal communication, he continued to struggle when he had to express himself in writing. As he had throughout his life, he preferred to speak through visual images. This small pencil sketch offers a rare glimpse of the rich world of culture and ideas which he absorbed and transmuted in creating his art. In his painting, this visual communication took on a subtlety: details, shapes, colors, postures, scale, and specific juxtapositions join to convey many levels of meaning.

CONSEQUENCES OF SUCCESS: 1936–1938

THE LATE 1930S saw the Hoppers' careers diverge ever more sharply. As Edward's professional recognition grew, nurtured by a network of male colleagues, his disdain for Jo's aspirations became even more galling. Tensions between them increased, played out sometimes violently in the automobile, which he defended against even her intermittent and long deferred designs. Through it all she kept caring deeply about his work, recording both the honors as they increased and the depressions as his quest for subjects became ever more arduous. Her chronicle of his distractions and laborious gestations lends an element of suspense to the story: what will he light on, what will catch his fancy, what will he manage to turn out, what picture come from some unexpected slant on a long familiar location or new take on such an old favorite as the world of the stage and screen? Will her energetic and mimetic collaborations spur him? Will she recover herself?

Part of the problem lay in Edward's own insecurity, which not even success could alleviate. In February 1936, filling out the entry form for the Whitney Museum's Second Biennial of watercolors and pastels, at the blank labeled "Prizes or Awards" he bristled and wrote: "Few indeed." Evidently he discounted the Purchase Prize at Worcester the previous fall. When he entered the first Whitney Biennial, he had been able to boast of the "Logan Prize in etching, Bryan Prize in etching, Baltimore Museum award."

If the signal of discontent was meant to alert the Whitney to Hopper's professional thin skin, it failed. The museum purchased *House on Pamet River* out of the Biennial but then, in April 1936, did an about face and proposed trading it for *House with a Big Pine,* also a watercolor, which Hopper sent to a second Whitney show called simply "1936."[1] Hopper wrote to the museum's director, Juliana Force, that he would be "very much disappointed" were this to happen, for *House on Pamet River* was the better work; in fact, he considered it "one of the very best" of his watercolors.[2] In the end, his judgment prevailed. The museum kept the work already purchased, but that alone.

Although times were hard, Hopper would not compromise artistic integrity. He rejected a proposal by the American Artists Group, a leading manufacturer of greeting cards, to let his etchings be mass-marketed. Similarly, even when such an old friend as Carl Zigrosser, then director of the Weyhe Gallery, invented a scheme to sell inexpensive "unsigned, unlimited edition impressions . . . at two dollars and seventy-five cents each,"[3] Hopper declined in terms that still bear the stamp of his old resentment against commercial art: "It does not seem to me as if it would be very profitable for the artist unless he could sell many thousands of prints. In order to make so wide an appeal the subjects and the treatment necessary would give the prints the character of pot-boilers—don't you think so?"[4] Years later, Zigrosser admitted: "We tried to slant the subject of the prints for popular appeal—pictures for the masses. . . . Our duality of purpose involved us in a certain amount of compromise, and as is often the case with half-measures, produced neither art nor popularity."[5]

Integrity also made Hopper refuse another opportunity to sell. To Wilbur Peat of the Indianapolis Museum he explained why he would not offer a drawing for acquisition: "Drawings are sometimes the most personal expression of a painter, but I do not think that is so in my case. Most of the drawings that I make are preliminary sketches and would have very little meaning or interest for anyone but myself. Under such conditions I don't feel that I have any drawings of sufficient interest to become part of a museum's collection."[6]

Meanwhile in the studio the couple had been busy. Toward the end of February he consigned to Rehn the only oil portrait he ever made of his wife, calling it *Jo Painting,* although a viewer unaware of the title might equally interpret the profile seen from the left side as a woman gazing at her own image in a hand-held mirror. Her upper arm actually points left toward the unseen canvas suggested by the title. Edward gave her the picture as an anniversary present in 1955; and in 1961 she told Brian O'Doherty, "I recall things he has done of people, double chins, latched right on to things they wouldn't like at all. He didn't do that this time to me."[7] The picture appears to have had a difficult gestation, for diary entries from a year earlier spoke of a portrait under way, of Jo's "misgivings about hair down and house robe," and of Edward's discouragement with the result.[8] In the interim, Hopper changed the robe to a dress with a brooch at the collar and altered the title in what looks like a gesture on his part to placate Jo by at least nominal acknowledgment of her identity as an artist.

After tying up loose threads at home, Hopper returned to the search for peculiar and dramatic ways of recasting familiar scenes in the street. At Columbus Circle he and Jo had frequented the second-story Chinese restaurant depicted in *Chop Suey*. Now he took a fresh look at the exterior of a movie palace, choosing a viewpoint from which the name on the marquis gets obliterated by a looming Victorian kiosk, a dark shape flanked by the vermilion letters "C . . . E." Behind and across the center of the composition runs the white facade of the theater with classical ionic capitals. Above this band on the left Hopper emphasizes billboards announcing "CANDY DRUGS SODA, HORTONS ICE CREAM," while beneath to the right huddle banal storefronts. The prominent signs recall Hopper's early commercial illustrations as well as paintings like *Drug Store* and *Chop Suey*. Evident also is Hopper's admiration for the work of John Sloan, who had earlier represented the exterior of a New York movie house. But in Hopper's ironic imagination, the classical architecture becomes a frame for the contrasts of old and new, commerce and entertainment, in urban life.

To the right, the bulky house of the theater rises in a regular pale green mass, its utilitarian form accentuated by a hint of decoration. Hopper decided to include the fire stairs on the right side of the building, making a visual pun about the cinema as escape, a function that he so often enjoyed when he was too blocked to paint. While individual films would continue to inspire Hopper, his fascination with "the movies" as a subject for his painting reached its peak during the late 1930s, when "Hollywood's technical supremacy" enabled America to dominate the world film industry.[9]

To the left, behind and above the theater, loom dark skyscrapers cut off from the vivid forms and messages of the foreground. A silhouetted traffic light in the immediate foreground makes a dark, modern counterpoint to the classical capitals of the facade. The choice of an unexpected viewpoint and the careful selection of elements dramatize the force of Hopper's imagination. He brought together disparate layers and strands of the urban landscape, pointing out the contrasts, dynamics, and ironies of the city. On April 18, Hopper consigned *The Circle Theatre* to Rehn.

The summer campaign had become the annual move to Cape Cod. Planning turned Jo's thoughts back to a long-frustrated aim. From the time of

their first car in 1927, Edward had managed to hold her to occasional practice driving. But in May 1936 she obtained her license, taking lessons in New
City from Andrew Youngberg, a "nice Swedish aviator," with an attitude so
unlike Edward's: "One did so nicely with him."[10]

Long since, Hopper had made the automobile his principal means of
searching for new subjects. If her new license seemed to threaten the routine,
in reality the weather that summer proved more of an obstacle. Edward was
able to eke out five watercolors: *House with a Rain Barrel,* on the bay side;
Near the Back Shore, some shacks on the ocean beach in Truro; *Toward Boston,*
the Truro railroad station; as well as *Spindly Locusts,* and *Oaks at Eastham;* yet
the constant rain kept forcing him to return later to get his skies. Jo complained that she painted "4 piddling watercolors . . . unsatisfying but better to
have done than not have done."[11]

Amidst his own difficulties, Hopper felt obliged to give a hand when
Ross Moffett came over from Provincetown with a problem. After all, Moffett had been a juror for Hopper's medal in Philadelphia and was a fellow
artist at Rehn's. Much less able to sell than Hopper, Moffett had taken the step
Hopper so adamantly ruled out, procuring a commission under the Federal
Arts Project to paint murals for the post office in Holyoke, Massachusetts.
Perplexed when it came to installation, he turned to Hopper, who had no experience with murals and scorned the Arts Project. Remembering that Guy
du Bois had painted murals for the Jumble Shop Cafe in Greenwich Village,
Edward took the trouble to write to Guy for the name of someone affordable
to install Moffett's work.[12]

Other distractions were more regular. Four summers in rented quarters
and two in their own house had given the Hoppers a circle of friends. Not
that Edward ever chatted, but Jo enjoyed company. Her commentaries often
mentioned their neighbors John and Katy Dos Passos.

Hopper had known Dos (as he was called) since the 1920s, when both
showed paintings at the Whitney Studio Club, but they only saw each other
regularly in the summers on Cape Cod. When Edward and Jo first arrived in
1930, Dos and Katy were already settled in their "little farm sunk in a lonely
and rather somber little hollow where," according to Edmund Wilson, who
visited from his house in Provincetown, "the occasional booming of bitterns
is the only sound to be heard."[13]

The friendship between Hopper and Dos Passos was kept alive by their
wives, who found immediate rapport in their shared passion for cats. Katy
kept dogs as pets and bred Siamese cats, which she never thought of as a business. She gave her cats names and considered them members of the family.[14]
One, Perkins Youngboy Dos Passos (named for John's editor, Maxwell
Perkins), not only caught Jo's fancy, but delighted Edward, who was moved

to make a sketch of Perkins. Years later, Jo recalled that Katy "could have been a Helen of Troy & disturbed all Truro but couldn't be bothered. Her Siamese took up with us when they flew to remote places leaving all their animals to a disinterested maid. So Perkins Youngboy Dos Passos selected us as his most abject slaves—the darling—most intelligent, loved to hitch & sang like a church organ."[15] The Hoppers even welcomed Perkins to their table, which they rarely did for human guests; the scene Jo describes recalls the earlier cartoon by Edward of Jo serving her cat Arthur at table, while Edward begs from the floor:

> We've been putting his dish at table with us—he sits on high stool—
> & eats like a little gentleman—doesn't snatch or leap out on table—or
> drag things off plate. We let him see what we eat & if he doesn't like
> it he is satisfied to let us eat. Only he gobbles his so fast—then he's
> ready for ours & E. always puts things on his plate. Tonight he got
> quite excited over the chocolate pudding til he got a taste of it—&
> found it most disappointing—found it resembled liver only in color.[16]

In what style Perkins dined at home is not clear. His two families, however, entertained each other very differently. The Hoppers always invited Katy and John for tea, although they were repeatedly asked back to dinner. Jo exclaimed over one such dinner party, noting in her diary: "What a marvelous meal & off Mexican dishes—cooking a fine art at that house. And such a delight, that house—Celophane curtains—canary yellow (Argentine Cloth) & canary sofa. Nice party."[17] To be sure, the Hoppers did not drink Dos Passos's home-brewed whiskey, if any was offered. Dos Passos recalled: "Lots of times we'd have tea with [Edward and Jo]. Then we'd have to leave and go some place else, and often I felt that Hopper was on the verge of saying something. But he never did."[18]

The friendship did not focus on politics, what with the Hoppers' conservatism and Dos Passos's sympathy for the left. A measure of their lack of real intimacy was the later admission by Dos that he never heard Edward express any political preferences, though he would guess him to be "a sort of McKinley conservative,"[19] which in fact zeroed in on the roots of Hopper's conservatism in the political climate of his youth, shaped not only by the Spanish American War but by the political campaigns that pitted McKinley's support for business and expansionism against William Jennings Bryan in the presidential elections of 1896 and 1900.

The Hoppers regretted being unable to register in 1936 "to vote against Roosevelt" because Edward's painting had kept them on the Cape, as Jo recorded, noting that Edward was "taking the election very seriously—he

finds Roosevelt a vain superficial man. On the screen he looks so terribly in-
sincere. I dislike his face almost as much as one disliked Wilson's."[20] Jo had
undergone a political transformation from the time before her marriage
when she illustrated for The Masses and many of her friends shared Dos Passos's politics. (Alfred Kreymborg had joined Dos Passos and others, in September 1930, on the Emergency Committee for Southern Political Prisoners,
set up in New York City under the direction of Theodore Dreiser.[21]) Given
the Hoppers' passionate antagonism to Roosevelt and the New Deal, it is
amazing that they were able to sustain a relationship with Dos Passos, who
later admitted: "It was somewhere during the years of the New Deal that I
rejoined the United States. I had seceded privately the night Sacco and
Vanzetti were executed [1927]."[22]

By late July of 1936, Hopper again fell prey to the sensation that there
were no more local scenes to paint. Although anxious about expense, he and
Jo decided to try Vermont again. The high prices and swarming tourists re-
pulsed them and "E. didn't find anything to do for a canvas until we were on
our way home, then he wouldn't stop. I made a watercolor of some black eyed
Susans in a tin can—an attempt at lifting oneself up by the boot straps."[23]

Back in Truro, the summer was over before he finally hit on a subject
near home for a new oil, which he identified as "just a house and shed done
directly from nature."[24] Jo conveyed more of the drama in his ultimate choice
and highly individual execution, describing it as "that old house on Pamet
River S. side—amazing old place—with every sort of excrescent hung on to
it—without rhyme or reason & yet on account of the slant of the barn, the tall
grass gone yellow . . . there is a mood of rich content—& peace—among its
shadows—sleeping in the late sunlight—sinking back into the ground—a
happy return to the dust."[25] She concluded: "I think E. has made a lovely canvas—for those who can see past the awful architecture & enter into its mood.
Disassociated from human significance its abstract pattern is very handsome—going in & out of planes, shapes, angles, textures. The things that
Braque has, plus."[26]

The picture inspired Jo again more than two decades later, when she
waxed even more metaphorical and romantic, personifying the subject as an
"old house that had suffered many forms of fancy in the way of turrets & what
nots, superimposed by people into whose hands it had passed—fairly burdened down by them—& quite pathetic sitting out its old age with eye lids
dropped & utterly relaxed & deserted."[27] In more prosaic realism, the local
paper reported that the subject was "a non-descript Summer cottage on
Pamet Road South" owned by Frederick Meier, a retired businessman, who
used the house only "occasionally."[28] A photograph taken of the site just after
Hopper painted it reveals that he not only chose a very particular viewpoint

but deliberately omitted an old apple orchard from the immediate fore-ground.[29] As he transformed this summer place inhabited by a businessman into an abstract pattern, his mind dwelt more on compositional problems than those of the Great Depression. Yet his satiric bent is manifest in the de-cision to foreground the back side, subverting conventions of what makes a good view. The hencoop and barn belonged to the productive life of the old farm in the rural America Hopper cherished. They become picturesque ruins in a countryside reduced to a vacation retreat for wealth gained in the city. It remained for Hopper to select a viewpoint and imagine a composition that bring such changes and ironies to light.

Jo remembered an idyll, with Edward sitting outdoors in the "peaceful setting there surrounded by grass grown high & perched off in the field at its left side" and she described how, in a magical moment, her husband paused

> in his work to step back & look at it from some 20 ft. or so, [when] a little bird came and perched on the stretcher near its left top corner & stayed a while, long enough for E. to call me to come see. Then there were 3 of us enjoying the peace & magic of the scene. When we got the canvas back in the studio, E. put in a glorious sky with big white clouds.[30]

Her contemporary records show, however, that the idyll turned into an ordeal:

> Poor Eddy has had such a dire time finishing his big canvas begun 2 months ago—& so interrupted by downpours & grey weather. The trees lost all their foliage & the sun changed its position so the long shadows all moved off in other places. He's had to wait for a sky. And when it came he was so tortured by mosquitoes—he standing in high grass & they getting up his nose even—nearly frantic—& sun in his eyes—couldn't see what he was doing or tell what it looked like until he got it in doors. But it is lovely.[31]

A year later she still recalled difficulties and gave a different account of the sky:

> E. was working on Cape Cod afternoon all thru Oct. except for one week of rain & fury during which all the trees lost their leaves or had them change color. Also the sun had gone so much farther south since he began the picture that the place looked different. I remem-ber the day he brought the canvas home with the most gorgeous blue sky & white clouds flying, tearing themselves in rush forward from

behind top of roofs—violent & stirring. But alas E. changed it—said the sky too important—& no matter how gorgeous & stirring—he not willing to sacrifice the house for the sky.[32]

No exaltation at finally getting a sky in spite of the physical obstacles, no sense of triumph in the quest, was allowed to outweigh Hopper's concentration on the formal values of the composition, the planes, lines, and shadows of the old coop and the angles of the looming barn and house and pillared porches. In the record book, Jo registered *Cape Cod Afternoon* with another metaphor, noting that the "shed goes in like entrance to a tomb—windows at L. of door with broken panes, some panes in, some out."[33]

Edward got done with his canvas none too soon. On November 3 a telegram abruptly called them to New York with news that burglars had broken into the studio: Jo's jewelry was gone, but not the art. Pulling themselves together, the Hoppers resumed their social routine. The diaries registered a spate of parties and featured a ritual tea for two artistic couples, Dorothy Lapham Ferris, a painter, and her husband Hugh, an architect, as well as Morris Kantor and Martha Rhyther Kantor, both painters, whom they knew from Cape Cod. Martha commemorated the ritual by painting *Tea at the Hoppers*. Even tea was too much entertaining, said Edward, since their parlor was his place of work.

The friendship between the Hoppers and the Kantors thrived for all their considerable differences in age, ethnic background, and politics. Morris, who was nearly twenty years younger than Edward, was a Russian Jewish immigrant. Already fifteen when he arrived in the United States, he never lost "his broad Yiddish accent."[34] In the early twenties, after studying with Henri and his disciple Homer Boss, Kantor became an abstract painter. In the thirties, however, after marrying Martha Rhyther, a New England painter, Kantor changed his style and began to work representationally once again. His subjects, "poetic evocations of the American past—early American houses together with the lives and the objects that occupied them,"[35] intersected with Hopper's own interest in American vernacular architecture of bygone eras. Martha's paintings, such as *Tea at the Hoppers,* contained charming autobiographical vignettes that must have appealed to Jo. On one such occasion, the men talked in the studio while Jo and Martha chatted in the bedroom. Much to the Hoppers' dismay, Edward learned that Morris supported Roosevelt.[36]

Immigrants to New York from the opposite direction, and now neighbors in Washington Square, Dorothy Lapham and Hugh Ferris came from the Midwest. Several years younger than the Hoppers, Hugh had graduated from architectural school in his native St. Louis and Dorothy had studied at the Art Institute of Chicago and then with Robert Henri, which cemented her bond with Jo.[37] After a brief stint in Cass Gilbert's New York office, Hugh became an architectural delineator, eventually celebrating the skyscrapers that Edward disdained.[38] When their daughter Jean was born, Dorothy interrupted her career as an cartoonist and illustrator for *Vanity Fair.* Continuing to work free-lance, she joined the kind of women's organizations that Edward belittled to Jo—the National Association of Women Artists, and Pen and Brush, finding exhibition opportunities and approbation. When Hopper's pal du Bois taught at the New School, Dorothy studied painting with him, something that Jo would not have felt free to do. At least once, the two women worked simultaneously on portraits of each other; at other times, they shared a model.[39]

In December 1936 the Whitney Museum purchased *The Circle Theatre* out of its Third Biennial and Rehn also sold an older oil, *Dawn before Gettysburg.* The Hoppers felt prosperous enough to continue employing Martha Falkner (who also worked for the Ferrises) to clean and to help out when they entertained at their trademark teas.

The holidays were even quieter than usual; the Ferrises came up on Christmas Eve, and Marion and the Rehns on Christmas Day. Edward's dealer was like family. During 1936, Rehn had sold three canvases and three watercolors for a total of $7,050, two-thirds of which was Hopper's income for the year. Reviewing the accounts, Hopper was so thrilled that he gave Rehn a watercolor, *Adams House,* on the spot.

After the ordeal of *Cape Cod Afternoon* and the shock of burglary, finding a new subject proved hard. There had been the distractions of the Whitney show and negotiations for the sale of *Circle Theatre,* also the bustle of entertainments and then a mysterious intestinal ailment of Jo's, diagnosed eventually as colitis, which required him to pitch in and nurse. When he escaped to the movies, what caught his fancy was not the usual fare of comedies, musicals, Westerns, gangsters, and detectives, but one of the new animated films, Walt Disney's *Three Little Pigs,* in which, wrote Jo, Edward especially liked the scene when the big, bad wolf tells the little captured pigs to say "Ahhh!" then stuffs an apple in each mouth and pops them in the oven.[40] Fleeing chatter and female rites, feeling housebound and hemmed in as once in childhood, the gruff man of few words unconsciously identified with a fantasy revenge.

All his prowling found him a new subject, *The Sheridan Theatre,* depicting the interior, this time, of a movie palace with its evocative dim lighting. In the studio Edward wanted to duplicate the dimness, so, by the second week in January 1937, as soon as Jo was getting over her colitis, she had to shut herself off in the little bedroom during the day to let him work in the dark. He was imagining a solitary blonde woman (described by Jo as a "Mae West effect") in a tight red skirt leaning provocatively against an interior balustrade. On January 18, he and Jo delivered the newly finished oil to Rehn. Again distraction intervened. Early in 1937, when President Roosevelt proposed changing the composition of the Supreme Court, the Hoppers' political fever hit a new high and they threw themselves into the general and acrimonious debate.[41] They believed that Roosevelt was trying to make the United States a dictatorship with his, for Jo, "villainous scheme to enlarge the Supreme Court so that he'd control that last stronghold of our national traditions."[42] Jo vigorously stigmatized the proposal in letters to New York's senators, Royal S. Copeland and Robert F. Wagner; she also wrote indignantly to senators from other states. She and Edward even purchased a radio, the better to hear reports on the vote. Jo also joined the National Organization for Hands Off the Supreme Court and tried to convince her friends to write protest letters. For the moment, she was completely distracted from painting by what she saw as an urgent need for political activism.

Given their attitudes toward the New Deal in general and Edward's belief that the federal arts project in particular only favored mediocrity, it is not surprising that he declined an invitation from the Treasury Department to submit sketches for the murals for the post office in Portland, Maine. He gave circumstantial reasons: the commission would keep him from doing other work for at least six months; he knew nothing about the techniques of mural painting; he would not be able to paint what he wanted. Jo thought that if he could choose his own subject, it would be a good thing to do, but of course, he never pursued the project.

Although Jo, too, was distracted in February, she fumed about Edward's inaction. Yet she reflected on her relative good fortune that his only vices were drinking too much coffee in the Automat and "doing word puzzles in the Evening Sun."[43] The Automat, like the movies, was a favorite haunt in sterile periods: in 1927, from just such experience of hanging out, he had painted *Automat*.

February was fallow, but on March 5 he began *French Six-day Bicycle Rider*. The subject had been simmering since December of 1935 when Jo complained to Marion that Edward was going repeatedly to the bicycle races at Madison Square Garden, just to see the same scene over and over again.[44] She was annoyed at the forty-cent tickets he indulged in, when, as she saw it, nothing came of it. At that time, he was stuck and unable to paint and she thought they should take a trip, perhaps to New Orleans, so he could work once again. It was one of the occasions when she simply misunderstood the often lengthy gestation that Hopper's creative process required. Very little of Hopper's time was actually spent painting.

When Lloyd Goodrich asked about the subject of *French Six-day Bicycle Rider* after its purchase by his sister and brother-in-law, the writers Frances and Albert Hackett, Hopper was unusually forthcoming.[45] Although unable to remember the name of the rider, whom he recalled only as "young and dark and quite French in appearance," he said: "I did not attempt an accurate portrait, but it resembles him in a general way. He was I think a member of one of the last French teams to win a race at Madison Square Garden."[46] Hopper added: "He is supposed to be resting during the sprints while his team mate is on the track or at the time when 'The Garden' is full in the afternoon or evening, when both members of a team are on full alert to see that no *laps* are stolen from them."[47] Hopper's uncommonly keen interest reflects the pleasure he took in bicycling as a boy as well as his enduring enthusiasm for French life and culture.

It was also in the spring of 1937 that the Carnegie Institute gave Hopper a one-man show in Pittsburgh. When they sent him a copy of the proposed catalogue text, he expressed his dissatisfaction with the statement that he had begun to etch under the "direction of Martin Lewis," which had been adapted from Barr's chronology in the catalogue for the 1933 retrospective: "This gives the impression that I studied under him—but such is not the case. Lewis is an old friend of mine. When I decided to etch, he who already had done some, was glad to give me some tips, on the purely mechanical processes, grounding the plate, printing etc."[48] Hopper protested that Lewis's work had not influenced his own: "[The] plates that he was making when he was telling me what he had learned about etching were reminiscences of his trip to Japan and he did not start his New York series until some time after I had started mine. His technique, point of view or selection of subject could not have, and did not influence my work in any way whatsoever."[49] As for the friendship, Jo once explained that Lewis and his wife, Lucille, had given the Hoppers up, "quite understandably. It has been too much of a blow to have E.H. so successful."[50]

An essay by the Carnegie's assistant director, John O'Connor, Jr., described Hopper's working methods:

His impression of an isolated house or interior of a room takes on a form in his imagination that appeals to him and he transfers his vision of it to canvas or paper. The transfer is made in as exact a way as is possible, and he eliminates all the incidents which may clutter up or distort the vision. After the form is achieved, the artist proceeds to fill it in with brush work which while modest and lacking in technical display, has a definite, sensuous quality, and in its smoothly, almost imperceptibly painted planes, conveys with a single color varieties of texture.[51]

The Carnegie was not alone in honoring Hopper. On March 22 he learned that his struggles the previous fall had been rewarded. *Cape Cod Afternoon* had made the trip to Washington, D. C., and won the first W. A. Clark Prize ($2,000) and a Gold Medal from the Corcoran Gallery of Art. The victory was sweet if one remembered that the jury's head, William J. Glackens, had been the power obstructing Hopper's path into the notorious show at the Armory in 1913.[52] The news came by telegram. Minutes later, on his way to the cellar to fill the coal scuttle, Edward ran into Floy du Bois, who shrieked with joy: "Guy has just got second prize at the Corcoran!" Jo later described Edward making a "wet blanket" response, "Yes, I know," then answering Floy's flabbergasted questions, "You must forgive me, because I got the first." He had seen Guy's name on the other telegram in the messenger's hand.[53]

The success in Washington demonstrated again how far Hopper had outstripped his oldest friend and first critical supporter. Hopper could take satisfaction that both won prizes, as long as he came in first, as he had in art school. When time came to fill out yet another entry form for a show at the Whitney, the 1937 Annual of Contemporary American Painting, he could write for Prizes or Awards "Corcoran 1st prize and medal," not the laconic "few indeed." He finished his canvas of the bicycle racer the day of the good news.

On March 26, the Hoppers drove down to Washington for a week to receive Edward's prize. All four winners were male and at the presentation ceremony, their wives were called upon to accept their awards. Jo years later still thought it worth recording that for the occasion she had worn her black velvet backless gown with a taffeta ruffle that she called a "Pierrot look"[54] (1920s fashions drew on the costumes of the commedia dell'arte, which influenced the poetry by Verlaine the Hoppers loved and served Edward in two paintings that framed his career). Jo vicariously shared the triumph, for the moment forgetting her own art.

Honor brought an unforeseen ordeal. Eleanor Roosevelt visited the Corcoran press opening and the photographers took her picture with the medalist. Mrs. Roosevelt, unaware of Hopper's attitude toward her husband and all his works, "declared outright that she didn't 'pretend to know anything about art,'" and she "voiced special appreciation of the judges' decision in awarding the first W. A. Clark prize" to *Cape Cod Afternoon,* sharing with the press and the unblinking artist "her pleasing discovery that she could really see the Hopper better when she walked off a little distance to view it."[55] This frank and practical appreciation must have left Hopper more tight lipped than ever.

More natural encounters were the rule that week, although fraught with ironies of another sort. One of the jurors, Richard Lahey, had been a friend since old times at the Whitney Studio Club and engineered Hopper's role in the printmakers society in 1927. The painter Theresa Bernstein had been close enough to warn Jo about the risks a woman ran in giving up her maiden name. Meeting them could only remind Jo how the male network supported Edward and how her career had trailed off.

On Easter Sunday, they drove down with Guy and Floy du Bois to Mount Vernon, and later attended a supper given by Forbes and Nan Watson. On Monday, Watson took them all to see murals by Reginald Marsh and George Biddle. The next day, they made a pilgrimage to the Phillips Memorial Art Gallery. Jo recorded their liking Renoir's *Luncheon of the Boating Party* (the painting inspired one of Hopper's last illustrations, the June 1925 cover of *Hotel Management*). She makes no mention of Duncan Phillips, who eleven years earlier had fallen in love with Hopper's work at Rehn's, praised his aesthetic in print, and purchased *Sunday*.

After the stimulus of recognition, new and revisited, and of friendships renewed, Hopper looked into his own memory to get going on a new canvas, *Five A.M.* He later explained its origin:

> The idea of the picture had been in mind a long time before I started to paint it, and I think was suggested by some things that I had seen while travelling on the Boston, New York boats on Long Island Sound. The original impression grew into an attempted synthesis of an entrance to a harbor on the New England coast. The lighthouse is a not very actual rendition of one near Staten Island in New York harbor.[56]

When Edward became discouraged with the canvas, Jo had to remind him that "there is always one stage in the middle of the work of every canvas where he feels that way about it."[57] Her advice helped, for he was then able to go back to work on his painting, which he would deliver to the Rehn Gallery on the fifteenth of May. It was there that they "christened" the picture *Five A.M.*

When Marion came to town in April, Edward took time off and accompanied her and Jo to see Helen Hayes in Laurence Housman's *Victoria Regina*.[58] (The celebrated actress and her husband, the playwright Charles MacArthur, lived just up the street from Marion in Nyack.) The diary from that spring also records that they saw Victor Wolfson's *Excursion,* Moss Hart and George S. Kaufman's *You Can't Take It with You,* and the 1936 film *Fire over England,* starring Vivien Leigh and Laurence Olivier.

Their interest in theater had been encouraged by Henri, but his influence was something that, in general, Hopper always showed eagerness to forget. *Scribner's,* for which Hopper had made the last of his illustrations, sent the critic Bernard Myers for an interview that provoked a quarrel: Edward did not wish to be identified as a follower of Henri; Jo, with her adoration of their former teacher, felt that Edward was ungrateful and had a swollen ego. Myers wrote that Hopper was "acknowledged as one of the most important American painters of our time."[59]

That spring, Jo attended a rally at Carnegie Hall protesting Roosevelt's Supreme Court initiative.[60] She proudly described it to John and Katy Dos Passos as her first political action, when she arrived on the Cape in early June and found that they were just back from Spain,[61] where Dos Passos had gone to work with Ernest Hemingway and Joris Ivens on a film about the Loyalist cause in the Civil War (his disillusionment with Hemingway and the Stalinists there eventually led to his break with the literary left).[62] The two couples now found some common ground in discontent with FDR, Dos Passos unhappy that the president would not intervene to stop the Fascists in Spain and the Hoppers angry that he was trying to control the Court at home.

Disturbing the peace in Truro, a letter arrived inviting Hopper to illustrate oceangoing vessels for *Fortune.* Hopper told the magazine's art editor that the request came too late since he was already settled in for the summer's campaign.[63] To be sure, anyone aware of his deeply seated resentment at everything connected with illustration would not have bothered to ask. For his part, he had no reason to insult *Fortune,* which had featured reproductions of his paintings in connection with an article on housing in February 1932 and a piece on lighthouses in January 1937.

Another invasion could no longer be put off. In July 1937 Marion finally made her visit to see the house her brother had designed with no provision for others. She slept on a cot in a makeshift guest room in the attic. It soon appeared that Jo had no monopoly on pent-up rage. Jo reflected on the wrath that Marion had been bottling up for thirteen long years: "Said she detested me at sight. Her mother has kept her in leash all these years. It's quite pathetic that she should have had this concentrated animosity bottled up & no good opportunity to let it off on me. These circumstances not altogether favorable—in my own house, at our own table, eating my nice chicken fricassee."[64] Edward, she wrote, "pussy footed about, scared to set off pit of dynamite either to R. or L. of him."[65] Looking back, Jo recalled that they had purposefully built their house with "one sole bedroom—deliberate decision—no provision for any in-laws." She recounted: "E.H. had gone about bowing this way & that, all the solicitude of one not wanting to stir up a volcano—but at last it did erupt—just so much smugness one could endure—then biff—the cover off."[66]

When Marion left, her shaken brother confessed that he could not yet work in the studio where she had stayed, because it was "too full of 'old home town,'" and would take a week or more to clear it out. He even admitted that he had been disagreeable. Jo reflected that the studio had become a living room and now it "seemed like it need disinfecting & incantations to make it a studio again."[67] August was already upon them before Hopper was finally able to get around to painting. As he had the previous summer, he turned to the house on the bay at the end of Depot Road, not far from his own home. Jo described the subject as "same greeny house down on Station road—full tide—house smaller than the one he did last yr. more flood tide."[68] This time he titled his watercolor *Mouth of the Pamet River—Full Tide.* He worked outdoors in the early mornings, racing against the waning flood tide. In a departure from his usual practice, but then it had been an unusual summer, he executed small paintbox-panel-sized studies for quick preliminary effects.

Yet another source of turbulence came from Jo, who by now had had her license to drive for more than a year and who kept insisting on getting to practice. On a trip to a local restaurant for lunch, her insistence led to "a little dispute over parking." Even when Edward allowed her to drive, she was humiliated by his repeatedly taking over when the time came to park. Stubbornly, she held out for her chance, whereupon Edward "hauled me out by the legs while I clutch the wheel—but he clawed at my bare arms & I all but sprawled on the road. Then he blames me that the audience inside peered out thru the windows."[69]

Even so Jo managed to maintain her supportive attitude toward Edward. Two weeks later, her belated fifty-fifth birthday present for him arrived: a ten-volume history of the Civil War, illustrated by Mathew Brady's photographs. Well aware of his inveterate fascination, Jo gave him a gift she knew he would treasure, and yet she regretted: "Now—goodbye painting. E. will have his nose in them . . . everything so beautiful, but so little one can lay hold of for a canvas."[70] The next day, Jo praised Edward for driving to Eastham "to get away from it all." The town, she saw, was no attraction, "so dumb, lacking in everything & flat. But it does show character to turn his back on the Brady pictures of the Civil War & all the text."[71]

As the summer drew to a close, Edward still lacked inspiration for an oil. The pattern of blockage was becoming endemic, certainly not helped by the tensions of Jo's driving and Marion's visit. In spite of previous failure, they resorted to Vermont. Arriving in South Royalton on September 4, they boarded for nearly a month at the White River valley farm of Robert and Irene Slater, for whom they developed a deep affection, remaining friends for life. Edward, feeling more enthusiasm, painted in watercolor *Route 14, Vermont* and several scenes along the White River. Jo made a watercolor portrait of the Slaters' seven-year-old son Alan, which she gave them in 1956. Irene let her know how thrilled they were and recalled: "I had forgotten how irked he looked because he had to pose. . . . You worked so hard on this picture—with Alan not wanting to sit, and Mr. H. making him laugh, and you struggling with both of them. I don't see how you turned out such a nice painting!"[72]

Reentering Cape Cod, the Hoppers visited a sailboat manufacturer at Buzzard's Bay. Jo told the salesman "not to wear himself out trying to sell E. a boat—because he was much too good a husband for his wife to take any chances on him in the high seas in one of those little things."[73] Truro proved cold and gray, but Hopper began a final watercolor, *Shacks at Pamet Head,* on Boylston Beach, painting in the afternoons about three o'clock. He disliked his results, but she wrote: "Oh dear . . . such grand organization—piling up of slats & roofs—he gets effects without the least exaggeration that any one else would be turning themselves upside down to achieve."[74]

Edward voiced a recurrent complaint about the difficulty of art: "the impossibility of rendering the vision of a scene—that each stroke on the paper destroys it more & more, commits him to something else—not what he wanted."[75]

Still without an oil painting to show for their summer, the Hoppers returned to New York and Jo reported going to openings at the Museum of Modern Art and the Whitney. She held a tea in the studio and gloated that although their guests stayed until 7:30 p.m., there was "not a drop of hooch for anyone."[76]

With Edward still stymied in his search for a new subject, Jo began promoting her own work with renewed energy. Before Christmas, she tried to sell or show her new watercolors, which she described as executed with a "loose treatment." While her flower pieces and portraits of children differed totally from his, she was also venturing similar motifs, such as *Cape Cod Hills.* The dealer Marie Sterner, who had included Jo's work in the American exhibition that she had organized for Paris in the summer of 1924, told her that she remembered her as a very talented young person.[77] Sterner however no longer organized shows, merely renting out her gallery space, which was no help. Jo also showed her work to Marie Harriman, Hudson Walker, and four or five other dealers without success. Fortunately, she did not have to live off of the sales of her paintings; she had her disability pension, and Edward's sales were recovering. In 1937 Rehn had sold four of Edward's oils and five of his watercolors for $7,225, two thirds of which was the artist's share, to say nothing of his prize money. But the inventory was not being renewed.

Jo's concern for herself resurfaced at the beginning of 1938, when opportunities seemed to open to get her work into two shows. Both juries included Edward, whose ties to the art network flourished even though he was not able to paint. He was invited to serve in Philadelphia for the 133rd Annual Exhibition of Oils at the Pennsylvania Academy of the Fine Arts, where he had won the medal in 1935, and for the First Biennial Exhibition of Contemporary American Painting at the recently founded Virginia Museum of Fine Arts in Richmond. Jo saw the network functioning in front of her eyes, when Arnold Friedman enlisted Edward to help him decide what to submit and to work for him on the jury. At this, Jo decided that she, too, should submit. Running into Leon Kroll, another of the Philadelphia jurors, she lobbied on her own behalf.

When James Chapin, again a Pennsylvania Academy juror, as in 1935, telephoned Edward, Jo teasingly threatened to "claw the eyes of your jury if they do not pass the canvas I'm sending."[78] Chapin reassured her that he remembered her work from the New Gallery fifteen years earlier, although he had assumed she had given up painting. On visiting the studio, he said he would be happy to include her *Cape Cod Hills* (exhibited as *Sandy Hills*), and wished all the work submitted would be as good. Jo remembered his as the only comforting words to come from any of the men with whom Edward associated. *Cape Cod Hills* was in the Philadelphia exhibition; the juror Hobson Pittman even sent word via Edward that he liked it. As for Edward, probably at Jo's insistence, he showed his 1936 portrait of *Jo Painting*. It was a choice that could only underline her resolve to revive her identity as an artist, and it complemented her participation in the show. The honeymoon was brief. Encouraged by her reemergence in Philadelphia, Jo submitted her *Dauphinée House* for the Virginia show, where Edward served as chairman of an all-male jury which included Bernard Karfiol, John Carroll, Daniel Garber, and Charles Hopkinson. In accepting the position, Hopper employed his usual self irony: "I assure you I have no executive ability whatsoever, and if the chairman's duties require anything more than counting votes, I will not shine brightly."[79] Before the jury met, Edward took to his bed for two days with what he called "body ache." Jo immediately wrote to Tom Colt, the director of the Virginia Museum, to warn him "so that he could be thinking of a likely substitute if it came to that," although she noted, "Edward sais he'll be all right."[80] She reported: "He has a doctor who is even more silent than himself, so beyond being a low thyroid—(so much leaked out) we know nothing."[81]

Dauphinée House was rejected at the jury's preliminary meeting. Although claiming to have voted for her work, a mortified Hopper never let the other jurors know that it was his wife's picture. Jo was furious: "I wanted . . . them all to know I painted!!—They needn't have voted for it— just looked at it with a momentary interest."[82] Alert jurors might have seen that Hopper too had painted a very similar *Dauphinée House*. He rationalized the museum's decision to invite certain painters and subject others to the jury: "There are perhaps certain painters who have to be included."[83] Clearly, his wife was not on his own preferential list. Seething with anger, Jo suffered another bout of colitis.

By February 20, she had recovered sufficiently to venture out, accepting a supper invitation by the Zorachs to celebrate the engagement of their son. Jo had always held up William's appreciation and promotion of his wife's art as the model of male open-mindedness.[84] Marguerite's work had also been rejected in Virginia, but Jo knew the outcome would have been different with William on the jury. The news that the jury awarded first prize to Eugene Speicher and Henry Lee McFee, two male artists from the Rehn Gallery, only emphasized how the system worked against women.

The following day, she summoned energy to go with Edward and the Ferrises to see Orson Welles's *Julius Caesar*. They all found "most striking" the modernistic production with its clear references to Mussolini and the threat to freedom from the Fascist menace.

Adding insult to injury Edward now traveled to the opening of the show he juried at the Virginia Museum, without taking Jo. From Richmond, he proceeded to Indianapolis for yet another jury at the John Heron Art Institute. It was the first time in the almost fourteen years since their marriage that he had left her for more than two or three days at a time. Under the circumstances she took it particularly poorly, feeling "bleak . . . low & lonely & sad & suspended."[85] Throughout her depression, she struggled to keep the fire in the stove burning (a job Edward usually managed) and had trouble staying warm enough. Bee Blanchard, long a widow, hardly helped by suggesting to Jo that this was a taste of how it felt.

Hopper had a good time. The Virginia Museum director, Tom Colt, who had met Jo in New York, wrote to her with humorous assurances about Edward's activities, explaining that he and his wife, Belle, "stood between him and the southern beauties."[86] Later, Hopper commented on the photograph of himself with the Richmond jury: "I look like a very gentle, harmless and much resigned old lady."[87]

When Edward returned from Indianapolis on March 2, Jo was greatly relieved, only to find that he was running a fever. He felt well enough to visit the doctor on March 7, but that afternoon he was too tired to accompany Jo to the Whitney's show of watercolors, prints, and sculpture.[88] The event became special for Jo when Lloyd Goodrich's wife, Edith, told her that she had seen her painting in the exhibition at the Pennsylvania Academy of the Fine Arts. (Goodrich was less generous; years later he admitted that he had never paid attention to Jo's painting.)[89]

On March 17, Jo talked Edward into attending a dinner at the Architectural League, where Hugh Ferris had assembled an exhibition of paintings of architecture since the fifteenth century, including *House by the Railroad*. They splurged, taking a taxi in the rain, because Edward insisted that they should spend their money on themselves rather than allow President Roosevelt to "throw it down a sewer."[90] Jo sat between their neighbor Walter Pach and Claude Bragdon, an architect and author known for his occult writings on the fourth dimension.

Jo lamented that Edward had not painted a canvas for nearly a year— since *Five A.M.* in April 1937. But on March 16, his travels by rail to jury shows began to bear fruit. He started the small canvas that became *Compartment C, Car 293:* Jo posed for the solitary figure sitting in a train interior "by night light in big pokey hat & hair down."[91] Hopper, who painted a view of the landscape at sunset seen through the train's window, once commented: "You know when you go by on a train, everything looks beautiful. But if you stop, it becomes drab."[92]

Both he and she had been suffering ailments that kept them from going out, so Edward hit on a subject that he could conceive and paint without further trips. Three days after making his initial sketches, he had the painting all blocked in. In the morning when Jo left to go shopping, he had only drawn in the image in blue, but when she returned, it was fully under way. He would finish the picture in just twelve days.

For the moment, Jo could no longer think about painting, for Edward was busy with his picture and did not want her in the studio. When they went to the Zorachs again, this time for tea, Jo was thrilled by their kindness about her work; yet without a studio of her own, she could only go to the movies, the theater, art exhibitions, or shopping with her friends. She and Dorothy Ferris went to see the Balthus show at the Pierre Matisse Gallery which Jo pronounced "unqualifiedly rotten." She returned the next day for a second view with Bee Blanchard, but found the work "repulsive—most unsympathetic & academic. What unspeakable children & good for nothing cat."[93] She even confronted Pierre Matisse, but felt that she got no satisfaction from him.

At the opening of George Picken's show at the Marie Harriman Gallery, Jo delivered a message from Edward to Mrs. Picken: he had made efforts on George's behalf with the Richmond jury. For Jo the errand could only rub in the slight, that Edward did nothing of the kind for her. She also recalled Marsden Hartley telling her that evening that "he had learned a lot from his present show at the Hudson Walker Gallery. Everyone of every generation had agreed on one point in his work—its strength, moral strength—the growth says he of long & terrifying experience."[94]

Jo and Hartley had a close mutual friend in Carl Sprinchorn, the painter whom she considered one of her most loyal supporters. One of the few other men whom Jo thought friendly to her work was James Chapin, who was visiting Edward when she returned from the Picken show. Chapin had been a

Edward Hopper, Jo Posing for "Compartment C, Car 293," *1938. Conté on paper,*
15⅛ × 22″ (13 × 55.9 cm.).

sympathetic juror in Philadelphia and now he actually asked to see her work
and acted sincerely concerned. The modicum of attention soothed her sufficiently that she put her pictures away again in peace.

Seeking to attract further notice, Jo gave a tea for Ella Mielziner, who
was leaving for Ireland. Her guest list comprised Guy du Bois's daughter,
Yvonne, who came with her husband, Houghton; Kenneth Miller's wife,
Louise; Ella's son, Kenneth McKenna; and Sprinchorn, who stayed for a late
supper. By entertaining the daughter and the wife of established male artists,
she hoped to get through to the men. The paintings she brought out included
Cape Cod Hills, just back from Philadelphia. In spite of Edward's hate for
these teas, especially when pushing Jo's work, which profoundly embarrassed
him, he helped by shopping for cakes.[95]

The next day, Edward went out with his sketchbook and Jo hoped that he
would begin a new canvas before his painting mood evaporated. But just after
he got back, Martin Lewis dropped by and after the visit a late snowstorm
blew in. Politics continued to distract. Both Edward and Jo wrote letters

protesting the "astounding pump priming expenditures of billions" by President Roosevelt. Edward wrote to Vice President John Nance Garner, who differed with FDR on the Supreme Court proposal and other issues, and also wrote to both New York senators.[96] Also there were the eternal openings to attend. There was Virginia Beresford's work at Marie Sterner's, Edwin Dickinson at Georgette Passedroit's, and Max Jacob at Mrs. Sullivan's.[97] Jo was cheered by an invitation to show at the Golden Gate exhibition in California. The curator, Roland McKinney, chose her *Chez Hopper,* which showed Edward's feet on their stove with his hat hung on the edge of his easel.

By the spring of 1938, the big 1929 Buick that replaced the original Dodge was costing too much to run. Even though Jo hated to give it up, they changed to a secondhand 1935 Buick that had a radio. The maiden voyage was a Sunday jaunt to Nyack, where Marion improvised a dinner of canned food. It was later that month, as they prepared to drive to Cape Cod, that their annual packing ritual escalated to levels beyond anything Jo had recorded before:

> He kept saying what he could see was tormenting me & I getting madder & madder. I get a sound cuff side of my face & he got his face scratched in 2 places. He complains that I lack playfulness, always tense & serious—all which are the obvious effects of trying to keep my nose above water in a struggle not to succumb to his efforts to negate my entity. Never does he say anything about me that isn't derogatory.... He doesn't want to extend his information in anyway that might cause him to alter his ultimatums.... Well it keeps one always tense, on the defensive—one doesn't play.... He knows quite well that it's like pushing a button to start up a tantrum & he keeps pushing it.... My good slip is torn at the knee—& new dress all dirty from floor where he held me down by his knee—& got his face well scratched—2 long scratches down his face—the face that other whiles I'm so fond of. And there's a black & blue bruise on my thigh.[98]

Jo had alluded repeatedly to biting and scratching. This time, her words cannot be passed off as figures of speech. The details are too material and exact. Edward obviously could provoke her, the more easily, no doubt, because of the temper, talked about in her family, that her mother refused to break.

When the packing ritual resumed and they stocked up on paint, canvas, and watercolor paper, Edward wanted to switch to Winsor & Newton, so Jo inherited his Rembrandt oils, including the zinc white, as Edward changed to lead white.[99] While they were packing, John O'Connor, who had written

Jo Hopper, Chez Hopper, *c. 1935. Oil on canvas, 36 × 29" (91.4 × 73.7 cm.).*

about Hopper for the Carnegie catalogue, came in search of pictures for a new exhibition; Edward's failure to suggest Jo provoked a new upsurge of resentment:

> He never has, never will dirty dog that he is. I'll never forget. Never. He understands so completely—has gone thru years & years of it. Went thru it at MacDowell Club shows, went thru it with Tittle—& he never forgets. Always he'd held it against Bellows, Kroll, Randall Davey, Tittle, Henri. He's had all the success of late years, but he's sour on those people. And I'm good and sour too this day when he sat there with his mouth shut. . . . Of course the more sour I get, the fewer pictures I'll do & that suits him fine. . . . The man on whom I've showered all my (far from passive) concern—is a prize hog. The realization of this is embittering me.[100]

On May 26, 1938, they embarked in the new car for the Cape. When Jo wanted to drive, violence broke out again, Edward going "crazy—started in shouting directions. Never can one learn to do anything when permitted only to follow directions, obey commands—military system when you're not allowed to drive or think at all. . . . Following orders brought us up near a post—& E. went wild, I thrown out of driver's seat & E. turned 100% gorilla for the next hour or so."[101]

Yet she did not give up. The fight continued into the next day with what she described as "violence à la gorilla."[102] More than a week later, she reflected upon life with Edward: "To exist at all, one must do battle. He sais insulting things about my mind, the impenetrable stupidity, the impossibility of me learning anything."[103] Lamenting his "revolting egotism," she commented: "It would have been a terrible thing for him to have had a child."[104]

Hopper's repression of Jo seemed to intensify as his own crisis of creativity dragged on. Jo tried to help by bringing down a failed canvas that had been consigned to the attic. The extremely self-critical Edward had started the picture three years earlier: a barn, a porch, and a male clam digger "sitting on edge of high grass," which he had given up in despair.[105] He told Jo that he loathed the painting. Dispirited, he returned to his habitual complaint that he had already painted everything that interested him on the Cape. In calmer moments he went sailing with a Cape friend, Reggie McKeen, and read his way through a one-volume edition of the complete works of Herman Melville, well suited to his love of nautical life and his concern with American themes in art.[106] Melville also had been promoted by Van Wyck Brooks, whom Hopper read and admired.[107]

More than ever discouraged about Edward's inability to work, the Hoppers went to Boston in early August to see a new doctor, B. H. Ragle, who put Edward in Massachusetts General Hospital for tests and found him free of the thyroid and pituitary problems for which he had been treated for years.[108] He gave Hopper the stimulant Benzedrine and vitamin C to treat his depression, fatigue, and lethargy.[109]

Buoyed by the new medication, Edward did some watercolors in late August, when he and Jo returned to South Royalton, where they again stayed at the Slaters' farm. Hopper painted *Sugar Maple, Bob Slater's Hill, First Branch of the White River, Rain on the River, Vermont Sugar House,* and *Windy Day* before a hurricane changed the landscape, forcing him to leave two works unfinished. When asked to comment on the circumstances in which he produced *First Branch of the White River,* he recalled: "I sat in a steep mountain pasture of Slater's looking down on this little stream, so very steep a hill that I had to prop up the front legs of my stool to keep from sliding down. Aside from that and the curiosity of the cows, the occasion was not momentous."[110] Jo fondly described the farm: "They had charming animals on the place. A calf named Nancy, with eyes like a Hollywood star used to lick E. Hopper's coattails & follow him about."[111]

Back on the Cape, Hopper painted a watercolor, *Crossing at Eastham,* in October; rainy weather forced him to finish the sky in the studio. Of another watercolor, *Cottages at North Truro,* Jo noted on November 6: "All that last watercolor of E.'s needs now is a sky. We drove all the way to N. Truro to see whether what on hand would do. E. decided not." They were again unsuccessful five days later, but eventually, Hopper got his sky and they could go back to the city.

In Washington Square, Jo suddenly found what she had desired for years. She was finally able to take over the rear studio on their floor at no extra cost, as new regulations prohibited renting it separately without its own bath. Once occupied by Rockwell Kent, it had no heat; yet, for the first time since leaving her quarters on Ninth Street in 1925, Jo had a space of her own.

Edward had now been living at 3 Washington Square since 1913, a quarter of a century. Although central heating was still to come, the Hoppers stayed in the famous old building by choice. They cherished the north-facing skylight and the open views to the south. Greenwich Village remained a vantage point for their ceaseless movements around the city, the invitations and openings, the escapes to plays and movies, the ever more urgent prowling in search of scenes. Not least, the rent suited their habitual frugality and Edward's protracted crisis, shrinking inventory, and fluctuating revenue, which in 1938 fell back to $4,750, with no prizes and the sale of only one watercolor and two oils.

THE STRUGGLE TO PAINT: 1939

AS 1938 WOUND to its end, neither Edward nor Jo was finding it possible to paint. His difficulty came from within, while she had only just found a studio again after thirteen years. Her old network had long since broken down, and her devotion to his career had not earned mutual and reciprocal support. If anything, his ridicule of his wife sharpened, fueled by his growing frustration. She had all she could do to keep from losing hope.

Once again he found an idea at the movies. In December 1938 at the Palace Theater, Hopper used dark crayon to draw the curtained entrance to one of the boxes. More than fifty sketches later, he would be ready to paint. Christmas briefly interrupted his progress, but by the day after the holiday, he was back at work. He went again to the Palace to collect more data and then returned to his studio, where he began to sketch out the set-up in charcoal on canvas. Jo, wearing slacks and with her hair hanging down, posed for him as a movie usherette. Except for mealtime interruptions, he worked day and night. On the thirtieth of December, he was still visiting movie theaters in the mornings and painting in the afternoons. The work in progress dominated their lives. They spent New Year's Eve quietly at home; Edward fell asleep before the arrival of 1939.

Edward Hopper, Study for
"New York Movie," *1939.*
Conté on paper, 11 × 15"
(27.9 × 38.1 cm.).

On New Year's Day, Jo commented:

E. in studio wrestling with a dark movie interior. It is such a difficult
subject. Dark is always so difficult. Not to be there to work as he
looks—& not even taken from any one theatre—bits from all of
them. So far it seems not so dark to me. Will get everything placed &
developed I suppose before he lets the dark descend. He would have
everything there & know where it is—the way we know where all
our things can be laid hold of in the dark. I keep well out of the way.[1]

The next day, Jo noted that Edward had a good day at work on his painting
and that she had stayed shut up in the bedroom.

That night, the Hoppers went to see Robert E. Sherwood's *Abe Lincoln in
Illinois.* They declared the cast inadequate and the play (which won a Pulitzer
Prize for 1938) disappointing, a judgment conditioned no doubt by their contempt for FDR, for whom Sherwood sought to create a mythic dimension in
the face of threatening war by evoking Lincoln's struggle with his own call to
greatness.[2] Hopper's cynicism about political figures was matched only by his

scorn for artistic reputations. On January 7, at dinner with Guy and Floy du Bois, who had a new duplex studio, the talk turned to William Glackens, who had chaired the jury at the Corcoran the previous spring when Guy and Edward placed second and first: the old man was certainly not "the greatest painter" in America, insisted Edward, although Jo vainly struggled to temper his asperity, as she always did in public, even among such intimate friends.[3]

Few contemporary artists held Hopper's respect. One who did, Charles Burchfield, was in town for his show at Rehn's and dropped by on January 9. For once, their visit was not interrupted by Jo, who busied herself with her women friends. When she saw the Burchfield show two days later, Frank Rehn, aware of her anger at not having a dealer for her own work, artfully diverted her attention by showing her Edward's portrait *Jo Painting,* then on view in the side room. Afterward, walking down Fifth Avenue, she passed the Grand Central Galleries, where there was an exhibition of Robert Henri. In the window, she saw her portrait. Remarking that it was good that she weighed some twenty-five pounds more now than she had then, Jo noted that Edward's portrait of her with the "bushy mane" was "much the finer." "Imagine—one's portrait in 2 places on 5th Ave. at the same time—the straining student in smock & britches & the wife who paints. Well, I'm glad to be the wife who paints."[4] The next day, she settled back into her role as model when she posed for the two moviegoers "in black hat with veil & fur coat, then little brown cloth hat with gala feathers & linen collar. They are to sit in the dark, but if any stray ray hits them they must be right."[5]

The Rehn Gallery loyally protected Edward's prices when Duncan Phillips put *The City* up for auction. Peggy Rehn attended the sale and bought the canvas for $310, noting that only dealers had turned up and there were no big transactions: a pastel by the famous Mary Cassatt had gone for just $200.

Before the Rehns could see the new work, Hopper suffered a last-minute crisis of confidence. On January 21, Jo noted that he had been at it since before Christmas and was "discouraged about the original idea, the raison d'etre, always escaping, evaporating with every stroke added—the distance increased, denied, made into something different," even though, she said, he was "getting depth, solidity."[6] Five days later, he once again had Jo pose out in their cold hall for the figure of an usherette holding a flashlight. On February 2, they delivered the newly titled *New York Movie* to the gallery, where the glee—it was "greeted like a newborn heir" said Jo—testified to acute awareness of how difficult it had been for Edward to work.[7]

In March, Hopper's early supporter Forbes Watson was to lecture at a luncheon at the Architectural League on government-sponsored murals around the country. Hugh Ferris invited them both, but Jo went alone. She feared that Edward would get into an argument because he did not believe "with the country on the verge of bankruptcy great sums should be spent that way—thousands to people like Kroll, Sterne, Schnakenberg & such like who have plenty without."[8]

Also in March, Burchfield came by again, while in town to serve on the jury for the World's Fair exhibition "American Art Today." He complained in his diary that Jo, as usual, "monopolized the conversation"; and he added unsympathetically, "Her grievance that day was that Hopper, according to her, had not only not voted for her picture at Richmond, but had failed to try to influence the other jurors in its favor. God help the artist who is married to another artist!"[9] Jo would have been happy to know that Burchfield at least recognized that she was an artist. Around this time Jo asked Stella Falkner, her cleaning woman's daughter, to pose for a portrait. Dorothy Ferris came over to share the young girl as a subject. Edward, more generous than usual, commented that if Jo could "superimpose some form on [the portrait] & keep what's there, it will be pretty good."[10] Although the girl returned twice, Jo never got a satisfactory likeness. But Edward sauntered in and made a drawing of Stella that Jo had to admire.[11]

Edward's benevolent disposition took an even more telling form when he gave Jo a birthday gift artfully contrived with evidence of their shared affection and culture. She was thrilled. He wrapped the package in brown paper tied with an old ribbon and placed inside white tissue paper sealed with a red paper bonnet cut-out, and inside that, a pocket-size French dictionary. To decorate the card, he cut pink paper to form wild rose petals and green paper to make leaves, and he added in limping verse:

> Jour de naissance, mars 1939
> Les orteils de Josie sont de rose
> Et elle aura le français
> Where ever she goes.

["Day of birth, March 1939. The toes of Josie are pink and she will have French wherever she goes," after the nursery rhyme "Rings on her fingers and bells on her toes, she will have music wherever she goes."] Also enclosed was fifteen dollars to buy a new dress.

In mid-March, Martin Lewis visited the studio: he was overweight and smoking heavily, perhaps reflecting his frustration at his lack of success. On March 30, Jo noted that Edward had "made sketches at a burlesque & is juggling his ability of attempting a canvas, but wants to see things more clearly—wants to make sure he is really interested before starting off."[12]

Edward Hopper, Portrait of Stella Falkner, *1939. Sanguine on paper, 21 × 16¼″ (53.3 × 41.3 cm.).*

As often in periods between paintings, Hopper was reading and he shared with Jo some of Paul Valéry's criticism of Baudelaire and Stendhal.[13] Valéry analyzed the influence of Poe on Baudelaire and the impact of Baudelaire on Verlaine, Mallarmé, and Rimbaud,[14] all of whom were familiars chez Hopper, where Edward's own thinking about aesthetics must have made some of Valéry's ideas seem quite cogent, especially his examination of the creative process and the conflicting claims of emotion and intellect on the artist. Valéry criticized Stendhal for trying "to be genuine to the point of falsity. The genuineness he strives to promote changes imperceptibly under his pen into a tone designed to appear genuine."[15] Valéry questioned: "How can we avoid selecting what is best out of the true we are working on? How can we avoid underlining, rounding off, touching up, adding color, trying to make it clearer, stronger, more disturbing, more intimate, more brutal than the model?"[16] He insisted that authors "selected" and that the result was "inevitably lighted, painted, and made up according to all the rules of the mind's theater."[17] The tension between selection and truth suggests what Hopper was getting at by saying that he put his personality into the "realism" of his painting. Valéry's metaphor of mind as a theater with its conventions intertwines with the centrality of theatrical imagery for Hopper's mind.

Edward's excursion into burlesque went no further, but on April 2, he made two sketches for a new canvas of the "bridle path in Central Park with the city outside & riders on the path." Jo was "excited over this new picture—sure it will be outstandingly fine."[18] The next day, he went up to West Seventy-second Street to sketch figures and horses, and the following day, Jo enthusiastically reported in her diary: "He's starting a new canvas—praise be. Had his sketches all stretched out and began charcoal sketch. This is the big event in this family!"[19]

On April 7, Hopper felt that he needed to "look up horses in old magazines." Jo noted that he "has a little book of horse anatomy" and that he had explained it to her. But Edward was having trouble with the picture and was returning to the park nearly every gray day to make sketches of details. Before he completed this canvas, he produced eighteen sketches. Jo noted: "After talk one day of ditching it, he goes right on. The color right now is very dull—I forbear mentioning it—hoping he will fight his way thru. I keep out from underfoot."[20]

Edward complained that he did not "see the thing clearly enough & that is what always happens if he starts anything before he has sharp enough interest & clear enough vision of what he wants to do."[21] By April 18, Edward's picture was "still pretty drab—but coming along. He scraped off paint making a line of white along back of horse in nearest foreground. E. not wanting to paint over & have underpainting come thru in later years. This line of white so effective. I'd be glad to see it left on—but E. no—indeed—that tricky & inconsistent too."[22] Edward remained discouraged and was fatigued by having to stand up to paint. His work was progressing very slowly.

On April 22, Jo noted that Edward was "out all morning looking at data & trying to keep up interest. The picture is making so many difficulties."[23] But the next evening, she wrote:

> E.'s picture has come on splendidly this week. . . . E. had been working 6 or 7 hours—& the rocks in that picture show it—form, color, solidity of the actual place. Unmistakably Central Park this time of year on a grey day. Almost the smell. Ground all scuffed in foreground—bridle path domain—barren, uninviting color. Some bare skinny trees have come out of the rock, to-day. He would construct the rock first & it is constructed. What thanks is he to get for doing the job so masterly? The horses too reek horse flesh. When one would expect the picture to be finished, there is certain to be 2 or 3 more weeks work due.[24]

Hopper worked hard to finish the picture by the end of April. On the 27th, giving in to pressure from Rehn, who wanted to show it the following week, he signed and varnished the canvas, calling it *Bridle Path,* and rushed to deliver it to the gallery. The very next day, Hopper went out looking for something else to paint. When it started to rain, he ducked into a movie house, his frequent escape and sometime solution to these recurrent quests. After the troubles he had just been through, he was in no mood to start anything without a clear vision of what he wanted to achieve. He did not begin another canvas before he and Jo left for the Cape.

In early July of 1939, Harriet Jenness died. It was she who had firmed up the Hoppers' courage to build in the first place and provided a roof till theirs was done. They drove to Chestnut Hill for the funeral.[25] For comfort, they turned to the Kantors. Morris had been the first to call when they arrived and Martha always hit it off with Jo.[26] Since Morris painted sites portrayed earlier by Edward, including South Truro Church, he may have seemed a kind of disciple as well as neighbor and friend.

Finding nothing new to paint near their house, Edward took to driving again. He had pushed down as far as Orleans before he came upon a location he felt he could use. Again he made sketches on the spot before going back to the studio to start what he later described as

> no exact transcription of a place but pieced together from sketches and mental impressions of things in the vicinity. The grove of locust trees was done from sketches of trees nearby. The doorway of the house comes from Orleans about twenty miles from here. The figures were done almost entirely without models, and the dry blowing grass can be seen from my studio window in late summer or autumn. . . . The dog is listening to something, probably a whippoorwill or some evening sound.[27]

His long-time friend Richard Lahey, the printmaker, filled in details:

> Edward was getting the dog painted and he was pretty well along with the whole composition—one day he decided to go down to the Truro Library and check the physical [identification] in the encyclopedia so as not to be at fault—There seemed to be no actual collie dog in Truro—or at least none that had come to his attention. When he returned with meager information from the library—they parked the car and there was this small miracle—just the type of dog that was wanted came out of the parked car ahead—with a child while the mother went in the nearby store to shop. Jo made friends with the children and dog—Edward got out his sketch book and pencil and while Jo held the dog with patting . . . Edward got his sketch.[28]

Edward Hopper, Study for "Cape Cod Evening," *1939. Conté and pencil on paper,
15 × 22⅛″ (38.1 × 56.2 cm.).*

Such congenial collaboration by Jo did not forestall the emerging
image of a deteriorating relationship between a man and woman. Hopper
had previously used the same metaphor of evening to suggest the end of a
romance in the etching he called *Summer Twilight.* In the painting the figures do not even look at one another. The dog, too, appears distracted, perhaps, as Hopper suggested, listening to a distant whippoorwill. The woman
appears angry, her posture tense and forbidding—a stance that suggests the
fury that Jo recurrently directed toward Edward. These figures appear to
be trapped in one another's moods; only the dog cocks its head alertly,
freely, toward something beyond. In the end, Jo and Edward engaged in
their usual fantasy about the scene, identifying the woman as "A Finn" and
trying out as titles *The Whippoorwill* and *After Supper* before deciding on
Cape Cod Evening.

Losing no time, by August Hopper was working on another round of
preparatory sketches, thirteen at least:

Ed is doing a fine large canvas in studio—sail boat, boys nude to the
waist, bodies all tanned, lots of sea and sky. It ought to be beauty.
Frank Rehn will be delighted. Everyone has wanted Ed to do sail
boats. He has only 2 or 3 weeks to finish it—and will need some fine

weather with rolling seas to go look at. Dense fog today but scarcely
any rain here either.[29]

Hopper finished *Ground Swell* on September 15. It was to be a season with
none of the watercolors that had been his staple. Five days later he and Jo left
the Cape, about a month earlier than they normally would.

In the aftermath of his 1937 show at the Carnegie Institute, Hopper had
been asked to serve on the jury for an international exhibition of paintings
there. Before the judging in Pittsburgh, festivities began in New York with a
cocktail party followed by dinner at the Rainbow Room. Homer Saint-
Gaudens, the director, was there, along with the other jurors: Eugene Speicher, Gerald Brockhurst (an English painter and etcher), and Hipôlito
Hidalgo de Caviedes (a painter from Spain), as well as Juliana Force of the
Whitney and the art critic Margaret Breuning. All together they took the
midnight train to Pittsburgh. (In August, when Hopper had corresponded
with the Carnegie, he had reminded Saint-Gaudens of his invitation for Jo to
travel to Pittsburgh with him: "I know that she has been looking forward to
going very much, and she would be little trouble. I might even bring her in a
dog basket."[30] The quip betrays his ambivalence and embarrassment.)

It was Edward's first "international" and he took the theme seriously, deciding to bypass his friends among the exhibitors—Burchfield, du Bois, and
Kantor—in favor of Maurice Utrillo, whose entry turned out to be less than
hoped for. Edward thought Burchfield's canvas was not one of his best; nor
did he feel strongly inclined to give the prize to du Bois or Kantor. Jo noted
that Edward was "falling over backwards to be unbiased, overstep his native
prejudices for work he didn't like at all."[31] In the end, the jury assigned first
prize to Alexander Brook, second to Yasuo Kuniyoshi, and third to Marc
Chagall. An honorable mention went to Raphael Soyer, with whom Hopper
would become well acquainted. True to form, Edward begged off giving a
speech at the close.

Jo was elated when Saint-Gaudens told her that he had seen her *Chez
Hopper* at the Golden Gate Exhibition in California. And back in New York,
she was thrilled to receive a questionnaire to fill out for *Who's Who in American Art;* the listing was probably prompted by her inclusion in two group exhibitions during the last two years.

The positive reinforcement in Pittsburgh motivated Jo to begin a painting of Edward's studio. Although Edward was not yet painting again, and,
she wrote, "had nothing in mind to start on," he still "felt an affliction to have
me working [there]."[32] He gave her only a week to finish and "retire to my
rear studio where I find nothing to work on but some still life of fruit & I don't
want to do still life at all."

The diaries report familiar rituals. Now Hugh and Dorothy Ferris came to tea with Reginald and Felicia Marsh. Felicia asked to see Jo's work and so the Marshes went into Jo's studio. When they rejoined the others, they found Edward showing the folk painting purchased years earlier. Jo viewed this as a competitive gesture by Edward, an attempt to undermine her paintings. Nonetheless, she felt "quite a thrill for Reggie Marsh to find them solid."[33] After the guests left, she unleashed her anger, but when Edward spent most of the next day away from home, she felt guilty and remorseful.[34] They took the Nyack bus together on November 3, to see Marion and take a short walk up the street to look at the grand house that belonged to the playwright Charles MacArthur and his wife, Helen Hayes, who was one of their favorite actresses.

The MacArthurs wanted to commission Hopper to paint a picture of their home. Jo noted that "E. has been trying to sidestep it, but Frank Rehn so wants E. to do it." After they spent nearly four hours studying it, she admitted, "I can see it will be very difficult to do—hard to get it simple enough. It will have to be the front—the back too cut up with staircases coming down from 2 sides & much doing with grounds: swimming pool expanse—then tennis court expanse & so on terrace after terrace down to the river & boat landing at edge. Interior charming."

Of their famous hosts she wrote:

> It was so nice to meet her, very simple, real genuine, like her work. She's very nice—& friendly & interested. After lunch Mr. McA. kept us at table talking about movies. He listened with so much interest to E.'s views & what E. said about a movie without any plot—a movie roving about the city, with the noises of the city, boats tooting, trucks rumbling, etc. E. so crazy about the great beauty of this city.[35]

The view from the opposite camp was less rosy, as Helen Hayes later confessed: "I had never met a more misanthropic, grumpy, grouchy individual in my life, and as a performer I just shriveled under the heat of this disapproval. I backed into a corner and there I stayed in the dark, lost. . . . Really I was utterly unnerved by this man."[36] She claimed that Hopper was "like a big hellcat of anger and resentment at the whole thing," remembering his protests: " 'I can't do this house. I don't want to paint this house. It does nothing for me. . . . There's no light and there's no air that I can find for that house.' "[37]

For a painter who had found nothing to paint since September, and who had been suffering from a dearth of new subjects for some time, Hopper's attitude was remarkable, yet only true to the form of his uncompromising and cantankerous independence.

On November 8, a resigned Hopper took the bus alone to sketch. Hayes recalled that he turned up unannounced; she only learned of his presence when her daughter exclaimed that there was a man outside making a picture: "I went to the window and sure enough, there was Hopper, grumpy as ever, sketching our house."[38] For Jo, his behavior was an embarrassment:

> I do wish I could change his attitude toward the job. It is a worthy enough house & he might get to seeing something in it. The worst of it is it is now so late in the season & it's getting cold. He'll have to make many trips up there to make sketches & it's such a distance to do that. He didn't want to go to-day at all but one could see the sense-lessness of further delay, when it was dimly unlit & we've had too much grey weather.[39]

The next day, which was bitterly cold but brilliantly sunny, Jo and Edward rode up together. Edward drew the house "from grounds in front," and then made a drawing for a detail of the facade. He felt so chilled that he went inside for a while. Jo noted: "Met [MacArthur's] mother. E. says she seems young & not a bit like Bessie Brewer's infered description with brogue."[40] Clearly the Hoppers had gossiped with Breuer, Henry Varnum Poor's wife, who was familiar with the neighborhood, picking up on the "Irish" theme. Edward went to it again the next day and "came back with such a fine sketch of house with branch of tree in foreground dangling from left top."[41] When it became clear that Hopper, after all his protests, was actually at work, Hayes recalled that "Charlie phoned Frank Rehn and said, 'How did you do that? What changed his mind?' And he said, 'Well, Jo and I have been working on him and after having an afternoon of Jo . . .' "[42]

Relaxing the pace a little, Edward went with Jo on some of their typical rounds. The Metropolitan Museum offered shows of photography and "Three Hundred Years of American Painting." Two days later, on November 14, Jo wore her "black lace Goya dress" when they went to the opening of a major exhibition at the Modern Museum: "Picasso: Forty Years of his Art."[43] They were amazed at Picasso's "prolificacy," which stood in such contrast to their own output, and liked the Blue and Rose periods, but precious little from the rest.

On November 16, Hopper finally stretched his canvas. Jo recorded a further lament about the house's lack of "sizable spaces":

> The walls cut up or all the rooms are too shallow, 3 or 4 parlors all in a row—windows & doors at ends so no stepping back any satisfac-tory distance from large picture. So this canvas can't be very large—

40 × 28 or so. E. is making it wider but scheming so that it can be cut off—foreground below & sky above. The view is close to house so as to keep roof angles bold & impressive. . . . He's taking it from his 2″ [2nd] sketch in crayon—which is a beautiful drawing. If the canvas can be successful, as full of mood as the sketch, it should be very fine. Besides it is helping E. a lot to have made this fine drawing at the very start when he was so bored & unwilling to undertake the project. . . . He squared off the canvas to reproduce sketch as closely as possible.[44]

Once he capitulated to the commission, the exacting method employed suggests that Hopper identified the project more with his earlier commercial art than with the personal and expressive aims of his mature aesthetic. He transferred his sketch to the canvas in as mechanical a way as he could, not looking for other, more creative solutions to the composition. On November 24, he and Jo were on the bus again, so he could check the color of the house and observe more details. Edward sat outdoors in the cold and made a drawing with color notations.

On December 8, Frank Rehn came to see the new canvas. Impressed, he encouraged Hopper to persist. When he left, Edward scrambled to get up to Nyack to see the house once more by daylight. Jo exulted that the picture looked better than the house, representing the "house clarified."[45] As the days grew shorter and Edward pressed on, she remarked that he became "cross & bothered because the daylight lasts so little time."[46] Still, he got up at five-thirty to get an early start, and by December 11, though still cross, he had painted the clapboards on the house.[47] By the 16th, Edward was nearly done. Jo commented, "They should like it—it has wonderful fidelity to all familiar details, but so enhanced by a vision of great clarity."[48] The next day, she noted that Edward was "cussing" her, the Rehns, and Helen Hayes for wanting him to include Hayes's daughter and French poodle in the picture. He did not give in. No figures intrude.

On December 21, the Hoppers took the finished painting to Rehn. The title was *Pretty Penny,* from the owners' name for their home. MacArthur phoned to say how pleased they were, and Jo fretted: "E. was so gruff—E. certainly not at his best over the phone & everyone else so cordial. I had so much wanted to invite them down to the studio."[49] Edward scotched that, insisting that his patrons would have no time; furthermore, they would "think we live in the uttermost poverty with the stove & the stairs & wouldn't think the picture could be worth its price."[50] Rehn asked twenty-five hundred dollars, more than half of Hopper's sales for the entire year.

For Christmas 1939, Marion came and Jo even cooked a chicken. In a rare gesture of regard and conciliation, Marion brought for Jo a brooch that had belonged to her mother. Valuing symbolism not at all, Edward professed to dislike the color and told Jo to give it back. For once resigned, she noted only that her husband was "so fussy about anything I wear."[51] (In fact, he did not like her in the bright colors that she loved, preferring that she dress entirely in black; even brown garments met his disapproval. When he particularly disliked some garment of hers, he "bought" it from her, to get it out of sight.)

Holiday spirit fared better when Jo persuaded Edward to bid on a little French desk at an auction house where they sometimes found antiques. She was delighted when his bid was high. Installing the new desk in their bedroom the last week of the year, Jo filled it with her possessions, while Edward moved her old desk to his studio. The changes inspired her to take stock of developments in Edward's working space since he had moved to the front studio in 1932. To her mind, her old desk merely added to the clutter and preempted the last free wall: "That room is fast losing all the old glamour it had the night before we moved in there from the rear studio. . . . Now that desk— so there is no longer any empty panel of white wall—that was the last."[52] The years of growth were over. Neither she nor he could imagine the turns and higher achievements, with harsher tensions and displacements, in store.

THE WAR BEGINS: 1940

AMIDST THE REPORTS of painting on Cape Cod, jurying in Pittsburgh, balking at a lucrative commission, the diaries take no immediate notice that on September 3, 1939, war was declared on Germany by Britain and
the Hoppers' beloved France. The previous European conflict had given
Hopper his anomalous flash of glory with the poster *Smash the Hun.* Now,
neither he—at fifty-seven—nor his private America would be likely to see
service. Yet the conflict soon quickened the sympathies of both Edward and
Jo and gradually began to revolutionize their professional world. The war
was to have an unforeseeable and far-reaching impact on the American art
scene, as vanguard artists, vilified and threatened, fled Europe and found
refuge in New York, where the newcomers attracted a large share of the attention from critics, galleries, collectors, and museums that had been flowing
to Americans like Hopper.

On the home front, conflict was endemic. Edward's attitudes once more
sparked Jo's commentaries when he prepared to send *Cape Cod Evening* to the
1940 Annual Exhibition of Contemporary American Art, which opened at
the Whitney on January 10:

> I am simply devastated over that frame. A very fine noble picture
> blotted out, absorbed by a wide heavy frame. A beautiful frame—

but deadly on that picture. Too overpowering, the 3 small scattered figures swallowed up. It's all nonsense this talk about the frame making no difference—& one not looking at the frame. The frame is part of the picture and is deciding as the light in which a picture is shown. Anyone knows what a hat will do to a woman—hat & all her clothes. They could all but destroy her, belie all her qualities. It is a great grief that E. will not have me around when he orders his frames.[1]

The frames on *Cape Cod Evening* and *Pretty Penny* "snuff the picture out," she added, so that they "scarcely look like Hoppers." She felt these works were her "children," as she often put it, and yet he shunned her advice.

Adding insult to injury, Edward chose this moment to launch one of his typical slurs on women artists, "Mary Cassatt got it all from Degas," setting off a dispute with Jo and an indignant sequel in the diary to the effect that Dorothy Varian, Peggy Bacon, and Marguerite Zorach were "better than plenty of men over there at that Whitney. . . . E. only too glad to have me left out. . . . Why don't I paint? Why indeed? On what—from out of what inner gladness?"[2]

As January dragged along without a new canvas on Edward's easel, Jo saw that he had Paul Valéry out of the library again, reading "Autres Fragments sur Mallarmé: Morceaux Choisis," with remarks on painting and the "intellectual invention" of the symbolist poet's last poem, "Un Coup de Dés." Edward was so taken that he sat down and typed out the essay. Going to return the book and get another Valéry, he braved the cold and walked to the library because his doctor had ordered exercise. For Jo he checked out, whether by request or not is unclear, a tome on psychiatry. More than a treatise, what she needed was a cease-fire, with a cessation of hostilities and some sign of appreciation for her painting. A slight thaw came by an improbable route, bringing with it a first sign that the events in Europe had caught the Hoppers' sympathies. Jo and Edward each agreed to contribute watercolors to a silent art auction organized for the benefit of Finnish Relief and Edward even told her that her watercolor "looked like a Raoul Dufy."[3] At the auction, she was cheered to see her Gloucester sailboats hanging next to his *Route 14, Vermont*;[4] and she was thrilled at the prospect that her work would be purchased by a real collector, only to find that the high bidder was Anne Tucker, her friend, while Edward's work had been acquired by the distinguished architect Philip Goodwin, himself not exactly a stranger, since he was a trustee of the Museum of Modern Art.[5]

The mail brought a fresh invitation from the museum, prompting Jo to reflect that she and Edward had been asked to every opening since the founding in 1929 and that "it's high time we joined"—which they did.[6] The show was featuring masters, past and present, from Italy. Jo, who had been there, gushed over Botticelli's *Birth of Venus,* giving Edward, who had never completed his grand tour, an opening for a contrarian riposte: "only another pretty girl picture."[7] The resort to verbal caricature betrays, as did his satiric sketches, some deeper stir.

The next day (January 26) Edward announced that he needed to go out to "meditate" a new picture. Jo, ever eager to help him get to work, even went into the kitchen early to give him dinner. Although it was a cold night, he was determined to take the El uptown. The following day Jo was gratified to see that "he has a black and white drawing of a man at a desk in an office & a girl to left side of room & an effect of lighting" and had gone out to buy canvas.[8]

The scene that Edward worked up with such dispatch after his brush with Botticelli features a curvaceous female alone at night with an uninterested male. Unlike the Venus, who assumes a modest stance, shielding naked virtue, Hopper's svelte secretary flaunts sexuality through a skin-tight blue dress. Yet in both compositions, wind gives palpable definition to the scene. Renaissance convention could represent winged gods with puffing cheeks propelling the advent of the goddess. In modern New York billowing curtains and flapping shades hint at seductions for the eye.

As the project progressed, so did the commentaries. By February 1 Jo was reporting:

> E. has his new picture drawn in charcoal. He is doing things with no end of preparation—had 2 highly finished crayon sketches. Seems to seek delays for beginning a canvas. It's a business office with older man at his desk & a secretary, female fishing in a filing cabinet. I'm to pose for the same tonight in a tight skirt—short to show legs. Nice that I have good legs & up & coming stockings.[9]

On February 5, they took time out to see a show at Rehn's by Henry Varnum Poor, whose application of paint struck Jo as stylish, causing Edward to say disparagingly that she was too carried away by the way paint was put on. Yet the sight of one of his watercolors hanging in the back room where his fortunes with Rehn began sent her into an affectionate reverie:

> It's a fine thing for me that I married that man. Even if I dance very little anymore. Oh yesterday, while E. painting, a most lovely Viennese waltz—Straus—came over the radio. E. left the easel & came to waltz with me—& did very nicely. I've insisted on his learning the waltz, very simple cut down to feeling the rhythm, one step & other

Edward Hopper, Study for "Office at Night," No. 1, *1940. Conté and charcoal with touches of white on paper, 15 × 19⅝" (38.1 × 49.8 cm.).*

leg brought up to meet the first one. . . . The music got E. & about he went. He's amazingly light on his feet when he dances."[10]

In dancing at least she had brought him far from his reticence long ago in Maine. It was Valentine's Day when the running commentary resumed: Edward had "been working on his office picture. It was dry so he took it off its first stretchers & put it on the stouter kind that cost a lot. Said the picture not finished but since he didn't feel as energetic he'd get that job done & paint when he felt more like it."[11] The next day, since he was not feeling well, she gave him breakfast in bed. Later, he "pulled his little canvas down low on the easel & sat down to work on it this afternoon, too bored to lie flat & rest his lengthy bones."[12]

Buoyed by the relative gladness of the previous month, Jo attempted a canvas of her own, a view of the bedroom fireplace done with the Rembrandt paints handed down from Edward. Both were still painting when she wrote on February 19: "The days are longer now & we both work until it is almost pitch dark. Each day I don't see how E. can add another stroke to his—& each day he goes right on & this picture becomes more palpable—not fussy . . . reduced to essentials . . . so realized. There is a little typewriter that could almost be stolen & carried away—& the room is a room."[13] When they took the finished work to the gallery on February 22, John Clancy, Rehn's assistant, suggested the title *Cordially Yours; Room 1506*. Edward proposed *Time and a Half for Over Time, Etc.* before they settled on *Office at Night*.

The new work was purchased by the Walker Art Center in Minneapolis, which years later elicited an explanation from the artist:

> The picture was probably first suggested by many rides on the "L" train in New York City after dark glimpses of office interiors that were so fleeting as to leave fresh and vivid impressions on my mind. My aim was to try to give the sense of an isolated and lonely office interior rather high in the air, with the office furniture which has a very definite meaning for me.[14]

In the back of Hopper's mind was his experience in 1913–1914 as an illustrator for the business magazine *System*. The theme of the office, which is not very common in the history of art, is one of the few in Hopper's mature work that did not occur in any of his boyhood drawings, although the book of Degas reproductions Jo gave him the year of their marriage included *The Cotton Exchange, New Orleans*. Hopper's debt to Degas's American scene is clear both in the sketches and in the painting, with its bird's-eye view of the floor tilted out toward the viewer. In several of his studies, Hopper rubbed out Degas-like details such as the framed picture hanging on the wall and the slat-back wooden chair in the lower left corner.

Hopper's own discussion of the painting went on to analyze it from the perspective of one of his most basic concerns:

> There are three sources of light in the picture:—indirect lighting from above, the desk light and the light coming through the window. The light coming from outside and falling on the wall in back made a difficult problem, as it is almost painting white on white, it also made a strong accent of the edge of the filing cabinet which was difficult to subordinate to the figure of the girl.[15]

This is the same painter who as long ago as 1907 had been impressed by Rembrandt's *Nightwatch* when he saw it in Amsterdam.

Simultaneously suggestive and ambiguous, *Office at Night* gives visual form to psychic and erotic tension between a sensual woman and a man who appears to ignore her. The viewer is cast by the artist as a voyeur, watching this nocturnal intrigue with the players caught unaware. At the conclusion of his commentary on the painting, Hopper cautioned: "Any more than this, the picture will have to tell, but I hope it will not tell any obvious anecdote, for none is intended."[16] Privately, however, Jo and Edward played their usual game of imagination: in the record book, Jo referred to the woman whose role she created as Shirley, noting she wore a "blue dress, white collar, flesh stockings, black pumps & black hair & plenty of lipstick."[17]

Jo's good mood heightened in March. An invitation came to submit her work for consideration for a juried show at the Philadelphia Art Alliance. She rushed to get a frame for a canvas, *Odor of Sanctity: South Truro Church,* that she had painted their first season on the Cape. Even more exhilarating, as her birthday approached, Edward gave in and agreed to buy oil to heat her studio, which had been too cold for her to use in winter. He couched his concession in mock religious language, to her surprise, "muttering 'Maybe it's God's will—maybe it is God's will that you should paint'."[18] At once she set to work on a still life, but then Edward tormented her, coming repeatedly to rebuke her for attempting "fashionable effects."[19] At least she was working: "Life seems a different thing to me these days since I've taken to painting again."[20]

The harmony was too good to last. The Art Alliance jury rejected Jo. She was in a sharp mood on March 25, when they went to a show by one of Edward's cronies who spurned her work and fawned on him.[21] Jo allowed that Arnold Friedman's landscapes were beautiful, but pounced on the figures as "good for nothing" and "repulsive."

One old pal whom Jo actually liked, perhaps because he had been so faithful and energetic in promoting Edward, returned to the scene in April: "Mon cher du Bois," wrote Edward, "Calme toi mon vieux, mets toi de nouveau au lit. Je ne suis pas pressé. J'espère que tu te trouveras mieux tout l'heure."[22] The signature was playful: "Votre tres devoué, E. Hopper (autrement dit le monstre)," the latter a sobriquet invented no doubt by Jo. The urgency that Edward disclaims regarded repayment of a loan, since a few months later he wrote Guy again: "I have received your check for twenty five dollars on account. Thank you."[23]

Not until April 17, almost two months since completion of *Office at Night,* did Jo observe Edward at work again with a drawing, and the next day she reported a "larger drawing of Gettysburg St. & rear of carts with canon," which she followed up: "E. went back to the Civil War drawing he's making carts dragging canon in long procession past white houses with head & neck of one horse entering from right, front to suggest the continuation of the long stream of tired men & beasts. It's a good drawing. Maybe there is to be a canvas."[24]

When the canvas materialized, Jo as the faithful record keeper knew exactly how it fit into the oeuvre: "The 2nd Gettysburg canvas is well under way."[25] She remembered the canvas of 1934, *Dawn before Gettysburg,* as well as their visit to the shrine in 1929 and her gift of the Mathew Brady photograph book. She registered progress and self-doubt on April 29: "E. worked from Early A.M. til dark—standing up. Has had the sky with dark cloud above, strip of robin's egg below—all scraped out—too heavy. The new sky not so impressive—sais he's painted this canvas only just to be busy. That is seldom his motive."[26] By May 6 the picture was causing physical strain: "E. still adding touches to Civil War canvas. It's amazing how long he can keep it going and it certainly grows richer. He has tied a cushion on a high stool, but finds he must work standing and gets so tired."[27] Delivered to Rehn on May 8, *Light Battery at Gettysburg* was not only the second, but the last of Hopper's paintings with such a specific historical theme.

At the end of May, the best winter clothes were stored and the car retrieved in Nyack, where Marion was facing the need for upkeep on the old house. The matter kept turning over in Edward's mind even in Truro, and he wrote her a painterly note:

> As to the color of the house—it might look very well without a different color for the trim. I have always disliked two colors on a house. . . . Why not have white. It is the most effective of all. I would not have the shutters too light a green, as it always fades and becomes more blue. I think a dark green is best, and looks very handsome against white.[28]

Designing his own house in Truro, he had opted for only white.

When Edward went sailing with Martha McKeen and her father, their neighbor Captain L. D. Baker, who let him take charge, Jo, perhaps thinking about the younger Martha, remarked of Edward: "He's always so poignantly faithful. What quality could be more cherishable."[29] They sought to repeat the previous summer's luck in Orleans, and an old house did prompt a sketch, which Edward destroyed in fear that it was "too much of a Burchfield." He still harbored resentment at the critics for calling him influenced by his old friend.

It was a season when both were painting, which inspired a revealing comment about Jo's effect on Edward's work and supplies a reason why their subjects, especially landscapes, are sometimes so alike: "Life is always so much more interesting around here when there is a canvas on the easel—either his—or mine. Not that one would expect him to find anything so stimulating for him to find one of mine starting up—except that he's so highly competitive. I've found that one way to give him a boost at getting started."[30]

As news of the war grew more preoccupying, Edward reacted with a characteristically individual stand in writing Guy: "We are evidently eye witnesses to one of those great shiftings of power that have occurred periodically in Europe, as long as there has been a Europe, and there is not much to be done about it, except to suffer the anxiety of those on the side lines, and to try not to be shifted ourselves."[31] In the same letter, he admitted: "It seems that I have no definite philosophy that would be a consolation in these times, but if I had one, it would be of no use to you, for you would not like it and no doubt would despise it."[32] But, he suggested, "Painting seems to be a good enough refuge from all this, if one can get one's dispersed mind together long enough to concentrate on it."[33] Such stoical attitudes were not for Jo, who "burst into tears among all the groceries in a store here in Wellfleet when she heard of the fall of Paris, and was patted and consoled by the grocer's wife, who I feel sure was much puzzled to know why anybody should actually weep over something happening so far from Wellfleet."[34] Together the Hoppers read firsthand reports of Nazi atrocities in Pierre Van Paassen's *Days of Our Years,* which Jo described to Dorothy Ferris as "truly harrowing, but so well written, so understandingly, that one feels as tho one had travelled much & had one's heart broken many times & was ready for anything."[35]

June came and went. Edward ranged ever farther in search. Only in mid-July during a hot spell and all the way down to Eastham did he spot something to sketch.[36] By mid-August Jo was reporting progress on a new oil:

> E. painted little grey house. It's taking so long & it isn't a bit like the find he made down Eastham back road. No good specially until the sun went down then it took on a dignity, ghostliness of color; something crustaceous in quantity. The 3rd dimension became insistent & the small trees at the sides became head & arms that reached out & swayed. E. isn't getting any of this & it isn't that he didn't see it. E sais one can't often, if ever, get just what one wants, it always turns out to be something different.[37]

What with the difficulty of finding subjects and his active engagement with producing oils, Hopper repeated his previous summer's abandonment of watercolor. Thus withdrawn from the medium that had been a forte, when he received an invitation to show at the California Water Color Society, he abdicated responsibility to his dealer. With no new work for two seasons, and nothing in mind, he wrote Rehn: "If you think it worth while you could choose any one that you can remember and think suitable."[38]

Without dissipating momentum, he focused on painting another oil. All the driving and searching now paid off with a unique subject, although, as

Edward Hopper, Study for "Gas," *1940. Conté on paper, 8⅞ × 11⅞″ (22.5 × 30.2 cm.).*

often, the idea had been circulating in his mind for years. On September 4, Jo wrote to Marion:

> Ed is about to start a canvas—an effect of night on a gasoline station. He wanted to do one for years. This is only his second canvas. Pictures come so hard this year. They used to flow along so much more easily.[39]

Several days later, she continued:

> Ed is struggling. It's a hard time to put one's mind on painting—and he's seen it all so often around here. He's doing a filling station—at twilight, with the lights over the pumps lit. And when we go to look at them—around here, they aren't lit at all. They're not wasting Elec. til it's pitch dark, later than Ed wants. He's painting in the studio entirely now. Lots more comfortable—but much harder to do. I'd hate it. When you are in front of the thing, its presence helps one.[40]

Keeping Marion posted, she wrote again after four days:

> Ed's canvas is coming on nicely. The pumps are shining red—and the lights above so bright and the trees dark beyond and a road going

Jimmy De Lory's Mobil Station, Truro, Massachusetts.

off in the distance. He gets so tired standing to paint but he can't work seated and get results that are effective at any distance.[41]

When it came time for an entry in the record book, Jo identified the man tending the pump as "the son of Capt. Ed Staples' burnt in train wreck returning from Cleveland Mus. show," creating an imaginary genealogy in Edward's oeuvre.[42] Hopper finished his canvas by the end of September and called it *Gas*. The rural filling station and its solitary attendant give new form to his concern with urban intrusion into the countryside; just on the horizon line he places the sign of the flying red horse, as if it would dart off into the sunset.

The owner of one of the stations Hopper studied remembers the couple well and prizes a reproduction of *Gas* inscribed by Hopper, "To our friend, Jimmy De Lory." He never saw Jo drive, though he recalls her as "a flighty little woman."[43] He does remember thinking what a "terrible driver" Edward was. It was a judgment that in his heart of hearts Edward shared. Once when he was unable to position his car over the work pit at the station and De Lory tried the maneuver himself, only to graze an advertising sign, Hopper growled: "You're a worse driver than I am."[44] The admission unmasks the mingled self-deception, bad faith, and crying need behind Hopper's long, adamant, and often violent adherence to the myth of male superiority behind the wheel.

The intense work of the summer reinforced Hopper's sense of professional identity and sensitivity to even potential attacks, as he showed in a letter in late September to the Art Institute of Chicago. The museum had acquired his 1938 canvas *Compartment C, Car 293,* which it persuaded him to discuss in writing. In preparation for a children's catalogue, the Education Department head, Helen Parker, recast his essay into simplified form and asked him to copy it out and sign it,[45] which he declined to do: "I know from experience that such chickens some times come home to roost. And such a statement attributed to me, falling into the hands of some sophisticated painters, who think none too well of my painting, it might cause me much annoyance in the future."[46]

His sense of professional identity also lies behind his refusal in October of a request from Lloyd B. Myers of the Bowman Deute Cummings Agency in San Francisco, who approached him after seeing his work in the Golden Gate International Exposition: "I know something of the difficulties," Hopper replied, "in adapting a personal point of view to the needs of advertising and do not feel inclined at this time to struggle with those difficulties. This is in no sense a criticism of advertising art, for many very effective things are being made for it."[47] He makes personal vision the nub of his denial, in keeping with his aesthetic. Having staked everything on the concept of individual autonomy, which he achieved late and through struggle, he rejected offers of patronage, whether commercial, personal or public, as less opportunity than restraint, unlike such contemporaries as Thomas Hart Benton, John Steuart Curry, and others.[48] Immune to anything as banal as anxiety over income in the eye of a depression, Hopper had had to be dragooned to paint for Helen Hayes the previous year.

The strain of painting steadily from mid-July late into September caused physical stress, as he wrote to his Boston physician: "I have been feeling very tired for the past week or so, which might be caused by my having stood on my feet every day from about nine in the morning until six at night, while painting. The dilation of the veins in my legs has been less noticeable since we have had the cooler weather."[49] Referring to the chaise longue he ordered from Macy's at the beginning of the summer,[50] he added, "I shall put my legs up like Lincoln whenever I get the chance."

As the 1940 presidential campaign heated up, so did the Hoppers' political fervor. Angrier than in 1936, this time they drove to New York and back just to register to vote against Roosevelt. Jo wrote to Dorothy Ferris that Wendell Willkie, Roosevelt's Republican opponent, "seems eminently eligible on all counts acceptable to both parties and to anyone not on the Roosevelt payroll. Edward says anyone but that jackass, even Shirley Temple."[51] Their rage was so ferocious that it dominated a visit by an old friend in November back in New York. Charles Burchfield dropped by on his way to Washington to jury an exhibition and noted in his journal that it had been "a disturbing visit, as they were rabid about the election and kept at me until I might [budge an] inch, and as a result we did not visit at all."[52] Nor were they in tune with other Rehn Gallery artists, such as Reginald Marsh, but especially Peppino Mangravite, who belonged to the far left Artists' Congress.

With an acquaintance less intimate than Burchfield, one was less frank. Edward liked to cover his tracks in politics as in art, and he managed to conceal the intensity and extent of his engagement and rage, if not his underlying bent, so that Lloyd Goodrich was bemused: "After all in the 1930's politics, in particular leftist social politics, was in the air, nobody could escape it—except Hopper! . . . Hopper never had any interest in politics. . . . I think he did, but he didn't express it. . . . But I sensed he was a Republican."[53]

Never so cryptic, when Jo wrote to the New York *Sun* in December 1940, complaining that the layout cut off an article on Islamic miniatures, she took the opportunity to praise the writing by Henry McBride and to lambaste FDR:

A lot one cares for Islamic Miniatures until the tour is conducted by some one who finds for us some relativity—the thing that makes H. McB., with no more Roger Fry, the most fascinating writer on his chosen subject that is provided today. . . . Well, when you get good Henry James style in a daily one resents having it chopped off with vicious rudeness. More Roosevelt Administration! Which reminds us that we rejoiced at his forthright stand agin New Deal prodigality & waste in his own field & with every blade of grass against him. Maybe not Every—the 2 of us cantankerous ones drove 600 miles just to register so that we might vote our protest—& self exile from the flock. So where we are practically White Russians at large in a world fast losing its appetite for such things.[54]

Gas was Hopper's entry in the Annual Exhibition of Contemporary American Painting at the Whitney that fall. At the opening, Lyonel Feininger charmed Jo. The expatriate modernist painter had returned to New York at the age of sixty-nine after a long period in Germany. He was a harbinger of the coming migration of artists from Europe. Surprised to learn that he was "really an American after all," Jo found him "so specially nice" that she called his wife the next day and invited them both to tea.[55] Improbably, Hopper and Feininger hit it off and became friends.

All told, 1940 had not been reassuring. At $3,866, the total sales only slightly bettered the year before, which had followed two progressive declines. Only four oils entered the inventory, and laboriously at that, again without new watercolors. October, November, and December produced nothing but politically impotent rage. Since the time of the retrospective, critics had been identifying loneliness as a distinctively American theme in Hopper. Solitude became a touchstone for reassessing his work of the 1920s and 1930s, forging the complexity and torment of his explorations into a serviceable commonplace for a thriving cultural traffic. The theme received new currency in 1940, "Loneliness of Big City Stressed by Artist: the pathos of the big city, the loneliness of the individual in an impersonal setting."[56] It was a voice from a small city in the heartland that reaffirmed Hopper's brand of American eye, just when it faced reevaluation in a New York made more cosmopolitan by the exodus from the European scene.

FAILED ODYSSEY: 1941

WHILE JO AND EDWARD were fuming, distracted, and facing bleak results, Frank Rehn was giving proof of the flair that carried him through the Depression with clients named Whitney, Rockefeller, Phillips, Crane, and Clark. The gallery led off the new year with "Early Paintings by Edward Hopper: 1907–1914," which opened on January 6, 1941. Not simply repeating the formula of his countless New Year shows of Hopper, Rehn had come up with a maneuver meant to capitalize on prestige and make up for the artist's inability to replenish stock. For Hopper, who had been coming more and more to rely on Rehn's judgment about what and where to show, it was a chance to redress old slights. Down from storage came eleven of the canvases painted so long ago in France, along with an even dozen painted during the ensuing, halting search for an American style and for recognition as an artist.

Their implication was not lost on a veteran Hopper watcher such as Jewell, who wrote in the *Times:*

> For at least a decade and a half, Hopper's style has seemed to epitomize the sort of plastic speech that, with augmenting assurance, is termed "American." Indeed, suddenly confronted with evidence, it may require some effort to adjust one's self to the fact that Paris has its place in the retrospective pattern of so American a painter's growth.[1]

For Hopper, who squirmed at reductive labels, one advantage now made itself felt. His "American" fame served to make critics at least acknowledge works ignored when shown by an obscure illustrator who was overshadowed by Henri and the pungent Bellows. Even these early tentative approaches caused less unease in an age schooled in styles as heterogeneous as Surrealism, abstraction, and Social Realism.

At least six newspapers took notice. Smugness tempted him to breach the armistice with Jo, gloating that her work was no good and even if she were to "have a show, no one would come."[2] Triggered by the insult, memories of her original hurt rushed into the diary: "A consummate ass—that's what I married. And a crook. Before we married didn't he write one museum to invite me, & said he'd bring another one over to my studio to see my work."[3] The spring of 1923 came back as clear as yesterday and she took comfort that before his letter had time to get to that museum, an invitation had come for her; but then her outrage returned that Edward introduced her merely as his wife to the second museum's curator, not mentioning that she was an artist.

The furies stirred up would not go away. Before a week was out they exploded in what Jo realized was an "awful fight":

> Great intensity on my part—interpreted by E. as obsession.... There was no peace here all that day. E. had to hear rehearsed all the meanness the accumulations of meanness directed against my work over a period of 16 yrs. Their memory perceived as in a viol [vile] meanness directed against my work & me as an artist, accounting for my inhibitions now. It was dreadful. And E. never yielding one foot. E.'s English to my Irish, his Grant to my Lee, he dominating male to me female. I got cuffed & could I but have reached, he'd have been bitten.[4]

What saved them was the fact that Jo had promised to go out to the theater with Dorothy Ferris, who told her there was nothing to do because all "men were definitely opposed to wives getting anywhere in art."[5] Afterward, as Jo was trying to doze off, she felt Edward's arms enfolding her; she was reassured, for as she confided to her diary, she loathed "there to be war between us."[6]

In the end, Rehn's scheme did not pan out. Only *New York Corner* of 1913, retitled *Corner Saloon,* inspired the Museum of Modern Art to propose an exchange for two watercolors from the 1929 trip south (*Charleston Doorway* and *Baptistery of St. John's*), donated by Mrs. John D. Rockefeller, Jr. The Modern, with *House by the Railroad* as the cornerstone of its collection, was adding depth, but that hardly accomplished what Rehn hoped. Neither he nor the artist would live to see a market for early Hopper.

§

A T   H O M E , the renewed armistice raised hope of getting beyond the doldrums that by now had been dragging on since the fall. What came to mind was an idea broached and dropped by Edward two years before that depended on Jo's customary readiness to aid his work. He would stage a new production in the studio and make Jo virtually star. On Valentine's Day he went to see a burlesque show. Some of his nearly thirty preparatory sketches were made at the Republic Theater, the home of Minsky's, one of the most scandal-ridden revues. At the time it was teasing Hopper's imagination, burlesque was a topic of vehement debate, denounced as "dangerous to the morals and welfare of the community" and about to be banned as "inartistic filth,"[7] with a puritanical shrillness that piqued Hopper's taste for forbidden views and stimulated the contrarian streak betrayed by his choice in 1925 of a subject such as *The Bootleggers.*

Two days after his evening out, Jo came upon Edward in the studio sketching a stripper.[8] He called on her to pose. Although it was freezing cold and drafty, he needed her in the nude. Heat came only from the coal stove; and she huddled as close to it as she could. In a trice she burned herself, but lodged no complaints. It was she, after all, when the question of hiring models arose, who laid exclusive claim to play all the parts in his dramas.

Jo by now was in her late fifties, but the attitude she struck was less the subdued stance of an aging wife than the flamboyant stride of a brazen sex kitten. The old actress knew how to fill the bill. How much her dramatic flair contributed to his work is evident from the close likeness he caught in preparatory drawings, even though one sketch also shows him adjusting Jo's petite proportions to those of the tall buxom redhead he wanted to paint. Moving from what he saw to what he desired to look at, he gave her the large erect breasts with bright red nipples that complement the highly rouged cheeks. In revising he also endowed her with the slender, taut body of a much younger woman. The home theatrical inspired a letter to Marion fit to raise spinster eyebrows and puritan ghosts: "Ed beginning a new canvas—a burlesque queen doing a strip tease—and I posing without a stitch on in front of the stove—nothing but high heels in a lottery dance pose."[9]

By February 25, Edward had sketched the figure on a canvas in blue. On March 9, Jo pitched in again to pose for hands, feet, and legs. Perched on a high stool to proffer one leg at a time, she balanced black and gold velvet bedroom slippers, musing on the result: "I declare it's curious how his draw-

Edward Hopper, Study for "Girlie Show," *1941. Conté on paper, 13¼ × 15″ (33.7 × 38.1 cm.).*

ing of legs look like my legs."[10] On March 26, she posed for the stripper's right foot, fortunately not the one scorched on the stove.[11] By the end of the month, the picture was far enough along that Edward was willing to show it off, at least when the person who dropped by was Chat Chatterton, with whom more than with anyone else he could joke in the manner of old chums. After two more days of work, it was ready for Rehn.[12] Jo had given everything she had to the performance and Edward responded as best he knew how. Their love of French was making them local characters; a clerk in Pierette's, their favorite bakery, said she knew Jo's husband because "he talks French."[13] For her birthday in March he had found her a small book of poems by François Villon and inscribed "a little card with gold fleur de lis ... pour la petite Josephine pour Vu qu'elle Soit sage" ("For little Josephine provided that she use good sense").[14] It was "la petite Josephine" whom he could hug in the dark, yet he qualifies the grateful rapprochement with a hint of reproach.

Hopper's conception of the dancer brings to mind the caricatures he made as a young man of prostitutes in Paris, placing the female form at a distance in a voyeuristic fantasy that avoids real intimacy with the woman and produces a disquieting sense of complicity in the viewer. Only his tender armistice with Jo and her responsiveness allowed him to shape a work that delineates their separate and irreducible roles, as male and female, actress and voyeur, each drawn to the other in an intimacy deep, indissoluble, and flawed.

The ritual of naming came up with *Girlie Show.* The canvas was delivered to the gallery on April 3. What happens next chez Hopper suggests how much had been invested in a collaboration that broke such a long dry spell, dramatizing their mutual dependence in the aftermath of so severe a clash. A brief drive to jury a show in Albany says only that the network goes on. Then a sudden and drastic break from habit signals how deeply they felt the letdown and a need to turn things around.

Right from their first purchase they had used the automobile in the quest for subjects. Now in their need they pushed the idea to a new extreme. Once before they had headed west, following Henri, Bellows, and Sloan by train to Santa Fe. This time the itinerary that unfolds from the diaries suggests the flexibility of the car and a more generic awareness of nineteenth-century artists and their heroic visions of the West. Frank Rehn added a practical note, enthusing Jo and not Edward: a list of clients to chat up en route across the plains as far as the coast.[15] On May 23, they packed up the Buick and started, Edward at the wheel. Three days later they crossed the Mississippi at St. Louis, where Rehn's list began with the young new director of the art museum, Perry Rathbone, who regretted his institution's lack of a Hopper. Jo chimed in to tell him about *Gas.* When he said he would look at it in New York, Edward growled, "It's no good!"[16]

The list took them across Missouri to Kansas City and the Nelson Art Gallery, where the director, Paul Gardner, showed off the Asian art collection. In Kansas at the Wichita Art Museum, they had a reunion with Hopper's *Five A.M.* In Dodge City, a lawyer they met by chance showed them his Indian arrowhead collection. Edward spotted on the office wall a mediocre reproduction from the Metropolitan Museum of a painting he liked by Homer Dodge Martin of the Hudson River School.[17]

More imposing memories from museum walls were on his mind. With a touch of the spirit of "Pike's Peak or bust," he drove steadily. The goal was Colorado Springs, which was famous for the Garden of the Gods, a geological spectacle of oddly shaped formations in red sandstone rising up like plants. When they had reconnoitered for three days and toured the art center, Edward declared that, after all, he saw nothing in the Rockies for him to paint. Actually looking at the vistas he had known since boyhood in the heroic renditions of a Bierstadt brought home to him his own more intimate bent. Mountains were not his meat in the Southwest and, here in Colorado, one of the great heroic subjects of the nineteenth century left him flat.

By June 4, they were wading in the Great Salt Lake. To Edward's disgust, Jo insisted on taking a tour of the Mormon Temple. As splendid as the scenery in Utah seemed, Jo registered frustration at her repeated failures to get Edward to paint. Other great scenes also failed to have the effect desired. Her chronicles check off the Grand Canyon and Las Vegas, where Nevada's new liberal laws permitting gambling and quick divorce did not tempt the Hoppers. When she praised the landscape, Edward turned to irony and put off work, opining that the mountains looked like "regular Arthur Davies" (the painter, who with Henri and Glackens was one of The Eight) and adding satirically: "Now all that is needed is some of those school teacher nudes 10 ft. high."[18]

Jo went to bed sick in Los Angeles, which Edward toured and described as "horrible."[19] Their Truro friend Ella Mielziner insisted they go to Hollywood to visit the avant-garde collector Walter Arensberg, who owned Marcel Duchamp's celebrated painting *Nude Descending a Staircase.* The collection was "Ultra Modern" and he was "perfectly charming—one of the most sympathetic people I have ever met,"[20] Jo vouched, saying that Arensberg promised to visit them in New York and "he loves stairs!" (She had in mind the climb at home up four flights with seventy-four steps.)

Arensberg, then sixty-three, had frequented Jo's old art-world friends, the avant-garde poets Kreymborg and Hartpence, in the *Others* group in 1916, and he reminisced with her about the dealer Joseph Brummer, who had encouraged her work. When Arensberg advised her to "remember this always," the bitterness welled up: "It has been my solace thru 17 years of sterility" (the length of her marriage). From Los Angeles, the trek led via Santa Barbara to Carmel, with a visit to the San Carlos Mission. The old buildings and the churchyard pleased both, one of Edward's few enthusiasms along the way. On seeking out another heroic vista made famous by Bierstadt, Yosemite, Edward complained about "the lack of clearness of atmosphere" in the West and the resulting lack of bright color and sharp lines. Proceeding to San Francisco, they exhausted Rehn's list with a visit to the director of the museum of art. On their own, they drove down to Palo Alto, where Edward, who had marveled at Jefferson's University of Virginia, thought Stanford looked most unpleasant.

Only on the way back up the peninsula did Edward at last find a subject. "He sat in the back seat," wrote Jo, "cursing constantly at smaller space in this car. . . . I in the front seat had the wheel in my way & nothing to prop up my watercolor paper—but we managed somehow."[21]

Edward himself recalled: "We stopped at a motel in San Mateo for a week or so, not wishing to stay in San Francisco, although we drove into the city a number of times. I discovered the house on a side street and thought it interesting, so made a watercolor of it while sitting in the car."[22]

In support, Jo found a new role: "A nice little boy came over to see what we were doing. . . . E. never wants to talk with anyone, but if you are actually doing their house, one has to be civil & so I talked with the little boy. When he heard that it bothered E. to have children collect, he stepped away & peeked in from back window. Later his mother came over to admire."[23]

Faced with uncertain weather, Edward put off finishing for two days. Jo recorded that he "finished sketch of that fine old house with 2 palm trees, now a negro rooming house. There has been little sun all week. He couldn't work yesterday, after we had stayed over for that purpose; so not wanting to stay around any longer . . . he decided to do what he could without sunlight—& after he got started there were glimpses of the sun occasionally."

In the end, Jo was greatly relieved. *House at San Mateo* meant they would not have to retreat from the whole adventure with nothing to show. Jo had also produced her version of the scene from her perch in the front seat. They both wished he had painted a larger watercolor, but Edward was eager to get out of California "alive,"[24] as he recalled: "San Mateo seemed a pleasant town and we found some good little restaurants on that death dealing main road that goes through it to San Francisco. One took one's life into one's hands to cross it on foot."[25]

Heading north to the Oregon beaches, they found an attractive cove where Edward began a small watercolor, *Oregon Coast*. Despite his recent difficulties, Jo was critical of this particular choice of subject:

> I don't see that E. has helped himself to a very likely composition. He's just that contrary, he would take something really stunning right under his nose. He's reducing it to a common denominator of any coastal scene. The reality is a picture postcard—what he's doing is any old picture postcard; one you'd especially never touch. I don't get the point. Of course he may do something to it tomorrow—but I can't see what.[26]

The next day Edward "sat high up and in full sun & wind but doesn't like what he got. He seems to care nothing for the really swell beach with mammoth rocks in such good composition too, make Garden of the Gods look like cheese."[27]

On July 2, they left for Portland, which attracted Edward because it reminded him of the city where he had painted in Maine. Home was on his mind. It was the moment to turn back. Across Oregon into Idaho Jo kept nagging him to stop and paint, but Edward drove and drove, gripped by a desire to get back that made no sense to her:

> Back to the Cape where . . . he's eaten up about everything & has the worst time trying to hatch material for a picture—& here, set down in magnificent plenty, he can only rush by. Inertia—that's one thing he's a victim of—& self-indulgence. . . . It's always so much like inducting oneself into a bay of cold water to get started at painting, it requires much effort.[28]

Her insistence provoked him to revert to attacks like the one on her art in January: "Vindictive slurring & deadly enough charges to hurl back at me—his technique of razzle-dazzle to change direction of one's interest. I'm familiar with this technique," she insisted, "& only concentrate with more fury—for his good."[29]

They managed to agree on visiting one famous attraction, which Jo described in a letter to Bee Blanchard's mother: "One of the most moving things for me was the sight in Yellow Stone Park of great big mamma bears with young daughters in tow sauntering about the roads, accepting ham sandwiches from tourists—and an elk near by quite undismayed—for this one place where man and beast walk the face of the earth in amity—a step toward the Garden of Eden."[30]

When Jo, with her fondness for animals, wanted to pet the bears, Edward refused to stop. Infuriated, she "put her feet up on the windshield in protest," at which he struck her: "I'll not have him feel he can use his great length of arm to cuff. Now he thinks 2 little scratches . . . on instrument board, were my doing. It's very possible they were. . . . I just don't know—if he cuffs—I'll scratch. What else is there to do—in protest."[31]

Jo reasoned with herself, "always found tall men exciting, not when they use that extra span of arm length to swat me tho." At his height and now weighing nearly two hundred pounds, Edward dominated any physical struggle. "But swatting isn't as bad as meanness. . . . His rule of reason always has a quality of tyranny in it—ego maximation—& I wearing myself to a bone to build it up—that it might crush me."[32]

Edward's repeated violence recalls and reenacts "the general depreciation of women as a sex" and "special depreciation of wives" that cause "the outrages they endure," which were denounced by the late-nineteenth-century English social reformer Frances Power Cobbe, who argued: "The common idea of the inferiority of women, and the special notion of the rights of husbands, form the undercurrent of feeling which induces a man, when for any reason he is infuriated, to wreak violence on his wife."[33] The common notions took on special virulence when fed by his insecurity about whether he could paint.

After Yellowstone, Edward's drive for home was stopped in its tracks by the sheer grandeur of the Wapiti Valley in Shoshone National Forest. The next day, July 9, Edward announced that he wanted to try for a watercolor "at the base of the Holy City rock formations," having decided to work where the Shoshone River cuts away at the bottom of these impressive dark red volcanic stone pinnacles, rather than from his usual place in the back seat of the car.[34] Taking courage from his example, Jo also determined to paint, but preferred to work in the car. Although he complained about having to park to suit her, she noted that he "brought home a fine start."[35] Returning to the site several days later, Edward did not feel like working as he had not slept well, which according to Jo meant that he had dreamt: "Neither of us ever have pleasant dreams."[36] He had been grumbling about the primitive accommodations: since they built their "perfect little house on the Cape," Edward had become "a tenderfoot," who "not only refuses to seek plumbing in the communal lavatories, but won't stand for dinginess & air of poverty too threadbare."[37] For her part, Jo was ready to "put up with scrubbed, patched poverty, do so sympathetically," if he could get the picture, which he finally did on July 15:

> Finished the fine watercolor of rocks—rock wall over the stoney Shoshone River. We stayed on for E. to finish it & every afternoon the sky clouded up & all but rained. Not that it would ever rain & be done with in this country. . . . When we got back to Holy City, the sky burned in splendor—but not for long. E. & bath went doggedly on— somehow. E. protected his watercolor during the rain fall—black oilcloth bag—& at it again, partly from memory. I'm so glad it's a fine one—to justify expense of our stay.[38]

Nothing else in Wyoming or South Dakota caught his eye and by July 17 Edward was "glad to be back to the familiar" crossing Wisconsin: he had missed the rapport he felt with his usual architectural subjects and found the Western deserts and canyons "too impersonal."[39] Curious, however, to see Lake Michigan, Edward imposed a detour through Gary, Indiana, where his slow driving on the way to the beach irritated two carloads of young men. As one honked at him from behind, he tried to pull over, almost colliding with the other, which was trying to pass him on the right. "Bastard!" he yelled, to Jo's consternation: "A man with his fine discriminations in the use of English has no business to talk Tobacco Road whenever he gets annoyed."[40] The "hicks" in the restaurant where they stopped for lunch also offended Edward, so they made "short work" of Indiana, only to find Columbus, Ohio, "utterly depressing" and Cleveland "a dingy dump."[41] None of the museums from Chicago down and across seems to have figured on Rehn's list. Jo registers only their stays in rooming houses, camps, or very cheap motels.

The haste of this last push reflected a specific agenda: on July 22 they made it to Nyack, in time to celebrate Edward's fifty-ninth birthday with Marion. The ten thousand miles and the sixty days in the car together added up in Jo's mind to "the rocky road of matrimony."[42] The next day they stopped off in Washington Square, then drove to Truro.

Morris and Martha Kantor saw the car and came to tell them that Peggy Rehn had died while they were away. The news shook Jo so deeply that she wrote at once to Frank and invited him to come and stay with them. Edward jeered, reminding her how violently she had refused his plan to invite his own mother and sister that first season in the house, just before his mother died, and she backtracked a little: "Well, we could give him our room for the first night anyway & if he didn't like our cramped quarters & my cooking, we'd plan something."[43] Waiting to hear from Frank, she caught up on correspondence, already idealizing their western odyssey for Bee Blanchard's mother as "a perfect trip";[44] indeed, by the end of August she wrote in her own diary of the "beautiful trip" with her "darling Eddy."[45] Not till September did Edward get around to writing Rehn himself and his reckoning was professional: "I did not do much work on the trip in the west, but got four water colors, two of which I think are pretty good,"[46] with no word of Rehn's list.

By the time he wrote to Rehn, he was painting in oil again, but the reentry had been painful and difficult, as Jo had foreseen and feared, merely plunging him back into the kind of state they had been trying to flee: "He's eaten up about everything & has the worst time trying to hatch material for a picture." The entire month of August passed with Edward still nervously cruising the roads: "Painted Cape so long now—it's increasingly difficult to dig up subjects."[47] Since depression always made him more hostile, the fights over driving broke out again, although they had been preternaturally absent from the diaries for most of the trip. He touched a new kind of low, not just the usual discouragement for her painting, but even snapping at her for singing and "uprooting my interest in the French language."[48] She philosophized on his "will to dominate completely" and her own nature, "such a queer choice to sharpen his claws on but a lesser hell cat would give no satisfaction to spend energy on."[49] Staking out a territory for herself in the bedroom, she withdrew and began to paint a small canvas.

Not till the end of the month was he able to do as much. On August 30 Jo found him in the studio, "making little crayon sketch of 2 sail boats & a house on the shore. Frank & everybody wants E. to paint boats. Something seems to keep him from doing them."[50] On September 4, Edward began work by stretching a canvas, which he found to his dismay was too narrow for the composition he had intended. He managed to get along by making smaller margins, but kept to his original proportions. That afternoon, he "propelled himself to easel & got busy with charcoal beginning. It came along fine. I went outside & said my prayers for the new picture. He hadn't done a canvas since last winter—the burlesque queen."[51]

Once he was able to paint, the tension eased. Edward even allowed Jo to "perch near the fire place with easel & get busy with goldenrod & white clusters."[52] Those were her happiest moments: "It's so nice to be working in the studio with Eddy. He's furious if he sees me watching him work before he's decided on changes."[53] Yet watch she did:

> I'm very excited about his canvas—& the charcoal layout has come along beautifully—tall sailboats one sailing parallel with a grassy hill—he wants the grassy edge of hill against white of road—meeting of shore of incongruous contacts & a summer cottage at right side of bluff—got a cupola—add a shock. . . . E. works on charcoal most of the day—& late this afternoon he went out & climbed to outlook—it was low tide—so not much inspirational in water—but when he got back & saw sketch with fresh eye, he much pleased.[54]

Jo noted that Edward had not been feeling well and found it difficult "to be working without the fact." But by September 10, he had the boats and the house "all very solid already."[55]

Having finished her paintings of the bedroom and the goldenrod, Jo moved to the hill outside their window, leaving Edward in the studio with his boats and house. In the spirit of their renewed armistice, he was stretching the new canvas for her, when she could not resist a rhetorical question, "Isn't it nice to have a wife who paints?" to which he replied, "It stinks."[56]

With his painting so well launched he felt he could report to Rehn: "Am working now on a canvas, which is not so bad."[57] Even the news of four watercolors was an improvement after two years with none. It came time to break off to drive to see his physician in Boston. The long trip west had come off without complications, so everyone was pleased, but the doctor suspected some sort of pituitary problem as the reason for Hopper's lack of energy.

As Jo continued painting her view from the hill, the autumn equinox came and went. Days grew shorter and cooler. One evening, when she was "almost frozen," Edward gallantly showed up just before sunset to help with her heavy paint box and easel. Protectively he put her to bed with a hot water bottle (which he jokingly referred to as his "rival"), leading her to reflect, "he actually likes me better when I'm sick in bed—away from greasy sinks & what they can do to me."[58]

Edward continued to work on his sky and to carry Jo's easel and paint box to and from the ridge. He finished his canvas on October 4, pleased, he said, that it was not "the picture of a supercilious painter."[59] Drawn from memory rather than observation, the house in *The Lee Shore*, with its distinctive conical roof and columned porch, recalls riverfront architecture in Nyack, especially the tall house next to the Hayes-MacArthur home, where two years earlier Hopper had sketched repeatedly on location for the commission that he resented so bitterly as infringing on his independence. Hopper's title is that of a concise and emphatically allegorical chapter in *Moby Dick*, which he had read in the summer of 1938. Melville evokes the ship "that miserably drives along the leeward land" to suggest the soul that must avoid her home harbor in order "to keep the open independence of her sea."[60]

On October 5, they drove to Provincetown so that Edward could search for another subject. He sketched the front fence of the Catholic church in back of the monument, but this never resulted in a painting. By October 11, however, he was stretching canvas for himself, and four days later, Jo noted that he

> went down to Eastham to have another look at house & barn formations he's had an eye on for years & has now started a canvas. It just doesn't look to me as though anything much could come of it this time—but I've been mistaken so often. He has a lot of pavement across front—forms are small & in nature it looks black & white. No color to notice—black roofs, white stretch of white house, dark bush, pale road, well—we'll see. He isn't bursting with enthusiasm—just forcing himself before going home.[61]

By October 25, Edward was at work on the sky of the new scene, which Jo described as: "house & barn profile as seen on way home going thru Eastham." She complained:

> Eastham his happy hunting ground & it's the least attractive township on the Cape & could be Westchester or N.J. almost & to think he has all these marvelous Truro hills stretched out all around us. No—they are too unusual—too off by themselves, of their own kind, unique. Most go to Eastham to get same old story. Can one beat that? And he hates Jersey & Westchester.[62]

Edward Hopper, Study for "Route 6, Eastham," *1941. Conté on paper, 10½ × 16"*
(26.7 × 40.6 cm.).

The work begun on the eleventh was finished the twenty-ninth. Jo was very
impressed: "It is a scene relived & absolutely convincing. It's amazing how he
could do it all from sketches & color notes. There is a beautiful bit of reserved
autumn coloring in grass."[63]

While he painted so intently, Edward was also reading. He would get "up
early to have his 'hour of prose' to read before I'm disturbing that world by just
being up." Once Jo found him poring over *Life* magazine and protested, why
did he bother with that "tripey" stuff. To fill up his head, he said: "it gets
empty." One book struck him as so important that he read from it aloud to Jo,
as he had when he found those passages in Valéry relating to his own ideas of
art. The writer in question was Van Wyck Brooks, to whom Jo wrote after the
war: "E. Hopper read me Indian Summer while he was painting his Route 6
thru Eastham (Cape Cod). It went right into that canvas. So that that picture
is rightfully dedicated to you. Your work has that life giving quality."[64] (She
added: "We have such overflowing national pride over your work. Ever since
years ago, as an avid art student one came upon your Henry James in the Dial,
one's ears have gone straight up at mention or sight of the name."[65])

Brooks's *New England Indian Summer: 1865–1915* dates to the year before
the painting and discusses authors and visual artists, including Hopper favorites such as Emerson, Henry James, Kipling, Winslow Homer, and
Robert Frost. One chapter that Edward read aloud to Jo dealt with the reclu-

sive personality of Emily Dickinson and how she transformed everyday New England in her imagination: "The familiar objects became portents and symbols. Here were the hills, the changing seasons, the winter light, the light of spring, . . . the lonely houses off the road, the village inn, the lamp-post that became, in the play of her fancy, sublime or droll." [66]

Hopper's absorption in Dickinson made its way into a letter Jo drafted for their neighbor Ethel Baker, who wrote songs: "Oh, E. has been reading about Emily Dickinson in New Eng. Indian Summer—& if you weren't gone—he'd have read for you in his large delight. As it is he tries to hang things poetic symptoms on to me." [67]

The summer that had opened with such a desperate quest was drawing to an idyllic close. Jo mused again on the mystery of their relationship and developed her theory: there had been plenty of women to marry in Nyack, she figured, but Edward wanted someone from his world of painters: "There must be a common background—paint, travel, French literature, on which to floor an adversary." [68]

Closing the house for the season on November 5, they left the following dawn for New York. Within the month they were approached by a young photographer and former painter, Arnold Newman, who decided to pose Hopper before a blank canvas, dressed in an elegant suit, standing pensively, arms held close, in one hand a cigarette, which, says Newman, he would not have suggested as a prop. "Hopper was very reserved—almost uptight," [69] adds Newman, who caught the inwardness and tenseness of his subject, even the difficulty of filling canvas. Other shots show Hopper attired more casually and looking more relaxed.

Newman's photo essay reflects Hopper's growing celebrity, since the photographer's other subjects in that busy year included John Sloan, Reginald Marsh, Marc Chagall, Fernand Léger, and Yasuo Kuniyoshi. Other evidence for Hopper's celebrity appeared in *The American Artist and His Times,* when Homer Saint-Gaudens represented him as something of a legend, even among the "Whitney Museum Moderns," on the basis of conversation at one of the "famous dinners" given by Juliana Force where the "Whitney crowd" agreed: "Edward Hopper is different, though he leads his simple life and paints his simple pictures just under the roof of number 3 Washington Square North. No one but Hopper can stretch such long legs before a stove and smile a bit sadly as he wonders where his next painting is coming from." [70] Saint-Gaudens added to the aura of legend: "No one but Hopper can write this: 'My aim in painting is always, using nature as the medium, to try to project upon the canvas my most intimate reaction to the subject when I like it most.' " [71] He praised Hopper for knowing "exactly what he wants to do in depicting his version of that famous American Scene," which he claimed in-

Arnold Newman, Edward Hopper in His New York Studio, *1941. Photograph ©
1995, Arnold Newman.*

cluded "catboats, cheap hotel bedrooms, the New York Elevated Railway ... and 'Lighthouse Hill.' "[72] Also in 1941, works by Hopper were
sought for their annual exhibitions by the Art Institute of Chicago, the Pennsylvania Academy of the Fine Arts, and the Cincinnati Art Museum.

When Jo bought the Hoppers' Christmas cards for 1941, she chose tiny
cards with an image of a petulant cat, whimsically sending them to anyone
who might meet criteria she described on one to the critic Henry McBride:
"On the chance of your being one of those graced by 'le sens de chat,' I've come
upon a litter of these & am showering them upon the deserving. You are under
that suspicion, along with Mark Twain, Sam Johnson, da Vinci & the like."[73]

In 1941 sales dropped to $1,560, their lowest point since 1933, in part be-
cause of the effect of his wife's death on Frank Rehn. Also, Newman's image
proved only too telling. All through November and into December the canvas in the studio remained blank.

NIGHTHAWKS: 1942

WHEN HOPPER FINALLY made his approach to the blank canvas in the studio, Jo and everyone else in New York were reacting to the Japanese attack on Pearl Harbor on December 7, 1941:

> Ed refused to take any interest in our very likely prospect of being bombed—and we live right under glass sky-lights and a roof that leaks whenever it rains. He refuses to make for any more precautions and only jeers at me for packing a knapsack with towels and keys and soap and check book, shirt, stockings, garters—in case we ran to race out doors in our nighties. For the black-out we have no shade over the sky light . . . but Ed can't be bothered. He's doing a new canvas and simply can't be interrupted! The Rehn gallery invites E. to remove some of his pictures to a store house so that the whole collection won't be in one place. Frank Rehn is very concerned and making many precautionary measures. I can't say I'm a bit panicy but I'm the kind that believes in precautions, and in a matter that everyone is concerned in, I can't see why anyone refuses to take an interest. Hitler has said that he intends to destroy New York and Washington. . . . It takes over a month for E to finish a canvas and this one is

only just begun. . . . E. doesn't want me even in the studio. I haven't gone thru even for things I want in the kitchen.[1]

He concentrated first on sketching, trying out variants of overall composition, alternative arrangements of architecture, diverse attitudes of figures, and even different slants on details such as coffee urns and condiment containers, producing all told some seventeen preparatory studies. To get the urns he went to the Dixie Kitchen, a coffeeshop where he and Jo often picked up a cheap meal.[2]

Tentatively he put it together in an elaborate sketch, which he further modified in the move to canvas, altering details for expressive edge. The sketch has the couple seated at the counter, turning toward one another with intimacy; the lone man a somewhat overpowering, isolated bulk at the center, his gaze falling toward the window; and the counterboy bent over staring down. Reflecting and focusing as he painted, Hopper made the couple look straight ahead, as if lost in separate reveries, raked by the harsh light that also picks out the man, yet reduces his bulk and emphasizes his isolation and posture of indifference, while the counterman cocks his head upward, in a gaze not connecting with the others.

By the third week in January, Jo reported to Marion: "Ed has just finished a very fine picture—a lunch counter at night with 3 figures. Night Hawks would be a fine name for it. E. posed for the 2 men in a mirror and I for the girl. He was about a month and half working on it—interested all the time, too busy to get excited over public outrages. So we stay out of fights."[3]

Years later Jo confirmed her invention: "I was the one who thought up its name: Nighthawks. E. & I did all the posing for figures except the young blond boy in charge of the counter & he is practically 'Capt. Ed Staples,' dreamed up by E. himself & perished with a car load of modern masterpieces in a R.R. accident."[4] Her witness to their renewed collaboration is confirmed by sketches for a figure wearing the belted safari jacket that she had purchased for Edward at Abercrombie & Fitch.

Jo's suggestion for a name stuck. The picture became a favorite with Edward, who confessed to liking it "very much. . . . [It] was suggested by a restaurant on Greenwich Avenue where two streets meet. Nighthawks seems to be the way I think of a night street."[5] Another interviewer gathered that the picture was "based partly on an all-night coffee stand Hopper saw on Greenwich Avenue in downtown New York, 'only more so.' "[6] To a query about loneliness in the picture, Hopper responded: "I didn't see it as particularly lonely. I simplified the scene a great deal and made the restaurant bigger. Unconsciously, probably, I was painting the loneliness of a large city."[7]

The scene recalls people sitting on stools at a counter that appear in an illustration Hopper did for *System* magazine (July 1916), or a waiter in a white coat with a man at the counter in *Associated Sunday Magazine* (1914). The illustrator captured the basic furniture and details of still life, such as the cash register, without the haunting mood.

The painting transcends any link to illustration. Hopper denounced "the invention of arbitrary and stylized design," while allowing that he "subjected, consciously or otherwise," "color, design and form . . . to considerable simplification."[8] Together the composition, content, and lighting betray Hopper's fascination with cinema, and also recapitulate features of earlier paintings such as *Drug Store,* where the electric light poured from a building and illuminated the nocturnal exterior, making visible the darker buildings across the street. So too, the "PHILLIES Am[erican] No 10" cigar sign belongs to the same popular culture as "Ex-Lax"; the red brick storefront across the street echoes the facade in *Early Sunday Morning;* the angled structure resembles that in *New York Corner,* renamed *Corner Saloon* just the previous year; and the counterman's alert but unfocused glance recalls the hint of mystery in *Cape Cod Evening,* with the distracted gazes of the human figures and the alert head of the dog.

Beyond his own earlier art, Hopper drew on sources such as Vincent Van Gogh's sinister *Night Café* (which had been exhibited in company with works of his twice, reproduced by his friend Pach in a book, belonged to his patron Stephen Clark, and was again on display in New York in January 1942); also the gangster movies popular in the 1930s; and Ernest Hemingway's "The Killers," a story Hopper so liked upon reading it in *Scribner's* for March 1927 that he wrote to the editor, praising an aesthetic that sounds rather like his own: "It is refreshing to come upon such an honest piece of work in an American magazine, after wading through the vast sea of sugar coated mush that makes up the most of our fiction. Of the concessions to popular prejudices, the side stepping of truth, and of the ingenious mechanism of the trick ending there is no taint in this story."[9] In its setting and mood of impending violence that creates suspense, "The Killers" has much in common with *Nighthawks.* The world of "The Killers" has echoes in Jo's title, "hawk" being a slang name for one that preys on others. The more innocuous "night owls" would have suggested a less ominous mood.

In *Nighthawks* Hopper created what would become his most famous image, arguably his masterpiece, pulling together with heightened intensity themes and forms that critics and the public had long responded to in his work. This unique power over the American imagination has a corollary in his behavior as he was executing the work. His cranky refusal to deal with the issues raised by the war and dramatized by Jo differs from the recalcitrance he would show when she tried to prick him out of depression to paint this or that church or that peak in the West. In this case, he was painting furiously with her loyal support, and she modeled as needed or kept out of his way. What he was denying with so much rigor was the anxiety created by the war. The depth of his need to submerge such fears surfaces unconsciously in his bullying concentration and the painting's exceptionally disquieting power.

While Edward was starting *Nighthawks,* Jo was shopping at Macy's for a new Bissell carpet sweeper to be a Christmas present for Marion, and offering to do a chicken if she came down on the bus. Blaming improper diet for a health problem that had been troubling her as long as seven or eight years, Jo entered St. Clare's Hospital on January 28, 1942, for an operation to remove painful hemorrhoids. Edward insisted upon getting her a semiprivate room rather than ward accommodations, and visited her daily. When her hospital bill, medicine, and taxi home a week later came to a hundred dollars, she reflected: "I'm ashamed to be such an unwilling expense to my good husband who needs a suit of clothes now."[10]

The truce soon broke down. On March 8, Edwin Dickinson, whom Jo had known for thirty years, probably from summers spent in Provincetown before her marriage, came to see her watercolors: To her astonishment and irritation, Edward insisted on chattering about a recent experience on a jury, then had the nerve to claim that Dickinson disliked her work and that he was only trying to be "cordial," something that he never did. She fought back in defense of her "poor little still born infants," and recorded the first serious blows since Yellowstone: "Well we went with this with considerable vigor after dinner—to the tune of my acquiring a good slap in the face & having my head banged up against a shelf in the kitchenette over the frigidaire. 'Afraid he'll kill me.' "[11]

She understood perfectly the reason for Edward's uncharacteristic loquacity: "E. always so slow, so silent, famed for his indifference to lapses in conversation, for pauses between gasps. . . . The minute any slight breeze blows in my direction—he must act immediately, kill it dead for all time. Can one wonder I'm still ill, that I've had hardly strength enough to crawl from chair to kitchen sink these last 7 or 8 yrs?"[12] Jo's temperament would not let her emulate Martha Kantor, who dealt differently with a similar situation: She "has the habit of asking so little & giving so much. . . . Some how she keeps on working. Doesn't waste her strength in bitterness."[13]

By St. Patrick's Day, Jo felt well enough to go with Edward to one of the openings she always enjoyed at the Museum of Modern Art, where an exhibition of Henri Rousseau had been organized by Daniel Catton Rich, the director of the Art Institute of Chicago, which had shown Hopper most recently the previous autumn. When Alfred Barr of the Modern "spoke enthusiastically of 'Gas,' " Jo told him he just had to go to Rehn's to see *Nighthawks*.[14] In the event it was Rich who went, pronounced *Nighthawks* "fine as a Homer," and soon arranged its purchase for Chicago.

The next day, for Jo's fifty-ninth birthday, Edward surprised her in the bath by singing "Happy Birthday," and giving her a present, Carl Van Doren's *Borzoi Reader.* Varying the ritual of the previous year, Edward cut out "a green tinsel paper cactus tree in desert soil," giving the legend a new fillip: "à la petite Xanthippe qui le bon Dieu, dans sa sagesse, m'a donné comme femme" ("to the little Xanthippe whom the good Lord, in his wisdom, gave me as a wife"). The wisdom he wished for her the previous year now belongs to God, while "the little" Jo is cast in the role of Socrates' wife, who was known as the "wife who is the hardest to get along with of all the women there are—yes, or all that ever were, I suspect, or ever will be."[15] Neither classical learning nor the slur on her personality implied by the prickly plant could spoil her pleasure at the attention. In the diary she called it the "duckiest homemade card." To celebrate, he also took her to see John Gielgud in J. B. Priestley's *The Good Companions,* where any implication of the theme of the nagging wife was overshadowed by her joy at his thoughtfulness.

Edward's ambivalent birthday signals betray another access of the hostility he always felt when unable to paint. It was not until April 7 that he broke through:

> E. is several days out at sea on a new canvas, praise be. It's the platform of a R.R. station with end of train at left side & baggage wagon truck at right. That car already looks heavy as lead—& steel & iron or whatever it is they're made of & this concrete platform all that solid. I think it's a dawn sky coming up over house tops beyond the tracks. The tracks are only indicated as yet. I'm expecting they will have their own particular gleam when he gets around to it. I can't remember what day he actually started on the canvas—he spent several days trying to locate canvas with a surface he liked that he believed strong enough.[16]

His response to her participative enthusiasm was typical, as she noted eleven days later: "E. always glad to get me out of house while he painting. Picture coming on fine—has made the tracks tracks. End of car rich in avoir du poids."

A whole history of slights to her work suddenly welled up in Jo at the funeral of Gertrude Vanderbilt Whitney on April 20. She and at least three other wives had to insist on their right to be seated up front with their artist husbands, who had been called to serve as honorary pall bearers—besides Hopper, there were Eugene Speicher, John Carrol, Guy Pène du Bois, and eight others. Whitney's Studio Club gave Hopper his first solo exhibition and so many venues through the years, but never exhibited, felt Jo, fair regard for an artist spouse. "True to the last," she grumbled, Mrs. Whitney even in death had imposed "the embargo on wives."[17] The loss of such a long-time supporter did not slow Edward. The next day, Jo noted that he "had changed his canvas—R.R. platform—onto heavier stretchers & had had a struggle over some wrinkles that had got into it. . . . It isn't finished yet but looks well along. One can never tell when he is through with a thing. It gets so much said by the 3″ or 4″ day—one marvels to see how much more intensity gets into it each day."[18] Hopper finished the painting, *Dawn in Pennsylvania*, on April 28.

Reluctant as he was to work under conditions that smacked of restraint, Hopper could not refuse one of his most faithful patrons and friends. Early in May, he and Jo went uptown to visit Bee Blanchard, so that he could get more data for the sketch of her old house that he had agreed to make for her book *The Life and Times of Sir Archie: The Story of America's Greatest Thoroughbred, 1805–1833*.[19] He made a watercolor on illustration board of Mowfield Plantation, which was her ancestral home in North Carolina on the Roanoke River.

A few days later, Jo noted that Edward was still at work on the watercolor, "old house with hedges & grounds among which somewhere lie the bones of Sir Archie."[20] But on May 8, she recorded that he had finished it and that "enlarging an old photo" was "nothing he liked doing," correctly judging that "he hasn't made it look a bit stylish . . . doesn't look like a Hopper."[21] When they delivered the watercolor to Bee several weeks later, they found that Edward's canvas *Corn Hill* had been displaced from its position over her fireplace by a portrait of Sir Archie.[22]

As the spring wore on without the arrival of Hitler's bombers, the war made itself felt in countless ways. Jo had to stand in line at a local school to get a card for sugar rationing and Edward had to wait for more than an hour for their gas rationing card.[23] Jo still worried that their skylights made them vulnerable.[24] Edward was solicited by James Thrall Soby to contribute a picture to a benefit for Soldiers' Entertainment and Art Projects. When Jo decided to offer something of hers instead of his, Edward said it would be refused; but Soby called and invited her to send it along. With Edward's help scraping paint where she wanted to change colors, she readied and sent *Chez Hopper II;* but she and two other women found at the opening that their works had not been hung.

On May 11, Frank Rehn called to say that the Art Institute of Chicago had purchased *Nighthawks,* paying for it in part with the smaller *Compartment C, Car 293*. Rehn told Edward that he had shown *Dawn in Pennsylvania* to Alfred Barr, who said he thought Hopper was "the most exciting painter in America," causing Jo to reflect: "One is glad that Barr can find the excitement latent in E's silent, austere, outwardly serene pictures."[25]

Bolstered by productivity and approbation, Hopper felt no urge to repeat the flight of the previous summer. Arranging to retrieve the car from the blocks where it wintered over in Nyack, they arrived in Truro on June 10, only to feel ever more urgently the effects of the war. To his physician in Boston, Edward wrote: "These complaints of mine seem pretty trivial, when men are being brought ashore right here at Provincetown, badly shot to pieces."[26] And he explained to Frank Rehn: "We are quite close to the war at sea here. The survivors of the vessel from Iceland that was sunk near here were brought into Provincetown and taken care of in one of the hotels. Some were badly injured."[27] Neighbors were standing watch at the local observation tower and blackouts were enforced. The Hoppers enlisted in a first aid course in Truro, which interested Jo more than Edward: "It's the only taste of social life I've had here nearby."[28] Hopper made a caricature of Jo with her friends (*Colonel Hopper SLICK BABY BRIGADE*) and dropped out. Then for each of the two weekly classes, he took her, drove home, then went back to get her, nine miles each time, or thirty-six miles per session, as if she did not drive and gasoline were not rationed.

Yet people would not want to use up their gas, he objected, when she wanted to celebrate their eighteenth wedding anniversary with a tea. Spending the anniversary alone, she took stock: "There are several things I've been clean pushed out of by his strutting superiority. . . . It's as though he had a no trespassing sign hung on them, which isn't his intention at all. But he came to feel sex, swimming, French—are his domain—Painting too—I've been crowded out of that too—almost. But I'm ready to fight."[29]

Then there was the driving he still refused her, and the risks he took swimming alone in rough weather, the "sheer egotism":

> Thank God I had learned to read & write before I became his wife— he'd have tried to prevent me acquiring even such a universal attainment. He hates my letters & so many people have liked them. He never wrote anything before we married—now he does articles even—with style & distinction. Why is he so unmercifully competitive—& why must I be always the arm to be defeated. I who think always in terms of we—or for him. He so gentle, so kind, patience, amusing & where it suits him, understanding & trying out on me a Hitler complex.[30]

Ignoring the war at home, Hopper volunteered to serve as an air raid warden, leaving Jo unhappy alone in the dark without a phone. "I've been

CDLONGL HDPPER
SLICK BABY BRIGADE

Edward Hopper, Colonel Hopper SLICK BABY BRIGADE, *1942. Pencil on paper.*

promoted since I saw you last," he wrote to Rehn. "I am to be an Air Raid Warden at Truro Centre [Fire Department], on duty for God and for Country every Thursday morning from four to eight o'clock. Hope I don't fall asleep on duty, and bring disgrace on my family and friends."[31] On his sixtieth birthday, July 22, a year to the day since getting back from the West, Edward fell into a depression. Jo found the strength to give him a "recital of all the glad things we have to be thankful for, the sizable accomplishment in work & well being."[32] Once again, he held her in his arms and went to sleep with further strife deferred.

As rationing began to hit home, Edward cut back on his customary cruises in search of subjects. He passed time building tool boxes and a work bench in the cellar, assembling lawn chairs, and making repairs around the house. He was also discouraged by the weather; that summer, it always seemed about to rain. Yet when further commercial offers came his way, he still declined. At the suggestion of the critic Thomas Craven, Reeves Lewenthal of Associated American Artists invited Hopper to participate in making advertisements for Lucky Strike cigarettes. They offered him a "journey to tobacco country to get the material" for his painting, "all expenses," and two thousand dollars.[33] Hopper immediately wrote to Rehn for his advice but noted:

> The proposition does not appeal to me very much, as I have been watching these advertisements for some time, and it seems to me that none of the men have been able to do anything good as pictures. This may be due to the restrictions imposed, or a lack of interest in the

subject, for they all seem to me to have been done in a mood of pot boiling boredom.[34]

Only a few days later, Hopper replied to Lewenthal, declining the offer: "You had better count me out of it. It appears pretty certain to me that I would not be able to please either the advertiser or myself. In view of that fact, I feel that it would be unwise for me to attempt to undertake the work."[35]

August was nearly over when late one afternoon Edward and Jo were out on a joint venture, seeking a subject, and he began a water color of *Cobb's House,* close by in South Truro. On September 5, Jo noted that he was "anxious to get off to paint at 4—watercolor down looking at side of Cobb's house."[36] Two days later she recorded that he "finished his watercolor down by side of their house with little locust trees."[37]

Trees had been a favorite motif of his since his first watercolors in Gloucester nearly twenty years earlier. Now the broken and rotting locusts in front of Cobb's inspired another watercolor, *Four Dead Trees.* On September 17, Jo reported:

> Edward began a second watercolor down near Cobb house but paper gets too soaked to work. He can't afford to use tires to go hunting down in his own particular happy hunting ground at Eastham—the one place on the Cape shorn of most all Cape glamour—it might be anywhere, except for the light & the tall grass. It's incredible what he has unearthed there. Now he's reduced to hunting down the lowest common denominator of Cape here at Truro where its special beauty is shown about in greatest richness—but he doesn't want this special beauty—too exotic, too special.[38]

Six days later, she noted: "E. works on watercolor of dead tree & pale high grass down on Cobb preserves."[39] On September 24, Edward was still trying to get a sky.

Hopper tried to start another watercolor over by the Jenness house on September 28, but, driven home by high winds, he retreated to his old birthday present, "pouring over Brady's Civil War 12 vols. of them," causing Jo to question: "Why ever did I give them to him to bury himself?"[40] When he made another effort to make a watercolor on October 1, working on their beach, he was routed by cold weather and "a late crop of mosquitoes."[41] The next day, he tried again unsuccessfully and finally attempted to work in the studio from memory, making trips back to look. Then he caught a cold and did not feel like painting.

As the Hoppers closed up for the season on October 20, talk in the neighborhood was that Hitler wanted the bay for a submarine base. What would become of their house, they wondered? Suppose the United States government requisitioned the Cape and took over their property. They felt compelled to take all of their summer clothes (which they usually left in the house) back to New York and departed in a state of great anxiety.

After a summer that was hardly a comeback, the fall brought new honor for *Nighthawks* when the Art Institute of Chicago dignified its new acquisition by awarding Hopper the Ada S. Garrett Prize. Hopper also took part in another round of fall group exhibitions, such as "Artists for Victory" at the Metropolitan Museum, where he showed *Gas* and the watercolor *Four Dead Trees* from the summer. His sales for 1942 had been good, a total of more than five thousand dollars, up dramatically from the previous year.

Yet 1942 also brought an attack. In *The Emergence of An American Art,* Jerome Mellquist identified Hopper as a pupil and a disciple of Henri, although he claimed, incorrectly, that Hopper's favorite teacher had been Kenneth Hayes Miller, and he argued that Hopper belonged "to a Puritan contingent at work in this country." Mellquist brought to light the fact that "Hopper was first sent to technical school to learn the trade of illustrating" and only then spent five subsequent years at the Chase school; the critic used this information to argue: "Hopper remains the illustrator in his paintings. It is significant that they are always recommended for reasons extraneous to the medium," and concluded that Hopper's paintings remained "cold."[42]

MEXICO: 1943

ON JANUARY 4, 1943, Hopper delivered to the Rehn Gallery a new oil painting, which provides mute evidence that the armistice of late summer held. Jo struck poses for each of the two female figures and marshaled an array of props. The seated matron with the piercing glance wears a plumed hat, fur coat, scarlet dress with a blue brooch, and sensible shoes on firmly planted feet. The younger blond woman, reading, wears a blue dress cut to above her elbows and knees, baring her arms and long legs that extend relaxed, slightly crossed, to feet scarcely wrapped in flimsy straps and balanced casually on spike heels.

For Jo there was plenty to do, since Edward made at least ten preparatory sketches and the attitudes and dress of the women figure largely. As he had for *Nighthawks*, Edward altered the sketches in the final work to emphasize separateness. Sketches show the matron in colloquy with her elegant male companion, but on the canvas the two look apart. A sketch shows a seated man gazing across the hotel lobby. In the painting, seated in his place, the young woman regards her book.

Also as in *Nighthawks*, architecture frames a scene in which light picks out figures theatrically and implies potential drama: there the two men in their respective detachments from the lurid woman, here the nuanced styles, postures, and positions of the two women in relation to the imposing male.

Edward Hopper, Jo Posing for "Hotel Lobby," *1943. Conté on paper,* 15 × 22⅛″
(38.1 × 56.2 cm.).

The architecture and dress in *Nighthawks* are plebeian, street vernacular, suggesting the kind of place in which the Hoppers habitually ate. Hopper endows the hotel with an architecture ornately classical, fluted columns and ionic capitals, and his figures are of commensurate class, more like the world of Rehn's clients, Hopper's collectors, or the comfortable hotels on the trips to jury various shows when the tab was paid by the host. The fur coat was Jo's, both a recurrent prop in the pictures and a fixture at the grand museum openings she loved. Filling out this scene of power and patronage, the picture framed in ornate gold on the wall depicts what Hopper himself refused to paint in the West—the heroic peaks and valleys captured by Bierstadt and others, which this context represents as a cliché. Identifying human restlessness with the American push for change, Hopper presents the hotel as a typical American building, as James had written in *The American Scene:* "a synonym for civilization, ... the American spirit most seeking and most finding itself."[1]

Hotel Lobby had scarcely been deposited with Rehn when a letter came from the social world that it evoked. Juliana Force, the legendary director of Gertrude Whitney's museum and hostess of "famous dinners," wrote Hopper to introduce the idea of an American Art Research Council, which was to collect information on important artists. Jo fired off a postcard, immediately asserting her role as a protagonist, Edward's "secretary," who for years had been "keeping a ledger including most of the data you are interested in concerning E. Hopper."[2] Edward was more circumstantial and less frank: "I have kept an accurate record of all my work done within the past twenty years, and have data not so reliable on most work done before that."[3]

The years of accurate records largely coincide with the period since marriage, when Jo was keeping the books. He was spelling out her practice when he specified that the records included only works that left the studio for sales, exhibitions, and some gifts. He added a caution that reflects his own frequent unsureness: "It would seem to me that one of the difficulties in compiling a record of a contemporary artist, would be in knowing how much to include, as all painters have many failures, unfinished works, and studies, that one might find unwise to include with the better things. Just where one can draw the line, would be hard to say."[4]

During the first week of March, Hopper traveled to Washington to serve as one of six jurors for the Eighteenth Biennial Exhibition of Contemporary American Oil Paintings at the Corcoran Gallery,[5] where his *Ground Swell* of 1939 was shown and subsequently purchased by the Corcoran. For Jo it was a harmonious trip, because her *Hills of Truro* was in the show.

As the weather warmed that spring, Jo began to invite acquaintances over to see her work, explaining that the oil heater had sprung a leak, so "I've had no use of my fine big studio all winter."[6] She nudged Henry McBride in a letter: "It's been too bitterly cold in my place until now—one drags one's own coal in #3 & E. Hopper has enough misery toting coal for the place where we live, I can't have him stoke grates or stoves in here too. . . . We keep vegetables in my studio all winter & I'm back underfoot in his. So now or never."[7] And since he had long been one of her favorite critics, she launched into a brief retrospective of her career:

> During the 25 years I've known you, I've always hoped there would be some occasion when you'd come upon my work. There was a chance you might like some of the watercolors. They were shown at that sprightly New Gallery with the Dufy's, Kislings & such like brought over by J. N. Rosenberg so long ago. Such swank to be let in. Also they were shown at Louis Bouché's Belmaison, the Sunwise Turn etc.[8]

In the margin perpendicular to this nostalgic history, she added, "mais où sont les neiges—" ("But where are the snows [of yesteryear]?"), paraphrasing the famous refrain from the same Villon who had been her birthday gift from Edward two years before.

> Then I married & the skies changed plenty. Friendly galleries folded up, & in this old painter's rookery, I poured tea to such neighbors as Kent, Du Bois, [Leon] Hartl, Ernest Lawson, while they talked art to my husband (E. Hopper) & to me—the weather! Swine—rats! Peggy Bacon would have known how to handle that.[9]

Proudly she informed McBride:

> Now I'm in possession of Kent's old studio, all mine. And on account of the good white walls, fine light—& the most comfortable deep chair, from which, out of the tail of one's eye one can see everything—I venture to stick my neck way out.

Yet, awed at her boldness, she undercut the invitation:

> Of course there are skads of reasons why this could never be—& I remember the millions of miles your feet have walked to feed or chastise the egoes of the tribe of us. This could well be a last straw. I have that last straw consciousness so well embedded (having this silly show when we should be packing for Mexico . . .)[10]

Winding down, she reflected:

> 57″ St. just doesn't want WIVES. So why ever should you be bothered either? But it's an Unquiet Grave—& how noisy. . . . You get them all, I dare say.

Signing off "Apologetically," she flared up again:

> So often I've written to chirp with glee over things you've said: re Hartley, lately, your attitudes toward the Roosevelt Administration farther back, a most splendid statement we adore you for; a recent Whitney etc.—but always what I would offer became so unworthy witless & longwinded that it went into the stove. E. Hopper never misses a word of your page. But this is my party. He's not even invited.[11]

No hint of a follow-up survives.

For once Edward did not carp at her exuberance, for he had thrown himself into a new canvas and needed her to create yet another telling role. In the wake of her burlesque dancer, and the calculated females of *Nighthawks* and *Hotel Lobby,* this time he wanted her to turn herself into what she pegged in the record book a "big strong girl in thin white dress, flesh showing thru of right upper leg,"[12] poised suggestively on a door stoop between austere columns while wind stirs the curtains of a partly opened window to one side.

Hopper produced at least three preparatory sketches, making adjustments of scale and proportions. In one he depicted the cornice of the doorway and other architectural details that he later chose to omit, when he compressed and narrowed his field to zoom in more closely on the figure of the girl. His drawings also reveal how he built up the female role, from the rather indistinct sketched outline to the painting, where Jo's dramatic flair shines forth in the attitudes and figure that suggest a temptress. Jo's springtime exuberance animates the role of a seductive young woman whose getup—red lips; jaunty hat; tight, almost bursting bodice; and blatantly transparent skirt—suggests the flamboyant allure of a prostitute. And where Jo fell short, Edward supplemented, as he had in *Girlie Show* the year before. In the background, he added the suggestion of a door ajar and the window, with their intimation of penetrable inner spaces, also the curtains slightly lifted and parted by the breeze, hinting at an illicit view, as wind and curtains do so often in the most erotic moments of Hopper's scenes. The fantasy that had just imagined Jo by night on the brazen stage, in the cheap diner, and amid the nice distinctions of a grand hotel, shifts to the play between cool, shadowy interior and the hot daylit street.

By May 8, Hopper had finished *Summertime.* Both he and Jo were free to pack. Gradually the previous summer they had been forced to realize that Truro was too difficult in time of war, between the rumors of U-boats and the stringencies of rationing, which put a crimp in Edward's cruising for subjects and even their comings and goings for daily needs. Since April they had been thinking of looking for subjects elsewhere, leaving the car on its blocks in Nyack, and reverting to travel by train.

Canada they had tried and fled in their first quest with the car. The American Southwest and West by train and car had been pretty much of a wash. Many artists went to Mexico. Marsden Hartley, Andrew Dasburg, and Mark Tobey had been attracted by the spectacular landscape and the exotic culture and people, none of which was Hopper's meat. He risked another arduous quest for minimal results. In Mexico he hoped "to do some painting," Hopper wrote to his physician. "My conscience troubles me somewhat about skipping away in this manner, but I have to keep on with my work and there will be more freedom of movement in Mexico than there will be here just

Edward Hopper, Study for "Summertime," *1943. Conté on paper, 8½ × 11"*
(21.6 × 27.9 cm.).

now."[13] He wondered if high altitudes might affect the medication he had
been taking since 1938. "I did pretty well last winter, as to health, and had no
lapses into periods of weakness. I have been taking the Betalin S [vitamin B₁],
and the Benzedrine steadily all the time."[14]

Leaving Pennsylvania Station on June 29, the Hoppers arrived in Mexico City on July 3, where they had reservations at the Ritz. Their choice of a
large, relatively expensive hotel reflected their uncertainty about what they
might expect to find. Jo wrote to Frank Rehn two days later: "We're all right,
trying to get acclimated. Mexico City far more expensive than N.Y.C.—at
least until one learns one's way around. But don't let that keep you from flying down."[15] Soon, however, she was referring to Mexico as "a land of great
exasperation."[16] Eventually, she concluded: "Mexico is a discipline for the
spirit. For every little thing they keep you waiting till you go crazy. They
bring the butter but no bread. Coffee gets cold while waiting for cream. . . .
Salt for the meat comes with the desert—if any."[17] Such French as they knew
was no help, and neither knew any Spanish: "Nearly no one speaks English,
but we manage," wrote Jo, describing how her acting skills came into use.
"Some are so bright at getting one's pantomime. Ed stands back & lets me play
monkey, but we usually walk out with what we go for & everybody shaking
hands & a fine time had by all. They can be very charming, those Mexicans."[18]

Settling in, the Hoppers ran into Katharine Kuh from the Chicago Art
Institute. She was "disposed to point out chief attractions north & south," said

Jo, "but E.H. always restless, just wanted always to get away. Wouldn't ride on local buses, expecting them to dispense small pox to say the least. Loathed all markets, baskets the bane of his life, silver so much junk."[19] Yet they did visit some attractions, making a day trip July 9 to Guadeloupe with its basilica and famous blue-mantled Virgin, the next day touring the famous floating gardens in Xochimilco (the subject of a mural by Miguel Covarrubias in the Ritz), also taking in the folkloric ballet, then making an excursion to the monastery of San Agustin Acolman and the Aztec pyramids. Years later, Hopper recalled the work of several contemporary Latin American artists, mentioning his admiration for Orozco; but when asked if the Mexican painter was great, he retorted, "Maybe, I don't know."[20]

If Edward had hoped for isolation, he must have been disappointed. Helen Hayes also turned up in Mexico City on her way to her vacation home in Cuernavaca. She had the satisfaction of telling Edward that *Pretty Penny,* the image of her Nyack house he had been so reluctant to paint, was about to be exhibited in Chicago. Graciously, she invited the Hoppers to visit her, but to Edward's way of thinking, Cuernavaca was nothing but a "damn art colony" and he would have none of it.[21] Jo's "chum," Dorothy Ferris, and her daughter had arranged to meet them in Mexico City. Jean Ferris recalls that Jo had a voice "like a little girl" and could be very gentle and nice, but was apt to be volatile. She and her mother spent time with Jo while Edward wandered around looking for something to paint; and Jean never forgot Jo saving table scraps to feed the starving cats.[22]

The car was missed, as Hopper wrote to Rehn: "We left Mexico City toward the end of July and have been in Saltillo ever since. It has a nice climate and is among some interesting hills. It is pretty hard to get near them or do much of anything without a car, but I have made a few watercolors, nevertheless."[23] Jo found it "much too hot to try to paint out. One should never come to Mexico without a car."[24] Saltillo, a small city located over five hundred miles north of Mexico City, is known for its finely woven serapes. In such an exotic setting, Hopper's concerns were basic: "It is a great relief to be here, where the nights are cool enough for comfortable sleep" (Saltillo is up about five thousand feet).[25] He added: "The food here, though, is a terrible let down after the Ritz in Mexico City. . . . To[o] much starch and too few vegetables and too little cooked. In plain language most of the restaurant food is lousy."[26] Jo concurred: "We have had only diet for billy goats since retracing our tracks back here to Saltillo."[27]

Still, Jo was warming up to Mexico, as she wrote to Rehn:

Eddy not crazy about Mexico. Too much noise. Dirt & noise—but we haven't been exposed to much dirt as yet. I'm delighted with the color of it & the charm of the people. One must watch out to do some trifling act of consideration for the old ladies with black shawls over their heads to lap up the lovely, lovely smile one gets—a smile—as it would seem—straight from the heart. I've never seen such marvelous faces, people in the street, Indian & Mexican. And so many beautiful girls sunkissed skins, such a glow about them.[28]

From the roof of the Guarhado House on Victoria Street, where they were staying, Hopper painted four watercolors. Jo explained why he had decided to work on the roof: "Among mts. doesn't mean you see any of them. They surround the place but there are always walls or towers or electric signs even, to shut out the view. E. sits out on our one story roof that affords more roofs & snips of things neither distinguished nor readily distinguishable & feeds upon that."[29] Lack of the car continued to trouble her: "It hasn't been easy to do anything without a car. Can't perch out in a blazing sun surrounded by young buzzards. The roof so far has yielded 2 watercolors finished & 2 on the way. It rains every afternoon at varying hours, so that slows up productions."[30]

In *Palms at Saltillo,* Hopper depicted a view of the pale adobe roof surface with trees and other buildings visible in the distance. *Saltillo Rooftops,* painted in late July, presents the view in a different direction, which features the rooftops against a backdrop of blue-green mountains. The chimney pots and pipes in the foreground are reminiscent of the prospect from the roof of Hopper's studio on Washington Square, suggesting that he sought something familiar in the midst of such a foreign setting. In August, he painted *Sierra Madre at Saltillo,* with rooftops and a utility pole before the majestic mountain landscape, and *Saltillo Mansion,* a nearby house with an elaborate cornice and decorative trim seen against the mountains.

On September 1, when the Hoppers left Saltillo for Monterrey, they had already been there by bus to explore. Jo had explained to Frank Rehn that Edward was "crazy about the mts. we passed on R.R. on way up to Mexico City—mts. around about Monterey. But he heard Monterey was hot so came here instead, 50 miles south of Monterey but high elevation so cool. People from Monterey & state of Texas swarm here."[31] She lamented: "He didn't bring any canvas or oil paints which is calamitous, because if it cools off enough to go to Monterey for 3 weeks in Sept. there is one gorgeous view from a hotel room window that I've unearthed & it's a crime not to do a sizable canvas of those mts. right out of window."[32] Jo had secretly brought along her own oil paints, which she was prepared to give Edward if he would only paint. When he stubbornly resisted her offer, she referred to him as a mule, adding, "Better mule than monkey I suppose."[33] He had determined to use only watercolor in Mexico. On September 5, when they were staying in the Hotel Monterrey, Jo was happy to see that Edward was working on a new watercolor "of some glorious mountains."[34] She happily reported to Rehn: "He sits at the window of our room at this hotel & with the greatest of ease gazes out. . . . It's blistering hot, this town, a little better in Sept., but he has a fine big electric fan on the ceiling over his head & after 3 days hounding the office we have the window screens removed so we can actually see out."[35] It was Jo who insisted that the screens be removed, for she knew that Edward, although he had said he would try to peer through them, would soon give up. Rather than worry about her own work, she clearly acted as his facilitator, arranging where and how he could best paint.

Hopper did produce two watercolors out of the hotel window: *Sierra Madre at Monterrey* and *Monterrey Cathedral.* In the former, he focused on the splendid shapes of the mountains, keeping rooftops to the lower portion of his composition; in the latter, he once again featured rooftops, along with the strong shape of the cathedral and its dramatic mountain backdrop. Since they were holding excursion tickets for the train, the Hoppers had to return to New York by the end of September. They longed to go to the Cape for October and the first half of November, but with gas rationed, they were unable to drive there.

From November 29 through December 23, the Rehn Gallery showed ten of Hopper's watercolors, including the six he had produced in Mexico. Henry McBride quipped that the artist was "unaffected by the politics of our fiery neighbor to the south. Probably he is not a communist. He doesn't paint like one," adding that the show "contained some of [Hopper's] best painting."[36] The critic for the *World-Telegraph* praised "the lyric freshness" of Hopper's watercolors; Royal Cortissoz commented that Hopper seemed "to have taken a new lease on artistic life."[37] Although the show was widely reviewed, the work did not sell very well. Earlier that fall, however, Alfred Barr had purchased *Gas* for the Museum of Modern Art. Hopper had reason enough to feel confident, and yet for the last three months of 1943 he did not paint.

WAR ON THE HOME FRONT: 1944

IN MEXICO, Jo had been self-sacrificing and supportive of Edward's work, yet back in their own surroundings she found herself bearing the brunt of his usual discontent as he reverted to his lethargic mode. Driven to one of her reviews of his attitude and her losses, her mind turned back to the time before her marriage and to an old supporter, Carl Sprinchorn. Wondering if she might be able to help Carl, at least, yet fearing that intervention by her might instead prove detrimental, she wrote to him about her loss of contact with the art world:

> For 20 yrs. I've been keeping my nose out of every thing, feeling if I am allowed to meet them it was a contract of some kind that I never try . . . [to] make anything out of it for myself & as you see I've come thru with absolutely *nothing*. On the fewest possible occasions when I've stuck my neck out the least bit, the meat ax fell on my head good & plenty.
>
> 20 years is a long time never to collect one crumb. And that's all right by E.H. too—which has the general effect of paralysis & the growth of fangs. Impotent fangs. A fine spiritual development, fangs. First pangs, then fangs.[1]

Jo's resentment subsided and she responded with her usual readiness when Edward was taken by the idea of yet another erotically charged canvas featuring her in the leading role. Again preparatory sketches show that they experimented with different scenarios. Variously the female figure seats herself on a bed, or comes to stand before an open window, or stands isolated in space looking away to allow detailed drawing from behind, which is the position reemphasized in the canvas, giving some cause to Jo's claim that Edward's favorite part of her anatomy was her "bottom." He endows her with red hair, yet her face looks more like Jo than many of the women in his pictures. In the final composition, he exposes her to morning light that pours through draperies pulled back from a window, through which appear two windows opposite with half-drawn blinds in a hint of peering eyes. *Morning in a City* was finished by April 3, and the gallery featured it in a group show in May.

In late June the Hoppers returned to Truro after nearly two years and passed two weeks coping with a broken pump, burst pipes, and squatters—mice and a three-foot blacksnake that Edward lifted on a shovel and carried outside. For once Jo made no effort to celebrate their wedding anniversary—

Edward Hopper, Jo Posing Nude. *Charcoal on paper, 15⅝ × 18″ (39.7 × 45.2 cm.).*

Edward Hopper,
Jo Posing for
"Morning in a
City," *1944. Conté
on paper, 22⅛ × 15″
(56.2 × 38.1 cm.).*

July 9, 1944, was their twentieth—although their neighbor Dad Stephens brought them a lemon pie. Jo was so touched that, most untypically for her, she actually invited him back to dinner several times.

The car, after two years on blocks, needed major repairs, requiring a trip to Boston. En route they stopped in Hyannis, where Edward sought medical attention for urinary problems, which the physician diagnosed as stemming from his habit of "standing in cold water before plunging in to swim."[2] He was ordered to take hot baths as a cure, and he soon developed the habit of taking off his trunks on their secluded beach and lying face down on the hot sand after a swim. After additional trips to Hyannis and Provincetown, both the car and Edward were in better shape, yet rationing aggravated a situation that Jo had seen only too often: he "drove around disconsolately, trying to work up to a canvas & everything so old & familiar nearby & scanty gas to go look beyond. He has such an uncanny attachment for Eastham, maybe the least interesting part of the Cape—while S. Truro is undoubtedly the most so for its curious glacial formations, its bareness, openness & sea beyond."[3]

Local talk focused on the war. Airplanes flew over at night and surveillance craft prowled by day. Blimps cruised overhead and flares illuminated the night sky. Food rationing led Jo to spend time struggling to master some local specialties: beach plum jelly, clam chowder, and clam pie. Their neighbor Frank Lombard showed her how to clam and his wife, Nettie, gave pointers on making jelly. Edward objected because he did not want Jo to become exhausted and cross.[4] On August 10, Hopper finally managed to stretch a canvas, for a new picture of a sailboat. Two days later, hoping for inspiration as well as pleasure, he went out for a sail with Martha and Reggie McKeen. On August 22, Jo reported that he was "working hard on sailboat canvas. Standing makes his long legs tired."[5] The next day the Hoppers dropped by the Lombard's so that Jo could find out why her "jelly would not jell." While there, they learned that the Allies had liberated Paris. Jo was ecstatic; that night when the airplanes flew over she reflected: "It's all rather thrilling."[6] The next day, Edward, who also still held great affection for Paris, made a special effort to buy *The New York Times*.

On August 30, Jo noted that Edward's canvas was nearly finished and that he was looking toward Orleans for something new to paint. On September 2, they went to Provincetown for the day so that he could get a good look at gulls for his sailboat picture, which was to be called *The Martha McKeen of Wellfleet:* "The line of them over Jos. A. Rick's fish house on R.R. wharf today were facing the right way, the wind not being in that direction."[7] The next day, Jo reported in her diary that Edward worked hard all day and that "the canvas is getting along fine—it's an all blue picture sea & sky—It might be E. himself at the rigger. . . . And the large waves. . . . E. says he cares nothing about painting violence in nature. He prefers potential strength."[8] On September 8, she worried that the canvas was not "moving very fast," because, insisted Edward, he was not "painting fact in this picture—but thought."[9]

For once his activity spurred her and she began a watercolor of some flowers given her by Ellen Ravencroft, an art school classmate who was now director of the Provincetown Art Association (and was trying to persuade Edward to show there). Jo, very soon dismayed by her watercolor, lamented: "How terrible if I'm not going to be an artist anymore!"[10] She dashed off a second letter to Sprinchorn, imagining her artistic plight in metaphors of motherhood, which she had never experienced herself: "I feel so utterly sterile, like I'd never paint again. That is what I get for letting myself get into trying a hand at beach plum jelly! It won't jell either. . . . It's simply fatal to get into that sort of thing. You get stretched out of your natural shape—then nobody wants you."[11]

Jo's frustration at her watercolor was matched by Edward's at his sailboat with gulls. On September 12, he went out looking for a different "picture on down Eastham way. No local sunlight local color charming in the grey light—what E. likes best."[12] When he put the sailboat aside, Jo thought: "Maybe he can get back to it & do something to it when he gets around to it."[13] He would not completely finish the picture until the following December, working in his New York studio, although on September 22, he wrote to Rehn: "I have one canvas (such as it is) finished but am hard put to get another and do not know just when we will get back to the city."[14] He later defended the title, *The Martha McKeen of Wellfleet:* "The young lady that the picture is named after has taken us sailing in Wellfleet harbor so often that the title has a sentimental value for us and Martha McKeen also. The title was given purposely to please her and I think it would make her feel badly if it were to be changed. There is no vessel with this name as far as I know."[15]

To Rehn he also reported on their recent hurricane: "The house here withstood the storm without any damage, but it certainly blew hard. They say 80 to 100 miles an hour here. A great many fine old trees have been destroyed on the Cape, but the damage to houses is not so great as one might expect."[16] On September 18, Jo noted that he had gone off to Eastham "to look again at a house he has designs on for composition."[17] She stayed behind to begin work on a canvas stretched two years earlier, a view of the studio interior as seen from the attic balcony. Hopper made a sketch of the house, but he found the location too far away to keep returning to, as was his preference. Jo lamented that he did not want to paint any of the houses in Provincetown that she found so charming:

> He cares only for the common denominator in houses, roads, etc. &
> is not beguiled by so much individuality. He no longer cares to work
> out from the thing, wants only to make sketches here & there & com-
> pare his own subjects in the studio which is much more comfortable,
> heaven knows. We know all about working in a cold wind or with
> mosquitoes or knats or nosee-ums plagueing the life out of one, & the
> publicity of working out too is so distracting, insufferable for E.[18]

Enjoying a relative armistice, both painted on into the autumn. Jo was busy at work on a still life of the top of her bureau (page 427), and he had begun a new canvas, which she described as "house & row of trees on right, broad road on left."[19] Having made four preparatory sketches, Edward worked in the studio with the shades all drawn, while Jo retreated to the bedroom, although she described it as "mighty inconvenient to try to paint in there, no room for easel & sun from 3 windows shining on canvas."[20] She was discouraged to find herself again painting still lifes, which Edward continually disparaged.

By October 7, Jo had finished two oils, but she reported that Edward's new canvas was "not going so briskly" and he was beginning to feel depressed.[21] Meanwhile, she set about painting their "little white settee (ex seat in sled or carriage), giddy braided rug & window & vertebrae of whale—another rug portrait just to get some bright color."[22] When she expressed doubts that her subject was too "pedestrian," he rubbed salt in the wound, asserting that "there is nothing but personality & no method is going to change, create or disguise that factor."[23]

That roused her old furies again, and she started to "rehash the outrage of his not caring or lifting a finger about my being left out all these years . . . from all the shows at the Whitney, considering such trash as they have made room for—& no room for . . . Marguerite Zorach, Martha Kantor or me."[24] Defending himself, Edward claimed the high ground, that he always took an "impersonal attitude." At that, Jo virtually exploded: "Impersonal—impersonal husband—then that makes me a whore."[25] Besides, she saw, his attitude was all of a piece: "A man who can't endure that women should paint, can no more easily endure that [they] should drive."[26] What he really wanted was "power" or control, which was why he had made her miserable all summer about driving. He insisted that she wait to drive until the car was fixed, but then never got it completely repaired. And when he did finally say she could drive to Provincetown, he spoiled her chance to be independent by taking the car out of the garage and turning it around, as if she were incapable of such an uphill maneuver on their sandy driveway. Seizing her chance while he was in the house, she tried putting the car back in the garage in order to start all over, but he came running and shouting, and the engine stalled. He "yelled like a mad man & while stalled . . . he leap thru the door after me & drags me out onto the grass with threats of extermination. He pulled up a stake to go for me, so I pulled up another & said I'd smash the windows if he touched me—his arms being so much longer than mine."[27] So she pointed out who had paid for their little house so he could have a good studio while she had to "sit out in the kitchen . . . to be out of the way" and said that "it was disgusting that I couldn't be allowed to use his miserable old car."[28] Then he did put the car back in the garage to let her practice getting it out by herself. But all the way to Provincetown he was "living thru every foot of the road, one would think one were driving over a different part of his body every few feet."

The psychology of power that Jo suffered under and saw for herself had been theorized in the *Independent Woman* by Geraldine Sartain five years earlier: "This consciousness of power that comes with successful handling of an automobile might even prove an important antidote for personality quirks. I wonder why psychiatrists don't recommend it to offset inferiority complexes. . . . It can make us feel infinitely more important than managing an egg beater."[29] Sartain's suggestion that women who could master driving an automobile might achieve biological and psychological equality with men touched upon some of Hopper's fears. Allowing Jo to drive fueled his insecurity as both a driver and a painter, and brought out his deep ambivalence toward women. Needless to say, Jo would have had more confidence about herself and painting if she had been able to master driving. Free to transport herself to locations that she wanted to paint, she would not have been so restricted by her husband's needs, tastes, and fears.

Driving, Jo vividly saw as she continued her diatribe, was just part of Edward's need to control the three "most important urges in life":

> Expression thru art, sex, & what ever driving might represent. E. has been implacable. He certainly knew all the subtle ways of killing the art instinct in me—the shock of learning that he had any such wish—way back—when we were first married—nearly did the thing so incredible, so unspeakably low down & so in direct contradiction of all his attitude before we married & he wrote to 2 museum directors commending my work—Imagine! Thereafter, & not too gradually appears the will to extinguish—the ghastliness of this one can't quite ever outlive.

From the "urges" for driving and art, she looked back over "the matter of sex," which she discovered only after their marriage and took years to sort out. It had taken Edward's physician to assure her that her instincts were natural, and a friend lent her

> a very fine book by some German specialist—in the light of which I find myself entirely normal. Imagine entirely normal, like any other woman, not a professional. It took about 5 yrs. to get E. to read this book. Not he, he knew everything. He had his mind made up & that was that. But now I could sass back—& plenty.[30]

Within two days, Edward raised one of his habitual flags of truce, sizing up her four canvases and allowing that he was "surprised that there should be as much skill—& good color."[31] Mollified, she slipped back into her supportive and participatory role, expressing awe at his "working persistently on lonely house on empty road, sitting in tall grass & not one other earthly thing except a few trees purposely not putting themselves forward"; there was, she saw now, a method to his madness. "It would seem almost a stunt to see how far one can eliminate & get only a mood. He early took the pink out of the grass so no one could find there any pretty color. . . . He isn't getting or going after anything specially alluring or exciting in the sky either."[32] She thought she would like a deer or a star in the picture (which was eventually titled *Solitude #56*), but that was her way, not Edward's.

In the end, he gave up on his picture and spent the last week of October scraping and painting the mullions of the big north studio window. He agonized through November into December before bringing himself to finish in the city either *Martha McKeen of Wellfleet* or *Solitude #56*. Holiday spirit suffered, as Jo wrote Marion:

> Not much jollity here with 2 old people and a restaurant dinner— not so hot. . . . Ed is well, thank goodness. He has been working on the 2 cavases he brought back from Cape and has helped them a lot. He's taking them up to the Gallery right now. Well—it will be a relief to have Xmas out from under foot. It's sort of sad. Enclose Ed's check.
>
> P.S. Ed got telegram saying he's elected to Institute of Arts and Letters—but he's not thrilled at all. Nothing comes of it, as far as he can see—purely honorary. High time, if you ask me.[33]

THE AESTHETIC DIVIDE: 1945

ONLY IN JANUARY of 1945 was Hopper at last ready to start prowling the city again. On the upper west side of Manhattan, one of the august buildings that front the park along Riverside Drive caught his eye. After making at least six preparatory sketches of tall windows around a curved bay, he gave a trademark turn of the screw, cropping to just above the cornices to draw attention to the central window, where through partially drawn draperies light picks out the statue of a woman agitated as if pursued.

August in the City, wrote Jo in the record book, "Painted in N. Y. studio April 16, '45 (finished). Winsor & Newton & Block colors . . . Poppy oil . . . Linen canvas, smooth prime of doubtful character. House & pavement in bright sunlight. . . . Pale yellow silk curtains, brownish bronze statue, female clothed." Meticulously and evenly she kept track of the materials, registered the resulting images and paradoxical title, which betrays her and Edward in the studio in the spring imagining a season in the city that they themselves rarely if ever saw. At the center, Hopper again invites a voyeuristic gaze through a window, only to expose not Jo in yet another erotic pose but the little bronze, imagined in an attitude that suggests a classical myth of rape.

Four days later, writing to a psychologist who had asked him to describe his own work, Hopper responded that every artist should "be constrained always to stop short of anything that would give the impression of extreme egotism," so that "the best I can do then is to give a sort of resumé of what I believe those who like it think about it":[1]

> I think they believe my work to be austere and simple, even to coldness, but at times not without a certain richness. They believe me to be not much of a colorist, which I think is true if one considers color for its own sake. However these last criticisms do not disturb me, as my intention in painting is far from giving form, color and design a place in my art as an end in themselves.[2]

He concluded: "I think they feel my work to be solid and having a personal element to which they no doubt respond for I feel that I have not a great deal else to interest them."[3] Such calculated understatement betrays, if not an extreme of egotism, at least the controlling style that made him so scrupulously selective, difficult in choosing subjects, and so domineering with his wife, yet also set him apart from artists who produced more copious, but often more uneven, bodies of work.

The egotism was evident in March, when Hopper attended a dinner under the racks of Dutch pipes at Keene's Chop House to honor Frank Rehn. All but one of the gallery's artists came, including Hopper's particular cronies Burchfield, Kantor, and Poor.[4] Peppino Mangravite, the organizer, and Henry Mattson were the life of the party, while Hopper kept pretty much to himself. Rehn was liked by Jo because he so devotedly promoted Edward's work, although at the time of the testimonial dinner the gallery showed no female artists.[5] On one occasion Jo remembered Edward suggesting that they "try to marry him [Frank] to Juliana Force" of the Whitney Museum, only to conclude that that "would be like marrying Santa Claus to Mrs. Machiavelli or Lucretia Borgia."[6]

Rehn's promotional energy and influence were responsible for the presence of Hopper's *Office at Night* in the seventy-fifth anniversary exhibition in May of the Salmagundi Club. Although the venerable Salmagundi on lower Fifth Avenue was not far from Washington Square, it was too academic for the tastes of Hopper, as an early initiate of the Whitney Studio Club; yet even though an outsider, he won the thousand-dollar prize.

At the death of Franklin Roosevelt, Jo unforgivingly wrote, "Nobody grief stricken here."[7] But when Germany surrendered, she and Edward cheered. Although the European war was over, meat and eggs were still hard to come by, and gasoline rationing was still in effect. Anticipating another trip to Mexico, in lieu of a drive to the Cape, Edward and Jo enrolled in weekly Spanish lessons. To motivate themselves they took on the assignment of memorizing passages from Cervantes.[8] When they ran into the Chattertons' daughter, Julie, on the street, Edward told her to ask her father if he wanted to go to Mexico with them next winter,[9] an usually social gesture for him and a measure of his deep fondness for Chat.

The war had made the Hoppers, like many Americans, more aware of cultural achievements at home. Jo recorded how much they enjoyed seeing landscapes by the painters of the Hudson River School on display at the Whitney Museum: she "was delighted at what for years we had snooted," admiring their "reverence for nature" and "amazing skill" and particularly liking the work of Thomas Cole.[10] Edward insisted on getting the catalogue as a reference for an article on realism that Guy du Bois was trying to persuade him to write.[11] On a return visit, she noticed how he warmed to Homer and Eakins: "He deserves to treat himself to them. Now his head will be in them for days."[12] Eakins was a lifelong enthusiasm of Hopper's: "Thomas Eakins who I believe is our greatest American painter . . . was an objective painter of almost photographic verisimilitude, but a profound personality speaks to us through his art, which used the facts of nature to express the 'cosmic.' "[13] When Hopper later asserted that Eakins was "greater than Manet" and called him a "great world painter,"[14] he verbalized the identity to which he himself aspired; he rejected the provincial term "American scene painter," which he did not consider himself to be.[15]

In May Hopper was inducted into the National Institute of Arts and Letters, and exhibited fourteen pictures in "Works by Newly Elected Members and Recipients of 'Arts and Letters Grants.' " On May 16, he went to the opening at the Brooklyn Museum of "American Watercolor and Winslow Homer," a show organized by Lloyd Goodrich that included nine examples of his work.

With all the gratifying commotion, Edward had done nothing since April, while Jo kept at it. Often he convinced her to accompany him to the movies; they saw Nunnally Johnson's *Keys of the Kingdom,* Elia Kazan's *A Tree Grows in Brooklyn,* Richard Oswald's *Portrait of Dorian Gray,* Peter Godfrey and Jack Gage's *Hotel Berlin.* When she was painting a view of the park from Edward's studio, he actually tried to sketch in hers but found it too dark. In the fall she had sent tips to Carl Sprinchorn with names of people to contact.[16] Now when Sprinchorn visited Los Angeles she gladly put him in touch with Roland McKinney at the Los Angeles County Museum, as well as Walter Arensberg, whom they had met in Hollywood.[17]

On June 10, Bertha Schaefer, an art dealer, looked at Jo's work and arranged for her to bring *Chez Hopper III* to her Fifty-seventh Street gallery. When Jo delivered the work two days later, she and Schaefer went off to see some shows. At Peggy Guggenheim's "Art of This Century" they saw a group show of women artists, including Nell Blaine, Buffie Johnson, Kay

Sage, and Irene Rice-Pereira. Jo did not like the abstract nature of the work and feared, correctly, that the abstract artists would soon want to show at Bertha Schaefer, leaving her canvas "quite friendless."[18] Meanwhile, as Jo worked away on her view of the park, Edward meddled. As in everything else, his views of style seemed calculated to cancel hers: "Said I'd get no brilliancy if didn't keep shadows simple & all one & tall house in back neutral & dark—after I made these corrections the whole thing looked dead, so had to wipe off as well as possible."[19]

When the Museum of Modern Art threw an opening party featuring its permanent collection on June 18, 1945, the Hoppers were there, proud to see his work included. Jo remarked especially on Loren McIver's *Votive Candles,* "Looks like real flame. Glad the Mus. has bought it. We told Barr & Mr. Wheeler. Later E. said we do not know what she has gone thru before getting her work taken up. How likely too. She is rather arrestingly plain. I liked her work right off, found it quite special & some thing akin to what I might once have gone after."[20] For Edward and Jo, who were then in their early sixties, this was an unusually strong response to the work of a younger artist.

On the way to the Cape in late June, the Hoppers stayed overnight in Connecticut with Guy and Floy du Bois in Stonington. Guy again tried to extract the magazine article on realism from Edward, who was "groaning over the prospect."[21] He was slower than Jo to realize the need for defense against the waves of abstraction that had been slowly rising throughout the war. Arrival in Truro did nothing to get him started again. Reading to each other became the preferred pastime: *The New Yorker,* especially its stories by Robert Coates; Emil Ludwig's *Mediterranean;*[22] E. B. White's short stories; and other books of history, fiction, and humor. Sometimes Edward read aloud while Jo did domestic chores such as darning his socks. They also continued to study Spanish. When Edward refused to help in the kitchen, Jo threatened to make him get all his own meals for a week. At this he coaxed her to cuddle with him on the studio chaise longue: "I guess the lion likes to be held by the lamb," he said, adding that he guessed she did not "need a lover after all." She had made a point of reading to him from Aldous Huxley's *Point Counter Point* about the "woman married to the scientifically disposed novelist who was so impersonal, so detached that she was practically thrust into the arms of a waiting vulture."[23] Driving home the message, she reminded him of a woman they knew who took a lover when her husband had "ceased to distinguish her from the table leg."[24]

It displeased Jo that Edward had lost his taste for painting outdoors. Of course, he told her, she could paint wherever she wanted; but he still refused to let her take the car and work in it. He would agree to drop her off somewhere, but then she had no way to get to a bathroom or to fend off the ticks.

Instead, Jo got out her watercolors and imagined painting the eleven-year-old daughter of the family who now rented the Dos Passos house. Edward did not begin anything during their first month on the Cape. Jo told him, "If he'd be willing to start on some factual statement from the thing itself, it might give him a start," but concluded that one could tell Edward "nothing, nothing at all."[25] Finally, hoping to spur him on, she got him to stretch a canvas for her and she started a picture of their fireplace and attic stairs.[26] Later she decided to paint him standing by the fireplace, but he only reluctantly and hurriedly posed.[27] He withheld the kind of participation she gave so freely, and she had great trouble getting the figure right.

They were out in the car on August 15 when the radio announced that the war with Japan was over:

> So glad not to have to hear it from voice of Roosevelt. Such a relief. Everyone so pleased with the successor who didn't even appear in person, just had message read. Amazing how everybody is united in satisfaction over the nonglistening, unasserting Truman—a sensible level headed man with a job to do, come in & clear up after that amazingly super spendthrift & his exceeding vanity.[28]

That night they could hear the celebratory ruckus all the way from Truro Center. Gas rationing ended (though tires were rationed until the end of the year) and Jo began to lobby again to drive. Even on shopping trips Edward always objected to her driving, yet she told herself: "Half the nation drives. I can't be less qualified than all these million women & won't be sold any belief in my competence to do what they all do tolerably well enough."[29] In fact, as early as 1940 *The New York Times* reported studies showing that women were as good or better drivers than men.[30]

In Edward, inflexibility went hand in hand with his lethargy and indifference. On August 23 he wrote to du Bois, declining to write the "American Realists" article: "It seems very difficult for me to get interested in it, although I have tried hard enough. The ideas that have come to me on the subject do not, for the most part, seem to hit the truth very closely. At any rate I can not seem to get into the thing."[31] "Perhaps," he explained, "one reason is that I have been worried about my painting, which has not even started up to this time."

The dry spell that began in April ended on August 29, when Edward stretched a canvas for himself and began the charcoal "layout" of a Provincetown night scene with lighted windows.[32] Two days later, when some unexpected visitors arrived, he surprised Jo when he "made no objection to taking them right in the studio with canvas begun in charcoal & sketches all around.

Usually he snatches everything away when anyone turns up"; and she took note that he "had charcoal drawing half covered by permanent blue in which he covers charcoal lines."[33] His alacrity was infectious. Jo started keeping close tabs, recording, in little less than a week, how the painting had taken

> a turn for the better. . . . E. went back to work in darkened studio. He has all the light shut off but what comes from upper half of big window. It was after 6 that I went in to see great strides had been made with the picture. He lit the rooms inside, what one sees under the dark awnings. It's yellow light, or the rooms look yellow & bright against dark outside; the Rooms sign stands out stark as it's meant to from front yard.[34]

Growing ever more involved, she registered changes four days later and began to second guess:

> He's made the dark sky lighter & lit some of the windows at side of bldg. It doesn't look as the little green light at side of door would show up much & it's so jewel-like & lovely in the reality. Maybe when he sees it again he'll try some more.[35]

As she put herself into his place, she reflected that for her part that summer, she had "produced nothing but fizzles." She toyed with doing a night picture of her own, but felt that making it would require the use of a car.

"Why don't I paint my own picture?" she asked herself the next day. "Why indeed? Why can't I want to? Maybe I am & it's his. I'm so impatient to have him keep at it. When I'm around he feels guilty if he retreats into a crossword puzzle." Suddenly she saw the meaning of her involvement: "It's so interesting to have something growing—one might almost say right inside one. Gestation is what it amounts to, what goes on in the studio—here or in N.Y. It's so a part of me too."[36]

By September 14 he had brought up the interior and put her in mind of Degas: "a house seen at night, a white house with street light full on it. But it's lit inside & that gives such an interest of the house as a shell containing interiors. Now it all so much reminds me for color of that Degas interior."

Still she had her sights set on that jewellike effect:

> Here the interest of the house has a jewel like effect, warm & glowing against dark exterior & there is a little green light at side of entrance that looks like a suspended jewel in the night. But E. isn't taking much interest in either of these elements. I was so tired wait-

ing for them to show up that I made polite inquiry. No—he isn't
going to make any d.——— John Sloan. He's interested in the light on
the facade & if he featured windows or little green light he'd have to
paint the whole outside darker to play up these other 2. No, & he isn't
going to do anything about featuring that little green jewel by dark-
ening the area surrounding it because that would give an effect of
modelling the wall in back & it's perfectly flat & he wants it to stay
flat.

That settled it, and she was forced to admit "it sure is hard to have 2 people
taking such keen interest in the painting of any one canvas."[37]
A few days later Hopper finished *Rooms for Tourists,* sooner than he or Jo
had expected, and still not going as far she would: "He hasn't put the name
on the sign under the electric light. I can't see how he can without spoiling the
effect of glare & ruin a handsome spot of light."[38] A remark that he made later
suggests that he heard but did not listen to Jo's advice: "Mrs. Hopper thought
I should let the landlady know what I was doing out there, but I didn't want
to intrude."[39]
After a trip to Hyannis on September 24, to repair the car and Edward's
glasses, he began "making little sketches" for a new painting.[40] On October 1,
he and Jo drove to Orleans and he "made drawing of house he means to use.
Tall, simple, dignified white house, as simple as they come, not the little Cape
Cod Colonial. He seems to steer away from these beguiling little darlings."[41]
The next day, he stretched a canvas and the day after that, he "drew in composition on canvas in charcoal. Now he finds he isn't quite ready to begin yet,
has to get clearer idea."[42] On October 9, the Hoppers drove to Orleans because Edward wanted "a grey day to look at trees without sun or shadow on
them."[43] They went shopping in Provincetown a week later, and Edward
"made a sketch of branches of elm tree with dripping foliage for his picture—
houses, white houses that look like white petunias."[44] Years later, Jo recalled
that she had "named that canvas & was very proud of myself, that just the way
those 2 houses look, upright, staid, yes purified there is a nice word to describe
them, 1 syllable & I can't recall it."[45] She also noted that there had only been
one house "in the fact but E. put in another—standing right at side of Route
6, no lawn, close to road with ciel blafard, palely loitering no sky, they loom
tall & pale & purified." Jo's emphasis on the "purified" quality of the canvas
that was eventually titled *Two Puritans* brings to mind Guy du Bois's earlier
insight that Hopper "turned the Puritan in him into a purist, turned moral
rigours into stylistic precisions."[46]
Through all the intense work of the fall, Edward was not feeling especially well. Jo noted that he "hates to go to bed because he dreams, always dis-

turbing dreams. With me right there too, it doesn't seem right that I couldn't stave off bad dreams. I wake him up if he seems uneasy, but there aren't any signs for me to know if he snores. I wake him up anyway."[47] One day, when a painting expedition was interrupted by unexpected car repairs, Edward "treated himself to a swivel screwdriver," telling Jo that "when ever he's depressed it helps to go buy a new tool."[48]

The Hoppers left Truro for New York on the morning of October 29, earlier than originally anticipated, because they had been invited to a luncheon at the National Institute of Arts and Letters. Membership in the Institute proved to be important to Hopper, for through it he became acquainted with intellectuals whose works he knew, such as Van Wyck Brooks, who was secretary of the Institute. Brooks and Hopper had a lot in common. Hopper admired Emerson, about whom Brooks had written two books. In *The Pilgrimage of Henry James* (1925), Brooks had dealt with what he saw as the dangers of expatriation.[49] In the face of growing cultural nationalism, Hopper had himself suffered from the lingering effects of his own brief sojourn in France. Brooks, who favored James's early works, claimed, "I have a holy mission to reinstate the despised and rejected *Washington Square.*"[50] Hopper too liked *Washington Square,* so much so that he felt the film based on the novel failed to do justice to James.

Both men felt the conflicts between the values of twentieth-century and Victorian culture. What has been said about Brooks, that he sought "the revitalization and transformation of the dominant American culture,"[51] might also be said about Hopper. Brooks's "youthful impulses toward aestheticism and pessimistic withdrawal"[52] have a parallel in Hopper's early fascination with French Symbolist poetry and its reflection in *Soir Bleu.* The mature work of both men became associated with cultural nationalism, Brooks becoming an eloquent spokesman for an American culture and Hopper's paintings becoming symbols of that culture. Like Brooks, who had published *The Flowering of New England* in 1936 and *New England Indian Summer, 1865–1915* in 1940, Hopper identified with New England; he chose to spend a third of each year there. Brooks wrote: "Americans could do anything but leave it alone. They liked to tease New England, but they were never indifferent to it. They could not have enough of Henry Adams, Santayana's *The Last Puritan* . . . their greatest tradition."[53] Brooks also shared Hopper's regard for the poetry of Robert Frost, to whom he assigned the "function to mediate between New England and the mind of the rest of the nation."[54] In *The Confident Years,* published in 1953, Brooks actually mentioned Hopper, claiming that Theodore Dreiser's prose vignettes in *The Colour of a Great City* "suggested Edward Hopper or Stieglitz's early photographs of battered old street-cars with teams of unkempt horses struggling through swirling winds and flying snow."[55] Surprisingly, Brooks failed to distinguish between Hopper's aesthetic and that of the more avant-garde photographer.

After the luncheon at the Institute, Edward joined Jo for an opening on West Ninth Street of work by William Glackens, whose widow, Edith, was very gratified that Edward had come. To Jo, the crowd seemed very much like that at a Whitney Museum party: she registered John Sloan and his wife, just back from Santa Fe, with no echo of Edward's summer curse "d.——— John Sloan." Edward also "met Walter Huston. They didn't get along any too well. E. strong in his praise of [the famous German actor] Albert Basserman, Huston noncommittal. E. said cold, unsympathetic like everything he does on stage & screen."[56]

Publicity flowered when *Hotel Lobby* won the Logan Institute Medal and a five-hundred-dollar prize in the Annual Exhibition of the Chicago Art Institute. A Chicago critic who had previously praised Hopper's work, C. J. Bulliet, wrote that though he "ranks close to No. 1 for me among all American painters . . . Mr. Hopper is getting a little lazy about the excellent formula he has hit. *Hotel Lobby* is typical Hopper, but Hopper that has lost something of its kick. Maybe Hopper is a drug that wears itself out on the patient."[57] At home, the waitress at the Dixie Kitchen restaurant proudly announced that she had read about Edward's honor in *Time,* and reproductions of *Hotel Lobby* appeared in *Art Digest* and *Art News.*[58]

The wave of abstraction, which aroused Jo's suspicions in June, registered a new advance in November, when it commanded the entire first floor at the Whitney Annual, relegating to the second floor Hopper's own *August in the City* and the work of other Whitney regulars, which were now "America Embalmed" protested Jo, declaring that it had become a misnomer for the Whitney to call itself a museum of American art. Two days later when Edward attended a dinner for the Institute of Arts and Letters, he sat next to Eugene Speicher, who agreed "that Whitney Show [was] a display of cowardice—afraid not to be le dernier cri."[59] Loyalty to the past surfaced at the personal level, too, when Edward learned that the Century Club was planning a show of "Henri's students who have attained eminence." Both he and Jo, who put aside old slights, felt that Arnold Friedman should be included, lest he "feel so hurt"; finally, Edward spoke to Guy du Bois who "got Gifford Beal on phone & learned they had decided in favor of Friedman."[60] After Speicher saw Friedman's current show of portraits, however, his name was dropped from the list. Neither Hopper nor any of the other men spoke of including any of Henri's female students such as Aileen Dresser, Amy Londoner, Lucy Bayard, or Jo.[61]

The slight set off a further round of reflection and comparison in Jo. Viewing sternly her watercolors, she saw a "collection of trees, children, a few pussy cats & lots of wasted paper, recording scenes à la Hopper influence, with life gone clean out of them, factual & empty."[62] Seeking to get to the bottom of how her aesthetic differed from his, she had tried, she said "to pin E down as to his larger purpose—extracting something to the effect that it is an attempt to crystalize a moment of time" or "the arrestation of a moment of time acutely realized."[63] Her disconsolate query could take little comfort from such aphorisms couched in the terse and judicious manner of his self-analysis for the psychologist in the spring and confirming the divergence in their styles brought out by their summer dialogue over the proper line to take in *Rooms for Tourists.*

Six days before Christmas, John Clancy called from the gallery to report that he had just sold *House with a Vine,* which Hopper considered "his best watercolor."[64] Sales for 1945 amounted to $2,020, little better than the previous year.

ANXIETY: 1946-1947

THE HOPPERS TROOPED downstairs with their neighbors on January 12, 1946, to see the victory parade on Fifth Avenue. Jo opted for the vantage point of a friend's apartment, while Edward could watch well enough from the curb, "holding up children to see parade til arms ached," this from a man who generally gave youngsters wide berth.[1] Yet the celebration seemed so grim, without enough music, Jo reflected, that she and Edward and their friends began to worry whether America was turning "into a militaristic state" where "the Army dominates our lives."[2]

The mood of apprehension infected the home front. Jo found need to reassure herself of her unflagging vigilance: "I never let anything slip. It must be understood, dissected, argued & understood on both sides. Interested or not, he's got to know my reactions. . . . Because we're bone of each other's bone, flesh of each other's flesh forever & ever, amen."[3] Her argumentative stance invited quizzical reflections from Edward, who was avidly reading a book borrowed from a friend of hers, *Kabloona*.[4] A study of Eskimo women, it recounts that they have no rights and are exchanged by men like any other property, yet manage to get the better of their men: "With the skill of actresses, the wives played their parts; and with the candour of provincial audiences, the husbands were taken in. There does not exist an Eskimo woman untrained in the art of wheedling . . . until the husband, worn down by her persistence, gives way."[5]

The drama of the sexes chez Hopper was about to reach a new height. In February, Edward showed *The Forked Road* (1934) in the Whitney Annual. Unaware of the date of production, Henry McBride praised the watercolor as "the best thing in some years by this artist. It contains no sleepy passages, if you know what I mean, and is animated throughout. It owes nothing to its subject, just a crossroad half buried in sand, with a few trees and weeds. It had to be very good or it would have been nothing, but fortunately it turned out good."[6] These annual shows at the Whitney always stirred up resentful memories in Jo:

> There is always an ill wind blowing from 8th St. on days of openings there—remember all the yrs. I've been practically on their door steps. . . . Wall flower complex . . . now the jazz is more raucous than ever. Of course I'm not the only victim of their boycott. . . . Certainly E. has never concerned himself in the least.[7]

This year she was especially vulnerable, as she explained in dense pages to Carl Sprinchorn that she finished on February 10.

> Grippe, flue . . . no reading for nearly 2 weeks. So one just lay there festering, stock taking on the brink of the grave, one foot in it—not the flue—just dull passage of years such a lot of them & what done with them. . . . Last week I about decided I'd sink right thru the mattress & if one didn't eat, one might manage it.—but after 2 days not eating, E.H. bribed & maneuvered me into delaying the experiment.[8]

Motivating her hunger strike, she hit Edward with the

> memory of a whole tribe of elephants—what he did in 1925, Aug. '33, Nov '38 etc. now '46 & all to the effect that since he had determined & succeeded in killing off such weakly spark as I had deluded myself into believing myself in possession of—the career had better go too—the easy way—right on thru the good comfortable mattress.

Her wrath modulated at the thought of "E. so uncomplaining, such a tender nurse—with me rending him limb from limb for his not sobbing like a baby that I've been left out of everything since the day I married him 21 years ago." But then the resentment welled again, since she knew Edward so well and reflected upon how he operated in the network, like the call to Guy du Bois on Arnold Friedman's behalf:

Didn't want me to have any spark, urge, what the hell call it—however feeble, pubescent, insignificant. . . . And it's about killing me. As we all know there has to be some loop hole, some inkling where things are brewing, who's gathering them in—& some word of commendation. E.H. has been in the thick of everything, but he'd see me dead before he'd want to let me in. . . . I can't bear to go on living with the bone of one's bone acting that way. Guy du Bois gets people there & trots out Yvonne's pictures—very nice pictures too. E.H. sais "but she's his blood, she's born du Bois." I only married a Hopper. A loathsome breed they are too.

Still bedridden, she resumed writing after a few days and turned to "remembering, as women do, everyone who has done kindness for them," but that had been before marriage. "Ever since, nothing but blight—just as E.H. wanted it for me. Maybe I'll go on another 2 day's hunger strike. I don't mind a bit, it's so easy." She underlines the new weapon in her arsenal, perhaps for future use, before attacking with powerful metaphors from the past the enigma of her attraction to Edward:

That Ego is so impenetrable. Those light houses are self portraits. At 2 Lights, Cape Elizabeth it was pitiful to see all the poor dead birds that had run into them on a dark night. I know just how they felt. That bright light on the top had deceived them—& no way they could think of to wring its neck.

Almost philosophically, she tries to cushion herself from the hurt with another barrage of metaphors:

Everyday we get cards from the galleries—"Come see me dance! Come see me dance!" The clodhoppers & gorillas! It's so silly to care. And that damned Whitney right around the corner. It was supposed to move away but it hasn't yet. . . . Bertha Shaefer has gone abstract. She seems to be having some pretty bad stuff & doesn't know the difference—but gets lots of publicity & I dare say is having a swell time riding crest of the wave.

By February 20, Jo was taking stock of the value of the hunger strike: "This the only thing that would impress E. at all. He didn't resort to his customary walking out of the room whenever I insisted on discussing my case—over the years."[9] In a quite new departure, Edward had even taken her "portfolio of watercolors up to inquire of Frank Rehn what he knew about possible galleries where they could get a nose in."[10] Rehn said he would include one or two in a group show, and his assistant, John Clancy, made some positive comments, but they had no concrete suggestions. Jo complained that the dealers Edith Halpert, Georgette Passedroit, and the Whitney's Juliana Force disdained all women artists. Bertha Schaefer had not sold *Chez Hopper III,* so she took it back.

Before her illness and the strike, Jo had recorded that Edward on January 27 was "going up town . . . & has found something to start on."[11] His movements had taken him as far as Ninety-seventh Street at Park Avenue, where the rail line to Grand Central passes from the viaduct over Harlem into the tunnel under Carnegie Hill. Four preparatory sketches survive. With some kind of truce declared, Jo resumed her usual attentiveness to Edward's work with a report on February 21 that he was "working on his underpass canvas in cold studio."[12] Two days later, she elicited an aesthetic rationale as to "why he doesn't want sharp gleam on his tracks running into his tunnel. It's because he wants the roadbed of the tracks to stay down low in the canvas. Feeling of hollow, deep below sheer cliffs, wall of buildings. Gleams on tracks would raise them. They go right into tunnels for 100 miles or so."[13] By March 1, *Approaching a City* had received its ritual entry in the record book, with a sketch by Edward. Jo's account is as punctilious as ever, giving no sign of her illness and rebellion. Only at the end, describing the signature, does something show: "Signature—most muleishly dimmed & concealed at lower R. alongside of R.R. tie."

Together they delivered the picture, and Jo recorded Rehn's reception: "Frank as usual very enthusiastic, altho it isn't a picture that will sell readily."[14] Hopper himself would tell one interviewer that the picture was just "improvised memories pieced together,"[15] although to another he gave a less obfuscating account: "I've always been interested in approaching a big city by train; and I can't exactly describe the sensations. But they're entirely human and perhaps have nothing to do with esthetics. There is a certain fear and anxiety, and a great visual interest in the things that one sees coming into the city."[16] Jo had been thrilled to see that Frank had hung one of her watercolors in the gallery. He called it "a honey," prompting Jo to kiss him in appreciation.[17] Other approaches to galleries brought no results.

In late February, Edward received a postcard from Nice, from an old friend who, in Jo's view, threatened to come to America. Jo worried: "Hope she won't furnish complications."[18] If the card came from Jeanne Chéruy, Jo might have remembered the name inscribed in the little volume of poetry by Verlaine that Edward had always kept, although it might have been disturbing enough to see a missive from any strange woman, especially French.

Following the contretemps in December, when Hopper recommended Friedman in vain, the Henri show at the Century Club featured the master with his favorite Bellows and only four of the surviving pupils—Hopper, du

Bois, Eugene Speicher, and Rockwell Kent. On March 7, at an all-male dinner before the opening, Hopper found most of the members old and boring, but he sat with his patron Stephen Clark, and met Paul Sachs, the influential Harvard professor and connoisseur. When he finally saw the show, Hopper thought it "dull," claiming that "an Eakins & a Homer would knock the spots out of everything there."[19]

Jo, meanwhile, submitted two watercolors to a jury for membership in the all-female Pen and Brush Club, only to be rejected. She was told to submit again in the autumn, but would not even consider it. Among the eight members of the jury were Dorothy Ferris, whom Jo imagined did not want her "encroaching on her domain," and another woman with whom Jo recalled having "a run in over Roosevelt last spring. I having let out that I thanked God devoutly that that menace had been removed by death." The club had no good painters, Jo consoled herself, and the "present show is pitiful. I'm well out of it."[20] But, since so many of her friends belonged to the club, she was very hurt and depressed at the rejection. Edward, calling the club "the last ditch of the Old Ladies Home for those who never at any time could get a nose in anywhere," offered his idea of consolation: "it might well be that some of them are reaping much satisfaction in being able—or being able to try to spite the wife of the famous E.H."[21]

Rejection by her natural allies made her see her alliance with Edward and her sense of herself in a new light: "To be the wife of such a great good man is not to be frustrated—not as a female, especially one with so little to commend her as such. . . . to be a better artist & incidentally a wiser, more comprehending female—& a lot more gracious one . . . to be grateful for the supreme gift that has been given & so little deserved."[22] Yet looking back, it was hard not to remember, if not all over again the searing hurts, at least the chronic domestic chill:

> As a companion E.H. lives to keep his nose in printed matter. Any printed matter even. He's up with the lark to drink print. . . . Any talk with me sends his eye to the clock. It's like taking the attention of an expensive specialist. He will listen long enough to make pronouncements, then willingly would he end that. Reopening the matter bores him. So this leaves me a rather lonely creature cut off by this boycott.[23]

§

ENCOURAGED BY THE ARTIST Edwine Behre, although discouraged by Edward, Jo mounted another show of her work in her studio, mailing homemade announcements and letters to her friends and to art critics such as

Henry McBride, Margaret Breuning, and Edward Jewell, hoping "not to be punished for vanity."[24] She wrote to Henry Schnakenberg: "There is a homemade one man show going on here in my studio. I haven't bothered you about it—expecting you'd be glad not to be bothered; an auspicious attitude on which to run a show. It ends Sun. It keeps one in, because always some people turn up & in a way it's been fun."[25]

Jo's efforts succeeded, to the extent that *The New York Times* printed a mention of her show.[26] Her most supportive friends came to see it. The artist Lou Chapin reminded her that she should only be concerned "to have painted them" and that "their destiny is in the hands of God."[27] The artist Maurice Becker and his wife, Dorothy, also visited. Jo was pleased when Maurice, whom she had known since the days when they were both Henri students, spent much time with her pictures and told her that "he loved them."[28]

Keeping tabs on responses, Jo was chagrined to hear no mention of her invitation from Edward's long-time admirer Jewell, whom they encountered on April 22, while visiting the Century Club to see "Henri and Five Pupils." The next day, however, Samuel Golden, who was publishing a new monograph on Edward's work, cheered her by suggesting that he might use her work on Christmas cards.[29] Other friends and acquaintances also showed up, most notably Marie Appleton from the Whitney Museum, which Jo particularly appreciated, noting that she had been "struggling for half a lifetime under the boycott of the Whitney."[30] Appleton told Jo that she remembered the freshness of her watercolors from the days of the Whitney Studio Club.

The show left Jo reasonably content, at least with the loyalty of old friends.[31] Edward's scoffing was only to be expected, especially since during March and April his own work was again stalled. What turns Jo to the diaries again is an acute recurrence of the old packing nerves. Jo felt that everything was left to her while Edward stopped to read the newspaper, study Spanish, and even work on crossword puzzles. When he decided that he did not want to take some article of clothing that Jo had carefully packed for Mexico, and refused to let her unpack it, she exploded:

Now for 22 yrs. I [have] practically never done anything to which he strongly objected. . . . So used is he to receiving this high consideration that he sees no room in court for me at all—& I'm not the kind to accept this for one minute & this no minute in history to try. This just another occasion. If he gets his way for all the sizable, important issues, I fight like a tiger for the little, absolutely inexpensive ones that to me, for one reason or another I find an importance—This one of them. Mind you, implying no outlay on his part of money, time, effort. . . . So the dynamite went off—& plenty. . . . I kicked, he swatted,

I stretched for a weapon to augment the length of my arm reach & he
dragged me across studio by my wrists & continued to swat while I
struggled & bit, bit hard right into one of the 2 hands that held me
tight & bit til he let go. I drew blood before he'd let go, he'd rather to
be bitten than let go, so my teeth went right on in & nothing else
would convince him of my utter exasperation & determination to up-
hold a principle. All very exhausting this interruption. So it was with
a bandaged hand that he packed the car & I can't see yet how it could
have been otherwise. No one who sees him, so saintly so patient could
realize what straights he could drive a person like me thru. I quite
willing to give up trip to Mexico, it was costing too much.[32]

Not casually, then, years later, did Jo tell Brian O'Doherty: "I once bit him to
the bone."[33]

The first trip to Mexico had been a relative success, although it might
have been better, they thought, with a car. Besides, rationing was over. Above
all, the anguish of searching for new subjects on the Cape was so certain that
it justified the risk of a new quest. Earlier than usual for a summer, they got
going on May 7. Battle broke out again the first night on the road because Edward insisted on having the window wide open all night, even though Jo
complained that she was "a block of ice."[34] Fortunately, the weather warmed
as they headed south; Edward insisted that he alone drive as they passed
through Maryland, Virginia, Louisiana, and Texas. In New Orleans, they
drove around the French Quarter and visited the cathedral and museums.
Edward looked at Civil War relics, which Jo dismissed as not very impressive. With their usual divergence in aesthetics, she regretted that he showed
no interest in painting the old quarter, which she found charming and he, too
picturesque.

Crossing the Laredo Bridge over the Rio Grande on May 16, they made
for their familiar haunts in Saltillo. Their hotel room opened onto a roof from
which they could paint, but the climate let them down. In spite of the high altitude, the heat was unbearable and the car that was supposed to free them
broke down; besides, they discovered that, even if the war was over, the local
supply of gasoline was short. Irritants that had been forgotten in New York
reasserted themselves: the food and "the lack of friendliness."[35] Jo complained
to Samuel Golden: "Mexico is truly maddening, the inefficiency & utter indifference & the fact that time does not exist."[36]

At least both were able to paint. Edward began work on a watercolor of
housetops, working after five, when the sunlight shifted to their roof. From
the same position, he painted three other watercolors depicting the *Church of
San Esteban* (an old mission church dating from 1592), a view with the movie

house *El Palacio,* and *Construction in Mexico.* He complained that the late afternoon showers were making it difficult for him to get his skies. He felt, he said, like a prisoner in Saltillo, obliged to wait for blue skies in the right light in order to complete his watercolors.

Jo painted a canvas of the cathedral tower and two other church roofs. Although she took issue with Edward's position that he cared not for color but values, she found that her own work often became too muddy.[37] He warned her not to be afraid of dark tones and to concentrate on solidity, bluntly declaring that she never had learned anything about painting.[38] When she finished her oil, he discouraged her from starting another, as they might soon be leaving town. So she painted a watercolor of the interior of the church of St. Esteban and made sketches of several of the local children.

Edward also showed a certain aptitude for Spanish. During one of their daily lessons at the Methodist school, their teacher lectured the gringo artists on aesthetics, advising them that one ought to wear clothing the color of one's hair, at which Edward managed to say in Spanish that since he had no hair, perhaps it would be becoming for him to wear no clothes.[39] On the whole, he grew progressively more glum, taking a dislike to the people, the architecture, and the climate; detesting the market, where the odor of unrefrigerated meat filled the hot air; and even expressing longing for the Canadian Rockies. Jo, on the other hand, began to enjoy herself and wanted to drive south, to Oaxaca.

The power of the disgruntled driver prevailed. Putting Saltillo behind on July 2, they pushed north as far as Wyoming, where they found a ranch in the Grand Tetons and stayed for ten days while Edward produced three watercolors: *Mt. Moran, Slopes of the Grand Tetons,* and *Jo in Wyoming.* In the latter, the setting and viewpoint make it clear that Edward was in his customary working position folded into the car's backseat. He shows Jo from behind, her diminutive figure perched in the front seat, her brush poised in making an image of mountains toward which her gaze darts, while through the windshield the road stretches to the horizon defined by green forests and blue peaks. Ten years earlier, he had portrayed her alert gaze and outstretched arm, but without context, so that his acknowledgement of her role as an artist seemed to come almost grudgingly, only with the title, *Jo Painting* (1936). Now he shows her sympathetically and fully in the role, in the spirit with which he nursed her out of her hunger strike and, finally getting the message, at least made a stab at promoting her work. It had taken tragic conflict and heroic travel to bring Edward to acknowledge in his own style her vision of herself, imposing of course, for once, his vision for her style.

The fears that drove them to Mexico and Wyoming were confirmed back on Cape Cod, where Edward lapsed into his all too familiar despair of sub-

Sidney Waintrob, Jo Hopper by Her 1946 Canvas "Church of San Esteban," *1955.*

Edward Hopper, Jo in Wyoming, *1946. Watercolor on paper, 13⅞ × 20″ (35.2 × 50.8 cm.).*

jects: "He's done so many around here, about eaten up everything."[40] On a visit to John and Katy Dos Passos in Provincetown, where they ran into Susan Glaspell, the feminist writer who had been kind to Jo before their marriage, he felt nothing but boredom.[41] He ignored Jo's praise of their Truro hills as a subject; nor would he let her use the car to paint them herself. Ruefully she took stock of the flower piece she had just produced: "garish color & no form. Stupid & vulgar."[42] Finally on September 23, Edward began to sketch a canvas, having worked on several drawings and diagrams over the last few days. Jo described the new picture as "a house & some fields." In the record book, the entry for *October on Cape Cod* shows her best austere ledger style, until the close, where she adds one of her personal asides: "Peace, quiet, 'no birds sing. Some day you will be quiet too.'—E.H.'s favorite Goethe (strictly off the record)."[43] The quotation, from Goethe's "Wanderers Nachtlied" ("Wanderer's Nightsong") is one that Hopper loved to recite in German, although he did not willingly advertise private preoccupations, especially with his own death, as suggested by the dying foliage of autumn.[44]

Another source of anxiety faced the Hoppers on their return to New York, where they learned that New York University had taken over their building from the previous landlord, Sailors' Snug Harbor. The university immediately raised rents by twenty percent and refused to give any lease renewals, "announc[ing] its intention of transferring its veterans' activities to Nos. 1 and 3" Washington Square North.[45] Jo observed in her diary that Edward had not been so depressed since the death of his mother.[46] For once, he was moved to speak to the press: "It's getting worse and worse. They're tearing studio buildings down and none are going up. We think it is inhuman and cruel to evict us from here. The University is supposed to be an educational institution, in sympathy with the arts. Is this the way to show it?"[47] He even donned an etching apron and posed with Jo by his press (which he no longer used and she had never tried) for a publicity photo captioned "Mr. and Mrs. Edward Hopper at their etching press."[48]

Thus began what Jo dubbed "The Battle of Washington Square, the long struggle against New York University" to remain in their home.[49] She launched an energetic epistolary campaign in which she accused the expansionist university, which was after the park and the surrounding property for its campus, of "Hitler-like aggression."[50] She described their home as "that famous old studio building where everyone has turned up at one time or another: Eakins painted a portrait, Paderewski gave a recital, Dos Passos wrote 3 Soldiers, Guy du Bois, Wm. Glackens, Ernest Lawson, Eleanor Wylie, Frank Harris, the 'Dial,' born on the 1″ floor, etc., etc."[51] Feeling that the struggle approached heroic dimensions, Jo reached for appropriate language from the classics, referring to the Trojans' loss of their homeland to the Greeks with quotations in Latin from the second book of Virgil's *Aeneid,* to the effect that even the enemy would weep at such a destruction.[52] She also echoed the opening of Horace's *Roman Odes,* claiming that the artists of number Three, like Horace, had an important role to play as teachers of the young; the unscrupulous university must not be allowed, she said, to turn these true teachers out of their historic homes.[53]

At a "conference" at the Office of Price Administration, from which the university had requested eviction notices, John Sloan stepped forward to defend Hopper and his neighbors, proclaiming, "No business should be allowed to throw out any people living in such premises. I regard the university as any other business," and cleverly pointing out, "Every eviction is crowding out service men."[54] It became clear at a hearing in March that the university intended to use the building for offices and classrooms, not housing.[55] In May the application to alter the interior of the building was denied by the Board of Standards and Appeals, but the uncertainty of the OPA ruling lingered into the following fall.[56]

Hopper's anxiety was momentarily deflected by his participation in the Whitney Annual, where he showed *Solitude #56,* completed two years earlier. Reviewing the show for the *Nation,* Clement Greenberg, the champion of Jackson Pollock and other Abstract Expressionists, expressed a liking for

Hopper's landscape, "despite the crudeness of its greens and the academic superficiality of its facture," going on to theorize:

> A special category of art should be devised for the kind of thing Hop-
> per does. He is not a painter in the full sense; his means are second
> hand, shabby, and impersonal. But his rudimentary sense of compo-
> sition is sufficient for a message that conveys an insight into the
> present nature of American life for which there is no parallel in our
> literature, though that insight in itself is literary.[57]

Greenberg's left-handed compliment must have made Hopper cringe:

> Hopper's painting is essentially photography, and it is literary in the
> way that the best photography is. Like Walker Evans's and Weegee's
> art, it triumphs over inadequacies of the physical medium. . . . Hop-
> per simply happens to be a bad painter. But if he were a better
> painter, he would, most likely, not be so superior an artist.[58]

The apologist of Pollock was not attuned to the relentless parsimony of ex-
clusions and reductions that distinguished Hopper's aesthetics.

Other critics involved with abstract art saw more in Hopper. Already in
October 1945, in the avant-garde journal *View*, its associate editor Parker
Tyler had published " 'Encyclopedism' of American Art," an article on Hopper that proved influential on others.[59] The managing editor of *View*, John
Bernard Myers, wrote in his journal for 1946: "Parker Tyler has taken um-
brage at what he considers my 'prejudice' against art by Americans. He
agrees with my idea that to speak of 'American art' is parochial and impre-
cise, but he then surprised me by urging me to really look at the work of Edward Hopper, a painter who he believes is first rate."[60] After a visit to the
Rehn Gallery, Myers concluded: "I realized that I hadn't really seen Hopper's
work, that I simply had lumped him with 'social conscience' artists like Reginald Marsh and Moses Soyer. It gradually dawned on me that Hopper's
painting is sophisticated and deeply felt."[61]

Distracted by the uncertainty of the future of number Three, Hopper did
not complete another picture until January 1947, when he painted *Corn Belt
City* in the studio. Jo described it as depicting a "little grey hot dog stand" with
a neon sign and a sandy-colored stream passing under a bridge. Tall buildings
with towers were visible in the distance, with treetops in the middle ground.
Seen against the evening sky were "Sailor boy & girl in green hot dog con-
sumers," while behind them stood " 'Jimmy' in white coat."[62] To absorb the
feel of the small cities, roadhouses, and motels of the Midwest, Hopper had his

readings in Sherwood Anderson, reinforced by the long drives to and from the West in 1941 and returning from Wyoming the previous summer.

For his next canvas, too, Hopper turned away from "The City" around him. On April 23, 1947, he finished *Pennsylvania Coal Town,* portraying a bald man with a rake in bright sun by a plain house, of a drabness relieved only by the light warming an ornate urn planted with green. The scene brings to mind Hopper's student sketch after Millet's *Man with a Hoe,* and represents the closest he ever came to expressing sympathy with the masses. Jo noted that the gray steps were "dark" and that the terrace was "sooty"; she identified the glum, lonely figure of a man as "a Pole," picking an immigrant ethnic working-class group of that region.[63]

Hopper's image evokes Anderson's *Marching Men* (1917). Set in a Pennsylvania town called Coal Creek, the novel, which Anderson dedicated "To American Workingmen," comments on the oppressive routine of workers' lives.[64] Anderson called the town "hideous . . . a necessity of modern life."[65] Hopper's painting of the man bent over the rake recalls Anderson's description: "An Italian who lived in a house on a hill side cultivated a garden. His place was the one beauty spot in the valley."[66] The novel recounts:

> When a strike came on he was told by the mine manager to go on back to work or move out of his house. He thought of the garden and of the work he had done and went back to his routine of work in the mine. While he worked the miners marched up the hill and destroyed the garden. The next day the Italian also joined the striking miners.[67]

The element that suggests "Italian" ethnicity was barely hinted in the preliminary sketch, but in the canvas it becomes a second focus. To share the stage before the otherwise dreary house, Hopper elaborates the urn into a warm terra cotta of classical style—an Italianate garden ornament—emphasized and illuminated by the same dramatic sunlight that shines on the bald man. Jo's identification of the man as "a Pole" recalls a reference to Polish immigrants in Anderson's novel: "In little Polish villages the word has been whispered about, 'In America one gets much money.' "[68]

Burton Rascoe, reviewing Anderson's *Winesburg, Ohio* in 1919, summarized the author's technique in a way that almost describes what Hopper later achieved in paint; he noted that the writer "frequently suggests rather than depicts; that he respects the imaginative faculty of his reader by refusing to be explicit where overtones of emotion are already invoked in the reader; that he is selective, indefinite, and provocative instead of inclusive, precise, and explanatory."[69]

The siege on their home by New York University was not deemed serious enough to preclude the annual summer campaign, nor did the previous year's experience dictate another heroic search. When Hopper finally broke out of the perennial doldrums of midsummer, the idea was closer to the works just completed in New York, looking out into America, than to anything specifically Cape Cod. He himself later claimed that the idea had been in the back of his head "for twenty years."[70] A couple on a front porch strikingly like that of his boyhood home in Nyack, "she standing out for matrimony," Jo remarked in the record book. Although dressed in 1940s fashion, the figures may draw on Edward's memories of his sister courting; in 1900, he produced a pen-and-ink drawing of a young woman who resembled Marion in the process of rejecting a cheerless would-be suitor. In the canvas, the couple, illuminated by a harsh electric light and shown leaning against the porch wall, are absorbed in an apparently distressing conversation. An irate scowl distorts this young woman's face, while her shoulders arch defensively like the back of a provoked cat. The use of posture communicates emotion as convincingly as in the old poster *Smash the Hun.* Her companion places his hand upon his chest in protest. The result is no mere summer idyll, but, as in Hopper's earlier etching, *Summer Twilight* of 1920, the portrait of a romance in crisis. The record book enters *Summer Evening* as painted in the Truro studio and completed on October 3, 1947.

Just before the summer's lone painting was done, news came that Katy Dos Passos was dead, and Dos in the hospital. Blinded by the setting sun while leaving the Cape, he had crashed into a truck, killing his wife instantly and losing an eye.[71] Jo and Edward drove to Provincetown to join the crowd that thronged Katy's funeral; what charming neighbors, Jo recalled, and thought of their last time together, when Katy gave her an inscribed copy of one of her books.[72] There was also a sad good-bye to their elderly neighbors, Nettie and Frank Lombard, who departed in failing health for an old-age home in Boston.[73] Jo was especially distressed at their loss, for Frank, ever practical and companionable, had taught her to go clamming and to bake clam pie.

Back in New York, Edward aroused himself from lethargy only to travel to Indianapolis in November, to serve on an exhibition jury, and that only because, Jo wrote Marion, he so loved to ride on trains.[74] Without Edward's knowledge, perhaps while he was out of town, Jo had gone to see the art dealer James Rosenberg, whose New Gallery had shown her work before she married. She subsequently wrote to thank him for looking at her watercolors and for giving her "excellent advice," which she lamented came "too late," because "life does things to one":

I keep these early pictures as sacred relics of a grace de coeur no longer in me. They have a certain "innocence et son noble orgueille" that has been outlived. I prize them myself but am amazed that anyone else should glimpse anything in them. Certainly not museum directors & the like. Especially since they miss out with anyone so wise and astute as E. Hopper—I keep these little bastards for myself. There can't be anymore like them.[75]

Later that month, Jo renewed another link to her more glorious past when the actor Sam Jaffe, from her Washington Square Players days, invited the Hoppers to see him performing in *This Time Tomorrow.*

As his depression dragged on, Edward often read from Robert Frost, "his favorite poet," whose poems Jo described as making "sense & the very good sense of an old Vermont Yankee."[76] Jo later admitted, "Verlaine got me long before Walt Whitman—such a silly snoot—never knew of Robt. Frost until E.H. initiated me."[77] She gave Edward a volume of Frost's poetry for Christmas 1947 and he immediately opened it and began to read aloud.[78] "I'm a great admirer of Frost," Hopper would tell an interviewer. "He's very pictorial, concretely pictorial for me. A poem like 'Come In,' or 'Stopping by the Woods in the Snow.' "[79]

They also sent a book of Frost's poetry for Christmas to their Truro handyman, Tommy Gray, with a note from Jo on Frost: "He is a delightful person. We have met him. He likes E. Hopper's work too. They are both such good American[s]—& they stand for good sense."[80] She gave Gray the following advice: "Any poem must be read slowly, because each single word counts for so much—no other word would do for the effect he produces—which is often a mood, a feeling for a place, its significance. Never dramatics, highly personal & mighty nice. You give him a chance."[81] The advice was not dissimilar to that concerning Hopper's painting given by one editor to another in *View.*

ILLNESS AND LOSS: 1948

THE SHOW OF Hopper's work that opened at the Rehn Gallery in January 1948 was the first since 1941, when early experiments got mixed reviews.
Now even the querulous Henry McBride wrote of "the best he has shown in
a long, long time; coolly, quietly built up in recognition of all the known rules
of picture-making but doing nothing to explain why the inhabitants have left
town without leaving . . . anything but the aura of intense loneliness—always
this artist's main theme."[1] Robert Coates, writing in *The New Yorker,* reviewed the exhibition along with one of Jackson Pollock at the Betty Parsons
Gallery, setting up a paradigm of two opposite poles of contemporary American painting. Coates observed that Hopper lifted his subjects out of their "or-
dinariness," creating "poetry and momentousness" and setting up "strange
overtones of suggestion."[2] Edward was pleased with this review.[3]

Frank Rehn proudly claimed that several thousand people visited the exhibition. Because of Hopper's scant production, three of the eight paintings
shown—*Nighthawks, Dawn in Pennsylvania,* and *Rooms for Tourists*—were
works sold years before and borrowed back for the occasion. Hopper admitted to the critic for *Time* magazine:

> I wish I could paint more. I get sick of reading and going to the
> movies. I'd much rather be painting all the time, but I don't have the

impulse. Of course I do dozens of sketches for oils—just a few lines on yellow typewriter paper—and then I almost always burn them. If I do one that interests me, I go on and make a painting, but that happens only two or three times a year.[4]

American critics—influenced perhaps by the wartime presence in New York of European Surrealists such as André Breton, Max Ernst, and André Masson—increasingly began to link Hopper's work to that movement, perceiving concealed moods and evocations. Carlyle Burrows wrote that Hopper's paintings dealt "with facts but do not exclude poetry."[5] Aline B. Louchheim insisted that Hopper's work was "not photographic," explaining that he had "selected, arranged, and ordered, but he lets what he feels emerge from what he sees."[6]

Other critics, responding to Abstract Expressionism, began to complain that Hopper was too illustrative. Emily Genauer commented: "It actually takes courage these days for an artist not to conform to the successful formulas of the abstractionists and surrealists."[7] Still, she attacked *Summer Evening* as an image "you could fit . . . to the text of any story in any woman's magazine."[8] Hopper rebutted: "I never thought of putting the figures in until I actually started it last summer. Why any art director would tear the picture apart. The figures were not what interested me; it was the light streaming down, and the night all around."[9] During this period, Hopper was often asked what he thought of nonobjective painting. To one such inquiry, he responded rather thoughtfully about a topic that increasingly distressed him:

> There is a school of painting called abstractionist or non objective which is derived largely from the work of Paul Cézanne, that attempts to create "pure painting" that is, an art which will use form, color, and design for their own sakes, and independent of man's experience of life and his association with nature. I do not believe such an aim can be achieved by a human being. Whether we wish it or not we are all bound to the earth with our experience of life and the reactions of the mind, heart, and eye, and our sensations, by no means, consist entirely of form, color and design. We would be leaving out a great deal that I consider worth while expressing in painting, and it can not be expressed in literature.[10]

At the time, Hopper dismissed abstract painting as merely "a temporary phase in art," claiming "it does not reflect life closely enough to endure for long." He added: "Abstract art is a very incomplete means of conveying great emotions, and all great art has expressed great emotion."[11]

Praise and controversy alike contributed to build Hopper's reputation. *Look* magazine polled sixty-eight "leading museum directors, curators of paintings and art critics" who voted Hopper one of America's ten best painters.[12] (Instead of pleasing Hopper, the poll, which placed him after John Marin, Max Weber, Yasuo Kuniyoshi, Stuart Davis, and Ben Shahn, probably annoyed him.) *Art News* would choose the Rehn Gallery exhibition as one of the five best one-man shows in New York that year, an honor Hopper shared with Alberto Giacometti, Jacques Lipchitz, Picasso, and Kurt Seligmann.[13]

§

AT THIS CRITICAL MOMENT in his career, Hopper was diverted by failing health. He entered New York Hospital on February 8 for prostate surgery. Before leaving for the hospital, he attempted to bring enough coal into the studio to enable Jo to keep the stove going. Initially, he did not want anyone except Frank Rehn to know about his illness—so Jo had to sneak through the building to cart off the ashes or haul fresh coal. Postoperative complications kept Hopper in the hospital longer than he had anticipated. When he was discharged on February 29, he moved into the Grosvenor Hotel, on lower Fifth Avenue at Tenth Street, to avoid climbing the seventy-four steps at Washington Square and to have a convenient private bathroom. Rather than spend an extra two dollars a day, Jo slept at home and visited him daily. Hopper's bleeding persisted and he returned to the hospital on March 6, to learn that he would eventually require two more procedures. He was not discharged until the third of April. He heard from many friends during his illness, including Lyonel Feininger, who wrote from New York's Mt. Sinai Hospital, where he too was undergoing surgery.[14]

During his enforced stay at the hotel, Hopper wrote to Carl Zigrosser, complaining about his ordeal. "Trying to get back to normal. I believe this is not considered a very serious operation, but the process of recuperation seems long and difficult. At least it has been with me."[15] Hopper was very demanding of Jo, who brought him meals and reading matter, and attended to him devotedly. She felt unappreciated, but she struggled to remain tranquil. Hopper did not venture the climb home until May 5. The very studio they were fighting so hard to keep had proven untenable during his illness.

Easily bored as convalescence stretched out, Hopper took the most pleasure in reading Van Wyck Brooks, Whitman, and Melville. His desire to take up the latter two at this particular moment was surely linked to his reading of Brooks's *The Times of Melville and Whitman*. Encouraged and stimulated by the literary critic's excitement, Hopper could ruminate about what constituted American culture. Brooks discussed his subjects as "writers of genius" working "in and about New York," giving Hopper a means to identify with them.[16]

He also loved *One Man's Meat,* a collection of short pieces by E. B. White, written between 1938 and 1943.[17] The pared-down style of White's writing suggests Hopper's parsimony. White's essays reflect on some of the same issues that concerned Hopper and informed his paintings, especially the mistrust of progress. For Hopper, who stubbornly clung to his vision of the past and steadfastly refused to embrace the skyscraper, the airplane, and other aspects of modern urban life, White's accounts of rural Maine were a tonic.

Later that month, the tedium was interrupted by an unexpected letter. Enid Saies, from whom he had not heard since 1907, when they parted in London, wrote to him from her home in Sweden after she saw his work reproduced in *Time.*[18] Could he be the same person whom she had known so many years ago in Paris? He responded with an outpouring of fond recollection, but a note of pride: "Those were my pictures that you saw in 'Time,' and very bad reproductions they were too."[19] In a manner remarkably forthcoming, he explained, "Paris saw me twice after I met you there," and recounted what he knew of the subsequent history of the family with whom they both had boarded. He then added:

> My last trip to Paris was in 1910, and all my traveling since then has been done here and in Mexico. I like our far west and we drive there now and then—a long drive of 3000 miles to the west coast, but worth the trouble of getting there. We like Mexico too, for all its dirt and its hatred of Americans. It's a long drive there too—over 2000 very tiresome miles through our south and through Texas which is larger than France.[20]

He also expressed concern at the political situation: "You in Sweden must be worried as to Russia's intentions—we are here in America and are fearing war again."[21] The threat of Communist expansion loomed large in Hopper's circle.

When Jo reminded Edward that on July 9 they would have accomplished a quarter of a century of matrimony, and suggested that they "deserved a Croix de Guerre—medal for distinguished combat," he agreed and proposed a coat of arms with a ladle and a rolling pin.[22] The violence of the previous year was far enough behind them to permit humor. His reconciliatory gestures and then vulnerability had made and kept relative calm. Without anger, she would return to her other realization, of the disparity in their social natures: "I need people & talk. E. so seldom deigns to talk—& only nonsense, good natured enough if it isn't about me driving, but the real thing, soul searching, he doesn't go in for—& I like that kind."[23]

On July 14, Edward and Jo left for the Cape. It was to be a summer of recuperation and reflection on friends lost. Jo would record that they both participated in a small exhibition at the post office of artists then living in Truro.[24] She also welcomed the few lavish dinner parties, since their own lack of refrigeration still held them to beans or canned pea soup at home.[25]

It had been October the previous year when Hopper last painted. Now Jo reported on August 10: "E. is anxious to get to work painting, he draws bits of things to embody his composition but hasn't yet shaped it to suit," and on September 1, they drove to Orleans, where he made a crayon drawing and later, on a side road in Eastham, she made a watercolor and he sketched a tree.[26] On September 7, Jo noted that Edward, who had stretched his canvas the day before, was "drawing in charcoal on a 30 × 40 canvas. It turns out to be a shop window; Praise be. It is chock full of promise."[27]

By September 9, praise turned to complaint: "E. still playing with charcoal drawing on canvas, not ready to commit himself to paint yet. He has curtains drawn & shades down in studio, so no place for me but kitchen chair or bedroom where nothing comfortable to sit on either."[28] Yet she did not "want to do still life—I can't take out the car—it's too cold outside or the wind blows too much & it's no good at all to paint in the kitchen or bedroom with [the] light all wrong."[29] Edward's penchant for aggressive jokes only aggravated the situation, when, after they ran into another artist couple from the Whitney Museum coterie, he said, "If Alexander Brook could stand Peggy Bacon, I guess I can stand you."[30] When they mentioned the death of Juliana Force, it reminded Jo of one thing: "She didn't like women."[31] Those were the hurts that surged through her letter to Sprinchorn after her hunger strike and that had been in remission, if only nothing stirred them again. The familiar resentments did begin to well up as Edward continued to isolate himself: "It's a most desperate thing to realize this. He couldn't spare any concern for someone else—it would rob him to disturb his self concentration to insist on the existence of another."[32] Yet the closure did more than merely reopen past wounds; it made her look back and appreciate even the trials of the trips: "Driving does feed one's instincts somehow. Covering distance is almost creative. Very therapeutic—Even if every part of the way is disputed, dictated, damned. An acquired skill is a satisfaction."[33]

Pulling herself together, Jo made do with the kitchen, taking out an old canvas that had the beginnings of a goldenrod bouquet, but substituting a vase of dried flowers. She planned to call the picture *Fleurs du Temps Jadis* ("Flowers of Time Past") in homage to her favorite Villon poem, "Ballade des Dames du Temps Jadis," ("Ballad of Ladies of Times of Yore"), thinking perhaps, too, of the way Villon identified women with flowers: "La royne blanche comme lis" ("The queen white as lily").[34] While Jo worked, she felt "as tho I'd come out of a long gloomy tunnel—Painting sure is a fine psychotherapy, even tho dead flowers might seem to be decadent."[35] Eventually, she added her beloved cat, Arthur, peeping around a curtain on the left, and the arch in Washington Square on the right, with a view of Truro in the background, changing the title to *Obituary* because dead flowers put her in mind of the past and death.

For a week, she had been "shut out of the studio by E.'s arrangement of light—everything shut up so light from upper part of big window only & that right on his canvas.... Can't read, desk in shadow which is too dark & no light on canvas anywhere but on his easel," so, on September 22, she celebrated: "E. has about finished his first canvas since last fall. It's a beauty. Shop window of a corner store with woods beyond."[36] She described his difficult struggle to realize what he wanted:

> E. lamenting "compromise of defeat" yesterday. I pinned him down to just what that meant. Well one never got what one started after, something steered him in another direction. What this time. He meant to have sturdy oak trees such as one sees on village streets—& he has locusts with spreading, curving trunks not what he wanted— these more decorative, more like pictures. But what they did for that bleak white store front when he put trunks in! Well they are compromise & defeat of the original intention. What kind of a store—he doesn't know ... can't do more about contents of window, would complicate.[37]

Responding to a request from the Whitney Museum for a painting for its annual exhibition, Hopper, with *Seven A.M.* in mind, wrote to Rehn: "I have just finished a canvas here that I think is good, but I do not think it will be back in time for the show."[38] He suggested that Rehn might submit something already at the gallery: "I should be more prolific but can't seem to make it."[39] When John T. Spaulding's collection was bequeathed to the Museum of Fine Arts in Boston, the institution sent Hopper photographs of the works. His comments on his early watercolors are telling: "They look better than I thought they would. I have been afraid to go to Boston to see them."[40]

Hoping against hope, Jo and Edward went out together in early October to scout for subjects, with results that led her to think back over their whole life in the place, and to testify again to their tenderness:

> Nothing seemed to crystallize into a picture. All impact of surprise is eliminated by years of familiarity. Nothing moves him to paint it. We have been ranging about these parts for 18 yrs. & he has produced many pictures, one has a sense of gratitude driving past.... They have supplied our sustenance all these years. But now he can no

Jo Hopper, Obituary, *1948.*
Oil on canvas, 24 × 20"
(61 × 50.8 cm.).

longer dig up material for new work. He had thought since he
couldn't do landscape, to do an interior he had had in mind for sometime. He got sketches down from attic & made some preparations,
but couldn't quite see the thing sufficiently to start. So he gave it up.
Was very depressed all day & kept wrapping me up in his arms. I'm
so distressed for him too. If there were anything I could do. I tried
my old trick of rigging up a canvas too & starting off—that often
starts him going.[41]

In the face of defeat, Edward turned for comfort to Jo with the gesture that
after battles had signaled truce. When the chips were down, she identified
with his pain. Since the clarifications of the previous year she had been if anything more devoted to supporting his work and she, if anyone, understood its
power and its source. When they reviewed the pictures in the recent monograph, she noted that "only a few of them had been done from the fact. The
fact is so much easier—than digging it out of one's inner consciousness. It's
such a struggle."[42] Hopper, clearly feeling pressure to produce something for
Rehn, drove to Wellfleet on October 16, "to see if he could force himself to do
a watercolor."[43] When he returned at dusk, it was with the start of a watercolor painted in Eastham: "an end of a church on the left & trees to the R."[44]
As she never failed to do, Jo marveled: "Eastham, of all the most unlikely
places for pickings & lo—it's always Eastham to which E. repairs—& such

good things he's unearthed—Route 6 thru Eastham, House with Big Pine water color . . . House at Eastham, Oaks at Eastham. And it looks more like Jersey than Cape Cod."[45]

Looking forward to seeing Olivier's film of *Hamlet,* Edward and Jo set out to read the play together.[46] On October 18, Tommy Gray, who had looked after the house, died of a heart attack, yet Edward returned to Eastham to work. After the funeral the next morning, while driving back down Route 6, he remarked to Jo: "Tommy Gray can't see this sunlight." He had said the same thing about Juliana Force after her death the previous September.[47] Light clearly signified the vitality of life itself for Hopper, although when asked about it by an interviewer, he would admit only that for him light and form meant more than color. "Light," he said, was "important, a means of conveying the structure of reality, a valuable weapon that allows the artist to convey his vision without having to fall short through lack of technical ability."[48]

On October 22, Edward, obviously anxious after Gray's sudden death, awoke Jo at four-thirty in the morning because his heart felt bad. They rushed to Cape Cod Hospital, but by then his symptoms had disappeared. When they got home, Jo insisted that he instruct her on running the water heater, the stove, and the furnace. As Jo worked frenetically to pack up their belongings, including their books, Edward dipped into the Sears, Roebuck and Company catalogue to calm his nerves, for once with no reproaches from Jo. Even if Hopper had wanted to return to Eastham to complete his watercolor, torrential rains kept him indoors until October 27. The next day he was working on it in the studio when he and Jo learned, in a letter from Bee Blanchard, that their dear friend Anne Tucker had died in her sleep. That winter an early supporter of Edward's work, Frank Crowninshield, had also died. Little over a year had passed since Katy Dos Passos was killed. Jo had felt herself with one foot in the grave the previous winter, and Edward had spent the spring in drawn-out convalescence. With a new layer of heaviness in their depression, they left the Cape for New York.

MELANCHOLY REFLECTION: 1949

HOPPER'S SUDDEN PANIC over his heart proved unfounded, but it was New Year's Day 1949 before he fixed on the new idea that became *Conference at Night.* On January 16, Jo posed "for hands of the tall straight saleswoman or head of filing dept."[1] That, evidently, was the last detail, for Hopper finished the painting that same day and delivered it to Rehn on January 18.

The setting of *Conference at Night,* with its strong theatrical light, was probably inspired by the movies, particularly the urban melodramas now known as film noir. The genre, with its potent dramatic scenes and generally pessimistic outlook on life, appealed to Hopper. In the record book, Jo identified two of the figures as "man on table in white shirt sleeves—Sammy. Deborah is blond, a queen in her own right."[2] She also described all three as "garment workers who were cooking up something" and wondered why Edward would celebrate such a meeting.[3] She speculated that he might have observed a similar scene from the El train, but Hopper later wrote in a letter: "The idea of a loft of business building with the artificial light of the street coming into the room at night had been in my mind for some years before I attempted it. And had been suggested by things I had seen on Broadway in walking there at night." It had, he added, not been easy to express his vision: "The attempt to give concrete expression to a very amorphous impression is

the insurmountable difficulty in painting. The result was obtained by improvisation, and from no known fact or scene."[4]

Hopper probably felt impelled to explain the genesis of this painting after
his major patron, Stephen Clark, returned the picture to Rehn because his
wife "found Conference looked too much like a Communist gathering."[5] Her
comment reflects the extremes of American paranoia in the early moments of
the Cold War, when the threat of international Communism seemed so insidious and vast that it might even render suspect paintings by such a staunch
conservative as Edward Hopper.[6] After a quarter-century of meticulously
recording Edward's pigments, supports, and every detail of his subjects, often
positing a drama and naming characters, it was just after the delivery of *Conference at Night* that Jo stopped for a moment to take stock of why she had decided not to do as much for herself:

> I might have kept something to record my own work, but it stepped
> out so little, it was not difficult to keep track of it. And that sad con-
> dition has improved not at all. A smaller ledger to keep track of
> where it had been turned down would only make the heart ache to
> look into, where as one can be unceasingly grateful & glad while
> turning the pages of E.H., purchased by museums, prizes etc.[7]

Yet the resentment was always festering, waiting for an occasion to well up:

> Of course, if there can be room for only one of us, it must undoubt-
> edly be he. I can be glad & grateful for that—But why couldn't he
> ever at all want to throw me a crumb? . . . He said once, with these
> conditions in reverse, he would have gotten out, not stayed to see it.
> This is my crown of thorns.[8]

With like memories stirring, she could hardly be sympathetic when Edward came home from a dinner at the Institute of Arts and Letters on January 21, to report John Sloan's disgust that Georgia O'Keeffe had been elected
to membership.[9] O'Keeffe belonged to the modernist coterie of Stieglitz, seen
with disfavor by Hopper and his friends, but Jo knew from long experience
that Edward neither respected nor encouraged women artists, whatever their
aesthetic persuasion. Two days later, when he went out of his way to attend
the opening of George Picken's show at Rehn's, loyally supporting a minor
male artist after belittling a woman such as O'Keeffe, Jo's resentment rose
toward the levels of the hunger strike, when she had denounced the art world
in metaphors of dancing: "I'm tired of running to shows. 'Come see me
dance, Come see me dance.' I dance too & no one comes to see me. All my life

I've gone to see other people's work. I'm tired & sick of it—out of it all my work has found no friends, no one to see that I'm invited to show. The years are many & long & the harvest none."[10]

Jo was still edgy the next day when Berenice Abbott visited the studio to photograph Edward. For a background, Abbott was intending to use some of Hopper's paintings, but Jo pointed out that she could get a better effect by using the stove and the cracked bare walls. As the photographer took numerous plates, Jo, inferring that she was inexperienced, insisted on having prints of each, and, when Abbott protested that these took a long time to do, Jo retorted that she had taken up an entire morning and used the studio of a very distinguished person.[11] Abbott had brought along examples of her cityscapes, to which Edward applied his own aesthetic standard, judging them short on personality.[12]

Before the photographer left, Jo insisted on showing her *Chez Hopper,* lest she claim that she herself had discovered the motif of stove, scuttle, and shovel suggested by Jo. When Abbott showed them her results, however, they were delighted, and happy with the print she gave them.[13] Eventually, she delivered two prints and accepted a copy of *Night Shadows* in exchange.[14] Abbott felt sorry for Jo, whom she viewed as "over-shadowed by a great painter," and she recalled that once Jo "realized that I was in no way after her husband," they actually struck up a friendship; Abbott returned to have tea with Jo the following summer.[15] The stove that Jo, through Abbott, turned into a symbol of sorts was in fact central to Edward's life, requiring to be fed by the coal he lugged in, and emptied of the cinders he carried out, and offering him a cozy place to read, which was how she described him in the diary toward the end of January, in his chair by the stove with his nose in his book on Eakins.[16]

The calm was short lived. The relative harmony since the hunger strike and the Mexican trip was fraying. No sooner had he finished, and uncertain what he would paint next, than he lapsed into his old habit of taunting her, leading her to feel her old sense of injustice coming back. On the first of February she exploded in the diary:

> E. is rushing me to movies because I'm so possessed by frustrations these days & he has to put up with plenty. How did he think he wouldn't—or more likely, he never gave it a thought, being absolutely selfcentered. It wouldn't have occurred to him that I'd never forget how I was always left out, negated by everyone he knew & I was meeting only his friends & being all sympathetic with them. He brags that everybody likes him much better than me & he doesn't do a thing to get them to. Only be great. People like you if you're great, even if you give them nothing, but cause for jealousy.[17]

This Nietzschean arrogance of his threw her into further self-reproach: yes, her work had become weaker:

> Time passing, passing, drop by drop of one's life's blood—hair graying, fashions changing, an entirely new slant on art rampant & 25 years of my life gone. . . . I've been deserted—left alone—in this field where we all have labored—& this partner . . . is in reality one prize hog. Too selfcentered even to be sadistic about it.[18]

Anger back in full force, she remembered, restated, spelled out the old accusations: Edward wanting to slam the door in her face, conspiring with other male artists by giving them inside data about exhibition juries, and letting them come to see her work only after they had been forewarned to be self-protective; recalling how Edward once took her brush and worked on a detail, when "he thought I wasn't making an apple solid enough," and afterward claimed that "he did it. I've never touched an apple since." Oh yes, there was Edward's crony, that Arnold Friedman standing in silence as she showed her watercolors to a collector; although he later purportedly told people that he thought Jo "was a much finer artist" than her husband, in front of Edward he held his tongue. And then there was the humiliating occasion when Edward conspired with the collector Edward Root in what she perceived as an attempt to embarrass her. Root posed her a "pedagogical problem," which she threw "back at him," while Hopper "even looked the monster he can be—an evil light in his eye—like one torturing an animal out of sheer exaltation."

Exhausted, she tried to help herself. Painting had seemed to her a kind of psychotherapy in the summer. In the next few days, she tried to start painting in Edward's studio, although she felt so insecure, in her anger and self-reproach, that she could only bring herself to work on brown paper so as not to waste the pristine canvas that Edward at least had had the good grace to stretch for her. To make matters worse, he kept warning her she would have to quit when he lowered the window shades to begin work on a new painting.[19]

If he had begun to work, it would have been better. Instead he lapsed into deeper depression on being told he would need further surgery. Trying to keep his mind off his troubles, for the next two weeks he went to the movies constantly, often dragging Jo along. She liked *Night Has a Thousand Eyes* with Edward G. Robinson, which they saw at Edward's old subject, the Sheridan Theater, but other films left her unmoved.[20] For her sanity, she needed to paint. Calmer by the third week of February, she looked at herself again. Yes, Edward had been hostile all those years ago, and his attitude was no better now. How often he had repeated that people did not like her, and she reflected with some accuracy: "I've probably changed. I used to have so many friends. But then, I've been seeing only his friends of late years. And people annoyed at him for turning them down on juries take it out on me. Naturally."[21]

Still casting about for relief from his depression, Edward picked up Jo's old copy of *La Vie de Jésus,* by the nineteenth-century French historian and critic Ernest Renan, which she had recently stumbled on in her trunk in the basement.[22] Renan's fictionalized portrait of the carpenter's son growing up in the Galilean landscape engaged Edward, and from time to time he chose passages to translate, reading aloud to Jo as he used to from Valéry's aesthetics.

With Edward's reading in mind, Jo wrote to praise J. Donald Adams for his argument that basic literacy once resulted from "wide spread reading of the Bible in the homes"; she mentioned Renan and admitted, "I regret to have missed this earlier culture, not made up for by Horace, Virgil & the like."[23] What Jo calls "this earlier culture," neither imbued by her family nor compensated by the Latin assigned at the Normal College, had been, of course, central to Edward's Baptist upbringing. It seems clear that his chance encounter with the old story, suavely repackaged in the language of his sophistication and his passion, stirred recollections of his roots. Three days later, on March 1, Jo confided in the diary her elation that Edward was acquiring "a sympathetic response to Jesus"; she was struck by his confession that "He finds Renan so much more moving than the Bible of old."[24] For Hopper such a flow of feeling, and openness of expression about it, were rare and no doubt facilitated by his anxiety about his health. The result was a further recovery of the past. On March 5, Jo noted that Edward had moved from Renan back to the Bible and was reading the New Testament.[25]

In the meantime the doctors decided that another round of prostate surgery would not be needed after all.[26] But Hopper's condition wavered, causing additional discomfort. At this point, Jo went so far as to hope that the very orneriness that provoked her resentment would actually come into play, if only to spur him to paint: "When he starts to try to work he is too worried about his prostate to concentrate wholeheartedly. I was hoping that with me working on park outside window, even using his easel, he'd be moved to clear me out & start himself."[27] On March 25, she found him reading Chaucer and "trying to make sketches to land idea. He gets tired so easily."[28] It was April 4 when she watched him begin painting "a little picture on a wood panel—a staircase going down to open door & hall lamp suspended. Said memory of a repeated dream of levitation, sailing downstairs & out thru door."[29]

On April 6, Hopper's doctor told him that a shred hanging from the urethral wall would have to be removed. The next day Jo noted that he was still "working on small panel—stairs down & outdoors into moonlight—but has so little heart to the work facing such uncertainty."[30] On April 9, he was at it again, but the next day a call came to say that a semiprivate room had become available. Jo packed and together they made their way down the steep steps and over to New York Hospital. Returning and climbing the stairs alone, Jo was devastated: "One of the meanest things is having to come home to the empty studio, yesterday & again to-day. There doesn't seem any thing to come home to."[31]

On the easel the small panel of "sailing downstairs and out through door" stood unfinished. The choice of material had been peculiar. Wood was a support he favored only much earlier in his career, particularly when he worked outdoors on Monhegan Island during the 1910s. The subject harked back even further. On the verge of leaving home for the city, he had sketched himself in cap and gown going out the doorway toward the distant peak marked "FAME." Now his preparatory sketch and panel both catch the banister and curtained door off the front hall in the Nyack house, but the drawing suggests a lamp outside, which Hopper canceled in the oil, preferring to emphasize distant heights that are indistinct and dark.

Hopper emerged relatively cheerful from this bout of surgery.[32] As he recuperated, Jo supplied him with books she borrowed from friends and from the library, including John Rewald's biography of Cézanne.[33] When Edward came home from the hospital, only two days of cooking for him sufficed to rekindle Jo's mood of resentment. She was "depressed about work & E.'s silent lack of concern—over the years—so sulked, went into back studio to be alone with my poor little bastards."[34] It was cold back there, but at least they were hers.

Toward the end of April, Lucy Bayard visited Jo and scolded her for complaining about Edward, that she was indeed blessed to have a husband "so faithful" and famous.[35] Jo took the advice to heart, for she did not like to feel angry and out of control. Shifting into her phase of self-reproach, she confessed she was "so little deserving," and worried that Edward's slow recovery was due to her "selfishly very depressed state regarding the outcast state of my work."[36] Yet she persisted in blaming herself and denigrating her work as "very picky, feeble & undistinguished."[37] She was sinking further into depression, when her old pal Bertram Hartman cheered her by offering to pose for a watercolor portrait.[38]

On Decoration Day Jo began a watercolor of a friend's garden, working outdoors on location on Tenth Street; Edward passed the holiday at home, going through old books and art magazines.[39] The warmer weather had let Jo make better use of her studio, with a display of twenty-one of her paintings, which she contemplated as the holiday came to a close:

> It occurred to me, that would be a pleasant place to die, sitting in that chair surrounded by a life's silly effort. The[y] sum up so much of

Jo Hopper, Portrait of Bertram Hartman, *1949. Watercolor on paper, 14 × 21″ (35.6 × 53.3 cm.).*

one. They're too nice to have been such friendless little Cinderellas. Not aggressive enough I suppose. Exhibition pictures require that quality before anything else. Then someone to acclaim them.[40]

In June, Edward felt strong enough to retrieve the car and make the drive to the Cape. For his birthday July 15, Jo gave him a copy of *Thomas Jefferson on Democracy,* selections from Jefferson's letters,[41] in which he marked the section headed "Why send American youth to Europe for education?"—a sketch rich in parallels to Hopper's own ambiguous affair with Paris:

He acquires a fondness for European luxury and dissipation, and a contempt for the simplicity of his own country. . . . He is led, by the strongest of all the human passions, into a spirit for female intrigue, destructive of his own and others' happiness, or a passion for whores, destructive to his health. . . . He retains, through life, a fond recollection, and a hankering after those places, which were the scenes of his first pleasures and his first connections.[42]

Jo, too, was reading, and risked parallels. She declared herself disappointed that the Kinsey report "doesn't tell what to do about it all, how teach children & that the important thing evaded while endless talk, talk, talk—rhetoric I should say."[43] Jo also reported reading Virginia Woolf's *A Room of One's Own,* where there were plenty of parallels: "Surely it is time that the effect of discouragement upon the mind of the artist should be measured";[44] or the attacks on the attitude that "the best woman was intellectually the inferior of the worst man";[45] and the "history of men's opposition to women's emancipation."[46]

Edward's own attitudes to Jo took a positive turn when sometime in midsummer, he actually offered to pose. Even more noteworthy, when she found that she had miscalculated and could not fit his feet in her picture, he made no complaint about stretching a larger canvas.[47] While he posed, and while she did her chores, Edward took to reading aloud to her again—sometimes songs from Shakespeare, Villon's *Ballade des Dames du Temps Jadis,* T. S. Eliot's essays.[48] Criticizing Eliot for his "triviality & essential lack of feeling," Edward turned again to Robert Frost and Jo reiterated her esteem for his work.[49]

In late August Edward and Jo visited Provincetown, but he did not want to stay long. She reflected that he was probably "depressed by all that crazy art flaunting itself," referring to the advent of the Abstract Expressionists, whom Edward dismissed as merely "a phase, passing phase."[50] The German émigré Hans Hofmann had been conducting a summer art school in Provincetown since 1934, but at this time his school was at the height of its influence. This was the summer of Forum '49, a program of lectures, debates, readings, and performances that took place at Gallery 200 on Commercial Street. Abstractionists exhibited their work and debated such subjects as "What Is an Artist?" At one of these events Adolph Gottlieb insisted, "The artist must take the risk of creating works that will not be recognized as art."[51] Hopper certainly disagreed, but Jo was less secure: "There's always a phase & if you do not fit in, you're out & it's so disheartening to be always out."[52]

The work of Oliver Chaffee, whom the Hoppers had known from art school days until his death in 1944, was featured in the show at Gallery 200, which was hailed as revealing "the roots of visual abstract work that had its beginnings in Provincetown not long after World War I."[53] This was the avant-garde world that Jo had known in the years before her marriage. Now, she was clearly associated with Edward's more conservative world, but regretted that she was not really a part of it. Perhaps had she not been married to Hopper, she might have tried to paint abstractly in order to be au courant.

Finally, on August 25, Hopper began sketching for his first canvas since January. Several days later, Jo exclaimed:

> E. has definitely started a canvas—the front of an old house with 2 figures in doorway & 2 dormer windows on 2" floor. He worked on it in middle of room while Linda [Beal, a neighbor's daughter, who posed for Jo] & I had worked on west side of room, no one in anyone's way. . . . Nice to have this studio come to life—at last. It may be that my painting E. & trying to do Linda started the wheels.[54]

They made a special trip to Provincetown so Hopper could look at gable ends; later, Jo noted: "E. is drawing in blue paint over his charcoal sketch & has me measured up against a door to see where a taller woman would reach in his picture."[55]

His newly benevolent mood, determined perhaps by his physical weakness and a greater sense of dependence, had made him more permissive than ever before about Jo's driving. On September 10 while driving in Wellfleet, she crumpled a fender of their car in a parking lot. There ensued "a day of calamity" that disturbed Edward's painting progress. He, "beside himself with rage," declared that this was the end of everything. Jo said she would sell the house (which she had paid for), but would never give him a divorce.[56] Edward drove to Hyannis, where repair was estimated at twenty-five dollars, which Jo said that she would pay herself. This hardly seemed worth a divorce. The next day, Edward lost himself in his painting, working all day. They spent the twelfth in Hyannis. While waiting for the car to be ready, they went to the movies to see *Madame Bovary.* Jo paid the repair bill of nineteen dollars out of the twenty-five that Edward had given her for new clothes. Edward strained a few muscles changing a flat tire on the trip home, and when, the next day, Jo drove him to Provincetown and back to consult a doctor, he yelled at her all the way.[57] The more he let her drive, the more incidents there were where "he had fits."[58]

It was September 21 before Hopper was able to get back to work on his painting, which in the meantime had changed. Jo now described a "woman at door of stark old house in bright sun."[59] Later, Jo would enter in the record book that Edward had painted this canvas, eventually called *High Noon,* in October, writing from memory rather than consulting her diary.[60] In addition to color details, she noted: "Female in stringy blue kimona open in front over possibly naked body, effect sloppy, but such a hot day!" In a postscript, she said that Hopper had made a little model out of heavy white paper to observe how light would fall on the corner of the house. (He once told an interviewer that the figure was very rarely the main emphasis in his work, but that he used the figure to augment the "emotional reaction of the moment."[61]) In this case Jo's chronicle shows rather clearly how he calculated and refined, eliminating one figure and elongating the survivor. Yet Jo reads the state of dress as "sloppy," with a note of practicality that diffuses any erotic charge; called once again to dramatize a fantasy for Edward, she understates it, for he endows the figure with an attitude worthy of the tragic eroticism of an Emma Bovary. It is remarkable, too, that Hopper here reverses the viewpoint of the wood panel, looking now from outside toward a doorway that frames a figure of ambiguous sexual allure.

Hopper creates this intense image of raking light after his own experience in the hospital and premonitions of death, which were no doubt put into perspective by the fact that he and Jo were reading Thomas Mann's *The Magic Mountain,* in which the hero learns to align himself with light and life through his exposure to death in a sanatorium. On October 24 Jo wrote to Carl Sprinchorn, who had lent them the book: "Carl dear, thank you so much for your Magic Mountain. We're having a tremendous experience, now nearing the end."[62] And again later: "I didn't half thank you for our pleasure in 'Magic Mountain.' We didn't find it a bit verbose. But I did find that one 'Return the Beloved' somewhat of a chore. We loved the Joseph & Egypt ones, Death in Venice & such short stories we've been able to get hold of."[63]

Hoping to get a watercolor before the return to New York, Edward set out for his favorite hunting grounds in Eastham. He had spotted a big white house with four tall trees, but decided it would not do after all.[64] Jo wanted to paint it, but he pushed on to Orleans and Chatham. Again he found nothing and refused to stop for views that attracted her. His rigidity provoked a new outbreak in Jo: "Heart . . . acting strangely. . . . Emotional combats, violent on both sides—are bad for both of us. It's all the same story—accusations, resentments, & downright devastating grief to know that with all his fine qualities, his goodness & blandishments, E. can be mean. The sources of all this are deeper than surface symptoms."[65] She had given up her exercise class the previous spring because of an undiagnosed condition that she surmised was either in her heart or lungs. Now she maintained that she could readily imagine "its source in my fits of rage over E.'s attitude toward my driving his car." Another old complaint resurfaced: "Sex is all for him too—so I retire from that, practically uncomplainingly."[66]

The Hoppers' perennial discord was often eclipsed by attention from friends, among them Davis and Elsa-Ruth Herron, who had moved into the former Lombard house and invited the Hoppers for dinner that October.

Davis, the son of a famous Social Gospel minister and the associate and brother-in-law of Elliot Cohen, an active Communist during the late 1920s and 1930s, had visited the Soviet Union and met with Trotsky in 1933. Like many intellectuals, however, Herron grew disillusioned with Communism; his brother-in-law became a virulent anti-Communist and the founder of *Commentary* in the 1940s.[67] Politics aside, the Herrons did share interests with the Hoppers; Davis both painted and played chess, and Elsa-Ruth loved to talk. After the Herrons, the Hoppers turned their attention to Constance and Henry Dauphinée (the neighbors whose Cape house they had both painted years earlier), staying overnight at their friends' winter home on the way back to New York.

The return to the city immediately revived Jo's concerns about her work. Hoping for a possible outlet, she made for the Riverside Museum, where Magda Pach, Theresa Bernstein, Lu Duble, and other friends were showing with the New York Society of Women Artists. Put off by finding the work "so plain," she intuited that there would be no place for her there.[68] That left her in the dilemma she had been lamenting, that with no real friends of her own she was forced back into Edward's inhospitable circles. Attending an opening for their old teacher Kenneth Hayes Miller at the Art Students League, she objected to everyone "swilling cocktails"; and a few days later she was reduced to gossip about another veteran, noting that at his show at the Hudson Guild, John Sloan "looked fine."[69] On November 11, Hopper met with Lloyd Goodrich at the Rehn Gallery to plan a retrospective at the Whitney Museum. Three days later, he finally delivered to Rehn the summer's canvas, *High Noon*. The next day he accompanied Jo up to the gallery so she could pick over some old frames that Rehn was discarding, even though the absence of any prospect of showing her work made it unlikely that she would need them.

The focus on Edward's circle continued. On November 22, there were Paul Cadmus's opening at the Midtown Gallery and Morris Kantor's at Rehn's. Although both artists were friends, Jo found the shows "too unintelligible."[70] The next day she noted that Edward was "playing with the idea of a little new canvas 20 × 30."[71] By the end of November, she found something to write about on returning from the opening at the Costaire Gallery of the Surrealist Pierre Roy:

> While I away E. free to paint in peace. He had canvas started drawn in oil. I amazed when found a mute figure stretched out full length on bed in back of the female figure. I won't have to go buy a new night gown for that creature. The stringy will do. Where E. going to get the boy friend? Maybe I could be used—since E. knows all there is to know he can elongate.[72]

Edward Hopper, Study for "Summer in the City," *1949. Conté and pencil on paper, 8½ × 11″ (21.6 × 27.9 cm.).*

The "stringy" blue kimono was a known quality for Jo, in which she had posed for *High Noon* and now imagined for the new picture, where her first thought is of the roles she may be expected to play. Her disaffection forgotten, she thinks concretely: Edward knows her so well that he can stretch her, which is what he had done with the woman in *High Noon*, too.

On December 3, Edward asked her to hurry back from the market so she could pose while the light was just right at noon. She undressed and donned a straggly nightgown, only to have Edward decide that he wanted a more husky figure.[73] But by December 6, he was making progress:

> E. has done something very advancing to that canvas this after-
> noon—put shadow in background that does much for deepening the
> room. He was saying regarding his buxom prima donna for whom I
> couldn't be used to pose: "C'est le propre des animeaux d'être triste
> après l'amour" ("It is the nature of animals to be gloomy after
> love")—a fine name for his picture. He says it could scare off buyers.
> The tall man stretched out head buried in the pillow is a swell piece
> of improvisation—with no model at all—those long bare legs and

feet—hot A.M. after a hot night in the city. But this is going to be another social consciousness picture. E. takes no active interest in social
welfare.[74]

As she had in *High Noon,* Jo reads in heat, careful, too, to distinguish "social
consciousness" from "social welfare," Edward's interest in personal psychology as opposed to political stress. On December 8, Edward surprised Jo by
having her pose for the legs of the man after all, which she had seen as a possibility from the first. He finished the canvas the next day and restretched it
onto heavier stretchers; on December 13, he delivered it to Rehn.

Jo described the painting as "Hot Aug. A.M. Husky blond wench in deep
rose night gown (possibly rayon)."[75] She also made extensive color notes. Edward and Jo called this painting *Triste Après l'Amour,* but in the record book
it was titled *Summer in the City.* Evidently, Hopper felt compelled to give the
painting a title that would not threaten its sale. There is, however, no question as to its theme—postcoital melancholy. The woman looks exceedingly
glum, and her male companion appears to be tense and unhappy as he buries
his head in the pillow. Jo's dissatisfaction with her sexual life with Edward
must have had mutual consequences that inform this painting, but if she had
any sense of identification with either of the figures, she did not indicate it either in her diary or in the record book.

Even the modest collaboration on the new canvas helped a return to
armistice, which was favored by the prospects that both would soon be showing, Edward in his Whitney retrospective and Jo her 1946 canvas, *San Esteban,* at the National Arts Club. At Christmas Jo put her little crèche on its
annual display in the studio, and on Christmas Eve they listened to Handel
and Tchaikovsky on the radio. As they sat together peacefully on their coal
box Edward kissed Jo.[76]

A RETROSPECTIVE YEAR: 1950

THE YEAR 1950 began with anticipation and preparation for Edward's retrospective, which opened at the Whitney on the ninth of February. This was his first one-man show at the Whitney and the first major New York museum exhibition of his work since the retrospective at the Museum of Modern Art in 1933. Jo, however, was angry that the curator had controlled the contents of the retrospective, because Edward was "too disgustingly timid to open his mouth, leaving it all to Lloyd Goodrich's taste."[1]

Escaping the pressure of the retrospective, the Hoppers went to the theater and the movies four times in nine days. For a Wednesday matinee of Carson McCullers's *The Member of the Wedding,* they obtained what they considered choice seats, the first row of the second balcony of the old Empire Theater, at $1.20 each.[2] They also saw Jean Giraudoux's *The Enchanted,* which they liked less than his *The Madwoman of Chaillot.*[3] At the movies, they took in *L'Affaire Blum,* which Jo pronounced "a more arresting story" than William Wyler's *The Heiress* (based on Henry James's *Washington Square*), which they saw twice for the sake of seeing their block on the screen—though Edward quipped that the film was "more Hollywood Sq. than Washington Sq."[4]

Anticipating the retrospective *Cue* magazine sent Emory Lewis for an interview. He described his "painfully shy" subject as "a handsome man in tweeds, with a nervous habit of constantly touching his chin and lips."[5] With a carefully calculated, "Nothing ever happens to us," Hopper promoted a myth, so the reporter informed the waiting world that "he and his wife live—with few visitors—in their three-room apartment, happy with each other"; and "he had the luck to be born of sympathetic and intellectual parents who thought his painting an excellent idea." More astutely, Lewis gathered that Hopper's views of trends in art reflected both amusement and confidence: "It will turn back to life again. When you deny representation, you limit yourself. Just another of those endless cycles." The journalist described Jo as "more gregarious" and as "a vivacious blonde who does her hair in the Twenties manner," noting that she "did most of the talking." He recorded her complaint that "Eddie is a bit of a hermit" and her comment, "Why, Eddie's father was so busy reading Montaigne, he didn't care."

On February 5, just four days before the retrospective opened, Hopper checked into New York Hospital to be treated for diverticulitis. Jo meanwhile took an advance tour of the exhibition. She was horrified: there were too many objects, and the best works suffered from the chronological installation. She reminded herself that Goodrich had been a good friend to Edward and his work, but:

> I went to that show expecting to be deeply moved. I was not. If moved at all—to exasperation at what had been done to defeat the beautiful show that could have been. There has never been anything of E's shown at Rehn's that I could have wished changed—all his shows there have been serene & beautiful I suppose it's like people stringing beads. Some will put together a beautiful necklace—others fail entirely. It's just not in L.G. to put together to make a result that is beautiful. He is dull & has no taste—scholastic, hardworking, but that's not enough for the impresario he fancies himself.[6]

Hopper, still in the hospital, was too weak to attend the opening, although his friends and fans turned out in force. Jo remarked on the presence of the critic James Johnson Sweeney and the painter Isabel Bishop, but what struck her most was the appearance of Hopper's patron Bee Blanchard, who wore "an amazing hat that sat on her head like a mast at full sail at 90 degree angle." At a party two days later, Lewis Mumford told Jo that in twenty-five or fifty years, Hopper would be "as famous as Van Gogh."[7] His esteem for Hopper had improved considerably since his mixed review of the 1933 show.[8] When Hopper finally saw the show on February 16, he was pleased. He had already had a positive response from Charles Burchfield, who visited him in the hospital after seeing the show.[9] Andrew Wyeth, who had traveled two hundred miles to see it, called and arranged to visit Hopper's studio. Both artists specifically admired *High Noon*.[10]

Hopper's reaction to all the attention was typically laconic.[11] When an interviewer for *Time* asked him about the show, his only comment was that the gallery seemed crowded with pregnant women. He quipped: "I guess they considered me a safe man to deal with."[12] He wrote to Flora Miller, the daughter of Gertrude Vanderbilt Whitney: "American artists must have the most sincere appreciation for the great opportunities your mother and you have given in making their work known to the public. For my own part I feel deeply as to the opportunity that you have given me to show my work in its entirety in the present exhibition."[13] He recalled his first show at the Whitney Studio Club (which he incorrectly remembered as having taken place in 1919 instead of 1920) and the many times he had shown at the museum since then: "I owe much to the Whitney Museum for the recognition that has come to me." He added diplomatically: "I think Lloyd Goodrich and Hermon More have done a fine job in organizing and hanging the show. It was done with great care and thoroughness." More than twenty-four thousand people saw the retrospective before it closed on the twenty-sixth of March, by which time Jo felt much better about it: "It's been such a happy episode, that so beautiful show & everything connected with it."[14]

Edward was once again in the limelight, but his reticence caused Jo to reflect: "Should think E. would be delighted—but no never sais anything to signify he is."[15] She herself was no doubt both proud and jealous. *New York Times* critic Howard Devree suggested that "Hopper's literary counterparts are some of the verse of Robert Frost and his New England predecessors and some of the novels of Sinclair Lewis and, possibly, Sherwood Anderson,"[16] which hit the mark (except for Lewis). The *Herald Tribune*'s Carlyle Burrows credited Hopper with a "clarity and poetry of mood," declaring his work "worthy of a lasting appreciation."[17] James Thrall Soby praised the "plastic discipline" that, he felt, combined "with a strong and tearless romanticism to dignify homely reality."[18] Margaret Breuning explained that "Hopper's realism is not a transcription of something seen. In his case that realism is produced by an adjustment through elimination or addition of detail which meets his response to the subject."[19] *Time* declared that "as a painter of the American scene, Hopper has only one peer, Buffalo's Charles Burchfield," and described him as "a high-domed, soft-spoken moose of a man" who "averages less than three oils a year."[20]

Burchfield proclaimed in *Art News:* "The art of Edward Hopper is destined to become a classic, like Homer's and Eakins' whose tradition he has so ably carried on. . . . There is a certain affinity with the watercolors of Winslow Homer, whose work Hopper is said to admire so much."[21] Burchfield knew his subject:

> Contrary to the case of many famous artists, it is unnecessary, or even impossible to ignore Hopper the man in studying his art. . . . With Hopper the whole fabric of his art seems to be completely interwoven with his personal character and manner of living. The simplicity of his work, its economy of means, its avoidance of ingratiating decoration all seems to stem directly from his almost ascetic make-up. Compared to other luxury-loving Americans, he demands very little of so-called creature comforts; the most modest of living quarters seem sufficient for him; there are no obvious self-indulgences. His is a life devoted to his art.[22]

Commenting on Hopper's "soft-spoken manner" and his "almost painful modesty about his art," Burchfield also spoke of the anguish Hopper experienced when he found himself blocked and unable to work:

> Into the career of every creative artist must come periods of complete sterility. Some learn to accept such times and to await with resignation the return of the impulse to paint. Hopper, however, suffers agony during his dormant periods, so important to him is his need to paint. Once, he told me, he became almost panic-stricken and thought he was through—and of course after that came some of his most important works.[23]

Only a few of the notices published were negative. Ralph Pearson, who had so stridently protested the first retrospective, crabbed that Hopper had "not yet learned the art of the picture."[24] Robert Coates, in *The New Yorker,* found fault with certain works that "become merely illustrative" and with Hopper's "penchant for portraying a scene through a window," but concluded that "at his best, he can invest the simplest subjects with a magic and mystery."[25]

When Coates, who wrote novels and stories in addition to art criticism, proposed to profile Hopper in *The New Yorker,* Edward and Jo hesitated.[26] Jo felt that the profiles were inevitably boring and insisted that Edward's "life has never been colorful. John Sloan's is, but his profile of John Sloan was also dull as dish water."[27] Edward initially refused to let Jo send her reply to Coates, prompting her to ask: "Is it possible he's grown into a publicity hound? He's had so much to feed on, must he go on feeding?"[28] Jo, adamantly opposed to this kind of "public Xray," worked on Edward to convince him to decline the offer; she mailed her refusal after a month.

To J. Donald Adams, then a contributing editor of *The New York Times Book Review,* Jo wrote, "My husband, Edward Hopper, was so pleased he handed me your page heavily marked,"[29] and she invited Adams to see the retrospective, "feeling this exhibition vindicated by much you say. Here innocence takes the form of light, a wonderful clarity vivifying in its impact, its highly communicable impact, technically equipped to flout obscurity."[30] She continued, not unlike a public relations text: "One finds something cheering in the Whitney's electing this once a dyed in the wool American—(after all the Whitney claims to be a Museum of American Art) at a time when all art is tottering on the brink of chaos."[31] Jo's efforts to call Adams's attention to Hopper's work paid off. He responded to her eccentric letter by going to see the exhibition and referring to it briefly in his column: "You might say that everything there is achieved by emphasis, whether on composition, color or form—or on light, as was recently exemplified in the Whitney Museum's retrospective of the work of Edward Hopper. No work of art can be successful . . . unless, by proper emphasis, it manages to communicate the thought or the emotion which brought it into being."[32]

Only *Newsweek* gave Jo a significant mention as an artist in her own right. Discussing Edward's "New York studio in one of the early-nineteenth-century brick houses on Washington Square—teeming with 'Hopper material,' " the critic reported: "His artist-wife is particularly annoyed by his refusal to paint anything that looks like a studio. 'Too arty,' he says. But she cannot understand how he resists all those familiar things—the plain white walls, his granduncle's mahogany chairs, the rush-backed chairs, and the pot-bellied stove. In desperation, she has painted the stove more than once."[33]

Even with such attention, Jo's pride in Edward's success was tinged with envy. She returned in her mind to his slackness on her behalf: "He shy—one can't afford such expensive luxury while someone else goes down for the last time. That shy doesn't fool me. . . . He knows his assets & how to collect from them & save himself any effort at all. It's a stage property."[34] Her swimming metaphor—the drowning person going "down for the last time"—gives a poignant twist to her distress, since swimming, like art, was something they shared and fought about on the Cape. But she returned as she had again and again to the liability of resentment: "With the coming of lonely old age it is not good to be piling up stores of bitterness. If I'm to be the old, old bag surviving his early departure, what thorn to lacerate in one's memory—since I have the memory of a mountaineer, God help me."[35]

As she had before when such memories became too powerful, she made a constructive effort on her own behalf, trying to arrange for the reproduction of one of her paintings, *The Kerosene Oil Lamp,* on a Christmas card: "The glass lamp, the antique mirror, the silver broach, silver lustre vase, Venetian beads, & subscription to the New Yorker are all birthday gifts gathered together on a bureau top on Cape Cod." And (on the same form) she described her "choice of subject matter" as "A former painter of flowers now painting dead flowers—& live pussy cat—also dormers & bell towers of Mexican churches & their interiors & child ballerinas."

When Hopper's retrospective traveled to the Boston Museum of Fine Arts, the Hoppers went to the opening; since Edward in the hospital had missed the festivities at the Whitney, this was his chance to bask. He and Jo had invited many Truro friends, and not a few showed up, proud of their famous neighbor. Jo wore "a silly new bonnet . . . good for rag doll but Ed chose it so I wear it! If it can be nailed or glued on."[36]

The show led to a feature in *Life* magazine. To Jo's delight, they were invited to a large party given by Henry and Clare Luce in their elegant penthouse. Shown in *Life* in an earlier photograph by Arnold Newman, Hopper, described as "a big (6 feet 5 inches), lumbering man," with a "frank and quietly brooding face,"[37] struck the pose of a business executive, elegantly dressed in his dark suit and tie and holding a cigarette. Standing before an unpainted canvas, he gave one the impression that he never got his hands dirty. By contrast *Life* had just featured Jackson Pollock with a Newman photograph that caught the artist in baggy paint-splattered work clothes, a cigarette dangling from his lips.[38] Of Pollock, *Life* demanded with some skepticism: "Is he the greatest living painter in the United States?," but Hopper was acknowledged as "a major American artist of the century."[39]

Life noted that Hopper's canvases sold for as much as "$5000 apiece," and commented: "No artist has portrayed the city with Hopper's severe and ungarnished power. A cool, precise man, Hopper has made his art a verbatim record of what he has seen and felt."[40] The biographical content of Hopper's paintings was suggested in the caption for his painting *Ground Swell,* depicting a sail boat: "Hopper grew up on the Hudson River where he learned sailing, the only sport that has interested him. He once built a boat, but it sailed so precariously that he had to sell it for scrap lumber."[41] Jo responded to the *Life* article with another access of rage.[42] She dwelt again on her failure to live up to her early promise as "the pretty little talent."[43]

To museum employees who worked on his show, Edward gave copies of his etchings. As he had to Berenice Abbott, he gave a copy of the etching *Night Shadows* to the photographer George Platt Lynes in exchange for prints of Lynes's photographs of him.[44] (Jo was amazed that Lynes succeeded in getting five good ones out of only eight tries.) Hopper had now found a new use for the old etchings, but lacked interest in pursuing the medium.

Jo Hopper, The Kerosene Oil Lamp (Gifts—Cape Cod Bureau Top), *1944. Oil on canvas, 24 × 20" (61 × 50.8 cm.).*

Although the myth of seclusion had been propagated in the popular press, the round of openings and encounters, as well as movies, kept up. There was Noel Coward in *The Astonished Heart,* which they thought immensely interesting; it starred Celia Johnson, who, Jo noted, was "so beguiling."[45] Yet the diversions did not calm Jo. The notice of a national competition at the Metropolitan Museum was her latest cause:

> I think I could have stood all this if I were not so closely involved in the fortunes of E.H.—& so excluded from participations & he, E.H. so content that this should be so. . . . It is most certainly undermining my feeling for him. How could it not? One can't forever throw all our light at a surface from which there is never any gleam reflected.[46]

When Daniel Catton Rich and Katharine Kuh of the Art Institute of Chicago came to tea on May 13, Jo had an opportunity to show them her work. But the purpose of their visit was to convince Hopper to come to Chicago to accept an honorary doctorate from the institute, an invitation he had previously declined (because he did not wish to bear the expense of travel for himself and Jo). Believing that "they are too hard-boiled to fancy my wares,"[47] Jo dismissed them both, accusing Kuh of being "a man's woman" and characterizing Rich as liking the art of the Magic Realist Ivan Albright.[48]

Before long the art network knocked at Edward's door again, inviting him to serve on the jury for the 1951 Corcoran Biennial, which provoked Jo: "I don't like so much of this playing God for him. Those thrown out will take it out on me. And E. doesn't say one word about taking one of my canvases. He'd be in a position to do this & tell them they'll be taking plenty worse."[49] When Edward did offer to get Jo invited, she initially refused, her pride wounded from past rejection: "No, I don't want him to do jury work so that I can get in, & I won't stand for him not inviting me with the . . . others who will be no better, he'll feel are no better—just so he can show off how he's such an honest man that he strikes down his wife to prove it & I pay for the demonstration."[50] It did not help matters when later that month *The New York Times* used "Edward Hopper's medium" as a crossword puzzle clue.[51]

Amid publicity, ill-health, and Jo, it had been a heady but not a productive spring for Edward. Nor were there prospects for change. In response to a request from the Whitney Museum, Hopper wrote at the end of May: "I shall certainly save one of my best pictures for the Whitney Annual. It's very likely that it will be my only new canvas, for I have painted but one this past winter. It's hardly probable that I shall paint more than one or two the coming summer."[52] Hopper saw his own lack of creative energy as typical of distinguished old men, for at the annual ceremony of the National Institute of Arts and Letters, he mockingly commented: "that funeral more lively than usual this time."[53] Though skeptical of pompous ceremonies, he approved of the induction of Andrew Wyeth, who was "a liked addition" in Jo's view.[54] Surveying the poets present, Hopper expressed interest in Carl Sandburg, Archibald MacLeish, and Robert Frost, who read during the program.

Kuh and Rich had prevailed in their mission to Washington Square, and in June, the Hoppers took a train to Chicago, where Edward received his honorary degree from the Art Institute, and then continued on to see the final stop of his retrospective at the Detroit Institute of Arts. They hated the "sooty dull grey black" walls,[55] but they liked the museum's director, Edgar P. Richardson, who, after showing them around the museum, took them home to dinner and put them on the night train for New York. Jo signed off: "E. loves to ride on trains. I can stand it."[56]

This latest round of honors left Jo in a funk again, until Edward thought of the magic words he had used the previous summer, "Want me to pose for you?" It was enough to start her painting again and cast him into the supportive role that she so often played for him.[57] They immediately moved into

Jo's studio to try out some poses, and then dashed out on a shopping expedition to buy her some stockings and him a new straw hat. She decided not to paint him in the new hat because "his skul is so handsome."[58] Not endowed with Jo's verve, soon Edward dozed off. Still, at the end of a week's work, Jo felt that at last she had gotten something; she kept at it and he came back a few times.

On the Cape that summer, Edward and Jo both read André Gide, their interest piqued by the publication of the last volume of his *Journal* and by the notoriety that followed his receiving the Nobel Prize in 1947. They liked Gide's nuanced prose and were drawn to his spiritual autobiographies, which paralleled Edward's exploration of his own disaffection in his painting and Jo's expression of her discontent in her diaries. There were parallels, too, between Gide, with his "use of personal and half-concealed symbols,"[59] and Hopper, who had sometimes portrayed his own emotions in such a fashion. And in the journals, Edward could recognize himself in the figure of the artist who often suffered from ennui and endured long periods of creative sterility; both men resorted to reading and to travel in search of something to budge the unwilling muse.[60]

Relatively early in the season, Hopper found an idea, as Jo reported on August 15: "It's the main street intersection in Orleans with A&P market outside, dress shop etc. We've been down there with E. making sketches while I made up to the beautiful big black A&P cat. He acts as tho he remembers me & tries to help by posing beautifully."[61] The next day Edward had his new picture drawn in. Jo noted: "It's not so exciting—yet!" and a day later, he had "the corner of Route 6 & the Main St. of Orleans . . . down in blue paint."[62] They returned to Orleans "to look some more at his corner at dusk. But it wasn't the right sky for his purposes. A lot of likely detail at that spot."[63]

Driving became as divisive as in the previous season. On a trip to the post office, Jo observed a teenager driving her grandmother's car:

> She 16—not born yet when I determined to master art of driving my husband's car. Just to think, 23 yrs. of battle, he determined I should not drive—using all his powers of meanness to sell me fear & discouragement. The meanness could slay one, if it hadn't so infuriated me. It's hard to realize that E. has no generous wish for anyone to succeed—& with me he has never wanted me to get anything, to get anywhere. It is a difficult situation I live thru—I a bird dog, again wrath prevents humiliation over the realization for a cat to find herself acting like a good dog.[64]

Cats were her totem, and here she was like a dog.

Yet she was getting through to Edward, getting more chances than ever to drive, and with mixed results. On the way back from one of their trips to Orleans for his picture, Jo veered sharply right to avoid an oncoming car. In alarm, Edward grabbed the wheel, and they ran into a guard post. He had intervened in this way on earlier occasions, and as in the past, he lost his head; he got out of the car, dragged Jo out and onto the ground, and created "quite a spectacle."[65]

Neither age nor illness nor deep bonds had managed to tame the violence. Jo's anger spilled over again in letters to Sprinchorn, as it had in the wake of her hunger strike in 1946:

> Last week, he grabbed the wheel out of my hands & ran into a post, bending it over & loudly blaming me. Then dragged me out of driver's seat—& all so publicly (cause I clung to the wheel & have black & blue spots to show his talons, post did nothing.) Not that I mind all this—this little sop to principle, I'll bruise for principles.[66]

The car caused tension again when Edward would not give a ride to friends who had parked and walked the long, rough, sandy road to the Hoppers' house, though night had fallen. Jo never thought for a moment that he would let her drive them back: "E. never enters into another's predicament, never takes his mind off of himself. That why I have to fight like a tiger for anything for myself—not regular routine. Why he can't teach. He refused to enter another person's mind to learn their reaction."[67]

On August 26, they drove to Orleans again for Edward to "get a sky." By August 31, *Portrait of Orleans* was nearly finished but he was still "waiting for a sky at all luminous before dusk." In what sounds a momentary armistice, Jo noted that she "posed for lone figure."[68] By the end of the first week in September, the truce seemed firmer. Jo was thinking of painting the view from their kitchen window to the south, with the clothesline blowing back of the lamp on their kitchen table. She noted that Edward had "given up finding an evening sky in Orleans, so faked one of his own. Brings picture together to get a sky."[69] She felt happy with both of them working, "he in studio—I in kitchen with one shade drawn to East. Every so often we'd stroll into see what other fellow doing." Whenever she saw herself on an equal footing with Edward, she was content.

Edward was unusually positive about Jo's painting, probably because he felt guilty about his behavior the day of the accident. He told her that she was "too loathe to use neutral passages to fortify bright areas & I'd better make hill neutral back of clothesline."[70] She also resurrected the portrait of Edward that she had worked on the previous summer, and he agreed to pose once again. Yet domestic peace, for Edward, always seemed to invite the kind of "blue jay pranks" that had been his trademark since boyhood: "What sadism to torture the faithful dog, bird dog, leaping after whatever he wants, or needs. His need to get back at me—for what ever it is I have that he hasn't. Why not pick what we have & share it?"[71] He could always "bask in the knowledge that he is Dr. E.H.—re. his contribution to Amer. Art" while she was just a "spitfire."[72]

It was the third week in September, when they learned from Carl Sprinchorn that Floy du Bois was dead.[73] Even the death of the wife of his oldest friend became a pretext for Edward to taunt Jo, telling her that Guy would marry again and "might enjoy a change."[74] Jo instead wrote Carl of the "great grief that has come to Guy du Bois" who "was so dependent on his fine wife. And one who regarded her memorable cooking as her very special art. Guy is a lost soul; at least for the time being. Edward comments, 'He'll marry again.' His need is so great, it is easily conceivable."[75] It had been Guy who remarked on Edward's need before his marriage to Jo. Very shortly Edward wrote a note of condolence to Guy that Jo described as "a cold fish of a letter."[76] He even invited her to add a postscript, although he was sensitive enough to realize that anything she wrote "would make him seem like a cautious deer on a chilly lawn."[77]

§

ON SEPTEMBER 26, Edward announced to Jo that he "had an idea." The next day they drove to Orleans so that he could "look at bay windows & doorways to match."[78] While there, they saw Michael Powell's film *The Red Shoes,* which brought happier memories rushing back to Jo's mind: "I got so excited about it, made one feel one had gone to a first night of Russian Ballet—or so long ago—Isadora or Yvette—or for that matter Wash. Sq. Players. Awakened memories make one's life to-day seem very dull & unallumined—but grateful for what one has had."[79]

Edward cut and stretched his canvas and then drew in the "layout."[80] Jo described the picture as "a bay window in profile & figure inside, also in profile. Window overlooking country," adding: "I don't dare ask more than is it to be day or night? Day."[81] Driving back from another trip to Orleans, where he searched for deciduous trees for his picture, Edward teased Jo: "You're never at peace. If only you were like that cow—she doesn't give a damn. You'd give plenty—all free. If you were penned in with a lot of them, you'd corrupt the herd. You'd be giving out banners! No rights—no milk!"[82]

Amused, two days later she cheerfully got out of bed at six in the morning to help him create his new scene.[83] She reports his stage directions and their mutual sense of theatrical play with exceptional detail, confirming and amplifying the other more oblique hints of how they did theater together in his studio. Edward wanted the sun to be "straight in her eyes leaning out inside window." She was too cold in the thin silk nightgown that he had chosen, but Edward wanted the look of a pink dress with short sleeves and a low neckline. "Sport shirts or slacks no good," she noted; "My hair too like a mop—so E. looking thru Life magazines for a hair-do." (Hopper's careful study of the images in *Life* explains why his paintings often seem so characteristic of their time. He insisted that Jo throw things out, but was not willing to part with cartons of old copies of *Life, The New Yorker,* and *Harper's.*[84]) As she posed, she asked if Edward wanted her to be thinking of a French poem about waking up in the morning, but he protested: "No, not at all. That woman doesn't know a word of French." Jo reflected, in line with her usual wry attributions of qualities to his characters, that indeed, she wouldn't know French if Edward were going to paint her, implying that his characters were supposed to be very American and his women neither sophisticated nor worldly.

Harmony broke down again as soon as the scenario was Jo's. When she planned a tea party for ten people on the eighth of October, he showed "complete selfishness—plus meanness."[85] Having protested the event itself, he would not lift a finger to help, not even offering, as he sometimes did, to buy cookies at the store. As the party broke up after dark, Jo wanted Edward to go out and illuminate the steep outdoor steps. He refused and said that their guests should look out for themselves. Edward "said [that] with such smugness—he wasn't much of a host—no hermits are good hosts."[86] "Hermit" was the image they had imposed on the press, not meant to be pushed so far in real life. Jo considered his behavior so unfeeling and irresponsible that she stopped speaking to him for several days—a punishment that he may have relished.

Jo was hardly soothed by learning that the jury for a regional show at the Metropolitan had rejected her submission, *San Esteban,* while accepting Edward's. He could count on two jurors, both Rehn men—his chum Burchfield and Ogden M. Pleissner. Also, he had awarded prizes to another juror, Yasuo Kuniyoshi. It was Burchfield in particular she resented, one whom she saw as "negating me as a painter. . . . I can remember when we had opposite walls at the Sunrise Turn years ago & he was such a bright spot."[87] She remembered, "One had such bright expectations—but with the coming of E. everything went dead. It took so long trying to make it out."[88]

They were on speaking terms again by October 12, when Edward finished *Cape Cod Morning,* rather pleased with it, confiding to Jo that it was better than *High Noon.*[89] The announcement led her to look back over their ups and downs during the painting: "He takes my upheavals philosophically— Would read me a story by Eliz. Taylor—current New Yorker about some difficult wife. E. saw constant parallels—but E. Taylor didn't show sufficient causations for her reactions."[90]

The boy who had been trained to see "parallels" to his life in what he read, from the parables in Sunday School to his father's applications of Montaigne, and the man who courted with love verses by Verlaine to marry a woman who was stocked with the grave examples of Horace and was quick to identify Villon's lost ladies with her dead friends, would have been attracted by the story's French title, "Gravement Endommagé," to read of an English couple on holiday in France after the war, with focus on the difficult personality of the wife, traumatized by her wartime experience: "What Richard needed was a holiday away from Louise, and what Louise needed was a holiday from herself, from the very thing she must always take along, the dull carapace of her own dissatisfaction, her chronic unsunniness."[91]

The parallels, as with so many of the texts they read, are stunning, only that Jo repeatedly and exhaustively recorded cause. Anything but consoled by his philosophy, that night as Edward slept, Jo was overcome by another cause for depression as she "lay awake . . . counting up, over the years all the people I've known on the Cape who have since died."[92]

No longer painting for herself or posing, she turned more and more of her energy to taking stock, until by the end of October she put together the fullest picture yet of their mutually contrastive ways:

> To-night E. said he was a watcher, I a participator. Oh no, no one could keep me from participating. Well 4 months on a remote sand hill with a watcher could explain why I'm the wild cat that I've become. One has to make so much of little—oh not little—the house, the hill, the thrilling sea, sunsets, flights of guls, winds—but E. so silent, so absorbed & elsewhere & knowing he thinks only of himself, won't give any of his thought, his concern. Said he's a hermit & hermits are never hospitable. He got that all settled, he recognizes no obligations. He accepts himself & upholds his conception. He doesn't want partnership, doesn't want sharing. Each get his own.[93]

Her expectations had been different, more like a woman's. She spits out the term: "I've spent these 26 years leaping after everything he wanted for him & so late to be convinced that that's all right by him—the way women do—do they? I despise that breed. I sure do, & find myself falling in that odious pattern—why wouldn't I be a she devil." Although Edward did provide "material things," she yearned for "the more special, emotional, dizzy & difficult—not even financially difficult or costly but highly personal in other ways extravagant & costly."

Packing up to leave made her think again of Katy Dos Passos, Peggy Rehn, Anne Tucker, her friends here on the Cape, all dead, and now Floy du Bois. In the end her list of those who were gone came to a total of 103, which, since it was Jo's list, included, besides poor Tommy Gray, thirteen animals and the privileged Siamese cat Perkins Youngboy Dos Passos.[94]

News of another loss awaited them in Washington Square, one that plunged Jo right back into her meditations on what a woman's role should be. Their neighbor Magda Pach had died. "What ever will happen to Walter?" asked Jo. "And Guy Pène du Bois. Both lost—along with everything else— their cooks. It will be sad to have Magda not down stairs anymore."[95] But Walter, Magda's husband, had "never much approved of me," she knew. "My influence could have been too contamination on an old fashioned German housewife whom he had snatched up before she had had chance to see how little of the old world ideals prevailed in N.Y. to-day regarding suppression of wives."[96]

"Now Magda is the second of the Euripides gang to go,"[97] added Jo, referring to the six women friends who met weekly—"rain or shine, no absences!"—to read the Greek tragedian.[98] Alert for parallels to their lives, Jo and her friends could not have read for many weeks without encountering awesome examples of male arrogance and women of power, "a constellation of strong women."[99]

As November stretched into December, Jo remarked the rising cost of living: a cup of coffee at the Coop, where they often ate, had gone up from five cents to ten and pie to twenty cents, "now not the inexpensive little excuse to escape drudgery of doing it ourselves."[100] Rather than spend money to heat her studio, she painted a picture of the bedroom fireplace with its grate and coal scuttle, shoving the bed against the door to make room for her canvas. Even then, she had to paint with the sunlight hitting her picture.

Once the season picked up in the art world, demand grew for Hopper's work, so much so that he was turning down invitations to exhibit, though he did not repeat his gesture of 1946 toward helping Jo reach an audience.[101] Meanwhile the number of abstract artists was greater than ever at the Whitney Museum Annual in December. Confronting the director, Hermon More, who had himself been a painter, they demanded to know why he had "gone right over to the other camp." Told that "he had to make a living,"[102] Jo responded that he could learn to live on less and be a painter again.

At a dinner of the American Academy of Arts and Letters, Hopper met a new member, William Carlos Williams: "E. quite likes him," Jo reported; "He told E. an amusing story" about his medical practice. Hopper shared with Williams the concerns expressed in his books, such as *In the American Grain* (1925) or *The Great American Novel* (1923). In the latter, Williams's comment that "The American background is America. If there is to be a new world Europe must not invade us. . ."[103] recalls Hopper's own 1927 call: "American art should be weaned from its French mother. . . . We should not be quite certain of the crystallization of the art of America into something native and distinct, were it not that our drama, our literature and our architecture show very evident signs of doing just that thing."[104] Hopper's statement suggests that he may indeed have read some of Williams's work by the mid-1920s, although Williams's own taste in contemporary American painting tended to favor artists more avant-garde than Hopper, such as Marsden Hartley, Charles Demuth, and others in the Stieglitz circle, about whom Edward and Jo read in Williams's autobiography.[105]

On December 28, the Hoppers went for a second time to Joseph L. Mankiewicz's film *All About Eve*. Edward, who thought it was the "best thing to come out of Hollywood," especially liked Bette Davis's portrayal of Margo Channing, a flamboyant, middle-aged actress who is exploited by the ruthless young Eve (Anne Baxter), who is on her way to fame.[106] Hopper, looking for parallels, may have found them in the character of the older actress, as he himself felt threatened by the younger abstract artists who had begun to displace his generation and realist style. Other parallels between the art and theater worlds are obvious: a drama critic, played by George Sanders, both promotes Eve's career and blackmails her to accept his advances, claiming, "We are very much alike, we have talent, unlimited ambition and no human feelings. We deserve each other."[107] It was a philosophy Jo might ruefully have recognized in Edward: Only be great. People like you if you're great, even if you give them nothing.

MEXICO AGAIN: 1951

JO PROTESTED to no avail. Edward accepted the Corcoran's invitation to head its Biennial jury and now, early in January 1951, he was making the rounds of the New York galleries with the director, "Bill" Williams,[1] to select artists, leaving Jo in the unaccustomed luxury of a heated studio with an open view of the towers of Judson Memorial Church to paint. Edward would be writing, too, as Jo explained in one of her fan letters to J. Donald Adams: "My poor husband is condemned to jury duty for the coming Corcoran show in Washington. He must also hatch some foreword for the catalogue & I think he'll be lifting some of your Charleston quotation re 'road of ancient centuries strewn with dead moderns,'" adding, "How beautiful of some one to say exactly what one wanted said. One clucks as over one's own chick."[2] The thought pleased her: "Why ever need it to have sprung out of one's own mouth, thereby only swelling one's own vanity. What a feeling of companionship to meet one's own thoughts in another. Emerson not withstanding. And your lovely Treasure Chest—Gide, Van Wyck Brooks, James, Valéry, Thomas Mann & now Henry Beston—so much of 'purest ray serene.'"[3]

Once the die was cast, Jo overcame her dislike for Edward's playing God. She leaned on him to include Carl Sprinchorn, and Edward "strained & strained his conscience," since he felt Carl's canvases at the Macbeth Gallery did not "stand out." Edward in fact found little in the galleries to like. He warmed to Edwin Dickinson's self-portrait and Paul Cadmus's painting of "a negro boy with his arm around a white girl," only to hear Williams say, "Would never do for Washington."[4] When Williams came to the studio to compile the results of their hunt, Jo was allowed to show him *San Esteban,* the one painting Edward had approved for the exhibition, and nothing else. It would look better alone, he said in his studio, "not surrounded by weaker sisters." Taking courage from her success on Sprinchorn's behalf, she also got him to admit Bertram Hartman, who had posed for her; but Edward drew the line when she also went to bat for Felicia Marsh. Jo saw it again, "They just don't want to know how well women paint."[5]

On January 22, Edward "made a draft for a new canvas"—a theater interior, *First Row Orchestra,* which reflected the expensive seats they enjoyed with Bill Williams, who took them to the theater four times while he was in New York. Four days after the sketch on paper, Hopper had the canvas drawn in charcoal; early arrivals, said Jo of the figures.[6] The next day, Edward had drawn the canvas in completely in blue paint.[7] When he took a break from painting a few days later, he and Jo went to see Marlene Dietrich and Emil Jannings in the movie *Blue Angel.*

By February 4, he was calling on Jo to dress up and pose. She did what she could to help, since he was having trouble working—it tired him to stand and paint for long periods of time—and yet he managed to make "some drawings of hands & feet while I posed in fur coat. Dug out old pumps with French heels for the purpose. Some how I never can fit myself into the poses he draws—but they are what he wants & can use what I do. What he does looks authentic enough, but I know they can't be done naturally."[8] He was pleased with his canvas when he finished it on February 20.

Collaborating with Edward always improved her sense of things, and now she reflected how she might have suffered worse husbands than he: Walter Pach treated Magda "as an overlord would a peasant on his domain . . . he would condition her to tremble at his wrath & swoon over any word of praise."[9] And she concluded that the fragile mental condition of the wife of Peppino Mangravite was a result of his domination: "Now I can see how her mind shook & broke thru contact with his Italian maleness. . . . How really strong a woman must be to survive such contact & all its complication. . . . Thank God I wasn't offered up to either of these two. Hard stolid egotism I've met, but no effort to reduce me to a beast of burden."[10]

Duty on the Corcoran jury took the Hoppers to Washington for six days at the end of February. At the National Gallery of Art, Edward became extremely enthusiastic on discovering Rembrandt's *Philosopher.* Although Jo had her one piece in the Corcoran show on sufferance, the rest of it was so discouraging that she thought a subversive thought: "Maybe there has to be an outbreak of the Abstract—something I had never realized before. San Esteban, an orphan child in hostile surroundings."[11]

Hopper had been procrastinating over his foreword for the Corcoran catalogue. Back in New York he set to work. Out of the usual painstaking self-examination came two dense paragraphs that were his longest formal statement of aesthetics since the 1930s, laying out a rationale for representational painting just when Abstract Expressionism was increasingly capturing the public's imagination. He did not view his own art as aesthetically conservative, and resented those who found his brand of realism reactionary. Still, he knew that he had written something unexpected, for he advised Bill Williams: "If you have not found my foreword suitable for publication, I shall not be offended, as I know it did not follow the usual run of such things."[12] He led off with a philosophical amplitude worthy of Aristotle and his beloved Emerson:

> Broadly stated, art is one's effort to communicate to others one's emotional reaction to life and the world.
>
> Misunderstanding has often been created in popular thought as to the valid use of the representation of nature's phenomena in this communication, and the meaning of the word life as applied to art. The word life has in some artists' minds a relation to those greatly despised words, story and anecdote, In that all life is gesture and all gesture can be the basis for story or anecdote, there cannot be the slightest gesture or mood of nature that does not in a sense create anecdote.[13]

Claiming that "the terms radical and conservative have almost no meaning as applied to the work of the individual in art," Hopper argued: "The true academician is the one who has nothing to say, and he may be found using any method, traditional or fashionable."[14] Jo thought the essay was "a fine piece of writing" which, she predicted, would be widely quoted.[15]

The jury, which Hopper chaired, consisted also of Lloyd Goodrich and Macgill James, assistant director of the National Gallery. They awarded the first Clark prize to Raphael Soyer for *Waiting for the Audition;* the second Clark prize to Philip Evergood for *Sunny Side of the Street,* a canvas depicting a teeming tenement district; the third prize to Richard Haines for *Prodigal Son;* and the fourth prize to Kay Sage for a Surrealist canvas titled *Nests of Lightning.*[16] The jury recommended that "in the future prize awards be abolished, and that the total funds now allotted for prizes should be used in purchasing works."[17]

§

THE WINTER HAD COME and gone. With the diversions of the jury behind him and no new painting on the easel, Edward fell prey to the discontent that fed his "blue jay pranks" at the expense of Jo. Soon he was trotting out his story about her career going nowhere because no one liked her work, which reduced her yet again to one of those moments when her work seemed destined to perish:[18] "The Whitney boycott has made ravages & not to me alone. Theresa Bernstein & Marguerite Zorach came in for it—but their husbands have stood loyally by them. That makes all the difference."[19] (Theresa Bernstein, at more than one hundred years of age and having recently received museum shows, awards, and other recognition, is still baffled at the Whitney's reluctance to show and acquire her work.[20])

Geared up to see Jean Cocteau's Surrealist film *Orpheus,* "2 or 3 times for the French," the Hoppers were disappointed. Jo tired after one viewing and noted that Edward "never did like Cocteau."[21] Faced with Cocteau's Gallic fantasy, he preferred the British realism of two films by Carol Reed: *The Third Man,* with Orson Welles, and *The Fallen Idol,* with Ralph Richardson.

When the Corcoran Biennial opened on the thirty-first of March, the Hoppers did not return to Washington. They were hardly surprised when Howard Devree in *The New York Times* sneered at the show: as Jo put it, what could you expect of an "ex shipping clerk."[22] She was cheered later in the month when the *Villager,* a neighborhood paper, reproduced her painting *San Esteban.* Edward saw it first and brought three copies home for her. Although she was thrilled to have a painting reproduced for the first time, she soberly noted how weak her eyes were becoming, a problem that can be seen in a deterioration of her handwriting in her diary.[23]

March, April, and most of May went by without a new idea. The Cape had long since become part of the problem, not a hope. Four years were plenty of time to forget the heat, and the smells, and the strain of the last Mexican campaign, and the precipitous detour to Wyoming, while the ledger was always there to testify that subjects to paint had been found. Health no longer preoccupied. On May 28, the Hoppers left New York for Saltillo, driving their "sacred" 1939 Buick.[24] Frugal as ever, they spent most of their nights in private houses or truck stops and took their meals at cheap restaurants and diners, or had picnics along the way.[25] Edward's driving caused a couple of minor accidents in the first four days, with short delays. They were back on location by June 10.

A couple of years later, Hopper explained to du Bois why they repeatedly returned to Mexico but did not visit him in France:

> I agree with you about the beauty of the buildings in France and one
> certainly sees nothing as impressive in Mexico. The great cathedral
> in Mexico City can not stack up with Notre Dame de Paris, or
> Chartres, or any of the others, but if you put a certain limited inter-

pretation on the two civilizations, there is perhaps not so much to choose from. Of course the Aztecs did cut the hearts out of their victims but then there was that horrible massacre of Saint Bartholomew's Eve and The Terror of 1793, when so many heads were lopped off. However I think that France has quite an edge on Mexico even so. . . . The thing is that to get to Mexico all you have to do is put your luggage in your car at the door and drive until you get there—as easy as that! Getting back into the States is somewhat more bothersome because of the U.S. Customs, but one can put up with it and one does not get seasick on the way.[26]

With their luck, they encountered another hot spell, breathing at high altitude seemed even more difficult than they remembered, and the food had not improved. Jo wrote to Rehn that it was not until eight days after they arrived that Edward "felt able to start looking about for watercolor, no canvas yet, not equal to it."[27] When he finally tried to work in watercolor, painting a view of the back of the facade of San Esteban, a sudden storm interrupted him. The attempt remained unfinished, abandoned in disgust when his sky went wrong.[28] Jo had to stop work on an oil of the hotel patio when Edward "got fed up with Mexico" and abruptly decided that they should leave.[29] In a heat wave, she reported, Edward "folded up as usual—he can't stand heat."[30]

The retreat began after just one month. On July 10 they left for Santa Fe, moved by Edward's sudden desire to see it again after twenty-six years. In a few hours they found the place "so changed for the worse after 25 yrs., that we were content with idea of Cape Cod & sped back there."[31] Santa Fe was "so cluttered & mangy" that it was "reminiscent of our own Coney Island."[32] To be sure, they "might have made some effort to see Mable Dodge [whose avant-garde salon had been the talk of New York in 1913] but that not in E.'s line—& if we had accepted any hospitality from her, E.'d have to bestir himself on behalf of any protegés she might send to him."[33] So they left, driving on through Las Vegas to Colorado, staying at shabby "camps," for which they paid about four dollars a night.

After six days of "sitting like a chow dog in the front seat," while Edward steadfastly refused to let her drive, Jo was fed up. She grabbed their big thermos and "said now I'm driver to this & dropped it out of the front car window."[34] While Edward walked back along the road to retrieve it, Jo seized the opportunity to move into the driver's seat and adjust the seat and the rearview mirror for her shorter stature. When Edward returned with the thermos, he found that it lacked its outer cover. As he went back to look for it, a car sped around the curve toward their car, which Edward had left with the motor running. Jo, not knowing what to do, concentrated on her "never failing standby over many years: Devine Love has met / And always will meet / Every human need!!"

Her prayer was better than her control of either the car or Edward, for at the last minute, the oncoming driver veered away, missing the ancient Buick by inches. Edward, who had watched all of this from down the road, made Jo go and look for the cap. By the time she found it, he had planted himself back in the driver's seat.

Back in New York on July 21, they left for Truro within a week, after stocking up on books from the library, particularly Henry James and Marcel Proust. Jo's eyes were tiring ever more easily, so Edward read aloud. They both found parallels to admire in the "lively problem in the history of taste," identified by Lionel Trilling in the hostile reviews of Henry James's *The Princess Casamassima*:[35] "Whoever wishes to know what the courage of the artist must sometimes be could do no better than to read the British reviews of *The Bostonians* and *The Princess Casamassima*. . . . James . . . was told by the reviewers that they were not really novels at all; he was scorned and sneered at and condescended to and dismissed."[36]

Hopper had been dealing with parallel issues in his essay for the Corcoran. Since the advent of Abstract Expressionism, his own work had suffered a similar fate: critics dismissing his mode of painting as mere "illustration."[37] Hopper may also have found parallels for his own aesthetics in Trilling's citation of Marianne Moore to the effect that "the special job of literature is . . . the creation of 'imaginary gardens with real toads in them.' "[38] Hopper's brand of realism was not verisimilitude, but the suggestion of reality conveyed through a simplified creation. When Trilling, responding to a critic's statement that nearly all of *Princess Casamassima*'s action "takes place on Sundays," writes, "What better setting for loneliness and doubt than Sunday in a great city?" he seems to evoke *Early Sunday Morning*.[39] Hopper, who recognized the autobiographical aspects of his own painting, would have appreciated Trilling's description of James's novel as "an intensely autobiographical book, not in the sense of being the author's personal record but in the sense of being his personal act."[40]

Hearing the voices of others brought them together; otherwise they found reasons to fuss. Edward insisted on keeping the windows wide open at night during a storm and Jo, who had been thoroughly chilled, resolved to stop wearing her "nylon Blashfield angel nightie" even though Edward "does like the feel."[41] She kept up her domestic defenses: "It's a great mistake to let anyone associate you with the cook stove & regular meals, [for] you soon lose any other identity."[42] After a month of relative harmony, Jo got to work on a 25 × 30 inch canvas that she had planned the previous spring. Entitled *Jewels for the Madonna,* it featured a "pussy cat Madonna & shrine," which she insisted was "far from blasphemy" for "cat people."[43] As she saw it, "Since the composition is a glorification of a pussy cat Madonna & Child, by Illa, one has to make them the kind to whom one would give beads & jewels & whatever one could lay one's hands on." She put the shrine together out of "all the beads in the world, a brass crocodile nutcracker, the skull of a gull, a scallop shell, some elaborate brooches and a yellow campaign button pen—'No Third Term'—from way back, and bouquets of dead grasses with a big cat tail at each side."[44] Edward said that her set-up "looked like something in a Penitente Church in New Mexico."[45] This quaint composition expresses Jo's most original style, her personal aesthetic, untainted by Edward's conception of what art should be. Yet his eye hangs over her, for even as she was working, she expressed trepidation that her painting would turn out to be "only another lady artist's still life."[46]

Although occupied with painting, Jo renewed her campaign to drive. Harking back to her strongest argument, she again threatened to sell the house unless Edward let her practice: "I was tired of being prisoner on this hill 2 miles from a bus & such 2 miles of deep sand & long hills to trudge over on foot."[47] When he did allow her to drive back from Provincetown, he let her go only ten or fifteen miles per hour.[48]

On September 17, Jo noted that Edward had "been making charcoal marks on a newly stretched canvas," but that he "complains he not really enough interested to do this one."[49] He was concerned enough about his sense of lethargy that he again consulted a physician, who prescribed vitamins ("beautiful amber and carmine things").[50] Six days later, he was "struggling to get new canvas started—having such a bad time. It is an open door with sea outside & strong pattern of light inside house. Looks like only a diagram as yet."[51] He was allowing her to work in the studio while he sketched out his canvas near the door opening out to the bay on the west side of the house. By the third of October, Hopper had made some important changes to his canvas: he had removed the steps outside the door and put the horizon back on the sea, which appears to come right up to the door in the final version. As the painting diverged from the concrete reality of their house, in Jo's opinion it was getting better and better, but it might be difficult to sell. Edward wrote to Frank Rehn: "I have finished a canvas am hoping to get another before we leave here." At the bottom of the letter, Jo added a note: "A queer one—could be called 'the Jumping Off Place'—we can't count on that one ever being sold—even by a wizard like you. I mention this so you won't be counting on it too much."[52]

Ten years later, an article on Provincetown artists featuring Hopper described the vista from his big studio window that "looks towards Province-

Jo Hopper, Jewels for the Madonna (Homage to Illa), *1951. Oil on canvas, 25 × 30″ (63.5 × 76.2 cm.).*

town ten miles away," and reproduced this canvas, *Rooms by the Sea,* identified only as "a view from his front door."[53] After the sterile spring and failed quest to Mexico, he had found a subject at home, rediscovering in Truro the theme of final departure—"the Jumping Off Place"—that had surfaced two years earlier during his illness when he painted the small wood panel of his boyhood home "out through door."

Jo meanwhile was confronting what she perceived as the failure of her *Jewels for the Madonna* and deciding that her last four paintings had also been "flops."[54] A visit that month from Walter and Helen Tittle had provoked Jo. In the nearly four decades since he and Edward had worked in adjoining studios, Walter had become bracketed as a portraitist of the socially prominent, which was, at least, an identity as an artist, something Edward had denied Jo: "After so many years of fiction . . . it is congenitally impossible for him to recognize the existence & needs of any one but himself. . . . It's so repulsive, my heart has withered & that's why all my pictures are born dead."[55] In the metaphors of sterility, she identified her sex and her art, frustrated by a man who never said "anything is good to praise it, or even recognize it, to admit it."[56] She felt a threat to the intimate ground of their relationship: "I'm not the least cuddly these days or at all responsive. He kills off all the deep emotion I had for him & his interests."[57]

A day or so after, when it was too dreary and rainy to paint, Jo read Edward a story from an old *New Yorker*.[58] They made themselves tea and "played at being polite." Jo put on her Mexican earrings and a big ring and they "talked French until we came to the word cookie & gateau wouldn't do."[59] In the gloom, thoughts of the dead came again: John Sloan had been like a landmark, and Magda, and Floy and Anne.

On the ninth of October, Henry Varnum Poor and his daughter Annie came to tea and reported a new artists' organization in New York made up of "objective painters trying to defend themselves." The group hoped to "get after" the Museum of Modern Art, "that has been no friend of anything but the nonobjective these days."[60] Henry gave them a copy of a letter Ben Shahn had written to the museum and told them that Raphael Soyer was "a central figure in this movement."[61]

Shifting away from herself, Jo had begun to fret that Edward was just sitting around reading, when Frank Rehn needed pictures to sell. As usual, she was full of ideas for him to paint, including the marquee of the Orleans cinema and the facade of the Lobster Pot restaurant, both of which he considered and rejected. She complained that once they returned all the Sartre, Proust, and Parkman to the library, Edward was absorbed in back issues of *Life* magazine and the *Boston Globe*.[62] Stymied, he even brought his unfinished watercolor from Mexico down from the attic and tried to fix the botched sky. Jo had also been expending a lot of time and energy trying to arrange for easements over neighboring properties so that they could run electric lines to their house. As they grew older, she worried more about health emergencies and the lack of a telephone, and felt that Edward cared very little about her fate should she outlive him.[63]

With nothing more to show Rehn, they returned to New York, where Jo promptly suffered a bout of colitis, which she attributed to "nerves."[64] Stressed by the readjustment to life in their cramped quarters, she also worried about the threat of an atomic bomb. (As she had after Pearl Harbor, she kept a rucksack packed for quick escape.) Edward, who scoffed at her war anxiety (as he had before),[65] had his chronic preoccupation. His Christmas present testifies that the normal affective-aggressive state prevailed: Arthur Rimbaud's poetry in French, inscribed: "la petite chatte qui découvre ses griffes presque tous les jours. Joyeux Noël, 1951."[66] ("To the little cat who bares her claws almost every day.")

PLANNING *REALITY:* 1952

THE LAST of the old teachers from the New York School of Art died in early January 1952. In Grace Church for the funeral of Kenneth Hayes Miller, Edward wondered "whether Kenneth had ever put his nose in there before," while Jo was thinking of him as a "distinguished" and "profoundly wise" man of "high discrimination."[1] A few days later, at the opening of a memorial exhibition for John Sloan at the Whitney, they saw many old friends "in their frames or moving about greeting each other."[2] Feeling like survivors of a happier past, "every one seemed so pleased at this opening, pleased at seeing familiar faces, familiar places treated so lovingly & in a familiar idiom and so understandable."[3] After several few years in which she and Edward had so often felt "puzzled & excluded," she found it especially pleasing to experience "the familiar life of our era—or of a slightly earlier one whose tradition we knew."[4]

Jo (and probably Edward too) was anxious that Flora Miller, Gertrude Vanderbilt Whitney's daughter, would take over the museum and might "not care to take advice from people like J. Sloan, who was there at the birth of the Whitney & guided her mother. What is there to keep her from taking the Modern Mus. as her model & join in with glorification of the chichi?"[5]

At home, Edward had been complaining of stomach pains after breakfast. "He is not suffering, only curious about cause. One doesn't like to disregard symptoms." A neighboring physician was "seeking causes which seem not to be heart, stomach, nor nasal, nor indicated in blood count nor sugar in urine. Prostate all right too," and trying to treat him with vitamins and digitalis ("no good") and hydrochloric acid (three drops).[6] Jo questioned whether she could be the cause of his illness and concluded: "I wouldn't want, I couldn't stand that it should hit him physically. Or any other way either. It would be my dedicated job to save him."[7]

Meanwhile, both of them were painting. He needed the afternoon light, leaving her free to use the studio in the mornings while she painted a canvas of their stove. The work was well along by February 22 when Jo reported Edward "working on Girl sitting up on bed looking out big window over red brick rooves. I posing occasionally."[8] Different occasions appear in four preparatory drawings, which reveal a typical evolution. At first a female figure with long hair leans close to a window, with a hint of erotic exposure as in certain earlier works, but then the hair is tightened into a bun and the figure withdrawn to a more reserved position on the bed, while the context is drawn more simply to convey the effect of penetrating and enveloping light. On the latest drawing Hopper penciled in exhaustive indications of colors and tonalities, suggesting a thorough and deliberate design. More than in many of his pictures, he preserved in the features a close resemblance to Jo, placing her in a powerful light yet concealing the fact that the "Girl" was now sixty-eight. He had brought his vision of light from the Truro studio in *Rooms by the Sea* to the bedroom in Washington Square in *Morning Sun*. From this time on, sunlight, in its imaginative association with life, became more and more his real subject. His longing for the values of the past began to give way to an intensified attempt to hold on to the present.

As Hopper lost old friends and colleagues to death, he began to discover affinities with a group of younger representational painters for whom he exemplified the best of what they saw themselves defending in an age dominated by Abstract Expressionism. Several months after he and Jo had first heard from Henry Poor about the group forming to protest the emphasis on nonobjective painting at the Museum of Modern Art, Isabel Bishop telephoned to invite Edward to a coming meeting.[9] Since Jo answered the phone, she took the occasion to tell Isabel that she, too, would enjoy the lively talk with the likes of Raphael and Moses Soyer, Reginald Marsh, Guy Pène du Bois, Leon Kroll, Yasuo Kuniyoshi, Chaim Gross, Jack Levine, William Gropper, Philip Evergood, Gladys Rockmore Davis, and Sol Wilson. When Isabel hesitated, Jo suggested that they only wanted "names," leading Isabel to insist that she was often the life of the party. At that point, Jo exploded with a protest that it was so awful to always be left out of everything, prompting Isabel to suggest that she take it up with her husband. Later, Jo regretted her

Edward Hopper, Jo Posing for "Morning Sun," *1952. Conté on paper, 12 × 19″ (30.5 × 48.3 cm.).*

outburst and Edward assured her that it would get her nowhere. He maintained that Isabel had succeeded because she had "such a good mind," causing Jo to ask what was wrong with her own.[10] Jo lamented her role "as a forever wallflower," and protested, "Why doesn't some merciful gardener come around & cut down the anguishing sight?"[11] She lamented: "Rejection has laid its mark on my soul—taking all sustenance from the making of pictures that could refute the justice of their being ignored."[12] When she proposed at least entering her work in the Washington Square street fair, Edward scotched even that, fearful that there could be publicity unfavorable to him.[13]

Edward went by himself to the meeting on February 25 at Sol Wilson's Sixth Avenue studio. To Jo he reported that of the fifteen artists who attended, he was one of only five "gentiles." Among the more numerous Jewish artists, Kroll was the old friend, a MacDowell Club regular who had also painted with Edward in Gloucester in 1912: he read the group a paper he had written for the College Art Association.

By February 28, Jo's rage and depression had grown so far as to be evident to others. The sculptor Lu Duble told her she was having "a manic depressive fit."[14] Duble convinced Jo to pack her watercolors in a portfolio and get Edward to take them to the dealer Maynard Walker, who, if he couldn't show them would know who could. When Edward resorted to his line that no one liked Jo's work, she snatched her watercolors and retreated to her unheated studio ("my private concentration camp").[15] Edward gingerly opened the door to his heated studio and proffered army blankets and electric heating pads. When she refused to budge, he gathered her up in an army blanket against her will and put her in a big chair in his studio. She declined to eat the supper that he had prepared and, in protest, slept on the edge of their bed, although she found the struggle "so wearing, devastating."[16] It had taken a second hunger strike, like the first in 1946, to move Edward. The watercolors, particularly those of cats and children, elicited some polite comments from Maynard Walker, but he declined to do anything with them and offered no suggestions, giving Edward the opening, which he took, to tell Jo over and over that the fault lay in her work.[17]

Edward, meanwhile, learned that he would be represented in the American pavilion of the Venice Biennale along with Stuart Davis, Yasuo Kuniyoshi, and Alexander Calder. Also, on April 8 and again on May 5, he attended meetings of the artists' protest group, which was planning to publish *Reality: A Journal of Artists' Opinions.*

Jo decided to take matters into her own hands if she could: "If one can't find any room at the bottom, I may as well try my chances at the top. The Mus. of Mod. Art ought to be more or less modern also in its approach to the prejudice against wives of painters."[18] Without Edward's knowledge, she made an appointment to show her work at the Modern, plotting to take a taxi uptown and pick up her two canvases that she had strategically placed with a friend nearby so that Edward would not notice. She chose to bring her oils *Jewels for the Madonna* and *Obituary,* as well as a portfolio of her watercolors.

Jo met with a Miss Bacon at the Modern, who informed her that it was museum policy to examine work carefully but to refrain from commenting upon it. She reminded Jo that the museum planned everything a year in advance. Jo liked her nice manner and felt placated for the moment.[19] From the Modern, she went on with her pictures to the Feragil Gallery where she left them overnight. When they showed no enthusiasm the next day, she took *Obituary* over to the Babcock Gallery, but found no interest there either.

Oblivious to Jo's discontent and initiatives. Edward had started to work on a canvas, which Jo described with her usual participatory interest as an "interior with 2 figures. E. posing for man at window who at present is a goodlooking enough guy but gives effect of being short. The female is chubby but tall not withstanding. The outdoor interest is taking definition & 3″ [3rd] dimension firmly established in & out."[20] Five days later, Jo noted that he was working on the male figure, and worried that he would "do something to mar his fairly good looks." She observed that Edward had moved the bureau to the left "so as to clear the profile of back of head."[21]

When Edward turned to Jo for her customary help, he was in for a surprise. She was not going to be her usual available self after all those taunts and humiliations. As he always did, even in hunger strikes, he found some way to soften her. Putting the humiliations behind, she recorded in some detail how she posed:

> Front hair down trying to look long & be a different hair do than I can supply beyond the ears because hair long only at sides which I pin up on top of head—pulled tight over ears. And I'm not the type he wants either. He wants a large creature able to hold her own with the man he has standing by a window with his back turned to her. She reads a book & wears my pink satin slip, grown old in the trunk because who wants to iron satin when I have one jersey & one nylon that get only washed.[22]

As work progressed she reported, "E. has changed the seated female in his canvas & the man grew younger,[23] and several days later she noted:

> Back by 4:30 to pose for E. who wanted satin slip for aged woman in Hotel Room by R.R.—sort of combination of earlier titles: Hotel Room & House by R.R. That would give critics something to help fill up comment. E. has the track showing right out window of run down or one never much run up hotel at side of R.R. tracks & these the people who stay there, a little sad albeit respectable.[24]

In the record book, she subsequently noted: "Emphasis on mood. Wife better watch husband & tracks below window,"[25] suggesting the man's desperate desire to escape, perhaps through suicide. Later, she commented that she found this painting "very depressing. The 2 figures are so frustrated, the man pulling on his neck tie & looking out of 3rd class hotel window on R.R. tracks."[26] The confession that the painting affected her strongly suggests that, unconsciously at least, she felt the parallels with her own marriage.

While Edward continued to meet with the *Reality* group at Sol Wilson's studio,[27] Isabel Bishop called and asked Jo if she could come and see her work. Jo found Bishop's compliments suspect and rejected the suggestion that she enter the Audubon Society juried show at three dollars an entry.[28] Jo's concern with showing her work gave way to a new anxiety when she finally had her eyes examined and discovered that she had "incipient cataracts" that might eventually require an operation; Edward assured her that they could afford it.[29]

When Jo initiated a correspondence with the poet Marianne Moore, and the two women developed a rapport by mail, Edward told her to forget about asking Moore to tea as she would not like Jo's work, since, as Jo noted, "she all Picasso & avant garde."[30] Here Edward was particularly out of line; Moore was friendly with Marguerite Zorach, with whom Jo was acquainted. Zorach had even painted a portrait of Moore and her mother, something Jo would have been thrilled to do. Little wonder if not long after, Jo described herself as "bitter with frustration & waspy of tongue & desperate of mood."[31]

As they approached their seventieth birthdays, the Hoppers really started to feel their age. One hot June day, Jo sadly looked over the banister to observe Edward slowly climbing their seventy-four steps. She noted: "He bends forward so far, holding on to the banister. I looked down on the top of his bare head. He feeling hot but wouldn't take off his wool sport coat to carry over his arm while making the long climb. . . . It doesn't seem that he does it so easily."[32]

When Reginald and Felicia Marsh came for tea, Jo took them into her studio to look at her work. Jo felt that their responses were polite and positive; Reggie even encouraged her to submit her painting of the Cape bedroom to the juried show at the Academy. Just at that moment, Edward intruded and began to distract them, showing his usual embarrassment at her showings, perhaps, too, his jealousy at anything that distracted her attention from him. (Similarly he had diverted Edwin Dickinson all those years before.) Marsh instead was boasting that a picture of Felicia's had just been very well received at the Whitney.[33] Felicia would have been in the Corcoran Biennial the year before had Edward not rejected Jo's campaign on her behalf.

Even a momentary encouragement from outside set Jo to looking again at the works gathered about her in the studio, which she was coming to see more clearly as reminders of her youthful accomplishment and possible monuments pointing beyond:

> They are really very nice, full of feeling & color & the youth of another day. They make me rather sad, this record of so much intensity & straining effort with so little strength to go on—nervously exhausted so much of the time, trying to exist on so little & do it with taste & possibly consideration. And where had it led one—professionally. They might be considered collectors items—if any day one were to collect the work of women painters who have married men whose work has achieved great recognition. Why doesn't some one do this—some feminist—or some one, make this collection in honor of his wife & give it to some female institution.[34]

Prescient to a fault, Jo's vision stands as a program and a reproach, two decades ahead of its time. Two days later, still thinking of this question of posterity, she denounced the diaries: "What trash this record is—never any intimate concern—it would take too much time."[35]

Rehn had arranged for twenty works by Hopper to travel to Venice for the Biennale. Reviews began to pour in by late June. Stuart Preston reported in *The New York Times* that "Hopper made the deepest impression. Foreigners recognized, and rightly, something authentically American in the pathos of his landscapes, a germ of loneliness which they detect in our literature. 'An American Chirico,' one critic called him."[36] Emily Genauer wrote that although usually preferring Stuart Davis for "the crisp, bold vigor of his design," in Venice she found in Hopper "a haunting mysterious, portentous air which somehow seems related to those early metaphysical paintings of empty, silent city squares done years ago by di Chirico."[37]

News of Edward's success even reached Truro, as *Time* magazine reproduced his work and other published reviews.[38] The Hoppers did not arrive on the Cape until the middle of July 1952. Continuing worries about his health and the knowledge that new subjects were so hard to come by there made them postpone their departure. By arriving late, Jo also hoped to avoid the season of wood ticks and to find the water warmer for swimming. When two men from the Cape Cod Art Association in Hyannis showed up unexpectedly while Edward was out, and asked to borrow one of his pictures for a forthcoming exhibition, Jo explained that they had none of his work on the Cape but offered them her painting of the *South Truro Church* instead. Thus, she came to show her work once again.[39]

Self-consciousness about the diaries resurfaced. Catching herself in a comment on the "thrilling sunsets—great ball of fire sinking into sea in the west," she queried: "Why ever do I record this other trivia? Sort of rendering an account of one's days—leaving out all the real rendering, what going on within. Cut off from human intercourse makes me very difficult for poor E. who so enjoys his inner life, he can get on fine without interruption by humans."[40] For once, she states an aesthetic similar to Edward's, separating the account of things seen from the "real rendering, what going on within."

Edward's contacts in the city with the realist protest led to socializing on the Cape with Sol and Dora Wilson. Neighborly contacts continued with Bob and Marie Stephens and Dick and Nell Magee. Edward even made a Conté crayon portrait drawing of Dick, an effusive gesture of friendship since he rarely did portraits.[41] On September 6, Hopper produced a crayon sketch and the next day pulled some stretchers out of the attic and prepared to paint once again. Jo with her usual attentiveness to the progress of his works reported that the picture "seems at present reading to be 2 figures sitting out in bathing suit in front of beach house."[42] A week later, he asked her to pose and she had to repress her old temptation to second guess:

> E.'s picture going fine. . . . E. has a touch of pink on a towel hanging on line at side of bath house, from which I deduct he's going to have the big ball of fire sink into the adjoining sea horizon—just what we look out at every day, but I can't believe he'll do anything so spectacular. He'll stop before he gets that far. Indeed, I'll not ask & set him against it.[43]

Getting started to paint often cleared Edward's petty hostility and freed him for intimacy. On the day he began his new canvas, Jo reported that he "gave me a pinch on the bottom thru my corduroy slacks & said 'You certainly are some baby.'" She observed happily: "We seem so calm & friendly tonight."[44]

Another of the innumerable exhibition juries interrupted the fall. On September 20 the Hoppers flew from Hyannis via Nantucket and Martha's Vineyard to New York, taking their first trip by plane. Jo had a good time and Edward was apprehensive:[45] They made the trip so Edward could serve, together with Charles Burchfield and Andrew Wyeth, as a juror for the watercolor section of a show of works on paper at the Metropolitan. (Reginald Marsh, John Taylor Arms, and Armin Landeck picked the prints for this exhibition.)

Jo was pleased that her watercolor portrait of the painter Bertram Hartman was selected. At a party at Roland McKinney's house, both Burchfield and Wyeth discussed the portrait with her. According to her account, they said that "no good heads had been sent in—a lot of conventional portrait commissions" and they found her work to have "character & likeness."[46] It appears that Edward, who showed his *Construction in Mexico,* a watercolor of 1946, had finally used his influence to Jo's advantage. He found it easier because of his long, close friendship with Burchfield and Wyeth's sincere admiration for his work.

The flight to New York had stalled progress on the new painting. Once back, Edward wrote to Rehn: "We arrived here without once crashing into either the water or the land. First stop New Bedford then Martha's Vineyard, Nantucket and Hyannis—as smooth as the train, but I'm still doubtful." Hopper never did come to enjoy flying, but he told Rehn: "Jo loves to fly. She thinks she's an angel, but we know better."[47]

In mid-October, Jo wrote to Bee Blanchard that Edward "has painted a beach scene & I'm doing a head of him & he poses like an eel."[48] About *Sea Watchers* Jo wrote in the record book: "Sheila and Adam; Irish girl, gentle, sweet, large & Yankee clam digger—very fine people—on New England coast for late swim. People inventions of E.H."[49] Hopper made at least three drawings for this canvas, one a detail of the girl, based on Jo, and two of the entire composition.

A letter that Hopper wrote to Rehn at this time betrays how adroit he was in using others to achieve his goals. When the *Instructor,* "a magazine for school teachers," requested permission to reproduce *Lighthouse at Two Lights* on its cover, he confided: "I don't think it will help me any to be reproduced on the cover, and I am easing them off by shifting the no to you. If you think otherwise, that's all right but I'd rather not do it. I have told them that you handle such matters for me, and they will write to you."[50] The tactic parallels his use of Jo as a screen against interviewers: not wishing to appear uncooperative, again and again he evaded interviewers' prying questions by having Jo interfere.

The Hoppers returned to New York on November 10, stopping en route to visit Ella Mielziner in Connecticut. When they delivered Edward's new canvas to Rehn on November 14, Jo noted, "The Yankee boyfriend not named yet."[51] As they planned to escape the cold New York winter by traveling south, they occupied themselves with openings and shopping in the city. (A reluctant shopper, Edward referred to Madison Avenue as "the gip St."[52]) Edward went to an editorial meeting of the protest group that was getting ready to publish *Reality.* On the second of December, the Hoppers attended the opening of the watercolor and print show at the Metropolitan. Jo was thrilled when she saw that her painting of Bertram Hartman (page 414) was hung in the first gallery with Edward's work.

The following week, they set out in the car for Arizona, thinking that they might continue on to Mexico and visit Oaxaca.[53] The heat that had spoiled their previous trip would not be a problem. Edward would not have to haul coal and Jo could get free of the cold in her back studio. She was so bored with Edward's silence in the car that she asked him to dictate comments for her diary. He begrudgingly offered occasional remarks such as, "Hanover Court House—think there was a battle here," dribbling bits from Civil War history.[54] Or, "Look at these damn women cops."[55] As they drove through North Carolina, Edward warmed at the sight of the motif that had dominated his recent works: "How fine to have this bright sunlight—brighter than in the N[orth] this season of the year."[56] As the weather changed, he again read with his painter's eye: "Well it's grey I don't like grey."[57]

Having no set itinerary, the Hoppers drove south through the Carolinas, and into Georgia, where Jo observed that the muddy banks looked like Indian red, right out of the paint tube. Their first destination, El Paso, Texas, where they spent a week, proved too cold at night. Edward wrote to Rehn that they were thinking of going on directly to Mexico, bypassing Arizona, which is what they did.[58] The yucca plants along the road inspired Edward to call them "the Pierrots among trees," pleasing Jo, who described "their gestures so whimsical, philosophic, stem dangling white lace hankies deliciously."[59] The casual exchange shows how thoroughly both Hoppers knew and loved the character out of French pantomime (originally from the *commedia dell'arte*).

Crossing the border, the Hoppers spent Christmas in Durango. The next day in Guanajuato they stayed at a delightful inn, Posada de la Presa. Pleased for once by Mexican food and needing to rest, they decided to stay for a while. They spent New Year's Eve there, enjoying a party for the guests, one of whom told them about a special place to stay in Mitla, run by Americans interested in anthropology. Edward wrote to Rehn, expressing relief that he had escaped the snow and reporting that he had not yet done any painting. He described Guanajuato as "a fine old city, but very much on the picturesque side," and concluded, "I do not know how long we shall stay here. We hate to leave to go further south because of the good food and comfort here."[60] Apart from those merits, he still found it the country he knew: "The same Mexico as before, peons on burros, dirty markets, poverty and narrow crowded streets."[61]

REALITY: 1953

IN GUANAJUATO, Edward spotted the top of a mountain to paint. When he was having trouble getting the foliage, tower, and reservoir below into his watercolor, Jo grew restless.[1] He talked of finishing and going on to Oaxaca, further south, where the weather would be warmer. In the end, he never got his sky. As late as the spring of 1954 the work was in his studio, still unfinished, according to Lloyd Goodrich and Rosalind Irvine, who reported that he had been afraid to spoil the picture. Taking courage in the course of the year, he delivered the completed work to Rehn in December 1954.

Leaving Guanajuato on January 12, the Hoppers were daunted by the rugged landscapes and the road curving among "peaks & chasms."[2] They stayed overnight on the outskirts of Mexico City, going on the next day to Mitla, outside Oaxaca. As they negotiated hairpin and corkscrew turns and the glaring sun, Jo recalled the tragic automobile accident that had cost John Dos Passos an eye and his wife.[3] Jo also feared running out of gas. Hopper later described the ride to Rehn as "all mountains from Mexico City through Puebla" and "not a drive I would care to take again."[4]

In Mitla, next to the Museo de Arte Zapoteca they put up at a hacienda, which Hopper described as "rooms connected with the museum founded by an American, he takes in a few professional people in this old hacienda. It is very charming and was built about 1720."[5] Although they visited the Zapotec ruins, covered in geometric mosaics that shimmer in the sunlight, nothing caught Edward's eye. Finding nothing he wanted to paint, he simply sat on the patio, bored, reading old *Reader's Digests*.[6] When they did go for a drive, Jo finally lashed out at his self-absorption and got him to start a sketch for a watercolor from a lower road overlooking a stony cliff.[7] The next day, Edward wrote to Rehn to inform him of his progress on *Cliffs near Mitla, Oaxaca:* "I did a watercolor in the last place that we stayed (Guanajuato) but I don't think much of it. I've started another which promises to be better."[8] That day, he began to add color to his sketch, which Jo said made him "more content."[9]

A couple of nights' rest gave him enough energy to drive the twelve miles to Oaxaca (a city with seventeenth-century baroque buildings from the colonial period). For once revealing some interest in local color, he produced a number of sketches of the indigenous people in Mitla and Oaxaca. But the cold weather and the rigorous conditions of the hacienda's communal bathroom made it seem necessary to think of moving on. While Edward was complaining about the dirt and disorder, Jo reported that "the Indians are charming & so intelligent."[10] Jo noted that Edward "seems so lacking in ambition regarding his own work."[11] On the thirtieth of January, when he put a sky on his Mitla watercolor, they were ready to flee Mexico and escape a flu epidemic that they feared was on the way. Edward, however, developed symptoms of a cold that left him feeling unable to travel.[12]

On February 6, when Edward began to feel better, he and Jo went to see the ruins at Monte Alban (a religious and funerary city dating from the third century A.D.). Climbing down into tomb chambers, they saw ancient wall paintings of sharply outlined stylized figures rendered in silhouettes and were fascinated to learn that the flat colors had been produced from insect dyes. Years later, when a journalist inquired about his opinion of Latin American architecture, particularly baroque, Hopper replied that he had not liked it much and commented: "I like the idea, though, of a large space on the facade without any decor, and then suddenly a very complicated motif in a corner. But I don't like the baroque very much. I did like the monuments of the pre-Columbians."[13] Another interviewer reported Hopper's interest in Zapotec Indian ruins and mentioned that he "put together a collection of arrowheads."[14]

The thirteen-year-old Buick delayed them for another five days for repairs,[15] while Edward suffered from his cold, unable to do anything but sit in a park. As they finally began their retreat, Edward would not hear of Jo's driving, so she filled the diary with what she now thought of as trivia—intricate details and observations on the vegetation, the animals, the topography, everyone they met along the way, and anything that occurred. As they raced toward Monterrey, by now a known quantity, Jo reckoned up their expectations and disappointments in a letter to Rehn: "It's all been grand but not exactly an escape from the cold—cold nights & no proper heat in houses—fire in fireplace in dining room—but bedrooms cold. E.—except for recent cold—well enough but lacking in ambition—turned Mexican, content to loll in patios with uneasy conscience."[16] At lunch, when they observed an "undistinguished pudgy looking male & woman with stern nose & short grey hair marcelled in prevailing mode," Jo commented, "Looks like George Washington," and Edward rejoined, "She's cut him down all right. And she'll not lie about it either."[17] In style this was still the boy who made caricatures of his overwhelming mother and browbeaten father. Those were roots he never outgrew.

As they crossed the border into Laredo, Jo's mood shifted toward the positive. Edward, having survived the ordeals, even mentioned returning to Mexico someday.[18] At their first American hotel, they were immediately annoyed that prices were in dollars and not pesos, for their money did not go nearly as far. After crossing Texas, Louisiana, and Mississippi, they headed north and arrived home on February 28.

The trip made Jo more tranquil, although the nub was what it had always been: "How remote all one's resentments appear right now, after Mexico & 3 mos. absence from the sight & thought of this life of rejection and my great compensation. E.'s big success—which is what I've wanted most & would readily have chosen. If only E. wasn't so terrifically self centered. Efforts to crash that hard shell have devastated me."[19] Edward turned down an invitation to serve on a jury in Los Angeles since it came too close to an already scheduled visit to Richmond. Approvingly Jo reflected: "Would have to fly & I can't have him fly that far alone. If there is to be any crash, I must be there too."[20]

On the ninth of March, Edward and Jo both attended a meeting of the artists' protest group: "The batch of painters banded together to preserve existence of realism in art against the wholesale usurpation of the abstract by Mod. Mus., Whitney, & thru them spread thru most of the universities for those who cannot abide not subscribing to le dernier cri from Europe."[21] She described meeting Sol Wilson (the host), Louis Bouché, Henry Poor, Jack Levine, Ernest Fiene, William Gropper, Raphael Soyer, Moses Soyer, Nicolai Cikovsky, and others. Hopper's manner smacked of the "New England Yankee" to one of the younger artists present, Joseph Solman. Amazed to hear that the great man "never took taxis," Solman blurted out, "I have the idea that you like Emerson," only to be stunned by Hopper's response: "Read him every day."[22]

Jo was pleased that Gropper, Poor, and Fiene welcomed her to the meeting. They had worked all year and promised to have a dummy of *Reality* by the very next week. It seemed that Edward had found her presence less objectionable than he made out at first. At the March 16 meeting, they "heard more discussion of how to get the pamphlet out,"[23] and approved the dummy.

On March 19, the Hoppers took the train to Richmond, where Edward would serve for three days on a jury for a show by local artists. His fellow jurors were the sculptor Jacques Lipchitz, and Gordon Washburn, the director of the Carnegie Museum in Pittsburgh. Hopper was given a small show of thirteen of his pictures to accompany the event. The local paper referred to him as "perhaps this country's leading exponent of realism."[24] Richmond artists Jewett and Jean Campbell recalled meeting the couple at the museum party: "Edward was seated at a bench with Jo standing over him doing all the talking."[25] Leslie Cheek, then the director, with whom the Hoppers lodged, recalls that "Mrs. Hopper was gracious and charming."[26] He did write to Gordon Washburn: "Your charming manners did much to make up for intentional deficiencies on the part of another member of the Jury."[27] Hopper or Lipchitz would fit the crime.

A few days after returning from Richmond, the Hoppers went to visit Guy du Bois before he and his daughter, Yvonne, left to live in France. Edward bought a drawing of himself that Guy had made in 1919 for twenty dollars and Jo got a white soup tureen to remind her of the wonderful dinners Floy had cooked.[28] Jo saw Guy's departure as the end of an era. She was not alone. Fellow callers included Lloyd Goodrich, Rosalind Irvine, and John Baur of the Whitney Museum. Goodrich asked Jo if Edward had told her that the Museum had tried to obtain one of her pictures for the last big Whitney show, but that the Hoppers had been away. Jo found him pompous and felt that he lacked credibility. When she sketched an imaginary graveyard, she placed him among the targets of her scorn along with the Pen & Brush Club, Isabel Bishop, Bessie Brewer [Breuer Poor], Alex Brook, and her old nemesis, Juliana Force, along with her bullying landlord, N.Y.U.

Jo's doubts about Goodrich's candor were well founded. Years later he not only discarded the works of hers she bequeathed to the Whitney, but when shown photographs of her pictures, claimed that he had not been aware that she painted so well. Seeing him there at Guy's brought to focus again the whole Whitney story:

> Well there has been enough heartbreak for me at the Whitney, a museum financed & run by 2 women, who hated women, so this Museum of Amer. Art was to catch men & negate women, let in a few homely ones to side step the omission being too marked. It so contrived by the great wealth behind it to acquire immense power. Not

Jo Hopper, Hic Jacet, *c. 1953. Pencil on paper.*

to be included in its shows, let alone collections, was to be ostracized in the art market. This a bitter experience for many so excluded.[29]

Once again she thought of her fellow victims—Marguerite Zorach, Felicia Marsh, Theresa Bernstein, and Helen Sloan. When she made an effort to thank Goodrich for his expression of interest, she could not conceal her sense of the reality: "Over the years I've learned that my poor little bastards—are little bastards & their very existence unmentionable."[30]

Edward forbade her to send the letter, an order she ignored because he refused any further discussion.[31] Her pride had stiffened with her participation in the last Corcoran Biennial and in the Metropolitan's watercolor show. She resented the Whitney's belated overtures, much the way that Edward had rejected the overdue offer of membership he had finally received from the National Academy of Design in 1932. Edward wrote du Bois to praise the drawing that he had just acquired: "It is a very stately and handsome head that you have drawn and that I now have. Only one with many years of experience in drawing could have made it, and we both admire it very much. It is now sitting on my easel, where there should be, but is not, a Hopper under construction."[32] Jo had hoped that Edward would express how sad they were that Guy was leaving America and how much he had meant to Edward's career. But Edward, to her dismay, said only, "Gratitude is a female virtue."[33] Seized by second thoughts about the letter she had defiantly sent to Goodrich, Jo wrote to Rosalind Irvine at the Whitney, thanking them both for considering her work and apologizing: after suffering "a 20 years' diet of hemlock," she had been "stunned"; she had to conclude, she added, that she cared "much more for people than for pictures," otherwise there would be more and better paintings.[34]

On the thirteenth of April, at a meeting at Sol Wilson's, they received the first copies of *Reality*.[35] Edward and Wilson were editors, along with Isabel Bishop, Alexander Dobkin, Jack Levine, Henry Poor, Joseph Solman, and Raphael Soyer. Edward had contributed a statement, which began:

> Great art is the outward expression of an inner life in the artist, and this inner life will result in his personal vision of the world. No amount of skillful invention can replace the essential element of imagination. One of the weaknesses of much abstract painting is the attempt to substitute the inventions of the intellect for a pristine imaginative conception. The inner life of a human being is a vast and varied realm and does not concern itself alone with stimulating arrangements of color, form, and design.[36]

Statement

Great art is the outward expression of an inner
life in the artist and ~~this inner life will~~ ~~can~~ result in his personal
vision of the world. No amount of skillful
invention can replace the essential element of
imagination. One of the weaknesses of much
abstract painting is the attempt to substitute the
inventions of the intellect for a pristine
imaginative conception.

The inner life of a human being is a vast and
varied realm, and does not concern itself alone
with pleasing or stimulating arrangements of
~~form~~ color, and form ~~and design.~~

The term life as used in art ~~is a term~~ something not
to be held in contempt, for it implies all of
existence and the province of art is to react to it
and not to shun it

Painting will have to deal more fully and
less obliquely with life and nature's phenomena
before it can ~~become~~ again great.

Edward Hopper

Edward Hopper, draft of statement for Reality, *1953.*

Jo took it upon herself to send copies to people who she thought would be interested, from Van Wyck Brooks to T. S. Eliot. Edward's list included Lewis Mumford and Lincoln Kirstein.[37] The group had pressured him into asking Mumford to contribute. When Mumford refused on the grounds that he was too busy writing a new book, Hopper replied in terms that reveal again how he brought the same scrupulous intelligence to writing as to painting: "It was with some embarrassment that I carried out the wishes of the editorial staff of 'Reality' in asking you to write for us, as I understand the amount of time and brain that can go into even a small well considered bit of writing."[38]

The cause of realism was betrayed, Jo thought, when Edward Root, an early supporter of Edward's, began to purchase the work of Abstract Expressionists: Root was "pretty far gone & goes ever more so, quite frisky over being exalted by possession of new gods. How I wish I could heard the discussion all this expos will provoke among good minds. I adore talk."[39]

The *Reality* group met on the twenty-seventh of April at Wilson's to celebrate the initial reactions to their initiative, including a favorable review by Emily Genauer in the New York *Herald Tribune*.[40] Jo felt that she got along fine at the meeting, which included three other women: Isabel Bishop, Gladys Rockmore Davis, and the sculptor Dorothea Greenbaum. They saw Reggie Marsh, who admitted that his wife, Felicia, was feeling so rejected that she refused to read their new pamphlet.[41]

On May 3, J. Donald Adams wrote about *Reality* in his column in *The New York Times Book Review*. When Raphael Soyer called to tell Edward about the favorable notice, he heard from Jo that she, having begun corresponding with Adams some two years earlier, had delivered the copy of *Reality* to his office. Writing to congratulate Adams on the column, she chirruped: "We knew you'd approve. That's why I carried it right up to your desk the minute it was born."[42]

On May 4, the Hoppers attended the funeral of Everett Shinn: "He the last of the 8 so thought we should go. They in a way our ancestors that 8: Henri, Sloan, Prendergast, Lux, Davies, Lawson, Glackens."[43] The year before it had been the funeral of their teacher and friend Kenneth Miller and the memorial for Sloan. Every death sharpened the sense of having lived and made a history—"our ancestors that 8"—their names as fresh as when they challenged the academy and their students cheered. For Jo, the name of Henri was always first. Now that the last of the ancestors was gone, she and Edward were the front line. The younger generation of abstract artists was bearing down on their heels.

Reality took up much of the Hoppers' spring. At the meeting of the editorial board on the fourth of May, Jo "let it be known that I had procured the splendid note of Reality in yesterday's Times Book Review only because I anxious to go on record as having contributed something because I want to be let in too."[44] She also reported how "several of them thought well of my asking if anyone had thought of the need to have the name copywrited. They hadn't thought of that yet, but thought that would have to be done, when they get the money."[45] Jo understood: "It's such a beautiful name & if it's becoming stylish why not some shoe polish, baking powder or worse grab out for it, not to say other magazines."[46] She reflected again how Edward was getting over his original embarrassment at having her at meetings. On the eleventh of May, they went to a meeting of the membership committee of *Reality*. A week later, they met again at Wilson's. Jo noted how "Jack Levine was bent on expansion. Sol keeping very quiet."[47] On May twenty-fifth, representatives from the *Reality* editorial board met at the office of the publisher, Sam Golden. Both Hoppers were there, along with Poor, Wilson, Soyer, and Abe Lerner, a book designer who served as the production editor. Golden agreed to finance the second issue if the artists could get it out before July, so that no momentum would be lost, but none of them was willing to work on it before the fall. They went on to Wilson's for their last meeting that season. No one wanted to be president or secretary of the group.[48] Later that summer, Edward would report to du Bois: "We've had a big response to 'Reality' from all over the country, backing us up in our effort—several thousand letters in reply. We'd appreciate it if you could find time to write a little more for us."[49] He told Mumford *Reality* "is having a large and sympathetic response from all over the country."[50] Years later Abe Lerner vividly recalled seeing the Hoppers at the *Reality* meetings:

> They were like many couples who have lived together a long time, emotionally dependent but sniping. Edward was spare, lean in his expressions, but he was aware every minute what was going on. He didn't look at you directly when he spoke. He looked stern; I don't think I ever saw him smile. Jo was a very nervous person. I never remember her being relaxed. Edward was nervous under his mask of taciturnity.[51]

On the easel, meanwhile, there still was not a Hopper under construction. When *Reality* did not suffice for an excuse, there were always the movies. Hopper went to see *Come Back Little Sheeba* and came rushing back to insist that Jo had to see it at once.[52] His urgency shows that again, as so often, he had noticed parallels: the story of a nagging wife who lives for the day when her lost dog will return home was too close to the Hopper family legend of Jo's lifelong nostalgia for Arthur, her strayed tom.

When Lloyd Goodrich invited Jo to bring two or three canvases to the Whitney for consideration for the next painting Annual, it was Edward who made the selection. Jo wanted *Obituary* (page 406), but Edward told her that it would not have "a chance of getting in," preferring instead her picture of the clothesline at Truro, the view of their fire escape, and her picture of the Judson church tower.[53] She concluded: "What E. has picked out to take over to the Whitney aren't the ones I like best. He knows they are a tough lot & not apt to fancy my little fancies."[54] He was particularly insistent that the museum would not like her cats and flowers.[55] Edward even applied the varnish to the canvases before delivering them to the museum.[56] Jo was elated when Goodrich called to say that the museum would show her *Fire Escape.*[57]

On the eighteenth of May, the Hoppers attended the funeral of Yasuo Kuniyoshi, whose work had been shown in Venice with Edward's and who belonged to the old network of juries and prizes. Afterward they stopped by the gallery to see Frank Rehn, whom they found too tired and thin.

On the third of June, a glorious, cloudless day, Rutgers University presented Hopper with an honorary doctorate of letters. Jo thought he looked quite stunning in his spreading robe and tasseled cap.[58] It was a day of festivities and ceremony: travel by train from New York, then lunch at the president's house, brief speeches of introduction by faculty members; neither Hopper nor his fellow recipient, General Albert Gruenther, was required to make an acceptance speech. The following week, the Hoppers traveled by train to Youngstown, Ohio, where Edward served on a jury at the Butler Art Institute. Jo later wrote to the director's mother to thank her for her hospitality, and excused her fascination:

> For me as a painter it has been a valued experience to see just how pictures meet a jury, something one should understand so as not to be too bitter when one's picture is thrown out. They surely look their worst all jammed in together, self conscious, scared, pitiful then when chosen & classed with the accepted, blossom right out & when hung on the wall become handsome & distinguished (or merely smug.) This experience of watching them make their appearance before a jury meant a great deal to me. That is why it was hard to tear me away.[59]

Mustering tact, since her husband had rejected a painting submitted by her hostess's son, the director, Jo waxed philosophical: "It's a great responsibility to be a juror. Too much like playing God. Who knows enough?" and she sounded a personal note, "I do wish E. Hopper had had another look at your son's picture. Seen in a mob of discarded elements is as bad as unfriendly light. Jury decisions are far too hasty for just appraisal. . . . Thank God E. Hopper isn't in politics. We'd fetch up in jail for oversight—& pigheadedness too."[60]

§

WHILE EDWARD THWARTED and denied Jo's capabilities in any sphere that he claimed for himself, he was only too happy to slough off on her the responsibilities in what he considered the female realm, notably for his sister, Marion. It was Jo who saw to it that the checks they contributed to her support arrived, Jo who did her shopping at Macy's, checked the sales for stockings, compared prices on carpet sweepers, and worried whether the bus trip would be too tiring at Christmas. Once Marion had vented her long-nursed jealousy after her mother's death, and made her peace offering from her mother's jewels, she grew more and more to depend on Jo for emergencies when she knew that she could not expect sympathy from her brother. In April 1953, Marion's cat, Mitzi, whom Jo referred to as "the Siamese center of her forlorn universe," was dying and would soon need to be buried. Jo was summoned up to Nyack to arrange everything.[61] In the middle of June, Edward and Jo spent three days in Nyack, where they always left their best winter clothes and other valuables. When Marion protested that she did not have enough room to store Jo's new coat, Jo was livid: "She is an ugly bitch. Well life has made her so. Too shut in a smug environment. Can't listen to anything about my life & interests but a monologist about her own. . . . I think I've been pretty decent to her. . . . Always glad to get back from there."[62]

Trying to put her studio in order, Jo came across old copies of *The New York Times Book Review* and *The New Yorker*. Discarding them and personal papers put her too much in mind of old days and old friends. She came across her early oil sketches, including two from the first year she had painted outdoors: a Venice street scene with a leaning tower and a Haarlem scene with the Grote Kerk in the back. "Now what to do with them?" she puzzled. "And a lot of Gloucester & Ogunquit, fortunately unframed. Where & when stow away—if there were only anyone to give to—like my beautiful old New Yorkers, who would take them out of my hands, but not into garbage can."[63] When Edward told her to discard all her old boxes of mementos without going through them, she balked: "I'm not going to throw away the evidence & banish memories of dancing with Clifton Webb & Dmetri Romanofsky, little one man show at the Vanderbilt Studios. Russian Ballet & Yvette etc. etc. All too vivifying, one having a life of one's own even as the mother of Arthur. I not yet the tail of a dog however celebrated by Rutgers."[64] Unlike Edward, Jo was in no hurry to depart for the Cape. Only recently had she been discovering that the spring allowed her to use her unheated studio to paint a little and to show her work to her friends: "The poor little bastards have their stronghold in that rear studio & from early April I can haul them out of their stacks & they can come to life for a short period before we close up & leave for the Cape."[65]

Age did nothing to alleviate the packing nerves that always preceded their trips and that were aggravated by Edward's incurable need to play his "blue jay pranks":

> Awful row yesterday—awful—actual combat. E. grabbed off my shoes, so went about barefoot until exhausted when fell on bed. Later E. crept in & so cautiously washed off soles of feet while I lay there. Then said much in common with him & Mary Magdalene. He always thinks of the most amusing tricks after having driven me to actual distraction & exhaustion—like the time he rushed in to rub away my "lumbago" rubbed & scrubbed, not concerned what part of back afflicted. His method of dealing with wild beast whose tail he has previously twisted. That just it—twisted tail until fury results, then the victim always the guilty one. Sadistic—he sure is—his way of relieving boredom?[66]

To fight boredom, they took with them to the Cape thirteen library books, with some titles implying the kind of parallels they looked for, others simply pet themes: *De la Palette à l'Ecritoire* by André L'Hote; *Discordant Encounters* by Edmund Wilson; *The Egoist* by George Meredith; *Viva Mexico* by Charles M. Flandreau; and Carey McWilliams's *North from Mexico*. For Jo there were J. Donald Adams's *Literary Frontiers* and *Chats de Colette* by Willy (Colette); for Edward, Robert E. Lee's biography by Frederick Maurice; and for good measure, the biography of Stendhal by Matthew Josephson and three volumes of short stories, as well as the autobiography *Si le Grain ne Meurt,* by their old favorite, André Gide. *The Egoist* tells of a woman trapped in a marriage with a selfish man whom she wants to leave; the theme is a running motif in Jo's diaries. Jo gave Edward two more books for his birthday: a collection of short stories from *The New Yorker* and an illustrated copy of Longfellow's *Evangeline* printed in 1860.[67]

Edward read aloud to Jo as she mended the mattress pad gnawed over the winter by field mice. *Viva Mexico* was so engaging that it made them think of trying again the next winter. As Jo observed: "E. loves travel better than anything else. One truly wants him to be happy."[68] Travel as an antidote to ennui was a theme shared with Gide. The reading did not suffice to relieve Edward's chronic ennui, as he told Guy du Bois: "It was good of you to write me such a long letter, but I'm afraid I can not equal it. You see while you have all Paris to feed your thought upon, all that I have is Cape Cod's sand and water. It's because I've so little to say that I have not written before."[69] By the end of the month, his silences were getting to her again, bringing back memories and resentment from years before: "No wonder I talk to saleswomen, laundrymen. I'm so bottled up. And traveling with him—what a treat. No comment our Grand Canon, Bridal Veil Falls, Zion—he just absorbs, goes on living his inner life, one doesn't exist. No wish to share—share—share? He share? Why should he share?"[70]

Once they had set up the house for the season, Jo as usual plotted to get Edward going: "If E. doesn't start on his own steam, I'd better get started my self, that would exorcise him. It always does. But what on Earth would I find to begin on? The grasses & flowers are long dead, I can't do hills without having the car & E. can't see that."[71]

On August 4, the Hoppers attended Dick Magee's annual birthday party at Cobb Farm. Ethel Lisenby, who was then the Magees' cook, fixed in her mind the picture of Edward sitting in a corner, at most quietly talking with one other person, while Jo flitted about.[72] Concerned with the fate of *Reality,* the Hoppers went to visit Sol Wilson in Provincetown on the sixth of July to deliver some copies that they had brought up from New York and to talk about the future. Jo noted that there "seemed no enthusiasm over admitting Geo. Biddle to group," and she remarked that Karl Knaths had dropped out, "afraid of losing grace at the Mod. Mus."[73]

When they got around to reading L'Hote's collection of essays by painters,[74] they especially liked what Vlaminck had to say about Picasso, which Hopper took the trouble to copy by hand, clearly in agreement that "Picasso a étouffé, pour plusieurs générations d'artistes, l'esprit de création, la foi, la sincérité dans le travail et dans la vie" ("Picasso has snuffed out, for several generations of artists, the creative spirit, the faith, the sincerity in work and in life").[75] Jo noted in her diary: "Picasso has no real identity, taken from everybody, everywhere, but nature had withheld any real identity to this blasphemous mocker."[76] In a related vein, Hopper would later insist: "The most important thing for the artist is that he should reach his own essence. This is what gives him strength." Rafael Squirru, who elicited this remark in an interview, concluded: "He resents Picasso because he finds him capricious, although willing to admit that in his capricious images there is power; but it is not the power that Hopper seeks. . . . What annoyed him about Picasso was his 'chicness' that would make him sacrifice the fingers in a human hand for the sake of elegance. In this he preferred Rembrandt."[77]

As the summer wore on, Jo renewed her attack on Edward's objections to her driving. Declaring, "This year this prohibition must be lifted," she had insisted on going out with him to practice.[78] She reminded him "how the English suffragettes had to destroy the mail to interrupt the Eng. policy of just muddling thru own objective."[79] She even got Reggie McKeen, the friend who often took Edward sailing, to take her out to practice. All through it, she knew that Edward enjoyed contradicting her, which meant that she could never be playful with him, and she was perfectly aware of the roots: "It all goes back to his having been a tease when he was a boy. He'd tease, enjoyed teasing & it never got licked out of him. Teasing the beginning of sadism. Egotism, sadism, domination of its own furtive kind. He loves no one." In a word, Edward was "kind of monstrous."[80]

By the last week of August, neither of them had been able to paint. As she recorded his difficulties in starting, she admitted that she, too, felt "empty." The problem as she saw it was that they had fought so much over her driving, yet the problem was deeper and perennial: "It is so hard for me to accept E.'s limitations. I can't take it. It's so lonely to have him so absorbed in just himself & so full of scorn & negation & no generosity or anything outgoing."[81]

Finally, on August 27, Edward started his first canvas of the year. What with travel and *Reality* and juries, he had procrastinated, pleading no time for what Jo described as "the proper isolation for pictures."[82] He had driven to Harwich several times "for architectural details,"[83] and now he was blocking out his idea in charcoal: "There is a man at a desk between 2 corner windows & views outside from both of them & a lot of side wall outside building when man sits—so it's interior and exterior. . . . I don't dare to ask, pry into anything premeditated, just watch with live interest, ready to go produce whatever needed."[84] She was ready to fill her accustomed role as prop mistress; seeing that this time she would not be needed as a model, she offered to get someone to model for the man at the desk, but realized "that E. doesn't want the man to be too important with so many side walls to intrigue. E. has to get data for that desk."[85]

In the interim, Jo was trying to read Virginia Woolf's *Jacob's Room,* which she found "fascinating," which suggests that she sensed parallels with her own aesthetics, parallels that emerge from her notes on Woolf's style: "It so like a female, realizing, jumping about among so many objects with such skill of saying a lot, covering the ground to much telling effect."[86] She could recognize and appreciate a distinctly feminine style in Woolf's writing, which makes it all the more tragic that she lacked the confidence to distinguish the feminine style in her most original work, that most distant from Edward's style. She too often fell prey to his disparagement, as when he dismissed her pictures by placing them in such sexist categories as the output of "Lady Flower Painters."

The last day of August saw an explosion. While backing up the car in Wellfleet, with Edward shouting instructions from the sidelines, Jo locked the bumper onto a street sign. The police appeared and Edward was furious.[87] The repair for the fender would come to eight dollars.[88] Now he had his excuse to cut off her latest campaign. In response, Jo tried one of her old tactics. She stopped speaking, although she was never sure of the ultimate effect: "How droolingly tender he is of a fender & how devastatingly hoglike toward all my feeling for him. How little he prizes what he got for nothing from me. In roads on my very soul. He, the ego hero, he could destroy—how great he is; he can destroy to prove male superiority, male dominance."[89]

On that subject, she voiced doubts for the first time, again getting at quirks rooted deep in his boyhood, as she had of late: "And he isn't male at all. He couldn't get anywhere on his male qualities, he'd measure well below par. Is that why he must prove to himself he is male, getting back at me that he never did have the physical strength of a husky male."[90]

Only from him could she have heard and sensed these feelings of inferiority. She had no way of knowing his early drawings of himself taking a beating from his boxing pal, but she takes stock again of their life and again sees parallels to his character built into his paintings:

> Life shared with E.H. has been a dull life, not with standing Mexico, Richmond, the Corcoran & Carnegie. It's been so exclusive his life—of course I've fitted in, what ever I had went into it. . . . All that is so splendid in him seems walled up in his own egocentricity. One gets so bruised against those walls—part of his consciousness out of which he builds the walls of his lighthouses. Let all flimsy feathery things beware![91]

Pain like that which produced her hunger strikes brings her again to the image of the lighthouse with dead birds. Yet she could see that his harshness was not just personal. She told herself that Edward treated everyone as a competitor, remembering his zest for winning and his delight in playing chess.[92] Ruefully she thought how Annette Chatterton, the wife of one of Edward's oldest friends, had once told her that she, Jo, had "humanized him."[93]

By the ninth of September, Hopper was still working on his canvas:

> It is making great strides. I've learned never to think anything doomed to flop. It's come to life—man working at desk inside window—sure enough interior established right off. Now white light on white wall of exterior. E. worrowing how to make left side of wall protrude from canvas . . . & make this wall a good perpendicula with roofs of houses opposite window out of which man looks straight ahead. What the man doing? Architect? Advertising layout man? Not N.Y.—Podunk, E. says.[94]

Hopper finished the canvas on the twelfth of September, although he still had no name for it. Jo suggested: "young man in airconditioned office" as a possibility.[95]

On September 13, late on a Sunday afternoon, just as the Hoppers were leaving for Wellfleet to pick up *The New York Times,* Henry Poor appeared with the news that Frank Rehn had suffered a stroke and was in the hospital in Gloucester.[96] The very next day they made the long trip to see him. To their relief, he recognized them, but he had trouble speaking, and they worried about his recovery.[97] Not only were they genuinely fond of Rehn, but Hopper had never had another dealer.

The trip made them fall "in love with Gloucester all over again, its very special character, like nowhere else. Houses large and formidable & solid standing up over the sea in bold outline, fit to contain history."[98] After visiting Rehn, they dropped by Our Lady of Good Voyage on Prospect Street, which both had painted: "One lit one's candle, dragged forth by E. who can take just so much."[99] The next day they sought out Rocky Neck, where they had painted watercolors together and laughed at the parallels to themselves in the puppet show that featured a "long & gangly frog" wooing a female mouse.[100]

Anxious to see what was happening at the gallery, they returned to New York City a month earlier than usual. At the opening (on October 14) of the Whitney's Annual Exhibition of Contemporary American Painting, which included both Edward's *Hotel by a Railroad* and Jo's *Convent across the Square through Fire Escape,* Jo felt in her element once again. She was proud to be included and she felt important because she was able to bring fresh news about Frank Rehn to all their friends. The next day, she and Edward visited the gallery, only to learn that Frank seemed to be worse.

Jo reported that Edward's canvas, "the man in concrete wall, doesn't look nearly so good away from Cape light"; he planned to work on it some more in the city.[101] Despite the difference between October light in New York and late summer light on Cape Cod, he managed to complete the work to his satisfaction and on October 28 delivered *Office in a Small City* to Clancy at the Rehn Gallery.

They had taken advantage of their absence to have their studios painted over the summer, but now they had trouble getting things back into place. Only a meeting of *Reality* to put together a second issue got them to dress up and go out. Someone, just back from Paris, reported that Jean Cassou, a famous critic at the Musée National d'Art Moderne, had admired Hopper's work, finding him the only truly American artist in "Twelve Modern American Painters and Sculptors," a show circulated in Europe by the Museum of Modern Art.[102]

Returning to the Whitney, Jo was interested "to observe how people skip to corner with my picture that seems pretty wan, light meat among all those eats-em-alive products."[103] That night, Edward wanted to walk home from the movies. Jo was apprehensive in the long, dark streets of Greenwich Village, having read in the newspaper of recent muggings on West Twelfth Street. She noted that Edward "doesn't walk so briskly either. Oh dear—he used to, now I go too fast for him."[104]

The next day, Edward yelled to Jo, "So—you're in the New Yorker!" Robert Coates had mentioned Edward, Jo, and Henry Varnum Poor as the three realists that he found acceptable.[105] Jo could do no less than pay yet a third visit to the Whitney. Meeting some friends, she reveled in her moment of glory. She recorded in her diary how Rosalind Irvine told her of hearing "the big, booming voice of Philip Evergood sounding out thru the room as he stood before my picture maintaining that that was what he called good painting!"[106] Jo was incredulous: "Imagine you. Could it be that he happened only to be standing & discussing something else? More likely, one would think. Why ever that big bruiser would fancy my painting—or another big husky, Robt. Coates singling it out too! It about the frailest I have too."[107]

Jo arranged to paint a canvas of the information desk at the Whitney Museum on Eighth Street just before their move to West Fifty-fourth Street the following spring. She worked on Mondays when the museum was closed and on mornings before they opened for the day. The painting was giving her trouble, and she asked Edward "if he wasn't curious to see what I was doing—but he said 'Oh, I know what it's like.' Well if it were he who was struggling over something with which I had had plenty of experience, I'd never have let him flounder & been crazy to do something to help."[108] She never failed to feel fresh surprise at every new proof of the depths of Edward's selfishness: "He didn't much want to pose for hands either & here I've posed for every female form that has appeared in his pictures for nearly the last 30 years—29 to be exact . . . tall, short, fat, lean, young, old, what a collection."[109] Finally, when she finished her canvas, he agreed to come help her decide if she should show it to the museum staff: "Oh, let them see. It's a cute little thing but has no guts."[110] By way of improvement, he counseled sacrificing color, her aesthetic, to build the drama of shadow and light.

At a general meeting of *Reality* on the evening of November 17 at Sol Wilson's, the group decided to seek an abridged version of Maurice Grosser's proposed article on art education in universities. Both Nicolai Cikovsky and Raphael Soyer mentioned seeing Jo's painting at the Whitney.[111] On the way home from the *Reality* meeting, she recorded, Edward held her arm: "How glad I am to be there for him to do this. It hurts that he should feel the need— if it is for steadying, but I shall want always to be there for that purpose"; at this, the thought returned of her own infirmity: "But my eyes aren't so good either. . . . I found my sight not so good at Macy's."[112]

With the arrival of the cold, Edward was discouraging Jo from working in her studio. Yet she remembered thirty years earlier when Edward was "in the farther back studio working there during dire weather with old gas stove surrounded by screens to keep heat in. Luck day I arrived to humanize those quarters fit only for a grizzly bear."[113] She recalled how only then did Edward get water in his studio, after Anne Tucker introduced them to the rector for Sailors' Snug Harbor, the old owner. Thoughts of Anne set off another of Jo's reveries about lost friends: besides Anne and her husband, Sam, she thought again of Henri, Sloan, Miller, Ambrose Webster, Magda, Peggy Rehn.

For once Jo could feel satisfied. She was in the Whitney Annual and mentioned in the press. "Max Weber had spoken in praise of" her picture, she learned from Marie Appleton, who worked at the front desk.[114] That she had made her mark and won respect in the circle of *Reality,* even Edward had conceded. Driving was not an issue, with the car on blocks in Nyack.

Yet there were too many memories and hurts. At the opening of a show of the work of Sidney Laufman, she spoke of her "predicament" with the artists Maurice and Lee Sievan. Later, she felt embarrassed enough to write to the couple: "Back home I was thoroughly disgusted to have croaked about me—me—who should have stayed home if I can't take 57th St. yet."[115] She wanted them to visit her studio, but had to explain that its unheated condition meant that they would have to postpone their visit until spring, when there would also be good daylight. Only then could she "have friends in for tea. My husband is such a hermit, all teas must be in my domain."[116]

After dragging its feet for years, the Metropolitan Museum was on the verge of opening a new American wing. The museum purchased *Office in a Small City* from Rehn's in time to hang it in the opening on December 17. Jo was taken aback to learn that the evening's glamorous entertainment was reserved for a show of French painting, but the curator, Robert Hale, invited the living American artists to his penthouse. Jo talked at length with Russell Lynes, the writer, only to realize that he was the brother of George Platt Lynes, whose photograph of her she had liked very much.[117] Among the others at the Hale party were Andrew Wyeth, Stuart Davis, and Jackson Pollock. Wyeth recalled that after Davis and Pollock had been arguing about issues concerning methods and techniques, Hopper "tapped Davis on the shoulder and pointed from the penthouse to the incredible light of the setting sun on the buildings. 'Can you ignore that?' he asked, going on to say: 'People are starved for content today.' " According to Wyeth, at least for a moment conversation stopped.[118]

For Christmas, the Hoppers invited Katherine Proctor to dinner at home. Jo displayed her little crèche in the studio, telling Proctor how it was "associated with Arthur's return—Xmas 1923" and adding, "Nice to have bits contributed by my darling Eddy of that long ago period—he part of it too."[119]

The year came to a close with new worry about Edward's health. On the advice of his doctor, he was going to have surgery for a hernia during January.[120] Looking back, Jo made a list of the good things that had come their way in 1953, adding a postscript: "May we always be together & when the time comes, go together to help each other enter upon the new."[121]

TAKING STOCK: 1954

IN 1954 it was with more than usual confidence that Jo performed her annual ritual of beginning a new canvas. Having no subject in mind, she pulled out her collection of old sketches to search for an idea. She also took courage to submit a canvas for a show at the Pennsylvania Academy of the Fine Arts. As for Edward, on the first of the year he took the Fifth Avenue bus to the end of the line for an exploratory look. Jo reflected that he "is beginning to worry about my easel getting in his way when he paints. Well that is fine if he is planning to start something. Poor lamb, he has such long waits before he finds anything he likes enough to do. Think he hoping to hit on an idea in bus today."[1]

A week later, Edward, reluctant to go out in the rain, sent Jo alone to a party at John D. Rockefeller's guest house, saying that she "always came home with eyes shining."[2] She reported, in fact, a great time, remarking the modern decor and contemporary art, even though she disliked what she saw. Among the guests she thought worth mentioning were artists Edwin Dickinson, Ben Shahn, Jacques Lipchitz, and Mark Tobey. The latter "spoke admiringly of E.H.—drew on his paper napkin a canvas of E. that he remembered seeing in Seattle—the Williamsburg Bridge I guess—he remember[s] the deep blue sky, the pink of the houses facing loop of the bridge & a white figure at a window."[3]

Edward, too, ventured out, for the opening of a George Grosz retrospective at the Whitney, although the art was not to his liking. In Jo's hearing he remarked, implying a contrast with his own indirection: "Fine satirists always want to be known as something else." He tried to avoid meeting Grosz, only to bump into him in the coat room.[4] To Jo's praise of the German émigré's caricatures, Edward retorted: "But you can't be that mad all the time."[5]

Jo was bitter when her painting was rejected by the jury at the Pennsylvania Academy of Fine Arts, though her resentment abated after she learned that Charles Burchfield had not been one of the jurors.[6] When she got her picture home, Edward pointed out that the work's new silver frame, which she had not really examined closely, was reason enough for the jury to pass it by.[7]

On January 18, the Hoppers attended another meeting of *Reality* at Wilson's. With the second issue about to appear, they talked of plans for a third. Jo observed that Edward "almost never opens his mouth. Sol Wilson is a good Solomon, what he said is always very wise."[8]

The fate of the Rehn Gallery was causing concern. After a dinner of the Society of Arts and Letters on January 22, Hopper had a chance to discuss the situation with Reggie Marsh. John Clancy was now managing the gallery, taking on new painters and giving them shows, "at the expense of the old members."[9] Edward told Jo that "Frank himself [was] not such a good picker of quality. How much less good will John be."[10] Jo was even less confident than Edward, who argued that she did not understand why Marsh, Burchfield, and he would "permit the several thousands due them be squandered on John's choice of talent," noting "John has none of the social grace or background of Frank R."[11]

Worries about the gallery had to yield to those at home. After a bout with the Internal Revenue Service, over failing to pay the new self-employment tax for three years, Hopper made his way once more to New York Hospital, this time for the hernia operation. Left alone, Jo regretted that she could not get to bed early because of doing "silly things" like writing in her diary:

> Heavens knows why I am impelled to keep records that could have interest to no one. I never reread. They're not specially about the life as he knows it of a great man. His life [is] so more or less uneventful as day by day record. He reads all the time, reads while I try to talk with him, do[es] crossword puzzles, enlarges his culture, contemplates silently himself, devoid of any generous concern for anybody else & for him all goes well. He wears a benign expression in public & everyone approves of the cut of him, tho his interest in them is of the slightest.... He shares nothing of importance to another's ego.... He's highly competitive—I win, you lose. He's fed on his victory over

me. And I never dreamed competition was to enter in our lives. I so deeply grateful for everything vainglorious that came his way & did everything to further his interests. What a blow to have it slowly dawn on me, he couldn't trump up any live interest in anyone but himself. In summing it all up, I realize with much bitterness I've been swindled of all the deeply human values. . . . Take[s] me & my efforts in his behalf entirely for granted. And in my own eyes, I'm humiliated. . . . While I am here alone. I feel all this. I can't bear that he, the leit motif of my life can be so ruthlessly selfish & egotistic. He pays the rent. . . . It hurts me so that he should be so limited in his own ability to include me in his own soul—make the effort of a partnership. . . . The sum total of his success is so without warmth, that the chill is destroying me—the chill of this realization. Some one of the I suppose lesser critics said his light had brilliance—but no warmth. This understanding struck me as psychic. Oh, I should bring him warmth, should I? And why? . . . Such thought of generosity outrages me— why ever breathe into such monster that which he is incapable. He is capable only of taking, other wise the line is dead.[12]

This latest regrouping of memory was so strong, that on Edward's second day in the hospital, January 28, she did not even go to see him; she had come down with a cold, but above all, her awareness had reached a new height.

Hopper had the first of two operations for his hernia in early February. Jo had seen him the day before, but she was not there when he was taken into surgery. He came through the operation in good shape, but two days later he was suffering the aftereffects. Jo found herself tending to him with devotion: "How could I stand the desolation if he were gone?"[13] On February 9, after the second operation, Jo suffered to see him in pain and realized that he was counting on her to be there. He kept wanting to hold her hand. Six days later, he was well enough to complain of boredom.[14] He was released from the hospital on February 17.[15]

Hopper's dependence on his wife throughout this ordeal did not make him more charitable about her painting. To Jo, "very sad" when the Martha Jackson Gallery, though advertising for artists, showed no interest in her, he could only say, "It's all in your work,"[16] forcing her to repeat: "He is without any human sympathy . . . to all intents & purposes, he is dead. As a human being he doesn't qualify."[17] With the hurt, driven ever more deeply home, transmuting resentment into the rudiments of biography, Jo virtually seethed:

I yearn to smash his glasses, something that would reach his complacency if only in a physical way. He owes everything to Guy du Bois

for liking his work—or wanting to like the work of an old schoolmate. Then Forbes Watson, looking about for something to write
about hit on E.H. Maybe it was Guy put him on to it. Both of these
very effective persons & E.H. was launched. They told the world
what to like.[18]

She especially regretted that she had been unable to exhibit her watercolors,
recalling a group of them that she had inadvertently left in storage in Nyack.
Coming back to her anxiety that she had "no one to leave them to," she consoled herself: "I rejoice they aren't lost—that would be the last straw!"[19]

It was only in June that Hopper finally found enough strength and concentration to paint again. When he presumed on their familiar pattern, and
called on Jo to pose, his nastiness of the winter had faded enough that she
agreed. While he worked away, Jo, referring to Virginia Woolf's book, wrote
to Rosalind Irvine of the Whitney inviting her over to "lap ice tea in this
'Room of My Own' that I have to enjoy only when heated by warm weather.
It's just too much labor to get coal dragged from the cellar to heat it."[20] She
added: "Grand if you could bring Lloyd, though well I know how busy you
both are. Edward is working on a new canvas, tell Lloyd."[21] Both Goodrich
and Irvine took her up on her invitation.

The predominantly gray picture that emerged did not please Jo, who, all
the same, entered into her usual interpretive game, identifying the woman as
a "blond girl with reddish blond hair in pink slip—polparot type."[22] More
than a year later, she again commented: "I can't bear pol parrot women & he
didn't need to make her that way. It just happened & when Lloyd G.
[Goodrich] came & said it looked like his sister, E. never fixed it altho the picture not finished & he could have given it one more shot which he probably
would have if L.G. had [not] looked in just then."[23] Jo was correct in her judgment that this painting is unresolved; the legs of the figure do not seem to
connect properly to the torso above. *City Sunlight* stands out as one of Hopper's weaker paintings of his mature period.

After a spring with so much of what she had called "real rendering, what
going on within," it was a relief for Jo to have the familiar trivia of the summer. In her best country newspaper style, Jo chronicled the presences at the
Edwin Dickinson home in Wellfleet, where the party included the abstract
artist Hans Hofmann and his wife, Mitz; the illustrator Edward Wilson and
his wife, Dorothy; their neighbor Davis Herron, and his wife, Elsa-Ruth;
Raphael Soyer, Edward's colleague on the *Reality* editorial board, and his
wife, Rebecca; the resident portrait painter Jerry Farnsworth and his wife,
the artist Helen Sawyer; and the poet Conrad Aiken, never as high on their
list as Frost.[24]

Two days later, after the Soyers came for tea, Jo described Rebecca Soyer as "a nice girl, just what one would have chosen for that saintly & sweet Raphael."[25] Soyer recalled that when he and Rebecca arrived they found Edward sitting in front of the house and "Jo sitting in the back."[26] He recorded Jo's explanation: "That's what we do all the time. . . . He sits in his spot and looks at the hills all day, and I look at the ocean, and when we meet there's controversy, controversy, controversy."[27] When Soyer inquired what Hopper was working on, he said: "I'm waiting for November when the shadows are longer and the landscape becomes more interesting, in fact, beautiful."[28]

News came in early July of Reginald Marsh's sudden death.[29] Hopper later sent an article about it to du Bois in Paris, commenting: "It seems odd that one built like a bull should go so soon. A simple nice boy."[30] They continued to worry about Rehn, who remained in the hospital after his stroke.

By now in their seventies, and twenty years in the house, the Hoppers still had not been able to obtain the easements necessary to run electric lines. One neighbor, Joan Colebrook, a writer who had purchased the former Dos Passos house, refused to give them permission. So they had to arrange to come from another direction, over a greater distance, passing over the railroad tracks. Despite the expense, Jo was adamant; she insisted that they needed a telephone for possible medical emergencies. They also longed for power for the water pump engine, a refrigerator instead of only their cellar's coolness, and for electric light. Jo complained of "getting tired stumbling about in the dark & doing all our night reading by kitchen lamp—& cooking in dark side room & washing dishes by candlelight & toting things down into dark cellar."[31]

In Wellfleet, the Hoppers ran into Bessie Breuer, who, true to her placement among Jo's tombstones of pet peeves, took it upon herself to insinuate to Edward that he and his wife vacation apart. Some nerve, thought Jo: "I snapped plenty when she tried to suggest to E. that we should have a vacation from each other. So that she could land in to snap up E. That her famed method—suggestion. She who stole the husband & broke up the home of his best friend years ago. She's a menace."[32] Jo now ignored the younger woman's accomplishment as a novelist and short-story writer.

Viewing the twentieth anniversary of the house as another occasion for taking stock, Jo described what it was like to live on the Cape with a man who was determined

> to do as little as possible so as to get back to his printed matter—his natural element, even as water to a fish & I'm exasperated—here alone on a remote sand bar with him with eyes glued to a page. Certainly he works—at routing things, at that he makes wide strokes & is thru with speedily so as to be back at his print, until he feels it's his

duty to eat, hungry or not, he must obey the clock. Then I'm to de-
vise what we can eat. The variety restricted with no refrigeration &
food 14 miles + round trip.[33]

Embroidering on the theme of the bookworm, she gave their inveterate game
of identifying with literary parallels a new and more comprehensive thrust,
breaking new biographical ground and throwing back Edward's barbed bon
mot that compared her with Socrates' shrewish wife:

> I'm so tired from the strain of all this. For 30 yrs. E. has argued every
> step of the way, argued & obstructed. In this he finds an unholy sat-
> isfaction. Thru me he gains the distinction of having the same kind
> of wife as Moliére, Socrates, Abe Lincoln, Horace Greeley etc. What
> those poor wives had to put up with from those damned egotists.[34]

Months later, Jo came across her record of an exchange with Edward.
Often she had referred to him as just an ugly duckling when she found him,
now she told him of "the Golden Swan—advice given young girl about to
marry—often young man not yet a golden swan she must make him one."

> I'm no golden swan—Moi—I'm a winged skunk.
> Someone we know called me your "dancing star."
> Oh, certainly, but one takes that for granted.[35]

Hurricane Carol hit the Cape on the last day of August, but without real
damage to the house. Just after the storm, the electricity began working and
they soon acquired an electric lamp for the bedroom, their first refrigerator,
telephone, and electric water pump. Telephones and electricity were already
spreading across America at the time of Hopper's birth in 1882. The basic
conveniences of the twentieth century caught up with him in Truro only at
age seventy-two in 1954. On September 11, Hurricane Edna struck. In anticipation, Dick Magee had brought over a battery-powered radio so that the
Hoppers could stay informed of the storm's progress. They watched as the
big north window in the studio bellied inward with the winds and were relieved that it held fast. As they mopped up the water that blew in around the
window sills and door jambs, they lost power and had to pull out the faithful
kerosene lamps that they had used for twenty years.

The Hoppers' initial misgivings about John Clancy's ability to carry on at
the gallery proved unfounded. By the end of 1954 alone, he had sold more
than thirty thousand dollars' worth of Edward's paintings, most of them that
summer. Hopper's work had attracted the attention of two major private col-

lectors and several museums. Joseph Hirshhorn bought four oils: *Gloucester Street, Eleven A.M., First Row Orchestra,* and *Hotel by a Railroad.* Roy Neuberger purchased the canvas *Barbershop,* and the watercolor *Gravel Bar, White River.* Hopper was particularly happy to have sold some of his older work, including the large *Barber Shop* from 1931 and *Gloucester Street* from 1926.

The sudden rise in sales did not quiet concerns about shifting critical fortunes. When George Stout, the director of the Worcester Art Museum, invited Hopper to show in "Five Painters of America," he replied:

> I hope though that in the publicity to be given this show there will be no reference to the "American Scene." There is a stigma attached to this designation in the public's mind, that implies a rustic lack of sophistication on the part of the art so called that is far from the truth.
>
> If one looks out of one's window in Ohio, Massachusetts, or California, and reports honestly what one sees and feels with one's personal vision of the world in command, that will be one's interpretation of the American scene. It is part of our daily existence. Even the mystics can not ignore it.
>
> This is a simplification of the matter, but it will do for now.[36]

In part he was still fighting battles of the thirties, when nationalism had been in vogue, but he may also have wanted to head off more recent writers, who had attempted to demonstrate a link between the program of "American Scene" painting and Nazi and Fascist art.[37]

As autumn came on and Edward showed no sign of any new ideas, Jo plotted again how to get him started. She proposed going to Orleans so that she could work on a watercolor of a tree, and he drove her with rare indulgence. More provocative still, she made new demands to drive, at which, though more grudgingly, he actually rigged some lengths of clothesline to guide her in learning to back the car into the garage. None of it stirred him to paint.

Departing early, the Hoppers returned to New York in mid-October, to be present for a television interview before the opening party of the Whitney Museum in its new location on West Fifty-fourth Street. When Hopper was asked "why he was accepted by both the traditionalists and the Museum of Modern Art," he responded: "That is true, and it's rather puzzling to me also," suggesting, "It may be that because my pictures have a basis of geometric design the advance guard accept me as one of them. I don't know how many do, but some do."[38] The broadcast elicited a letter from Chatterton, prompting Hopper to write his old school friend: "I am pleased that I am one of your favorite personalities on television. Perhaps it was the new Brooks coat that influenced you. The only tangible results so far is a bad cold in the head, that I seem to have acquired at the museum."[39]

Hopper continued to promote *Reality* and to work on the next issue. That December, he sent a copy of the second number to du Bois in Paris, writing proudly: "There has been a great response to 'Reality' with letters from all over the country in accord with one's point of view. I sent Bernard Berenson the first and second issues of 'Reality' and asked him if he would comment on them. He replied in a nice letter and sent me an article of his that had appeared in an Italian paper saying that I could use it for our magazine, in whole or in part. I think we shall use it."[40] With *Reality,* Hopper had successfully linked up with a group of younger artists who validated both his work and his principles. For him, the venture was a process of renewal.

PERSONAL VISION: 1955

IN OCTOBER 1954, Hopper had written to Chat: "I am thinking of getting a new car soon, and if I do I certainly will come to Poughkeepsie to show it off. I do not know when that will be though, for we may go to Mexico again before long."[1] In fact, he was loathe to replace his adored 1939 Buick, having jealously husbanded it against Jo's inroads and lovingly seen to having every fender she bent repaired. In the end he brought himself to acquire another used car in Nyack, although winter kept him from bringing it into the city at once to have the green glass windshield replaced.

On January 31, 1955, Jo and Edward attended a meeting of *Reality* at Sol Wilson's. The graphic designer Abe Lerner volunteered to do "all the editorial drudgery for nothing."[2] Joe Hirsch suggested that all of "the members of the Reality Group be required to send in answers to question. What kind of people we wished to be reached by my pamphlet."[3] Jo noted that Isabel Bishop opposed this suggestion, which she herself thought appealing. She was anxious that Bishop, whom she suspected of complicity in rejecting her grant application to the National Institute of Arts and Letters, still wanted to push her out of the group. Only later did it occur to Jo that the organization might not "want 2 Hoppers appearing on the same program," when it turned out that Edward had been awarded the gold medal for painting that year.[4]

Being chosen for the gold medal brought Hopper "much satisfaction," but as he wrote to Marc Connelly, the president of the Institute, it also brought anxiety regarding his acceptance speech: "I shall be scared stiff upon addressing all those faces, either critical or uncritical, as I have never before spoken to so many. Three or four at a time have been, heretofore, my limit."[5]

Hopper was the first painter to win the Institute's gold medal since 1950, when it had gone to John Sloan, and only the sixth painter ever to win the medal since its inception in 1909.[6] Henry Varnum Poor, who had nominated Hopper, with Burchfield and Bishop as seconders, explained his nominee's qualifications: "In a time of utmost confusion in contemporary painting, Edward Hopper has followed his own course with singular integrity, & with such clarity of design & intention that he stands now as a landmark in American painting."[7] Bishop enthusiastically called Hopper the "most outstanding living contributor to the art of painting in America."[8]

When another enthusiast, Richard Stark, a young plastic surgeon and amateur artist, asked Edward to comment on a monograph he had written, both Hoppers were dismayed. They had known Stark and his wife, Janet, since 1948, when Edward was a patient in New York Hospital. Jo noted that Stark "harping in his simplicity would think E. was a dolt—fatuous dolt. How obtuse not to realize he is highly sophisticated & extremely critical—not given to glibness."[9] She was particularly offended when she caught Stark putting "quotes about his own obnoxious paraphrases & negating all E.'s wit & terseness."[10] Jo wrote him to say as much, expressing surprise that he had not discovered that Hopper was a "complicated creature, & highly critical. . . . All E. wants is to slip by unnoticed, unchallenged, to go his own gait."[11] Stark, who was well-meaning if naive, must have been hurt by the Hoppers' severity, for he later declined to talk about his relationship with them.[12]

An interviewer for *Art Digest,* Suzanne Burrey, described the austerity of Hopper's studio: "The gray walls and high ceiling, a handsome coal stove with the black pipe casting a shadow against a smooth wall, an etching press, a wooden box and a large, heavy easel. . . . The rest of the room is furnished with early-American tables and chairs, antiques."[13] Jo told her that Edward "doesn't paint any of this. Nor the bedroom with its wonderful corners. I paint what he doesn't." Burrey contrasted Jo's studio ("a large, workable space of a room . . . filled with paintings. On her easel is a view over the rooftop of a Mexican church") with Edward's, where "nothing is on display. . . . There is nothing on his easel." Burrey made much of Hopper's "American individualism," "common sense," and unadorned "integrity."

On a bitter cold day in February, Hopper went to the American Museum of Natural History after they had listened to "Invitation to Learning on Walt

Whitman."[14] Jo was inspired to reflect about Whitman's intellect, always alert for parallels:

> It would seem he not so unsophisticated as he would let on—did a lot of reading of classics, etc. not confessed to—Leaves of Grass really his workshop from which the masterpieces evolved—or could be taken out in polished form from the matrix—he polished nuggets. Time & space his great concern—could realize them on a ferry boat—or an ocean liner. Could Ash Can School have derived from him? They would adore him. Mother Bird N. [Jo's mother, Mary Ann Nivison] had her reservations in front of the Alexander portrait [of Whitman].[15]

Jo was correct in her assessment that Whitman had been important for painters of their era, including her teacher Henri, whose taste for everyday reality won the sobriquet of "Ash Can School." Pertinent to Hopper was Henri's stress on Whitman's value as "autobiography—not of haps and mishaps, but of his deepest thought."

Meanwhile, Mexico was on the agenda again. The summer's reading outweighed the previous winter's chills, and now the prospect of avoiding the inevitable ceremonials of the Institute added a further lure. Jo stocked up on extra stretchers and canvas, purportedly for her, but actually she planned to coax Edward to paint the Sierra Madre. Before their departure, she wanted to make a provision in their will for someone to inherit their house on the Cape. She concluded miserably that there was no one who had helped her with her work in recent years, finally favoring Martha Kantor because she had "taste," but Edward preferred Julia Chatterton, the daughter of his old friend, even though Chat had never done anything for Jo's work. "It's quite sickening," she realized, "not to know any body at all of whom I have the memory of wanting some good to come to my poor little bastards. Hopper bastards—wall flowers—among such indifferent prima donnas."[16]

On February 23, the Hoppers attended the opening party for retrospective shows of Jack Levine and Hyman Bloom. Edward got very tired, but Jo felt much better at the chance to socialize with a group that she was proud to feel part of—the *Reality* crowd, who rallied for Levine, as a member of the editorial board.

When Edward went for a medical checkup to clear the way for their Mexican trip, his doctor remarked on the Hoppers' Christmas card, which depicted a choir boy with his neck raised in song. In what Jo described as "an unusual spirit of blythness," Edward had written on several, including those for the doctor and Lloyd Goodrich: "Peace on Earth, goodwill to men—& To

Hell with Women."[17] She knew the style only too well as that of the boy who teased. All that surprises is the equanimity of her response.

Because Edward contracted a bad cold, the departure for Mexico was delayed long enough to let them attend one last meeting of *Reality,* March 28. Fifteen or sixteen people came for a final review of the next issue before it was sent to press. A dispute broke out over two articles, one of them a protest piece by William Gropper, which Henry Varnum Poor feared might result in lost commissions for the *Reality* artists.[18]

On the last day of March, the Hoppers left for Mexico. They spent twenty-three days in Monterrey because Edward was weak and tired, and did not feel up to painting. When a local doctor changed his prescriptions, he began to mend, but the planned sojourn had to be curtailed. On the return trip, with Jo taking the wheel for the first time, Edward became so irritated that he tried to find a traffic cop to force her to stop driving. On May 1 they were back in New York, never to try Mexico again.

In anticipation of the gold medal from the National Institute of Arts and Letters, the art editor of *Time,* Alexander Eliot, projected an article. Taking the couple to lunch, he suggested that he might compare Hopper to T. S. Eliot, his uncle, at which Hopper objected that he "was much more enthusiastic about Robt. Frost."[19] In the end, Eliot wrote merely stressing Hopper's "deeply poetic view of the world," offering a corrective to common assumptions that he described: because Hopper's "sober realism is as different from the abstractionism now in fashion as it is from straight illustration, some abstractionists discuss him as a mere illustrator."[20]

It was Henry Varnum Poor who presented Hopper with the gold medal for distinguished achievement at the National Institute for Arts and Letters on the twenty-fifth of May. Even though the Institute offered to reimburse them for taxis, the Hoppers insisted on taking both a bus and the subway uptown to 157th Street and Broadway and back. Hopper wrote to Felicia Geffen, explaining, "My spending habits have been so conditioned by my early days, that I never take a taxi if I can get there otherwise."[21]

Poor's presentation began: "I have never known a man so sparing of words as Hopper nor a painter with a more spare use of paint, but this silent person and these sparse paintings both have a peculiar and powerful eloquence. Can integrity just in itself give off such beautiful and benign radiations that you feel them in your bones?" he asked, and answered: "I think it does when it occurs in such rare purity as in Hopper. This complete integrity, this utter honesty and lack of affectation, both in the man and in his paintings underlies everything else that can be said about Hopper."[22]

Having intended to avoid the public appearance by being in Mexico, Hopper had written a brief acceptance to be read by Poor:

The onus attached to the winning of medals in the arts, if not in war, often causes some hesitance in acceptance, a hesitancy not understood by the layman and perhaps construed by him as false modesty, or God knows what.

One cannot quibble with or refuse this crown of thorns, but accept the honor and generosity and the intention in which it is conferred, with gratitude to the members of the Academy and the Institute who liked my painting well enough to believe that I should receive this medal.[23]

In the event, Hopper just stood up and took a bow. Jo knew the attitude only too well: "How he has capitalized his being so shy—laying the burden of fetching everything to him by others who appreciate shyness but could weary of this labor for all the appreciating manifested by E.H. who so well realizes he needn't make any effort."[24] Her insight would prove ironically apt when the time came for Edward to reciprocate on behalf of Poor.

The Hoppers attended the last *Reality* meeting of the season at Joseph Floch's studio, where they went over new proof sheets and worked on layout. Jo noted that Maurice Grosser, with his article "Revolt of the Critics," was trying "to attract the attention of the Partisan Review."[25] Among the younger members of the group, the Hoppers felt closest to Raphael Soyer. They attended a dinner party at Soyer's house where Jo found his portrait of his Russian immigrant parents "a very sympathetic performance."[26] To reciprocate, on June 23, Jo held a tea party for Raphael and Rebecca Soyer and Germaine and Joseph Hirsch, which Soyer later described: "In Jo's studio there was a permanent, never-changing exhibition of her paintings—pictures of her small, crammed world, of Truro, flower pieces, interiors of rooms, and pictures of cats and pot-bellied stoves."[27] Since the Soyers were going to Cape Ann later that summer, Jo showed Rebecca her early watercolor of *Our Lady of Good Voyage* (page 170).

When the Hoppers took their car to Nyack for repairs and spent the night with Marion, the preacher of the Baptist church, where Marion was active and had become "a deaconess," dropped by to meet her famous brother. According to Jo, "E. had very little to say & went off to tend to car."[28] Edward's dislike of company was exceeded only by his disdain for religion and all its touts.

Picking up the mail that had been forwarded to Marion's house during their trip, the Hoppers found Bartlett Hayes's book *The Naked Truth and Personal Vision*. Hopper replied to Hayes, the director of the art gallery of Andover Academy: "I do not know what the 'Naked Truth' is, but I know that a 'personal vision' is the most important element in a painter's equipment, but it must be *communicated* [doubly underlined]."[29] Here Hopper reiterates what he saw as the purpose of his art and explains why he found abstraction so meaningless.

In her growing tendency to take stock, the repetition of a ritual like going back to Truro triggered a memoir that broke new biographical ground:

> After 31 yrs. of this state of heart, I have little joy of returning to this beautiful little house that has meant so much to us since we bought the hill & set the house on its top, overlooking the hills from one side, the east & on the west—the sea coming in & out over our very own beach—with full view of the sun, a huge flaming ball sinking down into the water on the horizon. . . . But there is nothing left in me with which to rejoice. He finds a way to do that to me. He resents that I should rejoice. He's a killer, that's what he really is. And that so greatly touted integrity applies only to the most obvious & material considerations. So often I'm the victim of that integrity—see the brave big creature kick his wife in the breast! He'll say anything to fit his argument & an argument is like a game, checkers, marbles, whatever—truth must fit his argument.[30]

In self-defense she had resorted to the temper that her mother had refused to break in the angry little girl: "I go in for outrage, could almost burst open with outrage & can condone violence in the defense of truth."[31]

As they were settling in, they noticed Goethe's *Wanderer's Nightsong,* reprinted by J. Donald Adams in his *New York Times Book Review* column, eliciting a letter to Adams for once not by Jo but by Edward, who wrote that he was "greatly pleased" to find the poem: "It has been an intense admiration of mine for a long time."[32] Hopper went on to mention what he considered the other two "finest poems of evening that I know": Robert Frost's "Come In" and "the verse from Verlaine's 'La Bonne Chanson' which begins, 'Un vaste et tendre / Apaisement / Semble descendre / Du firmament.' "[33] The latter he had quoted to Jo on the romantic Christmas card that he made for her in December 1923 before their marriage.

§

NEARLY A YEAR had passed since the one, mixed result of painting the previous summer. August was well along before Hopper finally settled on an idea, working into it with sketches on paper, without feeling any need to call on Jo. The work stretched on through September into October, causing Jo to confide more than once in her diary, "I'm not crazy about that one."[34] She did not provide her customary running commentary through the days and weeks as Edward drew the angled wall and harshly illuminated doorway that gradually came to highlight the female figure with its broad-brimmed red hat and electric dress that clings to full buttocks and stretches around a hip and knee bent forward above a foot thrust just over the threshold into a kinetic stance, anchored by stout arms positively folded under pneumatic breasts, deep cleavage, full red lips, rouged cheeks, and gold earrings that frame a negroid face.

Although Jo neither chronicled the progress nor claimed that she had posed, or even produced the dress, and shoes, and hat, she did her duty when the time came for the ritual of the record book, identifying the female figure of Edward's imagination: "South Carolina Morning . . . 'Dinah,' girl is a mulatto. Dress & hat red—not vivid, black pumps, thin nylons. House grey, shutters faded blue. Wall of front hall white."[35]

Although he was on the Cape, Hopper reached back to an experience from his 1929 trip to Charleston for the figure of the buxom woman. He described it not long after he finished the painting:

> We used to go along Folly beach. I remember you had to pay to get in. Sometimes I'd find a house I liked. There was this cabin back in the woods, and I stopped to sketch it. This mulatto girl came out of the cabin and she seemed interested in what I was doing. Then her husband came home. He was drunk or something and he was going to do something, I don't know what. I beat it.[36]

In Hopper's narrative version of the long-ago event, he identifies himself as an intruder, noticing that the erotically-charged object of his fantasy was attracted by his work, which he clearly perceived as an extension of himself.

The imaginative identification of the sultry figure in the painting as "Dinah" suggests that Edward and Jo had in mind the racial and sexual stereotypes of African-American women in folk songs that were popular around the turn of the century, such as "I've Been Working on the Railroad" ("Someone's in the kitchen with Dinah . . . strumming on the ol' banjo"), or in other familiar songs from minstrel shows. Drawings surviving from his childhood, depicting banjo players and other images of African-Americans, suggest that he was familiar with such popular entertainments. It has been suggested that the demeaning caricature of minstrel shows enabled white people to discharge fears of the "other" through humor, expressing simultaneous repulsion and attraction.[37]

The connection of the minstrel show to expressions of sexuality is echoed in Hopper's depiction of this African-American woman. There is a hint that large-bosomed women were objects of his fantasy in a comment he made when asked if it was an illustrator's convention "that all women are big-bosomed." He replied, "Remember what Balzac said? 'A cleft of prodigious breasts.' Maybe so. At least on the jackets of paperback novels. Actually, you know, American women are pretty flat-chested as a whole."[38]

Hopper revealed something about his perception of his new canvas soon after its completion. When Harold Harris, who had purchased *The Martha McKeen of Wellfleet,* stopped by with his wife, Leslie, and their children, Hopper took Harold in to see the this latest picture while Jo visited with the family outside. The Hoppers were especially pleased that Harris had purchased the earlier painting because Leslie was Martha McKeen's first cousin. While Edward never did welcome children in the house, still his behavior invites the inference that he saw his latest product as something man to man.

Ambivalence surfaced again when John Clancy asked about showing *South Carolina Morning* in the upcoming Whitney Annual at the end of October. Hopper hedged: "The picture does not please me very much and aside from that it seems to take a long time drying. I used a linseed oil that I have never used before, and it is still tacky about a month after I last worked on it. It would be risky to send it on to New York now."[39]

Silent about the strange woman on the easel, Jo did record a social engagement that ended by bringing out one of Edward's characteristic streaks. They were invited for dinner at the home of Davis and Elsa-Ruth Herron with the idea that the men would play chess after dinner. When Davis won the first two games, Edward insisted on a third, which ended in a draw at three in the morning. Jo and Elsa-Ruth had long since fallen asleep in their chairs in the next room of the cluttered house. Clearly Edward in adulthood, as in childhood, did not take lightly to losing games.[40] Driven to generalize, Jo concluded: "He is definitely sadistic & will destroy anyone in competition if they are obscure & defenseless."[41]

In late September Jo had spent a week painting a canvas of Cape vegetation, "goldenrod, seed pods, dusty miller & some asters," by the fireplace and little rush-bottom chair.[42] But the flowers kept dying before she could finish. To make matters worse, Edward peppered her with suggestions that struck her as inappropriate. She was after a "battle with the force of gravity," so left much of the canvas bare, while Edward argued for "a substantial enough chimney, bricks all functioning to hold the whole thing up."[43] The result, to her mind, was a flop.

While they were on the Cape, John Clancy was busy in New York. He sold *Hotel Room,* a large canvas of 1931, to Nathan B. Spingold, an important collector, who, he told Hopper, hung the picture "in his bedroom, which is quite large, and next to it is a Rouault and close by a Titian."[44] Clancy also assured Hopper of Alfred Barr's continuing respect and informed him that Barr had offered to take Hopper to see this collection when he returned to

New York. Hopper quipped: "I'm proud to be in such good company in Spingold's bedroom," and reflected, "It looks as if I would have to do some more big ones."[45] Clancy also reported good news on the critical front. Jacob Getlar Smith planned to write an article on Hopper for the magazine *American Artist*.[46]

On October 12, the Hoppers attended the church wedding of Jack Kelly, Jr., the son of their Cape handyman. Edwin Dickinson, whose house was also in Kelly's care, was there too. Jo later commented that Edward "skulked down stairs" outside, probably seeking to avoid having to greet people, and stood "among a lot of good looking cars."[47]

When the third issue of *Reality* arrived, Jo was devastated to see that she was still not listed as a member. She correctly asserted that it was she who had prompted J. Donald Adams to write about *Reality* in the *Times Book Review,* in effect launching the project. It was she who diligently promoted the publication by writing notes to so many important people and it was she who had suggested writing to Bernard Berenson.[48] She did not appreciate Edward's attitude that this was the way it should be.

Tension mounted. After a party at Dick and Nell Magee's, Jo noted that Edward "didn't find much to say during dinner. I'm afraid very bored. He can't enter in their transient interests or appreciate their friendly attempts to propitiate him. He speaks only when spoken to."[49] He may have been especially bored, for he seemed almost to be looking for a fight. He began to belittle Jo for taking time out to "scribble" in her diary.[50] The previous night they had fought over the arrangement of things stored in their attic. Edward wanted to dump out everything that Jo had so carefully accumulated without giving her time to go through her treasures. She retorted that she would "throw out the window all his Brady Civil War [books that she had given him] in wooden box if he threw out my pictures. I'm a born devil—and glad of it," she told herself.[51]

Jo turned to repainting a cheap frame for another of her flower pictures, a blue hydrangea, which won such unusually warm praise from Edward that she was led to suspect his motives: did he intend to distract her from wanting to take the car to seek subjects farther afield?[52] Given his often expressed contempt for flower pictures, she may have been right. Jo had brought from New York three canvases, hoping to show them to friends, if not in a gallery. But the summer gave way to autumn with no interest in sight.

On Armistice Day Edward went to bury their old cans in a remote spot near the swamp at the edge of their property. When twilight began to fall with no sign of him, Jo became alarmed and ran out to search. Trudging through the briars, she yelled "Eddie," at first getting no response. When she finally heard a faint answer but could get no reply to her repeated shouts of

"Where are you?" she panicked and ran back into the house to call Bob Stephens, who said he would be right there. Just as Jo was going out to search with a lantern and a length of old clothesline, Marie Stephens drove up with Edward in the car. He had heard Jo calling while he was pruning bushes along the road, but realizing that his voice could not be heard over the strong west wind, he just kept working. Jo, hoarse from screaming in the cold and looking, she said, like the Coast Guard with her ropes and lantern, was "mad as a hornet."[53]

His insouciance made her remember the time their sailboat capsized in Wellfleet harbor and he ignored her plea for help: "How safe am I out here in this wilderness? How feeble would be his efforts if I were to fall over a precipice?"[54] For not the first time she faced her dilemma: "I can scarcely stand E.H., but how possibly live without him."[55]

With electricity and a new gas stove, the house was now more comfortable than the studio in New York, with its seventy-four steps to climb and coal to haul. Lingering then until November 13, they had retrieved the fur coat and left the car in Nyack and were still unpacking and settling in when Sidney Waintrob arrived to photograph Hopper for the article mentioned by Clancy to appear in *American Artist*. Waintrob asked Edward to pose next to one of his paintings on his easel. Since all of Hopper's current work went immediately to the Rehn Gallery, he obligingly dug out a thirty-year-old canvas, *The Bootleggers* (page 194). Reconsidering a picture long forgotten, he told Waintrob: "Now I have another picture to sell." (In fact, he would sell it the next year.) Waintrob, who recalls that Jo told him "Nobody looks at my work," also photographed her in her studio standing by her painting *Church of San Esteban* (page 393).[56] He recalls that they were both quite pleased with his results.

Jo recorded that on Thanksgiving Day they were too tired and too busy "to do much about feasting."[57] Perhaps thinking that they were still away, no one had thought to invite them for the holiday. Contacts resumed on December 5, when they attended a meeting of *Reality* at Sol Wilson's, to decide whether to continue to publish the journal. While no one wanted "to bury the idea," no one volunteered any concrete future plans.[58] They had ungratefully kept off the list one person who had already given proof of ideas, zest, and gumption. But no, the project was left to expire. A week later, when Edward went to an editorial meeting at Maurice Grosser's studio on Fourteenth Street, only five members were there, including neither Wilson nor Henry Varnum Poor.[59]

Robert Frost read at the Academy of Arts and Letters on the eleventh of December, to the delight of Edward and Jo at hearing their favorites, which they knew well. At the party afterward Frost told Edward "that he was the one man there he most interested to meet."[60] (Frost seems to have forgotten an earlier meeting with the Hoppers, for Jo told Tommy Gray in 1947 that they had "met" the poet.) Frost asked Hopper if he was listed in the phone book and suggested that when he was next in New York he would like to come sit around their stove and talk. Jo may have told the poet about her painting of Edward reading his work and about his habit of sitting by their stove reading. Though no doubt thrilled at Frost's interest, Jo commented that Edward "had not lifted a finger as usual & he gets this."[61] Ever alert for aesthetic parallels with Edward, she recorded that Frost had said that "every poem is an exaggeration carefully trammeled to suit the mood."[62]

Years later, to the printmaker Richard Lahey, Hopper recalled the evening with revealing emphasis: "Robert Frost is a real person. When he

Josephine N. Hopper, Edward Hopper Reading Robert Frost, *c. 1955. Oil on canvas, 25 × 30″ (63.5 × 76.2 cm.).*

came down to deliver a speech at the Institute of Arts & Letters—and most of the members were there including myself—right after the speech he came down to greet me."[63] According to Lahey, Jo then interrupted and said: "Yes & he put his arms around you and embraced you and said 'You—Hopper . . . I was really talking to [you] throughout that speech of mine—I like your work very much.' "[64]

On December 12, Jo noted that Hopper had "painted some this A.M. but he's stuck for a dark street scene for outside the hotel window in what he's doing."[65] Edward had begun this "sizable" canvas (40 × 55 inches) the previous week, encouraged by the recent sales of *Barber Shop, Morning in the City,* and *Hotel Room,* three of his larger works. That night she observed that he had "gone to look about at dark facades in the side streets of the 30s—for a view out that hotel interior window. He has said he wanted this picture to be in the 30s—cheap hotel & the sort of people one sees there. One would expect them to be the sad sort, the tired, defeated sort who have to economize & do without glamour."[66]

Jo worried about Edward getting home safely. She reflected that their neighborhood had "been infected by thuggy looking people" and that someone had tried mugging one of their neighbors recently.[67] She lamented: "I don't like to have E. out alone after dark in the cold. Wolves are more active in the cold & dark & E. has no experience beating up anyone—occasional lurches at me wouldn't count."[68]

The next day Jo noted that Edward had done a lot of work on his new canvas, "that window filled with night. Last night he didn't like what he saw in the 30s—too lit up."[69] Hopper finished by the end of the year. Jo in the record book described the color and the content with the additional comment: "Hotel Window. . . . Whatever interests woman gazing out must occur offstage at left of canvas, distant enough to cast no light except on white pillar of stoop outside window. Picture definitely not called: 'Alone in the city at Night.' But why not?"[70] Hopper had made a preparatory sketch which included the figure of a man absorbed in reading a newspaper, seated just across the room from the woman. He commented about this painting: "It's nothing accurate at all, just an improvisation of things I've seen. It's no particular hotel lobby, but many times I've walked through the Thirties from Broadway to Fifth Avenue and there are a lot of cheesy hotels in there. That probably suggested it. Lonely? Yes, I guess it's lonelier than I planned it, really."[71] Beyond conscious planning, he had let the process of working bring out the loneliness from within. His reality, as always, was fabricated, not just from casual memories collected, but out of his personal vision. His every painting is an "exaggeration carefully trammeled to suit the mood."

TIME COVER STORY: 1956

IN JANUARY 1956 *American Artist* ran the long-projected article by
Jacob Getlar Smith.[1] The Hoppers were so delighted that they showed it to
Eddy Brady, the building handyman who had taken over the task of hauling
up coal for their stove; he sat down and read it on the spot, proud to know
Edward.[2]

Smith opened by setting Hopper apart from the ordinary artists who
would "adjust [their] artistic speech" rather than "follow their own paths,
popular or not." He linked Hopper to the "pungent idiom unmistakably
American" of "Bingham, Ryder, Blakelock, Eakins, Homer, Bellows, Sloan,
and Benton."[3] Certainly pleased to be associated with Eakins, Homer, and
Sloan, whom he himself prized, Hopper did not aspire to be compared to
Benton and his ilk: "The thing that makes me so mad is the 'American Scene'
business," he would say. "I never tried to do the American scene as Benton
and Curry and the midwestern painters did. I think the American Scene
painters caricatured America. I always wanted to do myself. The French
painters didn't talk about the 'French Scene,' or the English painters the
'English scene.' "[4] Still, Smith must have pleased Hopper when he singled out
what he perceived as a "strain of puritanism" and "a somberness, a realization
that existence is serious and at times desolate—that despite rigid demands,
out of every day percolates a radiancy, the haunting spell of life itself."[5]

The sense of well-being and accomplishment fed also on the year's first event at the Whitney—the opening on January 10 of a retrospective for Charles Burchfield, who had climbed the stairs so many times through the years to gossip, shared so many juries, often leaving Jo feeling slighted. Now she warmed to the celebration of a familiar world and echoed Edward in pronouncing it a "handsome show."[6] Still, Jo spent much of the evening lobbying for her own "little bastards." She snapped at Dorothy Miller because she and her husband, Holger Cahill, had left Jo out of an exhibition of Village artists that they had chosen for the New School for Social Research the previous November.[7] Edward introduced her to Eleanor Poindexter of the Poindexter Gallery, who told Jo that she would like to come and see her studio and would keep on her fur coat to endure the cold.[8]

In their confident and retrospective mood, Jo and Edward both were moved by the film *Marty* (a low-budget film distinguished by Paddy Chayefsky's screenplay), concerning the romance of two lonely people in the Italian area of the Bronx. It became a favorite with Edward, and Jo was so taken with it that she saw it for a second and third time with friends.[9] Not even the parallel with lonely romance was enough to preserve their domestic harmony. As so often when he was not painting himself, Edward fell to "intoning that no one likes my work.... Got so furious at [his] low down meanness. . . . I whacked his hand with an iron plate lifter from the stove & said I ready anytime he ready to wring my neck, I'd had enough."[10]

By the first of February, Jo recorded that Edward was "starting to cook up another canvas" so that he would be free, "if he feels so disposed [to] slack off on another safari to Mexico."[11] Five days later, she noted that he had "gone up in the W. 70's to look for an apt. stoop. . . . Nothing around here will do— here on own st. Wash. Sq. N. with the lovely white Georgian ones, not his idea at all. Always must be the common denominator. Everything about ourselves & our lives far too special."[12]

The next day, a cold and dreary morning, the Hoppers went uptown to attend the funeral of the artist Gifford Beal. Edward "went without argument, said he's known him for 50 yrs."[13] Beal, who was three years older than Hopper, was one of the last of the old classmates from the New York School of Art. He had just been a runner-up when the National Institute of Arts and Letters chose Hopper to receive its gold medal. He and Bellows had scored early success, leaving Hopper to come from behind. After the funeral, Hopper walked quite a distance with Jo, "looking for an old fashioned brownstone front with the rail of which has preserved its stone covering. Most we see have metal rails, the stone having crumbled probably."[14] Jo noted how they "found one or 2 stoops for E.'s consideration—not quite what he wants."[15] This shows again how clearly Hopper had his conception in mind before he began painting. The next day, Hopper again "went uptown to look at stoops in the lower West 80's."[16]

By the tenth of February, Jo observed that Edward "hasn't started his new canvas yet, goes over his sketches, gazes at book of Rembrandt reproductions, reads this & that."[17] Hopper, who admired Rembrandt's use of light and shadow, may have found a parallel for what he had in mind in the etching of *The Good Samaritan*. Both works depict figures in the elevated doorway of a building angled into space on the left side of the picture. Trees at the center of the composition meet the edge of the building in each.

By February twentieth, Jo noted that Edward "has the blue outline in of the new picture—don't know what it will be named—row of brownstone stoop, boy & girl. She's charming now with long hair & graceful. I'll be holding my breath lest in fear of having pretty girl . . . he'll do something awful to the face."[18] She knew his qualms about the facility to "do pretty girls,"[19] which he identified with illustration. When Jo came back from the theater on February 22, she was surprised to see that Edward "had been doing a lot of his new canvas. He has a blue sky rather sooner than usual."[20]

Even as Edward's work progressed, Jo was about to give up hope. Friends were constantly ill or dying. The spectacle of the new dealer, John Clancy, selling more and more of Edward's old canvases, carrying on and even outstripping the long, close relationship with Frank Rehn, who was still incapacitated by his stroke, made her think:

> But into this close corporation there was no room for me as an artist—nor is there any now. Nor anywhere else either. This year I've come to see there is no hope ahead—& something in me must die because what is the use of asserting an existence with no harbor for refuge—except that cold rear studio where at least my work can hang but no one is willing to take an interest or welcome it out into the light.[21]

This was her frame of mind when Edwin Dickinson called to inquire if Edward had any canvases to lend to a show traveling in France. Jo wanted him to recommend her picture, *Cape Bedroom,* particularly since he had nothing of his own to send. But he pointed out that she would have to get past Isabel Bishop as well, leading her to give up: "Now if I could remember—not to care—not to care at all. So soon we'll be dead."[22]

In a resurgence of her old entrepreneurial flair, Jo had left the *American Artist* article on Edward at the theater for Edward G. Robinson when she went with Ella Mielziner to see him perform in *Middle of the Night*.[23] Robinson, who had purchased Edward's canvas *Sun on Prospect Street* in 1940, called a few days later, saying he would like to visit the Hoppers. Jo recorded Edward's negative reaction, explaining his "not fancying the run down aspect of things here" and commenting, "Not that I mind, if we have time to slick things up, wash the white marble fireplaces, etc."[24]

At the next Whitney opening, a show of Morris Graves on February 28, Edward got so tired from standing that he "had to knock off painting" the next day.[25] He was on a veritable binge, since he had just finished the previous canvas around Christmas. He seemed to draw energy from John Clancy's enterprise in finding clients for early works. Also, seeing his backlog shrink may have impressed him with the need to provide new work for the gallery, which he very much wanted to support.

On the morning of March 4, Clancy called to inform Hopper that Rehn had died the night before. The funeral was set for the eighth, at the Church of the Ascension, and Jo volunteered to inform people, including the wives of Lloyd Goodrich and Alfred Barr. Yet in the diary, she continued to focus on the new painting, noting that Edward was working on the brownstone "stoops & railings bright pink in sunlight. Each day one thinks the picture done, but no—only become 'more so.' "[26] She added that Eddy Brady, who liked to observe Hopper's work in progress when he delivered their coal, had "complained that the girl's waste was too broad"; that Edward had gone out to get "more data on brown stone architecture detail"; and that further progress on the painting was delayed by the necessity of doing their income taxes.[27]

For her seventy-first birthday, Jo recorded the acquisition of a pink lace bra, "perishable & does nothing specially for me anymore than another layer of skin."[28] She described the bra as "a birthday present for E. & the most expensive thing of the kind I've ever owned."[29] Pride in dressing up and looking her best had been at the heart of their mutual performance. She also painted a self-portrait in the new bra.

On March 28, Hopper was "still working on his brown stoops in sunlight" and had justified various suspicions of Jo's, producing a new burst of biographical insight:

> He had such an attractive young thing perched on the railing but he's now made her much too old & determined to be perching on that rail & wearing her dark hair down on her shoulders. Now this the 3″ canvas where he's made his women so repulsive—their faces. The polparot face in City Sunlight & Italian female in 1″ Row Orchestra & now this one. They will just brand him as unsympathetic & hard & serves him right for his devastation repaid to me when I'm clawing on the bottom in utter desperation over my continued frustration: "It's all in your work."[30]

§

DEATH WAS WEIGHING ever more heavily on Jo. "Old friends keep dying off & I've made no new friends—so don't you dare let anything happen to you!" she wrote to Sprinchorn,[31] and she reflected on the plight of an elderly widowed friend: "God remember me when I'm a lone widow in a hotel room—if one can afford it—at 83—Everybody else will then be long dead. So much for neglecting to cultivate contemporaries. But I've had my sad experiences with contemporaries—they'll make passes at my husband."[32]

Having splurged on a gesture of conventional femininity for her birthday, Jo took more sober stock of herself as a woman: "Well I realize I'm neither young nor beautiful & my style's much the matter of opinion—it's individual, no question about that—if one likes that & its deviations from the generally accepted at a given time & place. . . . But no one would accuse me of laying myself out to catch men."[33] She then reflected about her taste in men in general and Edward, in particular:

> E. conforms to all my requirements, or most of them & I condone the rest. I used to say roughly "long, lean & hungry looking"—one need not look for unselfishness, it doesn't exist. Meanness I do not condone & E. can be really mean, eaten up with scorn & how I hate to admit it—on certain levels, smug—with the smugness of success. He lets on to be humble. He is not.[34]

When Ethel Baker from the Cape visited New York in late March, Edward showed her his new work.[35] From conception to completion, it had taken two full months, nearly double the time he had usually required in the past. He had made at least three working sketches, one of which had a second female figure as well as the male figure. Jo wrote in the record book: "Sunlight on Brownstones. . . . Early A.M. light on the West 80s (N.Y.C.) makes brownstones somewhat pink."[36] Later that year, Hopper told an interviewer:

> Brownstones are clotted in some sections of New York. Lots of them in the West Eighties, and the Park is right there. I went up there making sketches, nothing very definite, perhaps, a little bit of the park vague not accurate. The light is largely improvised. Is it as pink as I made it? I don't know. I had the idea quite a while. But not so long, I guess.[37]

In the midst of this remarkably productive period, in early April, Hopper's sister became ill. Edward and Jo rushed to Nyack to get her to a doctor, who diagnosed gallstones and a dangerous blood condition.[38] They found her house underheated as usual, with dysfunctional old water pipes. Jo complained because the house was so dark; Marion scrimped by using only twenty-five watt bulbs. Her cat was emaciated and sick. After one night, Edward, who heard ringing in his ears, decided that he had to get back to New York to see a doctor and to work on his taxes, but that Jo should stay with Marion. Jo, who found Marion so disagreeable, adamantly refused: "She & I make each other ill, we disturb each other so much."[39] She decided to allow Marion's noble friends at church to prove their idea of worthiness. Edward's doctor found nothing terribly wrong, but did reduce the amount of digitalis he had been prescribing, although he claimed that the drugs had been giving Edward more energy. With no further excuse to shirk his responsibilities and shift the burden to Jo, Edward went back to check on his sister and to see if her furnace was working in the face of an unseasonable snowstorm.

Meanwhile another argument over responsibility was brewing at home. Hopper had been asked to second the nomination of Henry Varnum Poor for the American Academy of Arts and Letters, but felt that he should decline to avoid the appearance of returning a favor. To Jo this was inexcusable: "I had no patience with that line of thought—side step benefiting anyone who benefited him—to wit penalizing one's benefactors."[40] The show of principle came, indeed, rather late, after the years of serving on juries that awarded prizes to those who had served on juries awarding prizes to oneself. Hopper made his case in a letter to Maxwell Anderson:

> I certainly believe Henry Poor should be honored for his intelligence and perception in art. As for my seconding his nomination I have the fear, and perhaps I am cowardly, that since he was one of those who proposed me for the Gold Medal for Painting, and wrote so well of me in the Presentation speech, and wrote in particular of my integrity, that I could easily be accused by the members, of a non-esthetic prejudice for him. Do not think, however, that I do not think highly of his ability.[41]

In the event, Poor's candidacy failed.

In addition to his loyal support of Hopper, Poor had been active in the *Reality* group, but the cause of realism and factional solidarity figured not at all in Hopper's considerations. On the very day of his letter Hopper attended a *Reality* meeting, attended by only seven members in all.[42] Maurice Grosser reread his long article and another issue was anticipated. On the seventh of May, *Reality* met again at Sol Wilson's with sixteen members present as well as some guests, including George Biddle, Edward Lanning, Byron Browne, and Ruth Gikow.[43] Browne was then working abstractly, but Biddle initiated talk of turning the publication into an artist's forum, giving "the enemy party" a chance to speak out. Jo thought that Biddle "could make trouble—letting him come in. It's amazing that this enterprise could have held up for 3 yrs. without dissension."[44]

Curious about the "enemy party," Jo went to hear the Abstract Expressionist painter Robert Motherwell speak at New York University in what she described as a "discourse on Mondrian. . . . Plenty of gobbledegook."[45] And she quoted something Edward had read about "either Renoir or Degas saying concerning some other painter given to discoursing, 'Oh—so now he paints with his mouth.' "[46]

Even before *Sunlight on Brownstones* could be framed, it was purchased by the Wichita Art Museum in Kansas, a week after Hopper had delivered it to the Rehn Gallery.[47] The Hoppers celebrated by going to see *Mister Roberts* and another film, *Rebel without a Cause.* For Jo, James Dean was "at once arresting";[48] but *Rebel* offered no parallels for Edward, whose own youth had been so tame. A few days earlier, the Hoppers had gone to see Henri-Georges Clouzot's *Les Diaboliques,* a sadistic story of murder that turns on a trick of plot, which Jo did not like because she felt that the ending was not explained.[49]

As the weather warmed, Edward liked to sit in Washington Square Park and watch chess games. He was complaining, however, of recurring stomach aches and a fever and feared the return of diverticulitis.[50] At his doctor's orders, he went on a liquid diet and started taking antibiotics, while staying in bed for several days. A week later, he was up, eating again, and made a brief excursion uptown with Jo to stop by the Rehn Gallery and see the Käthe Kollwitz show at Gallery St. Etienne. Jo found Kollwitz "tremendous—heartwringing that masterful drawing."[51] Here was a woman artist she could praise.

On the twenty-third of May, the American Academy of Arts and Letters inducted Hopper, Marianne Moore, Maxwell Anderson, Walter Piston, Lewis Mumford, and Andrew Wyeth into what Jo described as the "holyer than thou inner group,"[52] the Academy's fifty members, elected from its parent body, the National Institute of Arts and Letters. For the occasion, Hopper and Wyeth, then only thirty-eight years old and the youngest person ever elected, had their paintings on exhibition at the academy. At the party the night before the induction ceremony, the playwright Thornton Wilder had told Hopper how much he liked his work, adding that he would like to visit Edward and Jo in Truro.[53]

The new honor stirred a new wave of attention from critics and journalists. Alexander Eliot, who had already written about him for *Time,* invited Edward and Jo for dinner.[54] Selden Rodman came to interview him for a book of conversations with artists. Jo was outraged when "what was supposed to be a conversation turned out a quiz—or inquisition—with all the pounce of a district attorney. I simply can't stand anyone pushing my Eddie around—so I broke in & incurred the displeasure of the someone not expected of being such an egotist . . . a gangster intent on hunting down his prey."[55] Then, when Frank Crotty, of the Worcester (Massachusetts) Gazette, came to do an interview, Jo commented, "He's nice, intelligent but knows nothing about art."[56]

The Hoppers arrived in Truro on the first of July. In her diary for July 22, Jo noted, "Eddy's Birthday—& passed without a fight."[57] That day Edward received a letter announcing that he had been given the 1956–57 award of the Huntington Hartford Foundation: a thousand dollars and an invitation for him and Jo to make a six-month visit to the colony, which was a mixed blessing, thought Jo, since Edward "didn't favor either Calif. or community life."[58] As it later appeared, "E. didn't bite, but I asked around & heard such splendid reports that I got E. to consent, since we wanted to see the west coast road thru Mexico, we knew the one down from Loredo & the other one from El Paso, the middle one from Juarez."[59]

Meanwhile Jo found an opening. Nieta Cole, whose gallery was in Wellfleet, had written that she had included Jo's name in her list of artists for 1956. Jo sent her painting of *Petunias* and later took in seven small *pochades* or rapid sketches that she had made in her youth in Provincetown, Ogunquit, Gloucester, and Monhegan. They reminded her of "those seasons . . . full of heart throbs . . . those far distant days [when] one's life was so full of friends, we were all so happy together. Now I no longer have any—only acquaintances & friends of my husband." It led her to draw a contrast with the art world around her:

> As anyone a bit sophisticated knows the world of art is run by people who know nothing & care less about art. When quality becomes at all important, they have to be told. So they listen to those who have the audiences—the papers & the critics. And just who to-days writes at all well from any understanding. Publicity is the yardstick. Is it any wonder people stand on their heads to get publicity.[60]

As Edward occupied himself with repairs around the house, Jo lamented that "he looks fine, but complains of dreaming so much here. And none of our dreams are ever pleasing."[61] Yet Hopper had no professional reasons for anxiety. His critical reputation just kept growing. *Time* was making arrangements to photograph him for a cover story and *Art News* sent Parker Tyler, the film critic and poet, to do a feature for their annual.[62] The Hoppers liked Tyler, whom they discovered had written about Edward previously and was a devotee of Henry James.[63]

The flurry of excitement fed egotism and provoked Jo to new insights in her growing autobiography and biography: "I keep on digging & scraping in determined effort to extract blood from a stone, not willing to accept defeat & have always to sustain my grief alone," while Edward's enjoyment of her misery must give him "some special nourishment . . . because he had to see Bellows, Kent, du Bois & the rest of them blossoming out in high places during the years when he got nowhere. Now he can watch me taking what he endured."[64] The result, if understandable, left her disappointed of what she had expected in a husband: "Where is the protection, the concern, the wish to share what might have most value, regard of the good of my soul. What manner of companionship is here—of partnership. How could there be anything but bitterness."[65]

On the twenty-third of August, Bill Johnson, a researcher for *Time,* arrived to do an interview. Jo commented: "We felt rather annoyed at his thoroughness, but I right there to slip anything we felt too intimate that E. felt unable to handle by himself. E. didn't like the idea of interviewing Marion in Nyack. B.J. very nice & anxious not to offend."[66] Edward became quite anxious about "all the concern over his personal affairs" and concluded that since *Time* was not an art magazine, they had mostly "lay" readers "who'd want to count back teeth."[67] When Jo accused Johnson of such a tack, he assured them that the magazine only wanted to be accurate in its report. For his part, Edward wrote to Marion, telling her that *Time*'s researchers had "probed quite enough" and cautioned that if anyone tried to interview her, she should "tell them absolutely nothing about me or our family."[68] Responding to the Hoppers' sensitivities, Johnson switched the line of his questioning to focus on style in painting and events like the Armory Show. When he met with the Hoppers again, he brought his wife, Liz, to charm Jo. The strategy worked— Jo thought Liz was "a nice American girl & intelligent"[69]—and Johnson had some moments with his subject without Jo's intervention.

As for working, Hopper was bored. Jo had seen it before: "I'm convinced there is nothing more to be run upon hereabouts, he's done it all—& doesn't want to repeat himself. He's up a tree for subject matter so consoles himself or glad to justify himself, by just reading, reading incessantly in pure self indulgence."[70] They also went to the movies, driving all the way to Hyannis for a triple feature that included *Bus Stop* and *Moby Dick.* Jo especially liked *Moby Dick,* but remarked that Edward "always finds fault with every thing."[71]

"Concerning painting, neither of us has made one stroke," Jo complained to Carl Sprinchorn. "Edward only reads—& for me, I feel as tho it would be flying in the face of the Holy Ghost—each effort provokes only punishment. E. reminds me that no one likes my work which seems so difficult for me to believe. It's so friendly, one might expect simple souls to like it."[72]

Even Edward's carping mood did not deter Jo from looking again at the bright side—their little house, after twenty-two years so perfect; Edward diligent in taking care of it, enjoying it too, if not saying so; her trying not to "inflict" too many tea parties. Above all she prayed: "O God, God, so that he stays with me always—always—even if we do fight so much of the time. After all, it's to be expected, 2 such intense personalities, always together—happily with the same taste & sharing most convictions."[73] Edward, she groped for the truth again, "hasn't the emotional equipment to feel outside himself" and this "breaks my heart."[74]

By September 10, Hopper remained "stuck," or as Jo very succinctly put the dilemma: "Can't get any idea for picture. . . . His reputation is shooting sky high—but where is his work now so much needed?"[75] As so often, he was taking his books of Civil War photographs down from the attic and pawing through *The New York Times, Time,* and *Life.*[76] Jo made him share *The New Yorker* with her, by reading aloud. He fell again to taunting her about her "frustration" over her career and about having a "persecution complex."[77] The provocation pushed her to yet another overview of their biography:

> 32 yrs. on the surface so delectable & all this enmity & denying of natural sex. His abnormality could probably explain the whole thing. For years I listening to his efforts to prove all Amer. women low in sex capacity. Just what kind of sex capacity? And the Catholic Church variety—sneers, sneers. How categorize his variety—with nothing whatever for the normal human female. Recently when he spoke of my deficiency I let out and gave him a swift kick in the shin & glad I did. He stopped that sneer. That is the way to handle that.[78]

Yet even at this she undercut herself: "how wicked to feel quarrelsome."[79]

Out of the constant discord came Edward's next painting. He finally overcame his inertia on the twenty-third of September, and stretched a canvas. Two days later, Jo recorded that he had "his picture drawn in—an old man sitting outside his gas station & wife leaning out window. Far be it from him to put in that nice flying horse all lit-up-red."[80] She misses the sign that Hopper did put in *Gas.* By the second of October, Jo reported that Edward "had been working pretty steadily with the studio shades down & I keeping to the kitchen for light. He's getting what he wants fairly easily."[81]

When Johnson returned two days later, he saw the work in progress. Hopper remarked to him: "I don't like it much. Of course it isn't finished yet. But you can't tell. I had this sketch. I don't remember when I made it. Last spring, I guess. It wasn't any place in particular. Just an improvisation. Didn't think much of it then and don't now. But you have to do something."[82]

Jo noted that Johnson was "not slow to grab on to what dropped—I having mentioned the continuity of the road running parallel before or after edge of canvas—on & on across time & territory."[83] With her customary acuity and imagination, she drew the interviewer's attention to the suggestion of space and time beyond the present.

Four days later, she gave further proof of how her own mind was constantly interweaving present and and past, not only in their lives but in Edward's work:

> The white wall of the gas station will recall the white wall of Office in a Small City, where young architect could be the grim mouthed gas station manager, owner or what not. He has work to do on the wife inside house at window but the parallels of road swishing across canvas dive straight for Kingdom Come. The man sits in the sun bearing witness in quiet peace but the wife at the window is more vocal.[84]

Two days later, Jo focused on Edward's transformation of the female figure, as she had when she feared he would spoil the "pretty girl" in *Brownstones* that spring. Now she took her preoccupations to a new level of consciousness, when she observed that Edward was "making the most evil face on woman at window of filling station in his picture—a regular shrike, expressive of what he's feeling about me."[85]

For once she makes explicit the parallel between his art and their life. Having done so, in the record book, engaging in their usual ritual of fantasizing, she names the work and nails down the characters in terms that reflect her constant tension with her husband: "Four Lane Road. . . . Man sunburnt hair yellow, grey eyes, Anglo Saxon. . . . Woman alizarin waste, brown hair—finds his serenity a trial."[86] The play this time was real.

Meanwhile, Jo also recorded the ongoing interview and snatches of normal life. Davis Herron came over to play chess, which lasted till two in the morning, he and Edward each winning a game.[87] "I love to play chess," Hopper told Frank Crotty, "although I am not a good player." Asked whether she also played, Jo retorted: "I wouldn't waste my time. If I'm going to do anything, it'll be something creative."[88] On the fifteenth of October, Edward drove to Provincetown in search of a subject for a watercolor. The day was misty, not good for the light and shadow contrasts he favored, and his quest was unsuccessful.[89] Jo did not believe that he was ambitious enough to paint a watercolor before leaving.[90]

Andrew Wyeth telephoned to ask if he could add Hopper's name to the Committee of Arts and Sciences for the Eisenhower campaign. Although Jo commented that "they saw little good of art getting mixed up with politics,"

Edward Hopper, Study for "Four Lane Road," *1956. Charcoal on paper, 8½ × 11″*
(21.6 × 27.9 cm.).

Edward, who was never fond of the Democrats, agreed to serve after hearing that Leon Kroll was on a committee for the Democratic candidate, Stevenson. Others on this Eisenhower committee with Wyeth were Burchfield and Helen Hayes.[91] By the time Hopper lent his name, the presidential election was just days away.

The Hoppers left the Cape in late October, intending to prepare for a trip to the Southwest. Edward had reconsidered the offer of the Huntington Hartford Foundation and California was in the offing. In the 1956 Whitney Annual, which opened in mid-November, Hopper showed *Sunlight on Brownstones.* John Lamb, then a vice-president at Young and Rubicam, recalls meeting him at the opening party.[92] When he later wrote to Hopper, asking to purchase what Edward referred to as "a certain type of watercolor," he received the following reply: "I am sure I do not know when such a one will come to pass."[93] Jo added her own comment, apologizing for Edward's terseness and explaining: "My husband, a man of few words, doesn't explain that when one has said a great deal on a subject that interests one, there can come a time when one feels one has said all one can. Now, after a period, this interest can be revived & with it more to say. I'll see that you are remembered when this occurs."[94] Although Jo simply enjoyed people and liked corresponding, she also may have been unwilling to brush off a future buyer. The image Lamb sought was a lighthouse.[95] At this time, Hopper had two unsold watercolor versions of the *Lighthouse at Two Lights.* He had inscribed one of these to Jo, and one can only assume that either he did not consider the other successful or had forgotten he still had it.[96]

Although now aged seventy-four, Hopper set out to drive, reaching Pacific Palisades on December 9. They had planned to make the Huntington Hartford Foundation their base for explorations down the coast, but Jo later admitted, "Once there I really was too exhausted to drag on farther, the beautiful Fr. Lloyd Wright house & separate studio—even another studio for me, (which I turned back, not needing two & keeping someone else out) & delicious food we had then with their fine chef André in charge, so we just stayed on, a week at a time, then another month & another until June & most of our 6 months had past."[97] The first week Edward wrote to John Clancy: "We have ended up in this place and it's a very comfortable place to be. Good food here and good places to live in. I do not know how long we shall stay but it is so easy living here that it will be hard to break away."[98]

Jo recorded the details of their "splendid" temporary two-and-a-half-room home "with separate studio, out one door, in the other with no implications of feeding, sleeping or laundry anywhere about that good studio with lots of good shelves & one side the north, all glass slanted at an angle facing road—dead end & steep hillside with glorious clouds coming up from behind on cobalt sky."[99] She praised the hot shower in their "delux private bath." The accommodations were much more luxurious than those to which the Hoppers normally treated themselves while on vacation or those they had at home.

With all of their meals prepared by the staff, life was easy for Jo. Except for lunch, which was delivered in a basket at noon, meals were communal, giving her ample opportunity for conversation. This, however, was not so agreeable to Edward, who, she reported, "can't abide by community life. At meals he retired to farther end of table & wasn't at all sociable."[100] As for herself, she exclaimed: "What a God Send for me, not a stroke of house worry, pleasant people as much as one cared for, time went speedily."[101] She referred to Dr. John Vincent, the director of the foundation, as "Beloved John."[102]

Hopper received nothing but good news while he was in California. From Clancy he learned that his canvas *Four Lane Road* had been sold for six thousand dollars (the gallery's commission on such sales was a third).[103] Then he received the 1957 *Art News Annual* with Parker Tyler's article "Hopper/Pollock."[104] Declaring "Hopper's scenes are always composed rather than copied," Tyler emphasized the formal aspects of Hopper's art, viewing him as much more than a literal realist.[105] Hopper wrote to Tyler: "Your article . . . has been unusual in the sense that I think it is the first time my painting has been considered from a purely plastic point of view."[106] Tyler, with his strong interest in cinema, had noted, "Many of his works are like camera-shots consciously framed to give us a purified version of that strange blend of communicativeness and incommunicativeness that is 'Hollywood.' "[107]

That same month, the *Time* magazine cover story appeared, pointing out Hopper's historical significance by placing him in the tradition of American realists from John Singleton Copley to Thomas Eakins.[108] Alexander Eliot's article praised Hopper for having "opened a whole new chapter in American realism, painting a new world, never before pictured."[109] Although the publicity value of a *Time* cover was not lost on Hopper, both he and Jo were upset by the article itself. Jo thought it contained "belittling remarks," which made them feel betrayed by Johnson and Eliot.[110] She referred to the piece as "that so wretched Time article, making of E.H. a vulgarian or trying to."[111] She complained: "We are (I am) outraged at the vulgarity & falsity of their publication of E. Hopper—& they propose to make this source material for prosperity? E. Hopper has fine delicate hands & never cracked his knuckles! Nor does any of the people he ever painted—gas station attendants etc. That is definitely not the way he regards his world."[112] She deplored "the nefarious influence of 'Time' " and insisted: "It will only send him faster back into his Ivory Tower—where he sees with clairvoyant clarity the simplicity & sleeping beauty of his own reality. One is outraged at this effort to make him a mut among muts. He who with Horace, E. Hopper could always sing: 'Odi profanum vulgus et arceo' ['I hate the profane crowd and fend them off']."[113]

Aware of the Hoppers' distress over the piece, the assistant director of the foundation, Charles B. Rogers, wrote to *Time,* commenting: "Since Edward Hopper came to the Huntington Hartford Foundation recently, I've had an opportunity to learn that this reticent fellow has a good sense of humor, and is not always silent. He broke his silence in facing himself on your cover. To quote him on your article—"damn."[114] Jimmy De Lory, whose service station in Orleans Hopper had painted, wrote in to defend Hopper: "I disagree that 'the Hoppers go miles out of their way to get gas a fraction of a cent cheaper,' as they buy some of it from me and not at cut-rate prices. Mrs. Hopper appreciates our clean rest rooms."[115] Andrew Wyeth, however, loved the story, writing: "I think your article on Edward Hopper the most moving and understanding you have ever published. Many artists should read this."[116]

TOWARD RECONCILIATION: 1957–1958

LIFE IN PACIFIC PALISADES was so effortless that the experience helped to ease tensions between Edward and Jo. She had company and conversation, a place to paint, and no obligation to cook. He had tranquillity and plenty to read. He even managed to find a subject that he felt like painting. On February 18, he wrote to Clancy, "I've not done much considering the length of time we've been here: just an unfinished watercolor, but I hope to start a canvas soon."[1] By March 22, Hopper was uncertain whether to stay on in California, but soon gave in to the comforts of foundation life. Jo noted that he so disliked driving in Los Angeles that he preferred to remain "in the Canyon at Pacific Palisades, altho completely unimpressed by the rich green depths."[2] Responding in a minimal way to the new visual stimuli, Hopper reportedly commented: "The Pacific Ocean is sort of misty, grayish."[3]

While other guests pursued their work, Edward availed himself of the library. Jo later reported: "E. did one sizable canvas & one watercolor & read thru the nice library the rest of the time & enjoyed our neighbors, the birds, so tame, the charming deer & raccoons. I had a pet gopher, Gladys, the gopher took to us on her own—& a memorable big cat who put up with me, the darling. . . . The animals really are worth while."[4]

Among the other guests was Max Eastman, once the editor of *The Masses,* where Jo had published illustrations during the 1910s. Eastman had written some of the earliest articles on Freud and psychoanalysis to appear in the American popular press, and had published pieces in some of the magazines that commissioned Hopper's illustrations.[5] Of course, Hopper had no desire to reminisce about the days when he had had to illustrate to earn his living. Jo, who thought the two might get along well, reported that Eastman, who called on her husband to see his new canvas, got nowhere in conversation with him.[6] By the time he met Hopper, Eastman's once radical politics had shifted to the right; he despised Truman.[7] True to her growing sense of history, Jo recorded the names of their fellow guests. There was a poet, Charles Wagner, and a writer and editor, Charles Neider, who knew Thomas Mann and his family and "wrote well on them"; also Lily and Ernst Toch (an Austrian-born composer of Hopper's generation who also wrote about music); Esther Bates, the writer; Carl Carmer, also a writer, and his wife, Betty, who had been an illustrator and willingly posed for Jo; but then a couple of educators from Vermont who "knew the answers to everything," causing Edward to take "special exception."[8]

Charles Neider, who was an admirer of Hopper's work, recalls Jo as "a strange little lady . . . quite resentful of her husband's growing fame."[9] "She complained to anyone who would listen. She wanted recognition." Neider remembers Jo as "competitive" with Hopper, who, he said, indicated this to him with "a rather wry humor." He still remembers that she was "unconsciously amusing," recalling how when they lined up for dinner, she once asked him, "Can you tell me quickly what Proust was about?" Neider asserts that "to say Ed was not talkative is an understatement." He remembers a taciturn, quiet, and modest man with a stooped posture, "as if embarrassed by his height." Hopper, he recalls, "was difficult to engage in conversation" and "could be silent for the whole dinner." By contrast, Eastman was "the ladies' man and still very attractive."

While in southern California, the Hoppers renewed their friendship with Edna and Kenneth MacGowan, the drama critic, author, and former director of the Provincetown Players, whom Jo had known since her days as an actress. Jo recalled that MacGowan, who taught in the drama department at UCLA, "made time to do a lot for us."[10]

With Edward out of his studio so much of the time, Jo took the opportunity to paint there, producing oils and watercolors of views from the studio window. She painted several landscapes, the facade of their house, their Buick parked just outside, a red lily, and several portraits.[11] She also produced a few drawings. This was really an ideal environment for Jo; her only regret was that "none of my activities bred contagion in Eddy (as intended)."[12]

At the end of April, Hopper reported to Clancy, "Not much painting for me here this winter, but I have one good canvas 30 × 50, and an unfinished

Josephine N. Hopper, Buick in California Canyon, *1957. Oil on canvas, 32 × 22″ (81.3 × 55.9 cm.).*

water color."[13] *California Hills,* the watercolor, depicts a tall green hill with a sand bank at the ridge of a road on the right. On the other side of the composition is a "building of modern design," which Hopper said was a corner of one of the studios.[14] He was unable to complete the watercolor in California because, as Jo reported, "a most aggressive female," discovering that he had been on the cover of *Time,* "determined the hours when & where E. was working & descended on him—not withstanding the basic assurance that work was sacred & no intrusions to be tolerated."[15] As a result, he took this watercolor with him to Cape Cod that summer and managed to finish it there. As usual it was the sky that remained to be done.[16]

The canvas that Hopper painted in late February or March was called *Western Motel.* In the record book, Jo described the subject as a "Deluxe green motel room, mahogany bed, pink cover, dark red chair with blue robe." The female figure was a "haughty blond in dark red, her Buick outside window green."[17] In her diary, Jo described the painting, "with its front, that glass front of our fine Lloyd Wright guest house."[18]

With so much company and the frequent use of Edward's studio, Jo had little reason to complain. It is not surprising that, according to her own notes, she made "no winter account" in her diary.[19] Jo recalled that "it got too late to go to Mexico" and that Edward was "anxious to get to the Cape," driving all the three thousand miles of the return trip "with little sign of fatigue."[20] They left California on June 6 and arrived in New York on the nineteenth, concluding that "the East sure lets one down on energy" although their studio was "not so dirty as expected."[21]

Although they did not linger in the city, Jo managed to have a few dealers in to look at her work. One was Herman Gulack, who had immigrated from Latvia to the United States in 1922, at the age of thirteen. An artist himself, Gulack had studied painting with Moses Soyer and Philip Evergood. That spring, he had sent Hopper a catalogue of the first show at his new Greenwich Gallery at 71 Washington Place. The exhibition, which included Hopper's *Automat,* had been well received, drawing important young critics, such as Irving Sandler, and getting reviewed in *Arts* magazine.[22] It was accompanied by an ambitious catalogue, entitled *Fifty Contemporary American Artists,* for which Gulack had commissioned an essay from A. L. Chanin, a lecturer at the Museum of Modern Art.[23]

Back on the Cape by July 23, the Hoppers found themselves in the midst of their neighbors' woes. They went to Dick Magee's annual birthday party only to learn that Nell's eyesight had failed.[24] They were scandalized that Dad Stephens's son, Bob, had left his wife Marie after sixteen years of marriage, and had rapidly remarried. Jo commented that she had "taken this news hard, have been able to think of little else."[25] Even though she frequently counted among her blessings that Edward did not chase "the fluesies," she clearly identified with the "valiant" Marie.

Members of the *Reality* group also surfaced, including Joseph Hirsch and Raphael and Rebecca Soyer, who were renting on the Cape again. "Their frugality amused us," Soyer recalled. "They took us out to dinner in Truro ... not to any of the restaurants generally frequented by artists and their friends, but to 'Bill's,' a nondescript diner on the road," which Jo claimed had better food "than in any of the high-tone places."[26]

Davis Herron came over for the usual round of chess, but Jo forbade any more sessions lasting until the wee hours.[27] Charles Neider, whom they had just met in California, dropped by with his wife, Joan, and gave the Hoppers two of his books, to Edward the short stories of Twain, and to Jo a biography of Fanny Stevenson. Jo judged that Fanny was a "so much finer person—& artist—than husband Robt. Louis S[tevenson],"[28] as always seeing her own parallels with such artist-couples and with women cast into their husbands' shadows; she envied the recognition as partner (coauthor) accorded Fanny Stevenson.

Horace Snow, who owned the Shell filling station, also became friendly. When out driving around Truro, they would sometimes stop at the station so Jo could use the rest room. Horace's widow, Norma Snow, relates that the Hoppers gave them, as a wedding gift, a painting by Jo titled *Truro Hospitality,* which refers to those rest rooms. When the Snows came to tea for the presentation of the painting, Jo hesitated, saying, "I don't know, maybe it needs a few touches," only to have Edward speak up: "Jo, it's alright; you know that's all finished and you want to give it to Snowy."[29]

While Jo's paintings could be given away, Edward's were continuing to sell. He was selected for the Purchase Prize of two thousand dollars in the Fourth International Hallmark Art Competition and decided to send his new watercolor, *California Hills.* Hopper was surprised by the price, which was about three times the going rate. Still having the work with him on Cape Cod when he wrote to Clancy, he noted that to assure safe shipment, he was "packing it very carefully." He added: "The sky I put in the picture here seems very good for it."[30] That summer he also won the Salute to the Arts Award of the New York Board of Trade.

A surprising inquiry arrived from his important early patron Stephen Clark, asking whether the Rehn Gallery still represented him. Hopper answered, referring Clark to Clancy, and offering an unusual expression of gratitude: "I have always appreciated your having acquired my work in the past, and from the very first when few others were interested."[31] Hopper also wrote to Clancy, alerting him to an imminent visit from Clark and recommending his canvases *Western Motel* and *Hotel Room.*[32] Clark, in fact, acquired *Western Motel.*

The Hoppers left the Cape early to be in time for the October 17 benefit for the American Federation of the Arts at the Wildenstein Gallery. The exhibition, "The American Vision: Paintings of Three Centuries," featured *Early Sunday Morning.* At the opening gala, Clare Booth Luce told Jo that she would like to visit her studio the following spring.[33]

When George Biddle tried to reach Hopper to get his signature on a petition requesting the creation of a contemporary art wing at the Metropolitan Museum, Jo was instructed to fend off the phone calls.[34] Edward did not agree with the proposal, fearing that the Metropolitan would just end up showing more "gobble de gook"; nor did he trust Biddle, who sent out only the last page of his petition for signatures.

After all Jo's nagging, Hopper finally got her into an exhibition. When the Boston Public Library invited him to send watercolors for an exhibition traveling to India and the Philippines, he declined, but suggested his wife's work. He pointed out her recent exhibition history—the Metropolitan, the Whitney, and the Corcoran. Here was an exhibition that Hopper clearly did not care about, sufficiently remote and insignificant. The library accepted his suggestion, and she submitted three works to choose from: *Methodist Church, Provincetown; Three Children on Cape Elizabeth;* and *Mission,* showing an early sixteenth-century interior at Saltillo.[35]

As October was ending, Jo remarked that Edward "can't get started on large new canvas with figures—an interior."[36] The delay would be longer than they could imagine. On December 17, Edward had to return to New York Hospital for another round of prostate surgery, which left him uncomfortable and gloomy, remembering all too well the complications suffered after similar surgery ten years earlier. Jo was upset too that the hospital room for her "poor darling" was costing them thirty-two dollars a day.[37] Taking no chances, she lined up friends of the Catholic, Protestant, and Jewish faiths to pray for his safe recovery.[38] Edward, who was operated upon after six days of hospitalization, only began to regain his appetite five days later. He had lost a lot of weight and his recovery was slow.

By January 12, 1958, Hopper's doctor was concerned enough to schedule another session in the operating room. Days after this second surgery, Edward was busy signing some of his old drawings and watercolors that Jo had brought up so they could give them to his doctors. (The anesthesiologist, for example, had suggested that he would waive his fee in exchange for an inscribed drawing.[39]) Hopper told Jo that these old works "gave him the creeps."[40] In principle, he did not like to sell or exhibit his drawings and the old watercolors were probably ones of which he did not think too highly.

As Edward's condition improved, he began to feel bored. On January 23, he was sent home, where Jo diligently played nurse to her "sick boy,"[41] until his lack of appreciation began to get to her: "Sometimes as I look at him I regret having lifted a finger, he's all that self centered—his mind not big enough to include anything but himself sick or well."[42] He sat and read all the time—the same fare as ever, the old books, art books, old copies of *The New Yorker* and *The New York Times Book Review.* The latter especially galled, since these were the hoards he tried to make her discard.

Herman Gulack, who had visited Jo's studio the previous July, stopped by to choose some of her works for a spring show.[43] He selected ten—*Fire Escape, San Esteban, Obituary (Fleurs du Temps Jadis), Park outside Studio Window, Power of the Press (Blue Rocker), Cape Bedroom, Washington Square Bedroom, Chez Hopper II,* and *Cape Flowers*—but he told Jo that he liked all her pictures. She later recalled that Edward had actually named her canvas *Power of the Press,* about which she reflected: "I'm glad I put in that stack of newspaper and magazines beside little blue Fanny—that E.H. christened 'Power of the Press.' When it was shown at Herman's, the critic from the Villager spied her paper under the New Yorker & yapped with glee. Its photo carried off and that's how it appeared in their 25″ year Birthday issue."[44]

Jo was so excited about her show that she immediately ordered some frames from the Revel Picture Frame Company,[45] which sent Kenneth Lux out to her studio. He recalled her as "a real character out of books," wearing three sweaters in her studio, which was freezing cold and piled with cardboard boxes. To Lux, she seemed "tiny, prim, a little kookie, very vivacious." He recalled that "she spoke like the Good Fairy in the Wizard of Oz," "looked like a ballerina, wore ballet slippers and tip-toed around." Jo asked if Lux's wife kept things for a long time and pulled down a dress that she proudly proclaimed she had owned for twenty-nine years.[46] She herself wrote of keeping "long gloves of another age," "pitiful objects," making her ask herself "what strangling hold the past keeps on me? Is it that I never trust the future."[47]

When Gulack was late in having her pictures picked up for the show, Jo's paranoia took hold and she imagined a "greedy gang haunting him & tearing my work apart."[48] Nearly a week later, when he phoned to explain the delay in setting up his new gallery, she was greatly relieved and invited him to tea.[49] Gulack came and stayed on to play chess with Edward. Jo told him that her greatest interest in showing with him was not sales, but that she "just wanted my 'children' to have friends . . . good homes & appreciation."[50]

On March 4, Jo recorded that "My darling Eddy spent hours varnishing, hammering in keys to stretch out & nail in frames, tacking labels on the 9 canvases invited to Greenwich Gallery."[51] Thinking of possible publicity, she contacted Berenice Abbott for prints of her photograph of Jo with Abbott's cat, Gigi. Edward, who admired Abbott's work, said that this photograph was "a masterpiece & the most sympathetic photo I've ever seen."[52]

In the midst of it all, Jo was reading a book by Albert Ellis called *How to Live with a Neurotic.*[53] She sought the book out at the library "to find out how to get on with myself," but she concluded that she was "not nearly as neurotic as I suspected."[54] Finally, she realized that although Edward was "always complaining. I a neurotic—from this book I learn if there is any neurotic about here it's E. himself."[55] Ellis defined a neurotic as

> an individual who theoretically has the capacity to be effective, creative, and free from sustained or exaggerated anxiety and hostility. However, because he has one or more significant irrational, unrealistic assumptions—such as the philosophy that he must be universally approved, or that he should not be frustrated, or that it is terrible if he fails at something he would like to do—the neurotic

creates in himself, and then keeps sustaining by constant negative self-talk, various unpleasant and self-harming emotions.[56]

Jo may have related Edward's frequent inability to paint to Ellis's description; he had certainly taken the early rejection of his work to heart. Accustomed as she was to sniffing out parallels in her reading, she must have said "Ah Hah!" again and again as she conned the checklist of characteristics to look for in "recognizing emotional disturbance." She surely would have identified a parallel to Edward under the category "Shyness and withdrawal," which Ellis explained: "Believing that they may easily do the wrong thing and that others will spot their mistakes, numberless neurotics become shy and withdrawn, and retreat into various kinds of solitude. Constructively, they may follow useful occupations which demand solitude. . . . Destructively, they may merely avoid people."[57]

When Edward saw Jo's show at the Greenwich Gallery, he esteemed hers the only good work there, discounting the other exhibiting artists (Theodore Fried, Abraham Harriton, and Gaston Longchamp).[58] He even went so far as to write notes on ten of Jo's catalogues and send them to people in the press and museums. For the opening party on March 30, Jo's friends turned out, but Edward claimed it would have been "too much standing up & hand shaking for a convalescent," although he had already gained back ten of the fifteen pounds that he had lost.[59] Jo wrote to Marion, "I have such a beautiful serene wall, all to myself & the pictures feel they've gone to heaven."[60]

"A miracle in my life has come to pass," wrote Jo to Rosalind Irvine, calling the Greenwich Gallery "a lovely temple for the spirit," with Gulack "a most appealing young man for its high priest, shy, sympathetic, very intelligent, & incredibly he likes my work, liked it from the first sight of it."[61] She added, "I'm so thrilled . . . so pleased to see my pictures in this lovely peaceful sanctuary."[62] Gulack recalls that Jo, arriving at the gallery, would twirl around in delight.[63] She was ecstatic when her work was reproduced in both the *Christian Science Monitor* and in the the *Villager.*[64] The *Monitor,* noting her "personal style," commented: "Observantly and wittily, she paints domestic interiors, views screened through the fire escape of her apartment, genre compositions with cats, which make frequent entrance."[65] Identified as a former student of Robert Henri and Kenneth Hayes Miller, as well as the wife of Edward Hopper, Jo was credited with having "a substantial underpinning of good design" in her painting.[66]

Her only disappointment was that this recognition came so late, exclaiming "if everyone who could have liked them were not gone away—or dead & I'd be vindicated for feeling so agonized that my work was always left out & despised, sight unseen."[67] She commented that she recognized the effect that her pain had had on her marriage: "Agonized, the whole gamut of tragic frustration visited upon poor E. Hopper! And richly he deserved it! These male animals!"[68]

Jo was ebullient. Meeting Virginia Zabriskie, at the Zabriskie Gallery, which had a Joseph Stella show, she told the dealer that she "had known Stella & . . . he had been kind" to her work.[69] She showed Zabriskie photographs of her paintings and the reproduction in the *Monitor*.[70] Jo heard from Rosalind Irvine that she and Goodrich had seen the show and liked her pictures.[71] The critics Robert Coates and Parker Tyler both saw it as well.[72]

Shortly after Coates visited the Greenwich Gallery, he met Edward at a dinner of the Institute of Arts and Letters. He asked Hopper directly: "Why has your wife been hidden under bushes all this time?" Hopper replied: "She's very bitter about that," to which Coates responded: "My wife is bitter too. She writes."[73] Jo, who recorded this incident, described the two sarcastically as "big bruisers, victims of bitter wives," going off together.[74]

In February, John Lamb, who by then had purchased two of Hopper's watercolors, invited Edward and Jo to take a tour of his office at Young and Rubicam, and to be his guests for lunch. Hopper's interest was piqued and he wrote back, referring indirectly to his having read, with Jo, Vance Packard's *The Hidden Persuaders:*

> Thank you for the invitation to see your advertising agency. One hears such terrible things that the psychologists are saying about Madison Ave. that one would like to look in to see these dens of iniquity. From having met you I can not believe the worst. I should like to see your office but as it tires me to go out of the house, I am doing but little of that now. I go out mostly to see my doctor (surgeon).[75]

Lamb then urged the Hoppers to have lunch with him downtown. Invited to choose any place, they picked Young China, because the Waverly Inn was too far for Edward to walk. Hopper, who had been experiencing pain in his ankle, was using a cane. Afterward they went to Jo's show, where Lamb liked *Chez Hopper II,* but bought nothing.[76] When Gulack's wife stared at Edward's cane, he was quick to tell her it was not "for swank."[77] Lamb, like others before him, pegged Jo as a "sort of Billie Burke character, quick, energetic, flighty, in sharp contrast to Edward's reserve."[78] (The early character actress had played the Good Witch in *The Wizard of Oz.*)

Before the year was out, the Hoppers did visit Lamb and tour all eleven floors of Young and Rubicam. When asked what he thought of the agency, Edward replied with his Yankee economy: "So much for so little."[79] The encounter with commercial art must have brought back memories of the days when Hopper made laborious rounds to advertising agencies with his port-folio under his arm. Even when her show came down on May 13, Jo remained in fine spirits. For the moment, Edward, who had lent a hand, was "my good Eddy";[80] she felt it had been "one of the big events of my life."[81] Many friends had turned out—from notable artists like Edwin Dickinson to the woman who worked at the cafeteria that the Hoppers frequented on Tenth Street.[82] Her self-esteem was so much improved that she began to keep a ledger for her work like the one that she kept regularly for Edward.[83] She was thankful for the lovely space of the Greenwich Gallery, where she felt her paintings "thrived on the grace of God in its beautiful temple & its peace & lovely light & open space & at every angle its distinction of style."[84]

Gulack told Jo that he wanted to give her a retrospective the following January, but she was still too insecure to think about it much, anxious that the gallery might not survive or other obstacles might arise.[85] When the pictures were returned to her studio, Jo noticed that the dingy walls had last been painted twenty years earlier. In that ambience, her work had never looked its best. Only inertia or habitual thrift, not lack of funds, had prevented the Hoppers from maintaining a certain style.

On May 27, Edward bought stretchers to start a canvas 40 × 60". Jo noted that he felt anxious to work on it before leaving for the Cape.[86] By the second of June, he had his canvas drawn in charcoal. Jo found the "long diagonals driving from top left down on horizontal table tops in rows . . . very excit-ing."[87] She also noted a girl on the left, a man on the right, and revolving doors. But she observed with her usual caution: "I hated to inquire but find out it is day light."[88] After lunch at the cafeteria on Tenth Street, Hopper went up to the corner of Thirty-first Street and Fifth Avenue to study the doors of the Automat. This was his first canvas in nearly a year and a half, and Jo was encouraged that he felt he had the strength for it.

About this time, Hopper confided to an interviewer something about how he chose his subjects: "I look all the time for some thing that suggests something to me. Like Voltaire who once remarked, 'My book is finished; all I have to do is write it.' "[89] He liked, he said, to have a clear idea of the image of his painting before he started to work and, once he began, he liked to work continuously, "proceeding across the canvas in a methodical progression."[90] Jo added her own observation: "While he is working: 'everything else stops,' " asserting, not entirely accurately, "We don't do anything else when Eddie's painting a picture."[91]

As he worked on the new canvas, Jo was also painting. Her picture was a view of their hallway, with the banisters seen under the "green nimbus" of the electric light.[92] She felt that Edward's addition of "the houses close up thru window on left" changed everything and not for the better. She commented: "How true what he says about every stroke taking one farther from one's first intention."[93] The next day, she commented that Edward's "canvas had given him pause. Naturally he wants everything there installed in charcoal before he puts on a stroke of paint. He makes trips over to the nearby Automat on Bdway, but comes back tired."[94] Herman Gulack recalled running into Hopper at the Automat, sitting by a window with just a plate with two rolls. When Gulack asked if he would like a cup of coffee, he replied that he was only making believe to be a customer in order to observe the view through the window and across the street.[95] Hopper, having made sketches for the overall disposition of his composition, would then retain in his memory his impression of what he had seen.

By June 18, Hopper estimated that he needed another two weeks to finish. The blond girl was "certainly very voluptuous in the present stage of the picture,"[96] remarked Jo, adding that Edward "has been strengthening the bold white angle of the window in his restaurant against the dark building across the narrow street outside. Very startling, and the strong light coming in that annihilates the blond beauty . . . in the force of its glare."[97] She was impressed that he could make "the light on the walls and table tops so much more important" than the two figures.[98] Hopper's sketch reveals his earlier conception, which placed the two figures closer together and suggested contact between their eyes. Jo noted that Edward "finished *Sunlight in Downtown Cafeteria*" on the thirtieth of June.[99] In the record book, she added in quotes: "Eakins not interested in color," evidently recording Edward's comment.[100]

Hopper's patron Stephen Clark visited the studio on the first of July. With less than a day's notice, the Hoppers got up at dawn to "look ship shape." Clark, who requested that John Clancy send him the new canvas so that he could look at it at leisure, bought *Sunlight in a Cafeteria* for nine thousand dollars the following autumn.[101] Hopper wrote to him: "I'm very pleased that you have acquired my picture 'Sunlight in a Cafeteria.' I think it's one of my very best pictures."[102] Jo's comment shows precise awareness of differences between her aesthetic preferences and those of Edward and his patron: Clark was "much interested in E.'s light. Light & Space—the subject of this canvas. E. said—not large forms—because they fill up *space*. How true so that's why E. gives up those forms I liked so much, he more interested in empty space that is not empty—because filled with space consciousness."[103] Clark paid no attention to Jo's work, she said: wives' work was considered so much "damnation & Bitchery as far as he can see."[104]

As they were preparing to leave for the Cape, Walter Pach knocked on their door with the news of the death of Guy du Bois. He had been in ill health, they knew, back from France and living with his daughter in Boston. Jo recalled the "groom's man" at their wedding and thought that for once Edward managed to write an adequate condolence letter.[105] Right up to their departure on July 28, Jo was working on a new painting. That summer proved to be dreary, damp, and dark. When the sunlight was in short supply, Edward felt little energy and he produced no work at all; but Jo, with a possible show in the offing, managed to finish three small oils. She also reconsidered the merits of her painting of the *Old South Truro Meetinghouse* and took it back to New York.

By November 6, the Hoppers had returned to Washington Square. Thanksgiving Day they learned that Walter Pach was dead.[106] At his funeral the following Sunday, they noticed painfully that fewer and fewer of their old friends turned out, although they did see Edwin Dickinson and Van Wyck Brooks.[107] Jo learned from Herman Gulack that his brother's house, where he had his gallery, was up for sale. Still, he came and looked at her watercolors and wanted five or ten to sell. She was not willing to part with many of her early works, but Gulack agreed to show them as "not for sale" along with more recent works like her painting of marigolds from the previous summer on the Cape. Irving Gulack, one of his brothers who backed the gallery, was not thrilled with Herman's lack of enthusiasm about selling, rather than showing, works of art.[108] Herman, with his sweet and gentle personality, was anything but a hard sell.

Jo was in Gulack's Christmas show. She was disappointed, however, when she saw that the friends whom she had recommended to him—Maurice Becker, Lucy Bayard, and Dick Stark—had not sent their best work. She then took in two more early watercolors that she had unearthed—of the little dancer Margaret Van Epps.[109] The *Villager* described her work as "several fresh, uncomplicated water colors which dwell as airily as a summer breeze on moments of a children's play and on rural vistas. Black seldom appears in her palette, details are not belabored and the subject is left to speak for itself."[110]

On December 13, Hopper went back to New York Hospital for yet another prostate operation. The day following surgery, he got out of bed and collapsed on top of Jo. She was bruised, but thankful that she had caught him "to save his breaking a bone on furniture or radiator."[111] He came home from the hospital on December 21. By the end of the year, he had improved enough that Jo was feeling relieved and thankful. For a moment, she had her two wishes, his company and a gallery where she could show.

EXCURSION INTO PHILOSOPHY: 1959

WHEN GULACK RETURNED Jo's twenty-five pictures on January 17, 1959, she greeted them not as "bastards" but as her "jewels."[1] When she suggested painting Herman's portrait, Edward proposed that the two men could play chess, to keep Herman occupied. This was not Jo's ideal pose since they would be bending over. Although she accepted the idea, the portrait was never executed.

An article about Jo by Frank Crotty appeared in the February 1 issue of the Worcester *Telegram Gazette*. Although she liked the piece, she felt it served no useful purpose, for the Greenwich Gallery was closing and her April show was not to take place. The paper had reproduced Berenice Abbott's photo of Jo, but not Edward's tiny caricature of her as the "She Devil Angel" that they had given Crotty.[2] This was an image of Jo that Hopper had made more than once and that they both found amusing.

She was very pleased when Edward sent the article to Lloyd Goodrich, telling him:

> The Greenwich Gallery . . . has run out of luck, and has had to discontinue, which is too bad, as it was a very beautiful gallery. Jo was to have had a show there in April of this year, but that is off and this

Edward Hopper, Josie as a
She-Devil, *1956. Ink on
paper.*

article that is enclosed was publicity that was to have helped. This article was the result of an interview with her on her work . . . made last August on Cape Cod. It is headed by the best cat and woman picture I have ever seen—though it suffers much from reproduction on course newsprint paper.[3]

Time had lessened Hopper's embarrassment at helping promote Jo's work. To express their profound appreciation for what Gulack had done for Jo and their genuine fondness for him, the Hoppers each gave him an inscribed volume. Edward's was a small book of excerpts from Ralph Waldo Emerson's *Essays,* inscribed simply "To Herman Gulack from Edward Hopper." Jo, however, gave him a volume of Robert Henri's lectures called *The Art Spirit.* In it, she wrote: "For Herman Gulack, whom Robert Henri, because he loved the serious young, would have welcomed to his fold. But even at this later date, Herman feels the warmth & wisdom of the great master."[4]

The Hoppers learned that their landlord, New York University, was being forced by new city regulations to install central heating in their building.[5] The university had previously installed heat in the offices on the first floor, which, according to Jo, were "kept so hot they keep the door open onto the street—while we perish on the floors above. And all the back breaking work of coal & ash—thru distance too!"[6] But they adored their pot-bellied Murray Crane stove, which they had promised Berenice Abbott that they would never give to anyone else but her.[7]

On Easter Sunday, Jo and Edward attended services at the Church of the Ascension, and Jo remarked in her diary that she was "surprised that E. willing to go without argument."[8] For the moment, Hopper seemed to have mellowed in what he was willing to do to appease or even to please Jo, perhaps out of greater dependency due to illness and age. Jo noted how slowly he descended their stairs.[9] On the fourth of May, the Metropolitan Museum curator Theodore Rousseau and his wife visited the studio so the Hoppers could show them the sole painting they had ever collected, their American primitive *Calvin Howe and His Two Sisters*. Rousseau had no idea as to the artist, but, according to Jo, he "saw Ingres influence" and found "the seated child in foreground monumental."[10] Rousseau suggested that he send Albert Gardiner, a curator of American art, to look at the picture. He commented that Jo's pictures were "so gay," while his wife, who adored cats, spied the legendary Arthur peering around the curtain in *Obituary*.[11] Jo, who was pleased at these responses, noted that she "babbled of Marie Laurencin & her triumph over specific gravity."[12] Jo's interest in Laurencin and her own lack of interest in giving forms weight fit the whole picture of her distance from Edward's aesthetics.

Other visitors from the museum were not so charmed. It was not what Jo described as "our lovely house—falling plaster, awful floors, such halls—and stairs"[13] that discouraged Robert Beverly Hale, the curator in charge of contemporary art, and his wife, Barbara. When the Hales visited the Hoppers, they came under the mistaken assumption that they were to see Edward's work. Instead, they were presented with tea and Jo's, which, Barbara recalls, they did not like.[14]

Suddenly opportunities seemed to open for Jo. Mortimer Borne of the Connoisseur Gallery expressed interest.[15] Rosalind Irvine had selected *Cape Cod Bedroom* for the Whitney Annual.[16] When John Clancy and his wife, Winnie, came to see Jo's paintings, he surprised her by offering to "show them within a year."[17]

Hopper, who was suffering from shortness of breath, was not eager to get to the Cape that summer. Since Jack Kelly had died, the Hoppers had found no one to open and close the house.[18] Finally, Mike Howard, Kelly's brother-in-law, to whom they had written, agreed to help out.[19] In his weakened and more cooperative state, Edward even helped Jo sew one of her alteration projects on her "doll size Singer," rather than have her struggle with the machine.[20] The Hoppers reached Truro on July 9. Edward, feeling ill, was not even up to the effort of climbing down their cliff for a swim.[21] Mostly, he just sat indoors, immersing himself in books and magazines. He complained to Clancy, "We are having the most continued bad weather I've ever known here; rain, fog, mist and cloud, and almost no sun."[22] Jo reported in late July that "any effort drenches him in perspiration—a sign of weakness."[23] As for herself, she admitted that she "hadn't the energy to fight like a tigress to drive the car—after all these years. But in an emergency," she reassured, "I can. Even without the proficiency of frequent practice."[24]

Even if too tired to combat each other, Jo and Edward each managed to paint. Somehow, Hopper found the strength to produce a major canvas. On the seventeenth of August, Jo, telling Lloyd Goodrich that her note came from the "most private Bureau of Intelligence" and that it "may be intercepted," reported, "Health of E.H. some what improved, so after month's sterility, he starting canvas—man staring at spot of sunlight on floor & scandalous background. Did he kill her? Can't tell yet. This of course not his interpretation."[25] Elaborating on her fantasy, she revealed that once again she was playing a part in the process: "I'm so excited . . . this the 3rd day since start. He has me stretched out in back with not a stitch on—playing dead, if so required."[26] Jo eagerly reports playing a role again, after several years in which her reports of progress have continued to be vividly detailed, but make no further mention of her creating roles or even collecting props.

While Hopper was working, Frank Falacci, a reporter for the Boston *Sunday Globe* called to request an interview. Jo answered the phone and refused, telling him that Edward was "just recovering and has started to work again. . . . It is terribly hard work for him. . . . He simply must not be disturbed when he is working. He does not like to have even his train of thought broken. It's one of the reasons we live here, you know. . . . We are on the Cape Cod Bay side, quite isolated. . . . It helps."[27] Engaged by this reporter in conversation, Jo admitted: "Mr. Hopper, you know, is an introvert. I'm an extrovert. He is very shy of people." But she did describe both the house as looking "like an old fish house" and Edward's attire: "He usually wears a floppy panama hat, blue denims or corduroy trousers, a jersey and Greek sandals. If anyone comes to the house though, he kicks off the sandals, thinks they are too conspicuous. I can't get him into Bermudas, too tall."[28] Listening to Jo's end of the entire conversation, Edward corrected her occasionally, protesting that the house he had designed did not really look like a fish house.

Despite such uninvited interruptions, Hopper finished his new painting on the twenty-sixth of August, telling Jo that he thought *Excursion into Philosophy* might "be his best."[29] Jo first referred to this work in her diary as *Excursion into Reality,* describing it there as "with book of Plato on couch, resorted to on morning after episode with young woman who didn't wear Duncan Sandals—not that kind. She an addict to 4″ spikes, according to

Edward Hopper, Excursion into Philosophy, *1959. Oil on canvas, 30 × 40″ (76.2 × 101.6 cm.).*

E.H."[30] Jo wrote to Goodrich, telling him that the painting was "rather scandalous & he won't let people around here see it" and giving him the same information but explaining its origins:

> I said "a nice girl wouldn't have the soles of her feet so grimy."
> E. said: "I'm not sure she is a nice girl."
> But, said I, "soles of feet do get that way in Duncan Sandals."
> To which E.: "That girl doesn't wear Duncan Sandals. She wears 4″ spikes."

Jo, who wore the Greek-styled Duncan Sandals, which were made in Provincetown, concluded: "Guess I can't do anything more for that lassie."[31] Later, in the record book, she noted: "Real Hopper landscape out of window: A.M. Sun in blue sky touching green dune top, window sill, rug, man, leg of female in pink shirt & back wall. The open book is Plato, reread too late. Walls neutral greenish. Man in white shirt."[32] Jo explained to Goodrich: "Edward's picture came along easily. I'm so anxious for you to see. Edward thinks it his best. Maybe. It's a new note for him. I'm so happy he could do it. It's a valiant thing to fight down inertia, after so many months sterile & his supply of energy at low ebb."[33]

In her joy at Edward's recovery, Jo evidently failed to recognize that he had painted an image offering parallels to their own long-standing sexual tensions, focusing so brutally on the female's posterior and the discomfiture of the male. When Edward did offer his own interpretation, he made it clear that he meant to represent a stereotype of the sexually unbridled female. This he suggested pictorially by means of physique, posture, and partial undress; and he embroidered the sexual implication with his talk of her spike heels and being not "nice." It is a figure of sexual license, then, that he locates in an ascetic context, on a couch that could hardly be less sensual, next to a male depicted as at most slightly unbuttoned from the neck and quite abject, seated next to a book that lies, as if tossed there, on the edge, open so that in aspect it replicates the posterior cleavage behind.

The tossed volume, according to the record book, implies "Plato, reread too late." Now "Plato" may imply the concept widely known as "Platonic love," which directs passion away from specific beautiful objects toward beauty in the ideal. In Hopper's compressed narrative, "reread too late" would then imply a return to Platonic idealism only after experimenting with the specific attraction of sex, and finding it less than expected or hoped. The implication that abstinence would be preferable to a physical relationship would offer a parallel, with sardonic thrust, to Edward's own rejection of Jo's even tardy and limited sexual demands. In the Hoppers' fantasy narrative, a scandalous episode with a licentious female precedes the awakening to philosophy. Here in the back of their minds may be a parallel episode in Santayana's *The Last Puritan,* which featured among the volumes in the caricature *Le Rêve de Josie.* Santayana imagines a student discovered in his room at Harvard in "a licentious episode . . . in the arms of an actress,"[34] and overcome by regret that his behavior has hurt and offended his deeply religious tutor.[35] Discomfiture at the conflict between a free sexuality and traditional restrictive morality offers parallels with the experience of the Hoppers' entire generation in the turbulent passage between Victorian values and the liberalities of modern urban life.

In Hopper's portrayal, and interpretive fantasy, the female appears licentiously slack and the male tensely tormented. For her part, Jo virtually sang of Edward's victory over inertia. And still, as she interpreted his representation of the female, she felt that she, the old actress, to get into the part, would have to play dead. Intuitively she grasped the ultimate thrust of the relentless competitor with whom she engaged in the struggle of life.

Perhaps sensing that Edward had revealed his most intimate self in this picture, Jo wrote to Goodrich: "It may be that Edward won't stand for naming the new picture 'Excursion Into Philosophy.' You know E. Hopper. He'll call it 'Sunlight on the Floor' or something equally non-committal. But 'Excursion into Philosophy' is its true name, that's how he referred to it himself & I grabbed right on to it as perfect."[36]

The daring title entered the record book along with a poignant note: "On hearing about this canvas, Stephen Clark had come to see it. At old 5th Ave. address, he learned of gallery moving to E. 61st St., but when he got there, gallery locked, no one there. He wrote to tell us of his disappointment, and died a short time after that. It should have been his picture." Jo later wrote to Malcolm and Happy Chace, collectors in Providence, Rhode Island, who had purchased Hopper's *Four Lane Road,* telling them, "We'd love to hear what you think of Edward's Excursion into Philosophy. It's a new direction for E.H. & he was so pleased with it himself. Not for you darlings—it's a museum piece."[37]

Jo's own painting of that summer was a view of the north end of their home for which she reused her old title *Chez Hopper.* She described the thirty-by-twenty-five-inch canvas as "mostly dark window that makes that end of house. Pas grand chose—but E. says it has achieved 'presence.' "[38] At this time of harmony between them, Edward was much kinder in his criticism of Jo's work. She later recalled asking him on their front doorstep: "Isn't this good as Paradise?" to which he responded: "Better, no people, no harps."[39]

Despite Hopper's continued success and growing fame, he and Jo felt besieged by the incursion of the Abstract Expressionists and other supporters of abstract art. When they read in the conservative *Art Times* that Hale had purchased Jackson Pollock's *Autumn Rhythm* for the Metropolitan Museum for twenty-five thousand dollars,[40] the acquisition seemed like a death knell for American art as they knew it. After a dinner party at the Whitney, Jo had written to Rosalind Irvine, exclaiming, "We were so happy with the people at our table. . . . No fights over Picasso or anything."[41]

The Hoppers were fans of *Art Times,* a modest new publication edited by Philip Bisaccio and published by Billi Boros, both of whom had come to call. They were conservative in outlook, and their stand against abstraction appealed to the Hoppers. Jo had written a letter to the editor, exclaiming: "I'm so glad my husband subscribed to the Art Times. . . . The April issue . . . so succinctly states outrages that cry out for protest."[42] Several months later, Edward was moved to write: "I met Conrad Aiken at Orleans, Mass. a few days ago, and he said he had heard that 'The Art Times,' was in difficulty with its continued publication. It is too good to be allowed to die. I am enclosing a small contribution and I sincerely hope you can keep going."[43]

As Jo looked toward the end of another season, she surveyed her little domain in a letter to Marion, praising especially the "attic to absorb clutter [where] we keep all the suitcases and the plain impedimenta—as Caesar called his sinews of war."[44] On their return to New York, new warfare broke out over how to organize all their possessions in the crowded studios. Jo found that Edward challenged her every effort to get the job done, wearing her out in the process: "It has drawn me over spiked barriers, disrupted & tortured my mind to hang on to details & their disposition—the breath of life to E.H. is to wear one out, waste all one's vitality by argument, opposition—just for sake of hindrance. All highly sadistic."[45] She claimed that she did all "the real work, everything but actual hauling heavy weights."[46]

Forced again into taking stock, she reached for a new formulation of the paradox of their two characters. She found herself calling his behavior "cruelty," which one would not expect, yet it was also his brand of "ecstasy," he being "malignant to high degree,"[47] and she questioned whether his behavior pattern reflected

> a sex repression? Dire need of a victim—And I the bitch . . . fight back with tooth & claw if necessary. There are so many meaty little problems I'd like to discuss with some thoroughly understanding mind. So much is now understood, but with whom would one care to admit to extreme intimacy. It isn't that I seek justification for volcanic eruption on my part. Something in me supplies ample justifications. It always has in family relations—there is the will to fight back—resist any ideal of playing martyr—the most disgraceful degradation I can imagine. No indeed, I'm not the makings of a Hopper martyr. I doubt that his mother was ever either. She found so much of herself in me. So cute of her to say once—"Jo, you know neither of us was born Hoppers, we only married them." I had said, I always knew she was one of my people.[48]

§

IN EARLY DECEMBER, when a show of Edward's watercolors and etchings organized by the Currier Gallery of Art in Manchester, New Hampshire, traveled to the Rhode Island School of Design in Providence, the Chaces invited Edward and Jo to stay at their home. They went by train on the day before so that Edward would not "be too limp for all the standing around of a museum opening."[49] Jo explained to her hostess that although Edward "used to stalk about the city streets at all hours and for miles, [he] now gets tired after a few blocks! The effect of not so recent sojourns at the N.Y. Hospital."[50] But, she reassured, "Mr. Hopper isn't an invalid, it's only he gets tired more easily. He eats everything, one cocktail (if any) the limit, prefers not to smoke even." (Hopper had been a cigarette smoker, but had given it up when he learned of the illness of another smoker, the collector Otto Spaeth.[51])

Christmas 1959 gave some reason to celebrate. Jo was "getting a lift" out of being invited to show in the Whitney's "big annual" with Edward's "very handsome" new picture from the Cape.[52] Edward, for the first time in two years, did not spend the season in New York Hospital. Jo "dragged poor E. to 11 a.m. services at the Ascension," only to realize that he was very bored and would not want to go to church again soon.[53] Later, at the Christmas party of Alexander and Jane Eliot, the Hoppers spoke with the writer James Flexner, discovering yet another fan. Eliot gave Hopper a book of poetry inscribed to "the greatest painter of his time."[54] From that period he remembers Hopper wanting him to look at Jo's pictures, which somehow he never did. Reflecting on how he was conditioned by the prevailing biases, Eliot admits, "I was prejudiced, just not open to Jo's work."[55]

PROTEST: 1960

AS THE DECADE of the sixties opened, Edward Hopper was seventy-eight years old. On New Year's Day he stretched and placed on the hulking old easel a forty-by-sixty-inch canvas, for him an ambitious size. He started out "drawing in blue," and what he had in mind became clear enough by the fourth day to dispel some of the suspense: "It turns out to be a batch of Sun bathers—in street clothes—gazing out on an Arizona desert." Jo registered with approval his deliberate pace: "He says 'the way to do is to take plenty of time at the beginning.' How wise."[1] The blue outline sufficed to get her started embroidering a fantasy scenario out of their own past travels: "Sunlight on citizens in Tucson—or some such."[2] In three more days, the scene was filling out and she recognized the trademarks: "Shadows from camp stools or deck chairs very effective—shadows cast back of group, mostly men & light streaming on their heads."[3]

As she continued to look over his shoulder, he kept reiterating: "The time to take time is in the beginning—at start—to lay out . . . impeccable design so it won't be jostled or skimped later on."[4] Awed by the implication of what she was seeing, she wrote the Chaces on January 15 that Edward's work on such a large canvas was "assuring of his condition. He would not be tackling anything of that size if he were dying all over the place—too much high reaching while standing, I so glad." She flattered them by a comparison with their picture, then demonstrated again how well she had followed and understood his work:

> So far, not nearly so fine as 4 Lane Road. This a batch of people sunning themselves (not sunbathers with nothing on)—probably in Tucson, Ariz. with not a drop of water in sight—I don't yet know what he'll do with the sky. Not like him to do a noisy sunset—not he. I wait to see—so far there is only magnificent open space. He's good on space which isn't a bit easy. Clutter gives no trouble at all.[5]

When not engaged with the unfolding drama in the studio, Jo was trying to keep an eye on a real estate developer (who was also a Truro selectman) whom she suspected of being in cahoots with a crooked surveyor to usurp a right-of-way through their land. She was amazed that Edward was "taking this case so casually, jeers at my thinking there is such a thing as justice."[6] Jo was also fearful about New York University's plan to heat their studio with gas, which she considered unsafe. To Edward, who had painted right through the threats of German planes and Russian missiles, such matters hardly seemed to merit time away from the new work.[7]

On rainy days, when the light was too poor to paint, the Hoppers always turned to the movies, with especial predilection for French ones. On January 18, seeing Marcel Carné's *Les Enfants du Paradis,* they were so taken that they sat through a second showing. The setting in the Paris theater world of the 1840s transported them both into the past and played on their fascination with the stage.[8] The next day they saw Claude Chabrol's *Les Cousins,* where the anatomy of indulgences and weaknesses in modern society stirred anything but nostalgia. Drawing a parallel with her own experience, Jo thought the "sinister & tragic types would figure well at parties of Juliana Force."[9]

When the sun sent Edward back to his easel, Jo registered significant changes:

> Group of sun bathers grows more closely knit by their cast shadows chairs & legs & people's legs—effect of a phalanx pointed toward west too early for sunset yet. Phalanx could be some low slung animal gripping surface of the Earth against much tension from west— E. always keen on the surface of the Earth—its everlasting horizontal. I looking in vain for extravagances in the sky. Maybe none to be, just the horizontal triumphs—for miles & miles of prairie.[10]

Acutely she compared his design to the old Greek military formation, and evoked in large terms his instinct for the earth. A day later, she responded again vividly: "The canvas is doing well, one . . . sees a diagonal drive from sky, down into side & across the tall grass of prairie of something that pours down from above like sun rays . . . very striking design of darks—shadows of chair legs massed."[11]

People in the Sun was finished on February 4, the record book reports, giving the scenario a final twist: "People—tourists, color nondescript—hills & slate color (against light). Nobody the least distinguished, but great reality to the group of people, chairs & their shadows."[12] Hopper later remarked of this painting: "The idea was suggested by seeing people in Washington Square Park getting the sun—the park benches in the fall and winter. I changed the locale to a western setting. The greatest problem was to get as much feeling of sunlight on the figures without obliterating their individual character, also to keep the chairs' legs from being too insistent."[13] At a further remove, he offered more general considerations on what he liked to seek, emphasizing the sunlight that had given him so much impetus in his latest works:

> I like the long shadows of early and late sunlight, trying to paint sunlight without eliminating the form under it, if I can. It's very difficult to do. The form begins to obscure the light itself and destroy it. That is the way I feel about sunlight. I would like to do sunlight that was just sunlight in itself perhaps. But it has to be—sunlight has to be on some natural form. I did a picture and that was a problem that came up. . . . It was to be sunlight on these faces and figures, and predominantly sunlight, and it ended up by being the figures themselves with not too much sunlight on them.[14]

§

MEANWHILE, the Whitney's 1959–1960 Annual was causing consternation in critics such as Robert Coates of *The New Yorker* because of the scarcity of work by realist painters. Although Jo and Edward both were represented, they were appalled that most of the show comprised what they regularly referred to as "gobbledegook."[15] Still, Jo was elated to be included, thrilled because Coates mentioned her, and delighted that her *Cape Cod Bedroom* was also reproduced in the *Villager*.[16]

"Gobbledegook" also came under attack during a large party late in January given for *Art Times* at the lavish home on Central Park West of the painter John Koch. Some of the *Reality* crowd was present, including

Raphael Soyer, Maurice Grosser, and Jack Levine. Louis Bouché, whom Jo had known since he showed her work at the Belmaison Gallery in 1922, came in and gave her a hug and kiss, making her feel considered with "sincere affection as one of a chosen group."[17] Bouché addressed the guests later, effectively she thought, skewering people who sought status by switching even though they disliked abstract styles.

At the end of February, Jo showed *Obituary* (with Arthur) and *Jewels for the Madonna (Homage to Illa)* in a show called "The Cat in Art" at the Condon Riley Gallery. Observing the works of her acquaintances (Dorothy Ferris, Peggy Bacon, and Gertrude Nason), Jo noted that her own "looked blanched in the yellow light that left no color, so they receded into the wall—in that vile light. But," she assured herself, "it hardly matters in that hodgepodge."[18] At the opening party, Edward, who had come reluctantly, sat on a cushion in the corner, "too tired & disinterested to stir around"; he had made his disdain clear, "disposing of the cats with one wide glance on arriving."[19]

A similar attitude informs one of Hopper's caricatures, *Mrs. Kit Hopper's one man jury show,* where he imagined a mouse as the juror in a show entirely composed of portraits of Arthur, posing in various postures and costumes. The mouse-juror intently surveys the framed pictures from the vantage point of his baseboard hole.

Meanwhile, the threat of abuse on the Cape drove Jo to seek out a title lawyer. On March 1, with Edward's blessings, she took the train for Boston. The enforced leisure en route set her to thinking yet again about her relationship with Edward, who had just helped her onto the train:

> How wicked that we scrap so—that is I scrap—he says, not he scraps & true enough. But how other wise & it takes moments like this to realize he is the last word of perfection—with his patience, understanding, delightful humor, sheer goodness, good looks—really handsome & distinguished & was, before got to stooping full 6'4"+, as I measured him when we were married & rejoiced in this magnificent height . . . & as E. reminds me, he doesn't drink or chase the floozies.[20]

From this ideal portrait, her mind wandered to the actual landscape, where she perceived the views as "full of E. Hopper—shadows cast by underpass, sides, ends of house glorified, telegraph poles & car tracks running in endless horizontal & the heart-warming red bricks, the white line in center of roads . . . the ends of R.R. cars & baggage carriers."[21] Completely forgetting her reasons for resentment, she wound up in a flourish: "E.H. has made the nation conscious of its undiscovered beauties & the light that reveals America."[22]

Edward Hopper, Mrs. Kit Hopper's one man jury show, *1960. Pencil on paper,*
8½ × 11″ (21.6 × 27.9 cm.).

On return to New York the next afternoon, Jo saw that Edward was glad to have her back and decided that the trip "had been a diversion & good for both of us."[23] Taking responsibility made her feel confident and proud of herself, as she only too rarely did.

In the spring, *Art in America* printed a brief essay and short interview with Hopper by John Morse, prompting Edward to write: "The tape recording method of biography seems to give a factual intimacy that helps to reveal character, with the assistance of your sympathetic interpretation. I liked what you have said very much."[24] Morse, who conducted a completely superficial interview, did elicit from Hopper a terse description of his technique: "I have a very simple method of painting. It's to paint directly on the canvas without any funny business, as it were. I use almost pure turpentine to start with, adding oil as I go along until the medium becomes pure oil. I use as little oil as I possibly can, and that's my painting method."[25] Morse must have pleased Hopper when he predicted that "Hopper's paintings will definitely show increase in value for the simple reason that they are durably made, sincerely felt and superbly designed,"[26] asserting, too, "What makes Hopper's paintings durable in content is that they are much more than representations of recognizable, temporal objects. They are the expression of his thoughts and feelings about places and things—as he himself told me."[27]

Ever tardy in pursuit of technological innovation, only that spring did the Hoppers acquire a phonograph with a stock that included among others Beethoven, Tchaikovsky, and Schumann. The occasion was Jo's birthday, and they chose a lightweight machine that they could transport to and from the Cape. Jo hoped that the music "might stir E. to activity if he not too consumed getting everything to perform."[28] But when they played Strauss waltzes, Edward commented: "[They] are sad, so sad. I can't take too much of them."[29] Jo told this to Lloyd Goodrich, as if seeking to alert him to another whole realm of parallels beyond literature that merited scholarly exploration: "So E.H. does get them under the skin—& one might be getting dark strains of Strauss 'in them thar hills' & certain Hopper houses."[30]

At the end of March, the campaign against abstraction called the Hoppers once again to the home of John Koch, this time to compose a protest to the Whitney Museum over the emphasis give to Non-Objective art.[31] Jo recognized faces familiar from *Reality,* such as Raphael Soyer; Jack Levine and his wife the painter Ruth Gikow; Joseph Hirsch; and Ogden Pleissner. She recorded Henry Varnum Poor without further reference to the episode of his shabby treatment by Edward. Hopper was willing to take part despite the Whitney's sustained interest in his work. Jo was reluctant to complain, since she was happy to have been included in annual exhibitions since 1954, although she remembered the days of being "completely ignored" and feeling threatened: "I came right along with my husband, not leaving him for their devices—Mrs. Force always ready to grab & do her Circe act on him—naturally she'd hate me. She hated wives."[32] Citing the sorceress in Homer's *Odyssey* who seduced men and turned them into swine or fawning pets, Jo knew whereof she spoke: Force had conducted a well-known affair with Forbes Watson, while acquiring several examples of his wife Nan's work for the Whitney. Jo would not have been so willing to sacrifice Edward for the sake of her career.

Even as Hopper and the older painters were signing their protest to the Whitney, a group of younger painters had organized and were picketing in front of the Museum of Modern Art to protest its emphasis on abstraction. Although not directly involved, the Hoppers supported this action.[33] John Koch kept calling Edward to inform him about the MOMA protest.

During this period a new neighbor, the painter Paul Resicka, brought over his new wife, Gina Moscarella, to introduce her to the Hoppers. Jo, recalling that she too had come as a bride to the same old house, thought to herself that she hoped that "he'll know how to appreciate her."[34] Resicka recalls that Hopper, whom he first met in their subbasement when he offered to assist the older man carrying up coal, was "a Francophile who talked about Manet and Meryon" and was "very sophisticated."[35] He and Gina had tea at the Hoppers' on many occasions, "always in her studio," while Hopper kept his pictures turned to the wall. Resicka thought of Jo as "an amateur painter."

On May 4, the Hoppers returned to Koch's house with twenty-one other artists. The two protests were creating something of a stir, with articles appearing in several newspapers and journalists telephoning Edward for interviews, even at four in the morning, although Jo intercepted every call.[36] On May 19, Lloyd Goodrich and Jack Baur of the Whitney met with representatives of the group, including Hopper, Koch, Raphael Soyer, Levine, Gikow, and Poor.[37] On the eleventh of June, Jo wrote to Goodrich, telling him, "It is indeed beautiful to remember the way you handled the recent episode of that letter to the Whitney & showed how fine it is when people with deep attachments all together seek the truth & understanding. This incident is historic & heart warming in retrospect."[38] Jo tried to explain why she and Edward had been involved, given the recent support that they had both received from the Whitney: "E. Hopper was there because of his connection with 'Reality' & the survival of that principal is for him of intense concern. I there, to see that E. Hopper was not made vice president of anything. Because of his little strength, it must be well guarded."[39] She then expressed their appreciation:

> Edward, so silent, is deeply conscious of his debt to the Whitney over all these years & years. It all began there—the tall, solemn silent young man & his pictures of a blond Paris, so long ago. And so recently, at the last annual on 8th St., my 'Fire Escape' . . . so beautifully hung, and here at the last, the 1959, 60 Annual—my 'Cape Cod Bedroom' That gave me at long, so long last, a sense of being included. God love you and dear Rosalind for these happy occasions.[40]

§

JO HAD VIEWED her dealer, Herman Gulack, as giving her life legitimacy. At last, she could hold her head up high and be proud of herself as an artist. With Gulack's gallery gone, she reverted to her studio as exhibition space, appealing to Goodrich:

> But the light of late spring & summer is glamorous (even) in my studio just now. I have some new canvases, but who would come look? When it gets really hot, Edward will want to fly to the Cape—maybe not until July, so much packing to leave & take & when we get it all back—maybe Nov. before able to move again, my place will be icy

cold & gloomy, that College has found a way to side step furnishing
steam heat, city edict not withstanding.[41]

Taking advantage of the warm weather, Jo had Moses and Ida Soyer to tea.
She was pleased that Moses said "nice things about my work, especially liked
photo of Bertram H. portrait," and commented that her things "have the
charm of being humble."[42] Reflecting on her paintings in the bright light of
early June, she gave new voice to the consciousness of sadism that had been
surfacing over the previous decade:

> They are indeed highly autobiographical—I'm their mother, all
> right & deeply distressed that they are ignored—& break out of bit-
> terness at E. late last night & that creature cannot think or feel out-
> side his own hide & if any attempt is made to break thru, all the deep
> meanness of his soul comes out at me, I've married a sadist.[43]

Despite the unreserved enthusiasm felt en route to Boston, too much remained unresolved.[44]

Ida Soyer came to pose for Jo, who commented: "She is a beauty & quite
what I should be able to do well . . . but my start is just mud pie."[45] Ida had
belonged to the Neighborhood Playhouse, so she and Jo found much to share
about their pasts in the theater, initially making the act of painting secondary
to the social experience of their meeting. But on succeeding sessions, Jo began
to improve the portrait and, in several weeks, she was pleased by her results.

From the New York *Evening Post,* the Hoppers, as true film aficionados,
were delighted to learn that Alfred Hitchcock credited the idea for the house
in his film *Psycho* to looking at *House by the Railroad.*[46] Edward, who had
found so much inspiration in literature and the dramatic arts, was beginning
to repay the debt. Later that summer he told Clancy that Jo had written about
this to Stephen Clark, who had donated the painting to the Museum of Modern Art, "as Hitchcock had said The 'House by the Railroad' was the foundation for the weird house that was part of the film."[47]

Before the Hoppers left New York that July, they invited James
Flexner to visit both of their studios.[48] They had especially liked what he
had written about Edward in his *Pocket History of American Art:* "Hopper
had discarded Henri's romantic outlook and dramatic brushwork for a
firm, laconic realism. . . . Living in the same age, he has reached some of the
same conclusions as the Parisian masters. Like theirs, his art is moving and
forceful because it evolved from his own temperament and his own experience."[49] Flexner has recalled that Jo allowed him to sit alone with Edward
in his studio and that more than a half hour passed without either of them

speaking. Yet, despite the silence, Flexner said that he felt a kind of rapport with the artist.[50]

The Hoppers finally left for the Cape on the fourteenth of July. Jo confided in Goodrich her growing sense of the uniqueness, precariousness, and vulnerability of their lives:

> It is always with trepidation on my part when we pull off for that remote hill top over the sea lest I be left stark alone with all responsibility to face the inevitable, I so little wise or strong. On that high hill top, or this high house top on Washington Sq. We are exceedingly solitary here—or there. At times I'm scared—to be so detached.
>
> La vie est brève—
> Un peu d'espoir,
> Un peu de rêve,
> Et puis
> Bon soir[51]

The Cape was becoming more and more of a challenge for a couple less and less able to fend for themselves. After getting lost in Rhode Island, and again in Taunton, Massachusetts, in a tempestuous downpour, they decided to stay overnight in a motel in Eastham. Although only twenty-five miles from home, they were too tired to tackle opening the house. The next day, they drove on to Truro, only to find that the door of the house was swollen shut.[52] Their new handyman, Charlie Francis, could not be reached until the end of the workday, and it was six o'clock before they gained entry. A local art student helped them unpack the car and carry their belongings up the steep hill. These chores were not easy for people now in their late seventies: "so rattled, tired, E. argumentative & I ready to scratch & bite at all male reasoning that doesn't work."[53]

Rosalind Irvine of the Whitney, who was vacationing in Provincetown with her husband, Dick Snidely, came twice for visits. Jo had sent directions on one of the maps she often drew, advising: "Keep in the ruts on each side of grass" and cautioning, "If Dick has had no experience with sandy roads— you'd better let Edward meet you at P.O. to make sure you do not get stuck. So many do."[54]

Jo wrote to Carl Sprinchorn, "Edward, thank goodness, has been better since he came here—more strength & endurance. I, too, not dying all over the place."[55] Nevertheless, they bemoaned the "wretched" weather with "so little glorious sunlight."[56] By August, it was so cold that they could not swim and Jo was already sleeping in a flannel nightgown and bed socks. She felt besieged by the wood ticks and the encroaching real estate developer.

Edward was not willing to worry about their borders. Jo said that he re-minded her of Chekhov's *The Cherry Orchard* because "he won't let the sound of ax on trees in that cherry orchard bother him."[57] She concluded: "He's a good painter, but no talent even for survival—no business sense just takes for granted the law is there to rob & one can do nothing about it."[58]

In late August, Arnold Newman came to take photographs for *Horizon*. Edward trusted Newman, who had photographed him nearly twenty years earlier and who now meticulously made several visits to set up his shot, mov-ing furniture and studying the light. Newman got the Hoppers to observe and report to him exactly when the sun came up and whether the light would touch the northeast corner of their house.[59] On receiving the commission, Newman had been "cautioned that Jo considered herself as good a painter as Hopper." He recalled: "Jo kept getting into the picture. She wanted to be in it. She stood there and started prancing around. Suddenly it hit me. This was their relationship."[60] With a wide-angle lens on his four-by-five view camera, Newman caught Jo in the distance, while he focused on Edward in the fore-ground, seated on an antique bench in front of the great north window of their house.

On August 24, Jo recorded that Edward had begun a "canvas of the sides of 2 houses. From the sketch, charcoal on yellow paper—the 2 white fronts, going up in tall points, in contrast with dark roofs, make arresting uprights in dark canvas."[61] She was glad to see him at it again, for, as she put it, there was "nothing happening since last Jan. that he spent . . . doing Turists sitting out in sun in Tucson."[62] By now she actually welcomed the ritual: "Every-thing stops—I receive in the kitchen. Where else with only kitchen, bedroom & workshop."[63]

As intended, the phonograph had made the journey from New York and it was proving more important than anyone could have expected. Edward kept playing the Strauss waltzes again and again, even though he found them "so sad he can't take too much of them."[64] Always attuned to anything that affected his mood, Jo mused: "How glad I am we went thru great travail to get them into the house—at long last—and now they must help with this new 50 × 40—the high purpose of all this splendor of land & sea & of the enchanted perfection of our little house seem to be in operation when there is a picture on the easel."[65] Twenty years had passed since the time when waltzes came pouring out of the radio and Edward turned from his easel to whirl her around "amazingly light on his feet" in the steps she had made him learn.[66] Like the film images of old Paris, the waltzes brought back the past.

More than ten miles separated the Hoppers' hilltop from Provincetown, where their old school friends were long dead and the new art fashions were flourishing. Hearing a report of a workshop on abstract art, where someone claimed "that art came from the heart to the wrist," Edward expostulated: "It's not that easy. Art is like life itself, it's a lot of hard work."[67] The report came from a visitor, the poet Charles Wagner, whom the Hoppers had met at the Huntington Hartford Foundation. As she recorded Edward's outburst, she thought back to Louis Bouché's denunciation of opportunistic artists: "Too many of weak conviction anyway have got themselves on line for the band wagon. We've seen them do this—largely those who had nothing to say anyway & their work said nothing."[68] When Edward received an invitation to show in the next Corcoran Biennial, he wrote to Clancy expressing indifference about showing there, particularly, he noted, "If I am to be shown in a show preponderantly of abstractions."[69]

By the first of September Jo entered another report on the new picture: "Edward's new canvas is coming along famously. . . . I'm so glad to see him come back to his large forms. The 1″ [1st] drawing in was very impressive— the upper floors & roofs of the 2 adjoining houses in semi-profile give the sense to me of 2 tall ships coming in to dock, rising up with weight directed forward—purposeful."[70] This time the idea had led him to prospect and then invent: "After searching for trees somewhat in Orleans & not finding any special individual tree—didn't want either elms or pines—maybe sumac would answer—good in wind, needed them in good light—but didn't find what wanted, so now he has evolved his own masses of foliage for tree tops & heavy trunks."[71] Already he had communicated to her where he was heading: "He has to certify that what he's doing is 2″ [2nd] floor, well off the ground & I am keenly interested to watch how he's going to do that—push those upper stories up. By means of tree tops & trunks extending down off canvas. He sure has his problems. I know he'll do it. He always does."[72]

Hopper finished *Second Story Sunlight* on September 15. He later told Katharine Kuh that this painting was one of his favorites, explaining: "It shows the top stories of two houses with an upper porch and two figures, a young and an older woman. I don't think there was really any idea of symbolism in the two figures. There might have been vaguely; certainly not obsessively so. I was more interested in the sunlight on buildings and on the figures than in any symbolism. Jo posed for both figures; she's always posed for everything."[73] Despite the credit to Jo, their Cape neighbors, Marie Stephens and her then-adolescent daughter, Kim, each thought that she had inspired the youthful figure.[74] They argued that the young girl's ample bustline bore no resemblance to Jo's and more closely corresponded to their own. What they did not reckon with, of course, was Edward's demonstrated ability to transform the visible raw material into vision.

Hopper also offered the disclaimer that the work was only "an attempt to paint sunlight as white with almost no yellow pigment in the white," adding that "any psychological idea will have to be supplied by the viewer." He did leave open the possibility of a dimension of nostalgia: "But to paint light was not my initial impulse. I'm a realist and I react to natural phenomena. As a child I felt that the light on the upper part of a house was different than that on the lower part. There is a sort of elation about sunlight on the upper part of a house. You know, there are many thoughts, many impulses that go into a picture."[75]

Just after Hopper finished *Second Story Sunlight,* the journalist Frank Crotty and his wife came by and asked to see the new picture. When Mrs. Crotty inquired about its name, Hopper replied: "Toots." According to Jo, he later assured them "Toots [is] not a bad sort. Just a lamb in wolf's clothing."[76] Jo pointed out that, in fact, "Toots" was not wearing "very much."[77] In the record book, she described the older woman as "white haired, Gothic & Elderly" and again quoted Edward on "Toots," whom he described as "good Toots, alert but not obstreperous."[78]

James Flexner was so moved by *Second Story Sunlight* that he wrote to Hopper offering his interpretation:

> I felt both in the formal and emotional tensions of your painting a pull between restraint and the opulence of nature. Restraint represented by the peaked architecture and the old lady for whom all passion is spent; opulence, by the line of trees, the sky, and the marvelously buxom young lady sitting on the edge of the porch, not waiting for anything in particular, yet fertile and sure in the movement of the seasons to be fulfilled. I felt it was an allegory of winter and spring, life and death.[79]

Hopper was so impressed by Flexner's letter that he sent a copy to Lloyd Goodrich with a note stating: "Since I took the trouble of having a photostat made of it, it may indicate that I am not so modest as I am said to be."[80] Flexner found Hopper dismissive of his interpretation and "disagreeable"; he was stunned when Hopper claimed that the painting depicted a "tuberculosis sanatorium."[81] On the face of it, such a remark might be seen as offputting. Yet just such a retreat is the setting for Mann's *The Magic Mountain,* which the Hoppers had read with avid attention in 1949 at the time he was painting *High Noon.* In both paintings Hopper endows sunlight with particular resonance as the force of life.

Jo wrote to the Chaces in mid-September, complaining about the summer's travails: ticks, cold weather, and then Hurricane Donna that leveled their garage: "It lay flat down on our car so that it could not be extracted until just yesterday. So we've known no car, phone, no electric in the wilderness. But glad and grateful she left our big north window undamaged. . . . Hope to get the garage rebuilt. That car has always been so pampered. It could get sore throat staying out."[82]

That year the Hoppers returned from the Cape on October 10, earlier than usual, in order to register to vote in the presidential election. They also wanted to make sure that the reconstruction of their lobby would not result in the elimination of the dumbwaiter that they had been finding more and more essential for getting groceries and packages up their seventy-four steps. Jo recorded that she and Edward "had no use for either of the big parties & just couldn't bear either candidate—so much too young & at a time like this in the world's history." They shared the widespread fear that a Catholic president would allow his policies to be dictated by the Vatican. As was their habit, they voted for the Republican candidate, Richard M. Nixon, and were shocked when they learned of John F. Kennedy's election, which Jo called "the fatal news of the folly of the U.S."[83]

They did not accept an invitation to attend the inauguration because Edward was "not equal to the effort," and they missed hearing Robert Frost recite.[84] Despite their distrust of the new president, both were pleased when Jacqueline Kennedy arranged for the Museum of Fine Arts in Boston to lend Hopper's watercolor, *Houses at Squam Light,* for exhibition at the White House.[85]

On the home front, having lobbied against gas heat, the Hoppers were thrilled at the advent of steam, although put out by the need to move furniture to make place for three radiators. They could not bring themselves to part with their "adored pot-belly stove—our sacred altar that sent forth such good heat so graciously, glowingly, always so alive,"[86] which had been "47 years faithful to E and a Harvard poet before that," wrote Jo to Marion. She glanced up and acknowledged "the blizzard handsome outside our windows. . . . We have three parties this week—the house here looks like Bedlam."[87]

The Hoppers had not felt up to the party for Raphael Soyer's one-man show at the A.C.A. Gallery, and Edward wrote after a special trip: "I think it is a very fine show and it may be perhaps an influence on the younger painters who see it, in helping to turn the tide to a less superficial American painting. But the young are vain and without a long view of art, so perhaps they will not be influenced."[88]

In December 1960, *Art in America* presented Hopper with its annual award (a thousand dollars and a medal) "for an Outstanding Contribution to American Art." He was hailed by Stuart Preston in *The New York Times* as "the dean of American realist painting . . . an artist whose work through many years has succeeded in getting under the skin of American life in a unique way."[89] Preston said Hopper combined "a straightforward style with an austere, detachedly poetic point of view, which is remindful of the poetry of Robert Frost."[90] The award from *Art in America* stated: "He is respected equally by the realists for his uncompromising interpretation of this country's strengths and weaknesses, and by abstractionists, who admired the powerful designs inherent in his paintings."[91] Hopper, however, remained adamant. The abstractionists might view him favorably, but he did not respect their work and continued to protest their growing influence.

PRINTS AGAIN: 1961–1962

IN JANUARY 1961, Hopper wrote to thank Raphael Soyer for the gift of a book of Soyer's work: "I think the work has great sympathy without any sentimentality and you have achieved something which seems so easy to do, and is really so difficult, that is to fix the simple natural gestures of people in their daily activities."[1] Making explicit his long-held belief in the parallel between painting and writing, Hopper included his favorite quotation from Goethe, pointing out that it could "apply to painting and could interest painters who are not members of the new academy: 'The beginning and the end of all literary activity is the reproduction of the world that surrounds me by means of the world that is in me, all things being grasped, related, re-created, molded and reconstructed in a personal form and an original manner.' "[2]

Hopper now began to make preparations for an exhibition of his "complete graphic work" organized by his old friend Carl Zigrosser, then the curator of prints, drawings, and rare books at the Philadelphia Museum of Art. They had known one another since Zigrosser first showed Hopper's etchings at Frederick Keppel and Company in New York during the spring of 1917. Although the retrospective was to open only in the fall of 1962, there was much work to be done. Hopper realized that he had not kept a copy of each of his prints. He did have his original plates though, protectively covered in beeswax since 1927. He did not relish cleaning them himself, nor did he want to print them, although he had held on to his press, which now served only as a hat rack in his studio.

Zigrosser, a colorful character who sported a Van Dyck beard and a dramatic black cape, put Hopper in touch with Ed Colker, a printmaker who had trained in Philadelphia. Colker, a genial young man who had printed for the discerning collector Lessing Rosenwald, had a studio at 61 East Ninth Street, not too far from Hopper.[3] He cleaned and printed three plates for Hopper, making about six impressions of each image.

Hopper insisted that Colker obtain some umbria paper, which he found at Andrews Nelson Whitehead, a large New York paper importer. When Henry Pfeiffer, the president of the firm, learned who the paper was for, he delivered it himself in order to meet the artist. Hopper was evidently disappointed by the lack of intensity in the black ink used by Colker, who had taken the trouble to obtain it from Fred Weber, a specialist in Philadelphia. He preferred the richer black that he had used in the 1920s, which was known as Frankfort Black.

As Hopper waited patiently, Colker removed the aged beeswax and then printed the plates. Hopper noticed Colker's own prints about the studio, including some dedicated to various poets. Observing a plate on the poem "What Are Years?" by Marianne Moore, he asked Colker, "Did you ever meet her?" and commented: "Interesting woman. Spinster. Wore three-cornered hats." A plate on William Carlos Williams prompted the remark: "Interesting man. Might have had a Jewish grandmother." Hopper knew both writers from the National Institute of Arts and Letters, although he had frustrated Jo's budding friendship with Moore. Seeing another series on the Hudson River, Hopper recognized a view of Haverstraw, and commented: "That's Clove Road where the old trap rock company was. They used to send the clay down to Philadelphia on barges for brick making. I was raised near there." When Colker remarked that the Hudson and the Palisades must have had overpowering scale for a child, Hopper replied that people thought there was something psychological about his work, and then immediately denied that this was so.

Hopper wanted Colker to do trick wiping, instructing him to use his finger and a tissue on the inky surface to pull up some cloud grays in the background. Colker, realizing that every print would vary, told Hopper that he could not do it. In the end they compromised, with Colker pulling a few clean prints and a few with manipulated tone.

A week later, when the prints were dry, Colker delivered them to Hopper. Jo greeted him at the door of her studio, garrulously reporting that "Eddie" had told her that the Colkers' cat appeared to have "crossed over" like theirs (the legendary Arthur)—demonstrating responses to human signal and exchange. She expressed her disappointment in the lack of richness of the black ink Colker used, perhaps reflecting her husband's opinion, although Hopper wrote to Zigrosser that Colker made him "some good prints."[4] And she urged the printer to look at her paintings, which were stacked all around her studio. Colker was surprised to learn that Jo painted, since Hopper had not mentioned it. To him, Jo's work seemed skilled but appeared to be "second-rate Hoppers. . . . It worried me that I was suddenly seeing versions of what appeared to be a similar vision to Hopper's. It startled me." He recalls seeing mainly rooftops and views of New York City.

Colker was amazed that Hopper appeared to behave so differently in Jo's presence in the sparse but musty apartment. Rather than the grim, stolid presence he had witnessed in his studio, Hopper now seemed "boyish," trying to play down her criticism of the ink, remarking "aw shucks." Jo dominated the conversation, but Colker had the sense that this was "prearranged." He surmised that Hopper's "boyish manner" might have been calculated and that he preferred that Jo "took the heat for being involved in details." Still, Hopper was pleased enough with the results that he presented Colker with an inscribed copy of *Girl on a Bridge,* one of the three plates that he printed.

Not long afterward, when Colker saw Zigrosser and his colleague Dean McNulty at the Philadelphia Museum, they asked him how he had enjoyed his visit with Hopper. They teasingly asked if he had gotten to see Mrs. Hopper's work, later admitting that it was a well-known " 'rite of passage,' the toll-gate to pass through to see Edward Hopper."

From this period on, Jo frequently mentions their fears of mugging. When she went out to mail a letter, Jo was so afraid of being attacked that she insisted upon having Edward watch the steps until she returned safely.[5] When Edward went to a National Institute of Arts and Letters dinner, she arranged to have dinner at the nearby home of friends, so that he could pick her up on his way home. She wore a police whistle around her neck and even gave one to their neighbor Herdis Teilman.[6] Jo's increasing dependence on Edward is reflected in the letter she wrote to Dorothy Ferris just after the death of her husband, Hugh: "My heart aches for you, it does indeed. You will never again have to suffer so much. This is veritably an amputation."[7]

Doubt whether New York University would permit them to remain in their home also caused new anxiety. They were the last tenants at the top of what was now an office building for the School of Social Work (though there were still other tenants in the back part of the building, facing Washington Mews). Their isolation also increased their concern for their safety at night. Then, to their alarm, the office workers insisted on leaving the door to the street unlocked.[8] Jo wrote to the Chaces that this was just maliciousness on the part of the university: "Police disapprove but can do nothing. They believe that this is an effort of the college to get us out. Since there is no where else to go—after E.—being there 47 yrs., I try not to have jitters. That N.Y.U. is a low lot."[9]

That February, the Hoppers were drawn into a fierce controversy surrounding the *New York Times* art critic, John Canaday. A letter attacking Canaday signed by forty-nine noted artists, collectors, critics, and art historians (including Stuart Davis, Willem de Kooning, Hans Hofmann, Robert Motherwell, Harold Rosenberg, and other proponents of abstract art) was published in the *Times*. Among the statements that the group took exception to was Canaday's claim (September 6, 1959) that "the nature of abstract expressionism allows exceptional tolerance for incompetence and deception."[10] The Hoppers described the complaints against Canaday as from "the Enemy for everything that we relished most," when, to them, the critic was the "one ray of light in years."[11]

At John Koch's suggestion, both Edward and Jo wrote letters to the *Times*. More than six hundred people wrote such letters, and Edward's letter was one of the fifty-two chosen to appear in print. He wrote: "There have been, I believe, other efforts to silence John Canaday's voice, but heretofore they have failed. There are, I have heard, strong forces of money and influence against him, as there would naturally be, but I believe John Canaday is the best and most outspoken art critic the *Times* has ever had."[12] Canaday evidently considered Hopper's letter the best that he received.[13]

On March 4, the critic Brian O'Doherty visited the Hoppers to persuade them to appear on a show in his educational television series, *Invitation to Art*. Jo, who was impressed with O'Doherty, noted: "There was some interesting talk here—the young man—33—is intelligent & knowing & had some conception of what it's all about. He was bright enough to find some merit in my pictures since he landed in my studio in the midst of them. But soon as E. came, he lost interest in them & naturally E never referred to them."[14]

When Raphael Soyer invited the Hoppers to attend a meeting at the new Crystal Gallery concerning a projected show with a catalogue of drawings, Edward did not want to go, telling Jo that they would leave her out again. She recorded his reaction: "He didn't want to take a stand at defending me. Besides he didn't want anything to do with Isabel B. [Bishop] in it. It was an old Reality crowd: Jack Levine, Henry Poor, both Soyers, Evergood, [Edward] Melcarth & John Koch."[15] Because of Hopper's reservations, they stayed home and ate a steak dinner instead. Nonetheless, Hopper was extremely fond of Raphael Soyer, to whom he wrote in April, praising his work: "Both Jo and I liked very much your drawing of 'Lovers' that appeared in the Times Book Review recently. It is a very fine drawing and you have done so very much with so little means. I think it should go to a museum."[16] With Soyer, who had been a Social Realist in the 1930s, Hopper counted aesthetics more than politics. Thus he felt that he and Soyer stood on common ground, united against abstract art.

Several weeks later, the Hoppers did attend a meeting at the Crystal Gallery to voice their opinion about the proposed exhibition, which was to extend from Winslow Homer to contemporary work. As Edward had predicted, Isabel Bishop had taken on a position of authority and wanted to exclude Eugene Speicher.[17] John Koch and Ruth Gikow argued for including younger artists, which Jo felt was wrong, since "the future was theirs."[18] Jo finally concluded that there would be no place for her in this exhibition and lost interest in it.

From April 8 to 11, the Hoppers were in Boston, as the guests of the Museum of Fine Arts. Jo exclaimed to the Chaces: "They are putting us up as their guests at the Sheraton Plaza . . . & treating us as royalty. Imagine you! We'll be turned loose on Copley Square for the Museum & the Library—but I dare say they'll watch out to see that we're not trying on bargains in Filene's basement when it's time for their program to get underway."[19] Jo had no trouble adapting to being interviewed, although she claimed to be taken by surprise; and she reveled in dinner at the Harvard Club and "a nice intimate party" given by O'Doherty with Perry Rathbone, the director of the museum, and "Yvonne Pène du Bois, daughter of Guy Pène du Bois, Ed's old friend in the Henri Class."[20]

Hopper took the occasion of the O'Doherty interview to read and comment on the Goethe passage he had sent to Raphael Soyer: "This quotation is on literature, but it can be applied to painting. But I know that many contemporary painters will protest and show the greatest contempt for this quotation, but even so, I'm going to read it." Afterward he added: "To me that applies to painting fundamentally and I know that there have been so many different opinions on painting. Now, there will be many who protest that this is outmoded, outdated, but I think it's fundamental."[21]

After the taping, in which O'Doherty artfully drew Jo in at the end, the Hoppers watched themselves on television. Jo admitted that she and Edward were "not so happy for find[ing] ourselves greatly advanced in years. . . . Could it be that one actually does look like that & never guessed the awful truth. Now E. resents it too—resents being made older than he is."[22] To Marion, Jo confided that they were "horrified to find oneselves old as mummies" and complained that the light was "not well handled."[23]

Now that so many of their friends were somewhat younger than they, the Hoppers may have become more sensitive to appearing elderly. They continued to see associates from *Reality* and the subsequent protest group, such as Joseph Hirsch, Jack Levine and Ruth Gikow, and John Koch.[24] After the opening of Koch's show at the Kraushaar Gallery that April, Jo recorded meeting Sol and Dora Wilson, Edward Lanning, and her contemporaries William and Marguerite Zorach.[25] Jo called Koch "the greatest living master of skill, but here, skill plus," adding that his work had "the profundities of Rembrandt."[26]

When Koch came to Jo's studio to see her work a month later, he made her feel that he found merit in her pictures and was a "kindred spirit."[27] Edward took them out for lunch and they spoke about "the lasting outrage of the usurpation of non art, ubiquitous at museums, colleges, collections, everywhere—the press. So takes over & all the galleries, etc. etc." For Jo, the polemics against abstract artists as the villains of the art world allowed her to depersonalize the rejection of her work by the art establishment.

The Hoppers' hostility to abstraction even colored their view of the performing arts. When Ida and Moses Soyer took them to see Martha Graham dance, Jo pronounced the performance "all very interesting, extremely lively," but concurred with Edward's conclusion that Graham, who drew upon Abstract Expressionist art for some of her sets, was "saying nothing."[28] Edward "didn't even care for her design. He said it could have had dignity but it didn't," he was "never enthusiastic over dancing, but seems as though he has something there."[29] While mainstream art critics ignored Jo, the journalists of the Village were finding her worthy of copy. That May, Emeline Paige, who wrote the "Scoopie" column in the *Villager,* paid her a visit. Jo talked about doing books on Edward Hopper, on their venerable old building, and on her cat Arthur.[30] Emeline suggested that Jo try dictating into a tape recorder. This is Jo's first mention of a plan to put her diaries to use, and it suggests a motive for the increased reminiscing of her later years. In the back of her diary, she listed her three ideas: "I Life with E.H., II #3 Wash. Sq. North, III My Sainted Arthur & Titmouse Terrace." She considered the last proposal first, detailing the exploits of Arthur, who, despite his disappearance in 1925, remained vivid in her memory and mythology. She got as far as listing all the characters who should appear in her book, but if she made any further efforts, none has come to light.

When she and Edward attended the opening of "American Paintings, 1865–1905" at the Whitney on the twenty-third of May, Jo took note of being impressed in a list that included, among others, Eakins, Sargent, Alexander, Homer, Ryder, Whistler, Inness, J. Alden Weir, Childe Hassam, and Blakelock: "I went round with wet eyes so proud of our nation showing its humanity with breeding, quality, & nobility," she wrote, applauding the "absence of shock, vulgarity, brutality, exaggeration."[31] When they went back a week later, Edward was "not excited at all" and told Jo that he was "a better painter than any of them."[32] Ever on the lookout to find incentives for him, she thought: "Well, if he feels that way, maybe he can get started on a picture himself—to prove this to himself."[33]

Hopper made the effort to attend the American Academy of Arts & Letters because of the election of new members. He wanted to be present "to keep out any more de Koonings & the like."[34] Yet de Kooning both admired Hopper's work and shared his admiration for Courbet. Two years earlier, speaking privately to Irving Sandler about his own work, a picture suggested by the Merritt Parkway, de Kooning volunteered: "Hopper is the only American I know who could paint the Merritt Parkway."[35] Once, while drawing a sketch of a painting by Hopper (*Cape Cod Morning* of 1950) that he had seen in the Whitney, de Kooning told Sandler: "The forest looks real, like a forest; like you turned on it and there it is; like you turn and actually see it."[36] At the American Academy meeting, despite his dislike of speaking before a group, Hopper spoke out to insist that artists, not writers or composers, should decide on new artist members.[37] Jo recorded in her diary that Lewis Mumford later told her that he was glad "to hear rock bottom truth from E.H."[38]

After the celebrity of Jo's television appearance with Edward, John Clancy said that he would like to have a couple of her paintings at the Rehn Gallery.[39] He first picked out *South Truro Church* and her smaller version of the *Dauphinée House;* he also wanted her *Obituary,* but she would not part with it.[40] Instead, he took *Cape Cod Bureau, Tree Tops through Fire Escape,* and *Chez Hopper III,* with its coal scuttle and umbrella. Years later, Clancy admitted: "She wasn't a bad painter, but she was overshadowed by him. He was so great."[41] By now aged seventy-eight, Jo commanded much more attention and affection than she had wrested from the art establishment during her middle years. At last her association with Edward was counting for something positive.

The Hoppers left for Cape Cod in the middle of July, just as *Horizon* magazine published the promised feature article, "At the Tip of Cape Cod," by Robert Hatch. Arnold Newman's photograph of Hopper in front of his Truro house was captioned: "Its big window looks toward Provincetown ten miles away. Hopper—a man who values his privacy—does not regret the distance. Though probably the best-known painter on the Cape, he stays aloof from its art colony."[42]

By the end of September, the destroyed garage had been replaced, two-thirds paid for by insurance, and the couple were "starting out under a blue sky and in warm clothes to see if Ed can get started on a picture at long last."[43] He had not been able to start anything new since finishing *Second Story Sunlight* the previous September. When Edward began to paint on October first, he called on Jo once again to pose. Some of the six extant preparatory drawings reveal her actual proportions before he transformed them into the more erect and full figure he had in mind. Hopper later quipped to his dealer about the outcome: "That's Jo glorified by art."[44]

On October 14, Jo wrote to Clancy: "E.H.'s 60 × 40 is finished—all but the name. And that trollop is not such a bad sort." She added that Edward was "casting about now for a landscape. If he could start one at once before inertia sets in." In composing the entry for the record book, Jo virtually sketched a scenario, couching her account in language that reveals her sense of the painting process as theater and her own active part:

A Woman in the Sun. The Wise Tramp. Begun cold, very, very early Oct. 1. Tragic figure of small woman, blond, straight brown hair, grabs cigarette before shimmy shirt. Brightest note at R., off stage east (right). Path of light on floor thin pale yellow tinged with pale green. (Note that edges of streak ready to move as sun travels up in sky.) Streak of more distant light on side of dune facing east. Sky outdoors still muffled, so interior indiscriminate blue green. Black high-heeled shoes under bed. Cigarette & sad-face of woman unlit. Skin craving the warm therapy of this early light. E. H. called her 'a wise tramp'.[45]

Both Edward's paradoxical "wise tramp" and Jo's "trollop . . . not such a bad sort" encapsulate the ambivalence toward sexuality that prevailed chez Hopper. They had been partners and coconspirators in the drama of deep attraction and irreducible opposition that provoked and fed Edward's vision. In the end, both the passionate viewer and the passionate object were glorified in the art.

"Woman in the Sun brought back with us & snapped up at once before it reached the big Annual 1961 Whitney,"[46] recorded Jo. John Clancy sold *Woman in the Sun* to Frances and Albert Hackett, who had earlier purchased *French Six-Day Bicycle Rider.* When Jo learned that the Hacketts had replaced "that ugly stupid frame," she wrote Frances a scintillating analysis of aesthetics, rejoicing that the new frame was "just what I've been preaching: a narrow frame with the glint of pale metal over the canvas at top & bottom—that would do for her, as for us, what simple, expensive (or not) earrings could add to us, add light, sparkle, style."[47] She protested that their new framer, Mr. Heydenrik, had "imposed a *wide* stretch of *dark* wood around the metal strip," and she claimed that this darkened "the picture, sent it back into the 1880s, a gloomy period, before Impressionist light & airiness & gayity."[48]

In the meantime, Jo had completed a canvas of her own, *40 Steps up to Chez Hopper.*[49] She later wrote Marion: "I did a slouching portrait of Ed this summer 30 × 25 inches and a little one of our house—head on—on top of the hill with a long white rail leading up the hill to hang on to by day, or by night.

God forbid that anyone should acquire a broken hip making that climb either up or down. . . . Ed so little enthusiastic over that rail, but his hand is never off it now."[50]

The themes of infirmity, loss of weight, nagging fatigue, deaths of friends, and condolences to write multiply in Jo's reports, yet she also speaks of enjoying some recent acquaintances. Back in New York, Jimmy and Beatrice Flexner invited them to dinner with John Canaday and his wife, and Jo recorded their pleasure that the critic embattled in their cause was well sustained at home: "I'm glad that good wise man has such a lovely understanding wife. We're so happy about them. Surely, as they prophesy, the tide of the destiny of art in our time is about to turn."[51]

After Christmas, Jo evoked for Marion "the miracle of my little [Mary] Rogers' Creche that comes out every Xmas and is dedicated to Arthur, since it was all occasioned by him. A miracle too that Edward has replaced that 'maternity complex' I took out over that highly intelligent and responsive pussy cat."[52] Almost as a postscript she added, "We have reason to expect a good, yes (why not) happy (who cares for merry) New Year (we with our radiators also)."

§

THE WINTER OF 1961–1962 was their first full season with steam heat, and Jo's ecstatic and repeated praises bring home after the fact how harsh conditions had really been there on the top floor all those years, when her studio had been fit only to store vegetables in the winter and she burned herself while modeling in the nude when she huddled near the stove for warmth.

Not until April 1962 was Hopper able to begin work on a new canvas: "He started 55 × 40—white stone facade & female in office at R. Street going way back into depth way behind canvas at left."[53] When he released the painting to the gallery on May 16, Edward told Jo that he "did not know where he got the strength to do it, but he's certainly none the worse for the effort and would be glad to begin another if he could trap an idea."[54] In the record book, she did not provide even her customary catalogue of subjects and their tones, let alone any hint of participatory drama. In *New York Office,* Hopper featured a powerful vertical corner post drenched in sunlight that etches the horizontal crevices, dark and narrow, between building blocks. The center post and its twin on the right margin frame a broad plate glass window, behind which three progressively smaller light circles on the ceiling suggest a dark, receding depth, while in the middle, the sun highlights a blond woman, bare-shouldered, standing near a mute telephone, her head cocked, pensive, to read an oblong piece of paper that she holds out in sharp contrast to the dark. In the manner of a cinematic still, every detail suggests narrative to and from this moment, inviting the play of interpretive fantasy in the manner of Edward and Jo.

Just when Jo signaled the beginning of this work in April, offices had been on their minds: "1961—A season of turmoil, renovation for themselves by the College, arrival of the offices for Social Service Dept. What weird people."[55] No one records what the new arrivals in the School of Social Work thought of the eccentric old people in the garret.

In June, when the question "Is Modern Art Decadent?" was debated by John Canaday and Thomas Hess, a fellow-critic, in the sculpture garden at the Museum of Modern Art, the Hoppers were assigned seats in the front row, most likely, Jo figured, in the hope, which remained unfulfilled, that Edward would intervene.[56] At coffee afterward, the art historian and MOMA curator William Seitz asked, to Edward's consternation, to see Jo's work. This was still a sore point between them. Jo believed, as her friend Bertram Hartman had once quipped, that her husband was her "tallest handicap."[57] And she had considered the museum an "Evil Place," since it had once rejected her work.

The Hoppers pulled themselves together to travel to the Cape on July 2. Jo was suffering from one of her recurring bouts of colitis and Edward from a sprained hand. They learned that Dick and Nell Magee had both died over the winter.[58] The summer was uneventful until the end of August, when Edward began to work in watercolor, a medium he had ignored for years. Jo reported that he was painting "a clump of dark trees across road from Church of the Visitation in Eastham. He has tree & road but needs a good sky—so far only smooth blue."[59] It seemed like old times as he painted in the back seat, only now Jo in the front seat was altering his slacks. Because of rainy weather, he did not finish *Mass of Trees at Eastham* until September.

Even aged eighty and seventy-nine, Edward and Jo continued to contest the wheel. By now her ambitions had shrunk to mastering the art of backing out of their garage onto their sandy road to drive to the post office and back. Even that was too much for him. In September they had what Jo described as a "big, big row" with Edward "tormenting me on purpose, & I finally responding by breaking the wind shield because of big hole in it from way back."[60] Days later, during one of Jo's practice sessions in and out of the garage, "some oil fell onto the road & ignited with black top & took fire." Their fire extinguisher failed to work and by the time the fire department responded, their "cherished green Buick had given up its ghost."[61] The eight-year-old car was finished, but the argument over Jo's driving was merely postponed.

Early one damp October morning, Jo later recalled, they got up and went out hunting for a scene that Edward had in mind.[62] Finding a location, he produced two preparatory sketches and returned to the studio to paint: "Road and Trees. A morning sky, not very blue. Green trees with light on a few of the trees. Side of road green also," as Jo wrote sparely in the record book. The canvas is evocative for what it does not show, neither buildings nor figures nor angular forms, only the pale sky over three contrasting horizontal bands. Across the foreground runs a broad strip of warm gold varied into a suggestion of autumn grass in morning light; then the road, a narrow, stark ribbon of sand running left and right out of the frame; and above it the main mass of the woods, a backdrop from which two trees emerge in partial relief, highlighted by the early sun, which also picks out sparse verticals of trunks.

The composition, with its horizontal bands and backdrop of trees, bears a resemblance to Hopper's 1907 *Canal at Charenton,* inviting a comparison that reveals at once steadfastness of vision and a history. The young painter caught a park at noon, with light-filled trees and an inviting underspace, opened out and defined by solid tree trunks, where the light hints at borders and at company on civil paths. The old man uses marginal light to envision the road that has other business and leads elsewhere, against the uninviting, uncivilized woods edged by tree trunks that emerge like angry wraiths. The feel is that of an unsentimental, neutral to even menacing nature in the style of Robert Frost.

Just as the print retrospective was to open in Philadelphia, Goodrich telephoned Hopper to announce that the Whitney had scheduled another big retrospective for him in 1964. Jo commented: "This should encourage E. greatly. But he just takes it in his stride."[63] The decision to organize a Hopper retrospective came at a time when younger artists, especially among the Pop and Photorealist movements, were taking a renewed interest in realism and in one of its leading exponents. The print show opened before the Hoppers left Truro in mid-November, so they went down to see it toward the end of the month, asking Zigrosser to arrange for them to visit the Barnes Collection while they were there. Barnes's celebrated Renoirs would justify the trek to Merion, even if the Cézannes and Matisses were not to Hopper's taste.

Since his television interview, O'Doherty had kept in touch with the Hoppers. In December, Edward told him: "If anyone wants to see what America is, go and see a movie called 'The Savage Eye,' "[64] which was a 1959 documentary directed by Ben Maddow, Joseph Strick, and Sidney Meyers in the manner of cinema vérité, with a disturbing and singular view of urban American life and solitude quite parallel to Hopper's own. He had held to his vision long enough to see it return to the forefront of modern style.

LAST REHEARSAL: 1963–1964

IN JANUARY 1963, Marion developed heart flutter, causing Jo and Edward to make their laborious way to Sixth Avenue for the subway to the bus and the long ride to Nyack. The new crisis forced Jo to another stock taking: "No dodging fact M. & I do not like each other at all. For so many yrs. she has found satisfaction in giving me digs, mean digs & I've taken it, remembering that little enough for me to put up with since caring so little for her, it might annoy, but no deep hurt, specially now with her laid low, no time to snap back."[1] This, in spite of reams of chatty, sisterly letters with offers of shopping, concern about cats, a television at last, the need for a downstairs toilet, cleaning ladies, weight loss, costume jewelry, and pills.

Meanwhile Raphael Soyer, following Hopper's repeated signs of approbation, wrote to ask him to pose for a large group portrait, *Homage to Eakins*. Although most of those asked simply accepted, Hopper, with characteristic scrupulousness, inquired who else would be included and took it upon himself to warn Soyer: "You must know there are those who with only a mild interest in or in deference to Eakins, would like to be included, if only for the publicity it would give them."[2] Hopper's own admiration for Eakins was such that he boasted to Brian O'Doherty: "One of my paintings was swapped for an Eakins recently. That's coming up! [He's] greater than Manet."[3] When

Soyer inquired if Hopper had ever "done a self-portrait," he replied (inaccurately): "Only once, and according to Jo, so mean looking I never showed it."[4]

After their first two-hour session, Soyer analyzed in his diary his new subject: "There is a loneliness about him, an habitual moroseness, a sadness to the point of anger. His voice breaks the silence loudly and sepulchrally. He posed still, with folded hands on the table. . . . We hardly conversed."[5] The following session, intuiting what historians would later discover, Hopper commented: "I would think Eakins used photography to some extent in his paintings, but Goodrich says, 'No, he did not.' . . . I don't know."[6] He repeatedly expressed interest in the paint that Soyer used, commenting how he preferred lead white over zinc to avoid peeling. He revealed to Soyer that he had not yet painted that year and that he was bothered "like hell."[7] He added what any older friend would have known: "Jo and I go to movies a lot," mentioning *Long Absence, Twelve Angry Men,* and Jacques Tati's *Mon Oncle,* which he pronounced "a good satire on modern technology."[8] Another time, Hopper, whom Soyer described as looking "older, quite haggard," expressed his admiration for "a Dutch or Flemish painting" he had seen at a dealer's: "I don't know the artist's name. It was just a square, a beautiful sunlit pavement and houses—no figures."[9]

Hopper wrote thanking Soyer for a book on Renoir: "I am reading it with great interest. Your work is similar, as it has the same tender and human sympathy as Renoir's. But we know that this quality seems to have little or no significance with the so called avant garde painting of today."[10] Avoiding any political differences between himself and Soyer, Hopper saw the younger painter as an important ally in the battle against the domination of abstract art.

Jo began to feel otherwise. She described her reaction to Edward's posing for Soyer as "plenty rambunctious," noting that Soyer had "cooked up a scheme to get pretty well known people to pose for a 'Homage to Eakins' canvas & has begun with E.H. Claims he's doing Lloyd Goodrich, Edwin Dickinson & who ever? Now not just everybody will be crazy to further R.S.'s idea to glorify himself in getting people to pose for him in the name of Eakins, profits all to R.S. if he sells it with all the names."[11] She could only resent, too, the time Edward spent posing for Soyer when he so rarely posed for her.

With rising anger, she returned to the tactics that had served her at the time of her hunger strike. All one night in early February Jo sat up in a chair in her studio, pleased to be

> surrounded by good loyal friends, my framed canvases, they're nice to
> live with . . . even if not climatic as E. complains. And why not when
> he sais I'm definitely so much so. Maybe it's only when relaxed I can

Raphael Soyer, Portrait of Edward Hopper (Study for "Homage to Eakins"), *1963. Oil on canvas, 38 × 28" (96.5 × 71.1 cm.).*

get at it at all. When bursting with outrage, one can't go poking about of paraphernalia & soon too fatigued to stretch a canvas & if the outrage is precipitated by the one who always does the stretching, the situation is too awkward, yet how could one be all that beholden.[12]

As the old intransigence resurfaced, Edward again resorted to extraordinary means of conciliation. Long after dark, he appeared with a tray, bringing her dinner. She recalled that "it was the pink fringed paper towel doily that broke the resistance."[13] Edward had hand cut the towel with a ragged fringe so as to create a doily effect, just as he used to cut out colored paper flowers for her birthday cards.

Yet Jo felt her "own deep resentments" of Soyer growing as she placed on him the blame for keeping her off the masthead of *Reality*. She told Edward that he was posing for her "enemy" and that it was like "kicking me in the breast."[14] The slight from *Reality* rankled so deeply because Jo felt it was like the indignity she had suffered from Juliana Force. Jo never tired of finding new ways to express her scorn for Force because, in her role as director of the Whitney Museum,

> she hated wives & a wife that wouldn't drink. Wife of a tall handsome man, big reputation & wife who could be depended on to squawk (thoroughly) if she made passes at him. She'd destroy me she with all the power of that Whitney acting as sieve for all the talent that came there—so I was plenty boycotted for all the years that my generation was flourishing.[15]

As often in her deepest reveries of these last years, Jo moves from an immediate occasion back to reconstruct and revalue a whole chain of tensions and abuses, only to come back to the central enigma from which she begins and on which everything turns:

> Periodically, I've raved & raged. He like the Rock of Gibraltar. Nothing he can do. Doesn't like my work anyway—'a pleasant little talent.' But consider the hundreds, thousands with no kind of talent at all & thriving. He hiding under sneers at women's work. But there have always been some females in current shows. Then when Herman showed my work in 1958 & 9 so beautifully, the pictures sang out in happiness in his heavenly gallery.[16]

That show in that heavenly gallery had been her earthly paradise. The thought leads her to review their lives together and impending death:

desperate bitterness between us—a 39 yr. old bitterness, devastating for me. Hopper meanness & sadism & getting away with it. It's not the ostracism, the pitiful wall flower experience everybody taking it all in—I could take what the world heaves out, but it's effect on our relations—bone of bone & flesh of flesh rotting in bitterness & so many dying about us—Guy gone, Denys Wortman, Emma Bellows, both Speichers, both Rehns, Violet Organ—We should be huddling together. Huddling with bitterness—knives in my breast! What Katherine Mansfield said about marriage—the wedding ring a wall to shut out the world & the mean tricks & treachery of the world shut out. Hopper meanness & sadism prevailing to the end. Do I want to share his grave at the last?[17]

For public consumption, in further interviews with O'Doherty, the couple put on a more lighthearted face, although Edward complained: "Living with one woman is like living with two or three tigers," to which Jo retorted: "Can't you see why? This everlasting argument! He'd be up first to watch for the first thing I'd say in the morning and then be ready to disagree with it."[18] She had typical recourse to a literary parallel: "Like Carlyle with Jane. When he couldn't find anything else to complain about he complained about her breathing."

In Edward's presence Jo told Flexner that Edward wanted to paint another picture set in a movie theater, "but that they did not know how to get into one when it was, as he wished, shut and empty."[19] Flexner went to considerable effort to arrange this for Hopper and secured an offer from the president of one of the largest theater chains to make any of his theaters available, only to hear Hopper say "laconically that he had no intention of painting another theater picture."[20] Evidently, Hopper had his idea so clearly in his mind that his presence in an actual theater became unnecessary. During March and April 1963, he worked on the painting that he came to call *Intermission,* in which a solitary woman sits slouched in an ample armchair front and left in a theater. Without betraying whether she had posed or not, Jo very suggestively sketches a psychological profile:

E. H. says she is 'Nora'. She has brown hair, wears black dress & is seated in dull dark green chair, upholstered for great comfort. Pale light blue wall well muted. Light establishing the horizontal on warmish grey carpet of aisle. End of stage, white & solid (like lighthouse) under streak of pale yellow curtain. Nothing of the comfortably bleak lost on the highly conscious Nora, with strong long hands. She not the kind to slip feet out of long reasonably high heeled

pumps. E. says Nora is on the way of becoming an 'egg head'. An ef-
ficient secretary or prized chatelaine of big house.[21]

A surviving preparatory sketch reveals that Hopper initially considered placing another figure in the third row of the theater. Maintaining her solitude
keeps attention on her posture of inwardness and containment, which contrasts so strikingly with the erect and active females of the two previous years,
in *New York Office* and *Woman in the Sun*. Yet Jo also had what it took for the
role of high consciousness, missing nothing of the surrounding paradoxes of
their "comfortably bleak" lives and being herself quite the "egg head", as well
as the superb recording secretary (alert to spot a parallel with Edward's lighthouses) and even the chatelaine of their lofty retreats, as she saw them, in
Truro and Washington Square.

Having just completed a major painting, Edward, according to Jo, was
"amicable enough," when Emeline Paige and her feline "columnist," "Scoopy
IV," came to interview Jo in April, although he kept *Intermission* face to the
wall during the entire time.[22] He was more open to others when later that
month he and Jo attended the opening of Jack Levine's show at the Alan
Gallery. They had come to know Levine from working on *Reality* and
they liked his work, especially paintings called *The Last Waltz* and *Witches'
Sabbath*.[23]

In May the Hoppers attended three days of parties for the fortieth anniversary of *Time* magazine. On meeting Bette Davis, whom he had admired
in *All About Eve* and many other films, Edward declared that he considered
her "the greatest Amer. actress." For once the Nyack Yankee met his match.
She replied "So what."[24] At a dinner at the Waldorf on May 6, he sat between
his old friend John Dos Passos and Elizabeth Arden, whom he described to
his sister as "a great bore."[25] For Jo these parties were "a breath of life."[26]

On May 14, the Hoppers were in Boston again, where Edward received
an award from the St. Botolph Club and served as a juror for the Boston Arts
Festival. His fellow jurors for the New England Painting Competition were
Henry Varnum Poor and the Abstract Expressionist Robert Motherwell.
Poor felt he served as the "middle man" between their two extremes; peace
was achieved when the three decided to use the "Buffalo" method where each
juror had "to stand for his own selection."[27] For the catalogue, Hopper stated:
"No jury system is perfect, but this so-called Buffalo System is the best I have
been on."[28] Returning to New York, they attended the housewarming party
of the sculptor Chaim Gross and his wife, Renée, whom they knew from the
Cape.

O'Doherty visited the Hoppers in early June and they talked for two
hours. Jo recorded in her diary that Edward was "very shining about this &

that."[29] Catching Hopper's mood, O'Doherty asked whether he was a pessimist, provoking: "A pessimist? I guess so. I'm not proud of it. At my age don't you get to be? When I see all those students running around painting—studying like mad, I say 'What's the use?' It all ends the same place. At fifty you don't think of the end much, but at 80 you think about it a lot. Find me a philosopher to comfort me in my old age."[30] The theme took his mind back to the moment between rounds of surgery when he had been taken by Renan's *Life of Jesus*. Allowing that he read a lot of Emerson, he reflected: "Emerson's a very shrewd New Englander, but he's no help."[31]

In June, there was another death to absorb: a neighbor and Jo's close friend, the sculptor Bea Kroll Goldsmith, who was the sister of Edward's sometime painting companion Leon Kroll. A week later, Edward tried to cheer Jo up by inviting her and her friend Lucy Bayard out to lunch and to see Hitchcock's film *The Birds*. Thoughts of death had if anything intensified wholly Jo's concern for her work. When a collector telephoned saying he wanted to purchase a Hopper, Jo responded that there were only "females of the species available."[32]

That summer, Jo arranged for Marie Stephens to drive her from Truro to Boston on the last day of the Boston Arts Festival. There she was delighted to see two of her canvases on view, especially her *Cape Cod Bedroom* "looking frisky in [the] outdoor light."[33] Listed in the catalogue as being represented by the Rehn Gallery, she gave John Clancy an account of the festival: "There was a terrific downpour so we saw very little of pictures or people. The pictures each had the initial of the juror who had selected it. Mine had all 3 jurors. Politics of course—but who am I to protest. Motherwell is high priest of gobbledegook. And the more power to him if he did see that my Cape Cod Bedroom has color & it has design—the two factors most extolled by the abstract persuasion."[34] Her paintings were listed for sale at fifteen hundred dollars each.

For much of the rest of the summer, Jo was again troubled by threats of encroachments on their land. She was relieved that Edward felt well and she reported to Clancy "he is much stronger on the Cape."[35] He was not working, but as the Cape became quieter with the end of summer, he was sometimes better able to paint. He wrote to Clancy that O'Doherty was "working on and including me in a book to be called 'Ten Modern Masters'"; though clearly pleased, he questioned: "Who the hell knows who a master is?"[36] Edward discouraged Jo from holding any more tea parties, protesting, "Don't you like it here? So peaceful."[37] She gave in.

Just like the year before, it was October before he was able to start. In the midst of the new work, Hopper told O'Doherty, "It needs more white on the foliage outside" and reflected: "There's problems of positive and negative areas here on the right that I have to think about. A negative window with a positive tree outside. They're opposed to each other right there. . . . It's hard to counteract each other. . . . It's hard to paint outside and inside at the same time."[38]

He also took another tack with O'Doherty, saying that he had long been "intrigued by an empty room."[39] On this theme he embroidered: "I've always been intrigued by an empty room anyway. When we were at school, du Bois and Rockwell Kent and others debated what a room looked like when there was nobody to see it, nobody looking in even. Of course there might be a mouse somewhere. I'd done so much with the figure I decided to leave the figure out."[40]

No figure appears in two preparatory sketches that survive, yet Hopper also told his young friend: "I had a figure in the sketch, but the figure was too big."[41] At this Jo snatched the envelope containing the evidence and sat on it so it could not be shown, creating a suspicion of vanity, seeking to hide the evidence of aging that Edward caught in sketches and transcended in paint. The work in progress is also well documented in the photographs taken while it was under way. The result drew a terse note in the record book: "Sun in an Empty Room. Green bushes outside window. White light + uncompromising shadow. Stark."[42]

Actually visible in the painting, sunlight, late in the day or the season, penetrates the room and falls twice on the background wall, first at the center, casting a tall, bright strip on a built-out corner, then at the left edge, beyond the corner's shadow, falling again and casting a small, bright strip, so that the two uprights of light emphasized against the backdrop stand together, united by the light flooding the floor. People sometimes assume incorrectly that this picture was Hopper's last, for it seems to reduce reality to its barest outlines, affirming the ability to see sunlight that he associated with life itself. In passing from drawing to canvas, he eliminates the solitary figure from the sketch that Jo concealed, making it clear that he had no intention of just varying simply the series of compositions with lone females for which she had posed in these two years. All that remains is the intense focus of the eye on the play of light. The viewer, whom Hopper so often made party to skewed or ambivalent glances, here becomes coopted to a purified vision. It may be this that Hopper meant when, being asked by O'Doherty what he was after in this picture, he replied: "I'm after ME."[43]

This strategy of reduction suggests parallels with Gide, who had long been favored by Hopper for his preoccupation with shadows and absorbing shades, with the relationship between visual imagery and psychic needs.[44] A particular parallel appears in Gide's *Les Cahiers d'André Walter:* "Reduce everything to the ESSENTIAL—no phenomenal life, only the noumena—

Edward Hopper, Sun in an Empty Room, *1963. Oil on canvas, 28¾ × 39½"*
(73 × 100.3 cm.).

therefore no descriptions and the background neutral—to take place anywhere and at any time—to be outside time and space."[45] In glancing beyond
appearances to form, Hopper also comes back to reread Plato one more time.
Going now beyond the jarring polarity of the male and female figures in *Excursion into Philosophy,* here Hopper brings two figures back into a stagy relationship to each other, but now purified of flesh and made geometry, the small
and the large polarized and united, emanating from the same vital light.

Edward drove himself and Jo back to New York in the middle of November, when she was suffering from bouts of colitis and he from neck pain.
His doctor, who had prescribed a collar for Hopper to wear when he was
tired, had diagnosed a deterioration of the cartilage between vertebrae.

Through the autumn Jo chronicled their difficulties in a series of letters
to Carl Sprinchorn, beginning with her fears of returning to Washington
Square: "Could anything be worth all the trouble, all those 74 stairs, every
time we go to street level. And the long treck to the bath room down the hall

& I suppose the studio door should be locked when we leave it & bath room kept locked also. Such a lot of locking and unlocking when you have colitis too."[46] Jo suffered more in New York than on the Cape, and diagnosed her condition as "fatigue and outrage."[47]

By December she was reporting a serious retreat from what had enlivened her life: she had had to give up her practice of going to exhibitions and shopping uptown because even marketing once a week used up all her strength. In any case, she deplored the quality of the exhibitions, claiming "its too depressing to paint—more of the same—lone survivors."[48] She had one consolation, she confided: "It's such blessedness that Edward & I have each other. Surely I'll be allowed to go when he does. He gets so tired when he goes 2 or 3 blocks & we do not have the car here, use it only on the Cape."[49] Edward now walked with a cane, and Jo suggested that Carl, who himself had been quite ill, get one too. She also recommended a cat: "You may have found out that very special little miracles can occur. They certainly have for me. Arthur stayed until Edward came. They were devoted friends—then when not positively needed, & reassured that E. did very well, Arthur disappeared. Another commission maybe."[50]

As 1964 opened and their rounds of activities and circle of friends continued to diminish, Jo pursued her confidences to Sprinchorn: "Edward being such a hermit—& getting more so all the time."[51] He liked to listen to their radio, but she griped about "those loathsome personalities right in the room with us."[52] He started to take care of the cooking because she found that it was "easier to do without."[53] They went out very little. Jo told Sprinchorn that they had never even seen the Guggenheim Museum. They did occasionally go to see friends such as John and Dora Koch.[54]

In February, O'Doherty visited again and Jo, less reticent about drawings, showed him cartoons made by Edward of the two of them. She described Edward as "very relaxed & nonchalant & frank."[55] O'Doherty, whose affection for the Hoppers was genuine, had so won Jo's trust that she had spent the morning going through her file of old magazines and clippings in order to lend him some for his research.[56] Jo felt that O'Doherty, the physician turned writer, gave them nurturing advice; when they coughed, he told them they "must see a doctor."[57] On one occasion she suggested how his aesthetics matched theirs: "We love your being unceasingly wise. . . . With the poet there is always the surging flow of words, often like lovely star spangled yard goods that has need of shoulders to be fitted on. But with keen satisfaction we've seen you let certain brassy bones go naked & deservedly."[58]

Hopper learned that he had received the M. V. Khonstamn Prize for painting from the Art Institute of Chicago. They had chosen his canvas *Road*

Sidney Waintrob, Edward and Jo Hopper at the American Academy of Arts and Letters, *December 11, 1964.*

and Trees, painted only in 1962. Jo noted that Edward had remarked that "5 or maybe only 3 years ago they wouldn't have been giving that picture a prize; this turning the tide" was much to his satisfaction.[59]

Fatigue combined with concern about his first retrospective since 1950, and the intrusion of the event itself prevented Hopper from painting during the spring and summer of 1964. At the end of September, when he normally would be about to begin a canvas, the exhibition opened at the Whitney Museum, where it remained on view for two months. In anticipation, Hopper wrote to his sister, warning her not to even think of coming to the opening party: "This is one time in the year when I can meet museum directors, critics and collectors of importance and I shall have to devote all my time to them (and will have no time for you, Dr. Sanborn [the Baptist minister] and Beatrice)."[60] He explained that an opening was really "a cocktail party with hundreds milling around in a noisy crowd, looking at each other, often with dislike . . . quite a trying experience. . . . Jo's job will be to fight off autograph hunters."[61]

The Hoppers' personal guest list, sent to the Whitney, reveals a great deal about whom they considered important to their lives and his career.[62] Jo identified Clarence Chatterton as Hopper's "oldest, most valued friend." Besides friends and neighbors, such as John Dos Passos, "old friend, famous author," Jo listed various people in the arts whom they considered "very pro-Hopper," including, for example, Arthur Miller, whom she identified as a "great dramatist"; Lewis Mumford, whom she called a "fine critic" and an "architect authority"; Edward Durell Stone, whom she identified as the "architect of the Gallery of Modern Art"; and Thornton Wilder, whom she also described as a "great dramatist." (The Hoppers especially liked his Pulitzer Prize–winning play *Our Town,* with its depiction of small-town New England life.)

At the age of eighty-two, Hopper was still anxious about what the critics would say. The day before his opening, he remarked to John Canaday, "Tomorrow the knocks. Tomorrow the knocks."[63] He recalled the mixed critical response to the earlier retrospective when, much to his dismay, some compared his painting to illustration. He did not, of course, fear Canaday, who in fact underlined Hopper's uniqueness: "He has remained in the good graces of even the abstract painters, because, alone among American realists, he works in a way easily connectable with abstraction in the careful disposition, the inventive purity of his surface patterns."[64]

The veteran critic Emily Genauer puzzled over his place in American art, asking: "How could Hopper, never wavering even in his 83rd year, from pursuing his idea of realism, have turned out to be so close to abstraction?"[65] Younger critics added their praise as well. Hilton Kramer recognized Hopper's powerful "confrontation of American experience," while placing him in "the line of Eakins and Homer."[66] Brian O'Doherty celebrated Hopper's "vision which monumentalizes urban banality through means as geometric and solid as Cycladic masonry—given life by light moving across pictures in oblique trajectories."[67] Barbara Rose called Hopper's painting "superb," noting: "A comparison with Hopper's fluid terseness is one that Wyeth's academic pettiness cannot bear. Even Diebenkorn's abstractions in search of a story on which to hang themselves appear but virtuoso exercises beside the intensity of feeling conveyed in Hopper's precise stroking."[68] In an article titled "Edward Hopper and the Provincial Principle," the painter and critic Sidney Tillim wrote: "I am of the opinion that Hopper's Puritanism resulted in certain tensions that express themselves in particularly melancholy images which in turn may express a rather circumscribed view of art. At the same time his compensatory powers have been extraordinary.... Given the lag in the emergence of the provincial principle throughout the entire world now, it will simply be a question of time before his distinction is recognized abroad as it is in the United States."[69]

Hopper wrote to Lewis Mumford, whom he had gotten to know at the American Academy of Arts and Letters, expressing how gratified he was by Mumford's "thoughts" on his show: "The matter of staking out a territory in art is a puzzling problem and can be a subject for esthetic philosophy. The direction one's work takes is the inevitable concomitant of the painter's individuality (if he has any) and not a matter of conscious choice, as you know."[70] Mumford had thought Hopper a "good" painter at the time of his first retrospective in 1933, but now hailed him as one of the great.

To O'Doherty, Hopper confided that he found fault with the Whitney installation: "Some pictures lost impact because they were hung with so many others. It was hard to concentrate."[71] And he summed up his intention for his pictures, each of which he considered "an instant in time, arrested—and acutely realized with the utmost intensity."[72]

All in all, this retrospective had been encouraging. No longer strong enough to stand up for an opening party, Hopper sat in a chair while Jo stood to fend off the "autograph hunters."[73] She bragged to Sprinchorn that seventy thousand people saw the show. She and Edward saw no need to travel with it to Chicago, Detroit, and St. Louis, because they knew no one in any of those cities.

The exhibition brought Hopper a new wave of attention. He granted an interview to Rafael Squirru, a young Argentinian writer then living in Washington, D.C. When asked what advice he would give a young artist just starting out, he offered a characteristic one-word answer: "Work!"[74] Asked which period in art he preferred, Hopper gave what was for him an unusual response: "Maybe the Renaissance," only at once to pull back, "I don't know."[75]

As to his compatriots, Hopper reaffirmed: "Thomas Eakins, he is our greatest artist." At that Jo, whom Squirru described as a "delightful little woman, who could only be cast as one of the good fairies in the world of Grimm," interrupted: "How can you say that? How can you say that when Eakins was so mean? He used to make those young girls stand before him for hours and then he would paint them as if they were twenty years older. Do you think that is nice, making those poor young girls feel so dejected. Eakins was so cruel. How can you say he was a great artist?"[76]

When Jo spoke to Squirru, it sounded to him as if she "chirped"; he portrayed Hopper as staring into space and reflected rather trenchantly: "Somehow I have a feeling that he is rocking with laughter. That was a very funny remark on the part of his wife and he is enjoying it for all it is worth."[77]

The Hoppers must have liked Squirru, to speak openly with him in this manner. It is clear that they liked a good deal of what he had to say, particularly: "Many critics have recognized action painting as the first truly made-in-USA school of art. In this they are mistaken. It is Hopper who must be considered in that light, and in that light many movements, for example, Pop Art, find their strength, their backbone and their validity."[78] Hopper told Squirru about an incident that took place at the retrospective. When someone asked him, "Why are the people you paint always so middle class?" Hopper retorted, "I guess it is because there are so many of them," remarking that he was reminded of Lincoln's remark about the poor: "God must have loved them because he made so many of them."[79]

With the retrospective behind him, on Christmas day in 1964, Hopper began the canvas that Jo registered as *Chair Car* toward the end of January 1965:

> Glass of windows have opaque effect from light head on from outside of car. 4 patches of light, pale, on dark green floor. Upolstery heavy dark green, light touching white doilies on tops of chairs. Blond girl at front in black dress with lot of flesh color stockings. 3 other passengers not much defined. Walls & ceiling blue grey, not in sunlight except oblique patch on back wall from window farther back.[80]

The scene of a railroad parlor car harks back to Hopper's work as an illustrator, recalling more closely the perspective along the length of a car in the etching *Night, the El Train*. Railroads had fascinated him since the drawings of his youth and they returned in diverse paintings that evoke the paraphernalia of tracks, tunnels, signals, and compartments. In *Chair Car,* however, all such details fall away. The light, as Jo remarks, effectively isolates the compartment and the perspective carries the eye to a huge blank door. The blond girl does have showy legs, as Jo remarks, not shapely but bright. Her gaze bends intently to the book held out in her hands, face looking wrinkled and tired. The viewer's eye pursuing the patches of light along the carpet stops short at a pointed black pump against the green field and detours left to a hint of red dress and beady glare from a dark-haired head twisting back toward the self-contained reader. The paint is applied with a thickness that is uncharacteristic of most of Hopper's work.

The whole boxed-in situation and the potential story implied by the contrasting attitudes of the figures and the different directions of their eyes again prompt the play of interpretive fantasy. The obtrusive light suggests the harsh glare of the setting sun, which is a dreaded finale for a painter who equated the ability to see sunlight with life itself. (It was this blinding light at sunset that caused John Dos Passos to lose an eye, killing Katy, his wife.) The dark lady in red menaces the fair reader in black. The ill-defined door at the end looms.

FINAL CURTAIN: 1965-1967

IN JANUARY 1965, Hopper declined an invitation to attend Lyndon Johnson's inauguration. Never one to like Democrats, he explained to Marion he had heard it would be too tiring from friends who attended the inauguration of John Kennedy (which he had also had the honor to decline).[1] In June, he and Jo were taken by car to Philadelphia and housed in "a big hotel," so he could receive an honorary doctorate of fine arts from the Philadelphia College of Art with, Jo hastily jotted, a "big ovation by faculty, students & audience," to say nothing of the banquet after the ceremony, which they especially appreciated in the absence of much cooking at home.[2]

In his fashion Hopper kept in touch with his old friend Chatterton: "I wrote a reply to your letter of Jan. 19th but Jo said it was pompous and humorless, so at the risk of being thought pompous and humorless, I did not send it."[3] Jo invited Chat's daughter Julia to come and see her and her work, warning her to come early to have the sunlight: "E.H. never did a thing about lighting & so we're like a dingy cellar after daylight goes."[4] Telling Julia of her by now chronic colitis, Jo reiterated her charge that Edward's doctor had identified the cause as "fatigue & outrage!"—a diagnosis hailed by her as "God's truth at that."[5]

In March, Jo again confided in Sprinchorn that Edward got tired walking just two or three blocks, but that he was "doing fine—does those 74 steps up from the street, because he's now had a half century of practice."[6] She deplored his need to take taxis, which she considered "much of a concession to encroachment of time. Time that is so thievish."[7]

When the interview with Squirru came out, Hopper wrote to him: "I have read it several times. It is a more inclusive review than an art critic usually makes. That is good." He reflected: "There is a difficulty for the artist in such an intelligent critique. That if the subject of it is weak, he may unconsciously succumb to emulating it in his work. A possibility, though perhaps remote in my case. Mrs. Hopper says you are a romantic. Perhaps she is right."[8] Hopper seeks as ever the general principle, touching obliquely on his own situation, where it was less than ever clear if he would work again.

Jo was thrilled when O'Doherty included her *Chez Hopper* in an exhibition on lesser-known artists for the American Express Pavilion at the New York World's Fair. She described her picture as "long ridges of hills within the sight of Mrs. Scott's House, these hills going west to the sea with Chez Hopper, looking like an old fish house perched on the skyline."[9] Examples of Edward's work were shown in two other World's Fair exhibitions, "Four Centuries of American Masterpieces," held at the Better Living Center, and "The City: People and Places," in the New York State Pavilion. The collector Roy Neuberger, who owned *The Barber Shop,* accompanied the Hoppers to an opening party for the latter exhibition. He vividly recalled Jo's comment that she did not know why he was fussing so much about Ed when she was just as good an artist.[10]

§

IN MAY a burglar wearing a pink mask broke into the house in Nyack and, holding a hand over Marion's mouth, forced her upstairs. Jo advised her to open a checking account and took stock of their own vulnerability: "We sleep with an open window at head of a fire escape and dark park opposite—in an empty house. Bathroom out in hall—stairs to roof in front of studio door to hall. Edward impatient of any precautions with wallet stolen out of pocket three times, good overcoat also."[11]

With Marion failing and her housekeeper spending the Fourth of July in New Hampshire, Edward and Jo acted as nurses for a week, transported back and forth in his car by the Baptist minister, Arthayer Sanborn. Marion was taken to the hospital on July 16 and died the next day. On Sunday in a hard rain, Sanborn came for them and they stopped at the funeral home. Marion was buried on the twentieth in the family plot in Oak Hill Cemetery in Nyack, leaving "Edward the last in the line, every responsibility from way back & plenty."[12]

Apart from two trips back and forth by bus, Jo and Edward spent most of the next month and a half in Nyack, settling affairs and "breathing the dust of 100 yrs. in that old home."[13] Antique dealers had been courting Marion and sent flowers to her funeral; besides furniture, there were still three houses in the estate. To Jo it was left to sort through, finding the old photographs of Elizabeth Hopper, but unable to locate her solitaire, unearthing an "album quilt of 1850s done by the ladies of the congregation for our ancestor Griffiths . . . squares of colored cotton, including 3 cows, a horse, birds, flowers, an ark."[14] Marion had been "a pack rat like me. . . . She not so fond of me, but from across the grave, I felt her gladness I wasn't throwing out her treasures or selling the 100 yr. old birthplace, with everything the matter with it, naturally. Intriguing, like a stray pussy cat."[15] Jo complained that Edward left her to "do everything, drag, hawl, unwrap, wrap, wash hands 28 times a day, breathing in the dust of a century while he enjoyed gazing on a segment of the Hudson R. seen between the 2 receding rows of houses facing 2″ [2nd] Ave. where it ends with Chez Hopper."[16] His love for that open view had drawn him to the top floor of Washington Square and to the land in Truro overlooking the bay.

It was August 29 before the Hoppers were able to get to the Cape, and then only because they were driven by Eddy Brady, the handyman, their "trusty husky" as Jo called him, who traveled back to New York from Hyannis by Greyhound bus. Painting seemed out of the question, yet they hung on, even though Jo was always fearful that an early blizzard would cut them off.

When forwarded catalogues from Chat reminded them, two days before the opening November 1, that he was having a show at the Chapellier Gallery, Jo scribbled a note at the post office, "Darlings, We can't tell you how desolated we are not to get to your opening. If we were young enough to leap & drive like hell, we'd try, but élas, élas, E. H. stoops over a cane & I half blind. . . . Catalogue is handsome—so warm—*warmth* is so valuable—you & Annette certainly have that blessed quality." Edward more formally penned regrets, promised a visit on his return, and augured sales, "That is what we all wish about our work," adding philosophically: "Critical opinion has been inimical or silent on the work of most of our generation for the past forty years, so we never expect much from that area."[17] Treading delicately with respect to a friend who had achieved nothing comparable to his own success, Hopper shows that he still remembers the sting of early negative comments and certainly does not emphasize the precocious fame of their contemporary Bellows.

Through September and into October the easel before the tall north window stood empty, in the uncertainty of another canvas. Then an idea began to take shape. On Armistice Day in 1965, Edward signed the painting that Jo entered summarily in the book:

> The Two Commedians. Finished Nov. 10, 1966 in S. Truro studio. W. & N. Herger canvas, thick single white prime linen canvas—smooth as double would be, but less apt to crack than double. W. & N. lead white & colors. Linseed oil with turpentine. 2 white figures against dark stage, slightly green at R. (foliage).[18]

Jo embroidered in her diary for November 12, mimicking the ledger style in her pride that she, as well as Edward, had been at work:

> 2 canvases finished & signed yesterday
> E. H.   2 Commedians at Edge of proscenium—
>   2 small white figures against dark stage
>   stage—sturdy as a ship's bough
>   ± ⅛ of 29 × 40 picture.
> J. H.   Goldenrod & milkweed in glorietta peach can—
>   + painted yellow glass dishes 30 × 25.
>   Bambergers came to see yesterday.[19]

On November 14 she wrote Margaret McKellar at the Whitney Museum: "E. H. is bringing back a charming 29 × 40 canvas of a dark stage (and what a stage, strong as the deck of a ship) & two small figures out of pantomime. *Poignant,*" adding,

> We do hope all is well with you beautiful people—to whom we owe so much: you & Lloyd & Edith & dear lovely Marie—& the guards who watched over the pictures & counted noses as they came in with such satisfaction—the 75,000 of them. This recent close-up death makes one cherish one's living, see them as infinitely valuable—& here—now—right *now* & truly good & beautiful.[20]

To Goodrich, she later stated that the painting represented Edward and herself.[21]

As Hopper explored his idea, he drew the male figure leaping into the air while the other figure clambered up onto a small stage. In another drawing, he imagined the male graciously handing the female through an exit, with spectators appearing behind a low barrier. In the canvas, he raises both figures up to the solid stage, with its border of artificial woods, where they link

Edward Hopper, Two Comedians, *1965. Oil on canvas, 29 × 40" (73.7 × 101.6 cm.).*

hands and prepare to bow, their free hands poised as if about to gesture in deference to each other.

The comedians in their white costumes with ruffled collars recall Pierrot and Pierrette of the *commedia dell'arte,* which provided a frequent theme in the French symbolist poetry that Edward and Jo first quoted to each other in courtship.[22] Clowns were familiar from Watteau and such popular illustrations as those by Gavarni and Willette. Above all, only five years before, the Hoppers had been enchanted by Marcel Carné's classic film *Les Enfants du Paradis,* which tells of Jean-Gaspard Deburau, the nineteenth-century French actor whose renditions of Pierrot redefined understanding of the commedia.[23]

The haunting images of Paris in *Les Enfants du Paradis* triggered nostalgia. The young Edward had written home about the clowns and painted ladies he had seen in the "carnival" Mi-Carme in 1907. He had focused on the plight of Pierrot in his 1915 recollection of Paris, the monumental canvas *Soir Bleu,* where the brooding clown with large lips bears a striking resemblance to the artist himself. Hopper's sense of his own parallel with Pierrot reflects his consciousness of the loneliness the artist shares with clowns and other entertainers in their roles as outsiders.

By also presenting Jo as Pierrette, Edward pays homage not only to her cherished memories of her early acting career but to her active collaboration as his model. He allows her the recognition she had long sought, casting her as his partner, sharing the spotlight and the honor on the stage after a well-executed performance. The linked actors face the end together. On Saturday, November 13, late at night, Jo took stock in seven pages to Annette:[24] Edward the "perfect skunk about my acquiring great skill in manipulating a car" and her sight going, and he "so afraid he'll fall" and "stoops badly & breaks my heart. . . . Chat holds himself perfectly straight," no "compromises with that old man with the scythe"; then, "I'm a blond now & like it. And I'm sure you stay spry."

As for New York: "E. H. still does his 74 steps . . . had 52 years of practice . . . but its slowly & bent way over," and,

> All those grand studios turned into offices . . . neighborhood changed. We go out very little at night. And few people care to climb our stairs. . . . I have 30 ft studio also, full of my progeny. I find a certain comfort in it, a record of my life, here or there—relived—little bastards & not unrepentant. However, I've learned, lots of women can't help being more interested in people & life than in art. They must have both. Luckily, because Art can't be bothered much about the female—as we have occasion to observe. Of course you have had a beautiful daughter. . . .
>
> When E.H. goes I shall be alone upon Earth. He has not been greatly interested in people, we have no close friends. We feel that our little place here on the hill top is paradise—just every simple thing that we love best. Lovely long lines of hills to the East of us & the beach & the expanse of the sea to the West. . . . Not a breeze between here & Portugal that slights us on our bare hill—facing such glorious sunsets. Thrilling location, but not place to live alone in—if one were alone—in the dark with the sound of the sea: Made for Adam & Eve to fight it out in.

She wound to a close:

> With all this confession of what that old man with scythe has done to us, we want you to know we love you & thank God to have known you as one of the good things of our lives.
>
> That silent partner creature has gone to bed. He always hates what ever I write & will take no part in the way I say it.

§

ONCE THEIR "HUSKY" had brought them back, shepherding boxes up the dumbwaiter, Hopper kept his word and met Chatterton at the gallery, where, his daughter Julia remembers, the two octogenarians sat together in silence, contemplating the works.[25] In December, Edward's health continued to deteriorate, causing Jo to postpone planned surgery for her eyes. Edward experienced pain so severe that she called for an ambulance to take him to St. Vincent's Hospital for what turned out to be a double hernia operation.

It was July 16, 1966, when she wrote to Lucy Bayard describing Edward's plight:[26] "It's a matter of gaining strength. E. is afraid of falling if he tried to stand"; the other inhabitant of the semiprivate room had the window, the view, the air, and the light, leaving Edward behind the partitioning curtain: "It was my idea of hell."

Jo was desperate for someone to speak to. Over the telephone with the photographer Peter Pollack, whom she barely knew, she discussed Edward's illness: "He's never been undernourished. I once went to a doctor with him many years ago and the report about him read, 'large frame—well nourished.' I never worried after that, about my cooking or his health. But now he's sick—he won't do anything for himself and he's on his feet, walking—he's underweight so I'll have to be cooking things for him. And I hate to cook."[27]

Pollack recorded a long conversation in which Jo elaborated: "I'm real mean about the commissary act. I don't like to cook—I never did. But now it's my job. I've got to get strength back into his body."[28] When asked why she did not hire a cook and a nurse, Jo protested: "What? and have her and him both against me? I'll be able to see it in his eyes—he'll like it." She added candidly: "Of course we're on each other's nerves. I'm not a good Christian. I don't turn the other cheek. No, not I. I never forgive anything. My mother was a good Christian, she was the soul of patience. And, she lost out on every deal."[29]

Two days after this conversation, on August 27, 1966, Hopper received the Edward MacDowell medal for outstanding contributions to the arts. Lloyd Goodrich went to accept it and newspapers reported Hopper was much too ill to travel.[30] He was quoted as saying, "Recognition doesn't mean so much—you never get it when you need it."[31] (The award had previously gone to two writers Hopper especially admired: Thornton Wilder and Robert Frost.)

A week later, as Jo, whose cataracts were now complicated by glaucoma, was getting ready for her daily visit with Edward, she "slipped on sliver of floor wax" in the studio and broke her hip and leg, joining him in the hospital, where they remained for three months. She later wrote to her old friend Catherine Rogers that Edward visited her every day in her third-floor room, coming down in a wheel chair from the fifth floor. She recalled: "It was a strain, never the least privacy, no escape from personalities close as breathing, and their ghastly radios. E.H. never got over it." When Jack Levine and his wife, Ruth Gikow, visited them, Edward was grateful to learn that they had called on Jo first.[32] When they gave her a gift of talcum powder, Jo, feeling increasingly vulnerable, acted as if she thought someone in the hospital might steal it. When a stranger came to visit and introduced himself as an artist, Edward asked: "You got good light?"[33]

On their release from the hospital in early December 1966, they found daily life ever more difficult to manage: "We were both wrecks when we finally got back to our Paradise—here at #3—alone up 74 stairs."[34] She wrote to Sprinchorn a few weeks later: "E. has very little strength, always tired. Me, too, but have graduated from a walker—in the house, that is & stumble about the place watching out for what to reach for next. This condition is not helped by cataract in both eyes, with glaucoma, so can't operate on cataract."[35] They paid someone to market for them and someone else to clean, but Jo insisted on cooking herself, which she later claimed was "better than some one underfoot all the time. But I did have a broken leg and that got no rest."[36]

By April 28, 1967, Jo had recovered enough to attend a tea party given by Emeline Paige, the editor of the *Villager,* before she moved to Florida. The party was in honor of her "newest acquisition: the pot-bellied stove from the original Whitney Museum" on Eighth Street. She reported for the local paper of her new Florida town: "I gave a tea party for the stove and no one thought it strange—least of all the neighbor from three doors away on Washington Square North who arrived early and was almost the last to leave: Mrs. Edward Hopper."[37] Paige published a photograph of Jo seated smiling by the stove and quoted her: "Edward, she said, would love to have come . . . he knows the stove so well. Ours was somewhat smaller and was always called 'Mademoiselle.' This one—so handsome, isn't it?—you'll have to call 'Madame.' "[38]

Jo confided to Catherine Rogers that Edward's hernia operation was "not exactly successful, like darning an old sock, tissue too thin to hold."[39] Concerned that Edward was not getting enough to eat, Brian O'Doherty and his wife, the art historian Barbara Novak, tried to help out, but met with resistance from Jo. Novak asked Hopper if he knew that his work would soon be featured in the São Paulo Bienal. She was struck by his response: "You think it will amount to anything?"[40] Nine months after the operation, Hopper was back in St. Vincent's with heart problems. When he returned home very weak, Jo was unable to "lift, drag or haul an inch of him." Their "trusty husky" came to the rescue, showing, said Jo, the "strength and tenderness needed by a young child. It was beautiful for E.H. and for me. E. slept peacefully at night." To Rogers she described Brady's devotion as a miracle:

> Digitalis kills heart patients—it inhibits digestion while keeping the heart going and E.H. got thin as Ghandi and no strength at all. Had to be hauled up out of bed and to arm chair, shoved in his "cadillac" down hall to bathroom, fed and Oh so praised for any bite of food he could get down, all the arduous details of care for the very sick however sizable and rubbed down in alcohol, bathed, all so gently and expertly, by a person who had never done it before or will again for anyone else he doesn't love and feel positively sent by some higher power. I call it a beautiful miracle.[41]

§

HOPPER DIED in his Washington Square studio on May 15, 1967, two months short of his eighty-fifth birthday. To Rogers, Jo described the end:

> And when the hour struck he was home, here in his big chair in big studio—and took one minute to die. No pain, no sound and eyes sere and even happy and very beautiful in death, like an El Greco.

And she reflected:

> He didn't want to go and I thought maybe he would stay awhile longer under such good care. Then he left suddenly. One minute and gone! No waiting for me. We were alone there in late afternoon and he in his chair. No struggle, no pain, even gladly, and looked so beautiful![42]

Two days later, Hopper was buried in the family plot in Nyack, on a high ridge overlooking the Tappan Zee where he had sailed as a boy. Jo had no one to turn to to conduct the funeral but Marion's minister, Sanborn, whom she had pegged as a "13th disciple—he, such a husky, good looking football coach content to shepherd a flock of Nyack ladies . . . doing needed & often arduous practical good offices for them that would include going out in kitchen and making lunch for Marion," for which services she and Edward had paid him five hundred dollars from the estate.[43] The funeral was attended by Jo, John Clancy, Henry Varnum Poor, his daughter Anne Poor, Brian O'Doherty, Barbara Novak, Mrs. Clarence (Peggy) Day, and Lloyd Goodrich. Jo reported that the service was "very private, all done before and so forth, no hullabaloo and publicity, not Grace Church," thinking of the funerals they had attended for artists such as their old teacher Kenneth Miller. To another friend, she declared that those who attended the service were "all the people E.H. would want. Just a handful."[44]

Hopper's obituary made the front page of *The New York Times,* with a slightly garbled account of his career, claiming, for example, that he had painted in Spain and that he had "sold only two canvases" before his 1933 retrospective at the Museum of Modern Art, although, in fact, he had sold only two works before his one-man show at the Rehn Gallery in 1924.[45] Newspapers across the country reported his death. He was saluted as an American classic. *Newsweek* called him a "wonderful painter . . . a realist, a modernist, a romantic, a structuralist, a poet."[46] *Life* said that "Hopper distilled, more masterfully than any other artist of his time, a haunting look and mood of America."[47]

Hopper had lived long enough to see the critical revival of his art after its rebuff by many during the heyday of Abstract Expressionism. In March 1967, art historian William Seitz, who had written his doctoral dissertation on Abstract Expressionism, had announced that Hopper would be the key artist to represent the United States at the São Paulo Bienal opening in September. Seitz saw Hopper as "a bridge from the Ashcan School to the decade of pop art."[48] The younger artists in the exhibition included Jasper Johns, Roy Lichtenstein, Robert Rauschenberg, George Segal, James Rosenquist, Andy Warhol, and Tom Wesselmann. Seitz wrote in an evaluation for the Associated Press after Hopper's death that he "held a position of esteem among American artists that was unique, for he was highly regarded by advocates of both representational and abstract painting, and by avant-gardists as well as conservatives."[49]

Jo was left to fend for herself. She was ill, nearly blind, and entirely alone. Without family, she was totally dependent on her friends for company and assistance. In the weeks after the funeral, Dorothy Ferris, by then a widow for five years, contacted Jo. Describing what she saw as their tragic situations, Jo confided in Catherine Rogers, who was their mutual friend: "Dorothy Ferris phoned. Now we are both amputees. She has survived. But who wants to? I asked E.H. if he wanted me to come along. We've always gone together— up the Pyramid of the Sun and beyond Guadaloupe."[50]

She tried to occupy herself with paying bills and income taxes neglected by Edward during his illness. But, she confided, although "no matter how blind and lame it behooves me to get at it, . . . I seem to get nowhere." She complained of "dazed inertia." Jo knew that she should attend to probating the will and disposing of the dilapidated property in Nyack. She fondly recalled "some sweet bits of old furniture," but concluded that she was "all so alone and nearly blind," so that she "better let it alone." Deploring her lack of strength, she exclaimed: "Everybody gone!"

A month after Edward's death, Lila Harnett, a New York critic and collector who owned two of his watercolors, mentioned in a column an old letter from Jo referring to his paintings as "their children, and the people who buy them, (sort of) in-laws." Harnett reflected: "I wish she could know how proud we are to be in the family and how we grieve with her at this time."[51] When the column came to Jo's attention, she responded: "I've been meaning to write you but am driven into doing so by sheer loneliness, initiation into Les Amputees—as I call those selected for amputation—one half sliced off & bleeding. Wow. And Edward hadn't wanted to go. I said I'd go with him on this supposedly long trail. I was so tired maybe I could be let go. All these many years, I've always been along."[52] Jo concluded that she should remain behind to "invent places to put years' accumulations & nowhere possible to tuck anything to heave out; agonizing. We were both pack rats so 2 studios bulging."

To Emeline Paige in Florida, Jo complained of her poor vision and recounted her predicament and pain: she had her "eye operated on July 18," but "see much less than before anything done to eyes."[53] After the surgery she had spent "6 weeks at a nursing home where people left members of their family to die." Returning to the studio on September 18, she reported that the only walking she did was "around the house which I manage after a fashion." Her loss of sight was especially frustrating: "Can't sew—which is lamentable. Can't thread needle, even with devices. The main bother is scarcity of light. It is always dark & dull." And yet, Jo was glad to be "still here in our adored 2 studios, after all these years & no one throwing me out." She was grateful for Brady, who did her shopping. Referring to their mutual passion for cats, Jo fondly recalled to Emeline: "There was only one Arthur. He wouldn't have wanted to share with a pack. He & Edward did splendidly together. They both understood me. Not a lot of collision there either." Yet she admitted she felt "consumed by chaos, held back by my eyes."

As she struggled to cope with daily life, bills, and income taxes, her fears deepened of being alone in the studio at night. Her leg was slow to mend, and she felt like a prisoner; nor could she imagine being alone on the Cape. She no longer had a driver's license and even if she had, could not see to drive: "What was perfection together is a heart break alone."

All through this "time of problems & confusion,"[54] she continued to keep meticulous track of the whereabouts of her husband's work, and yet at least one major painting clearly listed as "in the studio" later turned up inexplicably in the hands of someone who in this period took the trouble to face the seventy-four steps.

Jo Hopper died on March 6, 1968, twelve days before her eighty-fifth birthday. Her husband of nearly forty-three years had been gone for less than ten months when she rejoined him as she had wished. Life without Edward was unthinkable. Life together, as she put it with telling parentheses, had been "perfection (of its own snappy kind)."[55]

BIBLIOGRAPHICAL NOTES

Complete citations for the sources used in this book appear in the end notes. The author has elsewhere published an extensive bibliography, exhibition history, Hopper's Record Books, and other reference data in *Edward Hopper: A Catalogue Raisonné* (New York: W. W. Norton & Co., 1995). Briefer bibliographies and good color reproductions can be found in the author's *Edward Hopper: The Art and the Artist* (New York: W. W. Norton & Co., 1980), *Edward Hopper* (New York: Crown Publishers, 1984), and *Edward Hopper as Illustrator* (New York: W. W. Norton & Co., 1979). For reproductions of Hopper's graphic work, see the author's *Edward Hopper: The Complete Prints* (New York: W. W. Norton & Co., 1979). Photographs by the author of many sites painted by Hopper are available in her *Hopper's Places* (New York: Alfred A. Knopf, 1985). For a more autobiographical account of creating the Hopper archive at the Whitney Museum of American Art and laying the scholarly foundations for a new understanding of Hopper, see the author's "Biography and Catalogue Raisonné: Edward Hopper in Two Genres," in *Biography and Source Studies,* 2 (New York: AMS Press, 1995).

ARCHIVAL MATERIALS

The following institutions are the main repositories of unpublished materials consulted for this book: American Academy of Arts and Letters, New York, New York; Amherst College Library, Amherst, Massachusetts (papers of George and Emma Bellows); Archives of American Art, Smithsonian Institution, Washington, D.C. (papers of Louis Bouché, Guy Pène du Bois, Samuel Golden, Edmund Graecen, Rockwell Kent, Leon Kroll, Richard Lahey, Elizabeth Novas, Henry Varnum Poor, Frank K. M. Rehn Gallery, Carl Sprinchorn, Walter Tittle, and Forbes Watson; diaries of Robert Henri; and other collections) Brandywine River Museum, Chadds Ford, Pennsylvania (*Scribner's* magazine papers); Milbank Memorial Library, Teachers College, Columbia University, New York (New York City Public School papers); Municipal Archives, Haarlem, Netherlands (Frans Hals Collection register); Hirshhorn Museum and Sculpture Garden, Smithsonian Institution, Washington, D.C. (Elmer MacRae papers); Archives, Hunter College Library, New York (Normal College of New York papers); Newberry Library, Chicago, Illinois (Arts Club of Chicago papers); University of North Carolina Library, Chapel Hill, North Carolina (Elizabeth Amis Cameron Blanchard papers); Van Pelt Library, University of Pennsylvania, Philadelphia, Pennsylvania (papers of Van Wyck Brooks, Lewis Mumford, and Carl Zigrosser); Randolph-Macon College, Lynchburg, Virginia; United States Office of Personnel Management, St. Louis, Missouri (Reconstruction Aide archives); Humanities Research Center, University of Texas, Austin, Texas (J. Donald

Adams papers); Alderman Library, University of Virginia, Charlottesville, Virginia (papers of John Dos Passos, Alfred Kreymborg, and Vachel Lindsay); Whitney Museum of American Art, New York, New York (Hopper's Record Books, Lloyd Goodrich's unpublished notes on his interviews with Hopper, letters to Goodrich, Rosalind Irvine, Flora Miller, and Margaret McKellar); Wittenberg University Library, Springfield, Ohio (Walter Tittle papers); Beinecke Library, Yale University, New Haven, Connecticut (letters to Robert Henri and Henry McBride). Other letters cited remain in the collections of the museums to which they were written. Many other papers, including the diaries of Jo Hopper, are in private collections. The author is currently preparing an edition of the papers of Edward and Jo Hopper.

NOTES

The locations of letters and other unpublished sources are given in the Bibliographical Notes under Archival Materials.

The author has preserved errors of spelling and syntax in the manuscripts of Edward and Jo Hopper, and in other unpublished documents cited.

INTRODUCTION

1 William Johnson, unpublished interview with Edward and Jo Hopper, October 30, 1956. The reporter who gave up was Robert Coates.

2 Jo Hopper, in Johnson interview.

3 Jo Hopper diary entry for March 29, 1950.

4 Jo Hopper diary entry for March 30, 1939.

5 Edward Hopper, quoted in Katharine Kuh, *The Artist's Voice* (New York: Harper & Row, 1960), p. 131.

6 Edward Hopper, quoted in Selden Rodman, *Conversations with Artists* (New York: Capricorn Books, 1961), p. 200.

7 Edward Hopper, "Notes on Painting," in Alfred H. Barr, Jr., *Edward Hopper: Retrospective Exhibition* (New York: Museum of Modern Art, 1933), p. 17.

8 Lloyd Goodrich, *Edward Hopper* (New York: Harry N. Abrams, 1971), p. 152.

9 For a commentary on the concept of spiritual autobiography, see Frederick R. Karl, *Modern and Modernism: The Sovereignty of the Artist 1885–1925* (New York: Atheneum, 1988), p. 172. Karl discusses European modernist artists as well, but does not consider Hopper.

10 Karl, *Modern,* pp. 173–75.

11 Paul Valéry, "Stendhal," in *Masters and Friends* (Princeton University Press, 1972), v. 9, p. 197.

12 Brian O'Doherty, "Portrait: Edward Hopper," *Art in America,* 52, December 1964, p. 69.

13 Jo Hopper diary entry for February 20, 1953.

14 Grace Glueck, "Art Is Left by Hopper to the Whitney," *New York Times,* March 19, 1971, p. 28.

15 Hilton Kramer, "The Hopper Bequest: Selling a Windfall," *New York Times,* March 28, 1971, sec. 2, p. 25.

16 John I. H. Baur to the editor, art department, *New York Times,* letter published April 25, 1971, sec. 2, p. 20, draft in Whitney Museum of American Art archives.

17 Josephine N. Hopper to Margaret McKellar, letter of January 20, 1964.

18 James R. Mellow, "The World of Edward Hopper," *New York Times Magazine,* September 6, 1971, p. 21.

19 Brian O'Doherty, *American Masters: The Voice and the Myth* (New York: Universe Books, 1988), p. 17.

20 Ibid.

21 Brian O'Doherty, "The Hopper Bequest at the Whitney," *Art in America,* 59, Summer 1971, p. 69.

THE ROOTS OF CONFLICT

1 For this information on Nyack, see Raymond J. O'Brien, *American Sublime: Landscape and Scenery of the Lower Hudson Valley* (New York: Columbia University Press, 1981), pp. 207–8.
2 Raymond Esposito et al., *South Nyack Centennial 1878–1978* (Tenafly, N.J.: Keystone Offset Printing, 1978), p. 3.
3 Barr, *Edward Hopper,* p. 9. Also reported in "Such Is Life," *Life,* 102, August 1935, p. 48.
4 Unidentified clipping, Nyack, N.Y., c. 1894.
5 "Native Nyacker's Paintings," *Rockland County Journal-News,* April 20, 1950, based in part on an interview with Marion Hopper.
6 "Such Is Life," p. 48.
7 Lois Saunier Carlson, conversation with the author, 1980, and unpublished memoir.
8 Years later Hopper claimed that his 1911 painting *Sailing* was inspired by "boyhood boating on the Tappan Zee." See *County Citizen,* April 3, 1963.
9 His friend's choice of the name Glorianna also has literary origins—in Edmund Spenser's *Faerie Queene,* where as the Queen of Fairy Land, she is the personification of glory and of Queen Elizabeth.
10 James Fenimore Cooper, *The Water-Witch, or, The Skimmer of the Seas* (New York: A. L. Burt Co., 1852), p. 167.
11 Ibid., p. 76.
12 Edward Hopper, in Johnson interview.
13 "Nyacker's Paintings."
14 Edward Hopper, unpublished taped interview by Arlene Jacobowitz, Brooklyn Museum, April 29, 1966; Jo Hopper also participated in this interview.
15 Jo Hopper diary entry for January 20, 1954.
16 Cornelius Burnham Harvey, ed., *Genealogical History of Hudson and Bergen Counties, New Jersey* (New York: New Jersey Genealogical Publishing Company, 1900).

17 Edward Hopper, quoted in Kuh, *Artist's Voice,* p. 135.
18 Jo Hopper diary entry for March 18, 1951.
19 Ibid.
20 Lois Saunier Carlson memoir.
21 See Louis L. Blauvelt, *The Blauvelt Family Genealogy* (Blauvelt-Demarest Foundation, 1957). Hopper was descended from Gerrit Hendricksen Blauvelt, who came to America in 1638.
22 See the census for 1855, which indicates that Charity, her father (Abraham Blauvelt), and three-year-old Garret were living in the ninth ward.
23 See Edward Hopper's birth certificate, State of New York, no. 8915.
24 "Death of G. H. Hopper Last Night," *Nyack Evening Journal,* September 19, 1913, p. 1.
25 Jo Hopper diary entry for March 25, 1950. Jo claims to have heard this description, which she contrasts to Edward's behavior.
26 For the earliest primary grades, the children attended Miss Dickie's, a school run by the sheriff's daughter and located near their home.
27 Jo Hopper diary entry for November 11, 1959.
28 Lois Saunier Carlson memoir.
29 Jo Hopper diary entry for July 19, 1955.
30 "Nyacker's Paintings."
31 Edward Hopper, in Johnson interview.
32 For some years, the Hoppers' receipts documenting these vacations have survived.
33 See Stanley Coben, *Rebellion Against Victorianism: The Impetus for Cultural Change in 1920s America* (New York: Oxford University Press, 1991), pp. 26, 31.
34 See Philip Greven, *Spare the Child: The Religious Roots of Punishment and the Psychological Impact of Physical Abuse* (New York: Alfred A. Knopf, 1991), pp. 6–7.
35 Ibid., p. 132.
36 Henry Steele Commager, *The American Mind* (New Haven: Yale University Press, 1950), p. 41.
37 Ibid., p. 43.
38 Edward Hopper, in Johnson interview.
39 Ibid.

40 Ibid.

41 Ibid.

42 Ralph Waldo Emerson, *Representative Men* (Boston: Houghton, Osgood & Co., 1879), p. 137. Hopper would later refer to five of the six men whom Emerson discussed. However, I know of no reference to Swedenborg.

43 Edward Hopper, "Notes on Painting," p. 17.

44 Ibid., p. 18. Ralph Waldo Emerson, *Works* (Boston: Houghton, Osgood & Co., 1879), v. 5, *Nature*, p. 18.

45 Montaigne, "Affection of Fathers," in *Essays, The Complete Works of Montaigne*, trans. by Donald M. Frame (Stanford: Stanford University Press, 1958), p. 288.

46 René Wellek, "The Nineteenth-Century Russian Novel in English and American Criticism," in John Garrard, ed., *The Russian Novel from Pushkin to Pasternak* (New Haven: Yale University Press, 1983), p. 243.

47 William Dean Howells, quoted in Wellek, "Nineteenth-Century Russian Novel," p. 244.

48 Henry James, "Ivan Turgenev," reprinted in Lyon N. Richardson, ed., *Henry James: Representative Selections with Introduction, Bibliography, and Notes* (Urbana: University of Illinois Press, 1966), pp. 38–39. The two essays that James published on Turgenev's work were published in collections that Hopper may have known: Henry James, "Ivan Turgenev," *North American Review*, 118, April 1874, pp. 461–8; and Henry James, *French Poets and Novelists* (London: Macmillan & Co., 1878). The subsequent piece on Turgenev appeared in the *Atlantic Monthly*, 53, January 1884, pp. 42–55, and was republished in Henry James, *Partial Portraits* (London: Macmillan & Co., 1888).

49 See Royal A. Gettman, *Turgenev in England and America* (Urbana, Ill.: University of Illinois Press, 1941).

50 See Kathryn Feuer, "Fathers and Sons: Fathers and Children," in Garrard, *Russian Novel*, p. 68.

51 See, for example, his reading of a quote from Goethe that he carried in his wallet for just such occasions. Edward Hopper, televised interview by Brian O'Doherty, WGBH-TV, Boston, April 10, 1961.

52 Edward Hopper, "John Sloan and the Philadelphians," *The Arts*, 2, April 1927, p. 169.

53 "Nyacker's Paintings."

54 Ibid.

55 Ibid.

56 Bernard Myers, ed., "Scribner's American Painters Series: No. 7—'Deck of the Beam Trawler *Widgeon*' by Edward Hopper," *Scribner's Magazine*, 102, September 1927, pp. 32–33.

57 Edmund Ollier, *Masterpieces from the Works of Gustave Doré* (New York: Cassell Publishing Co., 1887).

58 Itemized receipts exist documenting these items; private collection, copies with the author.

59 Joseph Pennell, *Pen Drawing and Pen Draughtsmen: Their Work and Their Methods: A Study of the Art with Technical Suggestions* (New York: Macmillan Publishing Co., 1920), reprinted (New York: Hart Publishing Co., 1977), p. 11 (written in 1889).

60 Lewis A. Coser, *Maurice Halbwachs on Collective Memory* (Chicago: The University of Chicago Press, 1992), p. 30. See also Howard Schuman and Jacqueline Scott, "Generations and Collective Memory," *American Sociological Review*, 54, June 1989, pp. 359–81.

61 Coser, *Maurice Halbwachs*, p. 25.

62 Commager, *American Mind*, p. 43.

63 Lawrence B. Davis, *Immigrants, Baptists, and the Protestant Mind in America* (Urbana: University of Illinois Press, 1973), p. 40.

64 Around the same time, Hopper also captioned *ANARCHISM*, a sketch of a male nude wielding a knife. For Hopper's later interest in the French anarchist Sébastien Faure, see page 65.

65 Drawing, Whitney Museum of American Art, Bequest of Josephine N. Hopper, 70.1557.41 recto. Hopper crossed out "sword" and "race" before choosing "horde" as his last word.

66 Coben, *Rebellion Against Victorianism*, 33.

67 Charles Darwin, *The Descent of Man* (New York: American Dome Library Co., 1902), p. 768.

68 Ibid., p. 778.

DEFINING THE TALENT

1 See *Brush and Pencil,* 4, no. 3, June 1899, p. 2. The address in this ad, 1295 Broadway, New York, is different from that on Hopper's receipts.

2 *Scribner's Magazine,* 26, October 1899, p. 36.

3 See *International Studio,* 8, September 1899, p. AD III.

4 He continued commuting for several years, as documented in "Nyacker's Paintings."

5 *Scribner's Magazine,* 26, October 1899, p. 36. Charles Hope Provost was the chief instructor and founder of the New York School of Illustrating, which later became the Provost School of Illustration (129 Sixth Avenue). In his 1903 book, *How to Illustrate,* he claimed the school was in its twelfth year, suggesting that he founded the Correspondence School of Illustrating in 1892.

6 Charles Provost, *A Treatise on How to Illustrate for Newspapers, Books, Magazines, etc.* (New York: Harvard Text Book Corporation, 1903), and *Simplified Illustrating* (South Orange, N.J.: M. R. Provost, 1911).

7 Provost, *Simplified Illustrating,* p. 7.

8 See Provost, *How to Illustrate,* title page, and Provost, *Simplified Illustrating,* p. 9, where he also lists the following as containing his work: *Collier's, Scribner's, New York Herald, New York World, Pearson's, Ladies World, American Queen, Paris Modes, Short Stories, St. Nicholas, Youth's Companion,* Munsey publications, *Life, Truth, Judge, Women's Magazine, Success, New York Evening Journal, New York Sunday Telegraph.*

9 Provost, *How to Illustrate,* pp. 161–62.

10 Homer Saint-Gaudens, *The American Artist and His Times* (New York: Dodd, Mead & Co., 1941), p. 273.

11 By 1910 a newspaper reported that Gibson was said to charge $1000 or more for a magazine cover: James J. Best, *American Popular Illustration: A Reference Guide* (Westport, Conn.: Greenwood Press, 1984), pp. 6–7.

12 Provost, *Simplified Illustrating,* p. 76.

13 See Sir Walter Besant, "One of Two Millions in East London," *Century Magazine,* 59, December 1899, with pictures by Joseph Pen-

nell and Phil May, whose East London Loafers appears on p. 228.

14 *Phil May's Sketchbook: Fifty Cartoons* (New York: R. H. Russell), 1899.

15 Edward Hopper to his mother, letter of July 26, 1900.

16 Documented by Nyack City Directory and Tremper's descendants, in conversation with the author.

17 For a reproduction of the 1900 Phil May sketch, see David Cuppleditch, *Phil May: The Artist and His Wit* (London: Fortune Press, 1981), p. 28. The original appeared in *Punch.*

18 C. K. Chatterton, "There Never Was a School Like It," unpublished manuscript edited from notes by the artist's daughter, Julia C. Van de Water.

19 Vachel Lindsay to his parents, letter of April 22, 1904.

20 Emory Lewis, "Painter Edward Hopper Has Show at Whitney," *Cue,* February 4, 1950, p. 16.

21 Other classmates were Arthur E. Cederquist, Oliver N. Chaffee, Lawrence T. Dresser, Julius Golz, Prosper Invernizzi, Edward Keefe, Warren T. Hedges, and John Koopman.

22 See Besant, "One of Two Millions." In the same issue, Arthur Keller illustrated S. Weir Michell, "The Autobiography of a Quack," pp. 290–98.

23 C. K. Chatterton, unpublished interview by Alexander D. Ross, November 7, 1970.

24 Walter Tittle, "Life—and the Pursuit of Happiness," unpublished autobiography, v. 1, chap. 13, p. 2.

25 Chatterton, interview by Ross.

26 Lolan C. Read, Jr., "The New York School of Art," *Sketch Book,* 3 (April 1904), p. 219.

27 Grace M. Mayer, *Once Upon a City* (New York: Macmillan Co., 1958), p. 421.

28 Ibid.

29 Chatterton, "There Never Was a School."

30 Read, "New York School of Art," p. 220.

31 Chatterton, "There Never Was a School."

32 Vachel Lindsay to his father, letter of November 3, 1903.

33 Ibid.

34 "From a Talk by William M. Chase with Benjamin Northrop of the Mail and Express," *Art Amateur,* February 1894, p. 77.

35 "A Talk on Art by William Merritt Chase," *Art Interchange,* 39, December 1897, p. 126.

36 Ernest Knaufft, "An American Painter—William M. Chase," *International Studio,* 12, January 1901, p. 151.

37 Ben L. Bassham, ed., *The Memories of an American Impressionist: Abel G. Warshawsky* (Kent, Ohio: Kent State University Press, 1980), p. 18.

38 Edward Hopper, unpublished interview by Bennard Perlman, June 3, 1962.

39 Walter Tittle, diary entry for September 7, 1902.

40 Tittle diary entry for October 28, 1902.

41 Guy Pène du Bois, *Artists Say the Silliest Things* (New York: Duell, Sloan, & Pearce, 1940), p. 75.

42 Ibid., p. 86.

43 Ibid., p. 84.

44 Tittle diary entry for November 7, 1902.

45 Course descriptions from the 1905 catalogue of the New York School of Art.

46 Vachel Lindsay to his mother, letter of December 13, 1903.

47 Vachel Lindsay to his father, letter of December 10, 1903.

48 Edward Hopper, in Johnson interview.

49 Robert Henri, *The Art Spirit,* compiled by Margery Ryerson (Philadelphia and London: J. B. Lippincott Co., 1923), p. 71.

50 Du Bois, *Artists Say the Silliest Things,* p. 83.

51 Henri, *Art Spirit,* p. 195.

52 Ibid., p. 55.

53 This is described by Rockwell Kent, in *It's Me O Lord: The Autobiography of Rockwell Kent* (New York: Dodd, Mead, & Co., 1955), p. 84.

54 Walter Pach, *Queer Thing, Painting* (New York: Harper & Brothers, 1938), pp. 42–43.

55 Henri, *Art Spirit,* p. 80.

56 Edward Hopper, quoted in O'Doherty, *American Masters,* p. 14.

57 Edward Hopper, interview by Arlene Jacobowitz, Brooklyn Museum, April 29, 1966.

58 Suzanne Burrey, "Edward Hopper: The Emptying Spaces," *Art Digest,* April 1, 1955, p. 9.

59 Tittle diary entry for March 1903.

60 Edward Hopper, "John Sloan and the Philadelphians," *The Arts,* 11, April 1927, pp. 174–75.

61 Mayer, *Once Upon a City,* p. 420.

62 Hopper, "John Sloan," p. 83.

63 Vachel Lindsay to his father, letter of November 3, 1903.

64 Vachel Lindsay to his parents, letter of March 29, 1904.

65 Tittle, *Pursuit of Happiness,* v. 1, chap. 14, p. 4.

66 Kent, *It's Me O Lord,* p. 83.

67 Ibid., p. 84.

68 Henri, *Art Spirit,* p. 104.

69 Tittle diary entry for May 21, 1903. Biehl was the last name of another of the students who went with Hopper to look at Rodin's work.

70 Pach, *Queer Thing,* p. 80. Ogiwara, whose name was then romanized as Moriye Ogihara, is the subject of an entire chapter in this book.

71 Yutaka Tazawa, ed., *Biographical Dictionary of Japanese Art* (Tokyo: Kodansha International), pp. 463–64.

72 Tittle diary entry for May 9, 1903.

73 Patrick Henry Bruce to Robert Henri, letter of February 4, 1904.

74 These prizes are recorded in Henri's diary for 1908.

75 *Sketch Book,* 3, April 1904, p. 233; his name was misprinted as Edward Hoppen. Susan Bissell was the faculty representative for the magazine.

76 Patrick Henry Bruce to Robert Henri, letter of July 5, 1904.

77 The earlier image is visible by X-ray.

78 Edward Hopper, in Johnson interview.

79 This team is described by Rockwell Kent, in *It's Me O Lord,* p. 84.

80 Ibid., p. 91.

81 Edward Hopper, in Johnson interview.

82 Patrick Henry Bruce to Robert Henri, letter of February 4, 1904.

83 Edward Hopper, in Johnson interview.

84 Charles H. Morgan, *George Bellows, Painter of America* (New York: Reynal & Co.,

1965), p. 42. Three of Emma Storey's dance cards are preserved in the Bellows papers.

85 Vachel Lindsay, unpublished diary entry for May 11, 1905.

86 Henri, *Art Spirit,* p. 188.

87 Emma S. Bellows, "A Diary without Dates," or "The Diary I Should Have Written," c. 1956, Bellows Papers.

88 Morgan, *George Bellows,* p. 43.

89 Edward Hopper to his mother, letter of January 25, 1907.

90 Tittle diary entry for May 29, 1905.

91 Bruce St. John, ed., *John Sloan's New York Scene 1906–1913* (New York: Harper & Row, 1965), p. 22.

92 Forbes Watson, "A Note on Edward Hopper," *Vanity Fair,* 31, February 1929, p. 107.

SEDUCTIVE PARIS

1 Edward Hopper to his mother, letter of October 30, 1906.

2 Edward Hopper to his mother, letter of November 9, 1906.

3 Cf. page 124: Guy Pène du Bois, unpublished *Diary,* pp. 178–79.

4 Edward Hopper to his mother, letter of November 16, 1906.

5 Edward Hopper to his mother, letter of November 23, 1906.

6 Edward Hopper to his sister, letter of November 29, 1906.

7 Louise Jammes to Ada Saunier, letter of December 1, 1906.

8 Louise Jammes to Elizabeth Hopper, letter of February 15, 1907.

9 Edward Hopper to his mother, letters of December 14, 1906, and January 25, 1907.

10 Edward Hopper to his mother, letter of March 17, 1907.

11 351 West 57th Street, where he sent her a postal card (Charity Hopper, Elizabeth's mother-in-law, may have been in residence in Nyack). According to the 1900 and 1910 census reports, this location was a boarding house. Elizabeth Hopper may have moved there to rest or for proximity to medical treatment.

12 Edward Hopper to his mother, letter of April 27, 1907.

13 Barr, *Edward Hopper,* p. 10.

14 Edward Hopper, in Johnson interview.

15 Edward Hopper to his sister, letter of November 29, 1906.

16 Edward Hopper to his mother, letter of December 8, 1906.

17 Edward Hopper to his mother, letter of April 1, 1907.

18 Edward Hopper to his mother, letter of May 11, 1907.

19 Edward Hopper to his mother, letter of May 26, 1907.

20 Lloyd Goodrich, notes of conversation with Edward Hopper, April 20, 1946.

21 Edward Hopper, quoted in O'Doherty, *American Masters,* p. 24.

22 Barr, *Edward Hopper,* p. 13. Hopper told Barr that he had no knowledge of Marquet, yet perhaps he saw his work and forgot his name.

23 Edward Hopper to his mother, letter of November 9, 1906.

24 Edward Hopper to his mother, letter of December 26, 1906.

25 Du Bois, *Artists Say the Silliest Things,* p. 110.

26 Barr, *Edward Hopper,* p. 10.

27 O'Doherty, "Portrait: Edward Hopper," p. 73.

28 Edward Hopper, in Johnson interview.

29 John D'Emilio and Estelle B. Freedman, *Intimate Matters: A History of Sexuality in America* (New York: Harper & Row, 1988), p. 210.

30 Known as the Tenderloin district, the neighborhood included the Haymarket, at the corner of 13th Street and 6th Avenue, where John Sloan depicted prostitutes in 1907. See Lloyd Morris, *Incredible New York* (New York: Random House, 1951), pp. 220–21.

31 See Suzanne Kinser, "Prostitutes in the Art of John Sloan," master's thesis, University of California at Berkeley, 1982.

32 Jerrold Seigel, *Bohemian Paris* (New York: Viking Press, 1986), pp. 39–42. The *grisette* also appeared in French classic literature, in an erotic tale by La Fontaine, *Contes,* I, *Joconde* (Paris, 1665), whose fables Hopper

read: "Sous les cotillons des grisettes / Peut loger autant de beauté / Que sous les jupes des coquettes . . . / Une grisette est un trésor . . ." Hopper might also have encountered the *grisette* in Alfred de Musset's "Mimi Pinson" (1845, in *Oeuvres Complètes,* Geneva, 1969, VII), and/or in Henri Murger's *Scènes de la vie de Bohème* (Paris: 1851).

33 Kent, *It's Me O Lord,* p. 91.

34 See Charles Bernheimer, *Figures of Ill Repute: Representing Prostitution in Nineteenth-Century France* (Cambridge, Mass.: Harvard University Press, 1989), p. 52.

35 George Augustus Sala, *Paris Herself Again in 1878–9* (New York: Scribner & Welford, 1880), pp. 3, 6–7.

36 See T. J. Clark, *The Painting of Modern Life* (New York: Alfred A. Knopf, 1984), pp. 115–16.

37 See, for example, Stanley Appelbaum, *French Satirical Drawings from "L'Assiette au Beurre,"* (New York: Dover Publications, 1978), pp. 126, 145, 147.

38 Jo Hopper diary entry for April 8, 1963.

39 Edward Hopper to his mother, letter of December 14, 1906.

40 See D. W. Brogan, *The Development of Modern France, 1870–1939* (New York: Harper & Row, 1966), p. 429.

41 Edward Hopper to his father, letter of May 7, 1907.

42 Ibid. See S. Faure, ed., *L'Encyclopédie anarchiste* (Paris, n.d.), 4 vols., trans. in George Woodcock, ed., *The Anarchist Reader* (Hassoch's, England: Harvester Press, 1977).

43 Edward Hopper to his mother, letter of February 8, 1907.

44 See Pach, *Queer Thing,* pp. 81–86.

45 Edward Hopper to his mother, letter of January 7, 1907.

46 Edward Hopper to his mother, letter of April 17, 1907.

47 Edward Hopper, in Johnson interview.

48 Edward Hopper to his mother, letter of February 19, 1907.

49 Edward Hopper to his mother, letter of March 3, 1907.

50 O'Doherty, "Portrait: Edward Hopper," p. 73.

51 Edward Hopper, in Johnson interview.

52 Ibid.

53 Ibid.

54 Edward Hopper to his sister, letter of April 2, 1907, and Edward Hopper to his mother, letter of April 1, 1907.

55 F. Berkeley Smith, *The Real Latin Quarter* (New York: Funk & Wagnalls Co., 1901), pp. 151–56.

56 Edward Hopper to his sister, letter of April 2, 1907.

57 Edward Hopper to his mother, letter of May 26, 1907.

58 Burrey, "Edward Hopper: The Emptying Spaces," p. 9.

59 Edward Hopper, quoted in O'Doherty, "Portrait: Edward Hopper," p. 73.

60 Edward Hopper to his mother, letter of December 29, 1906.

61 Enid M. Buhre (daughter of Enid Saies Buhre) to the author, letter of March 10, 1993.

62 Enid M. Buhre to the author, letter of March 4, 1993.

63 Edward Hopper, quoted in O'Doherty, "Portrait: Edward Hopper," p. 73.

64 Edward Hopper to Enid Saies Buhre, letter of June 17, 1948.

65 Author's telephone interview with Enid M. Buhre, Malmö, Sweden, February 28, 1993, and subsequent interviews in Lund, Sweden, April 1993.

66 Edward Hopper to his mother, letter of June 16, 1907.

67 Edward Hopper to his mother, letter of July 4, 1907.

68 Ibid.

69 Ibid.

70 Ibid.

71 Edward Hopper to Enid Saies Buhre, letter of June 17, 1948.

72 Enid M. Buhre, interview by the author, February 28, 1993.

73 Edward Hopper to his mother, letter of July 27, 1907, from Berlin.

74 Ibid.

75 Edward Hopper to his father, letter of August 2, 1907, from Brussels.

76 Edward Hopper to his father, letter of August 8, 1907, from Paris.

THE AMBIVALENT AMERICAN

1 In 1947, Hopper corrected a biographical text submitted to him by Lloyd Goodrich, marking "1908" over Goodrich's sentence: "From 1899 his winter home was New York."

2 Enid M. Saies to Edward Hopper, letter of 1907, from Darby, England.

3 Enid Saies Buhre to Edward Hopper, letter of May 23, 1948, from Malmö, Sweden.

4 Edward Hopper to Enid Saies Buhre, letter of June 17, 1948.

5 Arnold Friedman, "The Original Independent Show 1908," unpublished manuscript in the Museum of Modern Art, New York, n.p.

6 Ibid.

7 The seven other artists were Laurence T. Dresser, Edward R. Keefe, Howard McClean, George McKay (then deceased), G. LeRoy Williams, Harry Daugherty, and Stuart Tyson.

8 "The Eight Out-Eighted," *The Evening Mail,* cited in Morgan, George Bellows, p. 82.

9 St. John, *John Sloan,* pp. 204–5.

10 Edward Hopper, in Johnson interview.

11 "One Step Nearer to a National Art," *New York American,* March 10, 1908, p. 8.

12 Robert Henri, "Progress in Our National Art Must Spring from the Development of Individuality of Ideas and Freedom of Expression: A Suggestion for a New Art School," *Craftsman,* 15, January 1909, p. 387.

13 Edward Hopper to his mother, letter of March 24, 1909.

14 Edward Hopper to his mother, letter of April 16, 1909.

15 Edward Hopper, in Johnson interview.

16 Edward Hopper to Enid Saies Buhre, letter of June 17, 1948.

17 Edward Hopper to his mother, letter of April 29, 1909.

18 Edward Hopper to his father, letter of April 24, 1909.

19 Edward Hopper to his mother, letter of May 18, 1909.

20 Ibid.

21 Edward Hopper to his mother, letter of June 12, 1909.

22 Edward Hopper to Guy Pène du Bois, letter of December 14, 1954.

23 Edward Hopper to his mother, letter of May 29, 1909.

24 Edward Hopper to his mother, letter of June 7, 1909.

25 Edward Hopper to his mother, letter of June 16, 1909.

26 Edward Hopper to his father, letter of June 18, 1909.

27 See Eileen Bowser, *The Transformation of Cinema 1907–1915* (Berkeley: University of California Press, 1990), pp. 37–41.

28 Edward Hopper to his father, letter postmarked July 22, 1907.

29 Edward Hagaman Hall, *The Hudson-Fulton Celebration 1909, The Fourth Annual Report of the Hudson-Fulton Celebration Commission to the Legislature of the State of New York,* 1910, pp. 898–99.

30 Tittle diary entry for November 19, 1909.

31 Edward Hopper listed this early work in two separate record book entries, both made years after the work's completion. Book I, p. 50, gives no date, only "Painted in Amer[ica] bet. Paris trips," while Book II, p. 74, incorrectly dates this work as 1908. In conversation with Lloyd Goodrich, Hopper correctly recalled that the distant hill with buildings visible in the center was Montmartre in Paris.

32 *Bulletin of the Metropolitan Museum of Art,* 3, December 1908, p. 227, and discussed on p. 229, in the article "Principal Accessions." This painting would have been exhibited in the Accessions Room, which "changed each month at the time of the publication of the Bulletin."

33 Guy Pène du Bois, "Exhibition by Independent Artists Attracts Immense Throngs," *New York American,* April 4, 1910, p. 8.

34 For Henri, see William B. Homer, *Robert Henri and His Circle* (Ithaca: Cornell University Press, 1969), p. 244.

35 Edward Hopper to Enid Saies Buhre, letter of June 17, 1948.

36 Edward Hopper to his mother, letter of June 1, 1910.

37 Edward Hopper to his father, letter of July 4, 1910.

38 Ibid.

39 Edward Hopper to his sister, letter of June 9, 1910.

40 Edward Hopper to his mother, letter of June 16, 1909.

41 Entry form for the First Biennial Exhibition of Contemporary American Sculpture, Watercolors and Prints, Whitney Museum of American Art, December 4, 1933, to January 11, 1934.

42 Edward Hopper, quoted in Frank Crotty, *Provincetown Profiles and Others on Cape Cod* (Barre, Mass.: *Barre Gazette,* 1958), p. 34.

43 Edward Hopper, quoted in O'Doherty, "Portrait: Edward Hopper," p. 73.

IN SEARCH OF A STYLE

1 See *Trow's New York City Directory.* A comment made by Jo in her diary entry for March 22, 1948, may also offer a clue. When a salesman for the *Encyclopedia Britannica* telephoned, she asked if he wanted to be the "cause of a divorce here," a possible reference to Edward's disdain of encyclopedias, perhaps a result of his own sales experience. His friend the print dealer Ned Jennings, however, had been a Fuller Brush salesman.

2 James Chapin, interviewed by his wife, Mary Chapin, 1974. I am grateful to Brenda Billingsley, who is writing a biography of Chapin.

3 Edward Hopper, quoted in Alexander Eliot, "The Silent Witness," *Time,* December 24, 1956, p. 37.

4 Edward Hopper, quoted in O'Doherty, *American Masters,* p. 16.

5 "Panic Averted in Art Show Crowd," *New York Mail & Express,* April 2, 1910, p. 5.

6 Paintings in Oil and Pastel by James A. McNeill Whistler, Metropolitan Museum of Art, New York, March 15–May 31, 1910.

7 *County Citizen,* April 3, 1963.

8 See Edward Hopper Record Book I, p. 45.

9 Milton Cederquist, interview by the author, 1978.

10 Lawrence Gilman, "The MacDowell Club: A New Force in the Art Life of New York," *Critic,* June 1906, pp. 516 ff.

11 Homer, *Robert Henri,* p. 165.

12 Fredson Bowers and Nancy Hale, eds., *Leon Kroll: A Spoken Memoir* (Charlottesville: University of Virginia Press, 1983), p. 30.

13 James Chapin, interviewed by his wife, Mary Chapin, 1974.

14 Bowers and Hale, eds., *Leon Kroll,* p. 47.

15 Leon Kroll, *Leon Kroll* (New York: American Artists Group, 1946), n.p.

16 Edward Hopper, quoted in Kuh, *Artist's Voice,* p. 141.

17 Edward Hopper, conversation with Lloyd Goodrich, 1947.

18 Lloyd Goodrich recorded this in his notes and discussed it with the author.

19 Edward Hopper, quoted in Kuh, *Artist's Voice,* p. 135.

20 Milton W. Brown, *The Story of the Armory Show* (New York: The Joseph H. Hirshhorn Foundation, 1963), p. 65.

21 Ibid., pp. 66–67.

22 Edward Hopper, in Johnson interview.

23 Thomas F. Vietor (1871–1933), who bought *Sailing* the same year he married, lived at 787 Fifth Avenue, New York.

24 Edward Hopper to Walt Kuhn, letter of March 24, 1913; Elmer L. MacRae Papers.

25 Edward Hopper, in Johnson interview.

26 See Mindy Cantor, "Washington Arch and the Changing Neighborhood," in Mindy Cantor, ed., *Around the Square 1830–1890: Essays on Life, Letters, and Architecture in Greenwich Village* (New York: New York University Press, 1982), p. 48.

27 Tittle diary entry for January 17, 1914.

28 See O'Doherty, *American Masters,* p. 13.

29 H. Saint-Gaudens, *American Artist and His Times,* p. 171.

30 Jo Hopper diary entries for September 19, 1960, and c. May 1961.

31 Tittle diary entry for February 20, 1909.

32 Walter Tittle, "It's Good to Live," unpublished autobiography, p. 41.

33 Tittle diary entry for January 17, 1914.

34 Max Eastman, "Exploring the Soul and Healing the Body," *Everybody's,* 32, June 1915, pp. 741–50.

35 Guy Pène du Bois, unpublished diary, entry for November 30, 1918.

36 Edward Hopper, quoted in O'Doherty, *American Masters,* p. 13.

37 Edward Hopper, in Johnson interview.

38 Francis Browne, "Artist on American Art," *American Art News,* 12, November 8, 1913, p. 3.

39 Ibid. Browne, a Chicago painter, had been chosen to direct the American art section for the Panama-Pacific International Exposition of 1915 in San Francisco.

40 Anthony Slide, *The International Film Industry: A Historical Dictionary* (New York: Greenwood Press, 1989), pp. 119–22.

41 Edward Hopper, in Johnson interview.

42 Edward Hopper, quoted in O'Doherty, "Portrait: Edward Hopper," p. 77.

43 "Artist's Summer Resorts," *American Art News,* 11, June 21, 1913, p. 3.

44 Louise Tragard, Patricia E. Hart, and W. L. Copithorne, *Ogunquit, Maine's Art Colony: A Century of Color 1886–1986* (Ogunquit, Maine: Barn Gallery Associates, 1987), p. 19.

45 Ibid., p. 13.

46 Bernard Karfiol, *Bernard Karfiol* (New York: American Artists Group, 1945), n.p.

47 See "Frederick Palmer in Germany: My Day at the Front," *Everybody's,* 32, January 1915, pp. 72, 75, 78.

48 Guy Pène du Bois, "The Season's First Special Show," *Arts and Decoration,* 5, November 1914, p. 29.

49 Ibid.

50 "George Bellows at Montross's," *American Art News,* 12, January 24, 1914, p. 3. The critic Charles Caffin did not like Bellows's show.

51 "Strong Men at the MacDowell," *Evening Mail,* February 18, 1915, p. 10. "Art Notes," *The Evening Post,* February 20, 1915, p. 12.

52 Ernest A. Bell, *Fighting the Traffic in Young Girls or War on the White Slave Trade* (Chicago: L. H. Walter, 1911), pp. 183–84.

53 Ibid., p. 182.

54 D'Emilio and Freedman, *Intimate Matters,* p. 209.

55 Ibid., pp. 201, 208–9.

56 Ibid., p. 208.

57 Bell, *Fighting the Traffic,* p. 25.

58 D'Emilio and Freedman, *Intimate Matters,* p. 209.

59 Andre Fermigier, *Toulouse-Lautrec* (New York: Frederick A. Praeger, 1969), p. 126, mentions this image and that of "the muse of the fin-de-siècle period, at once tragic and comic, vulgar and refined" in Zola and other such diverse writers as Maurice Donnay, Jean Lorraine, Jules Renard, and Henri Lavedan.

60 Edward Hopper, in O'Doherty interview, WGBH-TV.

61 Guy Pène du Bois, "Exhibitions in the Galleries," *Arts and Decoration,* April 15, 1915, p. 238.

62 Guy Pène du Bois, "The American Paintings of Edward Hopper," *Creative Art,* 8, March 1931, p. 191.

63 See page 173.

64 Arthur Rimbaud, *Poésies* (Paris: Gallimard, 1960), p. 16, trans. by John Van Sickle.

Par les soirs bleus d'été, j'irai dans les sentiers,
Picoté par les blés, fouler l'herbe menue:
Rêveur, j'en sentirai la fraîcheur à mes pieds.
Je laisserai le vent baigner ma tête nue.

Je ne parlerai pas, je ne penserai rien:
Mais l'amour infini me montera dans l'âme,
Et j'irai loin, bien loin, comme un bohémien,
Par la Nature,—heureux comme avec une
    femme.

In the blue summer evenings, I'll go along the
    paths,
Pricked by ears of grain, to press the subtle
    grass:
Dreamer, I will feel its freshness on my feet.
I'll allow the wind to bathe my naked head.
I will not speak, I will not think at all:
But love will rise unbounded in my soul,
And I'll go far, quite far, a vagabond,
In Nature,—happy as with a woman.

65 Seigel, *Bohemian Paris,* p. 263. The enthusiasm for anarchism among some of the Symbolist artists and writers was not lost on Hopper, who had already sketched anarchists as a student.

66 Lloyd Goodrich, *Edward Hopper: Selections from the Hopper Bequest* (New York: Whitney Museum, 1971), without illustration here or in Goodrich's massive *Edward Hopper* (New York: Harry N. Abrams, 1971). The work was still unidentified when I went to the museum as curator of the Hopper Collection in 1976.

THE DETOUR THROUGH ETCHING

1 Nathaniel Pousette-Dart, "Editorial Comment," *Art of Today,* 6, no. 2, February 1935, p. 11.
2 Edward Hopper, quoted in O'Doherty, *American Masters,* p. 17.
3 C. K. Chatterton, quoted in Bennard B. Perlman, *The Life and Art of C. K. Chatterton* (New York: ACA Galleries, 1980), n.p.
4 Elsie Scott, interview by the author, July 9, 1976.
5 Homer, *Robert Henri,* p. 254 et passim.
6 Elizabeth Cornell Benton, letter to the author of April 29, 1979.
7 Bowers and Hale, eds., *Leon Kroll,* p. 33.
8 Edward Hopper, quoted in Archer Winsten, "Wake of the News. Washington Square North Boasts Strangers Worth Talking To," *New York Post,* November 26, 1935.
9 Edward Hopper to Frederick R. Mangold, letter of July 26, 1939, recommending Arnold Friedman for a teaching position at Black Mountain College.
10 Barr, *Edward Hopper,* p. 11.
11 [Guy Pène du Bois], "Walkowitz and Hopper," *Arts and Decoration,* 6, February 1916, pp. 190–91.
12 Tittle diary entry for April 13, 1916.
13 Walter Tittle, "Pursuit of Happiness," chap. 6, p. 1.
14 Tittle diary entry for January 1917.
15 "Henri et al. at MacDowell Club," *American Art News,* 15, February 17, 1917, p. 3. Dasburg refers to Andrew Dasburg.
16 Edward Hopper to A. N. Hosking, letter of March 7, 1917.
17 See Ralph Flint, *Albert Sterner: His Life and His Art* (New York: Payson & Clarke, 1927), p. 28. The initial meeting that led to the formation of the Painter-Gravers of America was held in Sterner's studio. Bellows and Leo Mielziner were among those present.
18 Edward Hopper to A. N. Hosking, letter of March 27, 1917.
19 Guy Pène du Bois, "Notes of Studio and Galleries," *Arts and Decoration,* 7, March 1917, p. 258.
20 Edward Hopper to A. N. Hosking, letter of April 7, 1917.

21 Rafael Squirru, "Edward Hopper," *Americas,* 17, April 1965, p. 14.
22 Edward Hopper to A. N. Hosking, letter of April 7, 1917.
23 Edward Hopper, quoted in O'Doherty, *American Masters,* p. 17.
24 Tittle diary entry for April 13, 1917.
25 Tittle diary entry for May 1, 1917.
26 See page 304: Jo Hopper diary entry for May 20, 1938. When Hopper was in Paris during the spring of 1907, his work was omitted from a show of Henri's students shown at the New York School of Art, although the organizers managed to include a painting by Patrick Henry Bruce, who was also in Paris. (See Perlman, *Robert Henri,* p. 78.)
27 Edward Hopper, in Johnson interview.
28 Jo Hopper to Alice Roullier, draft of letter of November 25, 1933, draft of actual letter sent to the chairman of the exhibition committee of the Chicago Arts Club, to which Hopper's 1933 Museum of Modern Art retrospective traveled.
29 Guy Pène du Bois, "Edward Hopper," *Living American Art Bulletin,* p. 6.
30 Edward Hopper, quoted in O'Doherty, "Portrait: Edward Hopper," p. 77.
31 Edward Hopper, in Johnson interview.
32 Henry McBride, "More on the Independents," *New York Sun,* May 13, 1917, reprinted in Daniel Catton Rich, ed., *The Flow of Art, Essays and Criticisms of Henry McBride* (New York: Atheneum Publishers, 1975), p. 127.
33 Edward Hopper to A. N. Hosking, letter of July 3, 1917.
34 Jo Hopper, in Johnson interview.
35 Carl Zigrosser, *A World of Art and Museums* (Philadelphia: Art Alliance Press, 1975), p. 131.
36 Tittle diary entry for April 26, 1918.
37 Guy Pène du Bois, "At the Galleries," *New York Evening Post Magazine,* May 4, 1918, p. 15.
38 Tittle, "Pursuit of Happiness," first version, chap. 22, pp. 1–4; the discussion that follows is based on this memoir.
39 Edward Hopper, in Johnson interview.
40 J. Edgar Leaycraft to Edward Hopper, letter of June 28, 1917, stating the cost of his

rent renewal at 3 Washington Square North for the year beginning October 1, 1917.

41 "Prize Ship Posters Join in Loan Drive," *New York Sun,* October 12, 1918, p. 9.

42 "Pete Shea, Poster Model, Joins Navy," *New York Sun,* August 15, 1918, p. 12. The next quotation is also from this source.

43 Matlack Price, "The Sun's Poster Contest Shows Arts Value in War," *New York Sun,* August 25, 1918, sec. 3, p. 8, includes a reproduction of Hopper's poster design.

44 Edward Hopper, in Johnson interview.

45 "True American Art Sought in Poster," *New York Sun,* October 12, 1918, p. 9.

46 Edward Hopper, quoted in "Pete Shea, Poster Model, Joins Navy."

47 Edward Hopper, quoted in "Maker of Poster Smash the Hun Is Visitor Here," *Portland (Maine) Evening Express and Daily Advertiser,* August 23, 1918, p. 20.

48 "No Fake Bohemian Can Join Penguins," *New York Sun,* January 8, 1917, p. 6.

49 Lawrence Hague, "In a Red Cross Art Factory," *New York Evening Post Magazine,* December 21, 1918, p. 14. Other artists known to be in this exhibition were Oscar Cesare, Mary Green, Maurice Sterne, Max Weber, Joseph Stella, Ernest Blumenschein, Robert Chanler, Albert Sterner, Modest Stein, F. R. Gruger, Bernard Gussow, Ernest Fuhr, Randall Davey, Boardman Robinson, William Zorach, Bertram Hartman, and Lee Conroy.

50 Louis Bouché Papers, Archives of American Art.

51 Tittle, "Pursuit of Happiness," first version, chap. 22, p. 3.

52 Jo Hopper to Alice Roullier, draft of letter of November 25, 1933.

53 The sales records for *Scribner's* are now in the Brandywine River Museum in Chadds Ford, Penn.

54 Gail Levin, *Edward Hopper as Illustrator,* (New York: W. W. Norton and Co., Inc., 1979), n. 319a/b.

THE DEEPER HUNGER

1 Du Bois diary, entry for November 30, 1918.

2 "Two Artists at Whitney Studio Club," *American Art News,* 18, January 24, 1920, p. 3.

3 Royal Cortissoz, "Random Impressions in Current Exhibitions," *New York Tribune,* January 25, 1920, p. 5.

4 Du Bois, *Artists Say the Silliest Things,* p. 189.

5 Edward Hopper, "Review of *Fine Prints of the Year, 1925*" by Malcolm C. Saláman (New York: Minton, Balch & Co., 1926), in *The Arts,* 9, March 1926, p. 173.

6 For both the Jacob Jordaens painting and Vincent Van Gogh's *Study of Cows, after Jacob Jordaens,* see the collection of the Musée des Beaux-Arts, Lille.

7 Edward Hopper, quoted in Kuh, *Artist's Voice,* p. 135.

8 Ibid.

9 "In Touchstone and Macbeth Galleries," *New York Herald,* October 24, 1920, sec. 3, p. 8.

10 Compare this to Bellows, who, according to Morgan, *George Bellows,* p. 224, had sold paintings for $12,500 in 1919 alone.

11 *The Fables of La Fontaine,* trans. Marianne Moore (New York: Viking Press, 1954), p. 210.

12 D'Emilio and Freedman, *Intimate Matters,* pp. 194–95.

13 Leo Marx, *The Machine in the Garden: Technology and the Pastoral Ideal in America* (New York: Oxford University Press, 1964), p. 29, discusses the parallel in American literature.

14 Carl Zigrosser, "The Etchings of Edward Hopper," in *Prints* (New York: Holt, Rinehart & Winston, 1962), p. 169.

15 This similarity was suggested to me by Stephen Saffron. The map, available at the Rockland County Historical Society, New City, New York, was drawn by L. R. Burleigh.

16 "The World of Art: Exhibitions for the Holidays," *New York Times Book Review and Magazine,* December 4, 1921, p. 5.

17 Edward Hopper, in Johnson interview.

18 Frank Knox Morton Rehn (1848–1914) was a member of the National Academy of Design and, for a time, president of the Salmagundi Club in New York. He special-

ized in marine and landscape painting. For further information on the dealer Frank Rehn, see Edna M. Lindemann, *The Art Triangle: Artist, Dealer, Collector* (Buffalo, New York: Burchfield Art Center, 1989).

19 Edward Hopper to Edmund Graecen, letter of November 28, 1921.

20 Edward Hopper to Marian Ragan, letter of February 10, 1956, Montclair Art Museum, New Jersey.

21 Henry McBride, "Art News and Reviews—Public," *New York Herald,* February 26, 1922, sec. 3, p. 5.

22 Recorded as a gift in March 1922 in Edward Hopper Dealers and Etchings Record Book, p. 68.

23 Edward Hopper, quoted in Burrey, "Edward Hopper: The Emptying Spaces," p. 10.

24 Edward Hopper, quoted in Archer Winsten, "Wake of the News."

25 Edward Hopper, quoted in Goodrich, *Edward Hopper,* p. 31.

26 David Lloyd, "Whitney Studio Club Show," *New York Evening Post,* April 29, 1922, p. 11.

27 Nathaniel Pousette-Dart, "Editorial Comment," *Art of Today,* 6, no. 2, February 1935, p. 11.

28 Guy Pène du Bois, "Edward Hopper, Draughtsman," *Shadowland,* 7, October 1922, pp. 22–23.

29 Virginia Spencer Carr, *Dos Passos: A Life* (Garden City, New York: Doubleday & Co., 1984), p. 191. They boarded with Elaine Orr Thayer, the former wife of Scofield Thayer, editor of the *Dial.* Jo Hopper later mentioned that this literary magazine promoting modern art was begun in the building, so the Hoppers probably were acquainted with Thayer.

30 "The Corcoran Biennial Exhibition Opens Today in Washington," *New York Sunday World,* December 16, 1923, p. 8E.

31 Edward Hopper to Maynard Walker, letter of January 9, 1937.

32 "Contemporary Etchers," unidentified clipping saved by Edward Hopper, January 1923.

33 "Studio and Gallery," *New York Evening Sun,* February 10, 1923, p. 9.

34 "George Hart and Edward Hopper," *New York Times,* February 11, 1923, sec. 7, p. 7.

35 Edward Hopper to Henry McBride, letter of February 19, 1923.

36 Edward Hopper to Carl Zigrosser, letter of April 2, 1923.

37 Translated excerpts from the following poems from Paul Verlaine, *Fêtes Galantes:* "Claire de Lune," "Pantomime," "L'Allée," and "Les Coquillages." See C. F. MacIntyre, *Selected Poems: Paul Verlaine* (Berkeley: University of California Press, 1948), pp. 53, 55, 59, 65.

THE LEADING LADY

1 In the 1880 New York census, Eldorado Nivison is listed as living with his family at 333 West 32nd Street. He is listed in the city directory as living at 316 West 32nd Street in 1881 and 1882. He is no longer listed in the city directory in 1883, the year of Jo's birth, but the family's address is listed on her birth report.

2 Moving from 312 West 20th Street, where the Nivisons were living at the time of Jo's birth, they lived at 320 West 18th Street, 313 West 42nd Street, 33 West 47th Street, 355 Eighth Avenue, 410 West 57th Street, and 131 West Street. In 1907, they moved to 939 Eighth Avenue.

3 Margaret McGrath is listed as living with the Nivisons in the New York census of 1880. She was just one year older than her sister, Nivison's mother.

4 Josephine Nivison, draft of undated letter of about 1921.

5 Jo Hopper, quoted in O'Doherty, *American Masters,* pp. 15–16.

6 She refers to herself as "Gallic and Celt" in Jo Hopper to Alice Roullier, early draft of letter of November 25, 1933.

7 In the 1920 census, Josephine Nivison stated that her father was born in Texas. Her brother, Charles Nivison, stated that his father was born in New York. It is possible that Eldorado had moved to New York at an early age and grown up there, thereby causing his son to think of him as born there. A Texas birth would explain the name Eldorado.

8 Jo Hopper diary entry for May 5, 1952.

9 In the city directories for 1880 to 1885, Eldorado Nivison listed himself as a musician; later, he usually identified himself only as a music teacher. Nivison claimed that she studied French with Mlle. Alice Bloom and dance with Catherine Rogers, a modern dancer. See Bettina Knapp and Myra Chipman, *That Was Yvette* (New York: Holt, Rinehart, & Winston, 1964), p. 287, for the identification of Mlle. Alice Bloom as Mlle. Alice Blum, who taught French language at Yvette Guilbert's School of the Theatre.

10 Jo Hopper, quoted in Frank Crotty, "Sharing Emotion with Others," *Worcester Sunday Telegram,* Feature Parade sec., February 1, 1959, p. 21. Jo Hopper diary entry for March 24, 1950.

11 Josephine Nivison, draft of undated letter of about 1921.

12 Jo Hopper diary entry for March 2, 1948.

13 Eddy Brady (handyman for the Hoppers' building), interview by the author, February 1977, and death certificate for Charles E. Nivison in the State Infirmary in Howard, R.I., dated March 19, 1931. See page 571 for a discussion of Eddy Brady.

14 Jo Hopper diary entry for August 3, 1951.

15 Jo Hopper, quoted in Crotty, "Sharing Emotion with Others," p. 21.

16 The census of 1900 lists Josephine Nivison as being at college; her career there is well documented in the Hunter College Archives.

17 See, for example, Elizabeth Vera Loeb Stern, "1870–1970: A History of Hunter's Splendid Century," *Hunter College Alumni Quarterly,* Winter 1970, pp. 13–21.

18 See the President's Annual Report for the years ending December 31, 1900, and December 31, 1901, which lists the students' grade averages and number of absences, Hunter College Archives, New York.

19 Jo Hopper diary entry for September 10, 1945.

20 See the 1904 yearbook, the *Wistarion,* published by the editorial staff of the Normal College *Echo,* Normal College, New York, pp. 52, 117, 155, 166, 177. In her senior year, she played Audrey, a country wench, in Shakespeare's *As You Like It,* and Fleur de

Lys, the maid of honor, in *In the Days of Charlemagne,* the Christmas play for 1904. In 1904, Jo was secretary of the dramatic club.

21 *Wistarion,* 1904, p. 52.

22 Normal College *Echo,* p. 35, signed "JVN 04" and listed on the contents page as well.

23 They appear in the *Wistarion,* 1902, pp. 65, 19, 58.

24 *Wistarion,* 1903, pp. 94, 96; p. 99 gives listing as one of the four special artists.

25 Thirtieth Annual Report of the Normal College for the year ending December 31, 1900 (New York, 1900), p. 37.

26 See the 6th annual *Wistarion,* 1901, n.p., which contains this photograph.

27 Jo Hopper diary entry for January 10, 1952.

28 Robert Henri, quoted in Bennard B. Perlman, *Robert Henri: His Life and Art* (New York: Dover Publications, 1991), p. 67.

29 Jo Hopper, in O'Doherty interview, April 10, 1961.

30 Jo Hopper, quoted in Frank Crotty, "Sharing Emotion with Others," p. 21.

31 See Hutchins Hapgood, *The Spirit of the Ghetto* (New York: Schocken Books, 1966, reprint of 1902 edition), p. 29.

32 The records of Nivison's career as a teacher in the New York City Public Schools are located in the Special Collections at the Milbank Memorial Library, Teachers College, Columbia University.

33 D'Emilio and Freedman, *Intimate Matters,* p. 190.

34 Ibid.

35 Ibid., p. 191.

36 Josephine Nivison signed the register to view the Frans Hals Collection on July 3, 1907. The register is now in the Municipal Archives, Haarlem, Netherlands. She listed landscape and portrait classes in Europe on her application for appointment as a reconstruction aide in 1918. Among the other students in the class that summer were Clara Perry, Louise Pope, Helen Niles, Elizabeth Fisher, and Hartman K. Harris.

37 Jo Hopper diary entry for January 10, 1952.

38 Jo Hopper, quoted in Frank Crotty, "Sharing Emotion with Others," p. 21.

39 Perlman, *Robert Henri,* p. 78.

40 See the United States Census of 1920.

41 Eddy Brady, in interview by the author, and death certificate for Charles E. Nivison.

42 Jo Hopper diary entry for January 1, 1954.

43 Jo Hopper to Marion Hopper, letter of September 3, 1935, and Jo Hopper diary entry for April 12, 1960.

44 D'Emilio and Freedman, *Intimate Matters,* p. 189.

45 See Mark Sullivan, *Our Times: The United States 1900–1925,* v. 4, *The War Begins, 1900–1914* (New York: Charles Scribner's Sons, 1932), p. 165.

46 Dorothy Norman, *Alfred Stieglitz: An American Seer* (New York: Random House, 1973), p. 116.

47 Jo Hopper diary entry for February 16, 1935.

48 Documentation for these two art schools is included in the papers Nivison completed in her application to become a reconstruction aide.

49 Lawrence Langner, *The Magic Curtain* (New York: E. P. Dutton & Co., 1951), p. 69.

50 The friendship of Kreymborg and Hartpence is discussed in Man Ray, *Self Portrait* (Boston: Little, Brown & Co., 1963), p. 45. See also Elizabeth McCausland, "The Daniel Gallery and Modern American Art," *Magazine of Art,* 44, November 1951, pp. 280–85.

51 Jo Hopper to Carl Sprinchorn, letter of February 10, 1946.

52 Others included were Julius Golz, Gilberta Goodwin, Hayley Lever, Harry Mathes, Ruth Mutcheson, H. Pendleton, Gus Mager, Paul D'Albert, Harry Berlin, Max Kuehne, Lucy Wallace, Jerome Myers, Middleton Manigault, Alexander Warshawsky, and Brod Nordfeldt.

53 "Little Paintings," *New York Times,* December 13, 1914, Magazine sec., p. 8.

54 *The Masses,* January 1917, p. 28.

55 For example, in the Fine Arts Supplement of the *Chicago Herald Examiner,* Saturday, May 25, 1918. "Roller Skating on the Gold Coast," and on Thursday, July 11, 1918, "Children of the Ghetto," by Josephine Nivison; *Saturday Magazine* of the *Evening Post,* August 1, 1916, sketch of four girls swinging, by Josephine Nivison, to accompany a poem by Robert Louis Stevenson; and the *New York Tribune* of Sunday, December 3, 1916, "At the Yellow Jacket," Josephine Nivison's sketch of "Henry Buckler as the Purveyor of Tea."

56 Jo Hopper diary entry for January 7, 1935.

57 Josephine Nivison to Robert Henri, letter of October 15, 1921.

58 The venture was organized in the winter of 1914 to counter the commercialism of Broadway. Its organizational meeting took place in Ida Rauh's studio.

59 For a discussion of Ida Rauh, see June Sochen, *The New Woman in Greenwich Village, 1910–1920* (New York: Quadrangle Books, 1972), pp. 16–18.

60 Alfred Kreymborg, *Troubadour: An Autobiography* (New York: Liveright, 1925), p. 209.

61 Walter Prichard Eaton, *The Theatre Guild: The First Ten Years* (New York: Brentano's, 1929), p. 22.

62 Langner, *Magic Curtain,* p. 96.

63 In the programs of these plays, her name is misspelled as "Josephine Nivisson."

64 Eaton, *Theatre Guild,* p. 24.

65 Jo Hopper diary entry for April 8, 1946; the encounter with a former fellow actor, Bobby Locher, at the Whitney Museum, prompted her to reminisce. See Langner, *Magic Curtain,* p. 71.

66 Lee Simonson, *Part of a Lifetime* (New York: Duell, Sloan & Pearcé, 1943), p. 28.

67 Jo Hopper, quoted in Crotty, "Sharing Emotion with Others," p. 21.

68 Jo Hopper diary entry for October 2, 1948.

69 Jo Hopper, in Johnson interview.

70 Nivison listed "landscape and portrait classes" in Provincetown with Webster on her application form to be a reconstruction aide for the U.S. Army.

71 Jo Hopper diary entry for October 2, 1944. Such rugs were also made as collaborations by her friends Bertram and Gusta Hartman, whom Nivison probably knew in Provincetown as well as in New York.

72 Jo Hopper diary entry for September 19, 1946, on the occasion of running into Glaspell at the home of John Dos Passos.

73 See Sochen, *New Woman in Greenwich Village,* p. 86, and Helen Deutsch and Stella Hanau, *The Provincetown: A Story of the Theatre* (New York: Farrar & Rinehart, 1931), pp. 7–8.

74 Jo Hopper diary entry for July 21, 1951.

75 Jo Hopper to Anne Tucker, undated letter of summer 1934.

76 Jo Hopper diary entry for July 18, 1951.

77 See Hutchins Hapgood, *A Victorian in the Modern World* (New York: Harcourt, Brace & Co., 1939), pp. 378–96.

78 Jo Hopper diary entry for April 12, 1960.

79 See Orrick Johns, *The Time of Our Lives: The Story of My Father and Myself* (New York: Octagon Books, 1973, originally published 1937), pp. 218–21.

80 Johns, *Time of Our Lives,* p. 218.

81 Josephine Nivison to Surgeon General W. C. Gorgas, letter of August 15, 1918. All of the following documentation of this job is located in the United States Office of Personnel Management, St. Louis, Mo.

82 Josephine Nivison to Surgeon General W. C. Gorgas, letter of August 18, 1918.

83 Addie Weihl to the American Red Cross, letter of July 25, 1918.

84 Arthur Warner to Miss Ellen L. Adee of the American Red Cross, letter of July 18, 1918.

85 Jo Hopper diary entry for March 13, 1948.

86 U.S. Army personnel form for Josephine Nivison.

87 Josephine Nivison to Major M. E. Haggerty, October 9, 1918.

88 Jo Hopper diary entries for September 26, 1935, and April 9, 1938.

89 Jo Hopper to Marion Hopper, letter of September 3, 1935. Jo Hopper to Carl Sprinchorn, letter of August 21, 1950, mentions that her mother was operated on for cancer.

90 Jo Hopper diary entries for September 3, 1935, and May 17, 1961.

91 Jo Hopper to Marion Hopper, September 3, 1935.

92 Jo Hopper diary entry for October 6, 1951.

93 Ibid.

94 Knapp and Chipman, *That Was Yvette,* p. 279.

95 Although Nivison was not listed in the program of *Guibour,* she vividly recalled this role in the televised interview with Brian O'Doherty, WGBH-TV, Boston, 1961. This adaptation of *Guibour* was by Anne Sprague Macdonald.

96 Harold Loeb, *The Way It Was* (New York: Criterion Books, 1959), p. 35.

97 Knapp and Chipman, *That Was Yvette,* pp. 286–87.

98 Edmund Wilson, *The Twenties: From Notebooks and Diaries of the Period,* ed. by Leon Edel (New York: Farrar, Straus, and Giroux, 1975), p. 89.

99 Ibid.

100 Jo Hopper, in O'Doherty interview.

101 Knapp and Chipman, *That Was Yvette,* p. 287.

102 United States Census, 1920, vol. 244, E.D. 708, sheet 1, line 37.

103 Knapp and Chipman, *That Was Yvette,* p. 287.

104 See Madge Jenison, *Sunwise Turn: A Human Comedy of Bookselling* (New York: E. P. Dutton & Co., 1923).

105 Loeb, *The Way It Was,* p. 4.

106 See Roberta K. Tarbell, *Hugo Robus (1885–1964)* (Washington, D.C.: Smithsonian Institution Press, 1980), p. 43.

107 Joseph S. Trovato, *Charles Burchfield: Catalogue of Paintings in Public and Private Collections* (Utica, New York: Munson-Williams-Proctor Institute, 1970), p. 37.

108 Lindsay Smith, ed., *I Shock Myself: The Autobiography of Beatrice Wood* (San Francisco: Chronicle Books, 1985), pp. 14, 17.

109 See, for example, "Reports 60 Cases of Diphtheria Daily," *New York Times,* February 20, 1920, p. 6, which notes that the "disease [is] reaching epidemic stage."

110 Aloha Hive, located on Lake Fairlee, was under the spiritual guidance of Reverend E. L. Gulick and his wife.

111 Jo Hopper diary entry for January 9, 1952, records Breuning's recollection.

112 Jo Hopper to Marion Hopper, letter of September 3, 1935.

113 Jo Hopper diary entry for January 10, 1956, and elsewhere.

114 Jo Hopper diary entry for September 19, 1960.

115 Jo Hopper to Carl Sprinchorn, letter of August 20, 1960.

116 Ibid.

117 Josephine Nivison, draft of letter to Board of Education, 1921.

118 This is documented by her employment records in Special Collections at Teacher's College and by various drafts of letters.

119 See Alf Evers, *Woodstock: History of an American Town* (Woodstock: Overlook Press, 1987), p. 479, and Tom Wolf, "Historical Survey," in *Woodstock's Art Heritage* (Woodstock: Overlook Press, 1987), p. 22.

120 Josephine Nivison to Robert Henri, letter of October 15, 1921. Subsequent quotes to Henri are also from this letter.

121 Robert Henri, "Mary Rogers," *International Studio,* May 1921, p. 81. In addition to the artists discussed here, Nivison also mentioned Florence Barkley, Carl Sprinchorn, Montfort Coolidge, Tommy (Van Vleet) Tompkins, and Lolly Forbes as her friends among Henri's former students.

122 Nivison to Henri, October 15, 1921.

123 Pamela M. Davis, "Maurice Becker, 1889–1975," in *City Life Illustrated, 1890–1940* (Wilmington: Delaware Art Museum, 1980), p. 32.

124 Nivison to Henri, October 15, 1921. The Canadian-born Shore had returned a year or so earlier from Los Angeles where she had settled. At about this time, she abandoned a Henri-influenced realist style to paint semiabstract canvases based on nature symbolism. In 1923, she returned to California, where she pursued a career as a modernist. See also Roger Aikin in *Henrietta Shore: A Retrospective, 1900–1963* (Monterey: Monterey Penninsula Museum of Art, 1986). By the late 1950s, Shore's career had fallen apart and she was institutionalized until her death in 1963 at the age of eighty-three.

125 See Edward Hopper Dealers and Etchings Record Book, p. 62.

126 Jo Hopper to Carl Sprinchorn, letter of May 24, 1960.

127 Jo Hopper diary entry for October 23, 1937.

128 "Old and New Pictures of Flowers Make Fine Effect at Belmaison," unidentified clipping saved by Jo Hopper.

129 James N. Rosenberg, *Painter's Self-Portrait* (New York: Crown, 1958), p. 56.

130 "Concerning the Painters," "Hundred Dollar Holiday Exhibition," *New Gallery,* New York, December 12, 1921–January 2, 1922.

131 *Evening World,* May 18, 1923.

132 Jo Hopper to Carl Sprinchorn, letter of February 10, 1946.

FIRST SUCCESS

1 James F. O'Gorman, *This Other Gloucester: Occasional Papers on the Arts of Cape Ann, Massachusetts* (Boston, 1976), pp. 93–95.

2 Crotty, "Sharing Emotion with Others," p. 22. Jo Hopper diary entry for July 8, 1941.

3 Jo Hopper diary entry for July 8, 1941.

4 Jo Hopper to Alice F. Roullier, letter of March 27, 1934.

5 Jo Hopper, in Johnson interview.

6 Ibid.

7 Ibid.

8 Jo Hopper diary entry for October 15, 1950, remarks upon Edward's reminiscence. Although there are many references to Hopper's interest in Verlaine, this is the sole reference to Emile Verhaeren, the Belgian poet who wrote under the influence of the French Symbolists.

9 Emile Verhaeren, *Les Heures Claires* (1896), *Les Heures d'Après-midi* (1905), and *Les Heures du Soir* (1911).

10 Amy Lowell, *Six French Poets: Studies in Contemporary Literature* (New York: Houghton Mifflin Co., 1921), p. 3. Lowell commented of Verhaeren that "newspapers and magazines are full of his fame, various publishers are issuing translations of his poems."

11 Barr, *Edward Hopper,* p. 11, suggests that Hopper was encouraged to try watercolor that summer by having won prizes for his etching. Jo later dismissed this suggestion as erroneous. See Jo Hopper to Alice Roullier, draft of unsent letter of November 25, 1933.

12 Edward Hopper, in Johnson interview.

13 Jo Hopper diary entry for July 9, 1938.

14 Jo Hopper, in Johnson interview.

15 Jo Hopper diary entry for September 16, 1953.

16 Edward Hopper, in Johnson interview.

17 Edward Hopper, in Jacobowitz interview.

18 For the author's photographs of Hopper's actual motifs, see Gail Levin, *Hopper's Places* (New York: Alfred A. Knopf, 1985).

19 Gordon W. Thomas, *East and Able: The Life Stories of Great Gloucester Fishing Vessels* (Gloucester, Mass.: Gloucester 350th Anniversary Celebration, 1973), p. 185.

20 For the history and lyrics of this song, see Theodore Raph, ed., *The Songs We Sang: A Treasury of American Popular Music* (New York: A. S. Barnes & Co., 1964), p. 29.

21 Jo Hopper diary entry for September 8, 1944.

22 Josephine Hopper, interviewed with Edward Hopper, by Arlene Jacobowitz at the Brooklyn Museum, April 29, 1966.

23 Ibid.

24 Ibid.

25 Elizabeth Luther Cary, reprinted from *New York Times,* November 15, 1923, in *Brooklyn Museum Quarterly,* 11, January 1924, p. 19.

26 Ibid.

27 Helen Appleton Read, "Brooklyn Museum Emphasizes New Talent in Initial Exhibition," *Brooklyn Daily Eagle,* November 18, 1923, p. 2B.

28 Royal Cortissoz, "A Fine Collection at the Brooklyn Museum," *New York Tribune,* November 25, 1923, p. 8.

29 Edward Hopper, in Jacobowitz interview.

30 Edward Hopper, in Johnson interview. Edward Hopper, in Jacobowitz interview. November 22, 1966.

31 Jo Hopper diary entry for October 12, 1944. No record of who these directors were has yet to come to light.

32 Paul Verlaine, *La Bonne Chanson* (Paris, 1870), trans. by John Van Sickle.

33 Edward Hopper to the Carnegie Institute, letter of February 21, 1924.

34 Jo Hopper, quoted in Crotty, "Sharing Emotions with Others," p. 22.

35 O'Doherty, *American Masters,* p. 16.

36 As recounted by Guy's daughter, Yvonne du Bois McKinney, unpublished memoir and interview with the author, 1978.

37 Edward and Jo Hopper, quoted in O'Doherty, *American Masters,* p. 25.

38 Edward Hopper Record Book III, p. 117, entry for Gloucester Beach, Bass Rocks.

39 Jo Hopper to Carl Sprinchorn, letter of February 10, 1946.

40 Jo Hopper, quoted in O'Doherty, *American Masters,* p. 16.

41 Jo Hopper diary entry for February 22, 1959.

42 Ibid. The celebrated French novelist shared Jo's love of cats; see Colette's *Dialogues de bêtes* (1904), in which her Angora cat converses with her bulldog, and *La Paix chez les bêtes* (1916), a collection of animal sketches.

43 Jo Hopper, quoted in O'Doherty, "Portrait: Edward Hopper," p. 74.

44 Jo Hopper to Ethel Parsons, letter of October 8, 1924.

45 Jo Hopper diary entry for December 2, 1941. According to Louis M. Dabney, Wilson's biographer, Wilson's marriage to his first wife, Mary Blair, was starting to go sour.

46 Jo Hopper, in Johnson interview.

47 Jo Hopper to Ethel Parsons, letter of October 8, 1924.

48 Ibid.

49 See Lewis A. Ehrenberg, *Steppin' Out* (Chicago: University of Chicago Press, 1981), p. 80.

50 Jo Hopper diary entry for October 12, 1944.

51 Ibid.

52 Jo Hopper diary entry for September 23, 1956.

53 D'Emilio and Freedman, *Intimate Matters,* p. 175.

54 Ibid., p. 176.

55 Ibid., p. 178.

56 Elaine Tyler May, *Great Expectations: Marriage and Divorce in Post-Victorian America* (Chicago: University of Chicago Press, 1980), p. 102.

57 D'Emilio and Freedman, *Intimate Matters,* p. 182.

58 Nancy F. Cott, *The Grounding of Modern Feminism* (New Haven: Yale University Press, 1987), p. 157.

59 Phyllis Blanchard and Carolyn Manasses, *New Girls for Old* (New York: Macaulay Co., 1930), pp. 179–80, quoted in Cott, *Modern Feminism,* p. 157.

60 Jo Hopper diary entry for November 11, 1959.

61 Jo Hopper diary entry for February 11, 1960.

62 Ibid.

63 This show was organized by the Art Patrons of America, Inc., directed by the art dealer Marie Sterner, who gave Sprinchorn a one-man show in 1922.

64 Paul Jamot, *Degas* (Paris: Editions de la Gazette des Beaux-Arts, 1924), p. 4, author's translation.

65 Edward Hopper, quoted in O'Doherty, "Portrait: Edward Hopper," p. 78.

66 His etching *People in the Park* (1919–1923) prominently features a baby carriage, and in *East Side Interior* (1922), there is a baby carriage visible at the left of the woman's sewing machine.

67 In Hopper's own account, in his 1956 interview with William Johnson, he claims that he was on his way to the C. W. Kraushaar Galleries when he stopped by Rehn's. Guy Pène du Bois's daughter, Yvonne du Bois McKinney, recalls that Mr. Kraushaar found Hopper's work "too stark," which seems more likely. Hopper would not have wanted to emphasize this rejection.

68 This account is based in part on Johnson's 1956 interview with Hopper and partially on the recollections of Yvonne du Bois McKinney. A separate and, I believe, less reliable account of this encounter was given by the elderly John Clancy and appears in Lindemann, *Art Triangle,* pp. 19–21. The watercolor in question was probably *House with a Bay Window,* which records show was purchased by Arthur Fowler.

69 Edward Hopper to Henry McBride, letter of October 10, 1924.

70 Garnett McCoy, "Charles Burchfield and Edward Hopper," *Journal of the Archives of American Art,* 7, July–October 1967, p. 10.

71 Ibid.

72 Ibid.

73 Ibid., pp. 10–11.

74 Rehn, however, never gave contracts to his artists.

75 *Sunday World,* October 19, 1924, p. E11.

76 Margaret Breuning, "Water Colors by Hopper," *New York Post,* October 18, 1924, p. 11.

77 Henry McBride, "Edward Hopper's Water Colours Prove Interesting—Also Sell," *New York Sun,* October 24, 1924, p. 4.

78 [Elizabeth Luther Cary], "Art: Exhibition of Water Colors," *New York Times,* October 19, 1924, sec. 10, p. 13.

79 Gerald Nachman, "Artist at 82," *New York Post,* November 17, 1964, p. 51.

GETTING ESTABLISHED

1 Tittle, "Pursuit of Happiness," vol. 1, n.p.

2 Jo Hopper diary entry for April 18, 1942.

3 Jo Hopper diary entry for January 6, 1951.

4 See Edward Hopper Dealers and Etchings Record Book, p. 80, which lists prints sold by E. P. Jennings to the Metropolitan Museum on May 27, 1925, and gives his address as White Plains, New York. Jennings went abroad in 1926, where he sold Hopper's work to the British Museum. Then, in late 1928, he returned prints to Hopper "before departing for Greece," after which no further sign of him appears in Hopper's records.

5 Jo Hopper Record Book, p. 68, and Edward Hopper Record Book I, p. 89.

6 Edward Hopper to John Andrew Myers, letter of March 19, 1933.

7 Like most of Jo Hopper's works, these two are lost; neither photographs nor record sketches are known.

8 Jo Hopper diary entry for March 14, 1948.

9 Jo Hopper diary entry for January 7, 1953.

10 Ibid.

11 Jo Hopper, in Johnson interview.

12 For an account of Jo Hopper taking in John Dos Passos's cat, see pages 286–87, and her diary entry for October 3, 1945.

13 Jo Hopper diary entry for May 24, 1948.

14 Jo Hopper diary entry for January 4, 1960.

15 Barr, *Edward Hopper*, p. 15.

16 Van Wyck Brooks, *John Sloan: A Painter's Life* (New York: E. P. Dutton & Co., 1955), p. 155.

17 Edward Hopper, in Johnson interview.

18 Jo Hopper diary entry for February 13, 1949.

19 For a description of what Hopper saw, see Vincent Scully, *Pueblo: Mountain, Village, Dance* (New York: Viking Press, 1975), pp. 193–205.

20 Jo Hopper diary entry for March 15, 1935.

21 Edward Hopper, in Johnson interview.

22 Edward Hopper to his mother, letter of July 27, 1925.

23 Jo Hopper diary entry for September 6, 1945.

24 Edward Hopper to his mother, letter of July 27, 1925.

25 *Time* magazine, February 16, 1925.

26 Edward Hopper Record Book II, p. 71, noted in 1956, at the time the painting was sold.

27 Robert L. Gambone, *Art and Popular Religion in Evangelical America, 1915–1940* (Knoxville: University of Tennessee Press, 1989), pp. 62–63. Hopper himself, working under the constraint of a commission for the Methodist foreign missionary magazine *World Outlook* (5, May 1919, pp. 12–13), had illustrated an article, Charles Stelzle, "Instead of John Barleycorn," on morally acceptable alternatives to the saloon.

28 Squirru, "Edward Hopper," p. 15.

29 John Maass to the author, letter of December 22, 1985.

30 Michael Quick aptly employed this phrase to describe George Bellows's use of Victorian settings and props in "New Thoughts on George Bellows," a paper given at the annual meeting of the College Art Association in New York on February 18, 1994. I am grateful to Quick for sharing his text with me.

31 Quick, "New Thoughts on George Bellows," sees such Bellows paintings as *Katherine Rosen* (1921) or *Lady Jean* (1924) as anticipating the development of Regionalism.

32 This is documented by the collection of ticket stubs that Edward saved, the titles of each play written on the verso.

33 Henrik Ibsen, *The Master Builder,* in *Six Plays* (New York: Modern Library, 1957), p. 505.

34 "The New Society Is Arranging Its Exhibit," *New York Sunday World,* January 3, 1926, p. 7M.

35 Lloyd Goodrich, "New York Exhibitions," *The Arts,* 9, February 1926, p. 98.

36 Joan Simpson Burns, *The Awkward Embrace* (New York: Alfred A. Knopf, 1975), pp. 176–77.

37 [Elizabeth Luther Cary], "Many Types of Art Are Now on Exhibition," *New York Times,* February 28, 1926, sec. 8, p. 12. Margaret Breuning, "Exhibitions of Contemporary American Artists Feature Lenten Week in Local Galleries," *New York Evening Post,* February 27, 1926, p. 9.

38 [Cary], "Many Types of Art Are Now on Exhibition," p. 12.

39 "America Today," *Brooklyn Daily Eagle,* March 7, 1926, p. E7.

40 Edward Hopper to A. P. Saunders, letter of March 19, 1928.

41 Edward Hopper to Frank Rehn, letter of July 6, 1926.

42 Bernard Myers, ed., "Scribner's American Painters series," no. 7, *Scribner's,* 102, September 1937, p. 32.

43 See Edward Hopper Dealers and Etchings Record Book, p. 62.

44 See Edward Hopper Record Book I, p. 65.

45 Duncan Phillips to Frank Rehn, letter of November 27, 1925.

46 Duncan Phillips, "Brief Estimates of the Painters," in *A Collection in the Making* (New York: E. Weyhe, 1926), p. 69.

47 Ibid.

48 Edward Hopper, in O'Doherty interview.

49 O'Doherty, *American Masters,* p. 20.

50 Sherwood Anderson, *Winesburg, Ohio* (New York: B. W. Huebsch, 1919).

51 Edward Hopper to Forbes Watson, letter of December 10, 1926.

52 Barr, *Edward Hopper,* p. 14.

53 Lewis Mumford, "Is the Skyscraper Tolerable?" *Architecture,* 55, February 1927, pp. 67–69, and "Botched Cities," *American Mercury,* 18, October 1929, pp. 143–50.

54 See also Merrill Schleier, *The Skyscraper in American Art,* 1890–1931 (Ann Arbor: UMI Research Press, 1986), pp. 93–94.

55 [Henry McBride], "Edward Hopper Adds to His Reputation," *New York Sun,* February 19, 1927, p. 16.

56 Frederick W. Eddy, *New York World,* February 20, 1927, p. 9M.

57 "Edward Hopper Frank K. M. Rehn Galleries," *American Art News,* 25, February 19, 1927, p. 10.

58 Helen Appleton Read, "The American Scene," *Brooklyn Daily Eagle,* February 20, 1927, p. 6E.

59 Royal Cortissoz, "The Architectural League," *New York Herald Tribune,* February 27, 1927, Sec. 6, p. 10.

60 Theresa Bernstein in conversation with the author, January 6, 1990, and in previous conversation.

61 Jo Hopper diary entry for March 3, 1964.

62 Jo Hopper diary entry for October 10, 1951.

63 November 29, 1926, they saw Jean Bart's drama *The Squall;* then they saw *The Captive* (a story of a lesbian, played by Helen Menken, costarring with Basil Rathbone) on December 3; *The Witch* (a drama by John Mansfield from the Norwegian by H. Wiers-Jensen) on December 6; *An American Tragedy* (by Patrick Kearney from the novel by Theodore Dreiser) on December 15; *The Constant Nymph* (by Margaret Kennedy and Basel Dean) on December 20; Sergei Eisenstein's film *Battleship Potemkin* on January 4; *This Woman Business* (a comedy by Benn W. Levy) on January 10; *Set a Thief* (a mystery melodrama by Edward E. Paramore) on February 4; and Maxfield Anderson's comedy *Saturday's Children* on March 3.

64 Daniel Blum, *A Pictorial History of the American Theatre 1900–1950* (New York: Greenberg, 1950), p. 183.

65 Lloyd Goodrich, "The Paintings of Edward Hopper," *The Arts,* 2, March 1927, pp. 134–38.

66 Edward Hopper to Lloyd Goodrich, letter of March 16, 1927.

67 Thus Goodrich never examined Hopper's commercial work and never wrote about it or its relationship to his development as an artist. As he explained to me, he never noted that Hopper studied with Chase, "because Hopper never mentioned it to me." Evidently, Goodrich never noticed the many early publications where Hopper had listed himself as having studied with Chase. My conversations with Goodrich extend over the years 1976 to 1984, during my tenure as curator of the Hopper Collection at the Whitney Museum of American Art, the museum from which Goodrich had retired as director.

68 Edward Hopper, "Books" (review of Malcolm C. Salaman, *Fine Prints of the Year,* 1925), *The Arts,* 9, March 1926, pp. 172–74.

69 Edward Hopper, "John Sloan," p. 172.

70 Ibid., pp. 177–78.

71 Edward Hopper, "Charles Burchfield: American," *The Arts,* 14, July 1928, p. 6. Ralph Waldo Emerson, *Essays,* First Series (Boston: Houghton, Osgood & Co., 1879).

72 Emerson, "Self-Reliance," p. 81.

73 William Wasserstrom, *Van Wyck Brooks* (Minneapolis: University of Minnesota Press, 1968), p. 16.

74 Van Wyck Brooks, quoted in Wasserstrom, *Brooks,* p. 14.

75 Edward Hopper, "John Sloan," pp. 169, 170.

76 Ibid., p. 170.

77 Ibid., p. 169.

78 Van Wyck Brooks, *The Pilgrimage of Henry James* (New York: Dutton, 1925).

79 Van Wyck Brooks, "Henry James: The American Scene," *Dial,* 75, no. 1, July 1923, p. 30.

80 See, for example, Lafcadio Hearn, *Glimpses of Unfamiliar Japan* (New York, 1894).

81 Jo Hopper diary entry for September 10, 1951.

82 See Virginia Scharff, *Taking the Wheel: Women and the Coming of the Motor Age* (New York: Free Press, 1991), pp. 32–35.

83 Michael L. Berger, "Women Drivers: The Emergence of Folklore and Stereotypic Opinions Concerning Feminine Automotive Behavior," *Women's Studies International Forum,* 9, no. 3, 1986, pp. 257–63.

84 Scharff, *Taking the Wheel,* p. 26.

85 Quoted in Scharff, *Taking the Wheel,* p. 32.

86 Quoted in Berger, "Women Drivers," p. 261.

87 Jo Hopper diary entry for January 13, 1941.

88 Jo Hopper diary entry for July 8, 1941.

89 Jo N. Hopper to Charles C. Cunningham, letter of March 31, 1957.

90 Jo Hopper diary entry for January 7, 1954.

91 Julia Chatterton Van de Water to the author, letter of March 26, 1980.

92 Jo Hopper diary entry for September 3, 1944.

93 Edward Hopper to Donald Adams, letter of August 7, 1955.

94 Edward Hopper to William Bender, Jr., letter of August 1, 1960. Budd (later Mrs. Katherine Proctor) gave singing lessons at Maxstoke. Her son, Tolman Budd, became a sculptor; see Edward Hopper to Katherine Proctor, letter of February 6, 1956, advising against sending Tolman to a European art school.

95 See Edward Hopper Dealers and Etchings Record Book, p. 62.

96 Jo Hopper to Carl Zigrosser, letter of October 26, 1927.

97 Flint, *Albert Sterner,* p. 29.

98 Edward Hopper to Pop Hart, letter of October 27, 1927, quoted in Gregory Gilbert, *George Overbury "Pop" Hart: His Life and Art* (New Brunswick, N.J.: Rutgers University Press, 1986), p. 120.

99 Edward Hopper, "Review of *Fine Prints of the Year, 1925,"* p. 173.

100 "The arrangement permits each member of the committee to invite two artists to show four prints of their own selection": press release for American Print Makers, Downtown Gallery, December 5, 1928. Other adherents were Rockwell Kent, John Sloan, Kenneth H. Miller, Walter Pach, Yasuo Kuniyoshi, Peggy Bacon, Boardman Robinson, Anne Goldthwaite, and Harry Wickey.

101 American Print Makers, Downtown Gallery, Third Annual Exhibition, December 10–31, 1929, lists Hopper as a member of the 1929–1930 committee. By 1929, Kent, Pach, and Robinson had been replaced by Ernest Fiene, Walt Kuhn, and Max Weber.

102 Kent, *It's Me O Lord,* p. 426.

103 Andrée Ruellan in an interview with the author, January 2, 1986, Woodstock, New York.

104 Jo N. Hopper to G. H. Edgell, letter of September 14, 1948.

105 J. Hyatt Downing, "The Distance to Casper," *Scribner's Magazine,* 81, February 1927, pp. 163, 167.

106 Edward Hopper, quoted in Goodrich, *Edward Hopper,* p. 31.

ON THE ROAD TO AMERICA

1 Stelzle, "Instead of John Barleycorn," *World Outlook,* p. 12.

2 Jo Hopper diary entry for August 11, 1954. The following quotation is also from this entry.

3 Edward Hopper to Charles H. Sawyer, letter of October 29, 1939.

4 Ibid.

5 See Joseph S. Trovato, *Edward W. Root: Collector and Teacher,* Fred L. Emerson Gallery, Hamilton College, Clinton, New York, 1982.

6 Edward W. Root, "To the Editor of the Press," *Utica Daily Press,* March 3, 1928, p. 9.

7 N. E. Montross to Charles Burchfield, letter of April 25, 1928, quoted in John I. H. Baur, *The Inlander: Life and Work of Charles Burchfield, 1893–1967* (Newark, Del.: University of Delaware Press, 1982), p. 150.

8 Edward Hopper, "Charles Burchfield," p. 6. Emerson, *Essays.*

9 Hopper, "Charles Burchfield," p. 10.

10 C. K. Chatterton, in interview by Alexander D. Ross, May 12, 1971.

11 Edward Hopper Record Book II, p. 35.

12 Fred G. Mories, a portraitist who worked in watercolor and charcoal, is listed in the

American Art Annual for 1924 as an illustrator who worked in Provincetown, Mass.

13 Jo Hopper diary entry for April 12, 1960. Jo Hopper diary entry for October 28, 1936. This earlier entry recounts that Edward danced to Brahms, not Beethoven.

14 Jo Hopper diary entry for April 12, 1960.

15 Ibid.

16 For a discussion of the connection of voyeurism and the cinema, see Laura Mulvey, "Visual Pleasure and Narrative Cinema," in Laura Mulvey, *Visual and Other Pleasures* (Bloomington: Indiana University Press, 1989), p. 17.

17 Anderson, *Winesburg, Ohio,* p. 150. Lawrence Campbell, "Hopper: Painter of 'thou shalt not,' " *Art News,* 63, October 1964, pp. 44–45, also suggested the similarity to this story.

18 Edward Hopper, quoted by Malcolm Preston in an unpublished interview, 1951.

19 Sherwood Anderson, *Many Marriages* (New York: B. W. Huebsch, 1923).

20 Kim Townsend, *Sherwood Anderson* (Boston: Houghton Mifflin Co., 1987), p. 200.

21 Edward Hopper to Forbes Watson, letter of December 16, 1928. The article, "A Note on Edward Hopper," appeared in *Vanity Fair,* 31, in February 1929, pp. 64, 98, 107.

22 Edward Hopper to Forbes Watson, letter of December 16, 1928.

23 Watson, "A Note on Edward Hopper," pp. 64, 98.

24 Hopper, quoted in Watson, "A Note on Edward Hopper," p. 98.

25 Watson, "A Note on Edward Hopper," p. 98.

26 Hopper to Watson, December 16, 1928.

27 Watson, "A Note on Edward Hopper," p. 98.

28 Ibid., pp. 98, 107.

29 Edward Hopper to C. C. Cunningham, letter of February 23, 1961.

30 Edward Hopper to Carl Zigrosser, letter of June 18, 1928, and Edward Hopper (in Jo's hand) to Carl Zigrosser, letter of December 8, 1928.

31 [Henry McBride], "Americanism of Edward Hopper," *New York Sun,* January 19, 1929, p. 10; [Helen Appleton Read], "Hopper Interprets America," *Brooklyn Daily Eagle,* January 20, 1929, p. E7.

32 See, for example, Margaret Breuning, "Exhibition of Watercolors at Brooklyn Museum Features the Week," *New York Evening Post,* January 26, 1929, p. 10M.

33 Edward Alden Jewell, "International & Other Exhibitions," *New York Times,* January 20, 1929, sec. 8, p. 12.

34 Ibid., 1929.

35 Edward Hopper to Forbes Watson, letter of January 22, 1929.

36 According to the Metropolitan, at some point in history this picture was overcleaned; I was told that it was not included in their catalogue because of concern that later overpainting might have been done by Hopper. In fact, there is no reason to suspect that he would have touched up the work, which he respected for its simplicity and historical value. For that matter, Hopper did not even repair damages to his own work, but regularly told museums to send such pictures to a conservator. On October 23, 1994, the Metropolitan sold this picture, which the Hoppers had bequeathed to them for the public's enjoyment, at Sotheby's, where it was purchased by a private collector.

37 The Whitney Studio Club held "Early American Art," the first exhibition of American folk art, in 1924.

38 Lena M. McCauley, "Renaissance in the South," *Art World Magazine: Chicago Evening Post,* April 17, 1928, p. 8. Cited in Martha R. Severens, "Charleston in the Age of Porgy and Bess," *Southern Quarterly: A Journal of Arts in the South,* 28, fall 1989, pp. 5–6.

39 This information is from the author's correspondence with Gertrude Wulbern Haltiwanger, September 1987.

40 For Hopper's comment, see page 488.

41 Jo Hopper to J. Donald Adams, letter of February 26, 1949.

42 Jo Hopper to Miss Masterson, letter of April 22, 1929.

43 Ibid.

44 Jo Hopper to Bee Blanchard, letter of July 14, 1930.

45 Ibid.

46 *Time, Capsule/1929* (New York: Time, Inc., 1967), pp. 173–74.

47 Jo Hopper to Miss Burchfield, letter of December 4, 1937. The following quotation is also from this letter.

48 Jo Hopper diary entry for October 12, 1944.

49 Quoted in C. F. MacIntyre, *French Symbolist Poetry* (Berkeley: University of California Press, 1961), pp. 14–15.

50 James Laver, *A History of British and American Etching* (New York: Dodd, Mead & Co., 1929), p. 150.

51 December 13, 1929–January 12, 1930. See *Nineteen Americans* (New York: Forum Gallery, 1990) for Frank Crowninshield's ballot and one of Barr's working lists.

52 Forbes Watson, "The All American Nineteen," *The Arts,* 16, January 1930, pp. 308–10.

53 Henry McBride, "Works of Nineteen Best American Artists Exhibited in New Museum's Second Show," *New York Sun,* December 14, 1929, p. 8.

RECOGNITION

1 Edward Hopper Record Book I, p. 58.

2 Quoted in Kuh, *Artist's Voice,* pp. 131, 134.

3 O'Doherty, "Portrait: Edward Hopper," p. 78.

4 Jo Hopper diary entry for September 1, 1960.

5 Jo Hopper to Marion Hopper, letter of July 5, 1936.

6 Horace Gregory, *The House on Jefferson Street: A Cycle of Memories* (New York: Holt, Rinehart & Winston), 1971, p. 165.

7 First by Forbes Watson, "In the Galleries," *The Arts,* 16, May 1930, pp. 626–27.

8 Jo Hopper to Forbes Watson, undated letter of April 1930.

9 Edward Hopper to Forbes Watson, letter of April 29, 1930.

10 Baur, *Inlander,* pp. 149–50.

11 Jo Hopper to Bee Blanchard, letter of July 14, 1930.

12 Aline B. Saarinen, *The Proud Possessors* (New York: Vintage Books, 1968), p. 264.

13 Jeremiah Digges, *Cape Cod Pilot* (Provincetown and New York: Modern Pilgrim Press and Viking Press, 1937), p. 209.

14 Jo Hopper to Blanchard, July 14, 1930.

15 Ibid.

16 Edward Hopper to C. K. Chatterton, letter of July 23, 1930.

17 Jo Hopper to Blanchard, July 14, 1930.

18 Jo Hopper to C. C. Cunningham, letter of March 31, 1951.

19 The lighthouse, known as Highland Light, was built in 1857, replacing the original of 1798.

20 Henry D. Thoreau, *Cape Cod* (New York: Thomas Y. Crowell & Co., 1907), p. 168 (reprint of 1865 edition). Arthur Wilson Tarbell, *Cape Cod Ahoy!* (Boston: Little, Brown & Co., 1932), p. 206.

21 Tarbell, *Cape Cod Ahoy!,* pp. 205–6. The ancient works were replaced by an electric motor in 1932.

22 Guy Pène du Bois, *Edward Hopper* (New York: William Edwin Rudge, 1931), p. 11.

23 Tarbell, *Cape Cod Ahoy!,* p. 244.

24 Jo Hopper to Blanchard, July 14, 1930.

25 Jo Hopper to Louise H. Burchfield, curator (sister of the artist Charles Burchfield), Cleveland Museum of Art, letter of December 4, 1937, states that *Hills, South Truro* was "the very first of his Cape Cod Series."

26 Jo Hopper to Blanchard, July 14, 1930.

27 Ibid.

28 Ibid.

29 Ibid.

30 Ibid.

31 Ibid.

32 Ibid.

33 Jo Hopper diary entry for June 30, 1961.

34 Ibid.

35 The *Provincetown Advocate,* March 21, 1940, p. 1, described the building as "a landmark famous throughout the Cape, known throughout the country, pictured by painters on hundreds of canvases," when reporting the church's destruction by fire after being hit by lightning. Artists who painted the church include Morris Kantor, Jerry Farnsworth, Edward Wilson, Bob Stephens, and Raymond Eastwood.

36 Jo Hopper to Louise H. Burchfield, December 4, 1937.

37 Tarbell, *Cape Cod Ahoy!,* pp. 216–17.

38 Jo Hopper to Bee Blanchard, undated letter of October 1930.

39 Ibid.

40 Jo Hopper diary entry for October 30, 1953.

41 Guy Pène du Bois, "America's Curious Predicament in Art," *Creative Art,* 11, September 1930, p. 33.

42 Ibid.

43 Ibid.

44 Ibid., p. 34.

45 Jo Hopper diary entry for January 10, 1935.

46 Edward Hopper's continuing admiration for Dutch painting is reflected in his enthusiasm for the film *Carnival in Flanders,* which he saw at least twice. Jo noted in her diary entry for January 10, 1941: "All the Dutch old Masters right out of their canvases—splendid production and so ably acted. We crazy about it."

47 Edward Hopper Record Book I, p. 59, entry for *Tables for Ladies.*

48 Jo Hopper diary entry for January 10, 1935.

49 Jo Hopper to Anne Tucker, undated letter of January 6, 1931.

50 Jo Hopper to Anne Tucker, undated letter of March 1931.

51 Edward Hopper, quoted in Johnson interview.

52 Jo Hopper annotation of May 27, 1953, on the verso of letter of March 17, 1931, from the museum's director, Roland McKinney, to Edward Hopper.

53 *Hotel Room* measures 5′ × 5′5″ and is much larger than works such as *Night Windows* at 29″ × 34″.

54 Jo Hopper diary entry for April 12, 1960.

55 Edward Hopper, "John Sloan," p. 171.

56 Du Bois, *Edward Hopper.*

57 Ibid., p. 8.

58 Ibid.

59 Edward Hopper to Guy Pène du Bois, letter of November 20, 1931.

60 See page 139: Edward Hopper, quoted in Goodrich, *Edward Hopper,* p. 31.

61 Forbes Watson, "The Rise of Edward Hopper," *Brooklyn Eagle,* November 5, 1933, p. 13.

62 Du Bois, *Edward Hopper,* p. 10.

63 Edward Hopper to Guy Pène du Bois, letter of November 21, 1931. The following quotation is also from this letter.

64 Edward Hopper to Wilbur Peat, letter of March 24, 1932.

65 Edward Hopper to Charles C. Cunningham, letter of March 21, 1935.

66 Jo Hopper to C. H. Edgell, letter of September 24, 1932.

67 Edward Hopper, quoted in O'Doherty, "Portrait: Edward Hopper," p. 80.

68 Ibid.

69 Edward Hopper, quoted in "Such a Life," *Life,* 102, August 1935, p. 48, and "Artist Edward Hopper Tells Story of 'Room in New York,'" *Lincoln (Nebraska) Journal & Star,* March 29, 1936, sec. C–D, p. 7.

70 Charles Burchfield, "Hopper: Career of Silent Poetry," *Art News,* 49, March 1950, p. 17.

71 Royal Cortissoz, "Some Modern Paintings From American and French Hands," *New York Herald Tribune,* November 27, 1932, p. 10.

72 "Modern Shuns Honor by Design Academy," *New York Times,* March 26, 1932, p. 15.

73 "Exhibitions in New York: The Spring Academy," *Art News,* 30, April 2, 1932, p. 9.

74 "Hopper Will Not Break Silence," *Art Digest,* 6, April 15, 1932, p. 13.

75 Henry McBride, "The Serene National Academy Remains Undisturbed by the Current Depression: Modest Spring Exhibition Seems Very Much as Usual," *New York Sun,* April 2, 1932, p. 34.

76 Frank Crowninshield, "A Series of American Artists: No. 3—Edward Hopper," *Vanity Fair,* 38, June 1932, pp. 30–31.

77 Edward Hopper to Guy Pène du Bois, letter of June 17, 1932.

78 Jo Hopper diary entry for January 9, 1941.

79 Edward Hopper Record Book II, p. 2.

80 Jo Hopper to Mary F. Williams, letter of September 5, 1958.

81 Edward Hopper Record Book II, p. 37.

82 Ibid., p. 36.

83 Jo Hopper to Bee Blanchard, letter of July 18, 1932.

84 Ibid.

85 Ibid.

86 Ibid.

87 Ibid.

88 Ibid.

89 Ibid.

90 Jo Hopper to Marion Hopper, letter of July 13, 1932.

91 Jo Hopper diary entry for February 11, 1960.

92 Jo Hopper diary entry for August 24, 1936.

93 Jo Hopper to Marion Hopper, letter of July 13, 1932.

94 Edmund Wilson, "The Crushing of Washington Square," October 12, 1927, reprinted in Edmund Wilson, *American Earthquake: A Documentary of the Twenties and Thirties* (New York: Farrar, Straus, & Giroux, 1958), pp. 93–94.

95 Ibid., p. 94.

96 Jo Hopper diary entry for April 26, 1941.

97 Jo Hopper diary entry for December 30, 1939.

98 Wilson, "Crushing of Washington Square," p. 94.

99 On June 25, 1933, Jo Hopper sent Guy Pène du Bois's book on Hopper to the Proctors with a note on a card (private collection) from Miss M. H. Wright's rooming house in Quebec: "He'll autograph it when we pass by next time."

100 Jo Hopper to Katherine Proctor, letter of June 24, 1933.

101 Ibid.

102 Jo Hopper diary entry for June 1933.

103 Jo Hopper undated diary entry for 1933.

104 Edward Hopper to W. G. Constable, letter of December 23, 1956.

105 Jo Hopper to W. G. Constable, postscript on letter by Edward Hopper, December 23, 1956.

106 Ibid.

107 Ibid.

108 Jo Hopper undated diary entry for 1933.

FIRST RETROSPECTIVE
AND THE TRURO HOUSE

1 Edward Hopper to Alfred H. Barr, Jr., letter of August 24, 1933.

2 Edward Hopper to Alfred H. Barr, Jr., letter of August 14, 1933.

3 Jo Hopper handwritten note on letter from Alfred H. Barr, Jr., to Jo Hopper, October 10, 1933.

4 Jo Hopper to Alice F. Roullier, letter of March 27, 1934.

5 "Modern Museum Holds Hopper Exhibition," *Art Digest,* 8, November 1, 1933, p. 19.

6 Ibid.

7 Edward Alden Jewell, "Aims and Attainments," *New York Times,* November 5, 1933, p. 12X; quoted in "Critics Differ on Hopper," *Art Digest,* 8, November 15, 1933, p. 12.

8 "Edward Hopper," *New York Herald Tribune,* November 5, 1933, sec. 5, p. 10; quoted in "Critics Differ on Hopper."

9 "Why 'Modern'?," *New Republic,* 77, December 6, 1933, pp. 104–5, letters to the editor from Ralph Pearson and Alfred H. Barr, Jr.

10 Edward Hopper, "Notes on Painting," p. 17, quoted in Ralph Pearson, "Why 'Modern'?," *New Republic,* 77, December 6, 1933, p. 104.

11 Pearson, "Why 'Modern'?," p. 104.

12 "New York Art Notes," *Christian Science Monitor,* April 2, 1923, p. 8.

13 "National Arts Club Exhibits Etchings," *Art News,* 22, December 22, 1923.

14 Barr, "Why 'Modern'?," p. 104.

15 Lewis Mumford, "The Art Galleries, Questions and Answers," *New Yorker,* 9, December 16, 1933, p. 62.

16 Helen Appleton Read, "Racial Quality of Hopper Pictures at Modern Agrees with Nationalistic Mood," *Brooklyn Daily Eagle,* November 5, 1933, p. 12 B–C.

17 Lewis Mumford, "The Art Galleries: Two Americans," *New Yorker,* 9, November 11, 1933, p. 78.

18 Ibid., p. 76.

19 Henry McBride, "Hopper's One-Man Show," *New York Sun,* November 4, 1933, p. 11.

20 Ibid.

21 Edward Hopper to Alfred Barr, letter of November 5, 1933.

22 Ibid.

23 Ibid.

24 Forbes Watson, "The Rise of Edward Hopper," *Brooklyn Eagle Magazine,* November 5, 1933, p. 13.

25 Ibid.

26 Ibid.

27 Eleanor Jewett, "Opposite Views of Art Shown in Club Exhibit," *Chicago Daily Tribune,* January 5, 1934, p. 15; C. J. Bulliet, "Hopper Poet of Solitudes Just Deserted," *Chicago Daily News,* January 6, 1934, p. 28.

28 Jo Hopper to Alice F. Roullier, letter of November 25 and 26, 1933.

29 Ibid.

30 Ibid.

31 Edward Hopper to Alice F. Roullier, letter of December 9, 1933.

32 Jo Hopper to Alice F. Roullier, letter of March 27, 1934.

33 Jo Hopper to Alice F. Roullier, draft of unsent letter of November 25, 1933. See also Barr, *Edward Hopper,* pp. 11, 19.

34 Edward Hopper, quoted in O'Doherty, "Portrait: Edward Hopper," p. 73.

35 Edward Hopper, "John Sloan," p. 170.

36 Jo Hopper diary entry for March 30, 1934.

37 Jo Hopper diary entry for April 3, 1934.

38 Jo Hopper to Alice Roullier, letter of March 27, 1934.

39 Jo Hopper diary entries for April 12 and 17, 1934.

40 Jo Hopper diary entry for April 18, 1934.

41 Jo Hopper diary entry for May 4, 1934.

42 Ibid.

43 Jo Hopper diary entry for May 5, 1934.

44 Ibid.

45 Jo Hopper to Bee Blanchard, letter of May 13, 1934.

46 Ibid.

47 A more conservative rival was the Cape Cod School of Art, which Charles W. Hawthorne conducted until his death in 1930.

48 Jo Hopper diary entry for September 23, 1948.

49 Edward Hopper, quoted in O'Doherty, "Portrait: Edward Hopper," p. 80.

50 Jo Hopper undated diary entries for 1934.

51 Ibid.

52 Jo Hopper to Bee Blanchard, letter of June 14, 1934.

53 Jo Hopper undated diary entry for 1934.

54 Jo Hopper to Bee Blanchard, letter of June 24, 1934. The following quotation is also from this letter.

55 Jo Hopper undated diary entry for 1934.

56 Jo Hopper to Blanchard, June 24, 1934.

57 Ibid.

58 Jo Hopper undated diary entry for 1934.

59 Jo Hopper to Bee Blanchard, letter of July 18, 1932.

60 Jo Hopper to Anne Tucker, undated letter of July 1934.

61 Jo Hopper to Marion Hopper, letter of August 23, 1934.

62 Jo Hopper to Bee Blanchard, letter of October 17, 1934.

63 Jo Hopper diary entry for August 30, 1934.

64 Edward Hopper to Homer Saint-Gaudens, letter of September 20, 1934.

65 Jo Hopper to Bee Blanchard, letter of October 17, 1934. The following quotations are also from this letter.

66 Jo Hopper undated diary entry for 1934.

67 Jo Hopper to Marion Hopper, letter of August 6, 1935.

68 Jo Hopper undated diary entry for 1934.

69 Jo Hopper diary entry for September 9, 1963.

70 This reflection recorded in Jo Hopper diary entry for February 2, 1937.

71 See Amy J. Wolf, *New York Society of Women Artists, 1925,* ACA Galleries, March 7–28, 1987.

72 Nathaniel J. Pousette-Dart, "Thomas Craven: Prophet, Surgeon or Undertaker," *Art of Today,* December 1934, p. 8.

73 See "Edward Hopper Objects," in *Art of Today,* 6, February 1935, p. 11.

74 "Edward Hopper Objects," p. 11.

75 "Editorial Comment" by Pousette-Dart in ibid.

76 O'Doherty, "Portrait: Edward Hopper," p. 80, gives Hopper's own translation.

77 Hopper surely also knew Longfellow's translation of this poem.

78 "Philadelphia Art Medals Awarded to New Yorkers," *New York Tribune,* January 27, 1935, p. 4.

79 Jo Hopper diary entry for February 5, 1935.

80 Jo Hopper diary entry for February 20, 1935.

81 Jo Hopper diary entry for February 11, 1935.

82 Jo Hopper diary entry for February 14, 1935.

83 Ibid.

84 Edward Alden Jewell, "In the Realm of the Abstract Trail," *New York Times,* February 17, 1935, sec. 8, p. 9.

85 Jo Hopper to Bee Blanchard, letter of October 17, 1934.

86 Anne Tucker to Bee Blanchard, letter written on verso of a letter Jo Hopper wrote to Anne Tucker on March 29, 1935, which Anne Tucker sent on to Bee Blanchard.

87 Jo Hopper diary entry for January 27, 1937.

88 Jo Hopper to Marion Hopper, letter of November 11, 1935.

89 Ibid.

90 Jo Hopper diary entry for March 17, 1935.

91 Jo Hopper diary entry for April 7, 1935.

92 Ibid.

93 Jo Hopper to Marion Hopper, letter of June 23, 1935.

94 Jo Hopper to Marion Hopper, undated letter of June 1935 and letter of June 23, 1935.

95 Author's interview with John Clancy, 1978.

96 Jo Hopper to Marion Hopper, letter of September 3, 1935.

97 "Art Finds Mark Worcester Show," *New York Times,* November 2, 1935, p. 13. The jury consisted of Charles H. Sawyer of the Addison Gallery of American Art, Dr. W. Irving Clark, Perry Cott, and Francis Henry Taylor, the director of the Worcester Museum.

98 William Shakespeare, Sonnet 73, in Hardin Craig, *The Complete Works of Shakespeare* (Chicago: Scott, Foresman and Co., 1951), pp. 483–84.

99 Archer Winsten, "Wake of the News: Washington Square North Boasts Strangers Worth Talking To," *New York Post,* November 26, 1935, p. 15. The following quotations are also from this article.

100 Jo Hopper to Marion Hopper, letter of December 5, 1935.

AN INTELLECTUAL SELF-PORTRAIT

1 Jo Hopper diary entry for March 7, 1935.

2 C. G. Jung, *Modern Man in Search of a Soul* (London: Kegan Paul, Trench, Trubner & Co., 1933), pp. 132–42.

3 Ibid., p. 18.

4 Jo Hopper diary entry for December 15, 1936.

5 C. J. Bulliet, "Artless Comment on the Seven Arts," *Chicago Daily News,* October 30, 1943, p. 7.

6 Edward Hopper, "Notes on Painting," p. 17.

7 O'Doherty, "Portrait: Edward Hopper," p. 75.

8 Jo Hopper to Marion Hopper, letter of July 5, 1936.

9 Jo Hopper diary entry for October 26, 1936.

10 George Santayana, *The Last Puritan* (New York: Charles Scribner's Sons, 1936), p. 3.

11 Santayana, *Last Puritan,* p. 5.

12 Ibid.

13 Ibid., p. 6.

14 Ibid.

15 Ibid.

16 Ibid., p. 7.

17 Joe Lee Davis, "Santayana as a Critic of Transcendentalism," in *Transcendentalism and Its Legacy,* ed. Meryon Simon and Thornton H. Parsons (Ann Arbor: University of Michigan Press, 1966), p. 166.

18 Edward Hopper, in O'Doherty interview.

19 Ralph Waldo Emerson, "The American Scholar," lecture of August 31, 1837, in *Works,* vol. 5 (Boston: Houghton, Osgood & Co., 1879), pp. 93, 95–96.

20 Santayana, *Last Puritan,* pp. 200–1.

21 Ibid., pp. 92, 171, 404, 552, 416, 518.

22 Ibid., pp. 314, 509.

23 See Joel Porte, *Representative Man: Ralph Waldo Emerson in His Time* (New York: Oxford University Press, 1979), p. 26.

24 Du Bois, *Edward Hopper,* p. 8. See also pages 238–39.

25 Warren I. Susman, *Culture as History: The Transformation of American Society in the Twentieth Century* (New York: Pantheon Books, 1973, 1984), p. 45.

26 Van Wyck Brooks, *The Wine of the Puritans,* reprinted in Claire Sprague, ed., *Van Wyck Brooks: The Early Years* (New York: Harper & Row, 1968), p. 38.

27 Van Wyck Brooks, "On Creating a Useable Past," *The Dial*, 64, April 11, 1918, pp. 337–41.

28 Du Bois, *Edward Hopper,* p. 8, and Susman, *Culture as History,* p. 45.

29 Hopper to Charles H. Sawyer, letter of October 29, 1939.

30 Edward Hopper, quoted in O'Doherty, "Portrait: Edward Hopper," p. 73.

31 Henry McBride, "Marsden Hartley Reappears: New England Artist Again at the American Place," *New York Sun,* March 28, 1936, pp. 331–32.

32 Squirru, "Edward Hopper," p. 14.

33 Ibid., p. 15.

34 Frances Brownell Burstein, "The Picture of New England Puritanism Presented in the Fiction of Henry James," Ph.D. dissertation, Boston University, 1964, p. 92.

35 Ibid., p. 291.

36 Henry James, *Roderick Hudson* (Boston: James R. Osgood & Co., 1875), p. 9.

37 Henry James, *Hawthorne* (London: Macmillan & Co., 1879). Reprinted in Richardson, ed., *Henry James: Representative Selections,* p. 49.

38 Henry James, "Emerson," from *Partial Portraits,* reprinted in Richardson, ed., *Henry James: Representative Selections,* p. 136.

39 Ibid.

40 Hopper, "John Sloan," p. 169. See also page 204.

41 Leon Edel, *Henry James* (Minneapolis: University of Minnesota Press, 1960), p. 41.

42 Even before he left for Europe, Hopper might have read James's earlier essays on New York, published in *Harper's Monthly Magazine* in February, March, and May 1906. See these reprinted as Henry James, *New York Revisited* (New York: Franklin Square Press, 1994).

43 Edward Hopper to his mother, letter of October 30, 1906.

44 Edward Hopper to his mother, letter of November 23, 1906.

45 Henry James, *The American Scene* (Harper & Bros., 1907), pp. 70, 105–6.

46 Ibid., p. 75.

47 Ibid.

48 Ibid., p. 110.

49 Edward Hopper, "Charles Burchfield," p. 7.

50 Marcel Proust, *Remembrance of Things Past,* 2 v., trans. by C. K. Scott-Moncrieff and Frederick A. Blossom (New York: Random House, 1932), p. 174.

51 Du Bois diary entry for September 11, 1924.

52 Henri, *Art Spirit,* p. 143.

53 Edwin E. Slosson, "Ibsen as an Interpreter of American Life," *Independent,* 60, May 31, 1906, p. 1253, reprinted in Michael Egan, *Ibsen: The Cultural Heritage* (Boston: Routledge & Kegan Paul, 1972), p. 451.

54 Hopper, "Notes on Painting," p. 18.

55 Jennette Lee, *The Ibsen Secret: A Key to the Prose Dramas of Henrik Ibsen* (New York: G. P. Putnam's Sons, 1907).

56 Ibid., p. 56.

57 Ibid., p. 51.

58 Ibid., pp. 88–89.

59 Ibid., pp. 99, 112.

60 Ibsen, *When We Dead Awaken,* in Henrik Ibsen, *Ghosts. A Public Enemy. When We Dead Awaken* (Baltimore: Penguin Books, 1964), trans. by Peter Watts, pp. 268–69.

CONSEQUENCES OF SUCCESS

1 He also showed *The Long Leg,* an oil painting.

2 Edward Hopper to Juliana Force, letter of April 27, 1936.

3 Aline Kister, "New Market Trends," *Prints,* 7, 1936, p. 32.

4 Edward Hopper to Carl Zigrosser, letter of January 31, 1936.

5 Zigrosser, *World of Art,* pp. 56–57.

6 Edward Hopper to Wilbur Peat, letter of May 26, 1936.

7 Jo Hopper, in O'Doherty interview.

8 Jo Hopper diary entry for February 14, 1935.

9 Louis R. Reid, "Amusement: Radio and Movies," in Harold E. Stearns, ed., *America Now: An Inquiry into Civilization in the United*

States (New York: Literary Guild of America, 1938), p. 22.

10 Jo Hopper diary entry for September 12, 1936.

11 Ibid.

12 Edward Hopper to Guy Pène du Bois, letter of June 9, 1936.

13 Carr, *Dos Passos,* p. 275.

14 See Carr, *Dos Passos,* p. 293.

15 Jo Hopper to Rosalind Irvine, undated letter of early March 1959.

16 Jo Hopper diary entry for October 28, 1936.

17 Jo Hopper diary entry for October 26, 1936.

18 John Dos Passos, quoted in notes from unpublished interview with William Johnson, October 30, 1956.

19 Ibid.

20 Jo Hopper diary entry for October 27, 1936.

21 Carr, *Dos Passos,* p. 277.

22 John Dos Passos, quoted in Carr, *Dos Passos,* pp. 306–7.

23 Jo Hopper diary entry for September 12, 1936.

24 Edward Hopper, quoted in Kuh, *Artist's Voice,* 1962, p. 131.

25 Jo Hopper diary entry for October 27, 1936.

26 Ibid.

27 Jo Hopper diary entry for September 19, 1960.

28 "Artist Found Prize Subject Outside Truro," *Cape Cod Standard-Times,* May 4, 1937.

29 Ibid.

30 Jo Hopper diary entry for September 19, 1960.

31 Jo Hopper diary entry for October 28, 1936.

32 Jo Hopper diary entry for October 23, 1937.

33 Edward Hopper Record Book II, p. 17.

34 Hilton Kramer, "Morris Kantor: A Passion for Painting," *New York Times,* February 10, 1974, sec. 2, p. 21.

35 Ibid.

36 Jo Hopper diary entry for January 18, 1939.

37 The following information on Dorothy Lapham Ferris (1887–1975) is from *Pen and Brush,* the newsletter of the Pen and Brush Club, 16 East 10 Street, New York City, October 1971, p. 3.

38 See Hugh Ferris, *The Metropolis of Tomorrow* (New York: Ives Washburn, 1929) and Carol Willis, "Drawing Towards Metropolis," in *Hugh Ferris* (Princeton, N.J.: Princeton Architectural Press, 1986).

39 Jo Hopper diary entries for February 1939.

40 Jo Hopper diary entry for January 23, 1937.

41 See James MacGregor Burns, "Court Packing: The Miscalculated Risk," in Don Congdon, ed., *The Thirties: A Time to Remember* (New York: Simon & Schuster, 1962), pp. 450–75.

42 Jo Hopper diary entry for February 9, 1937.

43 Jo Hopper diary entry for February 3, 1937.

44 Jo Hopper to Marion Hopper, letter of December 5, 1935.

45 Lloyd Goodrich to Edward Hopper, letter of August 29, 1944.

46 Edward Hopper to Lloyd Goodrich, letter of September 4, 1944.

47 Ibid.

48 Edward Hopper to John O'Connor, Jr., letter of March 12, 1937.

49 Ibid.

50 Jo Hopper diary entry for September 19, 1960.

51 John O'Connor, Jr., "Carnegie Traces Hopper's Rise to Fame," *Art Digest,* 11, April 1937, p. 14.

52 William J. Glackens had exhibited with Henri in "The Eight"; other jurors were the painters John Steuart Curry, Daniel Garber, William Paxton, and Richard Lahey.

53 Jo Hopper diary entry for September 19, 1960.

54 Ibid. See *Soir Bleu* (1914) and *Two Comedians* (1965).

55 See Leila Mechlin, "Paintings in Oil Seen at Corcoran," *Sunday Star,* March 28, 1937, part 1; "Mrs. Roosevelt Attends Preview of Art Exhibit," *Washington Post,* March 28,

1937, p. 11; "Edward Hopper's Cape Cod Wins a $2000 Prize," *Life,* May 3, 1937, p. 44.

56 Edward Hopper to Elizabeth Navas, letter of July 12, 1939.

57 Jo Hopper diary entry for April 27, 1937.

58 Jo Hopper diary entry for April 22, 1937.

59 Bernard Meyers, ed., "Scribner's American Painters Series," no. 7, *Scribner's,* 102, September 1937, pp. 32–33.

60 Jo Hopper diary entry for June 21, 1937.

61 Jo Hopper diary entry for June 20, 1937.

62 Carr, *Dos Passos,* pp. 365–75.

63 Eleanor Tracy to Edward Hopper, letter of June 11, 1937, and Edward Hopper to Eleanor Tracy, letter of June 14, 1937.

64 Jo Hopper diary entry for July 8–16, 1937.

65 Ibid.

66 Jo Hopper diary entry for September 9, 1963.

67 Jo Hopper diary entry for July 8–16, 1937.

68 Jo Hopper diary entry for August 5, 1937.

69 Jo Hopper diary entry for August 11, 1937.

70 Jo Hopper diary entry for August 24, 1937.

71 Jo Hopper diary entry for August 25, 1937.

72 Irene Slater to Jo Hopper, letter of July 20, 1956.

73 Jo Hopper diary entry for October 2, 1937.

74 Jo Hopper diary entry for October 25, 1937.

75 Jo Hopper diary entry for October 26, 1937.

76 Jo Hopper diary entry for November 14, 1937.

77 The show was at the Galerie de la Chambre Syndicale des Beaux-Arts, organized by Sterner for Art Patrons of America, Inc.; see page 183.

78 Jo Hopper diary entry for February 22, 1938.

79 Edward Hopper to Thomas Colt, letter of December 21, 1937.

80 Jo Hopper to Tom Colt, letter of February 14, 1938.

81 Ibid.

82 Jo Hopper diary entry for February 22, 1938.

83 Edward Hopper to Thomas Colt, letter of January 7, 1938.

84 In 1916, for example, Zorach shared his spot in the Forum Exhibition with his wife, the only woman in the exhibition.

85 Jo Hopper diary entry for February 26, 1938.

86 Thomas Colt to Jo Hopper, letter of March 3, 1938.

87 Edward Hopper to Thomas Colt, letter of March 26, 1938.

88 Dr. Sibley had made a house call first; the cause of Hopper's illness is not known.

89 Lloyd Goodrich in conversations with the author.

90 Jo Hopper diary entry for March 17, 1938.

91 Ibid.

92 Quoted in [Alexander Eliot], "A Certain Alienated Majesty," *Time,* May 26, 1967, p. 72.

93 Jo Hopper diary entry for March 29, 1938.

94 Jo Hopper diary entry for March 28, 1938.

95 Jo Hopper diary entry for April 10, 1938.

96 Jo Hopper diary entry for April 14, 1938.

97 Jo Hopper diary entry for April 25, 1938.

98 Jo Hopper diary entry for May 10, 1938.

99 Jo Hopper diary entry for May 18, 1938, indicates that they shopped for their art supplies at Rabinowitz in Manhattan.

100 Jo Hopper diary entry for May 20, 1938.

101 Jo Hopper diary entry for June 8, 1938.

102 Jo Hopper diary entry for June 9, 1938.

103 Jo Hopper diary entry for June 20, 1938.

104 Ibid.

105 Jo Hopper to Marion Hopper, letter of September 3, 1935; Jo Hopper diary entry for July 22, 1938.

106 Jo Hopper diary entries for June 11, 1938, and July 29, 1938 (identified incorrectly as Sept. 29).

107 Van Wyck Brooks, *Emerson and Others* (New York: E. P. Dutton, 1927), included a pioneering essay on Melville.

108 Jo Hopper diary entry for August 4, 1938.

109 The amphetamine Benzedrine, manufactured by Smith, Kline, and French, was not then a controlled substance and was commonly prescribed for "pep." Jo Hopper diary entry for August 6, 1938.

110 Edward Hopper to W. G. Constable, letter of January 26, 1939.

111 Jo Hopper diary entry for September 15, 1938.

THE STRUGGLE TO PAINT

1 Jo Hopper diary entry for January 1, 1939.

2 This is still clear today; for example, see Vincent Canby's review of the play's revival, "A Lincoln with an Agit-Prop Subtext," *New York Times,* December 12, 1993, p. 5.

3 Jo Hopper diary entry for January 7, 1939.

4 Jo Hopper diary entry for January 11, 1939.

5 Jo Hopper diary entry for January 12, 1939.

6 Jo Hopper diary entry for January 21, 1939.

7 Jo Hopper diary entry for February 2, 1939.

8 Jo Hopper diary entry for March 2, 1939.

9 Charles Burchfield diary entry for March 6–12, 1939. See J. Benjamin Townsend, ed., *Charles Burchfield's Journals: The Poetry of Place* (Albany: State University of New York Press, 1992), p. 564.

10 Jo Hopper diary entry for March 12, 1939.

11 Jo Hopper diary entry for March 18, 1939.

12 Jo Hopper diary entry for March 30, 1939.

13 Ibid.

14 Paul Valéry, *Leonardo, Poe, Mallarmé* (Princeton: Princeton University Press, 1972), v. 8, pp. 193–211.

15 Valéry, "Stendhal," in *Masters and Friends* (Princeton: Princeton University Press, 1972), p. 196.

16 Ibid.

17 Ibid., p. 197.

18 Jo Hopper diary entry for April 2, 1939.

19 Jo Hopper diary entry for April 3, 1939.

20 Jo Hopper diary entry for April 15, 1939.

21 Ibid.

22 Jo Hopper diary entry for April 18, 1939.

23 Jo Hopper diary entry for April 22, 1939.

24 Jo Hopper diary entry for April 23, 1939.

25 Jo Hopper to Marion Hopper, letter of July 8, 1939.

26 Jo Hopper to Marion Hopper, letter of June 16, 1939.

27 Edward Hopper, quoted in Goodrich, *Edward Hopper,* p. 129.

28 Richard Lahey Papers, "Reminiscences: Artists I Have Known."

29 Jo Hopper to Marion Hopper, letter of August 1939.

30 Edward Hopper to Homer Saint-Gaudens, letter of August 17, 1939.

31 Jo Hopper diary entry for September 28, 1939.

32 Jo Hopper diary entry for October 23, 1939.

33 Jo Hopper diary entry for November 6, 1939.

34 Ibid.

35 Jo Hopper diary entry for November 3, 1939. Charles MacArthur wrote (with Ben Hecht) such popular hits as *The Front Page* and *Jubilee.*

36 Helen Hayes, interview by the author, October 27, 1980, published in Gail Levin, ed., *Edward Hopper Symposium at the Whitney Museum of American Art,* "Six Who Knew Hopper," *Art Journal,* 41, summer 1981, p. 129.

37 Ibid.

38 "Helen Hayes Says Artist Edward Hopper Was Grumpy," *Arts and Antiques Weekly,* November 30, 1990, p. 10.

39 Jo Hopper diary entry for November 8, 1939.

40 Jo Hopper diary entry for November 9, 1939.

41 Jo Hopper diary entry for November 10, 1939.

42 Hayes, in Levin, ed., *Edward Hopper Symposium,* "Six Who Knew Hopper," p. 129.

43 Jo Hopper diary entry for November 14, 1939.

44 Jo Hopper diary entry for November 16, 1939.

45 Jo Hopper diary entry for December 8, 1939.

46 Jo Hopper diary entry for December 10, 1939.

47 Jo Hopper diary entry for December 11, 1939.

48 Jo Hopper diary entry for December 16, 1939.

49 Jo Hopper diary entry for December 21, 1939.

50 Ibid.

51 Jo Hopper diary entry for December 30, 1939.

52 Ibid.

THE WAR BEGINS

1 Jo Hopper diary entry for January 9, 1940.

2 Jo Hopper diary entry for January 11, 1940.

3 Jo Hopper diary entry for January 19, 1940.

4 Jo Hopper diary entry for January 22, 1940.

5 Jo Hopper diary entry for February 5, 1940.

6 Jo Hopper diary entry for January 24, 1940.

7 Jo Hopper diary entry for January 25, 1940. *Italian Masters* (New York: Museum of Modern Art, 1940).

8 Jo Hopper diary entry for January 27, 1940.

9 Jo Hopper diary entry for February 1, 1940.

10 Jo Hopper diary entry for February 5, 1940.

11 Jo Hopper diary entry for February 14, 1940.

12 Jo Hopper diary entry for February 15, 1940.

13 Jo Hopper diary entry for February 19, 1940.

14 Edward Hopper, "Office at Night," explanatory statement accompanying letter of August 25, 1948, to Norman A. Geske.

15 Ibid.

16 Ibid.

17 Edward Hopper Record Book II, p. 79.

18 Jo Hopper diary entry for March 8, 1940.

19 Jo Hopper diary entry for March 11, 1940.

20 Ibid.

21 Jo Hopper diary entry for February 2, 1937. The following quotation is from Jo Hopper diary entry for March 25, 1940.

22 Edward Hopper to Guy Pène du Bois, letter of April 11, 1940. "My dear du Bois: Calm yourself my old friend, get back in bed again. I'm not in a hurry. I hope that you will find yourself better soon. Your very devoted E. Hopper (also known as the monster)."

23 Edward Hopper to Guy Pène du Bois, letter of August 11, 1940.

24 Jo Hopper diary entry for April 18, 1940.

25 Jo Hopper diary entry for April 24, 1940.

26 Jo Hopper diary entry for April 29, 1940.

27 Jo Hopper diary entry for May 6, 1940.

28 Edward Hopper to Marion Hopper, letter of June 17, 1940.

29 Jo Hopper diary entry for July 6, 1940.

30 Jo Hopper diary entry for July 7, 1940.

31 Edward Hopper to Guy Pène du Bois, letter of August 11, 1940.

32 Ibid.

33 Ibid.

34 Ibid.

35 Pierre van Paassen, *Days of Our Years* (New York: Hilman-Curl, 1939). Jo Hopper to Dorothy Ferris, letter of July 31, 1940.

36 Jo Hopper diary entry for July 19, 1940.

37 Jo Hopper diary entry for August 12, 1940.

38 Edward Hopper to Frank Rehn, letter of August 29, 1940.

39 Jo Hopper to Marion Hopper, letter of September 4, 1940.

40 Jo Hopper to Marion Hopper, letter of September 13, 1940.

41 Jo Hopper to Marion Hopper, letter of September 17, 1940.

42 Edward Hopper Record Book II, p. 83.

43 Jimmy De Lory, interview by the author, July 29, 1991.

44 Ibid.

45 Helen Parker to Edward Hopper, letter of September 24, 1940.

46 Edward Hopper to Helen Parker, letter of September 29, 1940.

47 Edward Hopper to Lloyd B. Myers, letter of October 19, 1940.

48 For a discussion of Benton's corporate work, see Erika Doss, *Benton, Pollock, and the Politics of Modernism: From Regionalism to Abstract Expressionism* (Chicago: University of

Chicago Press, 1991), pp. 165–66 and 229–40.

49 Edward Hopper to B. H. Ragle, M.D., letter of September 30, 1940.

50 Edward Hopper to R. H. Macy & Co., letter of June 6, 1940.

51 Jo Hopper to Dorothy Ferris, letter of July 31, 1940.

52 Charles Burchfield journal, Burchfield Art Center, Buffalo, New York, quoted in Lindemann, *Art Triangle,* p. 70, n. 6.

53 Lloyd Goodrich, interview by Edna Lindemann, October 28, 1980, quoted in Lindemann, *Art Triangle,* p. 70. More recently, some art historians have strained to turn Hopper into an artist with a social message; they reinterpret his work in this context. See Gail Levin, "Edward Hopper," *New England Quarterly,* September 1988, pp. 475–79.

54 Jo N. Hopper, letter to the editor, *Sun,* December 21, 1940, Henry McBride papers.

55 Jo Hopper diary entry for December 8, 1940, recalling the opening of November 26, 1940.

56 Frank Sieberling, "Movie Scene Subject of Oil Painting: Loneliness of Big City Stressed by Artist," *Toledo Sunday Times,* July 14, 1940, p. 8.

FAILED ODYSSEY

1 Edward Alden Jewell, "Early Art Shown of Edward Hopper," *New York Times,* January 11, 1941, p. L18.

2 Jo Hopper diary entry for January 13, 1941.

3 Ibid.

4 Jo Hopper diary entry for January 19, 1941.

5 Ibid.

6 Ibid.

7 Bernard Sobel, *A Pictorial History of Burlesque* (New York: Bonanza, 1956), p. 184. In April 1942, Supreme Court Justice Aaron J. Levy used the phrase when he denied the application of a theater operator to reopen after the city had closed it down.

8 Jo Hopper diary entry for February 16, 1941.

9 Jo Hopper to Marion Hopper, letter of February 21, 1941.

10 Jo Hopper diary entry for March 9, 1941.

11 Jo Hopper diary entry for March 26, 1941.

12 Jo Hopper diary entries for March 31 and April 1 and 3, 1941.

13 Jo Hopper diary entry for April 18, 1941.

14 Jo Hopper diary entry for March 18, 1941.

15 Jo Hopper diary entry for April 26, 1941.

16 Jo Hopper diary entry for May 27, 1941.

17 Jo Hopper diary entry for May 29, 1941.

18 Jo Hopper diary entry for June 7, 1941.

19 Jo Hopper diary entry for June 12, 1941.

20 Ibid.

21 Jo Hopper diary entry for June 25, 1941.

22 Edward Hopper to Mrs. Alexander Albert, letter of February 4, 1955.

23 Jo Hopper diary entry for June 25, 1941.

24 Jo Hopper diary entry for June 27, 1941.

25 Hopper to Albert, February 4, 1955.

26 Jo Hopper diary entry for June 30, 1941.

27 Jo Hopper diary entry for July 1, 1941.

28 Jo Hopper diary entry for July 4, 1941.

29 Ibid.

30 Jo Hopper to Mary Amis Hooper, letter of August 5, 1941.

31 Jo Hopper diary entry for July 8, 1941.

32 Ibid.

33 Quoted in Carol Bauer and Lawrence Ritt, "The Work of Frances Power Cobbe: A Victorian Indictment of Wife-Beating," in Gordon W. Russell, *Violence in Intimate Relationships* (New York: PMA Publishing Corp., 1988), p. 20.

34 Jo Hopper diary entry for July 9, 1941.

35 Jo Hopper diary entry for July 10, 1941.

36 Jo Hopper diary entry for July 13, 1941.

37 Jo Hopper diary entry for July 8, 1941.

38 Jo Hopper diary entry for July 16, 1941.

39 Jo Hopper diary entry for July 17, 1941.

40 Ibid.

41 Jo Hopper diary entry for July 21, 1941.

42 Jo Hopper diary entry for July 22, 1941.

43 Jo Hopper diary entry for August 4, 1941.

44 Jo Hopper to Mary Amis Hooper, letter of August 5, 1941.

45 Jo Hopper diary entry for August 30, 1941, and elsewhere.

46 Edward Hopper to Frank Rehn, letter of September 17, 1941.

47 Jo Hopper diary entry for August 24, 1941.

48 Jo Hopper diary entry for August 17, 1941.

49 Ibid.

50 Jo Hopper diary entry for August 30, 1941.

51 Jo Hopper diary entry for September 4, 1941.

52 Ibid.

53 Jo Hopper diary entry for September 5, 1941.

54 Ibid. The next quotation is also from this source.

55 Jo Hopper diary entry for September 10, 1941.

56 Jo Hopper diary entry for September 14, 1941.

57 Edward Hopper to Frank Rehn, letter of September 17, 1941.

58 Jo Hopper diary entries for September 20 and October 25, 1941.

59 Jo Hopper diary entry for October 4, 1941. Jo recorded the canvas in the record book as *Lee Shore,* omitting the definite article; Hopper, however, called the painting *The Lee Shore* in both his 1945 monograph and his 1964 retrospective.

60 Herman Melville, *Moby Dick* (New York: Penguin Books, 1851; reprinted 1992), chap. 23, pp. 116–17.

61 Jo Hopper diary entry for October 15, 1941.

62 Jo Hopper diary entry for October 25, 1941.

63 Ibid. The following quotations are from the diary entries for October 25 and 30, 1941.

64 Jo Hopper to Van Wyck Brooks, letter of February 11, 1946, appended to letter of January 25, 1946.

65 Jo Hopper to Brooks, February 11, 1946.

66 Jo Hopper diary entry for October 30, 1941. Van Wyck Brooks, *New England Indian Summer: 1865–1915* (New York: E. P. Dutton & Co., 1940), pp. 326–27.

67 Josephine Hopper to Ethel Baker, draft of letter of November 2, 1941.

68 Jo Hopper diary entry for October 30, 1941.

69 Arnold Newman, interview by the author, September 8, 1993.

70 H. Saint-Gaudens, *American Artist and His Times,* p. 273.

71 Ibid.

72 Ibid., pp. 273–74.

73 Jo Hopper to Henry McBride, note inserted in Christmas card mailed December 24, 1941.

NIGHTHAWKS

1 Jo Hopper to Marion Hopper, letter of December 17, 1941.

2 Jo Hopper diary entry for March 24, 1959.

3 Jo Hopper to Marion Hopper, letter of January 22, 1942.

4 Jo Hopper diary entry for August 11, 1954.

5 Edward Hopper, quoted in Kuh, *Artist's Voice,* p. 134.

6 "The America of Edward Hopper," *Vogue,* 123, June 1954, p. 49.

7 Edward Hopper, quoted in Kuh, *Artist's Voice,* p. 134.

8 Edward Hopper, quoted in Goodrich, *Edward Hopper,* pp. 163–64.

9 Edward Hopper, letter to the editor, *Scribner's,* June 1927, p. 706d. Hopper may also have found one of the illustrations for "The Killers" suggestive. C. Leroy Baldridge depicted a counterman by a coffee urn that is almost a mirror image of that detail in *Nighthawks.* Hopper must have seen both the story and the illustration a second time after *Scribner's* reprinted them along with one of his own illustrations in its 50th anniversary issue in January 1937, 101, pp. 83 and 73.

10 Jo Hopper diary entry for February 8, 1942.

11 Jo Hopper diary entry for March 8, 1942.

12 Ibid.

13 Ibid.

14 Jo Hopper diary entry for March 17, 1942.

15 Xenophon, *Symposium,* 2, no. 10, trans. by O. J. Todd (Cambridge, Mass.: Harvard University Press, 1929), p. 547.

16 Jo Hopper diary entry for April 17, 1942. The following quotation is from Jo Hopper diary entry for April 18, 1942.

17 Jo Hopper diary entry for April 20, 1942.

18 Jo Hopper diary entry for April 21, 1942.

19 Elisabeth Cameron Blanchard and Manley Wellman, *The Life and Times of Sir Archie: The Story of America's Greatest Thoroughbred, 1805–1833* (Chapel Hill: University of North Carolina Press, 1958).

20 Jo Hopper diary entry for May 6, 1942.

21 Jo Hopper diary entry for May 8, 1942.

22 Jo Hopper diary entry for May 28, 1942.

23 Jo Hopper diary entry for May 12, 1942.

24 Jo Hopper diary entry for May 11, 1942.

25 Ibid.

26 Edward Hopper to B. H. Ragle, M.D., letter of July 6, 1942.

27 Edward Hopper to Frank Rehn, letter of July 4, 1942.

28 Jo Hopper diary entry for June 23, 1942.

29 Jo Hopper diary entry for July 9, 1942.

30 Ibid.

31 Edward Hopper to Frank Rehn, letter of July 10, 1942.

32 Jo Hopper diary entry for July 23, 1942.

33 Reeves Lewenthal to Edward Hopper, letter of July 27, 1942.

34 Edward Hopper to Frank Rehn, letter of July 29, 1942.

35 Edward Hopper to Reeves Lewenthal, letter of August 8, 1942.

36 Jo Hopper diary entry for September 5, 1942.

37 Jo Hopper diary entry for September 7, 1942.

38 Jo Hopper diary entry for September 17, 1942.

39 Jo Hopper diary entry for September 23, 1942.

40 Jo Hopper diary entry for September 28, 1942.

41 Jo Hopper diary entry for October 2, 1942.

42 Jerome Mellquist, *The Emergence of An American Art* (New York: Charles Scribner's Sons, 1942), pp. 293–95.

MEXICO

1 James, *American Scene,* p. 102. For a discussion of the hotel in James, see Peter Conn, *The Divided Mind: Ideology and Imagination in America, 1898–1917* (New York: Cambridge University Press, 1983), p. 40.

2 Jo Hopper to Juliana Force, postcard of February 15, 1943.

3 Edward Hopper to Juliana Force, letter of February 18, 1943.

4 Ibid.

5 The other jurors were Richard Lahey, Jerry Farnsworth, John Corbino, Bernard Karfiol, and the museum's director, C. Powell Minnigerode.

6 Jo Hopper to Mrs. Bull Tielman, draft of letter of spring 1943.

7 Jo Hopper to Henry McBride, letter of April 17, [1943].

8 Ibid.

9 Ibid.

10 Ibid.

11 Ibid.

12 Edward Hopper Record Book III, p. 3.

13 Edward Hopper to B. H. Ragle, M.D., letter of June 7, 1943.

14 Ibid.

15 Jo Hopper to Frank Rehn, postcard of July 5, 1943.

16 Jo Hopper to Frank Rehn, letter of August 19, 1943.

17 Jo Hopper to Frank Rehn, letter of September 5, 1943.

18 Ibid.

19 Ibid.

20 Edward Hopper, quoted in Squirru, "Edward Hopper," p. 12.

21 Jo Hopper to Rehn, September 5, 1943.

22 Jean Ferris Leich, interview by the author, July 11, 1988.

23 Edward Hopper to Frank Rehn, letter of August 14, 1943.

24 Jo Hopper to Frank Rehn, letter of September 5, 1943.

25 Edward Hopper to Rehn, August 14, 1943.

26 Ibid.

27 Jo Hopper to Rehn, August 19, 1943.

28 Ibid.

29 Ibid.

30 Ibid.

31 Ibid.

32 Ibid.

33 Ibid.

34 Jo Hopper to Rehn, September 5, 1943.

35 Ibid.

36 Henry McBride, "Attractions in the Galleries," *New York Evening Sun,* December 4, 1943, p. 4.

37 E[mily] G[lenauer], "At Rehn and Kraushaar's," *New York World-Telegraph,* December 7, 1943, p. 6; Royal Cortissoz, "Some Progressive Americans," *New York Herald Tribune,* December 5, 1943, sec. 4, p. 5.

WAR ON THE HOME FRONT

1 Jo Hopper to Carl Sprinchorn, letter of February 10, 1944.

2 Jo Hopper diary entry for July 11, 1944.

3 Jo Hopper diary entry for August 8, 1944.

4 Jo Hopper diary entry for August 10, 1944.

5 Jo Hopper diary entry for August 22, 1944.

6 Jo Hopper diary entry for August 23, 1944.

7 Jo Hopper diary entry for September 2, 1944.

8 Jo Hopper diary entry for September 3, 1944.

9 Jo Hopper diary entry for September 8, 1944.

10 Jo Hopper diary entry for September 10, 1944.

11 Jo Hopper to Carl Sprinchorn, letter of September 6, 1944.

12 Jo Hopper diary entry for September 12, 1944.

13 Jo Hopper diary entry for September 14, 1944.

14 Edward Hopper to Frank Rehn, letter of September 22, 1944.

15 Edward Hopper to Samuel Golden, letter of November 2, 1945.

16 Edward Hopper to Rehn, September 22, 1944.

17 Jo Hopper diary entry for September 18, 1944.

18 Jo Hopper diary entry for September 29, 1944.

19 Ibid.

20 Ibid.

21 Jo Hopper diary entry for October 8, 1944.

22 Jo Hopper diary entry for October 12, 1944.

23 Ibid.

24 Ibid.

25 Ibid.

26 Ibid.

27 Ibid.

28 Ibid.

29 Geraldine Sartain, "You and Your Car," *Independent Woman,* 18, May 1939, pp. 134–35.

30 Jo Hopper diary entry for October 12, 1944.

31 Jo Hopper diary entry for October 14, 1944.

32 Jo Hopper diary entry for October 23, 1944.

33 Josephine Hopper to Marion Hopper, letter of December 27, 1944. The National Institute of Arts and Letters was then the parent body that elected the fifty-member American Academy of Arts and Letters from its own membership. Today the two groups have been merged.

THE AESTHETIC DIVIDE

1 Edward Hopper to Dr. Roe, letter of April 20, 1945.

2 Ibid.

3 Ibid.

4 Henry Lee McFee lived in the Southwest. Present besides Hopper were Charles Burchfield, Morris Kantor, and Henry Varnum Poor, as well as Alexander Brook, John Carroll, Peppino Mangravite, Henry Mattson, George Picken, Eugene Speicher, Bradley Walker Tomlin, and Franklin Watkins. Rehn's assistant, John Clancy, helped to organize it.

5 Rehn did show the work of Helen Turner beginning in 1918 and, over the years, that of a few other women. In later years, he occasionally hung a work or two by Jo Hopper to soothe her feelings.

6 Jo Hopper diary entry for December 13, 1945.

7 Jo Hopper diary entry for May 18, 1945.

8 Jo Hopper diary entry for June 3, 1945.

9 Jo Hopper diary entry for June 5, 1945.

10 Jo Hopper diary entry for May 5, 1945.

11 Jo Hopper diary entry for May 16, 1945.

12 Jo Hopper diary entry for May 8, 1945.

13 Edward Hopper to Mrs. Frank B. Davidson, letter of January 22, 1947.

14 Edward Hopper, quoted in O'Doherty, *American Masters,* p. 11.

15 Edward Hopper, in O'Doherty interview.

16 Jo Hopper to Carl Sprinchorn, letter of November 3, 1944.

17 Jo Hopper to Carl Sprinchorn, postcard of May 27, 1945.

18 Jo Hopper diary entry for June 12, 1945.

19 Jo Hopper diary entry for June 11, 1945.

20 Jo Hopper diary entry for June 18, 1945.

21 Jo Hopper diary entry for June 30, 1945.

22 Jo Hopper diary entry for September 11, 1945.

23 Jo Hopper diary entry for July 22, 1945.

24 Ibid.

25 Jo Hopper diary entry for August 2, 1945.

26 Jo Hopper diary entry for August 15, 1945.

27 Jo Hopper diary entries for August 16 and 17, 1945.

28 Jo Hopper diary entry for August 15, 1945.

29 Jo Hopper diary entry for August 23, 1945.

30 Lewis Bergman, "Less Deadly Than the Male," *New York Times,* July 14, 1940, p. 10. Cited in Berger, "Women Drivers," p. 262.

31 Edward Hopper to Guy Pène du Bois, letter of August 23, 1945.

32 Jo Hopper diary entry for August 29, 1945.

33 Jo Hopper diary entry for August 31, 1945.

34 Jo Hopper diary entry for September 6, 1945.

35 Jo Hopper diary entry for September 10, 1945.

36 Jo Hopper diary entry for September 11, 1945.

37 Jo Hopper diary entry for September 14, 1945.

38 Jo Hopper diary entry for September 19, 1945.

39 Edward Hopper, quoted in "Traveling Man," *Time,* 51, January 19, 1948, p. 59.

40 Jo Hopper diary entry for September 24, 1945.

41 Jo Hopper diary entry for October 2, 1945.

42 Jo Hopper diary entry for October 4, 1945.

43 Jo Hopper diary entry for October 9, 1945.

44 Jo Hopper diary entry for October 17, 1945.

45 Jo Hopper diary entry for October 10, 1951.

46 Guy Pène du Bois, *Edward Hopper,* p. 8.

47 Jo Hopper diary entry for October 2, 1945.

48 Jo Hopper diary entry for October 18, 1945.

49 James Hoopes, *Van Wyck Brooks: In Search of American Culture* (Amherst: University of Massachusetts Press, 1977), p. 153.

50 Ibid., p. 154.

51 T. J. Jackson Lears, *No Place of Grace: Antimodernism and the Transformation of American Culture, 1880–1920* (New York: Pantheon Books, 1981), p. 258.

52 Ibid., p. 257.

53 Van Wyck Brooks, *New England: Indian Summer,* p. 542.

54 Ibid., pp. 542–43.

55 Van Wyck Brooks, *The Confident Years: 1885–1915* (London: J. M. Dent & Sons, 1953), p. 192.

56 Jo Hopper diary entry for November 2, 1945.

57 C. J. Bulliet, "Religious Trends Challenge Our Materialism in Chicago Annual," *Art Digest,* 20, November 1, 1945, p. 34.

58 "Artist's Choice," *Time,* November 5, 1945, p. 57; *Art Digest,* 20, November 1, 1945, cover; *Art News,* 44, November 1–14, 1945, p. 11.

59 Jo Hopper diary entry for November 28, 1945.

60 Jo Hopper diary entry for November 30, 1945.

61 Jo Hopper diary entry for December 17, 1945.

62 Jo Hopper diary entry for December 3, 1945.

63 Jo Hopper diary entry for December 11, 1945.

64 Jo Hopper diary entry for December 19, 1945.

ANXIETY

1 Jo Hopper diary entry for January 14, 1946.

2 Ibid.

3 Jo Hopper diary entry for January 22, 1946.

4 Jo Hopper to Carl Sprinchorn, February 10, 1946. (Edward borrowed the book from old friends of Jo's, the former Henri student Florence Dreyfous and her sister, whom they visited in Connecticut.) Gontran de Poncins, *Kabloona* (New York: Reynal & Hitchcock, 1941).

5 De Poncins, *Kabloona,* pp. 120–21.

6 Henry McBride, "Attractions in the Galleries," *New York Sun,* February 9, 1946, p. 9.

7 Jo Hopper diary entry for February 4, 1946.

8 Josephine Hopper to Carl Sprinchorn, letter of February 10, 1946. The following quotations are also from this letter.

9 Jo Hopper diary entry for February 20, 1946.

10 Ibid.

11 Jo Hopper diary entry for January 27, 1946.

12 Jo Hopper diary entry for February 21, 1946.

13 Jo Hopper diary entry for February 23, 1946.

14 Jo Hopper diary entry for March 1, 1946.

15 "The America of Edward Hopper," *Vogue,* p. 48.

16 Edward Hopper, interview by John Morse, *Art in America,* 48 (1960), p. 63.

17 Jo Hopper diary entry for March 4, 1946.

18 Jo Hopper diary entry for February 26, 1946.

19 Jo Hopper diary entry for April 6, 1946.

20 Jo Hopper diary entry for March 14, 1946.

21 Jo Hopper diary entries for March 26 and 16, 1946.

22 Jo Hopper diary entry for April 8, 1946.

23 Ibid.

24 Jo Hopper, diary entry for April 11, 1946.

25 Jo Hopper to Henry Schnakenberg, letter of April 26, 1946.

26 Jo Hopper diary entry for April 18, 1946.

27 Jo Hopper diary entry for April 20, 1946. This comment takes on particular irony given the eventual disposition of her artistic estate bequeathed to the Whitney Museum. See the Introduction, page xvi.

28 Jo Hopper diary entry for April 18, 1946. See also page 164.

29 Jo Hopper diary entry for April 23, 1946.

30 Jo Hopper diary entry for April 24, 1946.

31 Jo Hopper diary entries for April 25 and 26, 1946.

32 Jo Hopper diary entry for May 7, 1946.

33 Jo Hopper, quoted in O'Doherty, *American Masters,* p. 25.

34 Jo Hopper diary entry for May 8, 1946.

35 Jo Hopper diary entry for May 24, 1946.

36 Jo Hopper to Samuel Golden, letter of May 28, 1946.

37 Jo Hopper diary entry for May 31, 1946.

38 Jo Hopper diary entry for June 11, 1946.

39 Ibid.

40 Jo Hopper diary entry for September 21, 1946.

41 Jo Hopper diary entry for September 19, 1946.

42 Jo Hopper diary entry for September 21, 1946.

43 Edward Hopper Record Book III, p. 19.

44 See also page 266.

45 Mildred Faulk, "Washington Square Evictions Arouses Colony in Village," *New York Sun,* February 4, 1947.

46 Jo Hopper diary entry for April 17, 1947.

47 Faulk, "Washington Square Evictions."

48 Ibid.

49 Jo Hopper diary entry for April 17, 1947.

50 Jo Hopper to the Federation of American Artists, draft of letter of February 7, 1949.

51 Jo Hopper to George Harold Edgell, director of Museum of Fine Arts, Boston, letter of September 27, 1948. Actually, Dos Passos was living there in 1922, just after the novel was published, rather than during the period when he wrote it. Elaine Orr Thayer, the wife of Scofield Thayer, the editor of the *Dial,* lived on the first floor, in an open marriage arrangement. This explains the genesis of the magazine there.

52 Virgil, *Aeneid,* II, 1,7. "Conticuere omnes ... Myrmidonum Dolopumve ... duri miles Vlixi" ("All fell silent ... of the Myrmidons and Dolopes ... soldier of hard Ulysses").

53 Horace, *Odes,* 3.1.4. The poet took on the role of priest and teacher "virginibus puerisque" ("for girls and boys").

54 "Artists Make a 'Sentimental' Plea to OPA in Effort to Stay Eviction," *New York Times,* February 19, 1947, p. 27.

55 "University, Artists, Heard at OPA," *Villager,* March 6, 1947.

56 "Ruling of Board Stays Eviction," *Villager,* May 15, 1947.

57 Clement Greenberg, "Review of the Whitney Annual," *Nation,* December 28, 1946, reprinted in John O'Brian, ed., *Clement Greenberg: The Collected Essays and Criticism,* v. 2 (Chicago: University of Chicago Press, 1986), p. 118.

58 Ibid.

59 Parker Tyler, " 'Encyclopedism' of American Art," *View,* October 1945, p. 17.

60 John Bernard Myers, *Tracking the Marvelous: A Life in the New York Art World* (New York: Random House, 1983), p. 70.

61 Ibid.

62 Edward Hopper Record Book III, p. 21.

63 Ibid., p. 23.

64 Sherwood Anderson, *Marching Men* (New York: John Lane Co., 1917), p. 9.

65 Ibid., p. 38.

66 Ibid., p. 39.

67 Ibid., pp. 39–40.

68 Ibid., p. 155.

69 Burton Rascoe, *Chicago Tribune,* 1919, quoted in Walter B. Rideout, "Sherwood Anderson," in James J. Martine, ed., *Dictionary of Literary Biography,* v. 9, *American Novelists, 1910–1945* (Detroit: Gale Research Co., 1981), p. 23.

70 "Traveling Man," *Time,* 51, January 19, 1948, p. 60.

71 Carr, *Dos Passos,* pp. 455–61.

72 Jo Hopper to Marion Hopper, letter of October 6, 1947.

73 Ibid.

74 Ibid.

75 Jo Hopper to J. N. Rosenberg, draft of letter of December 16, 1947.

76 Jo Hopper to Tommy Gray, letter of December 22, 1947.

77 Jo Hopper diary entry for October 28, 1962.

78 Jo Hopper diary entry for December 25, 1947.

79 Edward Hopper, quoted in unpublished interview by Alexander Eliot and Joan Dye, reported by Joan Dye, at Charles French restaurant, May 19, 1955.

80 Jo Hopper to Tommy Gray, December 22, 1947.

81 Ibid.

ILLNESS AND LOSS

1 Henry McBride, "The Great Open Places: Edward Hopper Refuses to Notice the Overpopulation of the Town," *New York Sun,* January 16, 1948, p. 23.

2 Robert Coates, "The Art Galleries: Edward Hopper and Jackson Pollock," *New Yorker,* January 17, 1948, p. 57.

3 Jo Hopper diary entry for January 15, 1948.

4 "Traveling Man," *Time,* p. 60.

5 Carlyle Burrows, "Art of the Week: Some Stimulating Moods of Realism," *New York Herald Tribune,* January 11, 1948, sec. 6, p. 3.

6 Aline B. Louchheim, "Realism and Hopper," *New York Times,* January 11, 1948, sec. 2, p. 9.

7 Emily Genauer, "Courageously Realistic Oils Exhibited by Edward Hopper," *New York World-Telegram,* January 6, 1948, p. 12.

8 Ibid.

9 Quoted in "Traveling Man," *Time,* pp. 59–60.

10 Edward Hopper to Mrs. Frank B. Davidson of Richmond, Ind., letter of January 22, 1947.

11 Edward Hopper, quoted in "Self-made Artist Will Be Featured in American Group," *Cincinnati Times Star,* September 8, 1948.

12 "Are These Men the Best Painters in America Today?" *Look,* February 1948, p. 44.

13 "The Year's Best: 1948," *Art News,* 47, January 1949, p. 54.

14 Jo Hopper diary entry for March 20, 1948. The Hoppers had met Feininger and his wife three years earlier at a Whitney Museum opening.

15 Edward Hopper to Carl Zigrosser, letter of April 13, 1948.

16 Van Wyck Brooks, *The Times of Melville and Whitman* (New York: E. P. Dutton & Co., 1948).

17 E. B. White, *One Man's Meat* (New York: Harper & Brothers, 1944), p. 35.

18 Enid Saies Buhre to Edward Hopper, letter of May 23, 1948.

19 Edward Hopper to Enid Saies Buhre, letter of June 17, 1948.

20 Ibid.

21 Ibid.

22 Jo Hopper diary entry for September 1, 1948.

23 Jo Hopper diary entry for September 9, 1948.

24 Jo Hopper diary entry for September 15, 1949, recalls the show.

25 Jo Hopper diary entry for August 21, 1948.

26 Jo Hopper diary entries for August 10 and September 1, 1948.

27 Jo Hopper diary entry for September 7, 1948.

28 Jo Hopper diary entry for September 9, 1948.

29 Ibid.

30 Ibid.

31 Ibid.

32 Jo Hopper diary entry of September 13, 1948.

33 Ibid.

34 See "Ballade des Dames du Temps Jadis" from *The Testament,* which begins with a reference to "Flora la belle Rommaine," in *The Poems of François Villon,* trans. and intro. by Galway Kinnell (New York: New American Library, 1965), pp. 66–69.

35 Jo Hopper diary entry for September 15, 1948.

36 Jo Hopper diary entry for September 22, 1948.

37 Ibid.

38 Edward Hopper to Frank Rehn, letter of September 26, 1948.

39 Ibid.

40 Ibid.

41 Jo Hopper diary entry for October 14, 1948.

42 Ibid.

43 Jo Hopper diary entry for October 16, 1948.

44 Ibid.

45 Ibid.

46 Jo Hopper diary entry for October 18, 1948.

47 Jo Hopper diary entry for October 20, 1948.

48 Squirru, "Edward Hopper," p. 16.

MELANCHOLY REFLECTION

1 Jo Hopper diary entry for January 16, 1949.

2 Edward Hopper Record Book III, p. 29.

3 Jo Hopper to Marion Hopper, letter of January 1, 1949.

4 Edward Hopper to Elizabeth Navas, letter of June 28, 1952.

5 Jo Hopper diary entry for August 29, 1949.

6 The return of this painting took place soon after the Soviet blockade of Berlin and at the time of the Western powers' Berlin airlift. That July, the Senate ratified the North Atlantic Treaty Organization (NATO), which had been founded the previous April. At the same time, Communists were poised to take over China from the Nationalists.

7 Jo Hopper diary entry for January 20, 1949.

8 Ibid.

9 Jo Hopper diary entry for January 21, 1949.

10 Jo Hopper diary entry for January 24, 1949.

11 Jo Hopper diary entry for January 25, 1949. Jo first recorded her name as Bernice Adams.

12 Jo Hopper diary entry for January 25, 1949.

13 Jo Hopper diary entry for February 19, 1949.

14 Jo Hopper diary entry for March 12, 1949.

15 Berenice Abbott, telephone interview by the author, 1986. Jo Hopper diary entry for July 2, 1949.

16 Jo Hopper diary entry for January 26, 1949.

17 Jo Hopper diary entry for February 1, 1949.

18 Ibid.

19 Jo Hopper diary entry for February 6, 1949.

20 Jo Hopper diary entries for February 14 and 17, 1949.

21 Jo Hopper diary entry for February 19, 1949.

22 Jo Hopper diary entry for February 21, 1949.

23 Jo Hopper to J. Donald Adams, letter of February 26, 1949.

24 Jo Hopper diary entry for March 1, 1949. He told O'Doherty, *American Masters,* p. 15, "I like Renan's *Life of Jesus.*" See Ernest Renan, *The Life of Jesus* (New York: Modern Library, 1927). Hopper could have known of Henry James's interest in Renan, including James's review "Souvenirs d'Enfance et de Jeunesse," *Atlantic Monthly,* August 1883, which discussed *The Life of Jesus.* See Henry James, *Literary Criticism: French Writers* (New York: The Library of America, 1984), p. 636.

25 Jo Hopper diary entry for March 5, 1949.

26 Jo Hopper diary entries for March 2 and 3, 1949.

27 Jo Hopper diary entry for March 7, 1949.

28 Jo Hopper diary entry for March 25, 1949.

29 Jo Hopper diary entry for April 4, 1949.

30 Jo Hopper diary entry for April 7, 1949.

31 Jo Hopper diary entry for April 11, 1949.

32 Jo Hopper diary entries for April 11 and 12, 1949.

33 Jo Hopper diary entry for April 14, 1949. John Rewald, *Paul Cézanne: A Biography* (New York: Simon & Schuster, 1948).

34 Jo Hopper diary entry for April 20, 1949.

35 Jo Hopper diary entry for April 25, 1949.

36 Jo Hopper diary entries for April 25, 29, and May 3, 1949.

37 Jo Hopper diary entry for May 4, 1949.

38 Jo Hopper diary entry for May 10, 1949.

39 Jo Hopper diary entry for May 30, 1949.

40 Ibid.

41 Saul K. Padover, ed., *Thomas Jefferson on Democracy* (New York: Penguin Books, 1946).

42 Ibid., pp. 90–91.

43 Jo Hopper diary entry for August 9, 1949.

44 Virginia Woolf, *A Room of One's Own* (New York: Harcourt Brace Jovanovich, 1989 reprint of 1929 edition), pp. 52–53.

45 Ibid., p. 53.

46 Ibid., p. 55.

47 Jo Hopper diary entry for August 11, 1949.

48 Jo Hopper diary entries for August 11 and 18, 1949. Edward read Jo T. S. Eliot's essay on Baudelaire on this latter date.

49 Jo Hopper diary entry for August 19, 1949.

50 Jo Hopper diary entry for August 25, 1949.

51 See Dorothy Gees Seckler, "History of the Provincetown Art Colony," in *Provincetown Painters 1890's–1970's* (Syracuse, N.Y.: Everson Museum of Art, 1977), p. 65; for other information on this trend in Provincetown, see pp. 59–79.

52 Jo Hopper diary entry for August 25, 1949.

53 Seckler, "Provincetown," p. 65.

54 Jo Hopper diary entry for September 1, 1949.

55 Ibid.

56 Jo Hopper diary entry for September 10, 1949.

57 Jo Hopper diary entry for September 20, 1949.

58 Jo Hopper diary entry for October 19, 1949.

59 Jo Hopper diary entry for September 21, 1949.

60 Edward Hopper Record Book III, p. 31.

61 Edward Hopper, unpublished interview by Malcolm Preston, 1951, Truro, Massachusetts.

62 Jo Hopper to Carl Sprinchorn, letter of October 24, 1949. See also Jo Hopper diary entry for September 30, 1949.

63 Jo Hopper to Carl Sprinchorn, undated letter.

64 Jo Hopper diary entry for October 19, 1949.

65 Jo Hopper diary entry for October 20, 1949. The following quotation is also from this entry.

66 Jo Hopper diary entry for October 20, 1949.

67 Elsa-Ruth Herron, interviews with the author, July 1991 and earlier; see also Alan M. Wald, *The New York Intellectuals: The Rise*

and Decline of the Anti-Stalinist Left from the 1930s to the 1980s (Chapel Hill: University of North Carolina Press, 1987), pp. 57–58.

68 Jo Hopper diary entry for November 6, 1949, recapitulating November 3, 1949.

69 Jo Hopper diary entry for November 7, 1949.

70 Jo Hopper diary entry for November 22, 1949.

71 Jo Hopper diary entry for November 23, 1949.

72 Jo Hopper diary entry for November 30, 1949.

73 Jo Hopper diary entry for December 3, 1949.

74 Jo Hopper diary entry for December 6, 1949.

75 Edward Hopper Record Book III, p. 33.

76 Jo Hopper diary entry for December 24, 1949.

A RETROSPECTIVE YEAR

1 Jo Hopper diary entry for January 30, 1950.

2 Jo Hopper diary entry for January 16, 1950.

3 Jo Hopper diary entry for February 1, 1950.

4 Jo Hopper diary entries for January 26 and 27, 1950.

5 Emory Lewis, "Painter Edward Hopper Has Show at Whitney Museum," *Cue,* February 4, 1950, p. 16. The following references are also from this article.

6 Jo Hopper diary entry for February 8, 1950.

7 Jo Hopper diary entry for February 11, 1950.

8 Lewis Mumford, "The Art Galleries, Two Americans," *New Yorker,* 9, November 11, 1933, pp. 76–78.

9 Jo Hopper diary entry for March 8, 1950. Burchfield noted in his journal entry for February 14, 1950, that Hopper was "in good spirits." See Townsend, ed., *Burchfield's Journals,* p. 594.

10 Jo Hopper diary entry for March 10, 1950.

11 Jo Hopper diary entry for March 3, 1950.

12 "The Silent Witness," *Time,* December 24, 1956, p. 37.

13 Edward Hopper to Flora Miller, letter of February 26, 1950. The following two quotations are also from this letter.

14 Jo Hopper diary entry for March 26, 1950.

15 Jo Hopper diary entry for March 3, 1950.

16 Howard Devree, "Hopper Since 1907," *New York Times,* February 12, 1950, sec. 2, p. 9.

17 Carlyle Burrows, "Hopper: A Steady Climb to Eminence," *New York Herald Tribune,* February 12, 1950, sec. 5, p. 6.

18 James Thrall Soby, "Arrested Time by Edward Hopper," *Saturday Review,* 33, March 4, 1950, p. 43.

19 Margaret Breuning, "The Whitney Hails Edward Hopper," *Art Digest,* February 15, 1950, vol. 24, p. 10.

20 "By Transcription," *Time,* 55, February 20, 1950, p. 60.

21 Charles Burchfield, "Hopper: Career of Silent Poetry," *Art News,* March 1950, v. 49, pp. 15–16.

22 Ibid., p. 63.

23 Ibid.

24 Ralph Pearson, "A Modern Viewpoint," *Art Digest,* 24, March 1, 1950, p. 11.

25 Robert M. Coates, "The Art Galleries: Edward Hopper," *New Yorker,* 26, February 25, 1950, p. 77.

26 Robert Myron Coates was author of *The Eater of Darkness,* 1929; *Yesterday's Burdens,* 1933; *The Bitter Season,* 1946; *Wysteria Cottage,* 1948; and other works of fiction.

27 Jo Hopper diary entry for March 10, 1950.

28 Jo Hopper diary entry for April 16, 1950.

29 Jo Hopper to J. Donald Adams, letter of March 2, 1950.

30 Ibid.

31 Ibid.

32 J. Donald Adams, "Speaking of Books," *New York Times Book Review,* April 16, 1950, p. 2.

33 "Relentless Realist," *Newsweek,* February 20, 1950, p. 84.

34 Jo Hopper diary entry for March 19, 1950.

35 Jo Hopper diary entry for March 23, 1950.

36 Jo Hopper to Marion Hopper, letter of April 4, 1950.

37 "Edward Hopper: Famous American Realist Has Retrospective Show," *Life,* April 17, 1950, pp. 100–5.

38 "Jackson Pollock: Is He the Greatest Living Painter in the United States?" *Life,* August 8, 1949.

39 "Edward Hopper," *Life,* p. 100.

40 Ibid., p. 103.

41 Ibid., p. 104.

42 Jo Hopper diary entry for April 20, 1950.

43 Ibid.

44 Jo Hopper diary entry for April 28, 1950.

45 Jo Hopper diary entry for May 9, 1950.

46 Jo Hopper diary entry for May 11, 1950.

47 Jo Hopper diary entry for May 13, 1950.

48 Ibid.

49 Jo Hopper diary entry for June 2, 1950.

50 Jo Hopper diary entry for June 3, 1950.

51 Harold T. Bers, "Puzzles: Mosaic in Words," *New York Times,* June 18, 1950, p. 54.

52 Edward Hopper to Hermon More, letter of May 30, 1950.

53 Quoted in Jo Hopper diary entry for May 25, 1950.

54 Jo Hopper diary entry for May 25, 1950.

55 Jo Hopper diary entry for June 10, 1050.

56 Jo Hopper diary entry for June 11, 1950.

57 Jo Hopper diary entry for June 13, 1950.

58 Ibid.

59 Albert J. Guerard, *André Gide* (Cambridge, Mass.: Harvard University Press, 1969), pp. 37, 53.

60 For Gide's case, see Guerard, *André Gide,* p. 78.

61 Jo Hopper diary entry for August 15, 1950.

62 Jo Hopper diary entries for August 16 and 18, 1950.

63 Jo Hopper diary entry for August 19, 1950.

64 Jo Hopper diary entry for August 21, 1950.

65 Jo Hopper diary entry for August 29, 1950.

66 Jo Hopper to Carl Sprinchorn, letter of September 8, 1950.

67 Jo Hopper diary entry for August 22, 1950.

68 Jo Hopper diary entry for August 31, 1950.

69 Jo Hopper diary entry for September 7, 1950.

70 Jo Hopper diary entry for September 9, 1950.

71 Jo Hopper diary entry for September 13, 1950.

72 Ibid.

73 See Jo Hopper to Carl Sprinchorn, letter of September 20, 1950, for her response to this letter.

74 Jo Hopper diary entry for September 19, 1950.

75 Jo Hopper to Sprinchorn, September 20, 1950.

76 Jo Hopper diary entry for September 19, 1950.

77 Ibid.

78 Jo Hopper diary entry for September 27, 1950.

79 Ibid.

80 Jo Hopper diary entry for September 29, 1950.

81 Ibid.

82 Jo Hopper diary entry for October 3, 1950.

83 Jo Hopper diary entry for October 5, 1950.

84 Jo Hopper diary entry for October 4, 1950.

85 Jo Hopper diary entry for October 10, 1950.

86 Ibid.

87 Jo Hopper diary entry for October 11, 1950.

88 Ibid.

89 Jo Hopper diary entry for October 12, 1950.

90 Ibid. Elizabeth Taylor, "Gravement Endommagé," *New Yorker,* October 7, 1950, pp. 28–31.

91 Taylor, "Gravement Endommagé," p. 28.

92 Jo Hopper diary entry for October 13, 1950.

93 Jo Hopper diary entry for October 30, 1950. The succeeding quotations are also from this entry.

94 Jo Hopper diary entry for November 15, 1950.

95 Jo Hopper diary entry for November 12, 1950.

96 Jo Hopper diary entry for November 13, 1950.

97 Ibid.

98 Jo Hopper diary entries for October 22, 1951, and January 4, 1960.

99 See John Ferguson, *A Companion to Greek Tragedy* (Austin: University of Texas Press, 1972), p. 244.

100 Jo Hopper diary entry for December 12, 1950.

101 Jo Hopper diary entry for December 13, 1950.

102 Jo Hopper diary entry for December 18, 1950.

103 William Carlos Williams, *The Great American Novel* (Paris: Three Mountains Press, 1923), p. 47.

104 Edward Hopper, "John Sloan," p. 174.

105 Jo Hopper diary entry for April 15, 1952.

106 Jo Hopper diary entry for December 28, 1950. The film won Mankiewicz two Academy Awards, for script and direction.

107 Quoted in Richard Winnington, "Film of the Month: All About Eve," *Sight and Sound,* 11, January 1951, p. 374.

MEXICO AGAIN

1 Hermann Warner "Bill" Williams, Jr., director of the Corcoran Gallery, Washington, D.C.

2 Jo Hopper to J. Donald Adams, letter of January 14, 1951.

3 Jo Hopper to Adams, January 14, 1951. John Keats, *Works* (New York: Houghton, Mifflin & Co., 1899), p. 9, "On First Looking Into Chapman's Homer": "Yet did I never breathe its pure serene / till I heard Chapman...."

4 Jo Hopper diary entry for January 10, 1951. In the light of the recent controversy over showing Robert Mapplethorpe's photography at the Corcoran, the attitude reflected by this comment suggests that censorship has long been resorted to by this institution located in the midst of the nation's lawmakers.

5 Jo Hopper diary entry for January 13, 1951.

6 Jo Hopper diary entry for January 26, 1951.

7 Jo Hopper diary entry for January 28, 1951.

8 Jo Hopper diary entry for February 4, 1951.

9 Jo Hopper diary entry for February 13, 1951.

10 Ibid.

11 Jo Hopper diary entry for March 2, 1951.

12 Edward Hopper to Hermann Warner Williams, Jr., letter of April 3, 1951.

13 Edward Hopper, "A Statement by the Chairman of the Jury," Twenty-second Biennial Exhibition of Contemporary American Oil Paintings, Corcoran Gallery of Art, 1951, n.p.

14 Ibid.

15 Jo Hopper diary entry for March 4, 1951.

16 Florence S. Berryman, "Corcoran Gallery's 22nd Biennial Opens Today," *Sunday Star,* Washington, D.C., April 1, 1951, p. C3.

17 Statement of the jury signed by Hopper and the other members, dated March 1, 1951, recorded in Goodrich's hand.

18 Jo Hopper diary entry for March 22, 1951. Ironically, Jo predicted what the Whitney Museum would do to her work as soon as they got the opportunity. See the Introduction, page xvi.

19 Jo Hopper diary entry for March 22, 1951.

20 Theresa Bernstein, in conversation with the author, 1991.

21 Jo Hopper diary entry for March 22, 1951.

22 Jo Hopper diary entry for April 1, 1951.

23 Jo Hopper diary entry for April 12, 1951.

24 Jo Hopper diary entry for May 29, 1951.

25 Jo Hopper diary entry for July 17, 1951.

26 Edward Hopper to Guy Pène du Bois, letter of August 2, 1953.

27 Jo Hopper to Frank Rehn, postcard of June 18, 1951.

28 Jo Hopper diary entry for October 12, 1951.

29 Jo Hopper to Frank Rehn, postcard of August 1, 1951.

30 Jo Hopper to Carl Sprinchorn, letter of October 15, 1951.

31 Jo Hopper to Mrs. Crawford J. Campbell, postcard of May 26, 1951.

32 Jo Hopper diary entry for July 13, 1951.

33 Ibid.

34 Jo Hopper diary entry for July 17, 1951.

35 Jo Hopper diary entry for August 10, 1951.

36 Lionel Trilling, "Introduction," to Henry James, *The Princess Casamassima* (New York: Macmillan Co., 1948), p. vi.

37 For example, see Genauer, "Courageously," p. 12.

38 Trilling, "Introduction," p. xiv.

39 Ibid., p. xxviii.

40 Ibid., pp. xxx–xxxi.

41 Jo Hopper diary entry for August 18, 1951.

42 Jo Hopper diary entry for August 31, 1951.

43 Jo Hopper diary entry for September 11, 1951.

44 Jo Hopper to Marion Hopper, letter of October 6, 1951.

45 Jo Hopper diary entry for September 6, 1951.

46 Jo Hopper diary entry for September 23, 1951.

47 Jo Hopper diary entry for September 11, 1951.

48 Jo Hopper diary entry for September 17, 1951.

49 Jo Hopper diary entry for July 17, 1951.

50 Jo Hopper to Dr. Hiebert of Provincetown, draft of undated letter.

51 Jo Hopper diary entry for September 23, 1951.

52 Edward and Jo Hopper to Frank Rehn, letter of October 7, 1951. See Edmund Wilson, "The Jumping-Off Place," *New Republic,* 69, December 23, 1931, pp. 156–8, in which he describes a seaside hotel on the West coast where "the suicide rate is twice that of the Middle-Atlantic coast."

53 Robert Hatch, "At the Tip of Cape Cod," *Horizon*, 3, July 1961, p. 11.

54 Jo Hopper diary entry for October 3, 1951.

55 Jo Hopper diary entry for October 1, 1951.

56 Ibid.

57 Jo Hopper diary entry for October 2, 1951.

58 Jo Hopper diary entry for October 5, 1951. She read Rachel Louise Carson, "The Sea," from issues that had come when they were in Mexico (*New Yorker,* June 2, 1951, pp. 32–6 ff; June 9, pp. 34–8 ff; and June 16, pp. 35–8 ff).

59 Jo Hopper diary entry for October 5, 1951.

60 Jo Hopper diary entry for October 9, 1951.

61 Ibid.

62 The combination of history and literature in *The Oregon Trail* (1849) would have appealed to Hopper, but the recent publication (1948) of Parkman's lost *Journals* had probably caught his attention.

63 Jo Hopper diary entry for October 24, 1951.

64 Jo Hopper to Marion Hopper, letter of November 15, 1951.

65 Jo Hopper to Marion Hopper, letter of December 3, 1951.

66 Arthur Rimbaud, *Poésies* (Paris: Mercure de France, 1950).

PLANNING *REALITY*

1 Jo Hopper diary entries for January 6 and 10, 1952.

2 Jo Hopper diary entry for January 9, 1952.

3 Ibid.

4 Ibid.

5 Jo Hopper diary entry for March 2, 1952.

6 Jo Hopper to Dr. Hiebert of Provincetown, draft of undated letter.

7 Jo Hopper diary entry for February 9, 1952.

8 Jo Hopper diary entry for February 22, 1952.

9 Jo Hopper diary entry for February 20, 1952.

10 Ibid.

11 Ibid.

12 Ibid.

13 Ibid.

14 Jo Hopper diary entry for February 28, 1952.

15 Ibid.

16 Ibid.

17 Jo Hopper diary entry for April 28, 1952.

18 Jo Hopper diary entry for May 5, 1952.

19 Jo Hopper diary entry for May 6, 1952.

20 Jo Hopper diary entry for May 5, 1952.

21 Jo Hopper diary entry for May 10, 1952.
22 Jo Hopper diary entry for May 11, 1952.
23 Jo Hopper diary entry for May 14, 1952.
24 Jo Hopper diary entry for May 22, 1952.
25 Edward Hopper Record Book III, p. 45.
26 Jo Hopper diary entry for August 28, 1953.
27 Jo Hopper diary entry for May 12, 1952, and again for May 26, 1952.
28 Jo Hopper diary entry for May 10, 1952.
29 Jo Hopper diary entry for May 13, 1952.
30 Jo Hopper diary entry for June 5, 1952.
31 Jo Hopper diary entry for June 9, 1952.
32 Jo Hopper diary entry for June 16, 1952.
33 Jo Hopper diary entry for June 20, 1952.
34 Jo Hopper diary entry for June 25, 1952.
35 Jo Hopper diary entry for June 27, 1952.
36 Stuart Preston, "Art Survey by Nations," *New York Times,* July 20, 1952, sec. 10, p. 2.
37 Emily Genauer, "National Pavilions in Big Venice Biennial Exhibit Offer Surprises," *New York Herald Tribune,* June 29, 1952, sec. 4, p. 8.
38 Jo Hopper diary entry for July 27, 1952.
39 Jo Hopper diary entry for August 15, 1952.
40 Jo Hopper diary entry for August 20, 1952.
41 Jo Hopper diary entry for August 30, 1952.
42 Jo Hopper diary entry for September 7, 1952.
43 Jo Hopper diary entry for September 13, 1952.
44 Jo Hopper diary entry for September 10, 1952.
45 Jo Hopper diary entries for September 19 and 20, 1952.
46 Jo Hopper diary entry for September 20, 1952.
47 Edward Hopper to Frank Rehn, letter of September 28, 1952.
48 Jo Hopper to Bee Blanchard, letter of October 14, 1952.
49 Edward Hopper Record Book III, p. 47.
50 Edward Hopper to Frank Rehn, letter of October 21, 1952.
51 Jo Hopper diary entry for November 10, 1952.
52 Jo Hopper diary entry for November 18, 1952.

53 Jo Hopper diary entry for December 6, 1952.
54 Jo Hopper diary entry for December 8, 1952.
55 Ibid.
56 Ibid.
57 Jo Hopper diary entry for December 9, 1952.
58 Edward Hopper to Frank Rehn, postcard of December 17, 1952.
59 Jo Hopper diary entry for December 14, 1952.
60 Edward Hopper to Frank Rehn, letter of December 30, 1952.
61 Ibid.

REALITY

1 Jo Hopper diary entry for January 9, 1953.
2 Jo Hopper diary entry for January 13, 1953.
3 Ibid.
4 Edward Hopper to Frank Rehn, letter of January 21, 1953.
5 Edward Hopper to Rehn, January 21, 1953. The museum was then run by E. R. Frissel.
6 Jo Hopper diary entry for January 20, 1953.
7 Ibid.
8 Edward Hopper to Rehn, January 21, 1953.
9 Jo Hopper diary entry for January 21, 1953.
10 Ibid.
11 Jo Hopper diary entry for January 30, 1953.
12 Jo Hopper to Frank Rehn, John Clancy, and Margreta, letter of February 2, 1953.
13 Squirru, "Edward Hopper," pp. 11–17.
14 Crotty, *Provincetown Profiles,* p. 33.
15 Jo Hopper diary entry for February 11, 1953.
16 Jo Hopper to Frank Rehn, letter of February 17, 1953.
17 Jo Hopper to Rehn, February 17, 1953, and Jo Hopper diary entry for February 17, 1953.
18 Jo Hopper diary entry for February 18, 1953.
19 Jo Hopper diary entry for March 5, 1953.

20 Ibid.

21 Jo Hopper diary entry for March 9, 1953.

22 Joseph Solman, telephone interview with the author, April 19, 1992.

23 Jo Hopper diary entry for March 16, 1953.

24 "2 Exhibits at Museum on Friday," *Richmond Times-Dispatch,* February 8, 1953.

25 Jewett and Jean Campbell, interview with the author, January 10, 1989, Richmond, Va.

26 Leslie Cheek, Jr., interview with the author, January 10, 1989, Richmond, Va.

27 Leslie Cheek, Jr., to Gordon Bailey Washburn, letter of March 24, 1953.

28 Jo Hopper diary entry for March 23, 1953 [listed as December 23].

29 Ibid.

30 Jo Hopper to Lloyd Goodrich, letter of March 23, 1953. The text of this letter was copied out in full in her diary entry for that day. The author held regular conversations with Goodrich during the period 1976–1984.

31 Jo Hopper diary entry for March 24, 1953; letter received on file at the Whitney Museum.

32 Edward Hopper to Guy Pène du Bois, letter of March 26, 1953.

33 Jo Hopper diary entries for March 24 and 26, 1953.

34 Jo Hopper to Rosalind Irvine, letter of April 6, 1953.

35 Jo Hopper diary entry for April 13, 1953.

36 Edward Hopper, "Statements by Four Artists," *Reality,* 1, no. 1, spring 1953.

37 Jo Hopper diary entry for May 4, 1953.

38 Edward Hopper to Lewis Mumford, letter of May 12, 1954.

39 Jo Hopper diary entry for April 9, 1953.

40 Jo Hopper diary entry for April 27, 1953.

41 Ibid.

42 Jo Hopper to J. Donald Adams, letter of May 11, 1953.

43 Jo Hopper diary entry for May 4, 1953.

44 Ibid.

45 Ibid.

46 Ibid.

47 Jo Hopper diary entry for May 18, 1953.

48 Jo Hopper diary entry for June 1, 1953.

49 Edward Hopper to Guy Pène du Bois, letter of August 2, 1953.

50 Edward Hopper to Lewis Mumford, letter of May 12, 1954.

51 Abe Lerner, interview with the author, April 15, 1992.

52 Jo Hopper diary entry for May 8, 1953.

53 Jo Hopper diary entry for May 9, 1953.

54 Jo Hopper diary entry for May 10, 1953.

55 Jo Hopper diary entry for May 12, 1953.

56 Jo Hopper diary entry for May 11, 1953.

57 Jo Hopper diary entry for May 12, 1953.

58 Jo Hopper diary entry for June 3, 1953.

59 Jo Hopper to Mrs. H. A. Butler, letter of June 29, 1953.

60 Ibid.

61 Jo Hopper diary entry for April 13, 1953.

62 Jo Hopper diary entry for June 19, 1953.

63 Ibid.

64 Jo Hopper diary entry for June 23, 1953.

65 Ibid.

66 Jo Hopper diary entry for July 5, 1953.

67 Jo Hopper diary entry for July 22, 1953.

68 Ibid.

69 Edward Hopper to Guy Pène du Bois, letter of August 2, 1953.

70 Jo Hopper diary entry for August 24, 1953.

71 Jo Hopper diary entry for July 22, 1953.

72 Ethel Lisenby, interview with the author, July 24, 1991, Truro, Mass.

73 Jo Hopper diary entry for August 6, 1953.

74 André L'Hote, *De la Palette à l'Ecritoire* (Paris: Editions Correa, 1943).

75 L'Hote, "Article on Picasso by Vlaminck," p. 7 of Hopper handwritten transcript.

76 Jo Hopper diary entry for August 7, 1953.

77 Squirru, "Edward Hopper," p. 15.

78 Jo Hopper diary entry for August 24, 1953.

79 Ibid.

80 Ibid.

81 Jo Hopper diary entry for August 25, 1953.

82 Jo Hopper diary entry for August 27, 1953.

83 Ibid.

84 Ibid.

85 Ibid.

86 Jo Hopper diary entry for August 28, 1953.

87 Jo Hopper diary entry for August 31, 1953.

88 Jo Hopper diary entry for September 3, 1953.

89 Jo Hopper diary entry for August 31, 1953.

90 Ibid.

91 Jo Hopper diary entry for September 2, 1953.

92 Jo Hopper diary entry for August 31, 1953.

93 Jo Hopper diary entry for September 2, 1953.

94 Jo Hopper diary entry for September 9, 1953.

95 Jo Hopper diary entry for September 14, 1953.

96 Jo Hopper diary entry for September 13, 1953.

97 John Clancy to Edward and Jo Hopper, letter of September 15, 1953.

98 Jo Hopper diary entry for September 15, 1953.

99 Ibid.

100 Jo Hopper diary entry for September 21, 1953.

101 Jo Hopper diary entry for October 19, 1953.

102 Ibid.

103 Jo Hopper diary entry for October 22, 1953.

104 Ibid.

105 Jo Hopper diary entry for October 29, 1953.

106 Jo Hopper diary entry for November 8, 1953.

107 Ibid.

108 Jo Hopper diary entry for November 13, 1953.

109 Ibid.

110 Jo Hopper diary entry for November 17, 1953.

111 Ibid.

112 Ibid.

113 Jo Hopper diary entry for November 20, 1953.

114 Jo Hopper diary entry for December 5, 1953.

115 Jo Hopper to Mr. and Mrs. Maurice Sievan, letter of December 8, 1953.

116 Ibid.

117 Jo Hopper diary entry for December 17, 1953.

118 This account is based on Selden Rodman's journal, May–October 1956, in which he recorded his notes from an interview with Andrew Wyeth. The author is grateful to Selden Rodman for making his journal available.

119 Jo Hopper diary entry for December 31, 1953.

120 Jo Hopper diary entry for December 8, 1953.

121 Jo Hopper diary entry for December 31, 1953.

TAKING STOCK

1 Jo Hopper diary entry for January 1, 1954.

2 Jo Hopper diary entry for January 9, 1954.

3 Ibid.

4 Jo Hopper diary entry for January 13, 1954.

5 Ibid.

6 Ibid.

7 Jo Hopper diary entry for January 15, 1954.

8 Jo Hopper diary entry for January 18, 1954.

9 Jo Hopper diary entry for January 22, 1954.

10 Ibid.

11 Ibid.

12 Jo Hopper diary entry for January 28, 1954.

13 Jo Hopper diary entry for February 6, 1954.

14 Jo Hopper diary entry for February 15, 1954.

15 Jo Hopper diary entries for February 18 and 19, 1954.

16 Jo Hopper diary entries for February 23 and 25, 1954.

17 Jo Hopper diary entry for February 24, 1954.

18 Jo Hopper diary entry for February 25, 1954.

19 Jo Hopper to Marion Hopper, letter of April 25, 1954.

20 Jo Hopper to Rosalind Irvine, letter of June 16, [1954].

21 Ibid.

22 Edward Hopper Record Book III, p. 51.

23 Jo Hopper diary entry for October 24, 1955.

24 Jo Hopper diary entry for July 23, 1954.

25 Jo Hopper diary entry for July 26, 1954.

26 Raphael Soyer, *Diary of an Artist* (Washington, D.C.: New Republic Books, 1977), p. 250.

27 Jo Hopper, quoted in Soyer, *Diary of an Artist,* p. 250.

28 Edward Hopper, quoted in Soyer, *Diary of an Artist,* p. 250.

29 Jo Hopper diary entry for July 27, 1954.

30 Edward Hopper to Guy Pène du Bois, letter of December 14, 1954.

31 Jo Hopper diary entry for August 3, 1954.

32 Jo Hopper diary entry for August 5, 1954. See also "Bessie Breuer, 81, Novelist Is Dead," *New York Times,* September 28, 1975, p. 59. Jo Hopper diary entry for September 13, 1934, reveals that she once found Breuer "very exhilarating" and looked forward to the publication of her novel.

33 Jo Hopper diary entry for August 21, 1954.

34 Ibid.

35 Jo Hopper diary entry for February 21, 1955.

36 Edward Hopper to George L. Stout, letter of September 13, 1954.

37 See Lester D. Longman, "Contemporary Painting," *Journal of Aesthetics and Art Criticism,* 3, nos. 9–10, 1944, pp. 8–18, accompanied by a fold-out chart that places Hopper in a category he called "Programmatic Reactionism 1930–43 (Ideological; Nationalistic; Stylistic Reaction)." For a discussion of this absurd link of Hopper to Nazi art, see Gail Levin, "Edward Hopper and the Politics of Modernism," in *Edward Hopper* (New York: Gagosian Gallery, 1993), pp. 14–15.

38 Recalled in John Morse, "Edward Hopper," *Art in America,* 48, Spring 1960, p. 61.

39 Edward Hopper to C. K. Chatterton, letter of October 25, 1954.

40 Edward Hopper to Guy Pène du Bois, letter of December 14, 1954.

PERSONAL VISION

1 Edward Hopper to C. K. Chatterton, letter of October 25, 1954.

2 Jo Hopper diary entry for January 31, 1955.

3 Ibid.

4 Jo Hopper diary entry for February 6, 1955.

5 Edward Hopper to Marc Connelly, letter of January 1, 1955.

6 "Institute Medal Is Won by Hopper," *New York Times,* April 4, 1955, p. 38. Hopper had been elected by the members of the National Institute of Arts and Letters from a list of three candidates nominated by an award committee composed of members of the Department of Art. That year the other two artists nominated were Gifford Beal, Hopper's former classmate at the New York School of Art, and Franklin C. Watkins, another artist of the Rehn Gallery stable. Beal had been one of the five members who nominated Hopper in 1945 when he was first elected to membership in the Institute of Arts and Letters.

7 Archives of the American Academy and Institute of Arts and Letters.

8 Ibid.

9 Jo Hopper diary entry for February 6, 1955.

10 Ibid.

11 Jo Hopper diary entry for February 7, 1955.

12 Richard and Janet Stark, in interview with the author, 1985, New York City.

13 Burrey, "Edward Hopper: The Emptying Spaces," p. 8. The following references in this paragraph are also from this source.

14 Jo Hopper diary entry for February 13, 1955.

15 Ibid.

16 Jo Hopper diary entry for February 19, 1955.

17 Jo Hopper diary entry for March 11, 1955.

18 Jo Hopper diary entry for March 28, 1955.

19 Jo Hopper diary entry for May 19, 1955.

20 "Gold," *Time,* 1955, p. 72.

21 Edward Hopper to Felicia Geffen, letter of May 26, 1955.

22 Henry Varnum Poor, "Presentation to Edward Hopper of the Gold Medal for Painting," May 25, 1955, in Proceedings of the American Academy of Arts and Letters in the National Institute of Arts and Letters, 1956, pp. 34–36.

23 "Acceptance by Edward Hopper," Proceedings of the American Academy of Arts and Letters in the National Institute of Arts and Letters, 1956, p. 36.

24 Jo Hopper diary entry for May 24, 1955.

25 Jo Hopper diary entry for June 13, 1955.

26 Ibid.

27 Soyer, *Diary of an Artist,* p. 250.

28 Jo Hopper diary entry for July 1, 1955. She identified Arthayer Sanborn as Arthur Sandburn.

29 Edward Hopper to Bartlett Hayes, letter of July 4, 1955.

30 Jo Hopper diary entry for July 19, 1955.

31 Ibid.

32 Edward Hopper to Donald Adams, letter of August 7, 1955.

33 Ibid.

34 Jo Hopper diary entries for October 11 and 24, 1955.

35 Edward Hopper Record Book III, p. 53.

36 Edward Hopper, in Johnson interview.

37 See Eric Lott, " 'The Seeing Counterfeit': Racial Politics and Early Blackface Minstrelry," *American Quarterly,* 43, June 1991, pp. 223–54.

38 Edward Hopper, in Johnson interview.

39 Edward Hopper to John Clancy, letter of October 3, 1955.

40 Jo Hopper diary entry for September 15, 1955.

41 Ibid.

42 Jo Hopper diary entry for October 11, 1955.

43 Ibid.

44 John Clancy to Edward Hopper, letter of October 5, 1955.

45 Edward Hopper to John Clancy, letter of October 13, 1955.

46 John Clancy to Edward and Jo Hopper, letter of October 5, 1955.

47 Jo Hopper diary entry for October 12, 1955.

48 Ibid.

49 Jo Hopper diary entry for October 20, 1955.

50 Jo Hopper diary entry for October 24, 1955.

51 Ibid.

52 Jo Hopper diary entry for October 30, 1955.

53 Jo Hopper diary entry for November 11, 1955.

54 Ibid.

55 Ibid.

56 Sidney Waintrob, in interview with the author, October 31, 1993.

57 Jo Hopper diary entry for November 24, 1955.

58 Jo Hopper diary entry for December 5, 1955.

59 Jo Hopper diary entry for December 13, 1955.

60 Jo Hopper diary entry for December 11, 1955.

61 Ibid.

62 Ibid.

63 Edward Hopper to Richard Lahey, in Richard Lahey, "Artists I Have Known."

64 Ibid.

65 Jo Hopper diary entry for December 12, 1955.

66 Ibid.

67 Ibid.

68 Ibid.

69 Jo Hopper diary entry for December 13, 1955.

70 Edward Hopper Record Book III, p. 55.

71 Edward Hopper, in Johnson interview.

TIME COVER STORY

1 Jacob Getlar Smith, "Edward Hopper," *American Artist,* January 1956, pp. 22–27.

2 Jo Hopper diary entry for January 7, 1956.

3 Smith, "Edward Hopper," p. 23.

4 Edward Hopper, quoted in O'Doherty, "Portrait: Edward Hopper," p. 72.

5 Smith, "Edward Hopper," pp. 23, 27.

6 Jo Hopper diary entry for January 10, 1956.

7 Jo Hopper diary entries for January 10 and 25, 1956.

8 Jo Hopper diary entry for January 10, 1956.

9 Jo Hopper diary entries for January 21 and 30, 1956.

10 Jo Hopper diary entry for January 20, 1956.

11 Jo Hopper diary entry for February 1, 1956.

12 Jo Hopper diary entry for February 6, 1956.

13 Jo Hopper diary entry for February 7, 1956.

14 Ibid.

15 Ibid.

16 Jo Hopper diary entry for February 8, 1956.

17 Jo Hopper diary entry for February 10, 1956.

18 Jo Hopper diary entry for February 20, 1956.

19 Jo Hopper, quoted in O'Doherty, *American Masters,* p. 16.

20 Jo Hopper diary entry for February 22, 1956.

21 Jo Hopper diary entry for February 25, 1956.

22 Jo Hopper diary entry for February 27, 1956.

23 Jo Hopper diary entry for February 22, 1956.

24 Jo Hopper diary entry for February 28, 1956.

25 Jo Hopper diary entry for February 29, 1956.

26 Jo Hopper diary entry for March 5, 1956.

27 Ibid.

28 Jo Hopper diary entry for March 15, 1956.

29 Ibid.

30 Jo Hopper diary entry for March 28, 1956.

31 Jo Hopper to Carl Sprinchorn, letter of August 31, 1956.

32 Jo Hopper diary entry for March 28, 1956.

33 Ibid.

34 Ibid.

35 Jo Hopper diary entry for March 30, 1956.

36 Edward Hopper Record Book III, p. 57.

37 Edward Hopper, in Johnson interview.

38 Jo Hopper diary entry for April 5, 1956.

39 Ibid.

40 Jo Hopper diary entry for April 8, 1956.

41 Edward Hopper to Maxwell Anderson, letter of April 16, 1956.

42 Jo Hopper diary entry for April 16, 1956.

43 Jo Hopper diary entry for May 7, 1956.

44 Ibid.

45 Jo Hopper diary entry for April 20, 1956.

46 Ibid.

47 Jo Hopper diary entries for April 17 and 25, 1956.

48 Jo Hopper diary entry for April 25, 1956.

49 Jo Hopper diary entry for April 19, 1956.

50 Jo Hopper diary entry for April 27, 1956.

51 Jo Hopper diary entry for May 4, 1956.

52 Jo Hopper diary entry for May 23, 1956.

53 Ibid.

54 Jo Hopper diary entry for June 7, 1956.

55 Jo Hopper diary entry for June 1, 1956.

56 Jo Hopper diary entry for July 23, 1956.

57 Jo Hopper diary entry for July 22, 1956.

58 Ibid.

59 Jo Hopper to Carl Sprinchorn, letter of May 24, 1960.

60 Jo Hopper diary entry for July 22, 1956.

61 Jo Hopper diary entry for July 30, 1956.

62 Jo Hopper diary entries for July 24 and August 4, 1956.

63 Jo Hopper diary entry for August 8, 1956.

64 Jo Hopper diary entry for August 12, 1956.

65 Ibid.

66 Jo Hopper diary entry for August 23, 1956.

67 Ibid.

68 Edward Hopper to Marion Hopper, letter of August 24, 1956.

69 Jo Hopper diary entry for August 23, 1956.

70 Jo Hopper diary entry for August 25, 1956.

71 Jo Hopper diary entry for August 28, 1956.

72 Jo Hopper to Carl Sprinchorn, letter of August 31, 1956.

73 Jo Hopper diary entry for September 2, 1956.

74 Jo Hopper diary entry for September 12, 1956.

75 Jo Hopper diary entry for September 10, 1956.

76 Jo Hopper diary entry for September 18, 1956.

77 Jo Hopper diary entry for September 23, 1956.

78 Ibid.

79 Ibid.

80 Jo Hopper diary entry for September 25, 1956.

81 Jo Hopper diary entry for October 2, 1956.

82 Edward Hopper, in Johnson interview.

83 Jo Hopper diary entry for October 4, 1956.

84 Jo Hopper diary entry for October 8, 1956.

85 Jo Hopper diary entry for October 10, 1956.

86 Edward Hopper Record Book III, p. 61.

87 Jo Hopper diary entries for October 12 and 13, 1956.

88 Edward Hopper and Jo Hopper, quoted in Crotty, *Provincetown Profiles,* p. 33.

89 Jo Hopper diary entry for October 15, 1956.

90 Jo Hopper diary entry for October 17, 1956.

91 Jo Hopper diary entry for October 24, 1956.

92 John Lamb, in interview with the author, 1988.

93 Edward Hopper to John A. Lamb, letter of November 25, 1956.

94 Jo Hopper to John A. Lamb, on Edward Hopper letter to John A. Lamb, November 25, 1956.

95 John Lamb, in interview with the author, 1988.

96 Both of these watercolors were included in the Hopper Bequest to the Whitney Museum of American Art.

97 Jo Hopper to Carl Sprinchorn, letter of May 24, 1960.

98 Edward Hopper to John Clancy, letter of December 15, 1956.

99 Jo Hopper diary entry for July 22, 1957.

100 Ibid.

101 Jo Hopper to Carl Sprinchorn, letter of May 24, 1960.

102 Ibid.

103 Edward Hopper to John Clancy, letter of February 18, 1957.

104 Parker Tyler, "Hopper/Pollock," *Art News Annual,* 26 (1957), pp. 87–107.

105 Tyler, "Hopper/Pollock," p. 93.

106 Edward Hopper to Parker Tyler, letter of December 28, 1956.

107 Tyler, "Hopper/Pollock," p. 92.

108 "The Silent Witness," *Time,* 68, December 24, 1956, pp. 28–39.

109 Ibid., p. 28.

110 Jo Hopper diary entry for October 31, 1957.

111 Jo Hopper to Marion Hopper, letter of October 11, 1959.

112 Jo Hopper postscript on letter from Edward Hopper to W. G. Constable, December 23, 1956.

113 Jo Hopper to Constable, December 23, 1956.

114 Charles B. Rogers to the Editor, *Time,* January 14, 1957, p. 6.

115 Jimmy De Lory to the Editor, *Time,* January 14, 1957, p. 6.

116 Andrew Wyeth to the Editor, *Time,* January 21, 1957.

TOWARD RECONCILIATION

1 Edward Hopper to John Clancy, letter of February 18, 1957.

2 Jo Hopper diary entry for July 22, 1957.

3 Edward Hopper, quoted in "Silent Witness," *Time,* p. 39.

4 Jo Hopper to Carl Sprinchorn, letter of May 24, 1960.

5 For example, Max Eastman, "Exploring the Soul and Healing the Body," *Everybody's,* June 1915, pp. 741–50.

6 Jo Hopper diary entry for July 22, 1957.

7 Charles Neider, in telephone interview with the author, May 14, 1993.

8 Jo Hopper diary entry for July 22, 1957.

9 Charles Neider, in telephone interviews with the author, January 25 and May 14, 1993. The following quotations are also from this source.

10 Jo Hopper diary entry for July 22, 1957.

11 Ibid.

12 Ibid.

13 Edward Hopper to John Clancy, letter of April 28, 1957.

14 "Art World Honors Late Starter," *New York World-Telegram and Sun,* December 3, 1957.

15 Jo Hopper diary entry for July 22, 1957.

16 Edward Hopper to John Clancy, letter of August 29, 1957.

17 Edward Hopper Record Book III, p. 63.

18 Jo Hopper diary entry for July 22, 1957.

19 Jo Hopper, note on cover page of her diary for 1955, 1956, and July to September 1957.

20 Jo Hopper diary entry for July 22, 1957.

21 Ibid.

22 *Arts,* June 1957, p. 50. Irving Sandler signed the gallery's guest book, collection of Herman Gulack.

23 *Fifty Contemporary American Artists,* foreword by Herman C. Gulack, essay by A. L. Chanin on Greenwich Village as a center for artists (New York: Greenwich Gallery, 1957). Herman Gulack, in interview with the author, August 25, 1991.

24 Jo Hopper diary entry for August 5, 1957.

25 Ibid.

26 Soyer, *Diary of an Artist,* p. 250.

27 Jo Hopper diary entries for August 5 and 6, 1957.

28 Jo Hopper diary entry for August 12, 1957. See Charles Neider, ed., Fanny Osbourne Stevenson (Mrs. Robert Louis) and Robert Louis Stevenson, *Our Samoan Adventure* (New York: Harper, 1955). Charles Neider, ed., *Mark Twain: The Complete Short Stories* (New York: Hanover House, 1957).

29 Norma Snow, in interviews with the author, August 1991.

30 Edward Hopper to John Clancy, letter of August 29, 1957.

31 Edward Hopper to Stephen Clark, unsigned autograph draft of letter of September 14, 1957.

32 Edward Hopper to John Clancy, letter of September 14, 1957.

33 Jo Hopper diary entry for October 17, 1957.

34 Jo Hopper diary entry for October 23, 1957.

35 Jo Hopper diary entry for October 31, 1957.

36 Ibid.

37 Jo Hopper diary entries for December 18 and 21, 1957.

38 Jo Hopper diary entry for December 21, 1957.

39 Jo Hopper diary entry for January 22, 1958. The Hoppers later learned that his fee was automatically included in the hospital's charges.

40 Jo Hopper diary entry for January 14, 1958.

41 Jo Hopper diary entry for January 27, 1958.

42 Ibid.

43 Jo Hopper diary entry for January 29, 1958.

44 Jo Hopper diary entry for February 7, 1963.

45 Jo Hopper diary entry for February 3, 1958.

46 Kenneth Lux, in interviews with the author, August 21, 1991, and earlier.

47 Jo Hopper diary entry for June 8, 1958.

48 Jo Hopper diary entry for February 10, 1958.

49 Jo Hopper diary entry for February 26, 1958.

50 Jo Hopper diary entry for February 28, 1958.

51 Jo Hopper diary entry for March 4, 1958.

52 Jo Hopper diary entry for March 5, 1958.

53 Albert Ellis, *How to Live with a Neurotic* (New York: Crown Publishers, 1957).

54 Jo Hopper diary entries for March 6 and 9, 1958.

55 Jo Hopper diary entry for March 24, 1958.

56 Ellis, *How to Live with a Neurotic,* p. 67.

57 Ibid., p. 49.

58 Although all three artists were then obscure, Harriton had shown in 1917 in the Introspectives' show at the Whitney Studio.

59 Jo Hopper diary entry for March 30, 1958.

60 Jo Hopper to Marion Hopper, letter of April 22, 1958.

61 Jo Hopper to Rosalind Irvine, undated letter of spring 1958.

62 Ibid.

63 Herman Gulack, in interview with the author, August 25, 1991.

64 The *Villager* reproduced *Power of the Press* on April 17, 1958, and the *Christian Science Monitor* reproduced *Obituary (Fleurs du Temps Jadis)* on April 16, 1958.

65 Dorothy Adlow, *Christian Science Monitor,* April 16, 1958.

66 *Christian Science Monitor,* April 16, 1958.

67 Jo Hopper to Rosalind Irvine, undated letter of spring 1958.

68 Ibid.

69 Virginia Zabriskie, in interview with the author, August 1992, does not recall this encounter.

70 Jo Hopper diary entry for April 17, 1958.

71 Ibid.

72 Jo Hopper diary entries for April 26 and 29, 1958.

73 Jo Hopper diary notes, recorded after draft of letter to Lloyd Goodrich of June 11, 1960.

74 Ibid. Jo recalled this episode once again in her diary entry for February 7, 1963.

75 Edward Hopper to John Lamb, letter of February 26, 1958.

76 Jo Hopper diary entry for April 18, 1958.

77 Herman Gulack, in interview with the author, August 24, 1991.

78 John Lamb, in interview with the author, 1988.

79 Ibid.

80 Jo Hopper diary entry for May 13, 1958.

81 Jo Hopper diary entry for May 16, 1958.

82 Jo Hopper diary entries for April 25 and May 16, 1958. The Hoppers' neighbors on Washington Square came also, including the young artist Paul Resicka.

83 Jo Hopper diary entry for June 18, 1958.

84 Jo Hopper diary entry for May 16, 1958.

85 Jo Hopper diary entry for June 2, 1958.

86 Jo Hopper diary entry for May 27, 1958.

87 Jo Hopper diary entry for June 2, 1958.

88 Ibid.

89 Lester Cooke, "Paintings by Edward Hopper," *Russian America,* no. 3, July 23,

1958, typescript in Hopper archives at Whitney Museum of American Art.

90 Cooke, "Paintings by Edward Hopper," p. 7.

91 Cooke, "Paintings by Edward Hopper."

92 Jo Hopper diary entry for May 16, 1958.

93 Jo Hopper diary entry for June 7, 1958.

94 Jo Hopper diary entry for June 8, 1958.

95 Herman Gulack, in interview with the author, August 24, 1991.

96 Jo Hopper diary entry for June 18, 1958.

97 Ibid.

98 Ibid.

99 Jo Hopper diary entry for June 30, 1958.

100 Edward Hopper Record Book III, p. 65.

101 John Clancy to Edward and Jo Hopper, letter of September 9, 1958.

102 Edward Hopper to Stephen Clark, letter of September 1958.

103 Jo Hopper diary entry for July 1, 1958.

104 Ibid.

105 Jo Hopper diary entry for July 20, 1958.

106 Jo Hopper diary entry for November 27, 1958.

107 Jo Hopper diary entry for November 30, 1958.

108 Jo Hopper diary entries for November 30 and December 3, 1958.

109 Jo Hopper diary entry for December 7, 1958.

110 Hilary Dunsterville, "Art Reviews," *Villager,* December 24, 1957.

111 Jo Hopper diary entry for December 17, 1958.

EXCURSION INTO PHILOSOPHY

1 Jo Hopper diary entry for January 17, 1959.

2 Jo Hopper diary entry for January 28, 1959.

3 Edward Hopper to Lloyd Goodrich, letter of February 19, 1959. Goodrich telephoned and asked to keep the clipping (as per his handwritten notation on letter).

4 Jo Hopper to Herman Gulack, inscribed in Robert Henri, *Art Spirit.*

5 Jo Hopper diary entry for January 23, 1959.

6 Jo Hopper to Happy Chace, letter of December 9, 1959.

7 Jo Hopper diary entry for February 22, 1959. It was left in the studio when they died; it never went to Abbott.

8 Jo Hopper diary entry for March 29, 1959.

9 Ibid.

10 Jo Hopper diary entry for May 4, 1959.

11 Ibid.

12 Ibid.

13 Jo Hopper to Rosalind Irvine, undated letter of March 1959 (dated by Irvine).

14 Barbara Hale, in interview with the author, November 27, 1992, East Hampton, New York.

15 Jo Hopper diary entry for March 30, 1959.

16 Jo Hopper diary entry for June 4, 1959.

17 Jo Hopper diary entry for May 10, 1959.

18 Jo Hopper diary entries for June 21 and 27, 1959.

19 Jo Hopper diary entry for June 29, 1959.

20 Jo Hopper diary entry for June 28, 1959.

21 Jo Hopper diary entry for summer of 1959, written November 1959.

22 Edward Hopper to John Clancy, letter of July 22, 1959.

23 Jo Hopper to Rosalind Irvine, letter of July 28, 1959.

24 Ibid.

25 Jo Hopper to Lloyd Goodrich, postcard of August 17, 1959, mailed as a letter.

26 Ibid.

27 Frank Falacci, "Edward Hopper on Cape—But Prefers Isolation: Portrait of Artist As Drawn by Wife," *Boston Sunday Globe,* August 23, 1959.

28 Jo Hopper, quoted by Frank Falacci, "Edward Hopper on Cape."

29 Jo Hopper diary entry for summer 1959, written November 1959.

30 Ibid.

31 Jo Hopper to Lloyd Goodrich, letter of September 23, 1959.

32 Edward Hopper Record Book III, p. 39.

33 Jo Hopper to Lloyd Goodrich, letter of September 23, 1959.

34 Santayana, *Last Puritan,* p. 442.

35 Ibid.

36 Jo Hopper to Lloyd Goodrich, letter of September 23, 1959.

37 Jo Hopper to Mr. and Mrs. Malcolm Chace, January 15, 1960.

38 Jo Hopper diary entry for summer 1959, written early November 1959.

39 Jo Hopper diary entry for February 11, 1960.

40 Jo Hopper diary entry for May 12, 1959.

41 Jo Hopper to Rosalind Irvine, undated letter of early March 1959.

42 Jo Hopper to the Editor, letter in *Art Times,* 1, no. 11, May 1959.

43 Edward Hopper to the Editor, letter in *Art Times,* 2, no. 3, October 1959.

44 Jo Hopper to Marion Hopper, letter of October 11, 1959.

45 Jo Hopper diary entry for November 11, 1959.

46 Ibid.

47 Ibid.

48 Ibid.

49 Jo Hopper to Happy Chace, letter of November 22, 1959.

50 Ibid.

51 Ibid.

52 Jo Hopper to Marion Hopper, letter of December 19, 1959.

53 Jo Hopper diary entry for December 25, 1959, written January 4, 1960.

54 Jo Hopper diary entry for January 4, 1960.

55 Alexander Eliot, in interview with the author, August 24, 1991.

PROTEST

1 Jo Hopper diary entry for January 4, 1960.

2 Jo Hopper diary entry for January 8, 1960.

3 Jo Hopper diary entry for January 7, 1960.

4 Ibid.

5 Jo Hopper to Happy and Malcolm Chace, letter of January 15, 1960.

6 Jo Hopper diary entry for February 11, 1960.

7 Jo Hopper diary entry for January 8, 1960.

8 Jo Hopper diary entry for January 18, 1960.

9 Jo Hopper diary entry for January 19, 1960.

10 Jo Hopper diary entry for January 20, 1960.

11 Jo Hopper diary entry for January 21, 1960.

12 Edward Hopper Record Book III, p. 71.

13 Edward Hopper to Lee Nordess, draft of letter (in Hopper's hand), July 30, 1962.

14 Edward Hopper, interview by Aline Saarinen, *Sunday Show,* NBC, New York, 1964.

15 Jo Hopper diary entry for January 3, 1960.

16 *Villager,* December 31, 1959.

17 Jo Hopper diary entry for January 22, 1960.

18 Jo Hopper diary entry for February 29, 1960.

19 Ibid.

20 Jo Hopper diary entry for March 1, 1960.

21 Ibid.

22 Ibid.

23 Ibid.

24 Edward Hopper to John D. Morse, letter of March 8, 1960. John Morse, "Interview with Edward Hopper," *Art in America,* 48, spring 1960, pp. 60–63.

25 Morse, "Edward Hopper," p. 62.

26 Ibid.

27 Ibid.

28 Jo Hopper diary entry for March 30, 1960.

29 Jo Hopper to Lloyd Goodrich, draft of letter of June 11, 1960, included in diary after entry for February 11, 1960. Also noted in Jo Hopper diary entry for August 24, 1960.

30 Jo Hopper to Lloyd Goodrich, draft of letter of June 11, 1960.

31 Jo Hopper diary entry for March 31, 1960.

32 Jo Hopper diary entry for April 3, 1960.

33 Jo Hopper diary entry for April 22, 1960.

34 Jo Hopper diary entry for May 1, 1960.

35 Paul Resicka, in interviews with the author, July 1977 and May 10, 1993.

36 Jo Hopper diary entry for May 1, 1960.

37 Jo Hopper diary entry for May 18, 1960.

38 Jo Hopper to Lloyd Goodrich, draft of letter of June 11, 1960, recorded in diary after entry for February 11, 1960.

39 Ibid.

40 Ibid.

41 Ibid.

42 Jo Hopper diary entry for May 31, 1960.

43 Jo Hopper diary entry for June 1, 1960.

44 Jo Hopper diary entry for June 2, 1960.

45 Jo Hopper diary entry for June 6, 1991.

46 Jo Hopper diary entry for June 16, 1960. Archer Winsten, "Rages and Outrages," *New York Evening Post,* June 13, 1960, p. 41.

47 Edward Hopper to John Clancy, autograph draft of letter of September 7, 1960.

48 Jo Hopper diary entry for July 1, 1960.

49 James Flexner, *Pocket History of American Art* (New York: Pocket Books, 1950), p. 96.

50 James Flexner, in interview with the author, September 13, 1991.

51 Jo Hopper to Lloyd Goodrich, letter of June 11, 1960. ("Life is brief— / A little hope / a little dream / And then Good night.") The verse Jo quoted is from Léon Montenaeken, "Peu de Chose," in *Anthologie du Parnasse Contemporain* (Brussels: 1887), ed. by Alphonse Lemerre. The verse was later adapted for the song "Petite Pensée," composed by Natalie Townsend in 1918. See Gustave Charlier and Joseph Hanse, *Histoire Illustrée des Lettres Françaises de Belgique* (Brussels: La Renaissance du Livre, 1958), p. 392.

52 Jo Hopper diary entry for August 8, 1960, and Jo Hopper to Mr. and Mrs. Richard Snidely, letter of July 18, 1960.

53 Jo Hopper to Mr. and Mrs. Richard Snidely, letter of July 18, 1960.

54 Jo Hopper to Mr. and Mrs. Richard Snidely, letter and map of July 18, 1960.

55 Jo Hopper to Carl Sprinchorn, letter of August 20, 1960.

56 Ibid.

57 Ibid.

58 Ibid.

59 Jo Hopper diary entry for August 24, 1960.

60 Arnold Newman, in interview with the author, September 8, 1993.

61 Jo Hopper diary entry for August 24, 1960.

62 Ibid.

63 Jo Hopper to Mr. and Mrs. Malcolm Chace, letter of September 16, 1960.

64 Jo Hopper diary entry for August 24, 1960.

65 Ibid.

66 Jo Hopper diary entry for February 5, 1940.

67 Jo Hopper diary entry for September 1, 1960.

68 Ibid.

69 Edward Hopper to John Clancy, letter of August 3, 1960.

70 Jo Hopper diary entry for September 1, 1960.

71 Ibid.

72 Ibid.

73 Edward Hopper, quoted in Kuh, *Artist's Voice*, p. 134.

74 Conversations between the author and Marie Stephens, August 1977, and Kim Stephens, August 1991.

75 Edward Hopper, quoted in Kuh, *Artist's Voice*, pp. 135, 140.

76 Jo Hopper to Mr. and Mrs. Malcolm Chace, letter of January 18, 1961.

77 Ibid.

78 Edward Hopper Record Book III, p. 73.

79 James Thomas Flexner to Edward Hopper, letter of May 13, 1961, quoted in James Thomas Flexner, in Gail Levin, ed., *Edward Hopper Symposium,* "Six Who Knew Hopper," p. 134.

80 Edward Hopper to Lloyd Goodrich, letter of May 18, 1961.

81 James Thomas Flexner, in Gail Levin, ed., *Edward Hopper Symposium,* "Six Who Knew Hopper," pp. 133–35.

82 Jo Hopper to Mr. and Mrs. Malcolm Chace, letter of September 16, 1960.

83 Jo Hopper diary entries for November 8 and 9, 1960.

84 Jo Hopper diary entry for January 30, 1961.

85 Jo Hopper diary entry for April 21, 1961.

86 Jo Hopper diary entry for November 30, 1960.

87 Jo Hopper to Marion Hopper, letter of December 13, 1960.

88 Edward Hopper to Raphael Soyer, letter of December 6, 1960.

89 Stuart Preston, "Art: Award to Hopper. Quarterly Honors Dean of U.S. Realist Painting—Other Displays on View," *New York Times,* December 16, 1960, p. 45.

90 Preston, "Art: Award to Hopper," p. 45.

91 "The *Art in America* Annual Award," *Art in America,* December 1960, p. 3.

PRINTS AGAIN

1 Edward Hopper to Raphael Soyer, letter of January 2, 1961.

2 Ibid. Quotation from Goethe to Jacobi, Frankfurt, letter of August 21, 1774, in *Letters from Goethe* (New York: Thomas Nelson & Sons, 1957), p. 41.

3 The following account is based on the author's interview with Ed Colker on April 15, 1992.

4 Edward Hopper to Carl Zigrosser, undated Christmas card.

5 Jo Hopper diary entry for January 30, 1961.

6 Jo Hopper diary entry for February 26, 1961.

7 Jo Hopper to Dorothy Ferris, letter of February 8, 1962.

8 Jo Hopper diary entry for January 30, 1961.

9 Jo Hopper to Mr. and Mrs. Malcolm Chace, letter of January 24, 1961.

10 The letter appeared on February 26, 1961. It is quoted in John Canaday, *Embattled Critic: Views on Modern Art* (New York: Farrar, Straus and Co., 1962), pp. 219–23.

11 Jo Hopper diary entry for February 26, 1961.

12 Edward Hopper, quoted in Canaday, *Embattled Critic,* p. 231.

13 Jo Hopper diary entry for March 24, 1961, and *Time,* March 11, 1961.

14 Jo Hopper diary entry for March 4, 1961.

15 Jo Hopper diary entry for March 28, 1961.

16 Edward Hopper to Raphael Soyer, letter of April 12, 1961.

17 Jo Hopper diary entry for April 18, 1961.

18 Ibid.

19 Jo Hopper to Happy and Malcolm Chace, letter of April 6, 1961.

20 Jo Hopper to Marion Hopper, letter of April 23, 1961.

21 Edward Hopper, in O'Doherty interview.

22 Jo Hopper diary entry for April 8–11, 1961.

23 Jo Hopper to Marion Hopper, letter of April 23, 1961.

24 Jo Hopper diary entries for April 12 and 14, 1961.

25 Jo Hopper diary entry for April 16, 1961.

26 Jo Hopper diary entry for April 14, 1961.

27 Jo Hopper diary entry for May 19, 1961.

28 Jo Hopper diary entry for April 26, 1961.

29 Ibid.

30 Jo Hopper diary entry for May 9, 1961.

31 Jo Hopper diary entry for May 23, 1961.

32 Jo Hopper diary entry for May 31, 1961.

33 Ibid.

34 Jo Hopper diary entry for May 23, 1961.

35 Willem de Kooning in 1959, quoted in Irving Sandler, "Conversations with de Kooning," *Art Journal,* 48, fall 1989, p. 217. The Merritt Parkway connects Fairfield County, Connecticut, with New York State; completed in 1940, it constituted one of the earliest attempts to contend with America's new fixation on the automobile.

36 De Kooning, quoted in Sandler, "Conversations," p. 217.

37 Jo Hopper diary entry for May 23, 1961.

38 Ibid.

39 Jo Hopper diary entries for May 23 and June 15, 1961.

40 Jo Hopper diary entry for June 15, 1961.

41 John Clancy, quoted in Levin, *Edward Hopper Symposium,* "Six Who Knew Hopper," p. 128.

42 Robert Hatch, "At the Tip of Cape Cod," *Horizon,* July 1961, 3, no. 6, p. 11.

43 Jo Hopper to Marion Hopper, letter of September 29, 1961.

44 John Clancy, in interview with the author, 1980.

45 Edward Hopper Record Book III, p. 75.

46 Jo Hopper diary entry for April 17, 1962.

47 Jo Hopper to Frances Hackett, letter of December 17, 1962.

48 Ibid.

49 Jo Hopper to John Clancy, postcard of October 14, 1961.

50 Jo Hopper to Marion Hopper, letter of December 8, 1961.

51 Jo Hopper to Beatrice and Jimmy Flexner, letter of January 16, 1962.

52 Jo Hopper to Marion Hopper, letter of December 27, 1961.

53 Jo Hopper diary entry for April 17, 1962.

54 Jo Hopper diary entry for May 16, 1962.

55 Jo Hopper diary entry for April 17, 1962.

56 Jo Hopper diary entry for June 3, 1962. This was for the NBC show called "The Nation's Future."

57 Jo Hopper diary entry for June 3, 1962.

58 Jo Hopper to Marion Hopper, letter of July 19, 1962 (added on to a letter by Edward Hopper).

59 Jo Hopper diary entry for August 25, 1962.

60 Jo Hopper diary entry for September 13, 1962.

61 Jo Hopper diary entry for September 18, 1962.

62 Jo Hopper diary entry for February 28, 1964.

63 Jo Hopper diary entry for October 15, 1962.

64 Edward Hopper, quoted in O'Doherty, "Portrait: Edward Hopper," p. 76.

LAST REHEARSAL

1 Jo Hopper diary entry for January 18–23, 1963.

2 Edward Hopper to Raphael Soyer, letter of January 7, 1963.

3 Edward Hopper, quoted in O'Doherty, "Portrait: Edward Hopper," p. 70.

4 Soyer, *Diary of an Artist,* p. 75.

5 Ibid., p. 70.

6 Edward Hopper, quoted in Soyer, *Diary of an Artist,* pp. 71–72. See Susan Danly and Cheryl Leibold, *Eakins and the Photograph* (Washington: Smithsonian Institution Press, 1994).

7 Soyer, *Diary of an Artist,* pp. 70–71.

8 Edward Hopper, quoted in Soyer, *Diary of an Artist,* p. 72.

9 Ibid., p. 74.

10 Edward Hopper to Raphael Soyer, letter of February 20, 1963.

11 Jo Hopper diary entry for February 11, 1963.

12 Jo Hopper diary entry for February 7, 1963.

13 Jo Hopper diary entry for February 11, 1963.

14 Ibid.

15 Ibid.

16 Ibid. Entry also notes that as a result of the show in 1958, the Whitney invited her to be in their next Annual, the *Monitor* reproduced her work, *The New Yorker* came and wrote to her, and the critic from *Arts* came as well. Her

next show of watercolors and *pochards* in December 1959 was during a press strike, Edward's hospitalization, and a blizzard. Then, to Jo's sorrow, the gallery closed.

17 Jo Hopper diary entry for February 11, 1963.

18 Edward and Jo Hopper, quoted in O'Doherty, "Portrait: Edward Hopper," p. 75.

19 James Flexner, quoted in Levin, ed., *Edward Hopper Symposium,* "Six Who Knew Hopper," p. 134.

20 Ibid.

21 Edward Hopper Record Book III, p. 81.

22 Jo Hopper diary entry for April 7, 1963.

23 Ibid.

24 Jo Hopper to Marion Hopper, letter of May 7, 1963.

25 Edward Hopper to Marion Hopper, letter of May 7, 1963.

26 Jo Hopper diary entry for May 7, 1963.

27 Henry Varnum Poor, journal entry for May 20–21, 1963.

28 Edward Hopper in "Jury Statements," in Boston Arts Festival, Boston, 1963, n.p.

29 Jo Hopper diary entry for June 5, 1963.

30 Edward Hopper, quoted in O'Doherty, "Portrait: Edward Hopper," p. 72.

31 Ibid., p. 73.

32 Jo Hopper diary entry for June 22, 1963.

33 Jo Hopper diary entry for July 14, 1963. Her second painting was *Victorian Fireplace.*

34 Jo Hopper to John Clancy, letter of August 19, 1963.

35 Ibid.

36 Edward Hopper to John Clancy, letter of September 27, 1963.

37 Jo Hopper to Carl Sprinchorn, letter of January 14, 1963.

38 Edward Hopper, quoted in O'Doherty, *American Masters,* p. 26.

39 Ibid.

40 Edward Hopper, quoted in O'Doherty, "Portrait: Edward Hopper," p. 80.

41 Edward Hopper, quoted in O'Doherty, *American Masters,* p. 26.

42 Edward Hopper Record Book III, p. 83.

43 Edward Hopper, quoted in O'Doherty, *American Masters,* p. 26.

44 Guerard, *André Gide,* pp. 53–54.

45 André Gide, *Les Cahiers d'André Walter* (Paris, 1891), quoted in Guerard, *André Gide,* p. 56. See also André Gide, *Oeuvres complètes,* ed. Louis Martin-Chauffier (Paris, 1932–39).

46 Jo Hopper to Carl Sprinchorn, letter of October 22, 1963.

47 Ibid.

48 Jo Hopper to Carl Sprinchorn, letter of December 16, 1963.

49 Ibid.

50 Ibid.

51 Jo Hopper to Carl Sprinchorn, letter of January 14, 1964.

52 Ibid.

53 Ibid.

54 James Biddle to Edward Hopper, letter of January 9, 1964.

55 Jo Hopper diary entry for February 6, 1964.

56 Ibid.

57 Jo Hopper diary entry for February 28, 1964.

58 Jo Hopper to Brian O'Doherty, undated letter.

59 Jo Hopper diary entry for February 28, 1964.

60 Edward Hopper to Marion Hopper, letter of September 14, 1964.

61 Ibid.

62 Jo Hopper to Margaret McKellar, letter of August 29, 1964.

63 John Canaday, "The Solo Voyage of Edward Hopper, American Realist," *Smithsonian,* September 1980, p. 127.

64 John Canaday, "Art: Edward Hopper, American Realist 55 Years," *New York Times,* September 29, 1964, p. 47.

65 Emily Genauer, "Edward Hopper at Whitney," *New York Herald Tribune,* September 29, 1964, p. 15.

66 Hilton Kramer, "Edward Hopper: An American Vision," *New Leader,* 47, October 12, 1964, p. 23.

67 Brian O'Doherty, "Edward Hopper," *Newsweek,* December 1964, reprinted in Brian O'Doherty, *Object and Idea: An Art Critic's Journal 1961–1967* (New York: Simon and Schuster, 1967), p. 43.

68 Barbara Rose, "New York Letter: The Hopper Retrospective," *Art International,* November 25, 1964, v. 8, p. 52.

69 Sidney Tillim, "Edward Hopper and the Provincial Principle," *Arts,* November 1964, v. 39, p. 31.

70 Edward Hopper to Lewis Mumford, letter of October 29, 1964, Lewis Mumford Papers, Van Pelt Library, University of Pennsylvania, Philadelphia.

71 Edward Hopper, quoted in O'Doherty, *Object and Idea,* p. 42.

72 Ibid.

73 Jo Hopper to Carl Sprinchorn, letter of March 3, 1965, erroneously dated 1964.

74 Edward Hopper, quoted in Squirru, "Edward Hopper," p. 12.

75 Ibid.

76 Jo Hopper, quoted in Squirru, "Edward Hopper," p. 14.

77 Squirru, "Edward Hopper," p. 14.

78 Ibid.

79 Edward Hopper, quoted in Squirru, "Edward Hopper," p. 15.

80 Edward Hopper Record Book III, p. 85.

FINAL CURTAIN

1 Edward Hopper to Marion Hopper, letter of January 21, 1965.

2 While in Philadelphia, they saw their friends Ruth and Ben Wolf.

3 Edward Hopper to C. K. Chatterton, letter of January 30, 1965.

4 Jo Hopper to Julia Chatterton, letter of March 29, 1965.

5 Ibid.

6 Jo Hopper to Carl Sprinchorn, letter of March 3, 1965.

7 Ibid.

8 Edward Hopper to Rafael Squirru, letter of April 14, 1965.

9 Jo Hopper to Miss Williams, letter of April 9, 1965.

10 Roy Neuberger, in conversation with the author, November 1984.

11 Jo Hopper to Marion Hopper, letter of June 1, 1965.

12 Jo Hopper to Margaret McKellar, letter of November 14, 1965.

13 Jo Hopper, undated diary entry for 1965.

14 Ibid.

15 Jo Hopper to Margaret McKellar, letter of November 14, 1965.

16 Jo Hopper diary entry for August 7, 1965.

17 Edward Hopper to C. K. Chatterton, October 29, 1965.

18 Edward Hopper Record Book III, p. 89.

19 Jo Hopper diary entry for November 12, 1965.

20 Jo Hopper to Margaret McKellar, letter of November 14, 1965.

21 Goodrich, *Edward Hopper,* p. 154.

22 For other examples in modernist painting, literature, theater, ballet, opera, music, and film, see Martin Green and John Swan, *The Triumph of Pierrot: The Commedia dell'Arte and the Modern Imagination* (New York: Macmillan Publishing Co., 1986).

23 Ibid., pp. 4–6.

24 Jo Hopper to Annette Chatterton, letter of November 13, 1965.

25 Julia Van de Water, in conversation with the author, March 26, 1980.

26 Jo Hopper to Lucy Bayard, letter of July 16, 1966.

27 Peter Pollack record of conversation with Jo Hopper, August 25, 1966.

28 Ibid.

29 Ibid.

30 "Edward Hopper to Be Honored," *Sentinel,* Keene, N.H., August 11, 1966, p. 1; "Ill Hopper Awarded MacDowell Art Prize," *New York Times,* August 15, 1966.

31 "MacDowell Medal for 'Most Modest' Artist," *Transcript,* Peterborough, N.H., September 1, 1966.

32 Jack Levine, in interview with the author, September 9, 1985, New York City.

33 William Pellicone to the Whitney Museum, letter of January 24, 1977.

34 Jo Hopper to Catherine Rogers, letter of June 4, 1967.

35 Jo Hopper to Carl Sprinchorn, letter of December 27, 1966.

36 Jo Hopper to Catherine Rogers, letter of June 4, 1967.

37 Emeline K. Paige, " 'The Villager' Editor Moves to North River Shores," *The Stuart News,* Stuart, Fla., August 3, 1967, p. 1B.

38 Ibid.

39 Jo Hopper to Catherine Rogers, letter of June 4, 1967. Unless otherwise indicated, the following references are also from this letter.

40 Barbara Novak, in interview with the author, April 29, 1994. Mrs. Clarence (Peggy) Day recalled bringing homemade soup and custard to Hopper the night before he died. See Grace Deschamps, "Truro Tales," *Provincetown Advocate,* June 3, 1971, p. 2.

41 Jo Hopper to Catherine Rogers, letter of June 4, 1967.

42 Ibid.

43 Jo Hopper diary entry for 1965.

44 Jo Hopper to Emeline Paige, letter begun October 6 and completed November 7, 1967.

45 "Edward Hopper Is Dead at 84; Painter of the American Scene," *New York Times,* May 17, 1967, p. 32, continued from p. 1.

46 Jack Kroll, "I Want to Paint Sunlight," *Newsweek,* May 29, 1967, p. 88.

47 "Edward Hopper," *Life,* May 26, 1967, p. 36A.

48 William Seitz quoted in "Painting: A Certain Alienated Majesty," [Alexander Eliot], *Time,* May 26, 1967, p. 72. "For São-Paulo—Some Pop, Lots of Hop (per)," *New York Times,* March 19, 1967, sec. D, p. 29.

49 William C. Seitz, "An Evaluation: Edward Hopper, Painter of the American Scene," *Sun,* Lowell, Mass., May 28, 1967.

50 Jo Hopper to Catherine Rogers, letter of June 4, 1967.

51 Lila Harnett, "Week End in New York," *Citizen Herald,* Newburgh, N.Y., May 24, 1967, p. 21.

52 Jo Hopper to Lila Harnett, letter of June 18, 1967.

53 Jo Hopper to Emeline Paige, letter of October 6, 1967. The quotations that follow are also from this source.

54 Jo Hopper to Lila Harnett, letter of June 18, 1967.

55 Ibid.

ACKNOWLEDGMENTS

Since I began to work on Edward Hopper in the summer of 1976, many more individuals and institutions have contributed to my efforts than it is possible to name here. The Andrew W. Mellon Foundation provided funding for the initial three years of my research for a catalogue raisonné and later, in 1987–1988, enabled me to take part in a year-long seminar on biography with Kenneth Silverman at New York University. Progress resulted from the year in which I held the Durant Chair of the Humanities at Saint Peter's College, where Dr. George Martin provided a supportive environment and I benefited from the ideas and enthusiasm of the participants in the faculty seminar I conducted on Hopper. The National Endowment for the Humanities gave aid at a crucial moment. The Rockefeller Foundation accorded me the privilege of residency at Villa Serbelloni in Bellagio, allowing a major push toward completion. Fellow members of the ongoing Biography Seminar at New York University have offered encouragement.

My research has had the benefit of the superb resources and able staffs of many institutions. Especially helpful were the Archives of American Art, the library of the National Museum of American Art at the Smithsonian Institution, the library of the University of Virginia, and the Beinecke Library at Yale. I am grateful to David Ross, director of the Whitney Museum of American Art, for facilitating the reproduction of works from the Josephine N. Hopper Bequest.

Over the years, many people who knew or met Edward and Jo Hopper have generously communicated with me, among them Berenice Abbott, Perry Anthony, Stella Falkner Barnette, Elizabeth Cornell Benton, Theresa Bernstein, Jean Bellows Booth, Eddy Brady, Jean and Jewett Campbell, Lois Saunier Carlson, Milton Cederquist, John Clancy, Leslie Cheek, Edward Colker, Tess Daisey, Jimmy De Lory, Joan Dye, Judith Shahn Dugan, Alexander Eliot, Etta Falkner, Lawrence and Barbara Fleischman, James Flexner, Charles Francis, Janet Thornley Francis, Edith and Lloyd Goodrich, Herman Gulack, Barbara Hale, Gertrude Wulbern Haltiwanger, Joel and Lila Harnett, Helen Hayes, Elsa Ruth Herron, William I. Homer, Jacques Howlett, Virginia Jenness, William Johnson, Dorothy Bosch Keller, Jack Kelly, Leon Kroll, John Lamb, Abe Lerner, Jack Levine, Jean Ferris Leich, Ethel Lisenby, Kenneth Lux, Yvonne Pène du Bois McKenney, Charles Neider, Roy Neuberger, Bennard B. Perlman, Malcolm Preston, Emeline Paige, Perry Rathbone, Paul Resicka, Selden Rodman, John B. Root, Andrée Ruellan, Arthayer R. Sanborn, Irving Sandler, Lois Saunier, Elsie Scott, Lee Sievan, Clyde Singer, Irene Slater, Robert Slater, Helen Farr Sloan, Norma Snow, Raphael and Rebecca Soyer, Kimble Stephens, Marie Stephens, Jane Bouché Strong, John Thornley, Helen Tittle, Gladys and Paul Todd, Julia Chatterton Van de Water, Bud Waintrob, Bill and Diana Worthington, and Virginia Zabriskie. I am grateful to each for sharing their experiences and helping to make the Hoppers come alive.

Along the way I have met with innumerable forms of encouragement, courtesy, and help, which I gratefully acknowledge. Regretting that no such list can ever be as full as I would like, I wish to mention in particular Cynthia Adler, Ann J. Anderson, Matthew Baigell, Evelyn Barish, Brenda Billingsley, Suzaan Boettger, Gerald D. Bolas, Phyllis Braff, Frederick R. Brandt, Sharon Brysac, Enid M. Buhre, Mindy Cantor, Mary Ann Caws, Mary Chapin, Geoffrey Clements, Lurana Cook, Lewis M. Dabney, Alan Dugan, Betsy Fahlman, Donald Fanger, Nancy Freeman Ferguson, Jane Freeman, Linda Freeman, Marjorie Freytag, Elizabeth Fuller, Barbara Dayer Gallati, Larry Gagosian, Jeannette D. Gehrie, William Gerdts, Bernd R. Gericke, David Goodrich, Philip Greven, Helen A. Harrison, Leata Hasler, Mary C. Henderson, Lawrence Heyl, Glenn Horowitz, Janet Hutchinson, E. J. Kahn, Thomas A. Kane, Frederick R. Karl, Willa Kim, Carole Klein, Bettina L. Knapp, Janet Le Clair, David Levy, M.D., Pat Lynagh, Don Lynch, Richard Macksey, Betty Magill, Thomas P. Magill, M.D., Madeline F. Matz, Paul Mees, Dara Mitchell, Lorette Moureaux, Robert L. Mowery, Eleanor Munro, Mary Murray, Percy North, Roger Randolph North, Marlene Park, Erica Passantino, Ron Peck, Robert Pincus-Witten, Ronald Pisano, Michael Quick, Carrie Rebora, Jacqueline Risset, Julie Rizzato, William Rubin, Stephen Saffron, Catherine Schear, Howard Schuman, Charles and Lenore Seliger, Susan Sheehan, Roberta K. Tarbell, Diane Tepfer, Judith Tick, Thayer C. Tolles, Louise Traeger, Ruth O. Trovato, Joyce Tyler, Barbara Wolanin, Laurel Weintraub, Virginia Weygandt, Breene Wright, Frank Wright, Milton Wright, Chris Yang, and Judith K. Zilczer.

I wish to single out Anton and Joan Schiffenhaus and Laurence and Betty Schiffenhaus for their generosity, encouragement, and trust. My work has been generously and ably counseled by Harriet Pilpel, Carl D. Lobell, and Gloria Phares. Barbara Novak and Brian O'Doherty have given me proof of the warmth and intelligence that won the hearts of the Hoppers. To Arnold Newman and Sidney Waintrob I am grateful for the acute humanity of their photographs and their frank recollections of their subjects. Ellen K. Levy read early drafts and offered a painter's perspective. My colleagues Eloise Quinones-Keber and Virginia Smith offered unfailing support.

At Knopf, I appreciate the early and unwavering enthusiasm of the managing editor Kathy Hourigan. To my editor Susan Ralston, I owe many good suggestions, patience, and above all sustained belief in the value of this project. I also wish to thank Amanda Gordon for her cheerful assistance, Carol Devine Carson for the jacket design, and Iris Weinstein for the interior design, as well as Susan Chun, production manager; Debra Helfand, production editor; Laura Zigman, promotion manager; and Kathy Zuckerman, publicity manager.

This book is joyfully dedicated to my husband, John Babcock Van Sickle, who deserves credit not only for his unflagging interest and enthusiasm, but for his unique contributions which have been collaborative in the best sense. He has supplied remarkable insights at every level, literary acumen, translations, editorial improvements, and above all, good cheer at sharing our home with the Hoppers for so many years.

INDEX

Abbott, Berenice, 410, 514, 520, 522
Abbott's House, 199
Abe Lincoln in Illinois (Sherwood), 308
abstract art, 267, 378, 383, 539, 546, 548, 555
    artists' group to protest emphasis on, 444,
    446, 448, 457–8. *See also Reality*
    Hopper on, 401, 460, *461, 462*
Abstract Expressionists (Abstract Expres-
    sionism), 401, 415, 438, 462, 500, 526,
    546, 578
A.C.A. Gallery, 541
ACT I, ACT II NECK, THE ESCAPE, 24,
    25
Adams, J. Donald, 412, 425, 436, 462, 487,
    490
Adams House, 291
adolescence of Edward Hopper. *See* child-
    hood and adolescence of Edward
    Hopper
Adventure (magazine), 108
advertising work, 48, 73, 79, 87
    refusal of requests to do, 329–30, 355–6
aesthetics (aesthetic philosophy), 39, 41–3,
    48, 486–7
    in Hopper's foreword for 1951 Corcoran
    catalogue, 438
    Valéry on, 311
"Affection of Fathers" (Montaigne), 15
African-Americans, 20, 488–9
Aiken, Conrad, 477, 526
À la Route au Theatre, 196
Albright, Ivan, 428
All About Eve (film), 435
Aloha Hive (religious camp), 163

American Academy of Arts and Letters,
    499, 500, 549, 564
American art. *See* national art
American Art Association (Paris), 60
American Artist (magazine), 490, 491, 494
American Artists Group, 284
American Art News, 95, 97, 111, 128, 202
American Art Research Council, 360
American culture, 402. *See also* American
    literature; cultural nationalism;
    national art
American Etchers Salon at Brown-Robert-
    son Galleries, 138
American expatriates, 205, 278, 382
American Express Pavilion (New York
    World's Fair), 570
American Federation of the Arts, 512
American folk art, 221
American Landscape, 132, 135, 209
American literature, 200, 205, 402. *See also*
    specific authors
"Americanness," 197
American Place, An (gallery), 253
American Print Makers, 209–10
American Red Cross, 115, 121
"American scene," 202, 234, 280, 377, 480, 494
American Scene, The (James), 279, 359
American Society of Independent Artists,
    First Annual Exhibition of (1917), 114
American subjects, 41, 75, 85, 94, 129, 200,
    211. *See also* national art
American Village, 89, 96, 108, 114, 201
À Mlle. Jo. Noel 1923 (Christmas card), 173,
    174

Anarchism, 20, 21
anatomy, 35
Anderson, Maxwell, 499, 500
Anderson, Sherwood, 200, 218, 397, 423
Anderson Galleries, 139, 141, 189, 196
Anderson's House, 199
Andover Academy, teaching exhibition for
    (1939), 215
Andreyev, Leonid, 157
angle. *See* perspective
Anshutz, Thomas, 39, 48
Antick, The (MacKaye), 156
Apartment Houses, 189
appearance, Edward Hopper's, 47, 125,
    219–20, 232, 239–40
    as adolescent, 12–13, 26
    du Bois on, 124
    personal characteristics of, 168
Appleton, Marie, 209, 390, 472
Approaching a City, 388
Après-midi de Juin, 66
Après-midi de Printemps, 129
Architectural League, 300
architecture, 131, 139, 280, 288, 359
    American vernacular (native), 217,
        279–80, 290
    Latin American, 456
    photographs of architectural details, 67,
        114
    skyscrapers, 201, 228–9, 247, 281; James
        on, 279
    Victorian houses, 131, 139, 169–70, 185,
        195, 234–5, 279–80
Arden, Elizabeth, 559
Arensberg, Walter, 338, 377
Armory Show (1913), 89–90
Arms, John Taylor, 452
art critics. *See* critical reactions to Hopper
Art Digest, 242, 252, 383
Arthur (Josephine Hopper's cat), xi, 163,
    165, 168, 171, 175–6, 196, 463, 473, 548,
    551, 563, 579
    disappearance of, 190
    Mrs. Kit Hopper's one man jury show and,
        532, 533
articles and reviews by Edward Hopper
    The Arts, reviews and articles for, 204–6,
        216, 253, 279
    Corcoran Gallery of Art, essay for (1951),
        436, 438, 441

du Bois's request for article on realism,
    377–9
    Reality, statement in, 460
Art in America, 533
    award from, 541, 542
Art Institute of Chicago, 115, 142, 188, 329,
    347, 351–3, 383, 563, 565
    Chicago Society of Etchers at, 128
    honorary degree from, 427–8
Art News, 383, 402, 501
Art News Annual (1957), 506
Art Nouveau, 73
"Art of This Century" show (1945), 377–8
art press, nationalist campaign in, 94. *See
    also* critical reactions to Hopper; *specific
    publications, critics, and reviewers*
Arts, The (magazine), 197, 200, 203, 204, 216
Arts and Decoration (magazine), 97, 108
art schools and teachers, 113
    New York School of Art. *See* New York
        School of Art
    New York School of Illustrating, 27–9
Arts Club of Chicago, 255
Art Society (Utica, New York), 215
Art Student, The (Henri), 150, *152*
Art Students League, 39, 43, 46, 154
art supplies, 17, 27, 303, 484
Art Times, 526–7, 531
Ash Can School, 138, 484
Ash's House, 222
Associated American Artists, 355
Associated Sunday Magazine, 89, 350
Atget, Eugène, 67
Atlas-like figures, 81–2, 86
At Valley Forge, 20
Audubon Society, 449
August in the City, 375, 383
Automat, 201, 292, 511
Automat restaurants, 292, 517, 518
automobiles. *See* cars and driving
"Autres Fragments sur Mallarmé: Morceaux
    Choisis" (Valéry), 321
Autumn Rhythm (Pollock), 526
Aux Fortifications, 141, 197
Avery, Milton, 167
awards won by Hopper. *See* prizes and
    awards won by Hopper

Back of Freight Station, 244
Bacon, Peggy, 140, 321, 361, 404, 448, 532

Bailey, Temple, 122
Baird, Peggy, 159
Baker, Captain L. D., 250, 326
Baker, Ethel, 346, 498
Balcony, The (The Movies), 212
Balthus, 301
Baltimore Museum of Art, 238
Balzac, Honoré de, 63, 148, 489
Bandbox Theatre, 156
Bangor, Maine, 198
Baptist church (Baptists), 5, 12, 20, 39, 49, 52, 69, 72, 79, 134, 175, 180, 222, 278, 412, 486, 570
Baptistery of St. John's, 222, 334
Barber Shop, 240, 480
Barn at Essex, 223
Barnes, Bert Edward, 116, 117
Barnes Collection, 553
Barr, Alfred H., Jr., 4, 55, 107–8, 191, 201, 225, 251, 268, 274, 351–4, 366, 489–90
    1933 retrospective and, 253–5
Barrymore, Ethel, 47
baseball, 11, 22, 46, 91
Basserman, Albert, 383
Bates, Esther, 509
Bathers, 115
Baudelaire, Charles, xii, xiii, 46, 161, 225, 311
Baur, John (Jack), xv, 458, 535
Bayard, Lucy, 413, 519, 560, 575
Bay Window, The, 127, 139
Beach, Sarah E., 150
Beal, Gifford, 34, 183, 383, 495
Beam Trawler Seal, 171
Beau Desert (Saverney, France), hospital at, 160
Becker, Dorothy, 390
Becker, Maurice, 164, 390, 519
Beckwith, J. Carroll, 35
Bedell, Ralph, 4, 25, 263
Behre, Edwine, 389
Belcher, Hilda, 45
Belden, Susie, 153
Bell, Edith, 47
Bell, Ernest A., 98
Bellows, Emma (née Story), 46, 47, 104
Bellows, George, 34, 46, 74, 85, 87, 89, 96, 97, 104, 105, 108, 111–13, 141, 183, 186, 195, 238, 254
    death of, 188–9

Belmaison Gallery of Decorative Arts, 141, 165
Benda, Wladyslaw Theodor, 45, 121
Benton, Thomas Hart, 171, 330, 494
Berenson, Bernard, 481, 490
Beresford, Virginia, 303
Berge, La, 89, 173–4
Berlin, 1907 visit to, 71
Bernstein, Aline, 165
Bernstein, Theresa, 115, 167, 203, 265, 295, 418, 439
Beston, Henry, 436
Bible, the, 412
bicycling, 31, 292–3
Biddle, George, 295, 467, 499–500, 512
Bierstadt, Albert, 31, 338
biography, xii
Birth of Venus (Botticelli), 322
Bisaccio, Philip, 526
Bishop, Isabel, 422, 446, 449, 458, 460, 462, 482, 483, 546, 547
Bistro, Le (The Wine Shop), 80, 86, 87, 129
"black and white modeling," 40–1
Blackhead Monhegan, 129
Blackwell's Island (Hopper), 85–7, 90, 217–18
Blackwell's Island, East River (Henri), 85
Blaine, Nell, 377
Blanchard, Elizabeth Cameron (Bee), 186, 223, 230, 232, 244, 258–62, 261, 264, 268, 300, 301, 342, 353, 407, 422, 452
Blanchard, Phyllis, 182
Blauvelt, Abraham, 8
Blauvelt, Lillian, 11
Blauvelt, Marie, 8
Bloom, Hyman, 484
Blum, Alice, 162
Boats (Josephine Hopper), 202
boats, sailing, and nautical scenes, 18, 30, 40, 85–8, 96, 110, 115, 169, 170, 223, 269, 295, 314–15, 342–3, 370, 426
    cat boat Hopper built as a youth, 4–5
Bob Slater's Hill, 305
bohemian life, 51, 58, 60, 67, 93, 101
Bootleggers, The, 193, 194, 195, 196, 282, 491
Borne, Mortimer, 522
Boros, Billi, 526
Boss, Homer, 34, 154
Boston, 89, 96, 160, 186, 211, 244, 249, 257–8, 295, 305, 330, 343, 354, 369, 398, 405, 518, 532, 536, 547, 559–60

Boston Arts Club, 197

Boston Arts Festival (1963), 559

Boston Museum. *See* Museum of Fine Arts, Boston

Boston Public Library, 512–13

Boston *Sunday Globe,* 523

Botticelli, Sandro, 322

Bouché, Louis, 121, 140, 165, 174, 183, 222, 457, 532, 539

Bourgeois Gallery, 109

Bowman Deute Cummings Agency, 329

Bow of Beam Trawler Widgeon, 202

boxing, 25, 32–3, 46, 78–9

Boyce, Neith, 159

Boys' Yacht Club, 4

Boy with a Sword (Manet), 40

Brady, Eddy, 494, 497, 571, 577, 579

Brady, Mathew, 20, 246, 256, 297, 326

Bragdon, Claude, 301

Breton, André, 401

Breuer, Bessie. *See* Poor, Bessie Breuer

Breuning, Margaret, 163, 187, 315, 390, 423

Briar Neck, 88

Bridge, The, 94

Bridge, The, Blackwell's Island (Bellows), 85

Bridle Path, 282, 312–13

Brief Estimates of the Painters (Phillips), 200

Brill, A. A., 93

Brinley, Daniel Putnam, 59

British Steamer, 87

Brockhurst, Gerald, 315

Brook, Alexander, 315, 404, 458

Brooklyn Daily Eagle, 253, 254

Brooklyn *Eagle,* 197

Brooklyn Museum, 164, 188, 377
    watercolors exhibit (1923), 171–2

Brooklyn Society of Etchers, 136, 139
    First International Exhibition of Etching organized by (1922), 139

Brooks, Van Wyck, 165, 205, 277, 305, 382–3, 402, 436, 462, 519
    New England Indian Summer: 1865–1915, 345–6

Browne, Byron, 499

Brown-Robertson Galleries, 138, 139, 141

Bruce, Helen Kibbey, 59, 60

Bruce, Patrick Henry, 34, 45, 48, 59, 60, 77

Brummer, Joseph, 190, 338

Brush and Pencil (magazine), 27–8

Brussels, 71

Bryan Prize for the Best American Print, 142

Budd, Katherine. *See* Proctor, Katherine

Buggy, The (House on a Hill), 131, 195

Buick in California Canyon (Josephine Hopper), 509, *510*

Bull Fight, The, 104, 115, 116, *117,* 128, 136

bullfights, 82–3

Bulliet, C. J., 255, 274–5, 383

Burchfield, Charles, 162, 187, 230, 234, 242, 253–5, 309, 310, 315, 326, 331, 376, 422–3, 432, 452, 475, 483, 495, 505
    Hopper's article on (1928), 216, 253
    on Hopper's work, 423–4
    Pousette-Dart on Hopper and, 265–6

burlesque, 310, 335

Burly Cobb Hen Coop and Barn, 231

Burly Cobb's House, 231

Burns, Tommy, 79

Burrey, Suzanne, 483

Burroughs, Bryson, 238

Burrows, Carlyle, 401, 423

Butler Art Institute, 464

Cadmus, Paul, 418, 437

Cahiers d'André Walter, Les (Gide), 561–2

Cahill, Holger, 495

Caillebotte, Gustave, 66, 89, 201

Calder, Alexander, 448

Calder, Stirling, 196

California
    1941 trip to, 338–9
    1956–1957 stay in, 506, 508–10

California Hills, 510, 512

California Water Color Society, 327

Calvin Howe and His Two Sisters (anonymous), 221, 243, *245,* 522

Camel's Hump, The, 240

Campbell, Jewett and Jean, 458

Camp Nyack, Greenwood Lake, 31, 32

Canaday, John, 546, 551, 552, 565

Canadian National Exhibition, 136

Canal at Charenton, 553

Canal Lock at Charenton, 67

Cape Ann Granite, 217

Cape Ann Pasture, 217

Cape Bedroom (Josephine Hopper), 496, 513

Cape Cod, Massachusetts, 233, 243, 244, 249.
    See also Truro, Massachusetts
    light shadows in, 258
    sunsets on, 259

Cape Cod Afternoon, 290, 294

Cape Cod Art Association, 451

Cape Cod Bedroom (Josephine Hopper), 522, 531, 560

Cape Cod Bureau (Josephine Hopper), 549

Cape Cod Evening, 313–14, 350
  frame for, 320–1
  study for, *314*

Cape Cod Hills (exhibited as *Sandy Hills*) (Josephine Hopper), 232, 298, 299, 302

Cape Cod Morning, 431–2, 549

Cape Cod Sunset, 256

Cape Elizabeth, Maine, lighthouse at Two Lights on, 207, 208

Cape Flowers (Josephine Hopper), 513

Capron House, 249

Captain Ed Staples, 213, 329, 349

Captain Kelly's House, 240, 243

Captain Strout's House, 208

Captain Upton's House, 208

caricatures, 30
  of Arthur (Jo's cat), 176
  in childhood and adolescence, 15, 25–6
  of Josephine Hopper: *Colonel Hopper SLICK BABY BRIGADE,* 354, *355*; *The HOUSE THAT JO BUILT,* 259, *260*; *Jo's "Cellar-way" Studio at Provincetown years ago,* 157, *158*; of married life, 176–9, *177–80*, 183, 192, 196, 237; for tenth wedding anniversary (1934), 261, *261*
  Mrs. Kit Hopper's one man jury show, 532, *533*
  self-, 26, 47–8, 93, 106, 274, *274*
  of sexually available women in Paris, 61, 108, 140, 337

Carmer, Betty, 509

Carmer, Carl, 509

Carné, Marcel, 530, 573

Carnegie Institute (Pittsburgh)
  1924 international exhibition at, 173–4
  1937 one-man show at, 293
  1939 international exhibition at, 315

Carroll, John, 299, 352

cars and driving, 303, 364, 369, 482
  1941 cross-country trip, 337–42
  Edward as bad driver, 328
  first car, 206, 208
  Josephine Hopper and, 206, 208, 224–5, 283, 285, 297, 304–5, 372, 373, 378, 379,

404, 416, 429–30, 439–40, 442, 467, 468, 523, 552
  women in the 1920s and, 206

cartoons, 22, 25. *See also* caricatures

Cary, Elizabeth Luther, 171, 187, 197

Cassatt, Mary, 309, 321

Cassou, Jean, 470

Cat Boat, The, 170, 209, 210

cats, 286–7. *See also* Arthur

C. C. Phillips and Company, 48

Cederquist, Arthur E., 86, 140, 174

Cederquist, Milton, 86

Central Park (New York), 312

Century (magazine), 30, 35

Century Club, 383, 388–9

Cervantes, Miguel, 29, 376

Cézanne, Paul, 58, 59, 109, 135, 401, 413

Chabrol, Claude, 530

Chace, Malcolm and Happy, 526, 527, 529, 540, 545, 547

Chaffee, Oliver N., 77, 415

Chagall, Marc, 315

Chair Car, 567–8

Chanin, A. L., 511

Chapellier Gallery, 571

Chapin, James Ormsbee, 85, 87, 267, 299, 301–2

Chapin, Joseph Hawley, 122

Chapin, Lou, 390

Chaplin, Charlie, 47

"Charles Burchfield: American," 216, 279

Charleston, South Carolina, 221–2

Charleston Doorway, 222, 334

Charleston Slum, 222

Charlestown Tree (Josephine Hopper), 217

Charlottesville, Virginia, 223

Chase, Dorothy, 37

Chase, William Merritt, 33–8, 40, 43, 90, 204

Chase School of Art, 33, 34, 43

Chatterton, Clarence K. (Chat), 34, 35, 36, 79, 103, 108, 111, *124*, 208, 217, 230, 336, 376–7, 480, 565, 569
  portraits by Hopper of, 125, *127*

Chatterton, Julia, 484, 569, 575

Chatterton, Margaret Antoinette (Annette), 208, 217, 469

Chayefsky, Paddy, 495

Cheek, Leslie, 458

Chekhov, Anton, 538

Chéruy, Jeanne, 142, 144–5, 167, 168, 173, 280, 388
 drawings of, *143, 144*
Chez Hopper (Josephine Hopper), 303, *304*, 315, 410, 570
Chez Hopper II (Josephine Hopper), 353, 513, 516
Chez Hopper III (Josephine Hopper), 377, 388, 526, 549
Chicago Arts Club, 186
Chicago *Herald Examiner,* 155
Chicago Society of Etchers, 115, 128
childhood and adolescence of Edward Hopper, 3, 10–13
 ancestors, 5–8
 art, 13, 16–26
 boating, 4–5
 drawings made during, 16–18, 20–3, 25, 35, 37
 father's influence, 13–16
 intellectual and literary interests, 13–15
 oil paintings, 18
 pranks, 10, 22
 recreation and family outings, 11–12
 school, 10–11, *13*, 25
 Sunday school, 12
children (and Edward Hopper), 106, 136, 184, 339, 489
Chop Suey, 172, 221
Christian Science Monitor, 515
Christmas cards
 1923, 173, *174*
 1955, 484–5
Church of San Esteban (Edward Hopper), 391
Church of San Esteban (Josephine Hopper). See San Esteban
Cikovsky, Nicolai, 457, 471
Cincinnati Art Museum, 347
cinema. *See* movies
Circle Theatre, The, 285, 291
Cité, La, 129
City, The, 201, 229, 309
City Roofs, 247
City Sunlight, 477
Civil War, American, 20, 198, 221–3, 256, 297, 325–6
Civil War, Spanish, 296
Civil War Campground, 198
C. K. Chatterton on Mohegan, 127

Clancy, John, xvi, 269, 324, 384, 388, 470, 475, 479, 489, 496, 506, 512, 518, 522, 523, 549, 560, 577
Clancy, Winnie, 522
Clark, Stephen C., 186, 198, 225, 227, 350, 389, 409, 512, 518, 526, 536
Clark Prize, 141, 294, 438
Cleveland Museum, 188
Cliffs near Mitla, Oaxaca, 456
Clouzot, Henri-Georges, 500
Coates, Robert, 378, 400, 424, 471, 516, 531
Cobb, A. B. Burleigh, 230
Cobbe, Frances Power, 340
Cobb's Farm, 233
Cobb's House, 356
Cocteau, Jean, 439
Cold Storage Plant, 249
Cole, Nieta, 501
Cole, Thomas, 80, 377
Colebrook, Joan, 478
Coleman, Glenn, 34, 46, 74
Coles Phillips, Clarence, 48
Colette, 176, 466
Colker, Ed, 544, 545
Colonel Hopper SLICK BABY BRIGADE, 354, *355*
Colorado Springs, 337
Colt, Tom, 299, 300
Come Back Little Sheeba (film), 463
commedia dell'arte, 573
commercial art, 18, 29, 72, 81–2, 84–5, 107, 114. *See also* advertising work; illustrations; movie posters
Committee of Arts and Sciences (for the Eisenhower campaign), 504–5
Communism, 366, 403, 409, 418
Compartment C, Car 293, 301, *302,* 353
 essay on, 329
competitiveness, Edward Hopper's, 169, 316, 326, 354, 469, 475–6, 489
composition in art, 39, 40, 43, 215
 Summer Interior, 80–1
Conan Doyle, Arthur, 29
Condon Riley Gallery, 532
Confederate Museum (Richmond, Virginia), 223
Conference at Night, 408–9
Confident Years, The (Brooks), 382
Connah, Douglas John, 33–4, 38, 45, 153
Connelly, Marc, 483

Connoisseur Gallery, 522
Construction in Mexico, 392, 452
Content, Marjorie, 162
Convent across the Square through Fire Escape (Josephine Hopper), 464, 470, 471
Cook, George Cram "Jig," 158
Coolidge, Mountfort (Monty), 87, 160
Cooper, James Fenimore, 4
Coquelin, Contant-Benoit, 65
Corcoran Gallery of Art, 360, 460
    1923 Biennial at, 140–1
    1951 Biennial at, 428, 436–8
    1960 Biennial at, 539
    essay for (1951), 436, 438, 441
    Gold Medal from, 294
Corn Belt City, 396
Corn Dance, 191
Cornell, Elizabeth, 105–6
Cornell, Joseph, 105
Corner, A, 127, 128, 132
Corner Saloon. See New York Corner
Corn Hill, 233, 353
corporal punishment, 12
Corsi, Jimmy, 37–8
Cortissoz, Royal, 128, 138, 171, 202, 242, 366
Cottages at North Truro, 306
Cottages at Wellfleet, 249
Cotton Exchange, New Orleans, The (Degas), 324
Country Gentleman, The (magazine), 109, 111, 115
Courbet, Gustave, 48, 58–9, 549
Cousins, Les (film), 530
Cow on Monhegan, 115
cows, 130, 135–6
Cows and Rocks, 130, 135
Cox, Kenyon, 43
Craven, Thomas, 355
Creek at Hogencamps, The, 31
critical reactions to Hopper, 97, 98, 196–7, 366, 376. *See also specific critics, reviewers, and publications*
    1924 watercolors, 186–7
    1927 Rehn Gallery show and, 201–2
    1929 Rehn Gallery show and, 220
    1964 retrospective and, 565–6
    early paintings show and (1941), 333–4
    etchings, 141–2
    Museum of Modern Art restrospective (1933) and, 252–6

sexuality and, 99
    Venice Biennale and (1952), 451
    Whitney retrospective (1950) and, 423–5
cropping, 141, 184, 199
Cropsey, Jasper, 31
Crossing at Eastham, 305
Crotty, Frank, 501, 520, 540
Crowninshield, Frank, 219, 225, 243, 407
Cruikshank, Colin, 92
Cruikshank, Eva, 182
Crystal Gallery, 546, 547
Cubism (Cubists), 219, 253
cultural nationalism, 382. *See also* national art
Cuniffe, Miss, 53, 54, 69, 83
Currier Gallery of Art (Manchester, New Hampshire), 527
Curry, John Stewart, 330, 494
Custom House, Portland, 208–9
C. W. Kraushaar Art Galleries, 127, 185

D. & R. G. Locomotive, 191
Dahl-Wolfe, Louise, 243
dancing, 46, 115, 157–8, 218, 322–3, 548
Daniel, Charles, 154
Daniel Gallery, 154
Darwin, Charles, 22, 206
Dasburg, Andrew, 191, 362
Daugherty, Harry, 75
Daumier, Honoré, 48, 195, 238
Dauphinée, Constance, 244, 418
Dauphinée, Henry, 244, 418
Dauphinée House, 244, 299
Dauphinée House (Josephine Hopper), 244, 299, 549
Davey, Florence, 191
Davey, Randall, 87, 110, 113, 115, 183, 190
Davidson, Jo, 60
Davies, Arthur B., 74, 121, 162, 462
Davis, Bette, 435, 559
Davis, Gladys Rockmore, 462
Davis, Joe Lee, 276
Davis, Stuart, 90, 154, 167, 448, 451, 472, 546
Davis House, 199
Dawn before Gettysburg, 256, 291, 326
Dawn in Pennsylvania, 352–3, 400
Day, Mrs. Clarence (Peggy), 577
Day after the Funeral, 188, 189
Days of Our Years (Van Paassen), 327

Dead Tree and Side of Lombard House, 240

dead trees, 169

Dean, James, 500

death
of Edward Hopper, 577
thoughts about, 560

Decadents, French, 46

Deck of a Beam Trawler, 171

Degas (Jamot), 183

Degas, Edgar, 40, 81, 109, 127, 203, 258, 324, 380
concealment of his personal life, 183–4
influence on Hopper, 184

de Kerstrat, Yvonne, 60

de Kooning, Willem, 546, 549

Delaunay, Robert, 57, 104

Delaunay, Sonia, 104

De Lory, Jimmy, 328, *330*, 507

demi-mondaines, 57, 61, 63, 80–1. *See also*
prostitutes

Demoiselles d'Avignon, Les (Picasso), 101

Demuth, Charles, 154, 159, 165

depression, 12, 116, 217, 246, 305, 342, 355, 395, 399, 406, 411

Derain, André, 67

Descent of Man, The (Darwin), 22

Deserted House on Mountain, 31

Detroit Institute of Arts, 428

Deux Pigeons, Les, 132, 133–4, *134,* 137, 144, 145

Devree, Howard, 423, 439

Dewing, Thomas W., 92

DeWint family, 5

Diaboliques, Les (film), 500

Dial (magazine), 165, 219

Dickens, Charles, 16, 29

Dickinson, Edwin, 303, 351, 437, 450, 474, 477, 490, 496, 519, 555

Dickinson, Emily, 346

Dickinson, Preston, 154

Disney, Walt, 291

Dobkin, Alexander, 460

Dodge, Mabel, 93, 159, 191, 440

Dodsworth (Lewis), 256–7

domestic chores, 177, 231–2, 244, 246, 262–6, 441, 575, 576

Don Quixote, 103, 127

Doré, Gustave, 17

Dories, The, Ogunquit, 96, 108

Dos Passos, John, 140, 174, 286, 288, 394, 398, 565
political views of, 296

Dos Passos, Katy, 286, 287, 296, 394, 398

Downs, Frank, 206

Downtown Gallery (New York), 210

Doyle, Sir Arthur Conan, 16, 29

drawings, 251, 513. *See also* caricatures; illustrations; prints
declination of offer to buy, 284
in Paris (1906–1907), 63
pen-and-ink: of childhood and adolescence, 18, 25; in Paris (1906–1907), 63;
for poems by Poe, 46
youthful, 16–18, 20–3, 25, 35, 37

dreams, 272, 274, 381–2

Dreiser, Theodore, 200, 288, 382–3

driving. *See* cars and driving

Drug Store, 210–11, 282, 350

Dry Dock Dial. See Morse Dry Dock Dial

Dryer, Rufus J., 87

Duble, Lu, 418, 447

du Bois, Floy, 125, 128, 294, 295, 378
death of, 431

du Bois, Guy Pène, 34, 39, 45, 52, 59, 73, 75, 77, 81, 89, 93, 99–100, 108, 112, 121, 123, *124,* 125, 128, 133, 145, 183, 185, 246, 286, 295, 315, 325, 352, 377, 378, 383, 387–9, 439, 466, 478, 481
on 1920 one-man show, 129, 130
as champion of Hopper's work, 74, 87, 97, 108, 112, 123–4, 128, 140, 234, 476–7
death of, 518–19
death of wife of, 431
departure for France (1953), 458, 460
as editor of *Arts and Decoration,* 97, 108, 112
on etchings, 115–16
on Hopper's character, 124–5, 129
marriage of Edward and Jo Hopper and, 175
monograph on Hopper (1931), 238
Montross Gallery show and (1914), 96–7
portraits by Hopper of, 125, 126
on Puritanism, 97, 238–9, 276–7, 280
on *Road in Maine,* 97
on *Soir Bleu,* 100, 101

du Bois, Yvonne, 302, 458, 547

Duchamp, Marcel, 90, 109, 338

Du Côté de Chez Swann (Proust), 280
Dufy, Raoul, 321
du Mond, Frank Vincent, 35, 39
Duncan, Isadora, 155, 182
Dunlavy, Maurice, 257, *261*, 261–2
Durand-Ruel, 109
Dureyea, Hetty, 47, 206
Dutch heritage and ancestry, 3, 5, 6–8, 239
Dwight, Mabel, 140

Eakins, Thomas, 39, 92, 377, 518, 548, 554, 567
"Early Paintings by Edward Hopper: 1907–1914" show (1941), 333–5
Early Sunday Morning, 18, 227–30, *228*, 350, 441, 512
easel built by Edward Hopper, 187, *188*, 258
Eastham, Massachusetts, 327, 344, 370, 371, 404, 406–7, 417
Eastman, Max, 93, 99, 155–6, 508–9
Eastport, Maine, 198
East River (New York), 85, 193, 213, 217
East Side Interior, 138, 142, 165
East Wind over Weehawken, 257
Echo (school magazine), 149–150
Eclair (Société Française des Films et Cinématographes), 95
Eddy, Frederick W., 201
Edel, Leon, 278
Edward Hopper Boxing with Wallace Tremper, 32–3, *33*
Edward Hopper Reading Robert Frost (Josephine Hopper), 492, *492*
Edward MacDowell medal, 575
Eglise Evangélique Baptiste (Paris), 49
egotism. *See* selfishness
Eiffel Tower, 56, 57
"Eight, The," 74–5, 90, 338, 462
Eight Male Figures of Different Nationalities and Occupations, 23
Eisenhower, Dwight D., 504–5
Eleven A.M., 201, 216–17, 480
Eliot, Alexander, 485, 500, 507, 528
Eliot, Jane, 528
Eliot, T. S., 415, 462, 485
Ellis, Albert, 514–15
El Palacio, 392
El Station, The, 75

Emergency Committee for Southern Political Prisoners, 288
Emerson, Ralph Waldo, 14–15, 41, 91, 216, 276, 278, 382, 457, 521, 560
puritanism and, 276–8
"Self-Reliance," 204, 216
Emperor's Ghost, The (Bailey), 122
Enchantment of Don Quixote, The (illustrated by Doré), 17
Enfants du Paradis, Les (film), 530, 573
entertaining. *See* social life and entertaining
Ernst, Max, 401
Essex, Massachusetts, 223
etching(s), 102, 109, 115, 142, 167, 170, 189, 252, 293, 426. *See also* prints
of 1919–1920, 125–8
of 1921, 132–8
1922 exhibition of, 139–40
of 1923, 141–2, 172
1926 exhibits of, 197
Hopper on, 130, 139
origin of Hopper's interest in, 102–3
European influence, rejection of, 205. *See also* national art
Evening, the Seine, 112, 115
Evening Wind, 132–3, 136, 137, *137*, 138, 139, 142, 252–3
Evergood, Philip, 438, 471, 546
Everybody's (magazine), 85, 93, 96
Excursion into Philosophy, 276, 523–6, *524*, 562
Exhibition of Independent Artists (1910), 81
Exhibition of Paintings and Drawings by Contemporary American Artists (1908), 74–5
EX-LAX, contretemps over, 210–11

Falacci, Frank, 523
Falkner, Martha, 291
Falkner, Stella, 310
"Fantastic Art, Dada and Surrealism" show (1936), 274
Farmer's Wife (magazine), 102, 104, 111
Farm House at Essex, 223
Farnsworth, Jerry, 477
Fathers and Sons (Turgenev), 15
Faure, Sébastien, 65
Federal Arts Project, 286
Feininger, Lyonel, 60, 331, 402

feminists, 155, 161, 182

Feragil Gallery, 448

Ferris, Dorothy, 290, 291 300, 301, 310, 316, 327, 330, 334, 364, 389, 532, 545, 578

Ferris, Hugh, 290–1, 300, 310, 316

Ferris, Jean, 364

Field, Hamilton Easter, 95, 165

Fiene, Ernest, 457

Fight, The Bull, 127

fights and violence between Edward and Jo Hopper, 303–5, 334, 340, 342, 351, 372, 390–1, 417, 430, 466, 490, 527, 552

figure, the, renewed interest in, 139, 140

Fille de Joie, 61, 62

films. *See* movies

financial affairs, 113. *See also* sales of art
    in 1915, 104, 105
    in 1919, 125
    in 1920, 131
    in 1923, 172
    in 1928, 220
    prize won for poster (1918), 117, 118, 120
    rent, 117

Finnish Relief, 321

Fire Escape (Josephine Hopper), 513

First Branch of the White River, 305

First Row Orchestra, 437, 480

Fisher, Elizabeth, 71

Five A.M., 295, 337

Flandreau, Charles M., 466

Flaubert, Gustave, 16, 75, 416, 417

Flexner, Beatrice, 551

Flexner, James, 528, 536–7, 540, 551, 558

Flint, Ralph, 209

Floch, Joseph, 486

flowers, 165, 169, 205, 241, 259, 264, 298, 370, 404–5, 426, 464, 467–8, 486, 489, 490, 513

Folly Beach, 222

Fontainebleau, 77

Forain, Jean-Louis, 81, 238

Force, Juliana, 128, 209, 229, 284, 315, 346, 359, 376, 388, 404, 407, 458, 534, 557

Forked Road, The, 264, 386

Fort Sumter, 221–2

Fortune (magazine), 296

Fortuny y Carbo, Mariano, 37

40 Steps up to Chez Hopper (Josephine Hopper), 550

Forum '49, 415

Four Dead Trees, 356, 357

Four Lane Road, 506, 526
    study for, 505

Fox, William Henry, 171

frames (framing), 184, 217, 320–1, 324, 359, 418, 475, 490, 514, 550

France, 112, 122, 135, 145, 239, 320, 433, 439–40, 458. *See also* French subjects; Paris
    Edward Hopper in, 49–71, 76–9, 82, 382
    Jo Hopper in, 153, 159–60

France America Corporation, 125

Francis, Charlie, 537

Fraser, John, 186

Frederick Keppel and Company, 112, 115, 141, 543

Freight Car at Truro, 240

Freight Cars, Gloucester, 217, 230

French ancestry, 5, 16, 147, 203, 239

French art, 37, 40, 48, 66, 89, 129, 184, 201, 203, 219, 238, 239

French illustration, 81

French language, xvii, 54–5, 63, 77, 98, 100, 106–7, 145, 148, 162, 168, 172–3, 175–6, 189, 272, 310, 336, 342, 439, 444

French literature, 14–16, 41, 46, 55, 61, 124, 133, 144–5, 148, 161, 168, 173, 176, 225, 280, 311, 346, 412, 432, 444

French people, 63, 65, 98, 388

French Six-day Bicycle Rider, 292–3

French subjects, 75, 80, 84, 87, 94, 98–101, 112, 122, 125, 128–9, 132, 134, 135, 203, 233
    at 1920 one-man show, 128–30
    Parisian caricatures, 61, 108, 140, 337

Freud, Sigmund (Freudian theory), 93, 272, 274, 277

Friedman, Arnold, 74, 265, 299, 325, 383, 386, 411

From Williamsburg Bridge, 213

Frost, Arthur Burdett, Jr., 59

Frost, Robert, 136, 189, 382, 399, 415, 423, 428, 487, 491–3, 541, 542

Fry, Roger, 165

funeral for Edward Hopper, 577

Gaîté Montparnasse (du Bois), 75

Galerie de la Chambre Syndicale des Beaux-Arts (Paris), 183

Gallery 200 (Provincetown), 415

Garber, Daniel, 299
Gardiner, Albert, 522
Gardner, Paul, 337
Gare d'Orléans, 66
Garner, John Nance, 303
Garrett Prize, 357
Gas, 328, 331, 337, 357, 366
   study for, *329*
Gateway and Fence, Saint Cloud, 67
Gavarni, 238
Geffen, Felicia, 485
Genauer, Emily, 401, 451, 462, 565
George L. Dyer Company, 140
Germany, poster art in, 120
Gettysburg, Pennsylvania, 223, 256, 325–6
G. H. Hopper Dry Goods, 8, 25
Giacometti, Alberto, 402
Gibson, Charles Dana, 29, 114, 121
Gide, André, xiii, 429, 436, 466, 561
Gifford, Sanford Robinson, 31
Gikow, Ruth, 499, 534, 535, 547, 576
Gimbel's department store, 117
Girl Asleep, A (Vermeer), 201
Girlie Show, 335–7
Girl on a Bridge, 141, 545
Glackens, Edith, 383
Glackens, William, 74, 86, 89, 92, 294, 309,
   383, 462
Glaspell, Susan, 158, 394
Glebe, The (magazine), 154
Gloucester, Massachusetts, 87, 88, 198, 470
   1923 summer in, 167–70
   1924 summer in, 174–5
   1926 summer in, 199
   1928 summer in, 217
Gloucester Harbor, 88, 94, 96
Gloucester Society of Artists, 167
Gloucester Street, 199, 201, 480
Goethe, Johann Wolfgang von, 14, 30, 266,
   276, 394, 487, 543
Golden, Samuel, 390, 463
Golden Gate Exhibition, 303, 315
Goldman, Emma, 254
Goldsmith, Bea Kroll, 560
Golz, Julius, Jr., 74, 85, 110
Good Harbor Beach, Bridge at Bass Rock
   (Kroll), 88
Goodrich, Edith, 300
Goodrich, Lloyd, xiii, xv, 101, 197, 293, 300,
   331, 377, 418, 421, 422, 438, 455, 458,

460, 463, 477, 484, 520–1, 523, 525, 534,
   535, 537, 540, 553, 555, 577
"The Paintings of Edward Hopper"
   (1927), 203
Goodwin, Philip, 321
Goodyear, William H., 171
Gorge de Franchard, 77
Gottlieb, Adolph, 415
gouache, 18
Goya y Lucientes, Francisco José de, 40, 78,
   83, 112, 317
Graduate, The (newspaper), 25
Graecen, Edmund, 34, 48, 59, 138
Graff, William V., 139
Graham, Martha, 548
Gravel Bar, White River, 480
Graves, Morris, 497
Gray, Tommy, 399, 407, 492
Great Depression, 227, 250, 271, 289
Great Eastern, 18
Great God Arthur, The, 176, 177
Greenbaum, Dorothea, 462
Greenberg, Clement, 395–6
Greenwich Gallery, 511, 519, 520
   Josephine Hopper's show at, 514–17
Greenwich Village, 92–4, 103, 107, 128, 153,
   155, 159, 160, 163, 168, 177, 180, 247,
   286, 306, 471, 495, 548
Gregory, Dorothy Lake, 263
Gregory, Horace, 229, 253
Griffiths, Elizabeth Lozier, 5, 7, 16
Griffiths, Joseph W., 5, 7
Grisette, La, 61
Gropper, William, 457, 485
Gross, Chaim, 559
Gross, Renée, 559
Grosser, Maurice, 471, 486, 499, 532
Grosz, George, 475
Ground Swell, 314–15, 360, 426
Guanajuato, Mexico, 454–6
Guggenheim, Peggy, 377
Guggenheim Museum, 563
Guibour (miracle play), 161
Guilbert, Yvette, 99, 161–2
Guillaume, Albert, 81
Guinney Boats (Josephine Hopper), 197
Guinney Fleet in Fog (Josephine Hopper),
   199
Gulack, Herman, 511, 513, 515, 517–21, 535
Gulack, Irving, 519

Hackett, Frances and Albert, 293, 550
Haines, Richard, 438
Hale, Barbara, 522
Hale, Robert Beverly, 472, 522, 526
Hall, G. Stanley, 151
Halpert, Edith, 210, 388
Halpert, Samuel, 59, 154
Hals, Frans, 37, 48, 58, 71, 79, 236
Haltiwanger, Gertrude Wulbern, 222
Hamlet (film), 407
Hapgood, Hutchins, 159
Harnett, Lila, 579
Harper's (magazine), 17, 18, 29, 432
Harriman, Marie, 298
Harrington, Gertrude P., 150
Harris, Harold, 489
Harris, Hartman K., 71
Harris, Leslie, 489
Hart, George "Pop," 209, 210
Hartley, Marsden, 154, 191, 277, 301, 362
Hartman, Bertram, 162, 165, 413, *414*, 437,
    452, 552
Hartman, Rosella, 265
Hartpence, Alanson (Lance), 154, 338
Harwich, 468
Haskell's House, 186
Hassam, Childe, 136–7, 185, 242
Hatch, Robert, 549
Haunted House, 198
Haworth, Edith, 47
Hawthorne, Nathaniel, 29, 278
Hayes, Bartlett, 486
Hayes, Helen, 295, 316–18, 330, 344, 364, 505
    Hopper commissioned to paint house of
        (*Pretty Penny*), 316–18
health of Edward Hopper, 191, 224, 299,
    300, 305, 330, 363, 369, 407, 422, 445–6,
    473, 499, 500, 522, 523, 528, 562,
    569–70, 575, 576
    age, effects of, 450
    eyesight, 439
    fatigue and lethargy, 224, 237, 343, 442
    hernia operations, 473, 475, 476, 575, 576
    prostate operations, 402, 411–13, 513, 519
Hearn, Lafcadio, 205, 206
Heiress, The (film), 421
Hemingway, Ernest, 296, 350
Henri, Robert, xvii, 34, 39–48, 70–2, 74, 75,
    81, 82, 83, 84, 85, 87, 104, 105, 108, 110,
    111, 115, 120, 140, 162, 164, 190, 196,

    204, 237, 254, 281, 291, 295, 296, 304,
        309, 357, 462, 484, 521
    The Art Student, 150, 152
    Century Club show (1946), 383, 388–9
    death of, 224
    etchings and, 112–13
    Hopper on, 41–3
    Josephine Hopper and, 150–1, 237–8
    MacDowell Club group shows and, 86
Henri School of Art, 154
Henry Ford, 170
"Henry James: The American Scene"
    (Brooks), 205
Heron Art Institute, 240
Herron, Davis, 417–18, 477, 489, 504, 511
Herron, Elsa-Ruth, 417–18, 477, 489
Hess, Thomas, 552
Heyward, DuBose, 221
Hic Jacet (Josephine Hopper), *459*
Hidalgo de Caviedes, Hipôlito, 315
Highland Light, 231
High Noon, 416–19, 423
High Road, 240
Hill and Houses, 208
Hills of Truro (Josephine Hopper), 360
Hills, South Truro, 231
Hirsch, Germaine, 486
Hirsch, Joseph, 482, 486, 511, 534, 547
Hirshhorn, Joseph, 480
historical subjects, 256, 326
History of British and American Etching, A
    (Laver), 225
Hitchcock, Alfred, 536, 560
Hodgkin's House, 217
Hofmann, Hans, 415, 477, 546
Hofmann, Mitz, 477
Holland, 1907 visit to, 70–1
Hollenbeck, Webb P., 34
Homage to Eakins (R. Soyer), 554
Homer, Winslow, 20, 95, 97, 171, 256, 377,
    424, 547
honesty. *See* sincerity
Hood, Thomas, 29, 63
Hook Mountain, Nyack, 31
Hoover, Herbert, 218
Hopkinson, Charles, 299
Hoppen, Andries, 7
Hopper, Charity Blauvelt (great-grand-
    mother), 7–8, 9, 55
Hopper, Christian (great-grandfather), 7, 9

Hopper, Edward
  as celebrity or legend, 346
  death of, 577
  early life of. *See* childhood and adolescence of Edward Hopper
  funeral for, 577
  inability to paint, 262, 292, 297, 298, 424
  photographs of. *See* photographs of Edward Hopper
Hopper, Elizabeth (mother), 5, 6–7, 10, 12, 22, 25, 26, 48, 75, 90, 105, 267
  death of, 267–8
  health of, 267
  as insufficiently appreciative of Edward, 247
  Josephine Hopper and, 175, 234, 244, 262, 267–8
  letters from Edward to, 244; in 1900, 31–2; from New Mexico (1925), 192; from Paris (1906), 49–52, 54–5, 59, 69; from Paris (1909), 77–8
  Paris sojourn of 1906–1907 and, 49–54
  photographs of, *11*, 176
  public acclaim for son and, 266
Hopper, Garret Henry (father), 5, 8–9, 11, *11*, 12, 18, 20, 22, 26, 48, 49, 71
  death of, 90
  influence on son, 13–16
  intellectual and literary interests of, 13–15
  as male role model, 22, 25
  portrait of, 18
Hopper, Josephine Nivison (Jo), 47, 71, 95, 122, 146, 222
  1907 trip to Holland, 151, 153
  after death of Edward, 578–9
  aging, attitude toward, 246–7
  appearance of, 168
  as artist, 161, 163, 262, 283, 295, 367, 370–1, 373, 377, 379, 380, 383–4, 398–9, 434, 450–1, 489, 497, 517, 522, 557; 1946 show in her studio, 389–90; critical response, 166, 171, 515; Edward as model, 415, 428–31, 554, 555; Edward's negative attitudes and actions, 246, 264, 265, 334, 351, 372, 378, 386, 387, 392, 409, 411, 439, 447–8, 476, 495; exhibits, 154, 162, 163, 165–6, 171, 190, 512–13, 519, 528; first published drawings, 148–9; illustrations, 148–9, 155, *156*; *Jo Painting* (1936), 392; letter to McBride,

360–1; pastels, 174; Pen and Brush Club's rejection, 389; portrait of Edward, 550; promotion of her own work, 298–302, 304, 310, 447–8; resentment at lack of recognition, 265, 304, 367–8, 386, 409–11, 418, 425, 427, 428, 432, 443–4, 446–7, 460, 475, 496, 516, 548, 557; watercolors, 164–6, 169, 171, 199, 209, 217, 264, 288, 297–8, 321, 370, 383–4, 388, 389, 477, 509. *See also specific works, galleries, and museums*
  Arts Club of Chicago retrospective (1934) and, 255
  as art student, 151–4
  birthday card from Edward (1942), 352
  birthday gift from Edward (1939), 310
  birthday present to Edward (1937), 297
  Brooklyn Museum group exhibition (1923) and, 171–2
  Brooks's *New England Indian Summer* and, 345–6
  caricatures of, by Edward Hopper: *Colonel Hopper SLICK BABY BRIGADE*, 354, *355*; *The HOUSE THAT JO BUILT*, 259, *260*; *Jo's "Cellar-way" Studio at Provincetown years ago*, 157, *158*; of married life, 176–9, *177*–80, 183, 192, 196, 237; for tenth wedding anniversary (1934), 261, *261*
  cars and driving and, 206, 208, 224–5, 283, 285, 297, 304–5, 372, 373, 378, 379, 404, 416, 429–30, 439–40, 442, 467, 468, 523, 552
  cats and, 286–7; Arthur, 163, 165, 168, 171, 175–6, 190, 196
  Christmas card from Edward (1923), 173
  Christmas cards for 1941, 347
  Christmas present from Edward to (1951), 444
  clothes of, 259–60, 319
  cooking and other domestic chores, 177, 183, 231–2, 244, 246, 262–5, 370, 378
  Corcoran prize and, 294
  courtship of Edward and, 170–3
  cross-country trip and (1941), 337–42
  death of, 580
  death of friends of Edward and, 407, 434, 462, 498, 518–19
  Degas's strategy for concealing his personal life and, 183–4

Hopper, Josephine Nivison (Jo) (*continued*)
depression, 413, 447
diaries of, 248, 451, 475, 548
disability payments received by, 163–4
early life of, 146–9
on Edward Hopper's work, 199, 227,
235–6, 257, 288–90, 308, 343, 344–5,
371, 404–6, 412, 416, 431–2, 446, 448,
451–2, 487–8, 493, 495–7, 503, 504, 517,
518, 538, 551, 553, 572; *Approaching a
City,* 388; *Bridle Path,* 312; *City Sunlight,* 477; *Corn Belt City,* 396; *Excursion
into Philosophy,* 523, 524–6; fundamental character, 249; *Gas,* 328; *High Noon,*
416–17; *Intermission,* 558; *Light House
Village,* 224; MacArthur house commission (*Pretty Penny*), 316–18;
Nighthawks, 349; *October on Cape Cod,*
394; *Office at Night,* 322–4; *Oregon
Coast,* 339; *Pennsylvania Coal Town,*
397; *People in the Sun,* 529–31; *Rooms
by the Sea,* 442–3; *Rooms for Tourists,*
379–81; *Room in Brooklyn,* 241; *Ryder's
House,* 249; *Sea Watchers,* 452–3; *Second
Story Sunlight,* 539; *Seven A.M.,* 405;
Summer in the City, 418–20; *Sunlight in
a Cafeteria,* 518; *Two Puritans,* 381;
Western Motel, 510; Whitney retrospective (1950), 422; why his and her subjects are alike, 326
Elizabeth Hopper and, 175, 234, 244, 262,
267–8
fear of muggings, 471, 493, 545
at funeral for Edward, 577–8
Guilbert and, 161–2
health of, 162–3, 237, 291, 300, 386, 387,
444, 562, 575–6; 1942 operation, 351;
eyesight, 449, 471, 575, 579
Henri and, 150–1, 237–8
homeless and unemployed (1919), 160
hunger strikes of, 386–8, 392, 404, 409–10,
430, 448–9, 469, 555
Marion Hopper and, 234, 296, 465, 570–1
marriage to Edward, 174–5
The Masses magazine and, 155
Mexican trip (1943), 362–6
as model for Edward. *See* models,
Josephine Hopper as
Mories and, 218

names used by, 190, 197, 202–3, 272, 295
New Yorker profile of Edward opposed
by, 424–5
at New York School of Art, 47, 150–1
oil portrait of, 150–2, 284–5
personal characteristics of, 364, 463
photographs of, 263–4, *245,* 520; in 1955,
393; in 1964, *564;* as a young girl, *147;*
as a young woman, *148*
political views of, 287–8, 292, 330
portraits by, xvi, 414, 492
in Provincetown, 157–9, *158*
record keeping by, 183, 360, 409
relationship with Edward before marriage, 160–1, 168–74
relationship with Edward during marriage, 236–7, 261, 342, 346, 354, 385, 403,
433, 475–6, 479, 502, 538, 557–8; fights
and violence, 303–5, 334, 340, 342, 351,
372, 390–1, 417, 430, 466, 490, 527, 552;
hunger strikes, 386–8, 392, 404, 409–10,
430, 448–9, 469, 555; in late 1930s, 283;
power and control, Edward Hopper's
need for, 372–3, 376; sexual relationship, 178–83, 373, 503, 525
on Robert Frost, 399
as school teacher, 151, 153, 154, 156, 162,
163
as secretary to Edward Hopper, 255, 360
social life of, 177–8, 263, 286, 287, 290–1,
315, 331, 354, 403, 404, 410, 412, 432,
472, 551
Stieglitz and, 153–4
studios of: on Ninth Street, 163, 176, 190;
in Provincetown, 157, 158; at 3 Washington Square North, 306, 325, 360,
361, 465, 483, 486, 535
summer home in Truro and. *See* Truro,
Massachusetts, summer home in
theatrical pursuits of, 155–7, 161–2
on *Time* cover story, 507
in Truro, 230–3, 243–4; suspicious
stranger, incident with (1930), 232–3
as volunteer in World War I, 159–60
Washington Square Players and, 155–7
in Woodstock, 164–5
World War II and, 327
Hopper, Marion Louise (sister), 22, 90, 175,
233, 262–3, 268–9, 291, 295, 303, 316,

319, 326, 328, 335, 374, 465, 486, 502, 527, 541, 547, 550, 551, 565, 570
burglarized, 570
childhood of, 5, 10, *14*, 16
death of, 570
health of, 498–9, 554
Josephine Hopper and, 499
letters to, from Paris (1906–1907), 52, 53
photographs of, *14, 176*
visit to Truro house (1937), 296
Horace, 148, 395, 412, 433, 507
Horizon (magazine), 538, 549
horseback riding, 192, 312
Hosking, A. N., 109, 111, 112, 114, 115
Hotel by a Railroad, 282, 470, 480
Hotel Lobby, 358–9, *359,* 383
Hotel Management (magazine), 236
Hotel Room, 238, 489, 512
House at Dusk (House by Evening Park), 266
House at Eastham, 244
House at San Mateo, 339
House Back of Dunes, 244
House by a River, 130–1, 136
House by Squam River, 199
House by the Railroad, 135–6, 195–8, 227, 280, 281, 300, 334, 536
House in Italian Quarter, 186
House in Provincetown, 231
House in Tarrytown, 136
House of the Fog Horn, 223
House on a Hill (The Buggy), 131, 195
House on Dune Edge, 240
House on Pamet River, 264, 284
Houses at Squam Light, 541
HOUSE THAT JO BUILT, The, 259, 260
House with a Bay Window, 171
House with a Big Pine, 269, 284
House with a Rain Barrel, 286
House with a Vine, 384
House with Dead Tree, 244
Howald, Fernand, 154
Howard, Mike, 522
Howells, William Dean, 15
Hudson, Holland, 156–7
Hudson-Fulton Celebration, 79
Hudson River, 3, 80, 544
Hudson River School, 31, 80, 337, 377
Hugo, Victor, 15, 29, 54, 63, 113

humor (irony; satire), 93, 236, 253. *See also* caricatures
personal sense of, 45, 116, 218
self-satire, 21–2, 55, 84, 106
in youthful works, 21–3, 33
Hunter, Thomas, 148
Huntington, Madge, 47
Huntington Hartford Foundation, 501, 505–8
Huston, Walter, 383
Hutty, Alfred, 222
Huxley, Aldous, 378

Ibsen, Henrik, 29, 46, 47, 195–6, 275, 281
illness. *See* health of Edward Hopper
illustrated books, 17, 31
illustrated magazines, 17–18, 28–30, 81
illustration(s), 18, 20, 29, 34–5, 85, 91, 93, 94, 108, 296. *See also* advertising work; commercial art; drawings
as art student, 16
attitude toward work on, 113–14
conventions in, 91
for *The Enchantment of Don Quixote* (unpublished), 17
final sale of, 192–3
French, 81
Hopper on, 139
by Josephine Hopper, 149, 155, *156*
for magazines, 85, 87, 88, 89, 96, 102, 104, 108–11, 121–2, 125, 128, 192, 212. *See also specific magazines*
for *Melange* (yearbook of Lafayette College), 86
for New York Edison's *Bulletin,* 48
photographs used for, 114
Illustrator, The, 112
illustrator(s), 29, 30, 48, 87, 357
immigrants, 20, 22, 103, 146, 151, 236, 397
Impressionists (Impressionism)
American, 219
French, 59, 66, 75, 76, 89, 135, 203, 231
income. *See* financial affairs; sales of art
Independent Artists exhibition (1910), 85
Independent School of Art, 154
Indianapolis Museum, 284
Indian culture, in New Mexico, 191
individualism, 276
Ingres, 37

ink medium, 18. *See also* pen-and-ink drawings and sketches

ink wash, 30

insecurity (self-doubt; lack of self-confidence; feelings of inferiority), 25, 26, 33, 111, 126, 179, 326, 341, 373, 469

inspiration, 87–8, 249, 297, 370, 536

Institute of Arts and Letters, 374, 377, 382, 409, 482–3, 485, 500

Instructor (magazine), 453

Interior (Model Reading), 191–2

Intermission, 558

Internal Revenue Service, 475

International Exhibition of Modern Art (1913). *See* Armory Show (1913)

intimacy, theme of, 101, 116, 122, 132, 139, 142

introversion, 12

Invitation to Art (television series), 546

irony. *See* humor

Irvine, Rosalind, 455, 458, 460, 471, 477, 515, 516, 522, 526, 537

isolation (solitude). *See also* loneliness; shyness
Edward Hopper's personal, 177–8, 404, 515
theme of, 67, 100, 127, 136, 200, 201, 208, 210

Italian Quarter, 88, 171

Ivens, Joris, 296

Jacob, Max, 303

Jacob's Room (Woolf), 468

Jaffe, Sam, 399

James, Henry, 15, 205, 275, 277–80, 359, 382, 436, 441, 501
puritanism and, 277–8

James, Macgill, 438

James Mountain, Colorado, 190

Jammes, Louise, 49, 52–4, 68, 69, 76

Jammes brothers, 49, 76, 82

Jamot, Paul, 183

Japan and the Japanese, 45, 55, 65, 206, 223, 293, 338, 348, 379

Japanese prints, 36

Jefferson, Thomas, 414

Jenison, Madge, 162

Jenness, Harriet, 249, 257, 261, *261,* 313

Jennings, E. P. "Ned," 189

Jewell, Edward Alden, 220, 252, 267, 333, 390

Jewels for the Madonna (Homage to Illa) (Josephine Hopper), 441–3, *443,* 448, 532

Jewett, Eleanor, 255

Joan of Arc, 63, 65

John Heron Art Institute, 300

Johns, Orrick, 159

Johnson, Bill, 502–4

Johnson, Buffie, 377

Johnson, Jack, 78, 79

Johnson, Liz, 502

Johnson, Lyndon, 569

Jo in Wyoming, 392, 394

Jones, Robert Edmond, 159, 161

Jo Painting, 284, 299, 309, 392

Jo Posing for "Morning in a City," 369

Jo Posing Nude, 368

Jordaens, Jacob, 130

Jo's "Cellar-way" Studio at Provincetown years ago, 157, *158*

Joseddy at age of 6½, 184, *185*

Josie as a She-Devil, 520, 521

Josie lisant un journal, 183

Josie of Boston, The (Josephine Hopper), 190

Juin, 129

Jung, C. G., 93, 272, 274

juries at museums and shows, Edward Hopper on, 298–301, 315, 360, 398, 428, 436–8, 452, 457, 458, 464, 559

Kabloona (de Poncins), 385–6

Kandinsky, Vassily, 67, 90

Kantor, Martha Rhyther, 265, 290, 313, 342, 351, 376, 484

Kantor, Morris, 162, 290, 313, 315, 342, 418

Karfiol, Bernard, 90, 95–6, 105, 299

Keller, Arthur Ignatius, 34–5

Kelly, Jack, Jr., 490

Kelly Jenness House, 244

Kennedy, Jacqueline, 541

Kennedy, John F., 541

Kennedy and Company, 188

Kent, Rockwell, 34, 41, 43, 46, 74, 97, 110, 115, 141, 183, 197, 210, 254, 389

Keppel Gallery. *See* Frederick Keppel and Company

Kerosene Oil Lamp, The (Josephine Hopper), 426, *427*

Khonstamn Prize, 563

Kibbey, Helen, 59

"Killers, The" (Hemingway), 350
Kinsey report, 415
Kipling, Rudyard, 16, 29, 345
Kirstein, Lincoln, 462
Knaths, Karl, 467
Koch, Dora, 563
Koch, John, 531, 534, 535, 546–8, 563
Kollwitz, Käthe, 500
Kramer, Hilton, xv, 565–6
Kraushaar, John, 185
Kreymborg, Alfred "Krimmie," 154, 156,
    157, 159, 162, 288
Kroll, Leon, 86–8, 104, 106, 108, 113, 140,
    154, 174, 183, 299, 304, 505, 560
Kuh, Katharine, xii, 5, 363, 427, 428, 539
Kuhn, Walt, 121, 162
Kuniyoshi, Yasuo, 315, 432, 448, 464

Lady Jean (Bellows), 195
Lafayette College (Easton, Pennsylvania),
    yearbook of, 86
L'Affaire Blum (film), 421
La Fontaine, 133–4
Lahey, Richard F., 140, 174, 209, 210, 294–5,
    313
Lamb, John, 505, 516
Landeck, Armin, 452
Land of Fog, 94
LANDSCAPE AFTER HOPPER, 21–2
Landseer, Sir Edwin, 37
Langner, Lawrence, 157
Lanning, Edward, 499, 548
Larkspur (Josephine Hopper), 183
Last Puritan, The (Santayana), 275–7, 525
Laufman, Sidney, 472
Laver, James, 225
Lavoirs, Les, 129
Lawson, Ernest, 74, 462
Lee, Jennette, 281
Lee Shore, The, 342–4
Le Gallienne, Eva, 195
Leighton, Frederick Lord, 37
Lenox Library, 36
Lerner, Abe, 463, 482
Le Sueur, Eustache, 16
Le Sueur, François, 16
letters
    earliest surviving, 31–2
    to his mother, 244; in 1900, 31–2; from
        New Mexico (1925), 192; from Paris

(1906), 49–52, 54–5, 59, 69; from Paris
    (1909), 77–8
    to his sister, from Paris (1906–1907), 52, 53
Levine, Jack, 457, 460, 463, 484, 532, 534,
    535, 546, 547, 559, 576
Lewenthal, Reeves, 355, 356
Lewis, Emory, 421–2
Lewis, Lucille, 293
Lewis, Martin, 103, 135, 140, 174, 256, 293,
    302, 310
Lewis, Sinclair, 200, 252, 256, 423
Lewis Barn, The, 240
Lewis Farm, 231
Lewisohn, Samuel A., 225
Libby House, Portland, 208, 209
Liberal Club, 156, 159, 181
Liberty Street School (Nyack), 10
Life (magazine), 345, 426, 432, 444, 578
Life and Times of Sir Archie, The
    (Blanchard), 353
life drawing classes, 37, 39, 41, 42, 140. *See
    also* nude models
light, meaning of, 407
Light Battery at Gettysburg, 325–6
Lighthouse at Two Lights, 223, 453, 505–6
Lighthouse Hill, 207, 208
Light House Village, 224
Lime Rock Railroad, 198
Lindenmuth, Tod, 45
Lindsay, Vachel, 34, 36, 40, 43, 47, 95
Lipchitz, Jacques, 402, 458, 474
Lisenby, Ethel, 467
literature, 15–16. *See also* reading aloud, as
    pastime; *individual writers*
    American, 4, 14, 29, 41, 46, 200, 205,
        275–80, 402
    favorite authors, 275–81
    French, 13–16, 29, 46, 61, 100–1, 144, 168,
        173, 280, 311, 444
    German, 14, 30, 266, 276, 394, 487, 543
    Russian, 14–15, 41, 46
Little Cove Monhegan, The, 129
Locomotive, The, 136, 210
Locust Trees, 244
Loeb, Harold, 162
Logan Institute Medal, 383
Logan Prize, 142
Lombard, Frank, 244, 370, 398
Lombard, Nettie, 398
Lombard's House, 240

London, 1907 trip to, 69–70
Londoner, Amy, 47
loneliness. *See also* isolation (solitude)
   theme of, 81, 131, 236, 253, 255, 332, 400
Lonely House, The, 136
Longfellow, Henry Wadsworth, 466
Long Leg, The, 269
Look (magazine), 402
Lopokova, Lydia, 156
Los Angeles, 128, 130, 131, 132, 136, 338,
   377, 457, 508
Los Angeles Museum, 142, 188
Louchheim, Aline B., 401
Louvre, the, 279
Louvre et la Seine, Le (The Louvre and
   Seine), 66, 75, 81, 85, 129
Lowell, Amy, 162, 168
Lozier, Jacob, 16
Luce, Clare Booth, 426, 512
Luce, Henry, 426
Ludwig, Emil, 378
Luks, George, 74, 86, 171, 238, 254, 462
Luncheon in the Studio (Manet), 141
Luncheon of the Boating Party (Renoir), 295
"Lune Blanche, La" (Verlaine), 100, 173
Lux, Kenneth, 514
Lynes, George Platt, 426, 472
Lynes, Russell, 472

Maass, John, 195
MacArthur, Charles, 295, 344
   Hopper commissioned to paint house of
   (*Pretty Penny*), 316–18
Macbeth Gallery, 74
McBride, Henry, 114, 138–9, 142, 165, 186,
   187, 201, 226, 243, 253–4, 277, 331, 347,
   360, 361, 366, 386, 390, 400
MacDonald-Wright, Stanton, 60, 171
MacDowell, Edward, 86
MacDowell Club, group shows at, 86–7, 89,
   94, 98, 108, 109, 111, 113
MacDowell medal, 575
MacGowan, Edna and Kenneth, 509
MacKaye, Percy, 156
MacLeish, Archibald, 428
Macomb's Dam Bridge (New York), 268
Madame Bovary (Flaubert), 16, 75, 416, 417
Madame Cheruy, 143
Maddow, Ben, 553
Madrid, 1910 trip to, 82

Maeterlinck, Maurice, 156
magazines, 17–18. *See also specific magazines*
   of drawing instruction, 16
   illustrated, 18, 81
   illustrations for, 85, 87, 88, 89, 96, 102,
     104, 108–11, 121–2, 125, 128, 192, 212
Magee, Dick, 467, 479, 511, 552
Magee, Nell, 451, 552
Magic Mountain, The (Mann), 417, 540
Maine (battleship), 20, 30
Maine Coast, 132
Maîtres Humoristes, Les (illustrated by Guil-
   laume and Forain), 81, 238
male-female relationships. *See also* sexuality;
   women
   childhood and adolescence of Hopper
     and, 22, 25
   in Hopper's works, 22, 24–5, 101, 131,
     177–9, 241–2, 314–98, 420, 504, 525
Mallarmé, Stéphane, 311
Manet, Edouard, 37, 40, 48, 62, 78, 83, 109,
   135, 141
Mangravite, Peppino, 331, 376
Manhattan Bridge, watercolor of, 193
Manhattan Bridge and Lily Apartments, 198
Manhattan Bridge Entrance, 198
Manhattan Bridge Loop, 215
Mankiewicz, Joseph L., 435
Mann, Thomas, xiii, 277, 417, 436, 540
Mansard Roof, The, 169–71, 195
Man with a Hoe (Millet), 397
Many Marriages (Anderson), 219
Marching Men (Anderson), 397
Marin, John, 60, 121, 191, 253
Marquet, Albert, 59, 66
Marsh, Felicia, 316, 437, 450, 462
Marsh, Reginald, 295, 316, 450, 452, 462,
   475, 478
Marshall's House, 244
Martha Jackson Gallery, 476
Martha McKeen of Wellfleet, The, 370, 371
Martin, Homer Dodge, 337
Marty (film), 495
Masses, The (magazine), 155, 159, 164, 288
Mass of Trees at Eastham, 552
Masson, André, 401
Master Builder, The (Ibsen), 195–6
Masterpieces from the Works of Gustave Doré,
   17
Masters of Art series, 36

Masterson, Miss, 222
Matisse, Pierre, 90, 109, 301
Mattson, Henry, 376
Maupassant, Guy de, 41
Maurer, Alfred, 60
Maverick Festival, 164
May, Philip, 22, 30–2, 35
McFee, Henry Lee, 300
McIver, Loren, 378
McKeen, Martha, 326, 370, 371
McKeen, Reggie, 305, 370, 467
McKellar, Margaret, xvi, 572
McKenna, Kenneth, 302
McKinley, William, 20, 30, 287
McKinney, Roland, 303, 377
McNulty, Dean, 545
Meal Time, 177, *178,* 240
Meier, Frederick, 288
Melange (yearbook of Lafayette College), 86
Melcarth, Edward, 546
Melchers, Gari, 196
Mellow, James, xvi
Mellquist, Jerome, 357
Melville, Herman, 305, 344, 402
Meredith, George, 466
Merrymakers at Shrove Tide (Hals), 236
Meryon, Charles, 112, 125, 535
Methodist Church, Provincetown (Josephine Hopper), 513
Methodist Church Tower, 223–4, 231
Metropolitan Magazine, 87
Metropolitan Museum of Art, 36, 79, 80, 85, 221, 237, 238, 317, 357, 432, 472, 512, 526
    1952 watercolor and print show at, 452, 453
    national competition at, 427
    purchases of Hopper's works by, 189, 238
Mexico, xiv
    1943 trip to, 362–6
    1946 trip to, 391–2
    1951 trip to, 439–40
    1952 trip to, 453–7
    1955 trip to, 484, 485
Meyer, Josephine A., 157
Meyerowitz, William, 167
Meyers, Sidney, 553
Mielziner, Ella, 228, 302, 338, 453, 496
Mielziner, Jo, 221, 227–8
Miller, Arthur, 565
Miller, Dorothy, 495

Miller, Flora, 423, 445
Miller, Kenneth Hayes, 35, 37, 43, 109, 128, 151, 204, 357, 445, 462
Miller, Louise, 302
Millet, Jean-François, 37, 48
Minnigerode, C. Powell, 140–1
Minor, Robert, 155
Mirrielees, Edith, 93
Misérables, Les (Hugo), 15
Misinterpreted Command, A, 25
Mission (Josephine Hopper), 513
Mitla, Mexico, 455–6
Moby Dick (film), 502
Moby Dick (Melville), 344
Model Reading (Interior), 191–2
models, 37–40. *See also* figure, the; life draw-
    ing classes; nude models
    Josephine Hopper as, 191–2, 201, 203, 221, 238, 267, 277, 301, 309, 349, 368, 418–19, 431–2, 449, 452, 471, 549; *Cape Cod Morning,* 431–2; *Compartment C, Car 293,* 301; *First Row Orchestra,* 437; *Girlie Show,* 335–7; *High Noon,* 417; *Hotel by a Railroad,* 449; *Hotel Lobby,* 358, *359; Morning in a City,* 368–9; *Morning Sun,* 446, *447; New York Movie,* 307; *Nighthawks,* 349; *Office at Night,* 322; *Summer in the City,* 419–20; *Summertime,* 362
modernists (modernism), 88–9, 219, 252, 253, 278. *See also* abstract art
Moffett, Ross, 263, 267, 286
Molière, 30, 148, 281
Monet, Claude, 66, 109, 135
Monhegan Boat, The, 115, 127–8, 130
Monhegan Island
    as subject of paintings, 128
    vacations in, 110, 114, 118, 120, 125
Mon Oncle (film), 555
monotype prints, 38, 103
Montaigne, 13–15, 91, 148, 421, 433
Monte Alban, ruins at (Mexico), 456
Monterrey Cathedral, 366
Monticello (Jefferson's home), 223
Montross, Newman E., 216
Montross Gallery, 1914 show at, 96–7
Moonlight Interior, 139, 142
Moore, Marianne, 441, 450, 500, 544
Mora, F. Luis, 35
More, Hermon, 434

Mories, Fred, 218
Morning in a City, 368
Morning Sun, 446, 447
Morse, John, 533
Morse Dry Dock Dial, 108, 115, 117
Morton Gallery, 217
Moscarella, Gina, 534
Motherwell, Robert, 500, 546, 559, 560
Mouth of the Pamet River—Full Tide, 297
movie posters, 94–5
movies, 95, 201, 212–13, 218, 291, 295, 377, 408, 411, 421, 439, 463, 500, 502, 555. *See also specific movies*
Movies, The (The Balcony), 212
Movie Theatre—Gloucester (Josephine Hopper), 199
Mowbray-Clarke, John and Mary, 162
Mrs. Acorns' Parlor, 198
Mrs. Kit Hopper's one man jury show, 532
Mrs. Scott's House, 244, 267
Mt. Moran, 392
Muckrakers, 42–3, 85
muggings, fear of, 471, 493, 545
Mumford, Lewis, 201, 253, 422, 462, 463, 500, 549, 565, 566
murals, 309–10
  invitation to paint, 292
Museum of Fine Arts (Boston), 271, 405, 541, 547
Museum of Modern Art (New York), xiii, 248, 266, 274, 317, 321, 334, 351, 366, 378, 470, 536
  1929 exhibition at, 225–6
  1933 restrospective of Hopper's work: catalogue for, 251, 252, 254–6; installation of, 252; preparations for, 251–2
  artists' group to protest emphasis on abstract art, 444, 446, 448, 457–8
  House by the Railroad given to, 227
  Josephine Hopper's approach to, 448
  protest against emphasis on abstraction, 534, 535
music, 30, 65, 67, 78, 147, 155, 242, 310, 323, 385, 509, 534
Myers, Bernard, 296
Myers, Ethel Klinck, 47
Myers, Jerome, 162, 171
Myers, John Andrew, 189
Myers, John Bernard, 396
Myers, Lloyd B., 329

My Roof, 247
Mysteries of Paris (Sue), 61

Nason, Gertrude, 532
National Academy of Design, 46, 81, 121, 136, 141, 252, 460
  Hopper's refusal of membership in, 242–3
national art (native art; American art), 75, 94, 114, 203, 204–5, 220, 228–9, 239, 253, 276, 278, 396, 435. *See also* American subjects
National Arts Club, 128, 141, 188, 252, 420
National Association of Women Painters and Sculptors, 265
National Gallery (London), 70
National Gallery of Art, 437
National Institute of Arts and Letters, 377, 382, 428
  gold medal awarded to Hopper, 482, 485–6
National Organization for Hands Off the Supreme Court, 292
native art. *See* national art
nativist ideology, 20, 72, 75, 187, 202, 203, 204, 216, 219, 253, 280, 435
nature, harmony of man and, 14–15
Near the Back Shore, 286
Negro Cabin, 222
Neider, Charles, 509, 511
Neider, Joan, 511
Nelson Art Gallery (Kansas City), 337
Neuberger, Roy, 480, 570
neurotics, Ellis on, 514–15
New Deal, 271, 288, 292, 331
New England, 87, 96, 123, 136, 157, 183, 186, 198, 208, 213, 221, 223, 248, 277–8, 295, 346, 382, 423, 452, 457, 560, 565
New England Indian Summer: 1865–1915 (Brooks), 345–6
New England Painting Competition, 559
New Gallery, 165–6
New Jersey, childhood vacations in, 11–12
Newman, Arnold, 346, 426, 538, 549
New Orleans, 391
New School for Social Research, 495
New Society of Artists Seventh Exhibition (1926), 196
New Statesman, 206
Newsweek, 425, 578
New York City
  etchings of, 103, 115, 138

Paris compared to, 51, 52, 56, 279
  as subject, 75, 85, 90, 98, 103, 115, 130, 140,
    193, 196, 201, 213, 215, 217–18, 227–9,
    241–2, 247, 248, 266, 268, 269, 285, 322,
    349, 375, 408, 496, 498, 518, 551
New York American, 75, 81
New York Corner (retitled *Corner Saloon*), 98,
    189, 334, 350
New York Edison, 48
New Yorker, The, xi, xii, 378, 400, 426, 432,
    444, 465, 503, 514, 531
  Hopper's refusal to be profiled in, 424–5
New York *Evening Post,* 140, 155, 536
New York *Evening Sun,* 141
New York *Evening World,* 166
New York *Herald,* 131, 138
New York *Herald Tribune,* 242, 252, 462
New York Interior, 139, 140, 142
New York Mail and Express, 85
New York Movie, 309
  study for, 308
New York, New Haven, and Hartford, 240
New York Office, 551, 559
New York Pavements, 184, 196
New York *Post,* 269
New York Restaurant, 140, 141, 174
New York School of Art, xvii, 33–48, 74, 75
  Chase as teacher at, 35–7
  dances at, 46
  Henri as teacher at, 39–48
  Hopper as teacher at, 45–6
  Josephine Nivison at, 47, 150–1
  Keller as teacher at, 34–5
  Miller as teacher at, 35, 37
  scholarship won by Hopper, 45
  Sloan as teacher at, 48
  women at, 35–8, 43
New York School of Illustrating, 27–9
New York Society of Women Artists, 265, 418
New York *Sun,* 118, 201, 226, 331
New York *Sunday World,* 187, 196–7
New York Times, The, 154, 220, 242, 379, 390,
    428, 439, 546
  on etchings, 136–7, 142
  obituary for Edward Hopper, 578
New York Times Book Review, The, 462
New York *Tribune,* 128, 138, 155
New York University, xvi, 394–5, 398, 458,
    545–6
  central heating installed by, 521–2

New York *World,* 201
New York World's Fair (1964), 570
New York *World-Telegraph,* 366
Night Café (Van Gogh), 350
Night Has a Thousand Eyes (film), 411
Nighthawks, 349–53, 357–9, 400
Night in the Park, 131, 132, 136, 137, 210
Night Shadows, 131, 132, 136, 139, 210, 410,
    426
Night, the El Train, 115–16, 128
Nightwatch (Rembrandt), 71
Night Windows, 218–20, 238, 256
Nijinsky, Vaslav, 155, 165
Niles, Helen, 71
Nivison, Charles E., 147, 153
Nivison, Eldorado, 146, 147
Nivison, Josephine Verstille (Jo). *See*
    Hopper, Josephine Nivison
Nivison, Mary Ann, 146–7, 153, 159, 484
Nixon, Richard M., 541
Non-Anger man and Pro-Anger woman, 236,
    237
Normal College of the City of New York,
    148–9
North of Boston (Frost), 136
North Shore Arts Association, 167
North Truro Station, 231
nostalgia, 74, 84, 100, 123, 130, 131, 133, 135,
    173, 195, 463, 540, 573
"Notes on Painting," 281
Notre Dame de Paris, 129
Novak, Barbara, 576, 577
November, Washington Square, 248
Nude Female Model Posing in Class, 44
Nude in a Chair, 142
nude models, 37–40. *See also* figure, the; life
    drawing classes
nudes, 26, 35, 45, 60, 132, 139, 142, 201, 252,
    258, 335, 368–9, 549–50
Nyack, New York, 3–5, 79
  Saturday morning art classes in, 105
Nyack High School, 10, 25

Oaks at Eastham, 286
Oaxaca, Mexico, 456
Obituary (Fleurs du Temps Jadis) (Josephine
    Hopper), 404–5, 406, 448, 464, 513, 532,
    549
obituary for Edward Hopper in *New York
    Times,* 578

O'Connor, John, Jr., 293, 303–4
October on Cape Cod, 394
O'Doherty, Brian, xvi–xvii, 275, 284, 391,
    546, 547, 553, 554, 558–61, 563, 566,
    570, 576, 577
Odor of Sanctity: South Truro Church
    (Josephine Hopper), 325
Office at Night, 322–5, 376
    study for, *323*
Office in a Small City, 470, 472
Office of Price Administration, 395
Ogiwara, Morie, 45, 65, 206
Ogunquit, Maine, 95, 104, 157, 208
Ogunquit School of Painting and Sculpture,
    95
O'Keeffe, Georgia, 171, 228–9, 409
Old Church on New City Road, 31
Old South Truro Meetinghouse (Josephine
    Hopper), 519
Olympia (Manet), 40, 62
O'Neill, Eugene, 165, 221
one-man show, first (1920), 128–30
One Man's Meat, 403
On the Late Chinese War, 21
On the Quai: The Suicide, 63, *64,* 94
ON THE WATCH, 31
Open Window, The, 115, 116, 132, 133, 142
Oregon Coast, 339
Organ, Marjorie, 164
Orleans, Massachusetts, 313, 326, 381, 404,
    429–31, 480
Orozco, José Clemente, 364
Our Lady of Good Voyage, Church of
    (Gloucester), 169, 470
Our Lady of Good Voyage, (Josephine
    Hopper), 169, *170,* 486
Our Town (Wilder), 565
OUT INTO THE COLD WORLD, 26
Oxbow, The (Cole), 80

Pach, Magda, 418, 434, 437
Pach, Walter, 45, 59, 77, 109, 114, 301, 350,
    434, 437, 518, 519
Packard, Vance, 516
Paddock, Ethel Louise, 47
Paige, Emeline K., 548, 559, 576, 579
Painter-Gravers of America, First Annual
    Exhibition of the (1917), 112
Painting South Truro Church in the Wind,
    233, *233*

palette (Edward's colors), 240
    bright, 111, 241
    light, 66, 75
    in Paris (1906–1907), 55, 66, 67
    in Paris (1909), 76
    somber, 40, 48, 55, 132, 208–9
    tonalist, 85, 90, 94
Palms at Saltillo, 365
Pan-American Exhibition of Contemporary
    Paintings (1931), 238
*Parc de Saint-Cloud, Le (The Park at St.
    Cloud),* 67, 75, 129
Paris, 98, 99, 133, 280, 333, 403. *See also*
    French subjects
    1906–1907 stay in, 48–70; artistic influ-
        ences, 66–7; circle of friends and
        acquaintances, 59–60; descriptions
        and impressions of Paris, 49–52, 56–8,
        66–8; paintings, 55–6, 66–8; photogra-
        phy, 67
    1909 trip to, 75–80
    1910 trip to, 82
    American artists in, 60
    etchings of, 103
    impressions of, 279
    watercolor caricatures (of sexually avail-
        able women), 61, 108, 140, 337
Park Entrance, The, 132
Parker, Helen, 329
Park outside Studio Window (Josephine
    Hopper), 513
Parrish, Maxfield, 121
Passedroit, Georgette, 388
pastoral landscapes, 130, 135–6
Pavillon de Flore, Le, 76
Pearson, Ralph, 252–3, 267, 424
Peat, Wilbur, 284
Pemaquid Light, 223
Pen and Brush Club, 389, 458
pen-and-ink drawings and sketches. *See also*
    drawings; illustrations
    of childhood and adolescence, 18, 25
    in Paris (1906–1907), 63
    for poems by Poe, 46
Penguin Club, 45, 121
Penitente, La, 191
Penitente Order, 191
Pennell, Joseph, 18, 196
Pennsylvania Academy of the Fine Arts,
    132, 140, 189, 267, 347, 474, 475

133rd Annual Exhibition of Oils at (1938), 298–300

Pennsylvania Coal Town, 397

People in the Sun, 529–31

Perkins, Mrs. Daniel, 95

Perkins Youngboy Dos Passos (cat), 286–7

Perry, Clara, 71

personality of Edward Hopper, 168, 463
  Burchfield on, 424
  competitiveness, 169, 316, 326, 354, 469, 475–6, 489
  depression, 12, 116, 217, 246, 305, 342, 355, 395, 399, 406, 411
  du Bois on, 124–5, 129
  Helen Hayes on, 316, 317
  humor, 45, 116, 218
  introversion, 12
  loneliness and isolation, 177–8, 404
  sadism, 181, 261, 431, 466, 468, 489, 527, 536, 558
  selfishness (egotism) , 177, 181, 305, 375–6, 410, 430, 432, 433, 468, 469, 471, 475, 476
  shyness, 15, 282, 486, 515
  silence, 168, 287, 466–7, 509
  sincerity (truthfulness, honesty) , 97, 106, 129, 254, 276, 311
  Raphael Soyer on, 555
  Walter Tittle on, 116
  Forbes Watson on, 254

perspective (viewpoint; vantage point; angle), 67, 86, 89, 96, 114, 132, 184, 201, 417. *See also* voyeur, painter-viewer as

Petunias (Josephine Hopper), 183, 501

Philadelphia Art Alliance, 325

Philadelphia College of Art, 569

Philadelphia Museum of Art, 543

Phillips, Clarence Coles, 34, 48

Phillips, Duncan, 199–200, 225, 295, 309

Phillips Memorial Art Gallery, 295

Phil May's Singer, 31

Phil May's Sketchbook, 31

Philosopher (Rembrandt), 437

philosophy of art. *See* aesthetics

phonograph, 534, 538

photographs of Edward Hopper, 491
  in 1907, 68
  in 1915, 103
  in 1918, 119
  in 1919, 124
  in 1927, 207
  in 1938, 300
  in 1941, 347
  in 1953, 228
  in 1955, with *The Bootleggers, 194*
  in 1960, *ii*
  in 1964, 564
  by Abbott, 410, 514
  as a child, *13, 14*
  by Dahl-Wolfe (1932), 243, *245*
  in Henri's life class, *42*
  by Lynes, 426
  by Arnold Newman, 346, 347, 426, 538
  in Paris (1907), 68
  by Waintrob, 194, 491, 564
  by West, 263–4

photography, 20, 22, 67, 71, 95, 114, 117, 195, 220, 242, 246, 256, 288, 297, 317, 326
  Eakins and, 555
  in Paris (1906–1907), 67

physical appearance. *See* appearance, Edward Hopper's

Picasso, Pablo, 59, 101, 317, 402, 467

Picken, George, 301, 409

Picnic, The (Josephine Hopper), 183

Pierre Matisse Gallery, 301

Pierreuse, La, 61

Pilgrimage of Henry James, The (Brooks), 205, 382

Pissarro, Camille, 89, 201

Piston, Walter, 500

Pittman, Hobson, 299

Plato, 14, 525

Pleissner, Ogden M., 432, 534

Pocket History of American Art (Flexner), 536–7

Poe, Edgar Allan, 46, 311

Poilus, Les (Somewhere in France), 112, 115

Poindexter, Eleanor, 495

Point Counter Point (Huxley), 378

pointillism, 66

politics (political views), 195, 287–8, 292, 302–3, 308, 330–1

Pollack, Peter, 575

Pollock, Jackson, 400, 426, 472, 526

Pont des Arts, Le (The Bridge of the Arts), 67, 75, 129

Pont du Carrousel, 66

Pont du Carrousel in the Fog, 66

Pont-Neuf, Le, 129

Pont Royal, Le, 76, 132

Poor, Anne, 444, 577

Poor, Bessie Breuer, 317, 458, 478

Poor, Henry Varnum, 257, 263, 322, 376, 444, 446, 457, 460, 463, 470, 471, 483, 485, 499, 534, 535, 546, 559, 577

Poore, Dudley, 140

Pope, Louise, 71

Porgy (Heyward), 221

Port, The, 94

Portland, Maine, 208

   invitation to paint mural in, 292

Portland, Oregon, 339

Portland Head-Light, 208

Portrait of Bertram Hartman (Josephine Hopper), 413, *414,* 452

Portrait of Edward Hopper (Graff), 139

Portrait of Edward Hopper (Study for "Homage to Eakins") (R. Soyer), 556

Portrait of Jo, 213, *214*

Portrait of Mrs. Sullivan, 111

Portrait of Orleans, 430

Portrait of Stella Falkner, 310, *311*

portraits. *See also* self-portraits

   of Dick Magee, 451

   of Hopper: by Graff, 139; by Tittle, 116, *118*

   of Jo Hopper, 213–14, 284

   monotype, 38

   oil, 37

Portuguese Church, 188

posters, 115–21

   movie, 94–5

posture, 120, 398

Pousette-Dart, Nathaniel, 102, 140, 265–6

Power of the Press (Blue Rocker) (Josephine Hopper), 513–14

Prado museum (Spain), 78, 83

Prendergast, Charles, 162

Prendergast, Maurice, 74, 154, 162, 462

Preston, May Wilson, 87

Preston, Stuart, 451, 541–2

Pretty Penny, 318, 364

   frame for, 321

Princess Casamassima, The (James), 441

Print Makers of Los Angeles, 128

Print Makers Society of California, 142

prints (printmaking), 38, 111–12, 127–8, 130, 141, 284. *See also* etching(s); posters

   in 1927, 209

   1927 exhibit of, 210

   in 1928, 212

   1962 retrospective of, 553; preparation and printing, 543–5

   continuity between paintings and, 139

   first invitation to show, 114

   last, 212, 213

   monotype, 38

   prizes and awards won by Hopper, 238, 269, 294, 357, 376, 383, 482–3, 501, 512, 541, 542, 559. *See also specific prizes*

   for etchings (1923), 142

   for *Smash the Hun* (1918), 117, 118, 120

Proctor, Katherine Budd, 209, 248–9, 472–3

Proctor, William H., 248, 249

Prohibition, 193

Prospect Street, Gloucester, 256

prostitutes (prostitution), 42, 181–2, 236, 337, 362. *See also* demi-mondaines

   panic over "white slavery" (1908–1914), 98

   in Paris (1906–1907), 57, 60–3

   in *Soir Bleu,* 98, 101

Proust, Marcel, xiii, 275, 280, 441

Provincetown, Massachusetts, 230, 344, 370, 379

   Jo Nivinson's summer vacations in, 157–9, *158*

Provincetown Art Association, 159, 370

Provincetown Bedroom, The (Nivison), 165

Provincetown Players, 158, 165

Provost, Charles, 28–9

Psycho (film), 536

psychoanalysis, 93–4, 107, 158

Puck (magazine), 17–18

PUNISH LINE, THE: Where the Individualists in Public Schools Spend their Recess (Josephine Hopper), 155, *156*

Purchase Prize, 269, 283, 512

puritanism, 61, 81, 97, 238–9, 253, 275–8, 280, 566

   du Bois on, 276–7, 280

   Emerson and, 276–8

   Henry James and, 277–8

Quai des Grands Augustins, Le, 129

Quebec City, 248–9

Queensborough Bridge, 90

Quixote, Don, 103

Radford, Anne E., 160
Ragle, B. H., 305, 354, 362
Railroad, The, 94, 136, 209
Railroad Crossing, 136
Railroad Embankment, 244
Railroad Sunset, 225
Railroad Train, 75
Railroad Warning, 240
Rain on the River, 305
Rascoe, Burton, 397
Rathbone, Perry, 337, 547
Rauh, Ida, 155, 161
"Raven, The" (Poe), 46
Ravencroft, Ellen, 47, 370
Ray, Man, 121, 154
Read, Helen Appleton, 171, 202, 253
reading aloud, as pastime, 378, 415, 466, 503
realism (realist painters), 168, 195, 200, 220,
    242, 423, 441, 485, 531. *See also* repre-
    sentational painting
    du Bois's request for article on, 377–9
Reality: A Journal of Artists' Opinions, 448,
    449, 453, 457–8, 460–3, 467, 470, 471,
    475, 481, 484–6, 490, 491, 499–500, 511,
    534, 547, 557
    reactions to, 462
    statement by Hopper in, 460, 461, 462
Rebel without a Cause (film), 500
*Record of the Famous Fight between Phil May
    and Fatty Coleman* (May), 32
Redfield, Edward, 140–1
Red Shoes, The (film), 431
Reed, Carol, 439
Reed, John, 155
Regnault, Henri Alexandre Georges, 37, 62–3
Rehn, Frank K. M., 137–8, 215, 219, 238,
    291, 309, 327, 333, 337, 342, 348, 353–5,
    363, 376, 405, 442, 453–5, 464, 475, 560
    death of, 497
    health of, 470
    Josephine Hopper's works and, 387–8
    letters from Mexico to (1943), 364–6
    MacArthur house commission (*Pretty
    Penny*) and, 316–18
Rehn, Peggy, 210–11, 213, 309, 342
Rehn Gallery, 185–6, 189, 197, 210, 211, 213,
    217, 218, 225, 230, 257, 269, 284, 295,
    300, 309, 348, 358, 366, 402, 470, 512
    1927 exhibit at, 201–2
    1929 exhibit at, 220

1948 exhibit at, 400
    under Clancy's direction, 479–80
    concern about future of, 475
    "Early Paintings by Edward Hopper:
        1907–1914" show (1941), 333–5
    Josephine Hopper's works at, 549
    watercolors at, 185–6, 193
Reid, M. Christine W., 150
religion, 12, 21, 22, 193, 196, 486
    Emerson's view of, 14
Rembrandt van Rijn, 48, 71, 79, 324, 437,
    467, 496
Renan, Ernest, 412
Renoir, Pierre Auguste, 109, 135, 555
representational painting (objective paint-
    ing), 240, 444, 446. *See also* realism
Representative Men (Emerson), 14
Resicka, Paul, 534–5
retrospective exhibitions, xiii, 248, 251–6,
    421–6, 428, 565–6
Rêve de Josie, Le, 272, 273, 275, 282, 525
Revel Picture Frame Company, 514
reviews. *See* articles and reviews by Edward
        Hopper; critical reactions to Hopper
Rewald, John, 413
Rhyther, Martha. *See* Kantor, Martha
        Rhyther
Rice, Elmer, 221, 227–8
Rice-Pereira, Irene, 378
Rich, Daniel Catton, 351, 352, 427, 428
Richardson, Edgar P., 428
Richmond, Virginia, 223, 458
Rich's Barn, 240
Rich's House, 231
Rijksmuseum (Amsterdam), 71
Rilke, Rainer Maria, 162
Rimbaud, Arthur, 100, 101, 311, 444
Riverboat, 87
Riverside Drive (Manhattan), 375
Riverside Museum, 418
Road and Trees, 563, 565
Road in Maine, 96, 97, 129
Robinson, Boardman, 155
Robinson, Edward (Metropolitan Museum
        director), 238
Robinson, Edward G. (actor), 496–7
Rockefeller, Mrs. John D., Jr., 225, 334
Rockland, Maine, 198–9
Rockland Harbor, 198
Rocks and Houses, 96, 108, 129, 131

Rocks and Sand, 111
Rockwell, Norman, 95
Rocky Pedestal, 208
Roderick Hudson (James), 278
Rodin, François Auguste René, 45, 162
Rodman, Henrietta, 161
Rodman, Selden, xii, 500
Rogers, Catherine, 576, 578
Rogers, Charles B., 507
Rogers, Mary Gamble, 47, 164, 171
romantic movement, 278
Roofs of the Cobb Barn, 240
Roofs of Washington Square, 198
Room in Brooklyn, 241, 271
Room in New York, 241–2
Room of One's Own, A (Woolf), 415
Rooms by the Sea, 442–3
Rooms for Tourists, 379–81, 400
Roosevelt, Eleanor, 294
Roosevelt, Franklin D., 271, 287–8, 290, 292,
    296, 303, 330, 331, 376
Root, Edward, 215–16, 230, 254, 411, 462
Rose, Barbara, 566
Rosenberg, Harold, 546
Rosenberg, James, 165, 398
Rosenwald, Lessing, 544
Roullier, Alice F., 255
Rousseau, Henri, 351
Rousseau, Jean-Jacques, 41
Rousseau, Theodore, 522
Route 6, Eastham, 344–5
    study for, 345
Route 14, Vermont, 297, 321
Roy, Pierre, 418
Rubens, Peter Paul, 37
Ruellan, Andrée, 210
Rutgers University, 464
Ryder's House, 249

Sachs, Paul, 389
sacrament of sex, The (female version), 178,
    178
sadism (meanness; cruelty), Edward
    Hopper's, 181, 261, 431, 466, 468, 489,
    498, 527, 536, 558
safety, concerns about, 471, 493, 545
Sage, Kay, 377–8, 438
Saies, Enid Marion, 68–9, 70, 73, 76, 82,
    133–4, 403
Sailing, 85–7, 90

sailing. *See* boats, sailing, and nautical scenes
Saint-Gaudens, Homer, 29, 92, 264, 315, 346
Sala, George Augustus, 61–2
Salem, Massachusetts, 223
sales of art, 94, 110, 130. *See also* commercial
    art; *specific works*
  in 1920, 131
  in 1921, 136, 137
  in 1922, 139
  in 1923, 171, 172
  in 1928, 220
  in 1929, 225
  in 1930, 238
  in 1934, 265
  in 1935, 271
  in 1936, 291
  in 1937, 298
  in 1938, 306
  in 1940, 331
  in 1941, 347
  in 1942, 357
  in 1945, 384
  in 1954, 479–80
  etchings (prints), 126–7, 130, 189
  first sale of a painting, 90
  illustrations. *See* illustrations
  ledger kept to record, 90–2, 104
  refusal of opportunities for, 284
  watercolors, 185–6, 209
Salmagundi Club, 376
Salomé (Regnault), 62–3
Saltillo, Mexico, 364, 365, 391, 439
Saltillo Mansion, 365
Saltillo Rooftops, 365
Salute to the Arts Award, 512
Sanborn, Arthayer, 565, 570, 577
San Carlos Mission, 338
Sandburg, Carl, 428
Sandler, Irving, 511, 549
Sandy Hills. See Cape Cod Hills
San Esteban (Josephine Hopper), 392, 393,
    393, 420, 432, 437–9, 491, 513
Sanger, Margaret, 155, 181
Santa Fe, New Mexico, 190–3, 440
Santayana, George, 275–7, 382, 525
São Paulo Bienal, 576, 578
Sardeau Gallery, 139, 141
Sargent, John Singer, 37, 43, 45, 171, 548
Sartain, Geraldine, 372–3
satire. *See* humor; self-satire

Saunders, Arthur Percy "Stink," 198, 230

Saunders, Louise, 198

Saunier, Ada, 53

Saunier, Lois, 4, 10

Savage Eye, The (film), 553

Sawyer, Charles, 215

Sawyer, Helen, 477

Säyen, Lyman, 60

Scarlet Letter, The (Hawthorne), 278

Schaefer, Bertha, 377, 378, 387, 388

Schamberg, Morton, 60

Schnakenberg, Henry, 390

Schuman House, The, 240

Scott, Elsie, 104

Scribner's (magazine), 28, 121–2, 192–3, 295, 350

Scrub Pines, 240

sculpture, 45

   sketches of, 36

Sea at Ogunquit, 114

Sea Watchers, 452

Second Story Sunlight, 539–40

Seitz, William, 552, 578

self-caricatures, 26, 47–8, 93, 106, 274, 274

self-confidence, 35, 256. *See also* insecurity

self-evaluation, 376

self-image, 25–6, 47, 101, 148, 203, 272, 277

selfishness (egotism; self-centeredness), Edward Hopper's, 177, 181, 305, 375–6, 410, 430, 432, 433, 468, 469, 471, 475, 476

Self-Portrait (1925). *See Skyline near Washington Square*

self-portraits, 26, 47, 555. *See also* self-caricatures; *Skyline near Washington Square*

   of childhood and adolescence, 25–6

"Self-Reliance" (Emerson), 204, 216

self-satire (self-irony), 21–2, 55, 84, 106, 299

Seligmann, Kurt, 402

"Sensation" (Rimbaud), 100

Seven A.M., 405

sexuality (sexual themes; eroticism), 138, 488. *See also* voyeur, painter-viewer as

   1921–1922 etchings and, 132–5, 138

   in Anderson's *Many Marriages,* 219

   in *Soir Bleu,* 98–101

   in *Excursion into Philosophy,* 525

   Paris sojourn and (1906–1907) and, 51, 60–1

   in *Summer Interior,* 80

   transformation of American values, 98–9

sexual relationship of Edward and Jo Nivison Hopper, 178–83, 373, 503, 525

Shacks, 169

Shacks at Lanesville, 171

Shacks at Pamet Head, 298

Shadowland (magazine), 140

Shahn, Ben, 444, 474

Shakespeare, William, 14, 415

Shakespeare at Dusk, 269, 270

Shaw, George Bernard, 46

Shea, Pete, 117

Sheeler, Charles, 165, 228–9

Shepherd in the Distance (Hudson), 157

Sheridan Theatre, The, 291–2

Sherman and Bryan, 73, 79, 87

Sherwood, Robert E., 308

Shinn, Everett, 74, 462

Ship of the Great White Fleet, 30

Shore, Henrietta, 164

Shoshone National Forest, 341

shyness, 15, 115, 157, 168, 263, 282, 421, 425, 486, 515, 523

Sickert, Walter Richard, 59

Sierra Madre at Monterrey, 366

Sierra Madre at Saltillo, 365

Sievan, Maurice and Lee, 472

silence

   Edward Hopper's personal, 168, 233, 287, 466–7, 485, 509

   in Edward Hopper's work, 242, 249

Simonson, Lee, 157

sincerity (truthfulness, honesty), 97, 106, 129, 254, 276, 311, 483, 485, 487, 499

Sixteen East Gay Street (Bellows), 195

sketches. *See also* pen-and-ink drawings and sketches

   after other artists, 37

   for oil paintings, 215

   in Paris (1906–1907), 60, 61, 63

   of sculpture, 36

Skylights, 198

Skyline near Washington Square, 193, 281

skyscrapers, 201, 228–9, 247, 281

   James on, 279

   Mumford on, 201

Slater, Alan, 297–8

Slater, Irene, 297–8

Slater, Robert, 297, 305

Sloan, Dolly, 190

Sloan, John, 48, 74–5, 81, 86, 108, 111, 115,
155, 190, 216, 218, 240, 254, 278, 381,
383, 395, 409, 418, 424, 444, 445, 462,
483
Hopper on, 204, 381
Slopes of the Grand Tetons, 392
Smalley, Carl, 126, 131
Smash the Hun, 117–18
Smith, Jacob Getlar, 490, 494
Smith, John DeWint, 5, 6
Smith, Martha Griffiths, 5, 6
Snidely, Dick, 537
Snow, Horace, 512
Snow, Norma, 512
Soby, James Thrall, 353, 423
social life and entertaining, 177–8, 263, 286,
287, 290–1, 315, 331, 354, 403, 404, 410,
412, 432, 472, 551
Soir Bleu, 98–101, 99, 102, 116, 133, 280, 281,
573
Soldier Reading, 132
Soldiers' Entertainment and Art Projects, 353
solitude. *See* isolation
Solitude #56, 374, 395
Solman, Joseph, 457, 460
Somewhere in France (Les Poilus), 127, 131
Sourire, Le (magazine), 81
South Carolina Morning, 487–9
South Royalton, Vermont, 297, 305
South Truro, Massachusetts, 370. *See also*
Truro, Massachusetts
South Truro Church, 230, 233
South Truro Church, 232, 235, 235
South Truro Church (Odor of Sanctity)
(Josephine Hopper), 236, 451, 549
South Truro Post Office, 231
Soyer, Ida, 536, 548
Soyer, Moses, 457, 536, 546, 548
Soyer, Raphael, 315, 438, 444, 457, 460, 462,
471, 477, 478, 486, 511, 532, 534, 535,
541, 543, 546–7
*Portrait of Edward Hopper (Study for
"Homage to Eakins"),* 554–5, 556
Soyer, Rebecca, 477, 478, 486, 511
Spaeth, Otto, 528
Spain, 82–3, 104, 115, 191, 231, 296, 315
Spanish-American War, 20
Spanish language, 363, 376, 378, 390, 392
Spaulding, John Taylor, 186, 211, 405

Speicher, Eugene, 34, 86, 164, 300, 315, 352,
383, 389, 547
Spindly Locusts, 286
Spingold, Nathan B., 489, 490
Sprinchorn, Carl, 34, 74, 161, 165, 166, 301,
302, 367, 370, 377, 386, 417, 430, 436,
498, 502, 537, 562, 566, 569, 576
Springfield, Ohio, exhibition (1917), 111
Squam Light, 88, 89, 129
Squirru, Rafael, 467, 566–7, 570
Stark, Richard, 483, 519
St. Botolph Club, 197, 559
St. Francis Towers, 200
Steen, Jan, 8, 236
Steichen, Edward, 60
Stein, Gertrude, 59, 60, 93
Stein, Leo, 59
Stein, Michael, 59
Stella, Joseph, 109, 121, 165, 516
Stendhal, xii, xiii, 311
Stephens, Bob, 451, 511
Stephens, Dad, 369
Stephens, Kim, 539
Stephens, Marie, 451, 511, 539, 560
stereotypes, cultural, 20, 25, 52, 95, 99, 100,
122, 179, 236, 242, 488
of women, 22, 206, 525
Sterne, Maurice, 59
Sterner, Albert, 209
Sterner, Marie, 298
Stettheimer, Florine, 165
Stevenson, Fanny, 511–12
Stieglitz, Alfred, 153–4, 162, 382, 383, 409
still lifes, 37. *See also* flowers
stock market crash (1929), 225
Stokes, Frederick W., 92
Stone, Edward Durell, 565
Story, Emma. *See* Bellows, Emma
Stout, George, 480
Strange Interlude (O'Neill), 221
Strauss, Johann, 534, 538
Street in Paris, 94
Street Scene (Rice), 221, 227–8
Strick, Joseph, 553
Studio Readjusted, 176
studios, Edward Hopper's
at 3 Washington Square North, 92–3, 210,
259, 319, 483; burglary, 291; central
heating, 521–2, 530; Josephine

Hopper's painting of, 315; move into a larger space (1932), 247–8; New York University's attempt to evict the Hoppers, 394–5, 545–6
on Fifty-ninth Street (New York), 84
on Fourteenth Street (New York City), 46, 61
of Truro house, 258, 296–7
studios, Josephine Hopper's
at 3 Washington Square North, 306, 325, 360, 361, 465, 483, 486, 535
on Ninth Street, 163, 176, 190
in Provincetown, 157–8
Sue, Eugène, 46, 61
Sugar Maple, 305
Summer Evening, 131, 398, 401
Summer Interior, 80–1, 133
Summer in the City, 418–20
study for, 419
Summer School of Painting (Provincetown), 157
Summer Street, 111
Summertime, 362
study for, 363
Summer Twilight, 131, 133, 134, 314, 398
Sunday, 197, 199, 200
Sunday 1897 (Bellows), 195
Sun in an Empty Room, 561–2, 562
Sunlight in Downtown Cafeteria, 517, 518
Sunlight on Brownstones, 498–500, 505
Sun on Prospect Street, 256, 496
Sunwise Turn (bookshop), 162
Suppressed Desires (play), 158
Surrealists, 274, 334, 401, 418, 438, 439
Sweeney, James Johnson, 422
Symbolists, 225, 280
French, 46, 168, 272, 321, 382
symbols, 26, 81, 106, 120, 188, 195, 219, 225, 281–8, 346
System, the Magazine of Business, 87, 88, 324, 350

Tables for Ladies, 235–6, 238, 282
Tait, Agnes, 265
Talbot's House, 198
Tall Masts, 88
Taos, New Mexico, 191
Tappan Zee, 4, 31, 86
Tati, Jacques, 555

Taylor, Elizabeth (author), 432–3
Tea at the Hoppers (Martha Rhyther Kantor), 290
teaching (Hopper as teacher), 105–7
Hopper on, 106
Teilman, Herdis, 545
television appearance, 480, 546, 547, 549, 553, 554
Temple Gold Medal, 267
theater, 16, 47, 196, 203, 212, 221, 223, 256–7, 295, 300, 308, 334, 352, 399, 421, 437.
See also individual playwrights and plays
Josephine Hopper's involvement in, 155–7, 161–2
in Paris, 65
Theatre Guild, 196
There's a virgin—give her the works,' 179, *180*
THERES TROUBLE COMIN',' 19
THIS IS A COMIC PICTURE, 22
Thomas Jefferson on Democracy, 414–15
Thoreau, Henry David, 231
Three Birds on a Branch, 17
Three Children on Cape Elizabeth (Josephine Hopper), 513
Three Little Pigs (animated film), 291
Tillim, Sidney, 566
time, passage of, 280
Time (magazine), 403, 423, 451
cover story in, 501, 507
Tittle, Helen, 443
Tittle, Walter, 34, 38, 39, 42, 43, 45, 48, 92–3, 102, *103,* 109, 111, 112, 115, 121–2, 165, 189, 210, 304, 443
on etchings, 109–10
etchings by, 112–13
on personal characteristics of Hopper, 116
portrait of Hopper by, 116, *118*
Springfield, Ohio, exhibition (1917) and, 111
Tobey, Mark, 362, 474
Toch, Lily and Ernst, 509
Tolstoy, Leo, 15, 41, 46
Tony's House, 199
Touchstone Galleries, 131
Toulouse-Lautrec, Henri de, 238
Tourelle de la rue de la Tixéranderie (Meryon), 112
Toward Boston, 286

Train and Bathers, 132, 135–7
trains and railroad tracks, 280, 281, 301, 388, 428, 567
Tramp Steamer, 75
Tree, A (Josephine Hopper), 190
trees, 356, 539
Trees, East Gloucester, 199
Tree Tops through Fire Escape (Josephine Hopper), 549
Tremper, Wallace, 32–3
Trilling, Lionel, 441
Truro, Massachusetts, 230–3, 240, 243, 246, 249
  1936 summer in, 286
  gas station in, 328, *330*
  neighbors in, 263, 286
  summer home in, 248, 357, 487, 522–3, 537; cooking and other domestic chores at, 262–4, 370; design and construction of, 257–61; electricity for, 478, 479; Elizabeth and Marion Hopper's planned visit to, 262–3, 267, 268; entertaining in, 263, 286, 287; first year in, 263; hurricanes and, 371, 479, 540–1; rationale for investing in, 250; studio in, 258, 296–7
Truro Hospitality (Josephine Hopper), 512
Truro Station Coal Box, 231
truthfulness. *See* sincerity
Tucker, Anne, 223, 237, 262, 268, 321, 407, 472
Tucker, Sam, 223, 262
Tugboat at Boulevard Saint Michel, 66
Tugboat with Black Smokestack, 75
Turgenev, Ivan, 15, 46
Turner, Mary, 157
Twachtman, John, 185
"Twelve Modern American Painters and Sculptors" (1953), 470
Two Comedians, The, 572–4, *573*
Two Lights Village, 211
Two on the Aisle, 203, 206
Two Puritans, 381
Tyler, Parker, 396, 501, 506–7, 516
Type de Belleville, 61

unconscious, the, 93, 274, 277, 349
Une Demi-mondaine, 61, 75
United States Shipping Board Emergency Fleet Corporation, 116–17

U.S. Printing & Litho Co., 94, 95
Utrillo, Maurice, 315

Valéry, Paul, xii, xiii, xiv, 311, 321, 436
  "Autres Fragments sur Mallarmé: Morceaux Choisis," 321
Valley of the Seine, 80, 86, 87
Vallotton, Félix, 59
Van Dyke, Henry, 122
Van Epps, Margaret, 174, 519
Van Gogh, Vincent, 130, 350, 422
Vanity Fair (magazine), 219, 243
Van Paassen, Pierre, 327
Varian, Dorothy, 321
Vassar College, 105
Velázquez, Diego Rodríguez de Silva y, 37, 40, 48, 78
Venice Biennale (1952), 448, 451
Verhaeren, Emile, 168
Verlaine, Paul, 46, 100, 144–5, 161, 168, 173, 275, 280, 311, 399, 433, 487
Vermeer, Jan, 79, 201
Vermont, 163, 209, 246, 269, 288, 297, 305, 321
Vermont Sugar House, 305
Vesalius, 35
Victorian era (values), 3, 18, 27, 99, 134, 179, 182, 195, 206, 209, 382, 525
Victorian houses, 131, 139, 169–70, 185, 195, 234–5, 279–80
Vie de Jésus, La (Renan), 412
Vieille Femme, La (Rodin), 45
Vietor, Thomas F., 90
View (journal), 396
viewpoint. *See* perspective
Villager (newspaper), 439, 515, 519, 531, 548
Villon, François, 163, 336, 404, 415, 433
Vincent, John, 506
violence (domestic), 12, 283, 303–5, 328, 340–1, 372, 403, 417, 430, 487
Virgil, 395, 412
Virginia Museum of Fine Arts, 299, 300, 301, 457–8, 469
Viva Mexico (Flandreau), 466
Vlaminck, Maurice de, 467
Voltaire, 517
Vorse, Mary Heaton, 158
Votive Candles (McIver), 378
voyeur, painter-viewer as, 81, 101, 116, 133, 135, 218–19, 375
  Girlie Show, 337

Night Windows, 218
Office at Night, 324–5

Wagner, Charles, 509, 539
Waintrob, Sidney, *194, 393, 491, 564*
Walker, Hudson, 298
Walker, Maynard, 447, 448
Walker Art Center (Minneapolis), 324
Walkowitz, Abraham, 60, 154, 171
Wallace Collection (London), 70
Wanamaker, Rodman, 60
"Wanderer's Nightsong" (Goethe), 266, 487
Wapiti Valley (Shoshone National Forest), 341
Warner, Arthur, 159
Washburn, Gordon, 458
Washington Square (James), 382, 421
Washington Square Bedroom (Josephine Hopper), 513
Washington Square North, studio on, 92–3, 210, 259, 319, 483
  burglary, 291
  central heating, 521–2, 530
  Josephine Hopper's painting of, 315
  move into a larger space (1932), 247–8
  New York University's attempt to evict the Hoppers, 394–5, 545–6
Washington Square Players, 155–9, 196, 399
watercolors, 31, 173, 252, 321, 327, 384, 405, 513
  1924 exhibit of, 185–7
  of 1925, 191, 193
  of 1926, 198–9
  of 1927, 208
  of 1928, 217
  of 1929, 222, 223–4
  of 1930, 230–1
  of 1931, 240
  of 1932, 244
  of 1933, 249
  of 1934, 264
  of 1935, 269
  of 1936, 286, 291
  of 1937, 297, 298
  of 1938, 305
  of 1941, 339, 341
  of 1942, 353, 356
  of 1943 (in Mexico), 364, 365
  of 1946, 391–2

  in Brooklyn Museum group exhibition (1923), 171–2
  childhood, 18
  critical response to, 171
  new approach to (1923), 168–9
  Parisian caricatures (of sexually available women), 61, 108, 140
Watson, Forbes, 197, 200, 220, 229, 239, 254, 295, 309, 477, 534
  Vanity Fair article on Hopper, 219–20
Watson, Nan, 295, 534
Wearing Apparel, Textile and Fashion Show (Chicago, 1910), 81–2
Webb, Clifton, 34
Weber, Fred, 544
Weber, Max, 59, 171, 226, 472
Webster, Ambrose, 157, 258, 263, 267
Webster, Georgie, 258, 263
Weehawken, New Jersey, 257
Welles, Orson, 300
Wellfleet Bridge, 231
Wellfleet Road, 240
Wells Fargo, 111, 115
Wells Fargo *Messenger,* 104, 108
West, Davenport, 249, 263–4
West, Dorothy, 249
West, the, 1941 trip to, 337–42
Western Motel, 510–12
Weyhe Gallery (New York), 132, 136, 142, 188, 209
When We Dead Awaken (Ibsen), 281
Whistler, James Abbott McNeill, 36, 60, 84, 112, 205
  influence of, 85, 90
White, E. B., 378, 403
White, Trumbull, 85
Whitman, Walt, 41, 399, 402, 483–4
Whitney, Gertrude Vanderbilt, 128, 197, 238, 352, 353
Whitney, John Hay, 256
Whitney Museum of American Art, xv, 229, 238, 239, 242, 267, 283, 284, 377, 390, 405, 428, 434, 445, 458, 480, 495
  1937 Annual at, 294
  1940 Annual at, 320, 331
  1945 Annual at, 383
  1946 Annual at, 386
  1950 retrospective at, 418, 421–5
  1953 Annual at, 462–3, 470–2
  1956 Annual at, 505

Whitney Museum of American Art (*continued*)
  1959 Annual at, 522, 528, 531
  1964 retrospective at, 533, 565–6
  "American Paintings, 1865–1905" at, 548
  discrimination against women by, 265, 439, 458, 460
  Josephine Hopper's painting of information desk at, 471
  Josephine Hopper's works shown in, 463–4, 535
  protest against emphasis on Non-Objective art, 534, 535
  purchases of Hopper's works by, 229, 284, 291
Whitney Studio Club, 132, 139, 140, 188–90, 197, 202, 209, 217, 221, 423
  1920 one-man show at, 128–30
  1924 Members Exhibition of, 174
Whitney Studio Galleries, 222
Who's Who in American Art, 315
Wichita Art Museum, 337, 500
Wilder, Thornton, 500, 565
William A. Clark prize, 141, 294, 438
Williams, Bill, 436–8
Williams, G. Leroy, 75
Williams, William Carlos, 434–5, 544
Willkie, Wendell, 330
Wilson, Dora, 451, 548
Wilson, Dorothy, 477
Wilson, Edmund, 161, 177, 247, 286
Wilson, Edward, 477
Wilson, Sol, 447, 449, 451, 457, 460, 463, 467, 475, 548
Wilson, Woodrow, 248
Windy Day, 305
Winesburg, Ohio (Anderson), 200, 218, 397
Wine Shop, The. See Bistro, Le
Winsten, Archer, 269–70
Winter, Alice Beach, 167
Winter, Charles Allan, 167
Wistarion (school yearbook), 148–9, *149*
wit. *See* humor
With the Refugees, 121
Woman in the Sun, 550, 559
Woman with a Parrot (Manet), 40
women. *See also* feminists; male-female relationships; models; prostitutes; sexuality
  in the 1920s, 206
  African-American, 488–9

  attitudes toward, 25, 205, 206, 340–1, 415, 503; during childhood, 15, 16; stereotypes, 22, 206, 525
  in childhood household, 22
  college education and, 151
  in early drawings and sketches, 22, *24*, 25
  at New York School of Art, 35–8, 43, 47
  in Paris (1906–1907), 60
  Whitney Museum and, 265, 534
women artists, 377–8
  attitude toward, 205, 241, 265, 321, 388
Women's Christian Temperance Union, 99, 193
Wood, Beatrice, 162
Woodbury, Charles, 96
Woodstock, New York, 164–5
Woodstock Artists Association, 164
Woolf, Virginia, 415, 468, 477
Woolsonwood, Harry, 248
Worcester Art Museum, 269, 480
Worcester *Telegram Gazette,* 520
Works Progress Administration (WPA), 271
World Outlook (magazine), 212
World War I
  military draft in, 120
  propaganda poster in, 116–18, 120
World War II, 320, 327, 348–9, 353, 354–5, 370, 376
  end of, 379
writing, 200–1, 354, 379. *See also* articles and reviews by Edward Hopper; literature
Wyeth, Andrew, 423, 428, 452, 472, 500, 504, 507

Yawl Riding a Swell, 269
Yellowstone Park, 340
Yonkers, 189
Young and Rubicam, 516–17
Youngberg, Andrew, 286
Yvette Guilbert's School of the Theatre, 161

Zabriskie, Virginia, 516
Zapotec ruins, 456–7
Zigrosser, Carl, 115, 135, 142, 209, 284, 402, 543–5, 553
Zola, Emile, 16, 41, 63, 99
Zorach, Marguerite, 90, 159, 162, 265, 300, 301, 321, 439, 450, 548
Zorach, William, 90, 154, 159, 162, 300, 301, 548

TEXTUAL CREDITS

ILLUSTRATION CREDITS

A NOTE ABOUT THE AUTHOR

Gail Levin is an art historian who is internationally recognized for her scholarship on twentieth-century American art. The pre-eminent authority on Edward Hopper, she served as curator of the Hopper Collection at the Whitney Museum of American Art from 1976 to 1984, where she organized several major exhibitions and wrote eight books, including the catalogue raisonné of Hopper's work. Five other books have followed, two featuring her own photographs, which have been exhibited in museums and galleries around the United States. She received her doctorate in art history from Rutgers University and has been recognized with numerous fellowships and awards. Currently, she is Professor of Art History at Baruch College and The Graduate School of The City University of New York, and is completing a catalogue raisonné of Marsden Hartley, supported by a grant from the National Endowment for the Humanities.

A NOTE ON THE TYPE

This book was set in Granjon, a type named in compliment to Robert Granjon, a type cutter and printer active in Antwerp, Lyons, Rome, and Paris from 1523 to 1590. Granjon, the boldest and most original designer of his time, was one of the first to practice the trade of typefounder apart from that of printer.

Linotype Granjon was designed by George W. Jones, who based his drawings on a face used by Claude Garamond (c. 1480–1561) in his beautiful French books. Granjon more closely resembles Garamond's own type than do any of the various modern faces that bear his name.

Composed by North Market Street Graphics,
Lancaster, Pennsylvania
Printed and bound by
Quebecor Printing Martinsburg,
Martinsburg, West Virginia
Designed by Iris Weinstein